ONCE MORE UNTO THE SPEECH, DEAR FRIENDS

Monologues from Shakespeare's First Folio with Modern Text Versions for Comparison

VOLUME THREE: THE TRAGEDIES

ONCE MORE UNTO THE SPEECH, DEAR FRIENDS

Monologues from Shakespeare's First Folio with Modern Text Versions for Comparison

VOLUME THREE: THE TRAGEDIES

Compiled and Edited with Commentary by
NEIL FREEMAN

Applause Theatre & Cinema Books

Once More unto the Speech, Dear Friends
Monologues from Shakespeare's First Folio with Modern Text Versions for Comparison
Volume Three: The Tragedies
compiled and edited by Neil Freeman

Library of Congress Cataloging-in-Publication Data

Shakespeare, William, 1564–1616.
Once more unto the speech, dear friends : monologues from Shakespeare's first folio with modern text versions for comparison / compiled and edited with commentary by Neil Freeman.
p. cm.
ISBN-13: 978-1-55783-656-4 (v. 1)
ISBN-13: 978-1-55783-655-7 (v. 2)
ISBN-13: 978-1-55783-657-1 (v. 3)
ISBN-10: 1-55783-656-6 (v. 1)
ISBN-10: 1-55783-655-8 (v. 2)
ISBN-10: 1-55783-657-4 (v. 3)
1. Monologues. I. Freeman, Neil. II. Title.
PR2768.F74 2005
822.3'3—dc22
2005028249

Applause Theatre & Cinema Books
19 West 21st St.
Suite 201
New York, NY 10010
Phone: (212) 575-9265
Fax: (212) 575-9270
Email: info@applausepub.com
Internet: www.applausepub.com

Applause books are available through your local bookstore, or you may order at www.applausepub.com or call Music Dispatch at 800-637-2852

SALES & DISTRIBUTION
North America:
Hal Leonard Corp.
7777 West Bluemound Road
P. O. Box 13819
Milwaukee, WI 53213
Phone: (414) 774-3630
Fax: (414) 774-3259
Email: halinfo@halleonard.com
Internet: www.halleonard.com

Europe:
Roundhouse Publishing Ltd.
Millstone, Limers Lane
Northam, North Devon EX 39 2RG
Phone: (0) 1237-474-474
Fax: (0) 1237-474-774
Email: roundhouse.group@ukgateway.net

CONTENTS

ACKNOWLEDGMENTS

My grateful thanks to all who have helped in the growth and development of this work. Special thanks to Norman Welsh who first introduced me to the Folio Text, and to Tina Packer who (with Kristin Linklater and all the members of Shakespeare & Co.) allowed me to explore the texts on the rehearsal floor. To Jane Nichols for her enormous generosity in providing the funding which allowed the material to be computerised. To James and Margaret McBride and Terry Lim for their expertise, good humour and hard work. To the National Endowment for the Arts for their award of a Major Artist Fellowship; to York University for their award of the Joseph G. Green Fellowship, and to The University of British Columbia for their award of an canada Council SSHRC grant to help in proofing, as well as a Faculty Workstation Improvement Grant. To actors, directors and dramaturgs at the Stratford Festival, Ontario, especially Richard Rose and the late Michael Mawson; Repercussion Theatre, Montreal; Toronto Free Theatre (that was); the Skylight Theatre, Toronto and Tamanhouse Theatre of Vancouver. To colleagues, friends and students at The University of British Columbia, Vancouver; York University, Toronto; Concordia University, Montreal; The National Theatre School of Canada in Montreal; Equity Showcase Theatre, Toronto; The Centre for Actors Study and Training (C.A.S.T.), Toronto; The National Voice Intensive, Vancouver; Studio 58 of Langara College, Vancouver; Professional Workshops in the Arts, Vancouver; U.C.L.A., Los Angeles; Loyola Marymount, Los Angeles; San Jose State College, California; Long Beach State College, California; Brigham Young University, Utah and Hawaii, especially Craig Ferre and Robert Nelson; Holy Cross College, Massachusetts; Guilford College, North Carolina. To John Wright and Don Paterson, in their respective offices of Chairman and Associate Dean at U.B.C., for their personal support and encouragement. To Donna Wong-Juliani for her generosity and patient advice. To Tom Scholte and Rachel Ditor for their timely research assistance. To Alan and Chris Baker, and Stephanie McWilliams for typographical advice. To Jay L. Halio, Hugh Richmond and G.B. Shand for their critical input. To Frank Hildy, Director of the Shakespeare Globe Centre (USA) – Research Archives, and to Mark Rylance, Artistic Director of Shakespeare's Globe for their support and encouragement. To the overworked and underpaid proofreading teams who supervised the material from which this series books stem, Ron Oten and Yuuattee Tanipersaud, Patrick Galligan and Leslie Barton, Janet Van De Graaff and Angela Dorhman (with input from Todd Sandomirsky, Bruce Alexander Pitkin, Catelyn Thornton and Michael Roberts); Alexia Hagen and Samantha Simmonds for their work specifically related to the three audition volumes. And above all to my wife Julie, for her patient encouragement, courteous advice, critical eye and long sufferance!

SPECIAL ACKNOWLEDGMENTS

Paul Sugarman for initiating and supervising the production of the original material, indeed without his perseverance, patience, hard work well above the call of duty, encouragement, belief and friendship, none of the earlier material (*The Applause First Folio of Shakespeare in Modern Type* and the publication of the 36 individual plays under the collective title *The Applause First Folio Editions*) would ever have become a reality. Glenn Young, founder of Applause Books, for persisting with the first oh-so crazy scheme. Greg Collins especially (and Rachel Reiss) of Applause for their original struggles to turn other people's chaos into a practical and standardised reality. Shannon Reed – now a teacher and a burgeoning playwright, then of Applause – for suggesting the idea of a series of audition volumes and agreeing to and then laying in the foundations of this new approach; John Cerullo and Kay Radtke for supporting her; and especially Michael Messina and Brian Black (and designer Courtney Napoles) for taking over the project and sticking with it through all its trials and tribulations. And a huge thank you to the eagle-eyed proofreader cum editor Erin Herlihy whose exemplary diligence has saved me from many an embarrassing moment.

MASTER LIST OF SPEECHES

EIGHTY-SEVEN SPEECHES FOR WOMEN

for titles and page numbers, see the detailed listing in front of each play

Titus Andronicus (5), pages 28 - 46

Tamora	**Traditional & Today:** woman, old/young enough to have three adult sons	#4, #6, #7, #14
Lavinia	**Traditional & Today:** young woman	#11

Romeo & Juliet (11), pages 48 - 95

Nurse	**Traditional:** middle-aged woman or older **Today:** woman old enough to have breast-fed Juliet fourteen years ago	#18, #20
Mother	**Traditional:** middle-aged woman or older **Today:** woman old enough to have a daughter fourteen years ago	#19
Juliet	**Traditional & Today:** young woman, almost fourteen	#22, #23, #24, #27, #28, #29, #30, #33

Julius Cæsar (5), pages 96 - 122

Calphurnia	**Traditional & Today:** middle-aged woman and older	#10
Portia	**Traditional & Today:** middle-aged woman, sometimes younger	#20, #21, #22, #23

Hamlet (5), pages 124 - 156

Ophelia	**Traditional & Today:** young woman	#10, #12, #20, #21
Queene	**Traditional & Today:** woman old enough to have an adult son	#22

Troylus & Cressida (6), pages 158 - 189

Cressida	**Traditional & Today:** young teenage woman	#3, #5, #6, #7
Cassandra	**Traditional & Today:** young to middle-aged woman	#19, #20

Othello (11), pages 190 - 226

Æmilia	**Traditional & Today:** young woman, younger than her sister Adrianna	#13, #22, #26, #28
Desdemona	**Traditional & Today:** middle-aged woman, or younger	#4, #5, #14, #15, #23
Bianca	**Traditional & Today:** an attractive young woman of the town	#20, #21

Macbeth (8), pages 228 - 258

Lady Macbeth	**Traditional & Today:** young woman and older	#3, #4, #5, #8, #9, #11, #12, #26

Timon (0: however, see 'Speeches For Either gender, below), pages 260 - 286

King Lear (9), pages 288 - 320

Gonerill	**Traditional & Today:** early middle age and older	#2, #14, #16, #17
Regan	**Traditional & Today:** early middle age and older	#3
Cordelia	**Traditional & Today:** young woman	#4, #8, #28, #29

Coriolanus (8), pages 322 - 355

Volumnia	**Traditional & Today:** older woman with son and young grandson	#1, #2, #14, #15, #16, #23, #24
Valeria	**Traditional & Today:** female, any age	#3

Anthony & Cleopatra (9), pages 356 - 389

Cleopatra	**Traditional:** middle-aged woman, and older **Today:** early middle-aged woman, and older	#8, #9, #11, #22, #23, #24, #25, #26
Charmian	**Traditional & Today:** younger woman	#3

Cymbeline (10), pages 390 - 425

Imogen	**Traditional & Today:** young woman	#1, #12, #13, #14, #16, #17, #24
Queene	**Traditional & Today:** woman with an adult son	#2, #21, #22

FORTY-ONE SPEECHES (& MORE) FOR EITHER GENDER

for titles and page numbers, see the detailed listing in front of each play

Titus Andronicus (1), pages 28 – 46

Marcus	**Traditional:** older man, brother to Titus **Today:** could be played as Titus' sister	#3

Romeo & Juliet (11), pages 48 - 95

Chorus	**Traditional:** older male **Today:** any gender, any age	#1, #2
Prince	**Traditional:** older male with two adult nephews **Today:** any gender with two adult nephews	#3, #37
Benvolio	**Traditional:** young male **Today:** any gender	#6, #13
Frier Lawrence	**Traditional:** older male **Today:** any gender, any age	#16, #25, #31, #32, #36

Julius Cæsar(4), pages 96 - 122

Caska	**Traditional:** male, any age, often late middle-aged or older **Today:** any age, any gender	#9, #19
Decius	**Traditional:** male, any age **Today:** any age, any gender	#11
Murellus	**Traditional:** older male **Today:** any age, any gender	#18

Hamlet (1), pages 124 - 156

Priest	**Traditional:** middle aged man and older **Today:** any age, any gender	#24

Troylus & Cressida (0), pages 158 - 189

Othello (1), pages 190 - 226

Brabantio	**Traditional:** older male with adult daughter **Today:** any gender	#2

Macbeth (5), pages 228 - 258

Captaine	**Traditional:** military male, any age **Today:** with the above proviso, any gender, any age	#1

Macbeth (ctd.)

Rosse	**Traditional:** older male **Today:** any age, any gender	#24
Old Man	**Traditional:** old male **Today:** older person, any gender	#17
Lenox	**Traditional:** older male **Today:** any age, any gender	#15, #22

Timon of Athens (13), pages 260 - 286

Poet	**Traditional:** male, any age **Today:** any age, any gender	#2, #15, #16
Painter	**Traditional:** male, any age **Today:** any age, any gender	#14
Steward	**Traditional:** older male, any age **Today:** any age, any gender	#4, #5
{Lucius}	**Traditional:** male, any age **Today:** any age, any gender	#7
Apermantus	**Traditional:** older male **Today:** any gender, any age – often middle age or older	#9, #10
Senators (x3)	**Traditional:** male, any age **Today:** any age, any gender	#3a, #3b, #18, #20

Coriolanus (3), pages 288 - 355

Brutus	**Traditional:** male, any age **Today:** any age, any gender	#7, #11
2nd Servingman	**Traditional:** male, any age **Today:** any age, any gender	#19

Anthony & Cleopatra (2), pages 356 - 389

Soothsayer	**Traditional:** male, any age **Today:** any age, any gender	#4
Agrippa	**Traditional:** male, any age **Today:** any age, any gender	#7

Cymbeline (1), pages 390 - 425

2nd Lord	**Traditional:** male, any age **Today:** any age, any gender	#4

ONE HUNDRED AND SEVENTY-FIVE SPEECHES FOR MEN

for titles and page numbers, see the detailed listing in front of each play

Titus Andronicus (11), pages 28 - 46

Role	Description	Speeches
Saturninus	**Traditional & Today:** young man who becomes Emperor	#1, #5
Bassianus	**Traditional & Today:** young man	#2
Demetrius	**Traditional & Today:** young man	#10
Aaron	**Traditional & Today:** young or early middle-aged black male	#13, #15, #16, #17
Titus	**Traditional & Today:** older male	#8, #9, #12

Romeo & Juliet (15), pages 48 - 95

Role	Description	Speeches
Capulet	**Traditional & Today:** early or middle-aged male with young teenage daughter	#4, #7, #8, #9, #10
Paris	**Traditional & Today:** young man	#11, #12
Mercutio	**Traditional:** young man, probably older than Romeo & Benvolio	#5, #14, #15, #17
Romeo	**Traditional & Today:** young man	#21, #26, #34, #35

Julius Cæsar (14), pages 96 - 122

Role	Description	Speeches
Cassius	**Traditional:** early middle-aged man and older **Today:** male, any age	#1, #2, #3, #8
Brutus	**Traditional:** early middle-aged man and older **Today:** male, any age	#4, #5, #6, #7
Caesar	**Traditional:** older male **Today:** middle-aged male and older	#12
Antony	**Traditional & Today:** younger man	#13, #14, #15, #16, #17

Hamlet (19), pages 124 - 156

Role	Description	Speeches
Hamlet	**Traditional & Today:** young man	#1, #3, #5, #6, #8, #11, #13, #14, #15, #16, #18
King	**Traditional & Today:** younger middle-aged man or older	#2, #7
Ghost	**Traditional & Today:** middle-aged man or older	#4
Polonius	**Traditional & Today:** older male	#9, #17, #19
Clown	**Traditional:** early middle-aged man and older **Today:** male, any age	#23
Laertes	**Traditional & Today:** young man	#25

Troylus & Cressida (15), pages 158 - 189

Role	Description	Speeches
Troylus	**Traditional & Today:** young, perhaps teenage, male	#1, #8, #21
Pandarus	**Traditional:** older man **Today:** male, old enough to have an adolescent niece	#2, #4
Ulysses	**Traditional:** capable military male, middle-aged or older **Today:** male, any age	#9, #10, #12
Achilles	**Traditional & Today:** male, any age capable of military action	#11
Thersites	**Traditional &Today:** male, any age, often cast as a twisted form of a jester, though commentator might be a better description	#13, #14, #15
Æneas	**Traditional:** capable military male, middle-aged or older **Today:** male, any age	#16
Hector	**Traditional & Today:** young married man	#17
Nestor	**Traditional & Today:** older male commander	#18

Othello (17), pages 190 - 226

Role	Description	Speeches
Iago	**Traditional & Today:** early middle-aged (and older) military man	#1, #6, #7, #8, #9, #10, #11, #12, #17
Othello	**Traditional & Today:** early middle-aged military man	#3a, #3b, #16, #18, #19, #24, #27, #29
Rodorigo	**Traditional:** younger male **Today:** any age, usually middle-aged or younger	#25

Macbeth (15), pages 228 - 258

Role	Description	Speeches
Macbeth	**Traditional & Today:** younger middle-aged male and older	#2, #7, #10, #19, #20, #21, #27
King	**Traditional & Today:** older male (father of two young adult sons)	#6
Porter	**Traditional & Today:** male, any age	#13, #14
Macduff	**Traditional & Today:** younger middle-aged male and older	#16, #25
Banquo	**Traditional & Today:** younger middle-aged male and older	#6, #18
Malcome	**Traditional & Today:** a young man	#23

Timon of Athens (8), (or women in an adventurous production) pages 260 - 286

Role	Description	Speeches
Timon	**Traditional:** older male **Today:** male/female of any age	#1, #6, #8, #11, #12, #13, #17, #19

King Lear (21), pages 288 - 320

Character	Description	Speeches
Lear	**Traditional & Today:** older male	#1, #5, #18, #21, #22, #23, #26, #27, #30
Foole	**Traditional:** an older male, even though Lear frequently refers to him as 'boy' **Today:** male, any age	#15, # 20, #24
Kent	**Traditional:** older male **Today:** male of any age	#6, #7, #19
Bastard	**Traditional & Today:** young man	#9, #11, #13
Edgar	**Traditional & Today:** young man	#12, #25
Gloucester	**Traditional & Today:** older man with two adult sons	#10

Coriolanus (13), pages 322 - 355

Character	Description	Speeches
Coriolanus	**Traditional & Today:** late-young/early middle-aged military man	#4, #12, #13, #17
Menenius	**Traditional & Today:** late middle-aged man, and older	#5, #6, #8
Cominius	**Traditional & Today:** middle-aged and older military man	#10, #20, #21
Auffidius	**Traditional & Today:** late-young/early middle-aged military man	#9, #18, #22, #24

Anthony & Cleopatra (15), pages 356 - 389

Character	Description	Speeches
Cæsar	**Traditional & Today:** male, from young to early middle age (always younger than Anthony)	#1, #13, #18
Anthony	**Traditional & Today:** middle-aged man and older	#10, #12, #14, #16, #20, #21
Enobarbus	**Traditional & Today:** older military male	#5, #6, #17, #19
Thidias	**Traditional & Today:** male, any age	#15
Ventidius	**Traditional & Today:** military man of any age	#2

Cymbeline (14), pages 390 - 425

Character	Description	Speeches
Cloten	**Traditional & Today:** a young man	#3, #19, #20
Iachimo	**Traditional & Today:** a young to middle-aged male	#5, #6, #7, #8, #9
Posthumus	**Traditional & Today:** a young man	#10
Pisanio	**Traditional:** older male **Today:** male, any age, often middle-aged and older	#11, #15
Arviragus	**Traditional & Today:** young male	#23
Belarius	**Traditional & Today:** male old enough to be 'father' to two young men	#18
Cymbeline	**Traditional & Today:** male old enough to have a teenage daughter	#25

PREFACE AND BRIEF BACKGROUND TO THE FIRST FOLIO

WHY ANOTHER SERIES OF SOLILOQUY BOOKS?

There has been an enormous change in theatre organisation in the last twenty years. While the major large-scale companies have continued to flourish, many small theatre companies have come into being, leading to

- much doubling
- cross gender casting, with many one time male roles now being played legitimately by/as women in updated time-period productions
- young actors being asked to play leading roles at far earlier points in their careers

All this has meant actors should be able to demonstrate enormous flexibility rather than one limited range/style. In turn, this has meant

- a change in audition expectations
- actors are often expected to show more range than ever before
- often several shorter audition speeches are asked for instead of one or two longer ones
- sometimes the initial auditions are conducted in a shorter amount of time

Thus, to stay at the top of the game, the actor needs more knowledge of what makes the play tick, especially since

- early plays demand a different style from the later ones
- the four genres (comedy, history, tragedy, and the peculiar romances) all have different acting/textual requirements
- parts originally written for the older, more experienced actors again require a different approach from those written for the younger ones, as the young roles, especially the female ones, were played by young actors extraordinarily skilled in the arts of rhetoric

There's now much more knowledge of how the original quarto and folio texts can add to the rehearsal exploration/acting and directing process as well as to the final performance.

No matter how well prepared, no current soliloquy book deals directly with the bulk of these concerns. [1]

HOW THIS SERIES OF BOOKS MIGHT HELP YOUR EXPLORATION

This series is intended to help you explore your audition pieces theatrically, so that you can discover the extra details of humanity that the original texts automatically offer. Thus they do not provide much academic or comparative analysis; rather you will find in the commentary to each speech details and full discussions of the devices peculiar to that speech's genre and the age and gender of the character, so that the particular idiosyncratic characteristics each speech presents can be **practically** explored in and of themselves in whatever way you wish.

In the series as a whole, there are over 900 separate audition possibilities, some of which have been created by adding two or more consecutive shorter speeches from the same scene

- 301 in the Comedy Volume
- 298 in the History Volume
- 304 in the Tragedy Volume

about six hundred more than in any other series.

At the beginning of each play, the speeches are coded as suitable for women, either sex, or men; and approximate audition time is offered, with speeches ranging from twenty-five seconds to three minutes.

Each speech is made up of four parts

- a **background** to the speech, placing it in the context of the play, and offering **line length** and an **approximate timing** to help you choose what might be right for any auditioning occasion
- a **modern text version** of the speech, with unobtrusive symbols

[1] Though offering sensible basic guidelines as to how to use the original material, the recent publications of Patrick Tucker show the First Folio text only.

showing where editors have changed the original texts' sentence structure, capitalisation and spelling

• a **folio version** of the speech, with unobtrusive symbols showing where modern texts have intensified or diminished, added or removed punctuation

• a **commentary** explaining the differences between the two texts, and in what way the original setting can offer you more information to explore

Thus if they wish, **beginners** can explore just the background and the modern text version of the speech.

An **actor experienced in exploring the Folio** can make use of the background and the Folio version of the speech

And those wanting to know as many details as possible and how they could help define the deft stepping stones of the arc of the speech can use all four elements on the page.

THE FIRST FOLIO (for a list of current reproductions see Bibliography)

Late in 1621 or early in 1622 two men brought to the son of a somewhat disreputable printer an idea that was to change the face of literature and theatre for ever. The men were John Heminge and William Condell. The son, also a printer, was Isaac Jaggard. [2] The idea was to publish all the available plays written in whole or in part by the late William Shakespeare, who had died in 1616, and with whom they had been actors, business partners, colleagues, and friends for more than twenty years.

The end of 1623 saw the publication of the justifiably famed First Folio (F1). The single volume, published in a run of approximately 1,000 copies at the princely sum of one pound (a tremendous risk, considering that a single play would sell at no more than six pence, one fortieth of F1's price, and that the annual salary of a schoolmaster was only ten pounds), contained thirty-six plays.

The manuscripts from which each F1 play would be printed came from a variety of sources. Some had already been printed. Some came from the playhouse complete with production details. Some had no theatrical input at all, but were handsomely copied out and easy to read. Some were supposedly very messy, complete with first draft scribbles and crossings out. Yet, as Charlton Hinman, the revered dean of First Folio studies describes F1

> it is of inestimable value for what it is, for what it contains . . .
> For here are preserved the masterworks of the man universally recognized as our greatest writer; and preserved, as Ben Jonson realized at the time of the original publication, not for an age but for all time [3]

WHAT DOES F1 REPRESENT? [4] (the opening three bolded points being the most important considerations for this audition series)

• **texts prepared for actors who rehearsed three days for a new play and one day for one already in the repertoire**

• **written in a style (rhetoric incorporating debate) so different from ours (grammatical) that many modern alterations based on grammar (or poetry) have done remarkable harm to the rhetorical/debate quality of the original text and thus to interpretations of characters at key moments of stress.**

• **written for an acting company the core of which steadily grew older, and whose skills and interests changed markedly over twenty years**

• the texts having to be flexible enough to satisfy requests for private performances in the Inns of Court, private houses, and especially at Court

• represents a writing career of more than twenty years

---

[2] William, his father, had had a somewhat chequered reputation with fraudulent printing of theatre documents: two incidents had involved his publishing works by Shakespeare to which he was not entitled, and claiming works to be Shakespeare's which most definitely were not: William, nominally the head of the house of Jaggard, was blind and died before the Folio was published.

[3] Introduction to the 1996 photostat of the First Folio, *The Norton Facsimile,* page ix.

[4] All of what follows is discussed in great detail in the first seventy-two pages of *The Applause First Folio of Shakespeare in Modern Type.*

- presents thirty-six plays [5] [6]

- spaced over two monarchs, Elizabeth and James, the second of whom allowed for a greater deal of examination of the personal dilemma of those in authority, and the questioning of their mistakes

- for at least two thirds of Shakespeare's career, written for one permanent company that enjoyed huge aristocratic and, eventually, royal protection, thus ensuring it was always one of the few companies guaranteed a playing space in London

- played in two widely different spaces: at the beginning of Shakespeare's career, outdoor theatres in the less salubrious parts of London catering per performance to 2,500 spectators from all strands of society; by the end of his career, to a wealthier and socially more acceptable group of 700 per performance in an indoor theatre in the better part of the City of London

- for an audience whose make-up and interests likewise changed as the company grew more experienced

The whole is based upon supposedly the best documents available at the time, collected by men closest to Shakespeare throughout his career, and brought to a single printing house whose errors are now widely understood – far more than those of some of the printing houses that produced the original quartos.

TEXTUAL SOURCES FOR THE AUDITION SPEECHES

Individual modern editions consulted in the preparation of the Modern Text version of the speeches are listed in the Bibliography under the separate headings 'The Complete Works in Compendium Format' and 'The Complete Works in Separate Individual Volumes.' Most of the modern versions of the speeches are a compilation of several of these texts. However, all modern act, scene and/or line numbers refer the reader to *The Riverside Shakespeare*, in my opinion still the best of the complete works despite the excellent compendiums that have been published since.

The First Folio versions of the speeches are taken from a variety of already published sources, including not only all the texts listed in the 'Photostatted Reproductions in Compendium Format' section of the Bibliography, but also earlier, individually printed volumes, such as the twentieth century editions published under the collective title *The Facsimiles of Plays from The First Folio of Shakespeare* by Faber & Gwyer, and the nineteenth century editions published on behalf of The New Shakespere Society.

---

[5] Though appearing in an early quarto version (1609), Pericles did not appear in a Folio publication till the Third Folio of 1664. Three other plays attributed in whole or part to Shakespeare

a/ *Sir Thomas More*, finally collated from various manuscripts in 1911

b/ *The Two Noble Kinsmen*, the best regarded edition being the quarto of 1634

c/ the more recently proposed *King Edward III*, first attributed to Shakespeare in 1656

were never included in any of the first four Folios (1623, 1632, 1664 and 1685) and thus have not been included in this audition series. Similarly, though wonderful in and of themselves, none of the purely poetical works, e.g the *Sonnets*, *Venus and Adonis*, *The Rape of Lucrece* etc., have been included.

[6] it is the only source for eighteen plays, the better source for six more, and co-source for a further two — i.e. valued for twenty-six of the thirty-six plays presented: for the remaining ten, though most modern editors prefer the quarto versions of the play in some cases (*Troylus & Cressida* and *Titus Andronicus*), such choice is by no means universal: the differences between the two sets of texts are not always substantive either in plot or language used, but more often in what most scholars term the accidentals (the spellings, punctuation, and capitalisation). In some cases the differences are minimal (an almost identical sentence structure and positioning of major punctuation in both quarto and F1 *Merchant of Venice* for example); however, in certain plays (*Romeo & Juliet* and *Othello*), differentiations in single word usage are quite marked, occasioning serious choice by editors and readers alike. What F1 rarely contains are the oaths and blasphemies so common to plays written prior to the 1606 Acte to Restraine the Abuses of Players — in effect the Acte caused every such reference in any subsequent printed work to be removed. Thus every quarto, which were all printed prior to 1606, contained offensive matter, all of which were supposedly removed before the printing of F1 — not always successfully, as occasional references in F1's Hamlet show.

INTRODUCTION

So, congratulations, you've got an audition, and for a Shakespeare play no less.

You've done all your homework, including, hopefully, reading the whole play to see the full range and development of the character.

You've got an idea of the character, the situation in which you/it finds itself (the given circumstances); what your/its needs are (objectives/intentions); and what you intend to do about them (action/tactics).

You've looked up all the unusual words in a good dictionary or glossary; you've turned to a well edited modern edition to find out what some of the more obscure references mean.

And those of you who understand metre and rhythm have worked on the poetic values of the speech, and you are word perfect . . .

. . . and yet it's still not working properly and/or you feel there's more to be gleaned from the text, but you're not sure what that something is or how to go about getting at it; in other words, all is not quite right, yet.

THE KEY QUESTION

What text have you been working with — a good modern text or an 'original' text, that is, a copy of one of the first printings of the play?

If it's a modern text, no matter how well edited (and there are some splendid single copy editions available, see the Bibliography for further details), and despite all the learned information offered, it's not surprising you feel somewhat at a loss, for there is a huge difference between the original printings (the First Folio, and the individual quartos, see Appendix 1 for further details) and any text prepared after 1700 right up to the most modern of editions. All the post-1700 texts have been tidied-up for the modern reader to ingest silently, revamped according to the rules of correct grammar, syntax, and poetry. However, the 'originals' were prepared for actors speaking aloud, playing characters often in a great deal of emotional and/or intellectual stress, and were set down on paper according to the very flexible rules of rhetoric with a seemingly very cavalier attitude towards the rules of grammar, syntax, spelling, capitalisation, and even poetry.[7]

Unfortunately, because of the grammatical and syntactical standardisation in place by the early 1700's, many of the quirks and oddities of the originals have been dismissed as 'accidental' — usually as compositor error either in deciphering the original manuscript, falling prey to their own particular idosyncracies, or not having calculated correctly the amount of space needed to set the text. Modern texts dismiss the possibility that these very quirks and oddities may be by Shakespeare, hearing his characters in as much difficulty as poor Peter Quince is in *A Midsummer Night's Dream* (when he, as the Prologue, terrified and struck down by stage fright, makes a huge grammatical hash in introducing his play 'Pyramus and Thisbe' before the aristocracy, whose acceptance or otherwise, can make or break him)

If we offend, it is with our good will .
That you should think, we come not to offend,
But with good will .
To show our simple skill,
That is the true beginning of our end .
Consider then, we come but in despite.
We do not come, as minding to content you ,
Our true intent is.
All for your delight
We are not here.
That you should here repent you,
The Actors are at hand; and by their show,
You shall know all, that you are like to know.

(*A Midsummer Night's Dream*, speech #39)

In many other cases in the complete works what was originally printed is equally 'peculiar,' but, unlike Peter Quince, these peculiarities are usually regularised by most modern texts.

However, this series of volumes is based on the belief — as the following will show — that most of these 'peculiarities' resulted from Shakespeare setting down for his actors the stresses, trials, and tribulations the characters are experiencing as they think and speak, and thus are theatrical gold-dust for the actor, director, scholar, teacher, and general reader alike.

---

[7] See Freeman, Neil, *Shakespeare's First Texts*, distributed by Applause Books, New York & London: 2nd. edition. 1999.

THE FIRST ESSENTIAL DIFFERENCE BETWEEN THE TWO TEXTS

THINKING

A **modern** text can show

- the story line
- your character's conflict with the world at large
- your character's conflict with certain individuals within that world

but because of the very way an **'original'** text was set, it can show you all this plus one key extra, the very thing that makes big speeches what they are

- the conflict within the character

WHY?

Any good playwright writes about characters in stressful situations who are often in a state of conflict not only with the world around them and the people in that world, but also within themselves. And you probably know from personal experience that when these conflicts occur people do not necessarily utter the most perfect of grammatical/poetic/syntactic statements, phrases, or sentences. Joy and delight, pain and sorrow often come sweeping through in the way things are said, in the incoherence of the phrases, the running together of normally disassociated ideas, and even in the sounds of the words themselves.

The tremendous advantage of the period in which Shakespeare was setting his plays down on paper and how they first appeared in print was that when characters were rational and in control of self and situation, their phrasing and sentences (and poetic structure) would appear to be quite normal even to a modern eye — but when things were going wrong, so sentences and phrasing (and poetic structure) would become highly erratic. But the Quince-type eccentricities are rarely allowed to stand. Sadly, in tidying, most modern texts usually make the text far too clean, thus setting rationality when none originally existed, as with

Shylock: in the famous 'hath not a Jew eyes' speech, where the original onrush of four (quarto) or five (First Folio) sentences, suggesting a tremendous release and lack of control, has been turned into at least fifteen (sometimes sixteen, even seventeen) sentences of tidy grammatical correctness by most modern texts. Thus the ravings and anger of the original Shylock have been turned into the calm debate of a noble rational creature, a tremendous difference and one which has created a totally different arc/journey/character than, presumably, originally intended (Comedy Auditions, *The Merchant of Venice*, speech #21).

King Henry: in a speech set only in the First Folio, where alone after spending the night with his soldiers, he wonders aloud about the burdens laid upon any monarch, the highly irregular opening line structure is a wonderful testament to the struggle within him — a struggle eradicated by most modern texts that restructure the passage to create poetically correct (ten syllable) verse lines throughout. (History Auditions, *Henry V*, speech #14).

Mercutio: in the famous Queen Mab speech, despite both the good quarto (Q2) and the First Folio setting the speech as a mixture of prose and verse — with some meanderings in the order of what he is talking about, suggesting a character not necessarily in full control of himself (already drunk before the Capulet party perhaps) — most modern texts reset the speech as pretty verse throughout AND restructure the order of some of the lines to reconstruct a Mercutio in their own image, logical and gracefully verbal. (Tragedy Auditions, *Romeo & Juliet,* speech #14).

THE SECOND ESSENTIAL DIFFERENCE BETWEEN THE TWO TEXTS

SPEAKING, ARGUING, DEBATING

Having discovered what and how you/your character is thinking is only the first stage of the work — you/it then have to speak aloud, in a society that absolutely loved to speak — and not only speak ideas (content) but to speak entertainingly so as to keep listeners enthralled (and this was especially so when you have little content to offer and have to mask it somehow — think of today's television adverts and political spin doctors as a parallel and you get the picture). Indeed one of the Elizabethan 'how to win an argument' books was very precise about this — George Puttenham, *The Art of English Poesie* (1589).

A: Elizabethan Schooling

All educated classes could debate/argue at the drop of a hat, for both boys (in 'petty-schools') and girls (by books and tutors) were trained in what was known overall as the art of rhetoric, which itself was split into three parts

- first, how to distinguish the real from false appearances/outward show (think of the three caskets in *The Merchant of Venice* where the language on the gold and silver caskets enticingly, and deceptively, seems to offer hopes of great personal rewards that are dashed when the language is carefully explored, whereas once the apparent threat on the lead casket is carefully analysed the reward therein is the greatest that could be hoped for)
- second, how to frame your argument on one of 'three great grounds'; honour/morality; justice/legality; and, when all else fails, expedience/practicality
- third, how to order and phrase your argument so winsomely that your audience will vote for you no matter how good the opposition — and there were well over two hundred rules and variations by which winning could be achieved, all of which had to be assimilated before a child's education was considered over and done with.

In many ways this gave rise to what could be called the **ice-skating Shakespeare**, where you, as a speaker, awarded yourself points both for style as well as content

- with good content and good style you might give yourself a 100% score in each category, a perfect '6'
- with good content but boringly delivered you might give yourself 5.9 for content but only 1.5 for style
- while with poor content but excellently delivered, your score might be 1.2 for content but a triumphant 6 for style! — a fine example of audience-applauding-flim-flam-artistry at its very best!!

B: Thinking On Your Feet : i.e. The Quick, Deft, Rapid Modification Of Each Tiny Thought

The Elizabethan/therefore your character/therefore you were also trained to explore and modify your thoughts as you spoke — never would you see a sentence in its entirety and have it perfectly worked out in your mind before you spoke (unless it was a deliberately written, formal public declaration, as with the Officer of the Court in *The Winter's Tale*, reading the charges against Hermione). Thus after uttering your very first phrase, you might expand it, or modify it, deny it, change it, and so on throughout the whole sentence and speech.

Several modern acting dictums will serve to explain how this works today, in any form of script

- from the superb French director, actor and mime Jean Louis Barrault — "acting is staying in the ever-changing present"
- from the noted Shakespeare director, and for many years the highly regarded head of the prestigious Juilliard School (U.S.A.), Michael Langham — "characters have to speak aloud to discover exactly what it is they know and feel"
- from Rudi Shelley, for many years the mainstay of the acting programme at the famous Bristol Old Vic Theatre School (U.K.)— who

asked actors to ask once they've done or said something, "What happens next?"

- two wonderful acting truisms — "acting is reacting," and ask "**why** do you say, **what** you say, **when** you say it, **in** the way you say it"

And from the poet Samuel Coleridge Taylor there is a wonderful description of how Shakespeare puts thoughts together like "a serpent twisting and untwisting in its own strength," that is, with one thought springing out of the one previous. Treat each new phrase as a fresh unravelling of the serpent's coil. What is discovered (and therefore said) is only revealed as the old coil/phrase disappears revealing a new coil in its place. The new coil is the new thought. The old coil moves/disappears because the previous phrase is finished with as soon as it is spoken.

C: Modern Application

It is very rarely we speak dispassionately in our 'real' lives. After all thoughts give rise to feelings, feelings give rise to thoughts, and we usually speak both together — unless

1/ we're trying very hard for some reason to control ourselves and not give ourselves away. For example

- we want to ensure people listen to our arguments and are not distracted by any unnecessary emotion, so that they have to deal with the points we are making and cannot slough us off with the awful comment 'why don't we talk about this when you're feeling a little calmer/when you're not so worked up/when you're not so hysterical!'
- we simply have to control ourselves otherwise we'll lose face, or the way and/or the what of what we're talking about

2/ the volcano of emotions within us is so strong that we cannot control ourselves, and feelings swamp thoughts, and so, for example,

- we bellow with laughter
- we whoop with joy
- we scream with pain or fear
- we cannot contain our fury

3/ and sometimes, whether deliberately or unconsciously, we colour words according to our feelings. Think of Woody Allen in Annie Hall protesting his 'love,' 'lerve,' 'looove,' etc. for the character played by Diane Keaton, or the catch phrase or punch line of any TV personality or cartoon: while the spelling is horrific, the humanity behind the words so revealed is instantly understandable.

D: How The Original Texts Naturally Enhance/Underscore This Control Or Release

The amazing thing about the way all Elizabethan/early Jacobean texts were first set down (the term used to describe the printed words on the page being 'orthography'), is that it was flexible, it allowed for such variations to be automatically set down without fear of grammatical repercussion.

So if Shakespeare heard Juliet's nurse working hard to try to convince Juliet to set her sights on the Prince's nephew whom Juliet is being forced to (bigamously) marry, instead of setting the everyday normal

O he's a lovely gentleman

which the modern texts HAVE to set, the first printings were permitted to set

O hee"s a Lovely Gentleman

suggesting that something might be going on inside the Nurse that causes her to release such excessive extra energy.

Now the First Folio (and the second quarto too, for both well-regarded original texts set the text in exactly the same way) don't tell you, the actor, what is going on or how to play/say the moment, but the long-spelled 'hee's' and capitalised 'Lovely Gentleman' certainly guide you to where you might want to explore.

E: Be Careful

This needs to be stressed very carefully: the orthography doesn't dictate to you/force you to accept exactly what it means (it could be fear of being fired by Juliet's parents if she fails to persuade Juliet to marry Paris; it could be fear of Juliet herself; it could be extra wheedling because she knows Juliet loathes Paris; it could be embarrassment at having to persuade Juliet to this second marriage when she was a go-between for the first; it could even be an attempt to comfort Juliet in an attempt to get her to accept the inevitable). The orthography simply suggests you might want to explore this moment further or more deeply.

In other words, simply because of the flexibility with which the Elizabethans/Shakespeare could set down on paper what they heard in their minds or wanted their listeners to hear, in addition to all the modern acting necessities of character — situation, objective, intention, action, and tactics — the original Shakespeare texts offer pointers to where feelings (either emotional or intellectual, or when combined together as passion, both) are also evident.

So everyone when speaking, even messengers who know what they are going to say, shows signs of reacting to what they say as they say it, and reveals feelings about it, as with the Messenger obviously furious with the English nobles whose squabbling has left their generals facing almost certain defeat in France (History Auditions, *Henry VI Part I*, speech #1), and the most objective attempts at neutrality usually fail, as with Exeter reporting the deaths of two of his closest friends (History Auditions, *Henry V,* speech #17).

PRINCIPLES APPLICABLE TO ALL THE PLAYS

EXPLORING WHETHER YOU ARE IN CONTROL OR NOT

PRINCIPLES, PART ONE: A SILLY GUIDE TO THE DIFFERENT SORTS OF THINKING WITHIN A FIRST FOLIO/QUARTO SHAKESPEARE SPEECH

(just the ideas will be discussed here, examples will be shown in the section **Practical Exploration**, page 18)

A: NOW I'M IN CONTROL (something the modern texts always maintain)

This is easily seen, because though you are looking at an 'original' text

- the sentences appear grammatical (though not originally set with such grammatical niceties in mind)
- the phrasing is logical
- the line structure complies with the ten syllable pattern expected of 'regular' Shakespearean verse

TWO FORMS OF CONTROL MOST MODERN TEXTS USUALLY MAINTAIN

- the **expected I-am-in-control** character: the situation is normal, and you/your character appear to be handling it quite easily
- the **unexpected I-am-in-control** character: where, despite the fact the situation is anything but normal, you/your character still appear to be handling it quite easily — this is a fascinating one, because it suggests you have/your character has a wonderful sense of purpose or self-control, and should be truly applauded for remaining calm despite every provocation to the contrary

B: AND NOW I'VE LOST CONTROL — what the modern texts almost never maintain

You must be beware when modern texts alter the original texts' layout to be grammatically or poetically tidy (thus creating rationality which wasn't originally intended), not only because it ain't necessarily so but also because, just as maintaining control in a very difficult situation is of tremendous theatrical interest to your audience (and hopefully you), what is equally, perhaps even more, interesting is when the character does lose control.

In the 'original' texts this loss of control can be seen in four different ways

1/ THE SENTENCES ARE NOT GRAMMATICAL, BUT ARE

onrushed, i.e. ideas modern texts set as separate grammatical sentences F1 joins together in one longer sentence, connected by a grammatically incorrect comma, colon, semicolon, or no punctuation at all, as when Iago jams together in one sentence his hatred of Othello immediately onto the preceding seemingly casual discussion of cheating Rodorigo — a syntactically appalling conjunction most modern texts separate into two different grammatically correct sentences — creating rationality where the original text set momentary lack of control (Tragedy Auditions, *Othello*, speech #9)

or set as **very short sentences**, as if an idea is complete in and of itself without further elaboration, as with the opening five sentences of Constance's reaction to the appalling news that her son's legitimate claim to the English throne has been abandoned as a matter of political convenience (History Auditions, *King John*, speech #20); or Coriolanus' one word sentence of greeting ('Thanks.') to his fellow aristocrat busy with putting down a potential lower-class riot; or Edmund's exploration of his 'bastardy' as opposed to his brother Edgar being 'legitimate' (Tragedy Auditions, *King Lear*, speech #9)

2/ THERE IS SUDDENLY A HUGE AMOUNT OF EXTRA MAJOR PUNCTUATION (SEMICOLONS [;] OR COLONS [:])

suggesting that the mind is putting ideas together very explosively — and note this doesn't dictate how the ideas are to be spoken, for they could be uttered

with great control, as with Don Pedro who in order to punish Benedicke for challenging their mutual friend Claudio to a duel to the death, strips Benedicke of any illusions as to what Beatrice actually thinks of him (Comedy Auditions, *Much Ado About Nothing*, speech #16)

with much release, as when Falstaffe reveals plans to woo the two married women Mrs. Page and Mrs. Ford in order to gain access to their husband's wealth, (Comedy Auditions, *Merry Wives of Windsor*, speech #1)

3/ THERE ARE SUDDENLY A LOT OF EXTRA COMMAS (NOT SET BY MOST MODERN TEXTS)

as if the character needs either to split up thoughts into even **more tiny details**, as with Cymbeline when declaring opposition to Rome, even if it means war (Tragedy Auditions, *Cymbeline*, speech #25)

or needs the extra breaths **to control itself** before continuing, as with Rosalind when attempting to persuade Orlando of the foolishness of love (Comedy Auditions, *As You Like It*, speech #16)

4/ THE LENGTH OF THE VERSE LINE IS EITHER

longer than ten syllables, suggesting that the character's thoughts are running away with it as with Romeo, first seeing Juliet on the balcony, with both quarto/First Folio setting an exuberant 16 syllables

> It is my lady: O it is my love; O that she knew she were.
>
> (Tragedy Auditions, *Romeo & Juliet*, speech #21)

which most modern texts reset more politely as a regular ten syllable line plus a short six syllable one

> It is my lady: O it is my love;
> O that she knew she were.

shorter than ten syllables, suggesting that the character needs time to think or react, as with Lenox taking so many pauses in telling Macbeth of the peculiarities of the night following the murder of Duncan (Tragedy Auditions, *Macbeth*, speech #15).

THUS THERE ARE TWO FORMS OF LOSS OF CONTROL MOST MODERN TEXTS HARDLY EVER MAINTAIN

- once the situation is understood and seen as stressful, the **expected oh-my-gosh-I'm losing-it**-Shakespeare
- when the situation is understood and seen as fairly routine, the **unexpected oh-my-gosh-I'm losing-it**-Shakespeare

PRINCIPLES PART TWO: A SILLY GUIDE TO THE DIFFERENT SORTS OF SPEAKING WITHIN A FIRST FOLIO/QUARTO SHAKESPEARE SPEECH

(just the ideas will be discussed here, examples will be shown in the section **Practical Exploration**, page 18)

A: THE ICE-COLD SHAKESPEARE

this is when you and the character seem to be completely at ease with no excesses in capitalisation or spelling

the **expected** ice-cold Shakespeare is when you/your character are under no stress and can easily handle the given situation; everything is well under control — here the lack of excess reflects the ease of the moment e.g. most of the Sonnets

the **unexpected** ice-cold Shakespeare is when you/your character are under a great deal of stress, and the situation is proving very difficult to handle: unless you are very careful everything will spin out of control, and yet there are no excesses in spelling or capitalisation. This case suggests you are struggling to maintain an enforced calm in order to keep a lid on yourself/others or things in general, and succeeding, e.g., the just married Blanche in *King John* who speaks very carefully though torn apart by the impending battle between France and England (her husband is French and the uncle she owes fealty to is English).

B: THE EINSTEIN SHAKESPEARE

this is when you/your character's mind has to work very hard to come to terms with/fully understand the situation, or to explore the idea to its fullest, or to persuade yourself or others to a particular point of view — and in the text there are lots of capital letters, pointing to the key conceptual words you/your character needs defined, or understood, or acknowledged or explored.

the **expected** Einstein Shakespeare is when it is obvious your character has to work so hard because of the given circumstances, discovery, needs, or challenges facing it — e.g. much of Hermione's self-defence against her husband's unwarranted charges of treason in *The Winter's Tale*.

the **unexpected** Einstein Shakespeare is when despite the fact that the situation/circumstances/needs seem quite normal or even casual, nevertheless you/your character's mind is shown to be working very hard: (for those who enjoy their Monty Python, this could well be a case of 'my brain hurts, Brian'!) e.g. when *Romeo and Juliet*'s Mercutio analyses Tybalt's qualities, both silly and dangerous, for a skeptical Benvolio.

C: THE RUSSIAN SHAKESPEARE

this is when the text includes lots of long spellings, allowing the stress to come into the words, thus revealing the emotions (good or bad) underneath: (why call it Russian? Just a tip of the hat to the wonderful releases of temperament associated with that great nation, i.e. when you're happy, you're VERY HAPPY! and when you're sad, you're INCREDIBLY SAD!)

- the **expected** Russian Shakespeare is when you/your character are under obvious stress, the text shows it, and the listeners on- and off-stage expect such excesses, e.g. when *Midsummer Night's Dream* Lysander plights his troth after being transformed by Oberon/Puck's charm into 'Helen's knight.'

- the **unexpected** Russian Shakespeare is when you/your character are under no apparent stress, nevertheless the text displays lots of long spellings revealing a surprising release of very strong emotions — e.g. the King's fulsome praise of Helena in an attempt to persuade Bertram to agree voluntarily to marry her in *All's Well That Ends Well*.

D: THE VOLCANIC SHAKESPEARE

this is when the text is simply swamped with both long spellings and capital letters and you do not/cannot control yourself — this could be because of the delights of joy, laughter, love or the pain of fear, hate (and love)

the **expected** volcanic Shakespeare is when the situation is so overwhelming (whether for good or bad, and whether because of the circumstances surrounding you/your character, or because of your/the character's inner needs/desires) the text is swamped with releases, and such releases are understandable — e.g. Octavius Cæsar's ravings about Mark Anthony's dallying with Cleopatra in *Anthony and Cleopatra*.

the **unexpected** volcanic Shakespeare is when, despite the fact that the situation seems quite normal, or even casual, the text is nevertheless surprisingly swamped: here the excessive releases may not be what people expect, as with the 2nd Lord in *Cymbeline* listing the stupidities of the dysfunctional royal family, the effect of the unexpected can range from the appalling to the comic (indeed the wonderful book *The Craft Of Comedy*, by Athene Syler and Stephen Haggard, suggests much of the truly comic is based on the unexpectedly volcanic — viz. contrast, distortion, and surprise).

PRINCIPLES PART THREE: ELIZABETHAN/EARLY JACOBEAN CONSIDERATIONS MIGHT BE USEFUL WHEN EXPLORING THE ORIGINAL TEXTS

As discussed above in Elizabethan Schooling (page 6), the **plays are just as much about debate and discovery as poetry and emotion**. Thus no matter how purple the passage or how dense the text, there is always a reason for the complexity or simplicity in the characters' language and imagery. Thus it's important to **distinguish between the two strands that composed the English of the day, Anglo-Saxon simplicity** (single syllable words) and **European complexity** (multi-syllable words). Thus

Though you/your character can speak quite complex language, when you/your character speaks a line, or more, composed of monosyllables, as with Juliet's questioning of Romeo

> Doest thou Love [ ] ?
> I know thou wilt say I,
> And I will take thy word, yet if thou swear'st,
> Thou maiest prove false
>
> (*Romeo & Juliet*, speech #23)

your questioning/exploration/discovery is so immediate that you have no time for indulging yourself in words — you are being direct and honest.

However, when the opposite occurs, when though you/your character can speak quite simply but indulges in some wonderful many-syllable words, it would suggest that no matter what the situation, you/your character have time to enjoy not only what you say but the way you say it, as with Falstaffe's talking to the audience about the horrors of being thrown into the river Thames, with a wonderful final phrase

> The rogues slighted me into the river
> with as little remorse, as they would have drown'de a
> blinde bitches Puppies, fifteene i'th litter : and you may
> know by my size, that I have a kinde of alacrity in sinking:
>
> (*Merry Wives of Windsor*, speech #10)

After all 'I have a kinde of alacrity in sinking' could have been set as the more urgent and fearful monosyllabic 'a man of my girth sinks like a stone,' but the superb sound and sweep of Shakespeare's original phrasing has a much better ring to it, and smacks of the entertainer enjoying himself with his friends — here, the audience — at his own expense.

Of necessity, **your character has to be incredibly selfish** since scholars tell us

- there were only three days of rehearsal for any new play
- there was only one day of rehearsal for a remount
- the original actor was never given a full copy of the play, just their 'sides' (i.e. their character's speeches themselves and the cue line from whatever character preceded them and thus triggered/cued each speech)

Thus **the inner needs of your character are just as important as any other character on stage**, since that's all the original actor would have known. This means that

- in any two handed scene there are four different characters on-stage, the 'private you' and the 'public you,' the 'private other' and the 'public other,' thus
- when the 'public you' speaks, the next thought can reflect some sort of response from the 'private you' within
- this is especially marked whenever there is a solo speech, soliloquy, or aside.
- thus, your character must play its own needs and scene to the utmost and never play the other character's scene even if your character is subordinate to them status-wise: the scene is just as much, if not more so, about the messenger delivering the news as it is about how the leading characters receive it.

Overall, Shakespeare texts demand that an actor is capable of creating

- in the best sense of the word, a very selfish character capable of pushing its own needs to the utmost
- a character that can think quickly on its feet, constantly reassess what is happening to it, and respond/change direction, tactics, and argument accordingly
- a character that adores language; after all, Shakespeare himself is credited with inventing a myriad of new words and a wondrous series of phrases and maxims that are still in common use today.

EXPLORING THE TRAGEDIES

DECIDING WHETHER YOU ARE IN CONTROL OR NOT

PRACTICAL EXPLORATIONS PART ONE: COMPARING THE TWO TEXTS

(CLARITY OF THOUGHT: THE NATURE OF DEBATE)

(which will become much clearer as you explore each separate audition speech)

N.B. any words surrounded by square brackets [ ] point to a text difference between the original & modern texts

1/ FIRST, LOOK AT THE SENTENCES (the large-scale organisation of the speech)
Onrush; Analysis/Debate

AS A RULE OF THUMB

In general, when a period/full stop appears it indicates that one idea has been finished with and you/the character is moving on to something new. And because every Elizabethan was trained to explore an idea to it's fullest, sentences as first set in the original texts are often much longer than their modern counterparts, suggesting a much more focused and concentrated exploration, expression, and release.

WHEN THE SENTENCE STRUCTURES OF THE ORIGINAL AND MODERN TEXTS MATCH

If they do, if the original has not been restructured by the modern texts, then it would seem that the Elizabethan rhetoric is matched by modern grammar and, as far as the organisation of thinking goes, your character seems to be **rational** and in **self-control.**

WHEN THE SENTENCE STRUCTURES DON'T MATCH

A: WHEN THERE ARE **MORE** MODERN TEXT SENTENCES THAN ORIGINALLY SET

if you are faced with sentence(s) in the original text being split up into smaller units by most modern texts, then, as originally set, you/your character can be said to be in a state of **onrush**, that is your ideas are being piled one on top of another in a single much longer release than grammar would normally dictate, which leads to either

a fairly rational onrush: if at the point where the new modern sentence has been created, the original punctuation was either a colon, semicolon, question or exclamation mark, then your onrush can be seen as essentially rational, since the second idea, quite logical even if regarded as ungrammatical/non-syntactical by most modern texts, moves on with some control from the first, as with Cleopatra's hastening her preparation to meet her beloved Anthony - committing suicide by allowing herself to be bitten by poisonous snakes - lest one of her just deceased women, Iras, meets him first

This proves me base : *
If she first meete the Curled Anthony,
Hee'l make demand of her, and spend that kisse
Which is my heaven to have. *
Come thou mortal wretch,
With thy sharpe teeth this knot intrinsicate,
Of life at one untye : * Poore venomous Foole,
Be angry, and dispatch.

*N.B. * in the middle of the line, replacing a comma*

(*Anthony & Cleopatra*, speech #26)

where F's speedier two sentences confirm the resoluteness of her decision. Most modern texts expand the passage into four sentences as the asterisks (*) show, and thus reduce her determination more than somewhat. Try reading the passage as four separate sentences and then as two and you can feel the difference, not just intellectually understand it.

a somewhat irrational onrush: if at the point that the new modern sentence has been created the original punctuation was either a comma, or there was no punctuation at all, or, as here, the onrush is totally unexpected, then your onrushed connection is very fast, as the second grammatical idea springs almost unchecked from the first, and the effect/result is probably unexpected by your listener, and perhaps even by you yourself, as with the just magically enhanced Lady Macbeth's first greeting of her husband

Great Glamys, worthy Cawdor,
Greater [then] both, by the all-haile hereafter, *
Thy Letters have transported me beyond
This ignorant present, and I feele now
The future in the instant.

(*Macbeth*, speech #5)

where F's comma after 'hereafter' allows her to plunge on with her new-found sense of power and unstoppable abilities – a far more exciting moment for the actress than the grammatically correct two sentence setting of most modern texts.

B: WHEN THERE ARE **LESS** MODERN TEXT SENTENCES THAN ORIGINALLY SET

If several separate sentences in the original text are pushed together into larger units by most modern texts, then you/your character as originally set can be said to be in a state of **heightened analysis/debate**, in that your precise modification of ideas needs much more careful delineation than grammar will permit, or that, in some cases, you are working very hard and probably enjoying it. Thus there is

logical analysis/debate: provided that the shorter sentences of the original have some form of grammatical structure then you/your character can be seen to be proceeding rationally, if somewhat hyper-analytically or very carefully, as when Tamora, the Goth Queen and now Empress of Rome, deliberately lies about a supposed attack on her in order to justify the eventual execution of two sons of her bitter enemy Timon, the Roman general who not only captured her but also had her eldest son killed as a sacrifice to celebrate his victory

1 Have I not reason + thinke you + to looke pale.
2 These two have tic'd me hither to this place, +
A barren, detested vale you see it is.
3 The Trees + though Sommer, yet forlorne and leane,
[Ore-come] with Mosse, and balefull Misselto.
4 Heere never shines the Sunne, heere nothing breeds,
Unlesse the nightly Owle, or fatall Raven : . . .

with F's sentences numbered two through four above adding extra descriptive (melodramatic?) weight to the supposed horror of the place where the supposed indignities towards her were perpetrated far more effectively than most modern texts' jamming them together as one long generality

1 Have I not reason, think you, to look pale ?
2 These two have tic'd me hither to this place :
A barren, detested vale you see it is;
The trees, though summer, yet forlorn and lean,
[Overcome] with moss and baleful mistletoe;
Here never shines the sun, here nothing breeds,
Unless the nightly owl, or fatal raven ; . . .
(*Titus Andronicus*, speech #7)

As originally set, her fake report works in fast, small, ever increasing descriptive spurts of horror which play even faster without the added extra commas or heavier punctuation of the modern texts (shown as + in the F text) which unnecessarily slow down the 'horror' spurt opening F's sentences #1, #2, and #3.

illogical analysis/debate: when the shorter sentence of the original has no grammatical structure, or simply appears in the middle of an idea (and thus in the middle of a modern sentence), you/your character can be seen to be momentarily thrown by what he or she is discovering (the wonderful Northern English term for this is 'gob-smacked', i.e. you/your character has been metaphorically hit in the mouth), as with Enobarbus' still amazed recalling of the first sight of Cleopatra and her barge

I will tell you, †
The Barge she sat in, like a burnisht Throne
Burnt on the water : † the Poope was beaten Gold, *N.B. the † in the*
Purple the Sailes : and so perfumed that *middle of the line*
The Windes were Love-sicke.
With them the Owers were Silver,
Which to the tune of flutes kept stroke, and made
The water which they beate, to follow faster ;
As amorous of their strokes.

with F's totally appallingly non-syntactical extra sentence (marked *) and onrush (marked † twice) allowing for far more astonishment than the modern texts more rational repunctuation, viz.

I will tell you.
The barge she sat in, like a burnish'd throne,
Burnt on the water.
The poop was beaten gold,
Purple the sails, and so perfumed that
The winds were love-sick with them; the oars were silver, . . .
(*Anthony & Cleopatra*, speech #5)

One of the finest plays to explore from the viewpoint of sentence variations (with most modern texts setting both more and less than originally set) is Troylus and Cressida. Also, it is well worth remembering that in most of the Comedies and many of the Tragedies the trend is for most modern texts to create far more sentences than were originally set, thus establishing character rationality and self-control when often the exact opposite was shown in both Folio and quarto texts.

2/ THEN, LOOK AT THE MAJOR PUNCTUATION (the connecting spine within each sentence and speech)
Logical Connections/Emotional Connections

AS A RULE OF THUMB

As pointed out earlier, the major punctuation of an original text is not so much grammatical as oratorical/rhetorical. However, modern texts' punctuation is grammar and syntax based, and often the two systems clash. As a result

- key moments of passion and debate as originally set in F1
- as well as ungrammatical emotional moments when the situation is almost too much for the character to bear

are often altered by modern texts, substituting grammar for potential moments of human excitement or strain.

Thus, since the Shakespeare texts are based so much on the art of debate and argument, the importance of the major punctuation of the original texts must not be underestimated, for both the colon [:] and the semicolon [;] mark a moment of importance for you and your character, either for yourself/itself as a moment of discovery or revelation, or as a key point in a discussion, argument, ordebate that you/your character wishes to impress upon other characters onstage.

The far less frequent semicolons (;) suggest because of the power inherent in the point you/your character has discovered or argued, and no matter how logical that point may be, that the passion/emotional power of the moment causes you to become side-tracked, and you/your character momentarily either

- lose focus on the argument and fall back into itself
- can only continue the argument with great difficulty

As such, the semicolon should be regarded as an **emotional connection**, as with the prophetess Cassandra's farewells to her brother Hector prior to his unchivalric battlefield death at the hands of Achilles

O farewell, deere Hector :
Looke how thou diest ; x looke how thy eye turnes pale :
Looke how thy wounds [doth] bleede at many vents :
Harke how Troy roares ; x how Hecuba cries out ; x
How poore Andromache shrils her [dolour] forth ;
Behold [distraction], frenzie, and amazement,

(*Troylus and Cressida*, speech #20)

where the first semicolon as well as two of the last three (all marked ; x) are not set by most modern texts. However, as originally set, the four semicolons suggest that she becomes more and more trapped by the images of dreadful grief which will occur as a direct result of his death.

The more frequent colons (:) suggest that whatever the emotional power of the point discovered/argued, you/your character can continue with the argument. As such, the colon can be regarded as a **logical connection** in that you/your character are not side-tracked. It doesn't mean suppression of emotion, just refusal to give in to it, as with the Tribune (of the people, and a people's elected representative) Brutus' (scathing? distressed?) description of the crowds swarming to see the hated aristocrat Coriolanus

Your pratling Nurse
Into a rapture lets her Baby crie,
While she chats him : x the Kitchin Malkin pinnes
Her richest Lockram 'bout her reechie necke,
Clambring the Walls to eye him : x
Stalls, Bulkes, Windowes, are smother'd up,
Leades fill'd, and Ridges hors'd
With variable Complexions ; all agreeing
In earnestnesse to see him : seld-showne Flamins
Doe presse among the popular Throngs, and puffe
To winne a vulgar station : x our veyl'd Dames
Commit the Warre of White and Damaske
In their nicely gawded Cheekes, toth'wanton spoyle
Of Phoebus burning Kisses : x such a poother,
As if that whatsoever God, who leades him,
Were slyly crept into his humane powers,
And gave him gracefull posture

(*Coriolanus*, speech #7)

where the five colons add to the unstoppable build stemming from Brutus' fixation, four of which (marked : x) are most often replaced by three semi-colons (sometimes a dash) and a period by most grammatically minded modern texts – syntactical correctness perhaps, but the relentless hammer-blow logic of Brutus' release is thus more than somewhat diminished (especially since semicolons in an original text would suggest more emotion than control).

SURROUND PHRASES: THE LOGICAL AND THE EMOTIONAL SANDWICH (REPEATED MAJOR PUNCTUATION)

AS A RULE OF THUMB

With the roles of the major punctuation being so important in the debate process, denoting that you/your character have reached some important idea within the overall scheme of things, though such punctuation is usually lightly scattered throughout the text, occasionally a short passage of up to a line and a half [8] can be surrounded (i.e. started and finished) by such major punctuation. This suggests that the information so surrounded is of extra importance to you/your character, whether working out things alone in a soliloquy, or discussing matters with others on-stage.

A: OCCASIONAL SURROUND PHRASES

Sometimes these all-important surround phrases are linked/created by colons [:] **and can thus be called logical**, as with Polonius, doing his best to excite Hamlet with news of the acting-troop just arrived at the palace

> The best Actors in the world, either for Trage-
> die, Comedie, Historie, Pastorall : [Pastoricall] -Comicall-
> Historicall-Pastorall : Tragicall-Historicall : Tragicall-
> Comicall-Historicall-Pastorall : Scene [indivible], or
> Poem unlimited

(*Hamlet*, speech #17)

Sometimes the connection is far more emotional, when linked by the emotional semicolon [;] (see page ??), as with the severity of the warning from the Ghost of Hamlet's father telling Hamlet that, in his pursuit of vengeance against the murdering brother/uncle Claudius, Hamlet's mother, Gertrude, should not be harmed

> But howsoever thou [pursuest] this Act,
> Taint not thy mind ; nor let thy Soule contrive
> Against thy Mother ought ;

(*Hamlet*, speech #4)

where the warning is given extra emotional weight by the two surround phrases being created entirely by semicolons.

B: CONSECUTIVE SURROUND PHRASES

As the number of surround phrases increases, so the importance of what is being said is singled out even more for you/your character, whether light-hearted or serious (and, as shown here, question-marks [?] can help create the surround phrases too), as with Hamlet's unexpected self-definition to his two one-time acquaintances Rosincrance and Guildenstern, sent by his uncle and mother to spy on him

> What a piece of worke is a man! how Noble in
> Reason? how infinite in faculty? in forme and moving
> how expresse and admirable? in Action, how like an An-
> gel? in apprehension, how like a God? + the beauty of the
> world,+ the Parragon of Animals ; and yet to me, what is
> this Quintessence of Dust?
> Man delights not me ; [no],
> nor [Woman] neither ; though by your smiling you seeme
> to say so.

(*Hamlet*, speech #14)

C: OVERKILL: TOO MANY SANDWHICHES: CLUSTERS OF TOO MUCH MAJOR PUNCTUATION

Of course, as with clusters of other devices (notably capital letters or of 'funny' spellings – see pages 21–22 below), so occasionally there can be simply too much heavy punctuation crammed close together. As such, they can point to too much joy or too much pain - and it is obvious such an intensity of sustained release does not signify a mind at ease. Rather the repeated hammer-blows of such concentrated releases when taken to such excess could point to a possible brain-storm, even breakdown - as with the Soothsayer's warning to Anthony to stay away from Cæsar, where more than half the speech (the last three sentences) are composed of eight consecutive surround phrases

> But neere him, thy Angell
> Becomes a [feare] : as being o're-powr'd, therefore
> Make space enough betweene you.
>
> If thou dost play with him at any game,
> Thou art sure to loose : And of that Naturall lucke,
> He beats thee 'gainst the oddes.

[8] admittedly an arbitrary length, but, for all practical purposes on the rehearsal floor, this does seem to work

Thy Luster thickens,
When he shines by: I say againe, thy spirit
Is all affraid to governe thee neere him:
But he [alway] 'tis Noble.

(*Anthony & Cleopatra*, speech #4)

3/ FINALLY, LOOK AT THE COMMAS (the deft-dance & tiny details of the speech)
extra clarity; the need for self-control; speed and/or enthusiasm

AS A RULE OF THUMB

The first texts are not dealing with careful grammar. Rather they show how quickly a character's mind deftly dances from one thought to the next, this quick light 'dance' being part of daily Elizabethan speaking/writing life.

The comma marks the smallest part of the dance, the tiniest thought – as such, each comma must be explored because it marks a moving on to the next moment of definition/redefinition you/your character is in the process of discovering.

However, when finally spoken common sense (and heaven) forbid the comma be marked by an actual pause. All it needs is whatever small bending of the text may be occasioned by the new discovery or new thought the comma has created within you.

A: YOU SEE **MORE** COMMAS IN THE ORIGINAL WHICH HAVE SINCE BEEN REMOVED BY MOST MODERN TEXTS

Many modern texts omit them because they find them ungrammatical, but their value goes far beyond mere syntax into the very action of character and play, and the importance of these extra original commas cannot be stressed enough, for they show where you/your character needs new 'breath-thoughts' either

to make a meaning absolutely clear - as with Ophelia trying to tell her father Polonius what it was in Hamlet's strange behaviour that has so disturbed her

As I was sowing in my [Chamber],
Lord Hamlet with his doublet all unbrac'd,
No hat upon his head, his stockings foul'd,
Ungartred, and downe gived to his Anckle,
Pale as his shirt, his knees knocking each other,
And with a looke so pitious in purport,$_x$
As if he had been loosed out of hell,$_x$
To speake of horrors.

He tooke me by the wrist, and held me hard;
Then goes he to the length of all his arme;
And with his other hand thus o're his brow,
He fals to such perusall of my face,$_x$
As [he] would draw it.
Long staid he so,
At last, a little shaking of mine Arme:
And thrice his head thus waving up and downe;
He rais'd a sigh,$_x$ so pittious and profound,$_x$
That it did seeme to shatter all his bulke,$_x$
And end his being.
That done, he lets me goe,
And with his head over his [shoulders] turn'd,
He seem'd to finde his way without his eyes,
For out adores he went without their [helpe];
And to the last,$_x$ bended their light on me.

(*Hamlet*, speech #10)

where the seven extra breath-thoughts (marked ,$_x$) all highlight the tiniest of details burnt into her brain, especially towards the end of the third sentence.

or for you/the character to regain self-control or calm down - as with the tiny moments towards the end of an incredibly painful speech as Troylus comes to terms with what he is going to do following the ignoble battle-field murder of his brother Hector

Ile through,$_x$ and through you; & thou great siz'd coward:
No space of Earth shall sunder our two hates,
Ile haunt thee,$_x$ like a wicked conscience still,
That mouldeth goblins swift as frensies thoughts.

Strike a free march to Troy,$_x$ with comfort goe:
Hope of revenge,$_x$ shall hide our inward woe.

(*Troylus & Cressida*, speech #21)

where, though not regarded as grammatical by most modern texts and thus not set, F's three extra breath thoughts (marked ,$_x$) are a wonderful indication as to just how hard Troylus has to fight to maintain his composure.

Sometimes both reasons, the need for extra details and the need for self-control, exist side by side, as with King Cymbeline in his public defiance to pay Rome further financial tribute, even though refusal could lead to invasion by superior Italian forces

You must know,
Till the injurious Romans,$_x$ did extort
This Tribute from us, we were free.
Cæsars Ambition,
Which swell'd so much,$_x$ that it did almost stretch
The sides o'th'World, against all colour heere,$_x$
Did put the yoake upon's; which to shake off
Becomes a warlike people, whom we reckon
Our selves to be, we do.
Say then to Cæsar,
Our Ancestor was that Mulmutius,$_x$ which
Ordain'd our Lawes, whose use the Sword of Cæsar
Hath too much mangled; whose repayre,$_x$ and franchise,$_x$
Shall (by the power we hold) be our good deed,
Tho Rome be therfore angry.
Mulmutius made our lawes
Who was the first of Britaine,$_x$ which did put
His browes within a golden Crowne,$_x$ and call'd
Himselfe a King.
Thou art welcome Caius,
Thy Cæsar Knighted me; my youth I spent
Much under him: of him,$_x$ I gather'd Honour,
Which he, to seeke of me againe, perforce,
Behooves me keepe at utterance.
I am perfect,$_x$
That the Pannonians and Dalmatians,$_x$ for
Their Liberties are now in Armes: a President
Which not to reade,$_x$ would shew the Britaines cold:
So Cæsar shall not finde them.

I know your Masters pleasure,$_x$ and he mine:
All the Remaine,$_x$ is welcome.

(*Cymbeline*, speech #25)

where Cymbeline needs fourteen extra breath-thoughts in just twenty-five lines - some no doubt due to the risky act of defiance, others more likely as a result of the slow poison his second wife has been slowly administering to him (in order to gain sole control of the British throne).

B: YOU SEE **FEWER** COMMAS IN THE ORIGINAL, AND MORE COMMAS, WHICH HAVE SINCE BEEN ADDED, IN MOST MODERN TEXTS

Sometimes modern texts add commas where F has set no punctuation at all. This is usually done to clarify grammatical/syntactical relationships, but the unfortunate side-effect of these extra commas is that they often slow down you/your character's speed of thought or argument as originally set, as when Pandarus pushes to get his niece Cressida to join him at an advantageous spot so that they can watch all the (mostly young) Trojan soldiers returning from the day's battle. (The $^+$ indicates where most modern texts have added commas they thought syntactically necessary.)

Harke$^+$ they are comming from the field, shal we
stand up here$^+$ and see them, as they passe toward Illium,
good Neece$^+$ do, sweet Neece Cressida.

(*Troylus & Cressida*, speech #2)

The speed of the original speaks volumes as to his excitement – a speed slowed down enormously by most modern texts' addition of three extra commas (in the spots marked $^+$).

PRACTICAL EXPLORATIONS PART TWO: EXPLORING AN ORIGINAL TEXT BY ITSELF

(RELEASING YOUR THOUGHTS: i.e. SPEAKING WELL & MOMENTS OF BLURT)

(which will become much clearer as you explore each separate audition speech)

In real-life, as we speak, argue, or discover and as each new idea, nuance, or rephrasing of an already expressed idea hits us, so our vocal pattern changes. Sometimes we are exuberant throughout a phrase or sentence or two; sometimes we are very restrained over the same time-frame. Sometimes a word tickles our fancy and we play with it vocally, sometimes quite consciously or without really thinking, stretching and exaggerating or even compressing how we make it sound. Sometimes we are very precise in our choice of words so the other person understands exactly the point we are trying to make. Sometimes we are so emotionally moved (unconsciously rather than directly thinking about it) that we again stretch and exaggerate or compress how we make it sound, not deliberately, but as a gut reaction. And sometimes we are so moved that we both choose a word for precision and at the same time our subconscious colours our feelings as we release it.

To elaborate on what was briefly mentioned earlier, because of the enormous flexibility of the Elizabethan and early Jacobean orthography, all these things could be set down on paper without the tyrrany of grammatical and spelling accuracies and be recognised for what they could signify. Now this is not to say Shakespeare always did this deliberately - it's much more a matter of his artistic consciousness hearing a character intellectually moved, emotionally moved, passionately moved, in control, out of control, and as he was writing what he heard, the orthography of the period (not constrained by rigid rules of spelling, capitalisation, punctuation or grammar) allowed him to set down unconscious clues as to what was going on without having to think about it. And these unconscious orthographic clues would be automatically understood and responded to equally unconsciously (and perhaps sometimes deliberately) by his actors [9].

By looking at this unconscious orthography (these, as it were, extra theatrical/human clues, what we might call '**theatrical serendipity'**), and working backwards (what deconstructionists might call 'decoding') we can gain some idea as to '**what**' state a person might be in when they are speaking - never '**why**', that is up to each actor/director/reader/scholar to decide, and not really '**how**' either, for, having interpreted whether your character is in control or not, your chosen reasons why that character is in control will colour how you play that control or lack thereof. In other words, the original texts offer your more wonderful stuff for your rehearsal exploration.

Thus the following is not a manuscript which must be spoken a particular way. It is a map, which offers you clues for your journey - leaving you to make the decision what to do with your discoveries once you have found them.

1/ ICE COLD SHAKESPEARE

DO THE WORDS LOOK NORMAL TO YOU : i.e. DO YOU HAVE TOTAL CONTROL

Here the words look exactly the same as if they had been set in a modern text - there are no capitals, no peculiar (to our eyes) long or short spellings. The words are being spoken without any embellishment, any extra release. In other words you/your character are in a state of calm and being quite quiet - though whether this calm is justified by the ease of the situation or is something you have had to force yourself to do so that you don't lose control of yourself and/or the moment is up to each actor to decide.

Thus there is **the expected ice-cold Shakespeare,** where calmness is deliberate or not particularly surprising, as with Cassius' initial careful attempts to get Brutus to realise his name (and thus worth and reputation) is of as much political value as that of the potential tyrant Cæsar

Why should that name be sounded more [than] yours:
Write them together: Yours, is as faire a Name:
Sound them, it doth become the mouth [aswell]:
Weigh them, it is as heavy:

(*Julius Cæsar*, speech #3)

where the great care in making the statement is wonderfully broken by the excesses of the one phrase in the second line 'Yours, is as faire a Name'. And then there is Agrippa's very careful, self-protective, humbling final statement

---

[9] When I first started professionally in English weekly stock as an actor/director, experienced actors would term certain lines as moving, or standing, or sitting lines, and show me how the rhythm/sound of a particular line would lead them quite unconsciously to that action – and they were usually right.

Pardon what I have spoke,
For 'tis a studied not a present thought,
By duty ruminated.

(*Anthony & Cleopatra*, speech #7)

after dropping the bombshell suggestion that the two enemies, the Cleopatra-hugging sensualist Anthony and the very correct Octavius Cæsar, become allies - by Anthony marrying Cæsar's sister Octavia!

The unexpected ice-cold Shakespeare is where calm is present despite the disturbing circumstances, as with the amazing reoccurring unembellished moments as Macduff struggles to come to terms with the slaughter of his wife and children

I shall {dispute it like a man}:
But I must also feele it as a man;
I cannot but remember such things were
That were most precious to me: Did heaven looke on,
And would not take their part ?

(*Macbeth*, speech #25)

where the calm (only broken by 'feele' and the one phrase 'Did heaven looke on') speaks much to a man struggling to keep his feelings from swamping his verbal ability – that is, he is not denying his emotions, but endeavouring to control them.

2/ EINSTEIN SHAKESPEARE

ARE YOU FINDING QUITE A FEW CAPITAL LETTERS: i.e. ARE YOU DEFINING YOUR TERMS AND/OR SPEAKING YOUR MIND?

Being the selfish character that you are - after all you only know of your needs and predicament (as explained in Elizabethan acting considerations above, pages 11–12) - at times it is very important for you to define precisely for yourself and/or the audience (in a soliloquy) or others in a group scene (i.e. at least one other character apart from you), how you understand and want to deal with a particular moment, idea, or situation. Hence the capital letters. So when you find them in your speech, or in just certain parts of your speech [10], it's a nice clue to ask 'why am I using that word here. And this can even be asked when real names appear - after all you could have used an uncapitalised personal pronoun (you, he, she, they, them) instead.

The expected Einstein Shakespeare is where the situation demands careful argument and/or presentation, as with Portia's ferociously unrelenting attempts to get her husband Brutus to tell her who the men were that met with him in the dead of night (in fact, his co-conspirators in the plot to murder Cæsar)

I graunt I am a Woman; but withall,
A Woman that Lord Brutus tooke to Wife:
I graunt I am a Woman; but withall,
A Woman well reputed: Cato's Daughter.

Thinke you, I am no stronger [then] my Sex
Being so Father'd, and so Husbanded?

Tell me your Counsels, I will not disclose 'em:
I have made strong proofe of my Constancie,
Giving my selfe a voluntary wound
Heere, in the Thigh: Can I beare that with patience,
And not my Husbands Secrets?

(*Julius Cæsar*, speech #22)

With eighteen capitals (as opposed to just seven long spelled words) in eleven lines, it seems as though the intellectual-debating powers of her famed orator father have passed on to her and here she has no compunction about using them.

The unexpected Einstein Shakespeare is when an intellectual response is not the first thing the situation would seem to warrant, or a trait not normally associated with the character, or it suddenly kicks in out of nowhere, as with Mercutio's unexpected intellectual riff on the icons of love as the love-struck Romeo appears

Here comes Romeo, without his Roe, like a dryed Hering.

O flesh, flesh, how art thou fishified?
Now is he for the numbers
that Petrarch flowed in: Laura to his Lady, was a kitchen
wench, marrie she had a better Love to berime her: Dido
a dowdie, Cleopatra a Gipsie, Hellen and Hero, hildings and
Harlots: Thisbie a gray eie or so, but not to the purpose.

Signior Romeo, Bonjour there's a French salutation to your
French slop: you gave us the counterfait fairely last
night.

[10] Since capital letters traditionally start verse lines, rarely are such capitals included in any of the discussions here or in the texts below.

(*Romeo & Juliet*, speech #17)

for in addition to the eleven proper names seven more words are capitalised, making eighteen capitalised words in just eight lines (with only one long spelling) – a veritable maelstrom of quick intellectual invention and release.

As a result you will suddenly find moments during a speech when **the mind switches on or off,** i.e. there is a great deal of intellect which suddenly disappears or appears, as with Othello's sudden change in style in telling the full Venetian Senate how he and Desdemona grew close

Wherein I spoke of most disastrous chances :
Of moving Accidents by Flood and Field,
Of haire-breadth scapes i'th'imminent deadly breach ;
Of being taken by the Insolent Foe,
And sold to slavery.
Of my redemption thence,
And portance in my [Travellours] historie.
Wherein of Antars vast, and Desarts idle,
Rough Quarries, Rocks, [] Hills, whose [head] touch heaven,
It was my hint to speake.
Such was my Processe,
And of the Canibals that each [others] eate,
The [Antropophague] and men whose heads
[Grew] beneath their shoulders.

(*Othello*, speech #3b, sentences #3-6)

where the fourteen capital letters in twelve lines stress the factual content of the tales that captured her heart and imagination, but are followed by just six in the next nineteen (for this part of the text see the complete speech as set below, Othello, speech #3b) – a new sparseness that suggests that Othello's emotions arise to the fore once he begins to recall Desdemona's loving and generous reaction to his words.

And sometimes there is **swamping, i.e. clusters of/too many capital letters:** that is, occasionally there are just far too many capital letters within a small part of the speech, almost as if you/your character's mind is working too hard, or there are so many points to be made the intellect is close to crashing. In processing so much information there can be said to be a swamping of the mind, and you/the character are about to drown in a sea of overwhelming ideas, as with Banquo's unexpected joys in bird-watching

This Guest of Summer,
The Temple-haunting [Barlet] does approve,
By his loved Mansonry, that the Heavens breath
Smells wooingly here: no Jutty frieze
Buttrice, nor Coigne of Vantage, but this Bird
Hath made his pendant Bed, and procreant Cradle,
Where they [must] breed, and haunt: I have observ'd
The ayre is delicate.

(*Macbeth*, speech #6)

where something so simple wouldn't normally be sprinkled with so many capitals, unless great enthusiasm was at work – and the sudden lack of capitals in the last line and a half of the speech might well point to a sudden realisation of just how excessive he is being (perhaps occasioned by gentle laughter from those onstage with him?).

3/ RUSSIAN SHAKESPEARE

ARE THE WORDS SPELLED 'FUNNY' [11] : i.e. ARE YOU RELEASING OR CHOKING BACK YOUR FEELINGS

Being an emotional beast as you are (remember that the Elizabethan believed thought instantly created feelings/emotions, and feelings/emotions instantly created thought) and being excessively verbal, it's not surprising that feelings sometimes spill over into words and phrases. This is where word formations can be explored, for sometimes you will find even the simplest of words set in a normal twenty-first century spelling ('she') and a moment later in longer formation ('shee'), as with Shakespeare's version of St. Joan, a character known as la Pucelle (see History Auditions, Henry 6 Part 1, speech #2). And sometimes you will find the same word spelled in twenty-first century normality and then in a shortened version in the same sentence as with 'Country'/'Countrie', as when the Roman Volumnia trys to persuade her recently banished and now all-avenging son to spare Rome and Italy from the enemy forces he now leads

For how can we ?
Alas ! how can we, for our Country pray ?
Whereto we are bound, together with thy victory :
Whereto we are bound : Alacke, or we must loose

[11] See Appendix Two, Part Two, for words that are so similar in their original and modern spellings that for the purpose of your explorations they can be regarded as one and the same.

The Countrie our deere Nurse, or else thy person
Our comfort in the Country .

(*Coriolanus*, speech #23)

AS A RULE OF THUMB

Essentially the **longer** spelling suggests that you/your character has been emotionally affected by that word enough to set up a flurry of emotion within you somewhat more powerful than usual - though how you speak it is up to you, and releasing it can be great fun - as with Oliver's suggestion to Charles the Wrestler that, as far as Orlando (Oliver's younger and troublesome brother) goes, Oliver wouldn't mind if Charles were to 'brea**ke** his nec**ke**', the suggested extra (venomous? delighted?) alliteration offered by the 'ke' and the end of the two words being either an unconscious emotional release and/or a deliberate (conscious) witty delight for both you and your listener.

Shorter spelling suggests that for some emotional reason your reaction to the word is such that you, unconsciously, cannot give it full voice, or, consciously, you are deliberately choking the word back.

In many ways, the application of the modern dictum quoted earlier '**why** do you say, **what** you say, **when** you say it, in the **WAY** you say it', really applies here, for the shaping of the words themselves can add extra information to the rehearsal and performance process . Sometimes a single word (as the contentious 'Chaine' in *The Comedy of Errors*, initially bespoken by Antipholus of Ephesus for his wife, and then offered in a fit of pique to a local Courtesan) can point to a single moment of emotional impact. Sometimes the repeated placement of long-spelled words can suggest a flurry of energy at the end of thoughts and ideas (as with Sonnet #42).

But what is of even greater interest in the longer speeches (and thus in the audition speeches that follow) are those moments when suddenly a lot of extra spellings occur over a fairly concentrated passage.

The expected Russian Shakespeare is when the exigencies of the situation naturally lead to an emotional response, as when Lysander, recently transformed from his everyday self into a chivalric figure prepared 'To honour Helen, and be her Knight' overwhelmingly pleads his love suite to her, opening with

Look**e** when I vow I weep**e**; and vow**es** so born**e**,
In their nativity all truth appear**es**.

(*Midsummer Nights Dream*, speech not shown in this text)

or as in Cleopatra's fear of how she and her women will be subjected to close examination by the ordinary folk of Rome once Cæsar returns home in triumph with them in tow

In their thic**ke** breath**es**,
Ranke of gros**se** d**y**et, shall we be enclo**w**ded,
And forc'd to drin**ke** their vapo**ur**.

(*Anthony & Cleopatra*, speech #25, sentence #4)

where there are eight long spelled words in just two and a half lines.

The unexpected Russian Shakespeare is when an emotional response might be quite surprising, or unusually excessive given the circumstances or the relative unemotional lead-up to this sudden release, as with the normally phlegmatic and emotionally-controlled, even cynical, Caska and his sudden (frightened?) release in describing one of the most disturbing of the unnatural sights he saw walking through the streets during the storm

And there were draw**ne**
Upon a hea**pe**, a hundred gastly Women,
Transformed with their fea**re**, who swore, they saw
Men, all in fire, wal**ke** up and dow**ne** the stree**tes**

(Julius Cæsar, speech #19, sentence #6)

where there are six long spelled words in just three and a half lines.

WITHOLDING/CHOKING BACK

Of course sometimes there are moments when you can hardly speak, and words seem to our eyes short spelled, suggesting **restraint** (whether deliberate or no), perhaps it is **deliberate**, as with the Roman Octavius Cæsar, in the midst of his character assassination/dismissal of his nemesis Anthony who has been carousing in Egypt with, as Cæsar regards them, the lower classes

to sit
And keep the turne of Tipling with a Slave,
To reele the streets at noone, and stand the Buffet
With knaves that smels of sweate : Say this becoms him . . .

(*Anthony & Cleopatra* , speech #1)

where the three action derivated words ('Tipling', 'smels' and 'becoms') all underscore his utter rhetorical disdain.

Perhaps **unconsciously,** as with the very young husband Posthumus who has been tricked into believing that his beloved Imogen has been unchaste, even though they both swore faithfulness and abstinence

Me of my lawfull pleasure she restrain'd,
And pray'd me oft forbearance: did it with
A pudencie so Rosie,$_x$ the sweet view on't
Might well have warm'd olde Saturne;

(*Cymbeline*, speech #10)

where the extra breath-thought (marked ,$_x$) and the long spelling in the last line ('ol**de** Satur**ne**') throw the unconscious love he still feels for his wife into relief with the wonderful short-spelled phrase 'a pudenc<u>ie</u> so Ros<u>ie</u>'.

4/ PASSIONATE SHAKESPEARE LEADING TO VOLCANIC SHAKESPEARE

A: WHEN THERE IS A REASONABLE **BALANCE** BETWEEN CAPITALS AND 'FUNNY' SPELLINGS

Sometimes, especially when moved or stimulated, we/you/the character are, at one and the same time, emotional and intellectual in our responses, and . . .

AS A RULE OF THUMB

. . . that's what can be seen when spellings and capitals of the original text almost balance each other.

This indicates expected passion, quite understandable given the circumstances, as with Lady Macbeth, when she finally realises how she will be able to verbally manipulate her husband

High thee hither,
That I may powre my Spirits in thine Eare,
And chastise with the valour of my Tongue
All that impeides thee from the Golden Round,
Which Fate and Metaphysicall ayde doth seeme
To have thee crown'd withall.

(*Macbeth*, speech #4, sentence #5)

where the seven capital words and eight long spelled words underscore her complete understanding.

And of course there is unexpected passion when, perhaps after a relative period of calm, everything bursts through at once, sometimes in the most inappropriate circumstances, as, after much self-control, with Portia's sudden flurry as she decries her apparent status as a traditional wife rather than as Brutus' intellectual partner

Am I your Selfe,
But$^+$ as it were$^+$ in sort, or limitation?
To keepe with you at Meales, comfort your Bed,
And talke to you sometimes?

(*Julius Cæsar*, speech #22, sentence #2)

where the three capitalised words and the three long spelled words in three lines are a splendid indication of just how much she is now cutting loose (especially without the two extra modern commas, marked $^+$, slowing things down) in an attempt to get any response from him – a remarkable shift when compared to the relative calm of the early part of the scene.

B: ARE THERE FAR TOO MANY CAPITAL LETTERS AND 'FUNNY' SPELLINGS: CAN YOU NO LONGER KEEP YOUR PASSIONS IN CHECK

Inevitably, and especially in dramatic theatrical conflicts (at which Shakespeare was a master - both within a single individual, and between different individuals), there are moments (good and bad) when (we)/you/the character cannot turn the passion off, whether in excitement and joy or fear and disgust.

AS A RULE OF THUMB

In the original texts those moments are marked by far too many capitals and long spellings within a very short space of time, which of course leads to **the expected volcanic Shakespeare**, where the verbal excesses (emotional and intellectual) are only natural given the circumstances, as when Enobarbus begins to describe the magnificence of Cleopatra's barge

I will tell you,
The Barge she sat in, like a burnisht Throne
Burnt on the water: the Poope was beaten Gold,
Purple the Sailes: and so perfumed that
The Windes were Love-sicke.

With them the Owers were Silver, . . .

(*Anthony & Cleopatra*, speech #5)

where the nine capital words and five long spelled words in just five and a half lines pinpoint every tiny detail.

And since excesses often come at the most inappropriate of times, **there is also the unexpected volcanic Shakespeare**, where the circumstances rarely warrant such an explosive reaction, as with the 2nd. Lord's passionate discussion/dissection of the royal family whose idiot son (Cloten) he is forced to serve

That such a craftie Divell as is his Mother
Should yeild the world this Asse: A woman, that
Beares all downe with her Braine, and this her Sonne,
Cannot take two from twenty for his heart,
And leave eighteene.

Alas poore Princesse,
Thou divine Imogen , what thou endur'st,
Betwixt a Father by thy Step-dame govern'd,
A Mother hourely coyning plots: A Wooer,
More hatefull [then] the foule expulsion is
Of thy deere Husband.
[Then] that horrid Act [12]
Of the divorce, heel'd make the Heavens hold firme
The walls of thy deere Honour.
Keepe unshak'd
That Temple thy faire mind, that thou maist stand
T'enjoy thy banish'd Lord: and this great Land.

(*Cymbeline*, speech #4)

where there are twenty capital words and twenty long spelled words in just fourteen lines, his obvious discomfort heightened by the ungrammatical structure as noted in footnote #12.

---

[12] This and the next full line raise serious grammatical problems. Most modern texts do not reproduce the F1-3 but reset them as follows

Of thy deere Husband then (i.e. than) that horrid Act
Of the divorce heel'd make. The Heavens hold firm

The justification for keeping the F layout could be that the 2nd. Lord is undergoing such emotional turmoil that his rhetoric momentarily fails.

SUMMARY

BASIC APPROACH TO THE SPEECHES SHOWN BELOW
(after reading the 'background')

1/ first use the modern version shown in the first column: by doing so you can discover

- the basic plot line of what's happening to the character, and
- the first set of conflicts/obstacles impinging on the character as a result of the situation or actions of other characters
- the supposed grammatical and poetical correctnesses of the speech

2/ then you can explore

- any acting techniques you'd apply to any modern soliloquy, including establishing for the character
- the given circumstances of the scene
- their outward state of being (who they are sociologically, etc.)
- their intentions and objectives
- the resultant action and tactics they decide to pursue

3/ when this is complete, turn to the First Folio version of the text, shown in the third column: this will help you discover and explore

- the precise thinking and debating process so essential to an understanding of any Shakespeare text
- the moments when the text is NOT grammatically or poetically as correct as the modern texts would have you believe, which will in turn help you recognise
- the moments of conflict and struggle stemming from within the character itself
- the sense of fun and enjoyment the Shakespeare language nearly always offers you no matter how dire the situation

4/ should you wish to further explore even more the differences between the two texts, the middle column, the commentary, discusses sentence by sentence, and often phrase by phrase, how the First Folio has been changed, and what those alterations might mean for the human arc of the speech

N.B.
Occasionally seemingly similar words in each text will be bracketed. This highlights spelling differences, quite often vis-a-vis real names, both of places and people, e.g. 'Calais' (the modern version of the French town) and 'Callis'(the spelling often used at the time the Folio was set. Very rarely will the differences be noted in the commentaries, and it is suggested that actors or readers use whichever format appeals to them best.

HOW THE THREE COLUMNS WORK VISUALLY

SYMBOLS INSERTED INTO BOTH TEXTS

[ ] : set around words in both texts when F1 sets one word or phrase while modern texts, basing their choice on editorial glosses or alternative source texts (a quarto printed earlier than F1), set another

{ } : where some minor alteration has been made to the speech or the shape of an individual word originally set: this will only occur in a speech built up from two or more smaller speeches in the play, where, sometimes for clarification, a word or small phrase will be changed, added, or removed

{ψ} : again in the case of a speech built from two or more smaller speeches, this symbol shows where a sizeable part of the text has been omitted (e.g. before sentence #2 in the Messenger's speech, the first in Henry Six Part One)

xxxxxxxxxxxxx : indicates where one speech or part of a speech has been joined to the one that follows

shaded text: indicates where modern texts have altered F1's verse structure (changes in prose are not shown)

SYMBOLS INSERTED IN THE MODERN TEXT

MODERN CHANGES TO THE FIRST FOLIO SENTENCE STRUCTURE

†: marks where modern texts end a sentence and start a new one, though F1 extends the current sentence beyond this point

◊: marks where modern texts have continued a sentence, though F1 ends the sentence here and starts a new one after this point

°: marks where an F1 hyphen, suggesting both words have equal spoken weight, has been removed (&, rarely, -°, where a hyphen is added, suggesting a greater verbal connection than F1 might have intended)

MODERN CHANGES TO FIRST FOLIO CAPITALS

Δ: marks where F1 has set a capitalised word which has not been capitalised by modern texts (the importance of the F1 capital being it suggests that the word has been deliberately chosen, which in turn suggests that the character is capable of intelligent/intellectual process no matter how emotional the situation): the symbol will also be set when modern texts (rarely) create a capital not set in F1

MODERN CHANGES TO FIRST FOLIO SPELLINGS

* (* set high): marks where F1 has set a 'long-spelled' word that has been standardised by modern texts (the longer spelling of a word in F1 (e.g. 'shee' instead of 'she' as used by Joan la Pucelle in speech #4 of Henry Six Part One) suggests that, at the moment the word is said, the character is revealing some emotional feeling associated with that word (in this case, since Joan is talking about 'Gods Mother', her mentor, the longer spelling is hardly surprising)

* (* set low): marks where F1 has set a 'short-spelled' word which has been standardised by modern texts (the shorter spelling of a word in F1 (e.g. 'Tyrannie', 'perpetuitie', 'Skie', and 'Mortalitie', as used by Talbot ending lines 2-5 in speech #6 of Henry Six Part One) suggests that, at the moment the word is said, the character is, in speaking the word, holding something back – either an emotion associated with that word or feelings in general (in this case since the dying Talbot is talking to his dead son, the emotional withholding is hardly surprising)

SYMBOLS INSERTED IN THE FOLIO TEXT

PUNCTUATION REDUCED OR INCREASED BY MODERN TEXTS

since the Shakespeare texts are based so much on the art of debate and argument, the importance of F1's major punctuation must not be underestimated, for both the semicolon (;) and colon (:) mark a moment of importance for the character, either for itself, as a moment of discovery or revelation, or as a key point in a discussion, argument or debate that it wishes to impress upon other characters onstage

as a rule of thumb:

a/ the more frequent colon (:) suggests that whatever the power of the point discovered or argued, the character is not side-tracked and can continue with the argument - as such, the colon can be regarded as a **logical** connection

b/ the far less frequent semicolon (;) suggests that because of the power inherent in the point discovered or argued, the character is side-tracked and momentarily loses the argument and falls back into itself or can only continue the argument with great difficulty - thus, the semicolon should be regarded as an **emotional** connection

as such F1's major punctuation is not so much grammatical as oratorical and rhetorical: however, modern texts' punctuation is grammar and syntax based, and at times the two systems clash: thus key moments of passion and debate as originally set in F1, as well as ungrammatical emotional moments when the situation is almost too much for the character to bear, are often unwittingly altered by modern texts: hence the following key markings will be set

; **x** : indicating where an F1 (emotional) semicolon has been reduced or omitted by modern texts

: **x** : indicating where an F1 (logical) colon has been reduced or omitted by modern texts

; +: indicating where an F1 (emotional) semicolon has been set as something heavier (:, ., ?, !) by modern texts

: + : indicating where an F1 (logical) colon has been set as something heavier (., ?, !) by modern texts similar 'x' or '+' signs will be used when question (?) or exclamation (!) marks or commas (,) are likewise altered

→ : indicates that, though the original text has set two short lines for a single character, perhaps hinting at a minute break between the two thoughts, most modern texts have set the two short lines as one longer one

PUNCTUATION OMMITTED BY MODERN TEXTS (usually commas)

x : set where modern texts omit an F1 comma (or other punctuation): many modern texts omit commas because they are ungrammatical, but their value goes far beyond mere syntax into the very action of character and play: the importance of these extra F1 commas cannot be stressed enough, for they show where a character needs either

a/ an extra thought to make a meaning absolutely clear, or

b/ an extra breath to calm itself down

in the commentaries, these extra phrases will be referred to as **breath-thoughts**

PUNCTUATION ADDED BY MODERN TEXTS (usually commas)

+ : set where modern texts add a comma (or other punctuation) where F1 has set no punctuation at all: most modern texts add such commas to clarify grammatical/syntactical relationships: the unfortunate side-effect of these extra modern commas is that they often slow down the speed of the thought or argument F1 originally established

PROBABLE TIMING

(shown just before the speeches begin, set alongside the number of lines)
the # before the period refers to minutes, the # after to seconds - thus 0.45 = a forty-five second speech

SYMBOLS & ABBREVIATIONS INSERTED IN THE COMMENTARY

F: the First Folio

mt.: modern texts

F # followed by a number: the number of the sentence under discussion in the First Folio version of the speech, thus F #7 would refer to the seventh sentence

mt. # followed by a number: the number of the sentence under discussion in the modern text version of the speech, thus mt. #5 would refer to the fifth sentence

#/#, (e.g. 3/7): the first number refers to the number of capital letters in the passage under discussion; the second refers to the number of long spellings therein

within a quotation from the speech: / indicates where one verse line ends and a fresh one starts

TERMS FOUND IN THE COMMENTARY (part one)

OVERALL

1/ **orthography:** the capitalization, spellings, and punctuation of the First Folio

SIGNS OF IMPORTANT DISCOVERIES/ARGUMENTS WITHIN A FIRST FOLIO SPEECH

2/ **major punctuation:** colons and semicolons: N.B. the following is taken from the previous page since the Shakespeare texts are based so much on the art of debate and argument, the importance of F1's major punctuation must not be underestimated, for both the semicolon (;) and colon (:) mark a moment of importance for the character, either for itself, as a moment of discovery or revelation, or as a key point in a discussion, argument or debate that it wishes to impress upon other characters onstage

as a rule of thumb:

a/ the more frequent colon (:) suggests that whatever the power of the point discovered or argued, the character is not side-tracked and can continue with the argument - as such, the colon can be regarded as a **logical** connection

b/ the far less frequent semicolon (;) suggests that because of the power inherent in the point discovered or argued, the character is side-tracked and momentarily loses the argument and falls back into itself or can only continue the argument with great difficulty - as such, the semicolon should be regarded as an **emotional** connection

3/ **surround phrases:** phrase(s) surrounded by major punctuation, or a combination of major punctuation and the end or beginning of a sentence: thus these phrases seem to be of especial importance for both character and speech, well worth exploring as key to the argument made and/or emotions released+

SYMBOLS INSERTED IN THE FOLIO TEXT (CTD)

DIALOGUE NOT FOUND IN THE FIRST FOLIO

∞ : set where modern texts add dialogue from a quarto text which has not been included in F1

A LOOSE RULE OF THUMB TO THE THINKING PROCESS OF A FIRST FOLIO CHARACTER

TERMS FOUND IN THE COMMENTARY (part two)

1/ mental discipline/**intellect:** a section where capitals dominate suggests that the intellectual reasoning behind what is being spoken or discovered is of more concern than the personal response beneath it

2/ feelings/**emotions:** a section where long spellings dominate suggests that the personal response to what is being spoken or discovered is of more concern than the intellectual reasoning behind it

3/ **passion:** a section where both long spellings and capitals are present in almost equal proportions suggests that both mind and emotion/feelings are inseparable, and thus the character is speaking passionately

SIGNS OF LESS THAN GRAMMATICAL THINKING WITHIN A FIRST FOLIO SPEECH

1/ **onrush:** sometimes thoughts are coming so fast that several topics are joined together as one long sentence suggesting that the F character's mind is working very quickly, or that his/her emotional state is causing some concern: most modern texts split such a sentence into several grammatically correct parts (the opening speech of *As You Like It* is a fine example, where F's long 18 line opening sentence is split into six): while the modern texts' resetting may be syntactically correct, the F moment is nowhere near as calm as the revisions suggest

2/ **fast-link:** sometimes F shows thoughts moving so quickly for a character that the connecting punctuation between disparate topics is merely a comma, suggesting that there is virtually no pause in springing from one idea to the next: unfortunately most modern texts rarely allow this to stand, instead replacing the obviously disturbed comma with a grammatical period, once more creating calm that it seems the original texts never intended to show

FIRST FOLIO SIGNS OF WHEN VERBAL GAME PLAYING HAS TO STOP

1/ **non-embellished:** a section with neither capitals nor long spellings suggests that what is being discovered or spoken is so important to the character that there is no time to guss it up with vocal or mental excesses: an unusual moment of self-control

2/ **short sentence:** coming out of a society where debate was second nature, many of Shakespeare's characters speak in long sentences in which ideas are stated, explored, redefined and summarized all before moving onto the next idea in the argument, discovery or debate: the longer sentence is the sign of a rhetorically trained mind used to public speaking (oratory), but at times an idea or discovery is so startling or inevitable that length is either unnecessary or impossible to maintain: hence the occasional very important short sentence suggests that there is no time for the niceties of oratorical adornment with which to sugar the pill - verbal games are at an end and now the basic core of the issue must be faced

3/ **monosyllabic:** with English being composed of two strands, the polysyllabic (stemming from French, Italian, Latin and Greek), and the monosyllabic (from the Anglo-Saxon), each strand has two distinct functions: the polysyllabic words are often used when there is time for fanciful elaboration and rich description (which could be described as 'excessive rhetoric') while the monosyllabic occur when, literally, there is no other way of putting a basic question or comment – Juliet's "Do you love me? I know thou wilt say aye" is a classic example of both monosyllables and non-embellishment: with monosyllables, only the naked truth is being spoken, nothing is hidden

SPEECHES IN ORDER		TIME	PAGE
TITUS ANDRONICUS			
#'s 1 - 3: The Election			
1/ Saturninus	Noble Patricians, Patrons of my right,	0.30	29
2/ Bassianus	Romaines, Friends, Followers,	0.30	29
3/ Marcus	Princes, that strive by Factions, and by Friends,	1.30	30
#'s 4 - 9: The Revenge Of Tamora And Saturnine			
4/ Tamora	Stay Romaine Bretheren, gracious Conqueror,	0.55	31
5/ Emperour	No Titus, no, the Emperour needs her not,	1.35	32
6/ Tamora	My worthy Lord if ever Tamora.	1.30	33
7/ Tamora	Have I not reason thinke you to looke pale.	1.15	35
8/ Titus	Heare me grave fathers, noble Tribunes stay,	1.30	36
9/ Titus	Why 'tis no matter, if they did heare	0.45	37
#'s 10 - 12: Lavinia			
10/ Demetrius	Shee is a woman, therefore may be woo'd,	0.40	38
11/ Lavinia	Oh Tamora,/Be call'd a gentle Queene,	0.35	39
12/ Titus	Come, come Lavinia, looke, thy Foes are bound,	2.00	40
#'s 13 - 17: Aaron, And His Son			
13/ Aaron	Now climbeth Tamora Olympus toppe,	1.15	42
14/ Tamora	My lovely Aaron,	1.00	43
15/ Aaron	Sooner this sword shall plough thy bowels up.	1.15	44
16/ Aaron	'Twill vexe thy soule to heare what I shall speake :	1.00	45
17/ Aaron	{I am sorry} that I had not done a thousand more :	1.10	46

SPEECHES BY GENDER		Speech #(s)
SPEECHES FOR WOMEN (5)		
Tamora	**Traditional & Today:** woman, old/young enough to have three adult sons	#4, #6, #7, #14
Lavinia	**Traditional & Today:** young woman	#11
SPEECHES FOR EITHER GENDER (1)		
Marcus	**Traditional:** older man, brother to Titus **Today:** could be played as Titus' sister	#3
SPEECHES FOR MEN (11)		
Saturninus	**Traditional & Today:** young man who becomes Emperor	#1, #5
Bassianus	**Traditional & Today:** young man	#2
Demetrius	**Traditional & Today:** young man	#10
Aaron	**Traditional & Today:** young or early middle-aged black male	#13, #15, #16, #17
Titus	**Traditional & Today:** older male	#8, #9, #12

TITUS ANDRONICUS

#'s 1 - 3: The Election

1/ Saturninus **Noble Patricians, Patrons of my right,** 1.1.1. - 8
2/ Bassianus **Romaines, Friends, Followers,** 1.1.9 - 17

Background: Two brothers, rivals to succeed their father, the recently deceased Emperor of Rome, appeal to the public at large for their support. Each is supported by followers and 'drums and colours', suggesting the possibility of conflict. As the elder, Saturninus begins.

Style: both, public addresses in the open air to a large group of people

Where: unspecified, but a public square in Rome **To Whom:** a large group, comprised of Tribunes, Senators, and followers for each of the candidates

Speech 1, # of Lines: 8 **Probable Timing: 0.30 minutes**
Speech 2, # of Lines: 9 **Probable Timing: 0.30 minutes**

Modern Text

Saturnine as
1/ Saturninus

1 Noble Δpatricians, Δpatrons of my right,
Defend the justice of my Δcause with Δarms*; ◊
And, Δcountry*men, my loving Δfollowers,
Plead* my Δsuccessive Δtitle with your Δswords.

2 I [am his] first born* Δson*, that was the last
That ware* the Δimperial* Δdiadem of Rome,
Then let my Δfather's Δhonors* live in me,
Nor wrong mine Δage with this indignity*.

There is a marked difference between the two brothers. Saturninus is logical in sentence structure and in terms of spelling relatively self-contained. Bassianus is more openly passionate (the one long sentence scattered with extra spellings) yet still can make all the necessary logical stepping stones via the major punctuation.

- F's two sentence opening marks more clearly than the (longer) modern text Saturninus' clever appeal to two different classes, first the 'Noble Patricians', and only then the lesser 'Countey-men' in general
- the appalling incitement to civil war - 'Armes' and 'Swords' - seems determinedly intellectual (a 9 capital lead-up accompanied by just 3 long spellings)
- and the ensuing argument is all weighted on his father's merits (all four long spellings) rather than his own

First Folio

Saturnine as
1/ Saturninus

1 Noble Patricians, Patrons of my right,
Defend the justice of my Cause with Armes.

2 And + Countrey-men, my loving Followers,
Pleade my Successive Title with your Swords.

3 I [was the] first borne Sonne, that was the last
That wore the Imperiall Diadem of Rome : x
Then let my Fathers Honours live in me,
Nor wrong mine Age with this indignitie.

Modern Text

2/ Bassianus

1 Romans*, Δfriends, Δfollowers, Δfavorers* of my Δright,
If ever Bassianus, Cæsar's Δson*,
Were gracious in the eyes of Δroyal* Rome,
Keep* then this passage to the Capitol*,
And suffer not Δdishonor* to approach
Th'Δimperial* Δseat*, to Δvirtue consecrate,
To Δjustice, Δcontinence, and Δnobility;
But let Δdesert in pure Δelection shine,
And, Romans*, fight for Δfreedom* in your Δchoice.

- though one long sentence, F clearly outlines each stage of Bassianus' argument with the five pieces of major punctuation (4 x : and 1 x ;): sadly, few modern texts maintain them – thus removing his fine sense of oratory
- unlike his brother, Bassianus' capitals refer to the abstract values of 'Vertue','Justice', 'Continence', 'Nobility', 'Desert', and his plea to his own, not his father's, 'Right'
- the three key surround phrases that finish up the speech (starting from 'consecrate', ending the fourth line from the bottom) all point to Bassianus' love of Rome and democracy, and thus the honorable nature of his plea
- yet despite the intellect, the frequent long spellings – proportionately more than for his brother - show there are strong emotions burning within him

First Folio

2/ Bassianus

1 Romaines, Friends, Followers, →
Favourers of my Right : x
If ever Bassianus, Cæsars Sonne,
Were gracious in the eyes of Royall Rome,
Keepe then this passage to the Capitoll : x
And suffer not Dishonour to approach
Th'Imperiall Seate + to Vertue : x consecrate +
To Justice, Continence, and Nobility : x
But let Desert in pure Election shine; x
And + Romanes, fight for Freedome in your Choice.

3/ Marcus **Princes, that strive by Factions, and by Friends,** 1.1.18 - 45

Background: The politician Marcus Andronicus, brother (perhaps younger) to Titus, responds to speeches #1 and #2 above, informing the late emperor's sons of the people's choice.

Style: public addresses in the open air to two men on behalf of all present

Where: unspecified, but a public square in Rome **To Whom:** a large group, comprised of Tribunes, Senators, the emperor's two sons and their followers

# of Lines: 28 **Probable Timing: 1.30 minutes**

Modern Text

3/ Marcus

1 Princes, that strive by △factions and by △friends
Ambitiously for △rule and △empery,
Know, that the people of Rome, for whom we stand
A special* △party, have by △common voice*,
In △election for the Roman* △empery*,
Chosen Andronicus, △surnamed [Pius]
For many good and great deserts to Rome.

2 A △nobler man, a braver △warrior*,
Lives not this day within the △city △walls*.

3 He by the Senate is accited home
From weary △wars* against the barbarous Goths*,
That with his △sons*, a terror to our △foes,
Hath yok'd* a △nation strong, train'd up in △arms*.

4 Ten years* are spent, since first he undertook*
This △cause of Rome, and chastised* with △arms*
Our △enemies' pride; ◊ five times he hath return'd
Bleeding to Rome, bearing his △valiant △sons*
In △coffins from the △field,[1] ◊
And now at last, laden with △honor's* △spoils*,
Returns* the good Andronicus to Rome,
Renowned Titus, flourishing in △arms*.

5 Let us entreat by △honor* of his △name,
Whom worthily you would have now succeed*,
And in the Capitol* and Senate's right,
Whom you pretend to △honor* and △adore,
That you withdraw you, and abate your △strength,
Dismiss* your △followers, and as △suitors* should,
Plead* your △deserts in △peace and △humbleness*.

F's public address oratory has been reduced by modern text's jamming together of F's sentences #4-#6; also, F's orthography adds much to the understanding of the speech.

- with capitals outnumbering long spellings two to one (52/25), the speech is already a fine display of debate and precise argument
- this is even more enhanced when it's noted that 16 of the 25 long spellings are folded into words already capitalized – as if the force of the argument were giving rise to the accompanying personal release
- the colon at the end of the second line of F's first sentence has a fine 'announcing' quality to it ("now I have your attention, listen to what I'm going to say next"): modern texts completely wipe this out by replacing the colon with a comma
- the three separate F sentences #4-#6 allow Marcus to emphasise three separate points about his brother's accomplishments,
  - a/ the number of years he has served
  - b/ how many times he lost sons
  - c/ the fact that he has now brought great wealth to Rome with far more impact than the modern texts resetting of the whole as one eight line sentence

First Folio

3/ Marcus

1 Princes, that strive by Factions,$_x$ and by Friends,$_x$
Ambitiously for Rule and Empery : $_x$
Know, that the people of Rome$^+$ for whom we stand
A speciall Party, have by Common voyce$^+$
In Election for the Romane Emperie,
Chosen Andronicus, Sur-named [Pious],$_x$
For many good and great deserts to Rome.

2 A Nobler man, a braver Warriour,
Lives not this day within the City Walles.

3 He by the Senate is accited home
From weary Warres against the barbarous Gothes,
That with his Sonnes ($_x$a terror to our Foes)$_x$
Hath yoak'd a Nation strong, train'd up in Armes.

4 Ten yeares are spent, since first he undertooke
This Cause of Rome, and chasticed with Armes
Our Enemies pride.

5 Five times he hath return'd
Bleeding to Rome, bearing his Valiant Sonnes
In Coffins from the Field.

6 And now at last, laden with Honours Spoyles,
Returnes the good Andronicus to Rome,
Renowned Titus, flourishing in Armes.

7 Let us intreat,$_x$ by Honour of his Name,
Whom ($_x$worthily)$_x$you would have now succeede,
And in the Capitoll and Senates right,
Whom you pretend to Honour and Adore,
That you withdraw you, and abate your Strength,
Dismisse your Followers, and as Suters should,
Pleade your Deserts in Peace and Humblenesse.

[1] Q1 adds the following, rarely set by modern texts, "and at this day /To the Monument of that Andronicy/Done sacrifice of expiation,/And slaine the Noblest prisoner of the Gothes."

#'S 4 - 9: THE REVENGE OF TAMORA AND SATURNINE

4/ Tamora **Stay Romaine Bretheren, gracious Conqueror,** 1.1.104 - 120

Background: To offset the death of his two sons in the recent conflict, the Roman Titus is preparing to sacrifice the Goth Tamora's eldest son Alarbus. In the following, Tamora pleads, unsuccessfully, for her son's life to be spared.

Style: public address in the open air on behalf of all present

Where: unspecified, but a public square in Rome **To Whom:** Titus, in front of a large group, comprised of his four sons, daughter Lavinia, and brother Marcus; Tamora and her three sons; the emperor's two sons and their followers; Tribunes and Senators

# of Lines: 17 **Probable Timing: 0.55 minutes**

Modern Text

4/ Tamora

1 Stay, Roman* Δbrethren*!
2 Gracious Δconqueror,
Victorious Titus, rue the tears* I shed,
A Δmother's tears* in passion for her son*;
And if thy Δsons* were ever dear* to thee,
O* think* my sons* to be as dear* to me*!
3 Sufficeth not that we are brought to Rome
To beautify* thy Δtriumphs, and return*
Captive to thee, and to thy Roman* yoke*;
But must my Δsons* be slaughtered* in the streets*
For Δvaliant doings in their Δcountry's* cause?
4 O, ◊ if to fight for Δking and Δcommonweal*
Were piety in thine, it is in these. †
5 Andronicus, stain* not thy Δtomb* with blood!
6 Wilt thou draw near* the nature of the Δgods?
7 Draw near* them then in being merciful*: ◊
Sweet mercy is Δnobility's* true badge. †
8 Thrice-Δnoble Titus, spare my first-°born* son*!

Modern texts alter F's sentence structure on three occasions and in so doing create a far more melodramatic yet rational character than originally set. F's structure and orthography establish the more human dynamics of a high-status mother in pain.

• Tamora's F opening plea is far more speedy and direct without the extra comma and exclamation mark that modern texts add to the first line, especially when coupled with F's setting of the opening as one emotional sentence instead of modern texts' more rational two

• the mental and emotional struggle battling within her is clearly marked in three separate stages in the opening F sentence

a/ line 1 is essentially debate and public speech oriented (3/1), presumably to grab everyone's attention

b/ in the next two lines (speaking as a mother) feeling begins to swamp the intellect (2/3)

c/ and emotion floods the two remaining lines (1/7)

• and this struggle is seen again in the final F sentence, with the intellectually driven appeal inherent in the first line and half ('Nobilitie', 'Noble Titus' - 3/0) finishing emotionally once more (0/2 in the last phrase) as she pleads for her 'first borne sonne'

• her F struggle is more marked, for this last F sentence's somewhat ungrammatical blurt is split into a more controlled and rhetorical two sentence appeal in modern texts

• the single surround phrase " : Andronicus, staine not thy Tombe with blood . " is, whether consciously or not, remarkably prescient as regards the remaining action of the play, foreshadowing both her desire for revenge and the tragedies that befall the house of Andronicus

First Folio

4/ Tamora

1 Stay+ Romaine Bretheren,+ gracious Conqueror,
Victorious Titus, rue the teares I shed,
A Mothers teares in passion for her sonne: x
And if thy Sonnes were ever deere to thee,
Oh thinke my sonnes to be as deere to mee. +
2 Sufficeth not, x that we are brought to Rome
To beautifie thy Triumphs, and returne
Captive to thee, and to thy Romaine yoake, +
But must my Sonnes be slaughtred in the streetes, x
For Valiant doings in their Countries cause?
3 O!
4 If to fight for King and Common-weale, x
Were piety in thine, it is in these:
Andronicus, staine not thy Tombe with blood. +
5 Wilt thou draw neere the nature of the Gods?
6 Draw neere them then in being mercifull.
7 Sweet mercy is Nobilities true badge,
Thrice Noble Titus, spare my first borne sonne. +

5/ {Saturninus as} **Emperour No Titus, no, the Emperour needs her not,** between 1.1.299 - 337

Background: In a startlingly swift turn-around Saturninus, the emperor's oldest son, reneges on his agreement to accept Titus as the new emperor. In the ensuing fracas Bassianus offers Titus his support, but, for the good of Rome, Titus withdraws his candidacy in favour of Saturninus. All seems to calm, until Saturninus decides to take Titus' daughter Lavinia as his wife. Unfortunately she is secretly betrothed to Saturninus' younger brother Bassianus, who promptly steals her away. Though Titus' sons support Bassianus, Titus lays his support behind the new emperor, and in attempting to retrieve Lavinia for the emperor kills Mutius, one of his four remaining sons. In the uproar Titus demands of his remaining sons 'Traytors restore Lavinia to the Emperor', at which point the capricious Saturninus drops the following bombshell.

Style: public address initially towards one man, for the benefit of all present

Where: unspecified, but a public square in Rome **To Whom:** Titus, in front of a large group, comprised of his three remaining sons, daughter Lavinia, and brother Marcus; Tamora and her two remaining sons; the new emperor's brother and the two sets of followers; Tribunes and Senators

# of Lines: 32 **Probable Timing: 1.35 minutes**

Modern Text

5/ Saturninus

1 No, Titus, no, the Emperor* needs her not,
Nor her, nor thee, nor any of thy stock*. †

2 I'll trust by △leisure him that mocks me once, ◊
Thee never, nor thy △traitorous* haughty sons*,
Confederates all thus to dishonor* me.

3 Was none in Rome to make a stale
But Saturnine?

4 Full well, Andronicus,
Agree these △deeds with that proud brag* of thine,
That saidst I begg'd* the △empire at thy hands.

5 But go* thy ways*, go* give that changing piece*,
To him that flourish'd for her with his △sword. †

6 A △valiant* son*-in-law thou shalt enjoy,
One fit to bandy with thy lawless* △sons*,
To ruffle in the △commonwealth of Rome.

7 And therefore, lovely Tamora, Queen* of Goths*,
That like the stately [Phœbe] mong'st her △nymphs*
Dost over-shine the △gallant'st △dames of Rome,
If thou be pleas'd with this my sudden* choice*,
Behold, I choose thee, Tamora, for my △bride,
And will △create thee Emperess* of Rome.

8 {Speak, Queen of goths, dost thou applaud my choice ?}

9 And here* I swear* by all the Roman* △gods,
Sith △priest and △holy-water are so near*,
And △tapers burn* so bright, and every thing
In readiness* for Hymeneus stand,

F's prefix of 'Emperour' gives a clear indication as to how Saturninus regards both himself and his actions in the current situation: in renaming him as Saturninus modern texts remove this splendid clue. Thus F's running together as one sentence what most modern texts set as four (F #7, mt. #9-12), as well as F #5 (mt. two sentences #5-6,) speaks volumes as to his less than imperial style self-control (a major characteristic of his throughout the play).

• the surround phrases speaks volumes as to how Saturninus regards Titus and his family, as well as his own brother Bassianius who has stolen his supposed bride, Lavinia, Titus' daughter

" : A Valliant sonne in-law thou shalt enjoy : "

and the ungrammatical opening of F (#1-2) containing the following surround phrases speaks volumes to emotion barely held in check

" . Ile trust by Leisure him that mocks me once . "
" . Thee never : "

• F's Saturninus is often speedier than his modern counterpart, with at least eight occasions where modern texts slow him down by adding extra grammatical but action-wise unnecessary punctuation (marked '+'), especially as he starts his proposal to Tamora (F #6)

• in the less than controlled start, it's fascinating that the three most inherently outspoken attacks on Titus (F #1, #3 and #4) all display some form of mental control (3/2; 2/0; and 3/1 respectively), while the attack on Titus' sons (F #2) is more emotional (1/3)

• and this emotionality breaks forth even more as Saturninus rejects Lavinia (2/6 the first three lines of F #5)

• thus it's doubly startling that his sudden choice of Tamora as his bride starts out so mentally determinedly (13/5, F sentence #6)

• yet, true to his nature, this discipline cannot hold, and as he vows he will not return to the streets of Rome until they are married

First Folio

5/ Emperour

1 No + Titus, no, the Emperour needs her not,
Nor her, nor thee, nor any of thy stocke :
Ile trust by Leisure him that mocks me once.

2 Thee never : x nor thy Trayterous haughty sonnes,
Confederates all, x thus to dishonour me.

3 Was none in Rome to make a stale
But Saturnine?

4 Full well + Andronicus +
Agree these Deeds, x with that proud bragge of thine,
That said'st, x I beg'd the Empire at thy hands.

5 But goe thy wayes, goe give that changing peece,
To him that flourisht for her with his Sword :
A Valliant sonne in-law thou shalt enjoy : x
One, x fit to bandy with thy lawlesse Sonnes,
To ruffle in the Common-wealth of Rome.

6 And therefore + lovely Tamora + Queene of Gothes,
That like the stately [Thebe] mong'st her Nimphs
Dost over-shine the Gallant'st Dames of Rome,†
If thou be pleas'd with this my sodaine choyse,
Behold + I choose thee + Tamora + for my Bride,
And will Create thee Empresse of Rome.
[ ]

7 And heere I sweare by all the Romaine Gods,
Sith Priest and Holy-water are so neere,
And Tapers burne so bright, and every thing
In readines for Hymeneus stand,

I will not re-salute the streets of Rome,
Or climb* my △palace*, till from forth this place I lead*
espous'd my △bride along with me {.} {}

10 Ascend, △fair* △queen*,[Pantheon] .
11 Lords, accompany
Your △noble △emperor* and his lovely △bride,
Sent by the heavens for Prince Saturnine,
Whose wisdom* hath her △fortune △conquered . †
12 There shall we △consummate our △spousal* rites.

(mt. #9, the first seven lines of F #7, 9/8) so his underlying feelings break through once more to create a most passionate statement

- yet by the time he gives instructions to his Lords to accompany them he has managed to enforce mental discipline on himself once more (the last six lines of the speech - 12/5)

- and these rapid mood swings extend to smaller moments of release, with angry emotional releases ('goe thy wayes, goe give that changing peece') being offset by quite strong mental images (e.g. Tamora seen to 'over-shine the gallant'st Dames of Rome')

I will not resalute the streets of Rome,
Or clime my Pallace, till from forth this place,$_x$
I leade espous'd my Bride along with me,

Ascend + Faire Queene, →
[Panthean] Lords,[2] accompany
Your Noble Emperour and his lovely Bride,
Sent by the heavens for Prince Saturnine,
Whose wisedome hath her Fortune Conquered,
There shall we Consummate our Spousall rites.

6/ Tamora **My worthy Lord if ever Tamora,** between 1.1.428 - 458

Background: Though each of the emperor's sons now has the wife he desires, Bassianus Titus' daughter Lavinia, and the new emperor Saturninus the one time Queene of the Goths, Tamora, because of the early infighting (see background to speech #7), tensions are still running very high - especially between Saturninus and the family Andronicus. Bassianus has attempted peace-making overtures, which trigger the following from the new empress Tamora. One note: given that Titus is solely responsible for the death of her eldest son (see background to speech #4) it's not surprising that the apparent public generosity (sentences #1-3 and #8) is immediately undermined by her private shrewdly revenge-filled advice (sentences #4-7).

Style: initially a public address towards one man, for the benefit of all present, then as an aside to him

Where: unspecified, but a public square in Rome **To Whom:** her new husband, the emperor Saturninus, in front of a large group, comprised of Titus and his three remaining sons, daughter Lavinia, and brother Marcus; Tamora's two remaining sons; Bassianus and his and Saturninus' followers; Tribunes and Senators

# of Lines: 29 **Probable Timing: 1.30 minutes**

Modern Text

6/ Tamora

1 My worthy △lord, if ever Tamora
Were gracious in those △princely eyes of thine,
Then hear* me speak* indifferently for all;
And at my suit⁎, sweet, pardon what is past.

2 {ψ} The Gods of Rome for-fend
I should be △author* to dishonor* you ! †
3 But on mine honor* dare I undertake
For good Lord Titus innocence in all,
Whose fury not dissembled speaks* his griefs*. †
4 Then at my suit⁎ look* graciously on him;
Lose* not so noble a friend on vain* suppose,

When the modern texts restructured the earlier Tamora speech (#4 above) they turned a human speech towards oratory, here they turn a series of carefully planned stepping stones in the latter part of the speech (F #4-7) into a much more emotional pent-up release (mt. #5-6) and then wipe out the moment when she does crack.

- the two introductory F sentences, as befits a public appeal itself, start with full passion (6/4), but as she turns to the subject of Titus, the man who has just sacrificed her eldest son (F #3), so some emotion seems to break through (2/8), especially in the last three lines (5 of the 8 long spellings are in the last three lines), and though seemingly in support of Titus, given what follows next in her private manipulations of Saturninus this might be more her attempt to control her fury at having to speak in public seemingly on Titus' behalf.

- modern texts alter the nature of the appeal, for the longer F #3, suggesting a more onrushed plea, is split into a much more rational two sentence approach (mt. #3-4)

First Folio

6/ Tamora

1 My worthy Lord + if ever Tamora,$_x$
Were gracious in those Princely eyes of thine,
Then heare me speake indifferently for all : $_x$
And at my sute ($_x$sweet,$_x$) pardon what is past.

2 {ψ} The Gods of Rome for-fend,$_x$
I should be Authour to dishonour you . +
3 But on mine honour dare,$_x$ I undertake
For good Lord Titus innocence in all : $_x$
Whose fury not dissembled speakes his griefes :
Then at my sute looke graciously on him, +
Loose not so noble a friend on vaine suppose,

{ctd. over}

[2] *The Arden Shakespeare Titus Andronicus*, op. cit., suggests that the Q1 compositor (and presumably of F too) failed to realise that 'Panthean' is a building, the 'Pantheon': thus most modern texts repunctuate as shown

Nor with sour* looks* afflict his gentle heart.

{modern texts indicate #5-6 is spoken as an aside to Saturninus}

5 My Lord, be rul'd by me, be won* at last,
Dissemble all your griefs* and discontents . †

6 You are but newly planted in your △throne ;
Lest* then the people, and △patricians too,
Upon a just survey take Titus' part,
And so supplant [you] for ingratitude,
Which Rome reputes to be a heinous* sin*, ◊ †
Yield* at entreats,*; and then let me alone,
I'll find* a day to massacre them all,
And rase* their faction and their family,*,
The cruel* △father, and his traitorous* sons*,
To whom I sued for my dear* son's* life ; ◊
And make them know what 'tis to let a △queen*, ◊
Kneel* in the streets* and beg for grace in vain*.

7 Come, come, sweet Emperor* - come, Andronicus -
Take up this good old man, and cheer* the heart
That dies in tempest of thy angry frown*.

• however, once she addresses Saturninus privately (F #4) with the enormously politically astute first warning (subsumed into a larger whole in the modern texts and thus reduced in impact), the releases are few and far between (just 5/4 in seven lines), with

a/ the mental concentration reminding him of the dangerous principals involved ('Lord', 'Throne', 'Patricians', 'Titus' and 'Rome')

b/ the long-spelled words ('wonne', 'griefes', 'Least', and 'sinne') giving greater weight to the key points of her very shrewd political argument

• once she has advised Saturninus how to behave (carefully set as a separate sentence - #5 – by F) as she voices her plans for revenge (0/2 in the first two lines), so her feelings break through (1/5 in the last two lines), followed by . . .

• . . . two wonderfully ungrammatical sentences (F #6-7) when she finally snaps

• and as she moves back into public address mode (F #8) she shows an incredible ability to recover from the previous loss of control, for her speech now shows exactly the same passionate pattern as the opening two sentences of the speech (2/3 in three lines) – and whether this is the natural recovery of an accomplished villainess or the self-enforced recovery of an angry woman, the moment of transition offers the actress a splendid finish to the speech

Nor with sowre lookes afflict his gentle heart.

4 My Lord, be rul'd by me, be wonne at last,
Dissemble all your griefes and discontents,
You are but newly planted in your Throne, +
Least then the people, and Patricians too,
Upon a just survey take Titus part,
And so supplant [us] for ingratitude,
Which Rome reputes to be a hainous sinne.

5 Yeeld at intreats,+ and then let me alone : x
Ile finde a day to massacre them all,
And race their faction, x and their familie,
The cruell Father, and his trayt'rous sonnes,
To whom I sued for my deare sonnes life.

6 And make them know what 'tis to let a Queene. +

7 Kneele in the streetes, x and beg for grace in vaine.

8 Come, come, sweet Emperour, (x come x Andronicus x)
Take up this good old man, and cheere the heart, x
That dies in tempest of thy angry frowne.

7/ Tamora **Have I not reason thinke you to looke pale.** 2.3.91 - 115

Background: Though now empress of Rome, Tamora has maintained a lover, Aaron the Moore, from the days as Queene of the Goths. They have been discovered in a compromising situation by two of her perceived enemies, Titus' daughter Lavinia and her husband Bassianus, younger brother to Tamora's new husband, Saturninus: they threaten to tell Saturninus, 'for these slips have made him noted long,/Good king, to be so mightily abused'. Fortunately for Tamora, but not Lavinia or Bassianus, Tamora's sons Chiron and Demetrius appear, to whom she immediately tells the following lies (which eventually results in her sons killing Bassianus, and raping and mutilating Lavinia).

Style: as part of a six handed scene

Where: in the woods **To Whom:** in front of her lover Aaron, her sons Chiron and Demetrius, and Lavinia and Bassianus

# of Lines: 25 **Probable Timing: 1.15 minutes**

Modern Text

7/ Tamora

1 Have I not reason, think* you, to look* pale ?

2 These two have tic'd me hither to this place :
A barren, detested vale you see it is; ◊
The △trees, though △summer*, yet forlorn* and lean*,
[Overcome*] with △moss* and baleful* △mistletoe*; ◊
Here* never shines the △sun*, here* nothing breeds,
Unless* the nightly △owl*, or fatal* △raven ;
And when they show'd* me this abhorred pit,
They told me, here*, at dead time of the night,
A thousand △fiends, a thousand hissing △snakes,
Ten thousand swelling △toads*, as many △urchins,
Would make such fearful* and confused cries,
As any mortal* body hearing it
Should straight* fall mad, or else die suddenly.

3 No sooner had they told this hellish tale,
But straight* they told me they would bind* me here*
Unto the body of a dismal* yew,
And leave me to this miserable death !

4 And then they call'd me foul* △adulteress*,
Lascivious Goth, and all the bitterest terms*
That ever ear* did hear* to such effect; ◊
And had you not by wondrous fortune come,
This vengeance on me had they executed :
Revenge it, as you love your △mother's life,
Or be ye not henceforth call'd* my △children.

Yet again modern texts alter F's Tamora's sentence structure. While it may be logical to rework the end of F's sentence #2 into a larger whole (mt. #2), this interferes with her overworked attempts at scene setting the supposed horror of the event (and since the whole thing is a trumped up charge, interferes with her own private sense of fun perhaps?). Similarly, while resetting the two sentences ending the F text may be grammatically understandable, it reduces the extra (again perhaps fake) melodramatic oomph she has in the final F appeal for revenge, especially when the subtle variations in the orthography of F's #6 and #7 are added to the mix.

• unusually for Tamora, especially at supposedly crucial moments, here there are times where there is no embellishment, as if it takes her an effort just to tell her tale

"These two have tic'd me hither to this place,
A barren, detested vale you see it is . "
"And when they shew'd me this abhorred pit,"
"No sooner had they told this hellish tale,"
"And leave me to this miserable death . "
"And had you not by wondrous fortune come,
This vengeance on me had they executed : "

(again, perhaps the sign of a superb villainess acting out her role)

• that there are more long spellings to capitals is only to be expected (25/15), but it's interesting to see how the capitals fall into place in two major sets, with the supposedly (at least to most women) frightening images of sentences F #3-4 (11 of the 15) and then with the appeal to family loyalty in the last two lines of the speech, once she says she has been called 'Adultresse' and 'lascivious Goth'

• and with the sea of long spellings (2 in the first line; 5 in just two lines of F #3; 6 in the first two lines of F #4; 5 in the three lines of F #6) it's fascinating to see that there are none in her last F sentence, as she moves her sons to 'vengeance' (almost as if the game playing were now complete and no longer necessary)

First Folio

7/ Tamora

1 Have I not reason + thinke you + to looke pale. +

2 These two have tic'd me hither to this place, +
A barren, detested vale you see it is.

3 The Trees + though Sommer, yet forlorne and leane,
[Ore-come] with Mosse, x and balefull Misselto.

4 Heere never shines the Sunne, heere nothing breeds,
Unlesse the nightly Owle, or fatall Raven : x
And when they shew'd me this abhorred pit,
They told me + heere, x at dead time of the night,
A thousand Fiends, a thousand hissing Snakes,
Ten thousand swelling Toades, as many Urchins,
Would make such fearefull and confused cries,
As any mortall body hearing it, x
Should straite fall mad, or else die suddenly.

5 No sooner had they told this hellish tale,
But strait they told me they would binde me heere, x
Unto the body of a dismall yew,
And leave me to this miserable death. +

6 And then they call'd me foule Adulteresse,
Lascivious Goth, and all the bitterest tearmes
That ever eare did heare to such effect.

7 And had you not by wondrous fortune come,
This vengeance on me had they executed :
Revenge it, as you love your Mothers life,
Or be ye not henceforth cal'd my Children.

8/ Titus **Heare me grave fathers, noble Tribunes stay,** between 3.1.1 - 31
9/ Titus **Why 'tis no matter, if they did heare** 3.1.33 - 47

Background: Not only has Tamora succeeded in destroying Lavinia and Bassianus (see background to speech #7 above), she has successfully laid the blame for Bassianus' murder on two of Titus' remaining sons, Quintus and Martius. The two boys have been sentenced to death and are being escorted to their execution. Speech #8 deals with Titus' vain appeal in the public streets to the judges, which continues long after their exit. Speech #9 is a direct response to his eldest son Lucius' attempt to get him to see how low he has fallen in his distracted grief, 'you recount your sorowes to a stone. . . . no Tribune heares you speake'.

Style: speech #8 as public address; speech #9 as part of a two-handed scene

Where: in a public street **To Whom:** speech #8 initially to the senators and judges escorting his sons to their death; speech #9 to his one remaining son, Lucius

Speech 8, # of Lines: 27 **Probable Timing: 1.30 minutes**
Speech 9, # of Lines: 14 **Probable Timing: 0.45 minutes**

Modern Text

8/ Titus

1 Hear* me, grave fathers ! noble △tribunes, stay ! †
2 For pity* of mine age, whose youth was spent
In dangerous wars* whilst you securely slept ;
For all my blood in Rome's great quarrel* shed,
For all the frosty nights that I have watch'd,
And for these bitter tears* which now you see
Filling the aged wrinkles in my cheeks*,
Be pitiful* to my condemned △sons*,
Whose souls* [are] not corrupted as 'tis thought . †
3 For two and twenty sons* I never wept,
Because they died in honor's* lofty bed.

ANDRONICUS LYETH DOWNE, AND THE JUDGES PASSE BY HIM

4 For these [two] [3], △tribunes, in the dust I write
My heart's₊ deep* languor, and my soul's* sad tears* :
Let my tears* staunch₊ the earth's dry₊ appetite, ◊
My sons'* sweet blood, will make it shame and blush . †
5 O earth, I will [be°friend] thee more with rain*,

[Exeunt]

That shall distill from these two ancient [urns],
[Than] youthful* April* shall with all his show'rs* . †
6 In summer's drought I'll drop upon thee still,
In △winter with warm* tears* I'll melt the snow,

Once more the modern texts turns F's ungrammatical structure into something more orderly, taking a away the disturbed quality of the speech, especially when they split F's opening sentence into three: this, coupled with turning F's first two commas into exclamation points and adding two extra commas, totally alters how Titus starts his appeal.

- the long opening F sentence together with the already noted faster first line (slowed down in the modern texts by the added commas marked '+') along with the three extra breaths (marked , x) and the emotional content therein (3/11) speak volumes as to his lack of control as compared to earlier in the play
- his inability to think clearly could explain the ungrammatical context of F #2 and the start of #3, as more correctly rendered in mt.'s #4-5, as well as the peculiarly ungrammatical construction of the remainder of F #3
- the two surround phrases
  " : Let my teares stanch the earths drie appetite . "
  " . My sonnes sweet blood, will make it shame and blush : "
  reveal the depth of his sense of potential loss, modern texts slow down the opening line of this sentence by turning two F commas into exclamation marks and adding an extra comma
- and, as the final appeal to the long gone Tribunes is reached, whereas modern texts set three separate sentences (mt.. #7-9), F sets a much more direct single sentence plea

First Folio

8/ Titus

1 Heare me + grave fathers, + noble Tribunes + stay, +
For pitty of mine age, whose youth was spent
In dangerous warres, x whilst you securely slept : x
For all my blood in Romes great quarrell shed,
For all the frosty nights that I have watcht,
And for these bitter teares, x which now you see, x
Filling the aged wrinkles in my cheekes,
Be pittifull to my condemned Sonnes,
Whose soules [is] not corrupted as 'tis thought :
For two and twenty sonnes [4] I never wept,
Because they died in honours lofty bed.

ANDRONICUS LYETH DOWNE, AND THE JUDGES PASSE BY HIM

2 For these [ ], Tribunes, in the dust I write
My harts deepe languor, and my soules sad teares :
Let my teares stanch the earths drie appetite.
3 My sonnes sweet blood, will make it shame and blush :
O earth! x I will [be friend] thee more with raine +

[Exeunt]

That shall distill from these two ancient [ruines],
[Then] youthfull Aprill shall with all his showres
In summers drought : x Ile drop upon thee still,
In Winter with warme teares Ile melt the snow,

---

[3] some modern texts add 'two' to create pentameter; Qq/Ff do not : the original short setting once more suggests Titus is trying to maintain self-control
[4] many commentators point out that earlier (Act One Scene 1) Titus claimed 'one and twenty Valiant Sonnes ' had been killed in battle; either he is now confused, or has added to the list Mutius, whom he himself killed on stage

And keep* eternal* spring-time on thy face,
So thou refuse to drink* my dear* sons'* blood.

7 O* [reverend] △tribunes ! †
8 O* gentle, aged men ! †

9 Unbind* my sons*, reverse the doom* of death,
And let me say (that never wept before)
My tears* are now prevailing* △orators*.

10 Grave △tribunes, once more I entreat* of you - ◊

• indeed the emotional quality of the speech (9 capitals, 34 long spellings) suggests a man whose capacity for reasoning has been badly shaken; which throws the last unusually short one-line F sentence with its single capital letter into more relief, as if at the last moment he had regained some form of control

And keepe eternall spring time on thy face,
So thou refuse to drinke my deare sonnes blood.

4 Oh [reverent] Tribunes,+ oh gentle+ aged men,+
Unbinde my sonnes, reverse the doome of death,
And let me say (that never wept before)
My teares are now prevaling Oratours.

5 Grave Tribunes, once more I intreat of you.

Modern Text

9/ Titus

1 Why, 'tis no matter {ψ}, if they did hear*,
They would not mark* me ; [ ] if they did [mark],
They would not pity* me ; ◊ [yet plead I must,
And bootless unto them.] [5]

2 Therefore I tell my sorrows* [ ] to the stones, ◊
Who, though they cannot answer* my distress*,
Yet in some sort they are better [than]the △tribunes,
For that they will not intercept my tale . †

3 When I do* weep*, they humbly at my feet*
Receive my tears*, and seem* to weep* with me,
And were they but attired in grave weeds*,
Rome could afford no [△tribunes] like to these.

4 A stone is [soft as wax*], tribunes more hard [than]stones ;
A stone is silent, and offendeth not,
And △tribunes with their tongues doom* men to death.

• the emphatic single line F sentence #2 allows Titus a far greater explanation of his behaviour, no matter how outlandish it may seem

• the only (emotional) F semicolon (sentence #3) underscores the inevitable hopelessness of 'When I do weepe', especially when followed by a cluster of long spellings (7 in the next three lines)

• though the long spellings again outweigh capitals (3/15) there are passages of non-embellishment suggesting that Titus may be gaining a sense of calm, no matter how strange his new philosophy and course of action may seem to the others onstage, e.g. 'Why 'tis no matter'; 'Yet in some sort they are better than the Tribunes,/For that they will not intercept my tale'; 'Tribunes more hard [then] stones;/A stone is silent, and offendeth not,'

• two surround phrases reveal Titus' clear understanding of the hopelessness of the situation
" : oh if they did heare/They would not pitty me . "
" . A stone is as soft waxe,/Tribunes more hard then stones : "

• the two split lines opening sentence F #4 probably came about through too much text for the column, yet, as set, they allow Titus a moment of discovery and/or reflection as he makes the comparison

First Folio

9/ Titus

1 Why+ 'tis no matter {ψ}, if they did heare +
They would not marke me : x [oh] if they did [heare] +
They would not pitty me.
[ ]

2 Therefore I tell my sorrowes [bootles] to the stones.

3 Who+ though they cannot answere my distresse,
Yet in some sort they are better [then] the Tribunes,
For that they will not intercept my tale ;
When I doe weepe, they humbly at my feete
Receive my teares, and seeme to weepe with me,
And were they but attired in grave weedes,
Rome could afford no [Tribune] like to these.

4 A stone is [as soft waxe], →
Tribunes more hard [then] stones : x
A stone is silent, and offendeth not,
And Tribunes with their tongues doome men to death.

---

[5] most modern texts' setting is taken from Q

#'s 10 - 12: Lavinia

10/ Demetrius **Shee is a woman, therefore may be woo'd,** between 2.1.82 - 94

Background: Despite the fact that Lavinia is married to the emperor's brother, both Tamora's sons lust after her, and have come to blows as to who will actually have her. They turn to Aaron for advice, who, having asked the stark question 'Are you mad?', then asks the more practical question as to how they propose to 'atchieve her', triggering the following.

Style: as part of a three-handed scene

Where: unspecified, but probably in or near the palace **To Whom:** Aaron, in front of Demetrius' brother Chiron

# of Lines: 12 **Probable Timing: 0.40 minutes**

Modern Text

10/ Demetrius

1 She* is a woman, therefore may be woo'd,
She* is a woman, therefore, may be won*,
She* is Lavinia, therefore must be lov'd.

2 What, man, more water glideth by the Δmill
[Than] wots the Δmiller of, and easy, it is
Of a cut loaf* to steal* a shive, we know . †

3 Though Bassianus be the Emperor's* brother,
Better [than] he have worn* Vulcan's badge . †

4 Then why should he despair* that knows* to court it,
With words, fair* looks*, and liberality ? †

5 What, hast not thou full often struck* a Δdoe,
And borne her cleanly by the Δkeeper's nose?

Modern texts' resetting of F's two sentences as five creates a Demetrius working far harder to make his point than his original seemingly much more relaxed counterpart.

- his excitement is underlined by the preponderance of long spellings to capitals (8/14)
- the obviousness of his fixation is emphasised in his use of the unusually long-spelled 'shee' three times in the opening sentence, and the faster speed of the original throughout (which the modern texts slow by adding four extra pieces of punctuation – marked '+')
- his seemingly devil-may-care-approach to authority (lines 4-5 of F's sentence #2) and his casual approach to sexual infidelity (the last two lines of the speech) are emphasised by 5 of the 8 capitals scattered through the speech

First Folio

10/ Demetrius

1 Shee is a woman, therefore may be woo'd,
Shee is a woman, therfore may be wonne,
Shee is Lavinia + therefore must be lov'd.

2 What + man, more water glideth by the Mill
[Then] wots the Miller of, and easie it is
Of a cut loafe to steale a shive + we know :
Though Bassianus be the Emperours brother,
Better [then] he have worne Vulcans badge,
Then why should he dispaire that knowes to court it +
With words, faire lookes, and liberality : +
What + hast not thou full often strucke a Doe,
And borne her cleanly by the Keepers nose?

11/ Lavinia **Oh Tamora,/Be call'd a gentle Queene,** between 2.3.168 - 178

Background: As a result of Tamora's lies (speech #7 above), her sons have killed Lavinia's husband Bassianus. Tamora has then handed Lavinia over to the lustful Demetrius and Chiron (see speech #10 above) suggesting 'away with her, and use her as you will,/The worse to her, the better lov'd of me', which triggers the following.

Style: as part of a four handed scene

Where: in the woods **To Whom:** to Tamora, in front of Demetrius and Chiron, with the body of Bassianus, Lavinia's husband, close by

# of Lines: 10 **Probable Timing: 0.35 minutes**

Modern Text

11/ Lavinia

1 O* Tamora, be call'd a gentle Δqueen*,
And with thine own* hands kill me in this place !
For 'tis not life that I have begg'd* so long,
Poor* I was slain* when Bassianus died*.

2 'Tis present death I beg, and one thing more,
That womanhood denies my tongue to tell . †

3 O*, keep* me from their worse [than] killing lust,
And tumble me into some loathsome pit,
Where never man's eye may behold my body . †

4 Do* this, and be a charitable murderer.

- Lavinia's hesitency in appealing to Tamora can be seen in the two split lines opening the F text (where there was ample room to set the two lines as one, as most modern texts do)
- quite naturally her feelings are close to the surface in the first sentence (3/6) especially in the last line 'Poore I was slaine, when Bassianus dy'd' (1/3)
- and then, in true heroic fashion, she manages to restore a sense of calm, with just three long spellings in the remaining six lines

First Folio

11/ Lavinia

1 Oh Tamora, →
Be call'd a gentle Queene,
And with thine owne hands kill me in this place, +
For 'tis not life that I have beg'd so long,
Poore I was slaine, x when Bassianus dy'd.

2 'Tis present death I beg, and one thing more,
That womanhood denies my tongue to tell :
Oh + keepe me from their worse [then] killing lust,
And tumble me into some loathsome pit,
Where never mans eye may behold my body,
Doe this, and be a charitable murderer.

12/ Titus **Come, come Lavinia, looke, thy Foes are bound,** 5.2.166 - 205

Background: Titus has maintained the pretext of madness, and thus lured Tamora and her sons Chiron and Demetrius to his home. They believe they can continue their cruel mockery at his expense. However, once Tamora has left, a sane Titus and his relatives have seized and bound both sons, and now Titus explains very carefully what he intends to do.

Style: address to a small group

Where: Titus' home **To Whom:** initially Lavinia, in front of Chiron and Demetrius, and possibly Titus' relatives Publius, Valentine, and Caius

# of Lines: 40 **Probable Timing: 2.00 minutes**

Modern Text

12/ Titus

1 Come, come, Lavinia, look*, thy Δfoes are bound . †
2 Sirs, stop their mouths*, let them not speak* to me,
But let them hear* what fearful* words I utter.
3 O* Δvillains*, Chiron, and Demetrius ! †
4 Here stands the spring whom you have stain'd with mud,
This goodly Δsummer* with your Δwinter mix'd . †
5 You kill'd* her husband, and for that vile* fault,
Two of her Δbrothers were condemn'd to death,
My hand cut off and made a merry jest,
Both her sweet Δhands, her Δtongue, and that more dear*
[Than] Δhands or tongue, her spotless* Δchastity,
[Inhuman]* Δtraitors*, you constrain'd and forc'd*.
6 What would you say if I should let you speak*?
7 Villains*, for shame you could not beg for grace.
8 Hark*, Δwretches, how I mean* to martyr you . †
9 This one Δhand yet is left to cut your throats,
[Whiles] that Lavinia 'tween* her stumps doth hold
The Δbasin* that receives your guilty blood.
10 You know your Δmother means* to feast with me,
And calls herself* Revenge, and thinks* me mad.
11 Hark*, Δvillains*, I will grind your bones to dust,
And with your blood and it I'll make a Δpaste,
And of the Δpaste a Δcoffin* I will rear*,
And make two Δpasties of your shameful* Δheads,
And bid that strumpet, your unhallowed Δdam,
Like to the earth swallow her [own] increase.
12 This is the Δfeast that I have bid her to,
And this the Δbanquet she shall surfeit* on,

There is enormous potential for melodramatic grand guignol given the circumstances of the scene. And rather than falling into this trap by providing huge excesses of language, instead F hints at the horror of the scene with repeated awkwardness in Titus' thinking process – which goes a long way to re-establish his long tarnished dignity.

- certainly in the opening (and longer) F sentence Titus' feelings do break through as he brings Lavinia to face her tormentors and stops their mouths (2/5), but this is the only sentence where long-spellings outstrip capitalization
- the only other times the combination of spellings and capitals come together in a passionate mix are when he reminds Demetrius and Chiron how they ravaged Lavinia (the last three lines of F #2 - 5/4); as he starts to explain how he will 'martyr' them (the short four line F #5, 4/4); and the following even shorter two line F sentence (#6, 2/3) as he reveals that he knows of their mother's stupid disguise (and thus theirs)
- and the two simple surround phrases, no matter how bloody they may seem, again reinforce what is about to happen to them
  " : The bason that receives your guilty blood . "
  " : Lavinia come . "
- indeed, it seems that Titus is taking great care that Chiron and Demetrius understand exactly why they have been captured and what will happen to them, so his feelings seem to be well held in check both in the opening six lines of F's sentence #2 (as he begins to list their disgusting actions - 6/4), and from the start of F #7 till the last three lines of the speech (as he describes in detail what he's going to do with their bodies - 18/6)
- throughout, there at least eight extra F thoughts (marked ,$_x$), not punctuated as such by modern texts, as if Titus were taking great care that no tiny detail should escape their notice
- it seems his strain shows itself more in the way that thoughts are joined, for in the five cases where modern texts split into two sentences or more what F has set as one (mt. #1 and #2 from F #1; mt. #3, from F #2's first line; mt.#8 from F #5's first line; mt. #13

First Folio

12/ Titus

1 Come, come + Lavinia, looke, thy Foes are bound,
Sirs + stop their mouthes, let them not speake to me,
But let them heare what fearefull words I utter.
2 Oh Villaines, Chiron, and Demetrius, +
Here stands the spring whom you have stain'd with mud,
This goodly Sommer with your Winter mixt,
You kil'd her husband, and for that vil'd fault,
Two of her Brothers were condemn'd to death,
My hand cut off,$_x$ and made a merry jest,
Both her sweet Hands, her Tongue, and that more deere
[Then] Hands or tongue, her spotlesse Chastity,
[Inhumaine] Traytors, you constrain'd and for'st.
3 What would you say,$_x$ if I should let you speake?
4 Villaines + for shame you could not beg for grace.
5 Harke + Wretches, how I meane to martyr you,
This one Hand yet is left,$_x$ to cut your throats,
[Whil'st] that Lavinia tweene her stumps doth hold :$_x$
The Bason that receives your guilty blood.
6 You know your Mother meanes to feast with me,
And calls herselfe Revenge, and thinkes me mad.
7 Harke + Villaines, I will grin'd your bones to dust,
And with your blood and it,$_x$ Ile make a Paste,
And of the Paste a Coffen I will reare,
And make two Pasties of your shamefull Heads,
And bid that strumpet + your unhallowed Dam,
Like to the earth swallow her [ ] increase.
8 This is the Feast,$_x$ that I have bid her to,
And this the Banquet she shall surfet on,

For worse [than] Philomel you us'd my Δdaughter,
And worse [than] [Procne] I will be reveng'd . †

13 And now prepare your throats . †

14 Lavinia, come,
Receive the blood, and when that they are dead,
Let me go* grind their Δbones to powder small,
And with this hateful* Δliquor temper it,
And in that Δpaste let their vile* Δheads be bak'd*. †

15 Come, come, be every one officious
To make this Δbanket, which I wish [may] prove
More stern* and bloody [than] the Centaurs'* Δfeast.

[He cuts their throats]

16 So now bring them in, for I'll play the Δcook*,
And see them ready [against] their Δmother comes.

out of F #8's line 4; and mt. #15 from F #9's line 5) modern texts have recast as logical and disciplined in-control periods what were originally set as a fast linking commas

- in each of these cases F's far speedier connection of thoughts doesn't connect grammatically but is highly revealing either in terms of the urgency of the requested actions

For worse [then] Philomel you us'd my Daughter,
And worse [then] [Progne] I will be reveng'd,
And now prepare your throats : Lavinia + come.

9 Receive the blood, and when that they are dead,
Let me goe grin'd their Bones to powder small,
And with this hatefull Liquor temper it,
And in that Paste let their vil'd Heads be bakte,
Come, come, be every one officious, x
To make this Banket, which I wish [might] prove, x
More sterne and bloody [then] the Centaures Feast.

[He cuts their throats]

10 So now bring them in, for Ile play the Cooke,
And see them ready, x [gainst] their Mother comes.

#'S 13 - 17: AARON, AND HIS SON

13/ Aaron **Now climbeth Tamora Olympus toppe,** 2.1.1 - 24

Background: The first speech in the play for Aaron, Tamora's lover. As such, it is self-explanatory.

Style: solo

Where: unspecified, but probably in or near the palace **To Whom:** self, and direct audience address

# of Lines: 24 **Probable Timing: 1.15 minutes**

Modern Text

13/ Aaron

1 Now climbeth Tamora Olympus' top*,
Safe out of Δfortune's shot, and sits aloft,
Secure of Δthunder's crack* or lightning flash,
Advanc'd [above] pale envy's* threat'ning reach. †

2 As when the golden Δsun * salutes the morn*,
And having gilt the Δocean with his beams*,
Gallops the Δzodiac* in his glistering Δcoach,
And overlooks* the highest peering* hills :
So Tamora. †

3 Upon her wit doth earthly honor* wait*,
And virtue stoops* and trembles at her frown*; ◊
Then, Aaron, arm* thy heart*, and fit thy thoughts,
To mount aloft with thy Δimperial* Δmistress*,
And mount her pitch, whom thou in triumph long
Hast prisoner held, fett'red in amorous chains*,
And faster bound to Aaron's charming eyes,
[Than] is Prometheus tied to Caucasus.

4 Away with slavish weeds* and [servile] thoughts ! †

5 I will be bright, and shine in Δpearl* and Δgold,
To wait* upon this new made Δemperess*.

6 To wait* said I? ◊ to wanton with this Δqueen*,
This Δgoddess*, this [Semiramis], this Δ[nymph],
This Δsiren* that will charm* Rome's Saturnine,
And see his shipwrack* and his Δcommon°weal's*.

The modern text resetting of the F sentence structure turns what was originally a relatively uncontrolled personal release full of passion (delight perhaps?) into a far neater and tidier analytical exposition.

- the speech is extremely passionate (26/26 in twenty-four lines)
- the single surround phrase " : So Tamora:" sums up the sole focus of his world and hopes
- the two short moments where capitals and long-spellings don't match are the two emotional lines ending the long F sentence #1 with his unabated admiration for Tamora's current power (0/4), and the wonderfully intellectual self-assessment of how inextricably sexually bound to him she is (the last two lines of sentence #2, 3/0)
- the long eleven line opening F sentence all centers on Tamora and allows for a wonderfully passionate build: modern texts have broken it down into mt.. #1-2 and the first two lines of #3, thus reducing the release and drive, and further . . .
- . . . whereas in F sentence #2 Aaron focuses his attention purely on himself, the modern rewrite has split this focus and weakened his drive, the first two lines now being about Tamora and only then turning towards himself
- similarly, the onrush of F sentence #3 allows him his due moment of passionate celebration, whereas the modern texts that split it into #4-5 set up the response as far more calculating
- and the celebration of the unusually short F sentence #4 "To waite said I?" allows him a more pointed and concentrated moment in which to dream and revel before moving onto the sensuality of the last sentence: modern texts somewhat gut this by jamming F sentences #4-5 together

First Folio

13/ Aaron

1 Now climbeth Tamora Olympus toppe,
Safe out of Fortunes shot, and sits aloft,
Secure of Thunders cracke or lightning flash,
Advanc'd [about] pale envies threatning reach :
As when the golden Sunne† salutes the morne,
And having gilt the Ocean with his beames,
Gallops the Zodiacke in his glistering Coach,
And over-lookes the highest piering hills :
So Tamora :
Upon her wit doth earthly honour waite,
And vertue stoopes and trembles at her frowne.

2 Then + Aaron + arme thy hart, and fit thy thoughts,
To mount aloft with thy Emperiall Mistris,
And mount her pitch, whom thou in triumph long
Hast prisoner held, fettred in amorous chaines,
And faster bound to Aarons charming eyes,
[Then] is Prometheus ti'de to Caucasus.

3 Away with slavish weedes,$_x$ and [idle] thoughts,
I will be bright + and shine in Pearle and Gold,
To waite upon this new made Empresse.

4 To waite said I?

5 To wanton with this Queene,
This Goddesse, this [Semerimis], this [Queene],
This Syren,$_x$ that will charme Romes Saturnine,
And see his shipwracke,$_x$ and his Common weales.

14/ Tamora **My lovely Aaron,** 2.3.10 - 29

Background: This is the first scene that Tamora, recently married and promoted to empress of Rome, has alone with her lover Aaron. As such, it is self-explanatory.

Style: as part of a two-handed scene

Where: the woods **To Whom:** Aaron

# of Lines: 20 **Probable Timing: 1.00 minutes**

Modern Text

14/ Tamora

1 My lovely Aaron, wherefore look'st thou sad,
When every thing doth make a ^△^gleeful* boast?

2 The ^△^birds chant* melody on every bush,
The ^△^snake lies rolled in the cheerful* ^△^sun*,
The green* leaves quiver with the cooling wind*
And make a checker'd₊ shadow on the ground. †

3 Under their sweet* shade, Aaron, let us sit,
And whil'st the babbling₊ ^△^echo* mocks the ^△^hounds,
Replying shrilly to the well-°tun'd°^△^horns*,
As if a double hunt were heard at once,
Let us sit down* and mark* their [yellowing] noise*;
And after conflict, such as was suppos'd ◊
The wand'ring ^△^prince and Dido once enjoy'd,
When with a happy storm* they were surpris'd,
And ^△^curtain'd with a ^△^counsel*-keeping ^△^cave,
We may, each wreathed in the other's arms*
(Our pastimes done), possess* a ^△^golden slumber,
Whiles ^△^hounds and ^△^horns* and sweet ^△^melodious ^△^birds
Be unto us as is a ^△^nurse's ^△^song
Of ^△^lullaby₊ to bring her ^△^babe asleep*.

This speech brings into question how much sensuality/sexuality the original boy actor would be expected to bring to the role of the obviously besotted Tamora, and how. There are three of what many modern editors term as F accidentals that suggest enormous breaks in demeanor and intellect – the opening split lines, that suggest Tamora needs a pause somewhere before she can continue, and the most peculiar ungrammatical periods, one in the middle of a sentence (line 3, F #2) and the other interrupting a grammatical idea (the split between F sentences #2-3). Since the three accidentals are neither poetically nor grammatically correct, and were not set in the source text that preceded F, the quarto of 1594, no modern editor pays attention to them. Nevertheless, as a potential for exploring a character who cannot totally control herself, these irregularities could prove invaluable.

- interestingly, once the non-grammatical break between F #2-3 is passed, there is a total change in orthography, for, after the opening intellectually questioning tease (2/1), whereas sentence #2 was somewhat passionate (7/11 in ten lines), the remainder of the speech becomes amazingly strong in sensually intellectual imagery (14/6) as if the ideas themselves are giving her satisfaction and delight

- that she is moved by her images can be seen in the four wonderfully non-grammatical extra breath thoughts (marked ,ₓ) to be found in the last four lines, as if she were being carried away with the images and/or needed the extra breaths to control herself

First Folio

14/ Tamora

1 My lovely Aaron, → [6]
Wherefore look'st thou sad,
When every thing doth make a Gleefull boast?

2 The Birds chaunt melody on every bush,
The Snake lies rolled in the chearefull Sunne,
The greene leaves quiver.ₓ [7] with the cooling winde,ₓ
And make a cheker'd shadow on the ground:
Under their sweete shade, Aaron⁺ let us sit,
And whil'st the babling Eccho mock's the Hounds,
Replying shrilly to the well tun'd-Hornes,
As if a double hunt were heard at once,
Let us sit downe,ₓ and marke their [yelping] noyse: ₓ
And after conflict, such as was suppos'd. [8]

3 The wandring Prince and Dido once enjoy'd,
When with a happy storme they were surpris'd,
And Curtain'd with a Counsaile-keeping Cave,
We may⁺ each wreathed in the others armes,ₓ
(Our pastimes done)ₓ possesse a Golden slumber,
Whiles Hounds and Hornes,ₓ and sweet Melodious Birds
Be unto us,ₓ as is a Nurses Song
Of Lullabie,ₓ to bring her Babe asleepe.

---

[6] Ff's two short lines opening Tamora's speech reply (5/5syllables) allow a silent moment for them to embrace or kiss (or for Aaron to avoid embracing and/or kissing, hence the second short line): Qq/most modern texts set the pair of lines as one single line

[7] F 1-2 set a totally ungrammatical period, which, if it were to stand, might suggest the 'Snake' isn't the only thing that is quivering: Qq/F3/most modern texts omit the punctuation

[8] F 1-2 set a second totally ungrammatical period, which, if it were to stand, might well suggest Tamora is having to struggle to keep her passions in check: Qq/F3/most modern texts set a comma

15/ Aaron **Sooner this sword shall plough thy bowels up.** between 4.2.87 - 111

Background: Unbeknownst until the birth of the child, Aaron has sired a son on Tamora, and because of the child's colour it is obvious that he, and not her husband Saturninus, is the father. Fearful of reprisals, Tamora has had their son brought to Aaron with orders to kill it, an order seconded by both of Tamora's adult children. The following is triggered by Demetrius' 'Ile broach the Tadpole on my Rapiers point:/Nurse give it me, my sword shall soone dispatch it'. One note, perhaps the nurse is holding the baby, or even Aaron himself.

Style: address to two men, in front of one other person

Where: unspecified, but somewhere in or near the palace **To Whom:** Tamora's sons Demetrius and Chiron, in front of the Nurse who brought the baby, and the baby

# of Lines: 24 **Probable Timing: 1.15 minutes**

Modern Text

15/ Aaron

1 Sooner this sword shall plough thy bowels up.
2 Stay, [murderous] villains*, will you kill your brother?
3 Now, by the burning ^Δ^tapers of the sky*,
That shone so brightly when this ^Δ^boy was got,
He dies upon my [^Δ^scimitar's] sharp* point,
That touches this my first-born* son* and heir* !
4 I tell you younglings, not Enceladus,
With all his threat'ning band of Typhon's brood*,
Nor great Alcides, nor the ^Δ^god of war*,
Shall seize this prey out of his father's hands. †
5 What, what, ye sanguine, shallow harted ^Δ^boys* !
Ye white-[lim'd*] walls ! ye ^Δ^alehouse painted signs* ! †
6 Coal* °black* is better [than]another hue,
In that it scorns* to bear* another hue ;
For all the water in the ^Δ^ocean
Can never turn* the ^Δ^swan's black* legs to white,
Although she lave them hourly* in the flood. †
7 Tell the Empress* from me, I am of age
To keep* mine own*, excuse it how she can.
8 My mistress* is my mistress*, this myself *,
The vigor* and the picture of my youth :
This before all the world do I prefer*,
This maugre* all the world will I keep* safe,
Or some of you shall smoke* for it in Rome.

The control that the modern text Aaron seems to display throughout the scene is not supported by F's sentence structure and/or orthography. Though the opening three sentences match, once Aaron starts to heap the insults on the boys' heads (after the first colon of F sentence #4, start of mt. sentence #5), intellect gives way to highly personal feelings.

- there is a deceptive calm to the opening one line sentence (0/0), and even in the second equally unusually short F sentence [9] #2 with just the one long-spelled 'villaines' (an insult to which Aaron returns a little later): not surprisingly passion suddenly breaks through in sentence F #3 (3/4) finishing with a highly emotional cluster of long spellings 'my first borne sonne and heire'
- for a moment it seems as if Aaron can recover for, thanks to the classical allusions rife in the opening four lines of F sentence #4, intellect seems to dominate emotion (4/3)
- but the insult of 'young-lings', a reference at best to an inferior fish, at worst to something sexually unpleasant (spoiled by the modern text resetting the more recogniseable 'younglings') paves the way for Aaron's act of double defiance – the protestation that 'Cole-blacke is better than another hue' and refusal to follow Tamora's wishes to get rid of or kill the child ('to keepe mine owne'), and the remainder of the speech is highly personal (6/18 in 14 lines)
- and not surprisingly F (#4) sets this release of emotion as one long sentence, the drive of which most modern texts deflate by splitting it into four
- Aaron's act of defining the world as he sees it and will preserve it, i.e. an 'Empresse' (Tamora) is still his 'mistris' and his new born son is his sole concern is supported by the only surround phrases in the speech opening the first two lines of the last sentence, F #5, viz.
". My mistris is my mistris : this my selfe,/The vigour, and the picture of my youth : "

First Folio

15/ Aaron

1 Sooner this sword shall plough thy bowels up. [10]
2 Stay⁺ [murtherous] villaines, will you kill your brother?
3 Now⁺ by the burning Tapers of the skie,
That sh'one so brightly when this Boy was got,
He dies upon my [Semitars] sharpe point,
That touches this my first borne sonne and heire. ⁺
4 I tell you young-lings, not Enceladus⁺
With all his threatning band of Typhons broode,
Nor great Alcides, nor the God of warre,
Shall ceaze this prey out of his fathers hands :
What, what, ye sanguine⁺ shallow harted Boyes,⁺
Ye white-[limb'd] walls,⁺ ye Ale-house painted signes,⁺
Cole-blacke is better [then] another hue,
In that it scornes to beare another hue : ₓ
For all the water in the Ocean,ₓ
Can never turne the Swans blacke legs to white,
Although she lave them hourely in the flood :
Tell the Empresse from me, I am of age
To keepe mine owne, excuse it how she can.
5 My mistris is my mistris : ₓ this my selfe,
The vigour,⁺ and the picture of my youth :
This,ₓ before all the world do I preferre,
This mauger all the world will I keepe safe,
Or some of you shall smoake for it in Rome.

[9] Folio one line sentences are unusual in longer Shakespeare speeches (usually denoting that what is being said is so directly to the point that anything else is unnecessary and the speaker is hiding nothing), so it's of great interest the speech opens with two

[10] some modern texts suggest that Aaron seizes the child and/or draws his sword

16/ Aaron **'Twill vexe thy soule to heare what I shall speake :** between 5.1.62 - 85

17/ Aaron **{I am sorry} that I had not done a thousand more :** 5.1.124 - 144

Background: The following are two speeches of defiance by the captured Aaron. Speech #16 is triggered by the fact Aaron's offer to speak on the guarantee that his son's life will be spared is met with Lucius' reply 'if it please me which thou speak'st,/Thy child shall live, and I will see it nourisht', moving on to explain the pedigree of the child and then quickly elaborating in full his own and Tamora's role in the destruction of all the Andronici, Lucius' family. Speech #17 rejects any form of regret for what he has done.

Style: both addresses to one man in front of a large group

Where: both on the road to Rome **To Whom:** both to Lucius, in front of the army of the Goths

Speech 16, # of Lines: 19 **Probable Timing: 1.00 minutes**

Speech 17, # of Lines: 21 **Probable Timing: 1.10 minutes**

Modern Text

16/ Aaron

1 'Twill vex* thy soul* to hear* what I shall speak* :
For I must talk* of [△murders], △rapes, and △massacres,
Acts of △black* △°night, abominable* △deeds,
Complots of △mischief *, △treason, △villainies,
Ruthful* to hear*, yet piteously* [perform'd] . †

2 And this shall all be buried [in] my death,
Unless* thou swear* to me my △child* shall live.

3 {ψ} I know thou art △religious,
And hast a thing within thee called △conscience,
With twenty △popish tricks* and △ceremonies,
Which I have seen* thee careful* to observe,
Therefore I urge thy oath ; for that I know
An △idiot* holds his △bauble for a △god,
And keeps* the oath which by that △god he swears*,
To that I'll urge him : therefore thou shalt vow
By that same △god, what △god so'er* it be
That thou adorest and hast in reverence,
To save my △boy, to nourish and bring him up,
Or else I will discover nought to thee.

F's orthography opens up some quite surprising swings in mood and attitude not easily seen in the modern texts, all of which suggest several complex layers all vying for release, not just the ravings of a one dimensional figure of evil.

- the opening line is ferocious in its emotional release (0/4)
- the next three lines are full of intellectual savagery (8/4)
- and then, as the tantalizing blackmail finishes the longer F opening sentence ('let my child live and I'll tell you'), Aaron's personal needs come sweeping through (1/6), the only other passionate release (capitals and long-spellings virtually matching) coming in the two lines of incredibly insulting attack on Lucius' supposed religious beliefs (4/3 in just the two lines 6-7 of F #2)
- for the rest of the speech either an intellectual self-control is maintained (the opening three lines of F #2 as the question of religion is broached, 4/1), or the last four lines of the speech demanding Lucius vow to save the child, (3/0), or, and even more dangerously there are moments of very frightening non-embellished calm when Aaron is at his most demanding or incisive
  "And this shall all be buried by my death,"
  "Therefore I urge thy oath"
  "to nourish and bring him up,/Or else I will discover nought to thee"

First Folio

16/ Aaron

1 'Twill vexe thy soule to heare what I shall speake :
For I must talke of [Murthers], Rapes, and Massacres,
Acts of Blacke-night, abhominable Deeds,
Complots of Mischiefe, Treason, Villanies
Ruthfull to heare, yet pittiously [preform'd],
And this shall all be buried [by] my death,
Unlesse thou sweare to me my Childe shall live.

2 {ψ} I know thou art Religious,
And hast a thing within thee, x called Conscience,
With twenty Popish trickes and Ceremonies,
Which I have seene thee carefull to observe : x
Therefore I urge thy oath, + for that I know
An Ideot holds his Bauble for a God,
And keepes the oath which by that God he sweares,
To that Ile urge him : therefore thou shalt vow
By that same God, what God so ere it be
That thou adorest, x and hast in reverence,
To save my Boy, to nourish and bring him up,
Or else I will discover nought to thee.

Modern Text

17/ Aaron

1 {I am sorry} that I had not done a thousand more. †

2 Even now I curse the day, - and yet I think*
Few come within [the] compass* of my curse -
Wherein I did not some Δnotorious ill:
As kill a man, or else devise his death,
Ravish a Δmaid, or plot the way to do it,
Accuse some Δinnocent, and forswear* myself*,
Set deadly Δenmity between* two Δfriends,
Make poor* men's Δcattle* break*[11] their necks*,
Set fire on Δbarns * and Δhaystacks* in the night,
And bid the Δowners quench them with [their] tears*. †

3 Oft have I digg'd* up dead men from their graves,
And set them upright at their dear* Δfriends door*,
Even when their sorrows* almost was forgot,
And on their skins*, as on the Δbark* of Δtrees,
Have with my knife carved in Roman* Δletters,
"Let not your sorrow die, though I am dead."

4 [But], I have done a thousand dreadful* things,
As willingly, as one would kill a Δfly,
And nothing grieves* me heartily* indeed*,
But that I cannot do* ten thousand more.

The passion of the previous speech is just as marked here (15/22 in twenty-one lines), yet the switches are far more rapid and concentrated in smaller bursts than before.

- it's interesting to see the utter calm of the opening line quickly move into a much longer F sentence #1 where the remaining non-embellished lines, involving truly horrific images, viz.
  "{I am sorry} that I had not done a thousand more"
  "As kill a man, or else devise his death,"
  "Oft have I dig'd up dead men from their graves"
  "Let not your sorrow die, though I am dead"
  divide the sentence into at least four different rhetorical parts, each with their own speaking energy

- the bulk of the capitals fall into two particularly vicious clusters: more than half (8) in just 6 lines as Aaron begins to elaborate his attacks on the vulnerable, starting with 'Ravish a Maid' (starting line 6, F sentence #1), and 4 in the two lines describing what he would do with dead bodies he dug up (the next to last two lines of F #1)

- and the long spellings also fall into two patterns, either
  a/ in clusters, as with the 6 in the two lines of the following
  "Make poore mens Cattell breake their neckes,
  Set fire on Barnes and Haystackes in the night," &
  "foresweare my selfe "
  b/ often at the end of lines or phrases, as if the act of speaking leads to greater release as an idea is concluded/pushed home

First Folio

17/ Aaron

1 {I am sorry} that I had not done a thousand more:
Even now I curse the day, and yet I thinke
Few come within [few] compasse of my curse,
Wherein I did not some Notorious ill, +
As kill a man, or else devise his death,
Ravish a Maid, or plot the way to do it,
Accuse some Innocent, and forsweare my selfe,
Set deadly Enmity betweene two Friends,
Make poore mens Cattell breake their neckes,
Set fire on Barnes and Haystackes in the night,
And bid the Owners quench them with [the] teares:
Oft have I dig'd up dead men from their graves,
And set them upright at their deere Friends doore,
Even when their sorrowes almost was forgot,
And on their skinnes, as on the Barke of Trees,
Have with my knife carved in Romaine Letters,
Let not your sorrow die, though I am dead.

2 [Tut], I have done a thousand dreadfull things +
As willingly, as one would kill a Fly,
And nothing greeves me hartily indeede,
But that I cannot doe ten thousand more.

[11] since Qq/Ff set an eight syllable line, metrically minded commentators have suggested 'silly Cattle', or 'fall and break'

SPEECHES IN ORDER	TIME	PAGE
ROMEO & JULIET		
#'s 1 - 2: Theatrical Links		
1/ Chorus *Two households both alike in dignitie,*	0.45	50
2/ Chorus Now old desire doth in his death bed lie,	0.45	51
#'s 3 - 6: The Quarrel		
3/ Prince Rebellious Subjects, Enemies to peace,	1.10	52
4/ Capulet Content thee gentle Coz, let him alone,	0.35	53
5/ Mercutio Oh hee's the Couragious Captaine of Complements	0.45	54
6/ Benvolio {Tybalt} began this Fray,	1.15	55
#'s 7 - 10: The Rich Capulet Regarding Marrying Juliet To Nobility		
7/ Capulet What say {I} to {your} sute?	1.30	56
8/ {Capulet as} 1st Capulet Welcome Gentlemen,	0.45	57
9/ Capulet How now?/How now? Chopt Logicke? what is this?	1.55	58
10/ Capulet Come, stir, stir, stir,/The second Cocke hath Crow'd,	0.45	60
#'s 11 - 12: The Noble Paris		
11/ Paris Immoderately she weepes for Tybalts death,	0.35	61
12/ Paris Give me thy Torch Boy, hence and stand aloft,	1.00	62
#'s 13 - 17: Family And Friends About Romeo		
13/ Benvolio At this same auncient Feast of Capulets	0.40	63
14/ Mercutio O then I see Queene Mab hath beene with you.	1.40	64
15/ Mercutio This cannot anger him, t'would anger him	1.30	66
16/ Frier Lawrence Holy S Francis, what a change is heere?	0.50	67
17/ Mercutio Here comes Romeo, without his Roe, . . .	0.30	68
#'s 18 - 20: Family And Friends About Juliet		
18/ Nurse Faith I can tell her age unto an houre.	1.55	69
19/ {Mother as} Old Lady Marry that marry is the very theame	1.30	71
20/ Nurse Mistris, what Mistris? Juliet? Fast I warrant her she.	0.45	72
#'s 21 - 26: Romeo And Juliet, The Loving Beginning		
21/ Romeo He jeasts at Scarres that never felt a wound,	1.35	73
22/ Juliet O Romeo, Romeo, wherefore art thou Romeo?	0.50	75
23/ Juliet Thou knowest the maske of night is on my face,	1.10	76
24/ Juliet Three words deare Romeo	0.40	77

SPEECHES BY GENDER

		Speech #(s)
SPEECHES FOR WOMEN (11)		
Nurse	**Traditional:** middle-aged woman or older **Today:** woman old enough to have breast-fed Juliet fourteen years ago	#18, #20
Mother	**Traditional:** middle-aged woman or older **Today:** woman old enough to have a daughter fourteen years ago	#19
Juliet	**Traditional & Today:** young woman, almost fourteen	#22, #23, #24, #27, #28, #29, #30, #33
SPEECHES FOR EITHER GENDER (11)		
Chorus	**Traditional:** older male **Today:** any gender, any age	#1, #2
Prince	**Traditional:** older male with two adult nephews **Today:** any gender with two adult nephews	#3, #37
Benvolio	**Traditional:** young male **Today:** any gender	#6, #13
Frier Lawrence	**Traditional:** older male **Today:** any gender, any age	#16, #25, #31, #32, #36
SPEECHES FOR MEN (15)		
Capulet	**Traditional & Today:** early or middle-aged male with young teenage daughter	#4, #7, #8, #9, #10
Paris	**Traditional & Today:** young man	#11, #12
Mercutio	**Traditional:** young man, probably older than Romeo & Benvolio	#5, #14, #15, #17
Romeo	**Traditional & Today:** young man	#21, #26, #34, #35

25/ Frier Lawrence The gray ey'd morne smiles on the frowning night,	1.30	78	
26/ Romeo {I have not graced my} bed to night,	0.55	79	
#'s 27 - 30: Romeo And Juliet, Awaiting The Nurse			
27/ Juliet The clocke strook nine, when I did send the Nurse,	1.00	80	
28/ Juliet Gallop apace, you fiery footed steedes,	1.45	81	
29/ Juliet What storme is this that blowes so contrarie?	0.55	83	
30/ Juliet Blister'd be thy tongue/For such a wish,	1.45	84	
#'s 31 - 35: Romeo And Juliet, The Tragedy			
31/ Frier Lawrence Hold thy desperate hand:	2.30	86	
32/ Frier Lawrence Hold then: goe home be merrie, give consent,	1.35	87	
33/ Juliet Farewell:/God knowes when we shall meete againe.	2.10	88	
34/ Romeo No matter: Get thee gone,	1.15	90	
35/ Romeo O give me thy hand, . . .	2.00	91	
#'s 36 - 37: Final Words			
36/ Frier Lawrence I am the greatest, able to doe least,	2.00	93	
37/ Prince Seale up the mouth of outrage† for a while,	0.55	95	

ROMEO & JULIET

#'s 1 - 2: Theatrical Links

1/ Chorus ***Two households both alike in dignitie,*** Prologue 1 – 14

Background: The opening to the play (as set in the second quarto, and omitted by the folio).

Style: a self explanatory introduction to the play, set in the form of a sonnet

Where: the theatre **To Whom:** direct audience address

# of Lines: 14 **Probable Timing: 0.45 minutes**

Modern Text

The Prologue

2/ Chorus

1 Two households, both alike in dignity *,
In fair* Verona, where we lay our △scene
From ancient* grudge, break* to new mutiny*,
Where civil* blood* makes civil* hands unclean*. †

2 From forth the fatal* loins* of these two foes,
A pair* of star*-cross'd* lovers take their life;
Whose misadventur'd piteous* overthrows*
Doth with their death bury* their* △parents' strife.

3 The fearful* passage of their death-mark'd love,
And the continuance of their △parents' rage,
Which, but their children's end, nought could remove,
Is now the two hours* traffic* of our △stage; ◊
The which if you with patient ears* attend,
What here* shall miss*, our toil* shall strive to mend.

Written as a sonnet, the story is told emotionally (5/20) in four sections, (introduction/complications/crisis/summary - the first three sections being four lines each, the last set as two), yet the build of the two texts is very different. Most modern texts onrush the end of the speech, mt. #3 combining the crisis and summary, whereas F gains control by the end of the speech, after an onrushed difficult-to-control start - F #1 combining together the introduction and the complications. Therefore it's not surprising most of F's releases come in the middle of its onrushed first sentence.

- however, the speech opens calmly, with an unembellished first line (perhaps the ensuing story is difficult to share, with the final word 'dignitie' being short spelled)
- but even as the second line establishes the locale, the releases start (2/1), and then, spilling over the break between introduction and summary, the information of the 'ancient grudge' leading to the eventual fate of the 'paire of starre-crost lovers' is expressed via an enormous emotional release (0/10 in just four lines): and even after their deaths have been spoken of, the Chorus cannot regain self-control, for the acknowledgement that their 'death burie theur Parents strife' is still emotional (1/3, the last two lines of F #1)
- in comparison to the start of the speech, F #2's explanation that the story will be 'the two houres trafficque of our Stage' seems fairly relaxed initially (2/3), yet the fact that this is the crisis section of the sonnet and that the last two lines are expressed as surround phrases suggests that the Chorus might be working very hard to keep the appearance of control – fear of audience response perhaps – especially since the F #3 summary appealing that 'patient eares attend' is so emotional (0/4 in just two lines)

First Folio

The Prologue [1]

2/ Chorus

1 *Two households⁺ both alike in dignitie,*
(ₓIn faire Verona⁺ where we lay our Sceneₓ)
From auncient grudge, breake to new mutinie,
Where civill bloud makes civill hands uncleane:
From forth the fatall loynes of these two foes,
A paire of starre-crost lovers,ₓ take their life: ₓ
Whose misadventur'd pittious overthrowes,ₓ
Doth with their death burie theur Parents strife.

2 *The fearfull passage of their death-markt love,*
And the continuance of their Parents rage: ₓ
Which⁺ but their childrens end ⁺nought could remove:ₓ
Is now the two houres trafficque of our Stage.

3 *The which if you with patient eares attend,*
What heare shall misse, our toyle shall strive to mend.

[1] the Prologue, though set in Q1-4, was not printed in F1: the text here is taken from Q2

2/ Chorus **Now old desire doth in his death bed lie,** Act Two Chorus 1 - 14

Background: A short speech of plot advancement following the first meeting of Romeo and Juliet at the Capulet party.

Style: a self explanatory speech set in the form of a sonnet

Where: the theatre **To Whom:** direct audience address

# of Lines: 14 **Probable Timing: 0.45 minutes**

Modern Text

2/ Chorus

1 Now old desire doth in his death bed lie,
And young₊ affection gapes to be his △heir*;
That fair*, for which Love groan'd₊ for, and would die,
With tender Juliet match'd, is now not fair*.

2 Now Romeo is beloved, and △loves again*,
[Alike*] bewitched by the charm* of looks*;
But to his foe suppos'd he must complain*,
And she steal* △love's sweet bait from fearful* hooks* ! †

3 Being held a foe, he may not have access*
To breathe₊ such vows* as △lovers use to swear*;
And she as much in △love, her means* much less*
To meet her new-△beloved any where. †

4 But passion lends them △power, time means*, to meet*,
Temp'ring extremities with extreme* sweet*.

Once more set as a sonnet, most modern texts present a totally normal (4/4/4/2) linear structure. However, after a calm start – the almost unembellished opening two lines hinting at a new love – F moves into passion as the audience is told Rosaline is 'now not faire' when compared with Juliet (2/2 F #1's last two lines). Then, unlike the modern texts' continued rationality, F's remaining ten lines are totally onrushed, and, overall, full of emotional release (7/16). Interestingly, most of the emotional releases come at the end of each line, implying a certain rhetorical flourish as the information unfolds.

• thus, as the complications section starts, F 2's first line, 'Romeo is beloved', is informatively passionate (2/1), but, wonderfully, the remaining three lines of the section, both characters being 'bewitched', are highly emotional (1/6)

• rushing straight into the dilemma of their being unable to meet as normal lovers (because of their parents' enmity, a worthy subject for a crisis section) is still described passionately (3/5), and each time 'love' is mentioned it is capitalised ('Lovers', 'Love', and 'Beloved')

• which in turn rushes into the summary explaining that their 'passion' creates 'meanes to meete' – the accompanying emotion (1/4 in just two lines) perhaps suggesting that the Chorus is anticipates the bitter-sweet that is to follow

First Folio

2/ Chorus

1 Now old desire doth in his death bed lie,
And yong affection gapes to be his Heire,+
That faire, for which Love gron'd for+ and would die,
With tender Juliet matcht, is now not faire.

2 Now Romeo is beloved, and Loves againe,
[A like] bewitched by the charme of lookes: x
But to his foe suppos'd he must complaine,
And she steale Loves sweet bait from fearefull hookes:+
Being held a foe, he may not have accesse
To breath such vowes as Lovers use to sweare,+
And she as much in Love, her meanes much lesse, x
To meet her new Beloved any where:
But passion lends them Power, time, x meanes+ to meete,
Temp'ring extremities with extreame sweete.

#'s 3-6: The Quarrel

3/ Prince **Rebellious Subjects, Enemies to peace,** 1.1.81 - 103

Background: The ongoing quarrel between the two houses of Capulet and Mountague has lead to further street brawls involving innocent and angry citizens. This is their Prince's first on-stage attempt to prevent matters from getting further out of hand.

Style: group address in the open air

Where: public street **To Whom:** the Capulets, including the head of the family, his wife, and hot-headed nephew Tybalt; the Mountagues[2], including the head of the family, his wife, and hot-headed nephew Benvolio; citizens at large and members of the watch

# of Lines: 23 **Probable Timing: 1.10 minutes**

Modern Text

3/ Prince

1 Rebellious Δsubjects, Δenemies to peace,
Profaners* of this Δneighbor-stained Δsteel* -
Will they not hear*? -
2 What ho*, you Δmen, you Δbeasts !
That quench the fire of your pernicious* Δrage
With purple Δfountains* issuing from your Δveins*-
On pain* of Δtorture, from those bloody hands
Throw your mistempered* Δweapons to the ground,
And hear* the Δsentence of your moved* prince. [3]
3 Three civil* [Δbrawls], bred of an Δairy* word,
By thee, old Capulet, and [Montague],
Have thrice disturb'd the quiet of our streets,
And made Verona's ancient Δcitizens
Cast by their Δgrave beseeming Δornaments
To wield old Δpartisans*, in hands as old,
Cank'red with peace, to part your Δcank'red hate ;
If ever you disturb* our streets again*,
Your lives shall pay the forfeit of the peace.
4 For this time all the rest depart away. †
5 You, Capulet, shall go* along with me,
And, [Montague], come you this afternoon*,
To know our [farther] pleasure in this case,
To old Free-town*, our common judgment*-°place. †
6 Once more, on pain* of death, all men depart.

F's orthography suggests that the Prince has great personal difficulty in quieting the disturbance, while the final onrushed F #4 (split into three by most modern texts) suggests that, even though by F #3 he seems to have established self-control, in his final series of commands and warnings his control begins to slip once more.

- given the circumstances it's not surprising that unembellished lines are few and far between, the horror of civil chaos resulting in
  'Have thrice disturb'd the quiet of our streets,"
  plus the seriousness of
  "Your lives shall pay the forfeit of the peace. / For this time all the rest depart away: "
  the latter doubly weighted by being one of only two surround phrases in the speech
- his command Mountague and Capulet must report for hearings
  " : To old Free-towne, our common judgement place : "
  being set as a surround phrase might well suggest that a 'common judgement place' is not where two such worthies might expect to be summoned, and therefore could be construed as deliberate humiliation
- the initial (unsuccessful) command for attention is passionate (F #1, 4/3)
- to be followed by an equally unsuccessful intellectual attempt to shame them as 'Beasts' (the opening two and half lines of F #2, 5/3), while the last three lines, resorting to the threat of 'Torture' and identifying this as the third of 'civill Broyles, bred of an Ayery word,' becomes passionate once more (6/6, , the last three lines of F #2, and the first of F #3)
- and having got their attention, it seems the Prince has regained public and private control, at least for F #3's next six very factual lines describing the result of these 'Broyles' (8/1), only to become emotional again on the warning 'If ever you disturbe our streets againe," (0/2), followed by the two unembellished lines discussed above
- and control fades away throughout the onrushed F #4, the three lines telling the heads of the families that they will soon learn the Prince's 'pleasure in this case' being passionate (3/3), and the last two, with the potential insult of where 'judgement' will be pronounced and a further command on 'paine of death' for 'all men' to 'depart' turning emotional (1/3)

First Folio

3/ Prince

1 Rebellious Subjects, Enemies to peace,
Prophaners of this Neighbor-stained Steele,
Will they not heare?
2 What hoe, you Men, you Beasts,+
That quench the fire of your pernitious Rage,x
With purple Fountaines issuing from your Veines: x
On paine of Torture, from those bloody hands
Throw your mistemper'd Weapons to the ground,
And heare the Sentence of your mooved Prince.
3 Three civill [Broyles], bred of an Ayery word,
By thee+ old Capulet +and [Mountague],
Have thrice disturb'd the quiet of our streets,
And made Verona's ancient Citizens
Cast by their Grave beseeming Ornaments,x
To wield old Partizans, in hands as old,
Cankred with peace, to part your Cankred hate,+
If ever you disturbe our streets againe,
Your lives shall pay the forfeit of the peace.
4 For this time all the rest depart away:
You+ Capulet +shall goe along with me,
And+ [Mountague+] come you this afternoone,
To know our [Fathers] pleasure in this case: x
To old Free-towne, our common judgement place:
Once more+ on paine of death, all men depart.

[2] though referred to throughout as 'Mountague' most modern texts spell the family name as 'Montague': the variation will be herein noted by square brackets without further annotation

[3] most modern texts add a stage direction that all involved in the fighting throw/put down their weapons

4/ Capulet **Content thee gentle Coz, let him alone,** 1.5.65 - 74

Background: At the urgings of the neutral Mercutio, the Mountague Romeo and his friends have managed to gate-crash the enemy Capulet's party - mainly in the hopes to see his current love, Rosaline (see speech #2 above, and #13 below). Unfortunately the hot-headed Tybalt has seen through Romeo's disguise and has protested vehemently to the leader of the Capulets, Juliet's father, that Romeo should be taught a lesson, and to that end has sent for his sword. As the following shows, the older Capulet is much more sanguine.

Style: as part of a two handed scene in front of a much larger non-attentive group

Where: the main hall of the Capulet home **To Whom:** his nephew Tybalt, aside from the main body of the party

# of Lines: 10 **Probable Timing: 0.35 minutes**

Modern Text

4/ Capulet

1 Content thee, gentle Δcoz, let him alone,
A bears* him like a portly Δgentleman;
And to say truth, Verona brags of him
To be a virtuous and well govern'd youth. †

2 I would not for the wealth of all [this] town*
Here in my house do him disparagement;
Therefore be patient, take no note of him;
It is my will, the which if thou respect,
Show* a fair* presence and put off these frowns*,
An ill-beseeming semblance for a Δfeast.

Whether Capulet is warning Tybalt away from Romeo completely, or simply saying that Tybalt should not 'Here in my house do him disparagement' is up to each production to decide, but the careful unembellished quality of this line, coupled with the next two similarly unembellished lines, 'Therefore be patient, take no note of him,/It is my will, the which if thou respect,' suggest that Capulet is doing everything he can to maintain the public 'semblance for a Feast.', onrush or no.

- thus the opening three lines of rebuke of Tybalt and praise for Romeo (both perhaps galling to Tybalt) are intellectual (3/1)

- the following five of not 'Here in my house' and 'It is my will' are extraordinarily (icy? enforced?) calmly unembellished (0/1)

- while the last two lines, perhaps in support of pretence ('Shew a faire presence'), are slightly passionate (1/3) – the whole somewhat unusual for the normally effusive Capulet

First Folio

4/ Capulet

1 Content thee+ gentle Coz, let him alone,
A beares him like a portly Gentleman: x
And to say truth, Verona brags of him, x
To be a vertuous and well govern'd youth:
I would not for the wealth of all [the] towne, x
Here in my house do him disparagement: x
Therefore be patient, take no note of him,+
It is my will, the which if thou respect,
Shew a faire presence, x and put off these frownes,
An ill beseeming semblance for a Feast.

5/ Mercutio **Oh hee's the Couragious Captaine of Complements :** between 2.4.19 - 35

Background: Tybalt has challenged Romeo to a duel for daring to intrude on the Capulet's party (speech #4 above). Benvolio believes 'Romeo will answere it'. Mercutio, probably an ex-soldier, has no illusions about Tybalt's dueling skills, even though he mocks the book learning through which (the probably younger) Tybalt became accomplished.

Style: as part of a two-handed scene

Where: a public street **To Whom:** Benvolio

# of Lines: 14 **Probable Timing: 0.45 minutes**

Modern Text

5/ Mercutio

1 O*, he's* the △couragi-
ous △captain* of △compliments*. †

2 He fights as you sing
prick-song, keeps time, distance, and proportion ; he rests [me]
his minim* [rests], one, two, and the third in your bosom : the
very butcher of a silk button, a △duellist*, a △duellist*; a
△gentleman of the very first house, of the first and second
cause. †

3 Ah, the immortal* △*passado*, the △*punto reverso*, the
Hay !

4 The △pox of such antic*, lisping, affecting [phantasimes],
these new tuners of accent ! †

5 "[By] Jesu, a very good blade !
a very tall man ! a very good whore !"

6 Why, is not this a la-
mentable thing, △grand-sire, that we should be thus afflicted
with these strange flies, these fashion-△mongers, these
pardon-me's*, who stand so much on the new form, that
they cannot sit at ease on the old bench ?

7 O their bones, their
bones !

Mercutio's traditional flamboyance should not dupe readers to conclude his obvious taunting of Tybalt is simply one of exuberant disdain, for the large passages of unembellished phrases both about Tybalt and the new dandy he supposedly represents (the 'lisping affecting phantacies' who have no respect for tradition , i.e. 'the old bench') suggest a fixation beyond that of mere contempt.

- the first unembellished passage is about Tybalt himself
  "he fights as you sing pricksong, keeps time, distance, and proportion, he rests his minum, one, two, and the third in your bosom : the very butcher of a silk button,"
  while the rest deals with his type in general
  "these new tuners of accent . . . a very good blade, a very tall man, a very good whore . Why is not this a lamentable thing . . . that we should be thus afflicted with these strange flies . . . who stand so much on the new form, that they cannot sit at ease on the old bench."
- most of these releases come in the first sentence (9/5 in just six lines), from the passion of the opening surround phrase (3/4 in the equivalent of just one line) and, following the first unembellished passage, the highly intellectual put-down of Tybalt's dueling style (6/1, F #1's last three lines)
- but though F #2 is short enough to be seen as composed of two sets of surround phrases, the passion is somewhat restrained (2/1, suggesting an underlying seriousness perhaps), and the releases are even more controlled for the remainder of the speech (just 2/1 in the last five lines)

First Folio

5/ Mercutio

1 Oh+ hee's the Couragi-
ous Captaine of Complements : he fights as you sing
pricksong, keeps time, distance, and proportion,+ he rests [ ]
his minum [ ], one, two, and the third in your bosom : the
very butcher of a silk button, a Dualist, a Dualist : x a
Gentleman of the very first house+ of the first and second
cause : ah+ the immortall Passado, the Punto reverso, the
Hay . +

2 The Pox of such antique+ lisping+ affecting [phantacies],
these new tuners of accent : + [ ] Jesu+ a very good blade,+
a very tall man,+ a very good whore . +

3 Why+ is not this a la-
mentable thing+ Grandsire, that we should be thus afflicted
with these strange flies : x these fashion Mongers, these
pardon-mee's, who stand so much on the new form, that
they cannot sit at ease on the old bench . +

4 O their bones, their
bones . +

6/ Benvolio **{Tybalt} began this [ ] Fray ,** 3.1.151 - 175

Background: As a result of the challenge two young people have died: Tybalt has killed Mercutio (who was in part defending Romeo's honour after Romeo, newly married to Tybalt's cousin Juliet, had refused to fight) and in revenge a distraught Romeo has killed Tybalt. Since the Capulet Tybalt was killed by the Mountague Romeo, the Capulets are now demanding Romeo's death, and before giving judgement, the Prince has demanded of Benvolio 'who began this Fray?'. This is Benvolio's answer, his final words in the play.

Style: public address to one person, in front of a large group

Where: public street **To Whom:** the Prince, in front of the Capulets, including the head of the family and his wife; the Mountagues, including the head of the family and his wife; citizens at large and members of the watch

# of Lines: 25 **Probable Timing: 1.15 minutes**

Modern Text

6/ Benvolio {ψ}

1 {ψ} {Tybalt} began this [bloody] Δfray {,}
Tybalt, here slain*, whom Romeo's hand did slay ! †

2 Romeo that spoke him fair*, bid him bethink*
How nice the Δquarrel* was, and urg'd withal*
Your high displeasure; all this, uttered
With gentle breath, calm* look*, knees humbly bow'd,
Could not take truce with the unruly spleen*
Of [Tybalt] deaf* to peace, but that he Δtilts
With Δpiercing* steel* at bold Mercutio's breast,
Who, all as hot, turns* deadly point to point,
And, with a Δmartial* Δscorn*, with one hand beats*
Cold death aside, and with the other sends
It back to Tybalt, whose dexterity
Retorts it. †

3 Romeo he cries aloud,
"Hold Δfriends! Δfriends part!" and swifter [than]his tongue,
His [agile] arm* beats down* their fatal* points,
And 'twixt them rushes; underneath whose arm*
An envious thrust from Tybalt hit the life
Of stout Mercutio, and then Tybalt fled; ◊
But by and by comes back* to Romeo,
Who had but newly entertained Revenge,
And to't* they go* like lightning, for, ere I
Could draw to part them, was stout Tybalt slain*;
And as he fell, did Romeo turn* and fly*. †

4 This is the truth, or let Benvolio die.

Including the proper names that open the first two lines, Benvolio's attempt to maintain self-control lasts just two lines (4/1).

- the next four lines attempting to assure the Prince of Romeo's 'faire' behaviour is very emotional (1/6), until reaching Tybalt's return
- his description of the fight, placing the blame on Tybalt (with his 'unruly spleen') and exonerating Mercutio ('with a Martiall scorne'), becomes passionate (5/8, the seven lines to the second colon – where mt. #2 ends)
- F's onrush into what happened next suggests that Benvolio is very much caught up in the events he is reporting, and much less in control than the modern texts (which set a new sentence here) would suggest
- thus the one and half line reporting of Romeo's words (F's equivalent to the start of mt. #3) becomes factual once more (3/0), emphasising his peace-making appeal for them to act as 'Friends', which immediately turns emotional as Benvolio describes Romeo's coming between the combatants to beat 'downe their fatall points' (0/4 in just two lines)
- the description of Tybalt's actions (striking Mercutio, fleeing, and returning to face Romeo) becomes strongly factual once more (5/1 the last two lines of F #1 and the first two of F #2), as if Benvolio were once more laying all the blame on Tybalt
- the ensuing fight and killing of Tybalt is described emotionally (1/3)
- and at last with Tybalt's death, Romeo's flight, and Benvolio's offer to 'die' if what he has just reported is not 'truth, come the only surround lines in the speech

  " : And as he fell, did Romeo turne and flie : /This is the truth, or let Benvolio die. "

  the final three lines being monosyllabic - save for the three proper names - suggest that the images are seemingly burnt into Benvolio's mind
- the last line, 'the truth . . . or die' being unembellished - save for the capitalisation of his own name – suggests a very careful offer indeed, one with no time for extravagant images or justifications

First Folio

6/ Benvolio {ψ}

1 {ψ} {Tybalt} began this [ ] Fray {,}
Tybalt+ here slaine, whom Romeo's hand did slay,+
Romeo that spoke him faire, bid him bethinke
How nice the Quarrell was, and urg'd withall
Your high displeasure:x all this+ uttered,x
With gentle breath, calme looke, knees humbly bow'd+
Could not take truce with the unruly spleene
Of [Tybalts] deafe to peace, but that he Tilts
With Peircing steele at bold Mercutio's breast,
Who+ all as hot, turnes deadly point to point,
And+ with a Martiall scorne, with one hand beates
Cold death aside, and with the other sends
It back to Tybalt, whose dexterity
Retorts it: Romeo he cries aloud,
Hold Friends,+ Friends part,+ and swifter [then] his tongue,
His [aged] arme beats downe their fatall points,
And twixt them rushes,+ underneath whose arme,x
An envious thrust from Tybalt,x hit the life
Of stout Mercutio, and then Tybalt fled.

2 But by and by comes backe to Romeo,
Who had but newly entertained Revenge,
And too't they goe like lightning, for+ ere I
Could draw to part them, was stout Tybalt slaine: x
And as he fell, did Romeo turne and flie:
This is the truth, or let Benvolio die.

#'s 7 - 10: The Rich Capulet Regarding Marrying Juliet To Nobility

7/ Capulet **What say {I} to {your} sute?** 1.2.5 - 37

Background: Paris is nephew to the Prince. Despite modern texts' insistence, Capulet is not a lord, just very rich. Thus marrying his daughter into the Prince's family would be a wonderful coup. So, despite protestations as to Juliet's youth (described elsewhere as 'not fourteene'), Capulet is prepared to entertain Paris' persistent wooing.

Style: as part of a two-handed scene, with a servant in attendance

Where: public street **To Whom:** the County Paris, in front of a Capulet servant

# of Lines: 30 **Probable Timing: 1.30 minutes**

Modern Text

7/ Capulet {ψ}

1 {ψ} {W}hat say {I} to {your} suit*?

2 But saying o'er what I have said before,
My Δchild is yet a stranger in the world,
She* hath not seen* the change of fourteen* years*;
Let two more Δsummers wither in their pride,
Ere we may think* her ripe to be a Δbride.

3 Earth hath swallowed all my hopes but she,
She's* the hopeful* Δlady of my earth. †

4 But woo* her, gentle Paris, get her heart,
My will to her consent, is but a part;
And she* [agreed], within her scope of choice*
Lies* my consent and fair* according voice. †

5 This night I hold an old accustom'd Δfeast,
Whereto I have invited many a Δguest,
Such as I love, and you, among the store
One more, most welcome, makes my number more.†

6 At my poor* house look* to behold this night
Earth-treading stars*, that make dark* heaven light. †

7 Such comforts as do lusty young men feel*
When well-°apparell'd* April* on the heel*
Of limping Δwinter treads, even such delight
Among fresh Δ[female]* buds shall you this night
Inherit at my house; hear* all, all see;
And like her most, whose merit most shall be;
Which [on] more view*, of many, mine, being one,
May stand in number, though in reck'ning none.

8 Come, go* with me. †

9 Go*, sirrah, trudge about,
Through fair* Verona, find those persons out

Whether Capulet is genuinely kow-towing to a young man much higher in rank or is deliberately playing hard to get (for to marry his daughter to the Prince's nephew would be an enormous coup) is up to each actor to decide. Whatever the decision, the surprising unembellished portions of the text have a key part to play, as does the onrushed F #3 - split into five much more rational sentences in most modern texts).

- the first surprise is his opening unembellished response to the (perhaps too persistent) Prince's nephew's desire to marry Juliet
  "{W}hat say {I} to {your} sute? /But saying ore what I have said before,"
  no matter what the reason (perhaps the social gap between them - for Capulet is only described as 'rich', not a noble, and certainly not a Lord as some contemporary texts suggest) Capulet is forced to be careful in his denial
- then he recants, inviting Paris to see Juliet at the 'accustom'd Feast', but, again surprisingly, the invitation is also unembellished (tempting? o'er-reaching?)
  "Such as I love, and you among the store,/One more, most welcome makes my number more:"
- while the suggestion that Paris at least compare Juliet with other young women may come from false modesty, it's carefully unembellished yet again
  ". . . , even such delight/Among fresh . . . buds shall you this night/Inherit at my house: heare all, all see:/And like her most, whose merit most shall be: /Which one more veiw, of many, mine being one,/May stand in number, though in reckning none."
- the onrushed F #3 suggests a Capulet much less in control than his modern counterpart, and the very first line of F #3 goes a long way to explain why
  "Earth hath swallowed all my hopes but she,"
  the unembellished nakedness of it emphasised by being only a nine syllable line at most, suggesting that Capulet is moved, and needs a short pause before or after
- with the exception of the emotional description of Juliet 'Shee hath not seene the change of fourteene yeares' (0/4) the speech opens carefully (3/1, F #1-2)
- the agreement that Paris can woo her is very emotional (7/13, F #3's sixteen lines to the unembellished passage), though the invitation to the feast (F's equivalent of the opening two lines of mt. #5) is factual (2/0)
- and, after F #4's emotional first line and half of command to his less than competent servant (1/3), the final unembellished passage that ends the sentence, in turn heightened by the two extra breath thoughts (marked ,$_x$)

First Folio

7/ Capulet {ψ}

1 {ψ} {W}hat say {I} to {your} sute?

2 But saying ore what I have said before,
My Child is yet a stranger in the world,
Shee hath not seene the change of fourteene yeares,+
Let two more Summers wither in their pride,
Ere we may thinke her ripe to be a Bride.

3 Earth hath swallowed all my hopes but she,
Shee's the hopefull Lady of my earth:
But wooe her+ gentle Paris, get her heart,
My will to her consent, is but a part,+
And shee [agree], within her scope of choise,$_x$
Lyes my consent,$_x$ and faire according voice:
This night I hold an old accustom'd Feast,
Whereto I have invited many a Guest,
Such as I love, and you+ among the store,$_x$
One more, most welcome+ makes my number more:
At my poore house,$_x$ looke to behold this night,$_x$
Earth-treading starres, that make darke heaven light,
Such comforts as do lusty young men feele,$_x$
When well apparrel'd Aprill on the heele
Of limping Winter treads, even such delight
Among fresh [Fennell] buds shall you this night
Inherit at my house: $_x$ heare all, all see: $_x$
And like her most, whose merit most shall be: $_x$
Which [one] more veiw, of many, mine+ being one,
May stand in number, though in reckning none.

4 Come, goe with me: goe+ sirrah+ trudge about,
Through faire Verona, find those persons out,$_x$

Whose names are written there, and to them say,
My house and welcome on their pleasure stay.

"... find those persons out,x /Whose names are written there, and to them say,/ My house and welcome,x on their pleasure stay ."
might be a deliberate attempt to appear calm, enforcing a dignified control in front of Paris which is rarely evident with his other servants elsewhere in the play

Whose names are written there, and to them say,
My house and welcome, x on their pleasure stay.

8/ {Capulet as} 1st Capulet **Welcome Gentlemen,** 1.5.16 - 28

Background: The following is the opening speech of the Capulet feast and party, referred to in speech #7 above. Whether or not the party is designed to show Juliet off to the highest bidder, the speech suggests that Capulet regards himself as a Lady's man (reinforced by later comment from his wife, 'I you have bin a Mouse-hunt in your time').

Style: general address

Where: the main hall of the Capulet home **To Whom:** all invited to the feast

# of Lines: 13 **Probable Timing: 0.45 minutes**

Modern Text

8/ {Capulet as} 1st Capulet

1 Welcome, ^gentlemen ! †
2 Ladies that have their toes
Unplagu'd with ^corns*, will walk* [a bout] with you .†
3 Ah, my ^mistresses, which of you all
Will now deny to dance?
4 She that makes dainty,
She I'll swear* hath ^corns*. †
5 Am I come near* ye now?
6 Welcome, ^gentlemen ! †
7 I have seen* the day
That I have worn* a ^visor, and could tell
A whispering tale in a fair* ^lady's* ear*,
Such as would please ; 'tis gone, 'tis gone, 'tis gone .†
8 You are welcome, ^gentlemen !
9 Come ^musicians* play .†

MUSICKE PLAIES: AND THE DANCE

10 A ^hall, [a] hall !, give room*! and foot* it, ^girls*. †
11 More light you knaves, and turn* the ^tables up ;
And quench the fire, the ^room* is grown* too hot.

The exuberance of this speech, especially the three sentence Folio version versus the eleven sentence modern counterpart, belongs to the Capulet that audiences usually see throughout the whole play (14/17 in thirteen lines), though the excessive releases and five or six surround phrases are not always found elsewhere in such profusion, except when he is trying to keep up public appearances among equals or command those below him.

- the surround phrases/lines all point to the social presentation of himself, as with the tease
  ": Ah my Mistresses, which of you all/Will now deny to dance? She that makes dainty,/She Ile sweare hath Cornes : am I come neare ye now? "
  and the idea that he is too old to whisper 'in a faire Ladies eare'
  ": Such as would please : 'tis gone, 'tis gone, 'tis gone,/You are welcome Gentlemen, come Musitians play : "
  and the final instruction
  ": And quench the fire, the Roome is growne too hot. "

- the opening welcome is passionate (3/2, F #1) while F #2's tease of the ladies that immediately follows is emotional (1/3)

- F #3's almost locker-room humour as he returns to the men is once more passionate (5/5), though the regret that his flirting days are passed seems somewhat genuine, as the unembellished and monosyllabic 'Such as would please: 'tis gone, 'tis gone, 'tis gone,' seems to suggest

- the recovery, yet another welcome to the men and the first instructions to the servants (F #4's first two phrases) is totally intellectual (4/1), but this rapidly becomes emotional (3/6 the last two and half lines), perhaps suggesting that things may not be sitting as well with him as he would wish

First Folio

8/ {Capulet as} 1st Capulet

1 Welcome+ Gentlemen,→
Ladies that have their toes
Unplagu'd with Cornes, will walke [about] with you:
Ah+ my Mistresses, which of you all
Will now deny to dance?
2 She that makes dainty,
She Ile sweare hath Cornes: am I come neare ye now?
3 Welcome+ Gentlemen,+ I have seene the day
That I have worne a Visor, and could tell
A whispering tale in a faire Ladies eare: x
Such as would please: + 'tis gone, 'tis gone, 'tis gone,
You are welcome+ Gentlemen, +come Musitians play:

MUSICKE PLAIES: AND THE DANCE

A Hall, [ ] Hall,+ give roome,+ and foote it +Girles,
More light you knaves, and turne the Tables up: x
And quench the fire, the Roome is growne too hot.

9/ Capulet **How now? How now? Chopt Logicke? what is this?** between 3.5.149 - 195

Background: The good humour of Capulet's previous speech (#8 immediately above) soon dissipates when his wife tells him Juliet has refused to marry Paris. Once he has demanded 'Is she not proud?/ . . that we have wrought/So worthy a Gentleman', Juliet attempts to justify herself, answering 'Not proud you have,/But thankfull that you have:/Proud can I never be of what I [hate],/but thankfull even for hate, that is meant love'. The following is his response.

Style: direct one on one address in front of a small group

Where: Juliet's chambers, only recently vacated by her new husband Romeo **To Whom:** Juliet, in front of her mother and the Nurse

# of Lines: 38 **Probable Timing: 1.55 minutes**

Modern Text

9/ Capulet

1 How, [how], ◊ how, [how], ◊ chopp'd$_*$ △logic*? †
2 What is this?
2 "Proud", and "I thank* you," and "I thank* you not,"◊
[And yet "not proud," mistress minion you ?]
4 Thank* me no thankings, nor proud me no prouds,
But fettle your fine joints 'gainst Thursday next,
To go with Paris to Saint Peter's Church,
Or I will drag thee, on a △hurdle thither.
5 Out, you green* sickness* carrion ! †
6 Out, you baggage ! †
7 You tallow face !
8 Hang thee, young baggage ! disobedient wretch ! †
9 I tell thee what : get thee to △church a'Thursday,
Or never after look* me in the face.
10 Speak* not, reply not, do not answer* me !
11 My fingers itch . †
12 Wife, we scarce thought us blest
That God had lent us but this only* △child,
But now I see this one is one too much,
And that we have a curse in having her . †
13 Out on her △hilding !
14 God's bread, it makes me mad ! †
15 Day, night, [ ] work*, play,
Alone,$_x$ in company$_*$, still my care hath been$_*$
To have her match'd; and having now provided
A △gentleman of △noble △parentage,
Of fair* △demeans*, △youthful* and △nobly [lien'd],
Stuff'd$_*$, as they say, with △honorable* parts,
Proportion'd as one's thought would wish a man,

Though often played as a rant, much of F's orthography suggests a much quieter more controlled anger (whether this is out of a concern for the loss of social position if Juliet doesn't marry the Prince's nephew or an attempt to control his anger is up to each actor to decide).

- the onrushed F #13 also suggests, in finishing, that Capulet is not as controlled as his modern counterpart, who covers the same instruction in three more rational sentences

- the large number of unembellished lines point to his attempts to maintain control, starting with the opening 'How now?/How now?', and continunge
  "... proud me no prouds,/But fettle your fine joints 'gainst Thursday next,"
  "Or I will drag thee, . . . thither."
  ". . . out you baggage,/You tallow face. /Hang thee young baggage, disobedient wretch,/I tell thee what,"
  "My fingers itch, wife: we scarce thought us blest,"
  "But now I see this one is one too much,/And that we have a curse in having her:"
  "Gods bread, it makes me mad"
  "Alone in companie, still my care hath bin/To have her matcht, and having now provided"
  "Proportion'd as ones thought would wish a man,"
  "To answer, Ile not wed . . . :/I am too young, I pray you pardon me. /But, and you will not wed, Ile pardon you."/Graze where you will, you shall not house with me:"
  "/And you be mine , Ile give . . . :/And you be not, hang, beg, starve, die in the streets,/ . . . Ile nere acknowledge thee,/Nor what is mine shall never do thee good :/Trust too't,"

- the occasional surround phrase, either opening or closing sentences (both in F #9; ending F #5 and #10), or completely shaping sentences (F #3-4 and F #12) serve to either underscore the point he wants to drive home or mark an occasional burst of anger

- and the speech itself moves in surges of shifting releases, with the establishing of facts being highly emotional after the first moment of stunned unembellishment (1/4, F #3-4 and the first line of F #5), followed by the first intellectual attack 'proud me no prouds' (6/0, the remainder of F #5)

First Folio

9/ Capulet

1 How+ [now?]→
2 How+ [now?]
3 Chopt Logicke? what is this?
4 Proud, and I thanke you :$_x$ and I thanke you not.
[ ]
5 Thanke me no thankings, nor proud me no prouds,
But fettle your fine joints 'gainst Thursday next,
To go with Paris to Saint Peters Church: $_x$
Or I will drag thee, on a Hurdle thither.
6 Out+ you greene sicknesse carrion, +out +you baggage,+
You tallow face. +
7 Hang thee+ young baggage,+ disobedient wretch,+
I tell thee what,+ get thee to Church a Thursday,
Or never after looke me in the face.
8 Speake not, reply not, do not answere me. +
9 My fingers itch,+ wife: $_x$ we scarce thought us blest,$_x$
That God had lent us but this onely Child,
But now I see this one is one too much,
And that we have a curse in having her:
Out on her Hilding. +
10 Gods bread, it makes me mad: +
Day, night, [houre, ride, time,] worke, play,
Alone in companie, still my care hath bin
To have her matcht,+ and having now provided
A Gentleman of Noble Parentage,
Of faire Demeanes, Youthfull,$_x$ and Nobly [Allied],
Stuft+ as they say +with Honourable parts,
Proportion'd as ones thought would wish a man,

And then to have a wretched puling fool*,
A whining mammet, in her Δfortune's tender,
To answer, "I'll not wed, I cannot Δlove;
I am too young, I pray you pardon me."
16 But and you will not wed, I'll pardon you.
17 Graze where you will, you shall not house with me.†
18 Look* too't, think* on't, I do not use to jest.
19 Thursday is near*, lay hand on heart, advise. †
20 And you be mine, I'll give you to my Δfriend;
And you be not, hang, beg, starve, die in the streets,
For, by my soul*, I'll ne'er acknowledge thee,
Nor what is mine shall never do thee good. †
21 Trust to't*, bethink* you, I'll not be forsworn*.

• the further attacks on Juliet (F #7's 'Hang thee' and F #9's 'we have a curse in having her') are a mixture of intellect and unembellished control (5/2), interrupted by F #8's sudden flash of emotion in ordering Juliet not to answer back (0/2)

• and while he manages to regain some control during F #10's first four lines of somewhat unembeliished listing of how hard he has worked to find a good match (0/2), the struggle heightened by the pauses inherent in F's two (shaded) short lines (most modern texts remove the moment in setting one regular line by omitting some words, as shown)

• the ensuing three line description of Paris just explodes (8/4, frustration? anguish? or plain anger?)

• and then control is established once more, as he begins to repeat Juliet's refusal (2/1, the seven lines made up of the last four lines of F #10, F #11, the last line of F #12 and all of F #13), but as the onrushed final orders are given, so, for the first time in the speech, he finally turns to almost complete emotion (1/7), and exits, at least according to F, without finishing his sentence

And then to have a wretched puling foole,
A whining mammet, in her Fortunes tender,
To answer, Ile not wed, I cannot Love: x
I am too young, I pray you pardon me.
11 But, x and you will not wed, Ile pardon you.
12 Graze where you will, you shall not house with me:
Looke too't, thinke on't, I do not use to jest.
13 Thursday is neere, lay hand on heart, advise,
And you be mine, Ile give you to my Friend: x
And you be not, hang, beg, starve, die in the streets,
For+ by my soule, Ile nere acknowledge thee,
Nor what is mine shall never do thee good:
Trust too't, bethinke you, Ile not be forsworne

10/ Capulet **Come, stir, stir, stir,/The second Cocke hath Crow'd,** between 4.4.3 - 28

Background: Knowing that a potion given to her by Frier Lawrence will make it seem that she has died before the marriage (speech #32 below), thus preventing her from committing bigamy by marrying the unwished for Paris, Juliet has apparently submitted to her father's wishes. Today is the day of the wedding, and apparently there's much remaining to be done before Paris arrives.

Style: initially as part of a three-handed scene, and then to three or four servants

Where: Capulet's home **To Whom:** initially his wife and the Nurse, and then to three or four servants

# of Lines: 13 **Probable Timing: 0.45 minutes**

Modern Text

10/ Capulet

1 Come, stir, stir, stir ! the second Δcock* hath Δcrowed*,
The Δcurfew*- Δbell hath rung, 'tis three a clock* . †
2 Look* to the bak'd* meats*, good Angelica,
Spare not for cost.

3 Now, fellow, what [is]there?

4 Make haste*, make haste* . †
5 Sirrah, fetch drier Δlogs.
6 Call Peter, he will show* thee where they are.

7 {ψ} Good [faith], 'tis day.

[Music plays]

8 The County* will be here with Δmusic* straight,
For so he said he would . †
9 I hear* him near* .
10 Nurse ! †
11 Wife ! †
12 What ho ! †
13 What, Δnurse, I say !

ENTER NURSE

14 Go waken Juliet , go and trim her up,
I'll go and chat with Paris . †
15 Hie, make haste*,
Make haste*, the Δbridegroom* he is come already,
Make haste*, I say.

Again, though the three instructions to 'make hast' (note the F's short spelling of 'haste') as well as the opening 'Come, stir, stir, stir,' are usually bellowed, the F setting suggests a Capulet being much quieter (through clenched teeth perhaps), as if he were doing everything not to bellow – as if he were willing everything to go smoothly for just this once, for, as the (panicked?) last lines state, the noble 'Bridegroome' 'he is come already;' – presumably too soon.

- other almost sotto voce lines cover other instructions, as the short monosyllabic F #1 'Spare not for cost.'; the monosyllabic idea that for drier logs (the original presumably not good enough) the Servant should contact Peter 'he will shew thee where they are.'; and the yet again monosyllabic last minute instructions to get Juliet ready, 'go and trim her up', for he'll 'go and chat' with Paris
- though F #1 opens and closes with a semblance of (unembellished) control, the remainder of F #1 is highly passionate (5/6) - so much for self-control!
- Capulet does manage to keep emotions at bay in dealing with the need for 'drier Logs' and the initial recognition of it (already?) being daylight (3/1, F #2-5)
- however, with the realisation that 'Countie' (i.e. Paris) will 'be here . . . straight' any evidence of self-control disappears (3/3, F #6)
- though once more he seems to regain control in giving final instructions (to get Juliet ready and deal with Paris) and becomes factual once more (3/1, F #7)
- however, the final monosyllabic ' : Make hast I say . ' seems to take more effort than the rest, for it is the only true surround phrase in the speech

First Folio

10/ Capulet

1 Come, stir, stir, stir,+→
The second Cocke hath Crow'd,
The Curphew Bell hath rung, 'tis three a clocke :
Looke to the bakte meates, good Angelica,
Spare not for cost.

2 Now+ fellow, what [ ] there?

3 Make hast, make hast, sirrah, fetch drier Logs.
4 Call Peter, he will shew thee where they are.

5 {ψ} Good [Father], 'tis day.

[Play Musicke]

6 The Countie will be here with Musicke straight,
For so he said he would, I heare him neere,
Nurse,+ wife,+ what ho?+ what+ Nurse+ I say?+

ENTER NURSE

7 Go waken Juliet , go and trim her up,
Ile go and chat with Paris : hie, make hast,
Make hast, the Bridegroome,x he is come already: x
Make hast+ I say.

#'S 11 - 12: THE NOBLE PARIS

11/ Paris **Immoderately she weepes for Tybalts death,** 4.1.6 - 15

Background: Frier Lawrence, having secretly married Romeo & Juliet, is now being ordered by Paris to marry Paris and Juliet. In trying to head off the inevitable disaster the Frier has argued 'You say you do not know the Ladies mind ?/ Uneven is the course, I like it not'. The following is Paris' reply.

Style: as part of as two-handed scene

Where: Frier Lawrence's cell **To Whom:** Frier Lawrence

# of Lines: 10 **Probable Timing: 0.35 minutes**

Modern Text

11/ Paris

1 Immoderately she weeps* for Tybalt's death,
And therefore have I little [talk'd*] of Δlove,
For Venus smiles not in a house of tears*.

2 Now, sir, her Δfather counts it dangerous
That she [do] give her sorrow so much sway ;
And in his wisdom* hastes* our marriage,
To stop the inundation of her tears*,
Which, too much minded by herself * alone,
May be put from her by society*.

3 Now do* you know the reason of this haste*.

• Paris starts with quite an outburst (F #1, 3/3) taking as little time as possible to definitively spell out the background circumstances

• however, the two moments of defining the overwhelming reasons for the hasty marriage

"Now sir, her Father counts it dangerous/That she doth give her sorrow so much sway :"

and

" . . . May be put from her by societie ."

are completely unembellished (save for the word 'Father'), pointing to how calmly absolute Paris can be when necessary, and how little time he wastes in making his thoughts known

• yet, and quite naturally for a young man, his emotional self-control is not fully refined, for, though the first two lines of F #2 show no emotion (1/0), the remainder of the speech becomes somewhat so (0/4 in five lines) as he attempts to make Frier Lawrence understand that, because of the overwhelming facts and the wishes of those in authority for the marriage, no opposition will be tolerated

First Folio

11/ Paris

1 Immoderately she weepes for Tybalts death,
And therefore have I little [talke] of Love,
For Venus smiles not in a house of teares.

2 Now+ sir, her Father counts it dangerous
That she [doth] give her sorrow so much sway: x
And in his wisedome, x hasts our marriage,
To stop the inundation of her teares,
Which+ too much minded by her selfe alone,
May be put from her by societie.

3 Now doe you know the reason of this hast? x

12/ Paris **Give me thy Torch Boy, hence and stand aloft,** between 5.3.1 - 21

Background: The potion the Frier gave Juliet has worked well, and everyone believes that she has died on the morning of her wedding to Paris. Paris has come to mourn at the Capulet monument where her body has been laid to rest. This speech starts the scene, and as such is self-explanatory.

Style: as part of a two-handed scene

Where: outside the Capulet monument **To Whom:** his Page

# of Lines: 19 **Probable Timing: 1.00 minutes**

Modern Text

12/ Paris

1 Give me thy △torch, △boy. †
2 Hence and stand [aloof]. †
3 Yet put it out, for I would not be seen*. †
4 Under yond [yew] △trees lay thee all along,
Holding thy ear* close to the hollow ground,
So shall no foot upon the △churchyard tread,
Being loose, unfirm*, with digging up of △graves,
But thou shalt hear* it. †
5 Whistle then to me
As signal* that thou [hearst][4] something approach. †
6 Give me those flowers.
7 Do as I bid thee, go.

8 Sweet △flower, with flowers thy △bridal* bed I strew -
O woe, thy △canopy** is dust and stones! -
Which with sweet water nightly I will dew*,
Or wanting that, with tears* distill'd* by moans*. †
9 The obsequies that I for thee will keep*
Nightly shall be to strew thy grave and weep*.

[Whistle Boy]

10 The △boy gives warning, something doth approach. †
11 What cursed foot wanders this [way*] to night,
To cross* my obsequies and true love's [rite]?
12 What, with a △torch?
13 Muffle me, night, [awhile].

The modern texts' thirteen sentences suggest a very rational young man: F's six, especially the onrushed F #1 (usually split into six modern sentences) shows a very disturbed young man, at least at the top of the speech – until he settles into his self prescribed task of nightly worship.

- F #1's first line for the boy to leave is factual (2/0), while the further six lines of explanation and instructions become much more passionate (3/4, the next five and a half lines) until the very last (almost, save for 'signall') unembellished instruction that the boy should
"... whistle then to me,/As signall that thou hearest some thing approach,"
the attempted control somewhat undone by the ungrammatical final order, also unembellished, of 'Give me those flowers.'

- the first short sentence (F #2) 'Do as I bid thee, go.' is made even more powerful by being both monosyllabic and unembellished, immediately followed by the only surround phrase that underscores both the "why" and the pain and determination of his purpose '. Sweet Flower with flowers thy Bridall bed I strew : '

- as he begins to 'strew' the flowers, as with the first sentence, he starts out in control (3/1, F #3's first two lines), but then for the rest of the sentence he becomes emotional (0/5, F #3's last four lines), which spills into the 'Boy' giving 'warning, something doth approach' (1/2, F #4)

- and then his sense of control as seen in speech #11 returns, with two very precise short sentences taking charge of the situation to end the speech, the monosyllabic F #5 (1/0) and the unembellished F #6

First Folio

12/ Paris

1 Give me thy Torch+ Boy, hence and stand [aloft],
Yet put it out, for I would not be seene:
Under yond [young] Trees lay thee all along,
Holdingthy eare close to the hollow ground,
So shall no foot upon the Churchyard tread,
Being loose, unfirme+ with digging up of Graves,
But thou shalt heare it: whistle then to me,x
As signall that thou [hearest] some thing approach,
Give me those flowers.
2 Do as I bid thee, go.

3 Sweet Flower+ with flowers thy Bridall bed I strew:x
O woe, thy Canopie is dust and stones,+
Which with sweet water nightly I will dewe,
Or wanting that, with teares destil'd by mones;
The obsequies that I for thee will keepe,x
Nightly shall be,x to strew thy grave,x and weepe.

[Whistle Boy]

4 The Boy gives warning, something doth approach,
What cursed foot wanders this [wayes] to night,
To crosse my obsequies,x and true loves [right]?
5 What+ with a Torch?
6 Muffle me+ night + [a while].

[4] Q2-4/Ff = 'hearest', some modern texts = hears't (thus creating pentameter)

#'S 13 - 17: FAMILY AND FRIENDS ABOUT ROMEO

13/ Benvolio **At this same auncient Feast of Capulets** between 1.2.82 - 99

Background: Having promised his aunt and uncle that as regards Romeo 'Ile know his greevance or be much denide', Benvolio has discovered that Romeo is suffering the pangs of unrequited love. Then, having learned that Rosaline, the lady Romeo is being spurned by, will be at the enemy Capulet's party that night, Benvolio proposes an adventure.

Style: as part of a two-handed scene

Where: the street **To Whom:** Romeo

# of Lines: 12 **Probable Timing: 0.40 minutes**

Modern Text

13/ Benvolio

1 At this same ancient* Δfeast of Capulet's
Sups the fair* Rosaline whom thou so loves,
With all the admired Δbeauties of Verona. †

2 Go thither, and with unattainted eye,
Compare her face with some that I shall show,
And I will make thee think* thy Δswan a Δcrow.

xxxxxxxxxxxxxxxxxxxxxxxxxxxxxxxxxxxxxxxxxxxxxxxxxxxxxxxxxxxxxxxxxxxxxxxxxxxxxxxx

3 {ψ} {Y}ou saw her fair*, none else being by,
Herself * pois'd* with herself * in either eye;
But in that Δcrystal* scales, let there be weigh'd*
Your Δlady's* love against some other Δmaid
That I will show you shining at this Δfeast,
And she [shall scant show well] that now [seems] best.

Mercutio's later description of Benvolio as a hothead seems to be borne out by F's slight onrush, the two extra breath-thoughts (marked ,$_x$) in the last two lines and the (possibly) very strange last line.

- F#1's two unembellished lines 'Go thither and with unattainted eye, /Compare her face with some that I shall show,', supported by F #2's 'That I will show you, shining at this Feast' point to the possible seriousness of Benvolio's attempt to deflect Romeo's current impotent adulation (an attempt not to lose his friend/cousin to a woman perhaps?)

- while F #1 starts intellectually (5/2, first three lines) and moves into the unembellished calm discussed above, it ends passionately (2/1), and moves straight into emotion as he demeans Rosaline (0/4, F #2's first two lines), while the final suggestion that he can show Romeo women better than Rosaline is once more stoutly intellectual (4/2, the last four lines)

First Folio

13/ Benvolio

1 At this same auncient Feast of Capulets
Sups the faire Rosaline,$_x$ whom thou so loves: $_x$
With all the admired Beauties of Verona,
Go thither+ and with unattainted eye,
Compare her face with some that I shall show,
And I will make thee thinke thy Swan a Crow.

xxxxxxxxxxxxxxxxxxxxxxxxxxxxxxxxxxxxxxxxxxxxxxxxxxxxxxxxxxxxxxxxxxxxxxxxxxxxxxxx

2 {ψ} {Y}ou saw her faire, none else being by,
Herselfe poys'd with herselfe in either eye: $_x$
But in that Christall scales, let there be waid,$_x$
Your Ladies love against some other Maid
That I will show you,$_x$ shining at this Feast,
And she [shew scant shell, well[5]],$_x$ that now [shewes] best.

---

[5] F3 = 'And she'l shew scant well, that now shews best', Q2-4 and most modern texts = 'And she shall scant shew well:' F1 = 'And she shew scant shell, well,': the F1 reading seems due to compositorial error and should only be kept if the reader/actor wishes Benvolio to trip over his own tongue in his eagerness to prove his point!

14/ Mercutio **O then I see Queene Mab hath beene with you.** 1.4.53 - 95

Background: Though initially agreeing to go to the Capulet feast, Romeo is now backing out. At first teased unmercifully by his close friend Mercutio about being in love, Romeo attempts to justify himself through a dream. Being told by Mercutio that 'dreamers often lye', Romeo has quickly, wittily, and pointedly responded with 'In bed a sleepe while they do dreame things true', which triggers the following.

Style: a group address

Where: in the street **To Whom:** Romeo and the group, including Benvolio and 'five or sixe other maskers, torch-bearers'

# of Lines: 34 **Probable Timing: 1.40 minutes**

Modern Text

14/ Mercutio

1 O then I see Queen* Mab hath been* with you.

2 She is the Δfairies' Δmidwife, and she comes
In shape no bigger [than] [an] Δagot*-stone
On the forefinger of an Δalderman
Drawn with a team* of little [Δatomi]
[Athwart] men's noses as they lie asleep*. †

3 Her Δchariot is an empty* Δhazel*-°nut,
Made by the Δjoiner* Δsquirrel or old Δgrub,
Time out a mind, the Δfairies ΔΔcoachmakers. †

4 Her waggon-°Δspokes made of long Δspinners' legs,
The Δcover of the wings of Δgrasshoppers*,
Her Δtraces of the smallest [Δspider] web,
Her [collars] of the Δmoonshine's wat'ry Δbeams*,
Her Δwhip of Δcricket's bone, the Δlash of [Δfilm]*,
Her Δwaggoner a small gray-coated Δgnat,
Not half* so big* as a round little Δworm*
Prick'd from the Δlazy*-finger of a [maid].

5 And in this state she gallops night by night
Through Δlovers' brains*, and then they dream* of Δlove; ◊
[O'er] Δcourtiers' knees, that dream* on Δcur'sies straight*;
O'er Δlawyer's fingers, who strait [dream] on Δfees;
O'er Δladies' lips, who straight* on kisses dream*,
Which oft the angry Mab with blisters plagues,
Because their breath with Δsweet°meats tainted are.

6 Sometime she gallops ore a Δcourtier's nose,
And then dreams* he of smelling out a suit*;
And sometime* comes she with [a] Δtithe*- pig's [tail]
Tickling a Δparson's nose as a lies asleep*,
Then he dreams* of another Δbenefice.

7 Sometime she driveth o'er a Δsoldier's* neck*,

Q2-4/Ff print this speech as prose, Q1 prints a much shorter version of the speech in verse: most modern texts change the longer prose version to verse, thus spoiling the initial casualness of the major part of the speech, as well as undoing the switch in energy for the last four and a half lines of the speech which Q2-4/Ff do print in verse (as Mercutio focuses more and more on the ugly aspect of Mab). Also, though Q2-4/Ff print the shaded section as shown, most modern texts place it after 'they lie asleepe' in the fifth line of the speech, arguing that logically the description of the 'Chariot' should follow on immediately after that which draws it - this does, however, make the (not necessarily warranted) assumption that Mercutio is capable of being logical at this point in the play.

- thus, while the speech opens intellectually (33/11, F #1-3), both the extra breath thoughts (marked , x) and the less than logical progression of (shaded) thought suggest that his intellectualising is far more free-wheeling than most modern texts allow

- however, as he begins to focus in on the four of the groups Mab blesses with her dreams ('Courtiers' - twice -and 'Lawyers' – never Shakespeare's favourite people, together with 'Parsons', often a figure of fun, and 'Ladies') emotion starts to make more of a presence (11/5, F #4-5) as their not particularly finer qualities are listed

- the first reference to Mab and probably himself in the throes of battle (the 'Souldiers necke') is passionate (6/4, F #6's opening two lines to the first colon), but as he dreams of drink, 'Healths five Fadome deepe', and then awakes 'frighted' Mercutio becomes very emotional (2/7, F #6's next three lines)

- Mab and her dealings with horses and 'foule sluttish haires' are passionate (3/2)

- the few surround phrases underscore the effects Mab has on most of her dreamers, first the Lovers, Courtiers, and Lawyers

" : and then they dreame of Love . [On] Courtiers knees, that

First Folio

14/ Mercutio

1 O then I see Queene Mab hath beene with you.

2 She is the Fairies Midwife, & she comes in shape no bigger [then] [ ] Agat-stone, x on the fore-finger of an Alderman, x drawn with a teeme of little [Atomies], x [over] mens noses as they lie asleepe: her Waggon Spokes made of long Spinners legs: x the Cover of the wings of Grashoppers, her Traces of the smallest [Spiders] web, her [coullers] of the Moonshines watry Beames, her Whip of Crickets bone, the Lash of Philome, her Waggoner, x a small gray-coated Gnat, not halfe so bigge as a round little Worme, x prickt from the Lazie-finger of a [man].

3 Her Chariot is an emptie Haselnut, made by the Joyner Squirrel or old Grub, time out a mind, the Fairies Coach-makers: & in this state she gallops night by night, x through Lovers braines: x and then they dreame of Love.

4 [On] Courtiers knees, that dreame on Cursies strait: x ore Lawyers fingers, who strait: x [dreamt] on Fees,+ ore Ladies lips, who strait on kisses dreame, which oft the angry Mab with blisters plagues, because their breath with Sweet meats tainted are.

5 Sometime she gallops ore a Courtiers nose, & then dreames he of smelling out a sute: x & somtime comes she with [ ] Tith pigs tale, xtickling a Parsons nose as a lies asleepe, then he dreames of another Benefice.

6 Sometime she driveth ore a Souldiers

And then dreams* he of cutting ΔforeignΔ* throats,
Of Δbreaches, Δambuscadoes*, Spanish Δblades,
Of Δhealths five-°Δfathom* deep*; and then anon
Drums in his [ear]*, at which he starts* and wakes,
And being thus frighted, swears* a prayer or two,
And sleeps* again*. †
8 This is that very Mab
That plats the manes of Δhorses in the night,
And bakes the [Δelf]-locks in foul* sluttish hairs*,
Which, once untangled, much misfortune bodes. †
9 This is the hag, when Δmaids* lie on their backs,
That presses them and learns* them first to bear*,
Making them women of good carriage. †
10 This is she - ◊

dreame on Cursies strait : ore Lawyers fingers, who strait : [dreamt] on Fees "
and then with the 'Souldier' and the horses,
" : Of Healths five Fadome deepe, and then anon drums in his [eares], at which he startes and wakes ; and being thus frighted,sweares a prayer or two & sleepes againe : this is that very Mab that plats the manes of Horses in the night : "

• as he continues Mercutio becomes much more intense, switching to verse to explore love-making and its inevitable consequence: the deflowering is described emotionally (1/3 in the first two lines) while the pregnancy is handled via the only unembellished section of the speech, in which vein he would continue if Romeo did not interrupt him

necke, & then dreames he of cutting Forraine throats, of Breaches, Ambuscados, Spanish Blades: x Of Healths five Fadome deepe, + and then anon drums in his [eares], at which he startes and wakes; x and being thus frighted, sweares a prayer or two+ & sleepes againe: this is that very Mab that plats the manes of Horses in the night: x & bakes the [Elk]-locks in foule sluttish haires, which+ once untangled, much misfortune bodes,
This is the hag, when Maides lie on their backs,
That presses them, x and learnes them first to beare,
Making them women of good carriage:
This is she. x

15/ Mercutio **This cannot anger him, t'would anger him** between 2.1.6 – 41 (with some rearrangement)

Background: Having met and fallen for Juliet at the feast, Romeo has given his companions the slip. At Benvolio's urgings he and Mercutio have been searching for him. To provide a logical shape to the following, sentences #1-2, which in the play follow sentence #3, have been used to start the scene. In the play, the response is triggered by Benvolio's reaction to Mercutio's extremely graphic sexual imagery.

Style: as part of a two-handed scene

Where: close to the Capulet residence **To Whom:** to the in-hiding-somewhere-close-by Romeo, in front of Benvolio

# of Lines: 30 **Probable Timing: 1.30 minutes**

Modern Text

15/ Mercutio

1 This cannot anger him ; t'would anger him
To raise a spirit in his Δmistress'* circle,
Of some strange nature, letting it [there] stand
Till she had laid it and conjured it down*. †

2 That were some spite*.
3 My invocation
Is fair* and honest ; [ ] in his mistress'* name
{2 sections I conjure only* but to raise up him.
4 are reversed} Romeo! Δhumors*! Δmadman! Δpassion! Δlover ! †

5 Appear* thou in the likeness* of a sigh ! †

6 Speak* but one rhyme*, and I am satisfied;
Cry [] but "ΔAy me!", [pronounce], but "Δlove" and ["dove"],
Speak* to my gossip* Venus one fair* word,
One Δnickname for her purblind Δson* and [heir],
Young [Adam][5] Cupid, he that shot so [trim],
When King Cophetua lov'd the beggar-°Δmaid ! †

7 He heareth not, he stirreth not, he moveth not,
The Δape is dead, [and][6] I must conjure him . †

8 I conjure thee by Rosaline's bright eyes,
By her Δhigh forehead and her Δscarlet lip,
By her Δfine foot*, Δstraight leg, and Δquivering thigh,
And the Δdemesnes*, that there Δadjacent lie,
That in thy likeness* thou appear* to us !

9 Now will he sit under a Δmedlar* tree,
And wish his Δmistress* were that kind of Δfruit*
As Δmaids call Δmedlars*, when they laugh alone . †

There are many niggling variations to this speech, but in the main the F text is the one normally followed by most modern texts: nevertheless, even though a lot of the variations may only be offered by one text, they suggest fascinating possibilities for the speaker; thus all the variations that can be spoken and still make sense are square bracketed.

- in the shaded passage, F's two irregular lines (4/16 syllables) allow for a splendidly erratic Mercutio, especially as the long line could be a resumption (or summation) of his invocation: the poetically correct restructuring of the modern texts (9 or 10/11) creates normality where bizarreness may have been intended
- the speech starts very quietly but emotionally, as if Mercutio were resting from his first attempts to rouse Romeo (1/3, the four and a half lines of F #1); then comes the bizarre (mildly passionate, 1/1) shaded passage, as discussed
- although the first line of the onrushed F #3's appeal for Romeo to appear is highly intellectual (4/1), Mercutio's inability to settle down into any one mood is quickly seen, with the two line command to 'Appeare' and 'Speake but one rime' becoming emotional (0/3): yet the following the three line request to 'Cry . . . but Love' and then 'Speake' to 'Venus' turns passionate (5/3), only to be supported totally intellectually (5/0) by the next two lines of classical imagery ('Abraham Cupid')
- it's interesting that Mercutio's realisation of failure to rouse Romeo, at least so far, is completely unembellished ('He heareth not, he stirreth not, he moveth not,' which might suggest he is quite surprised
- which in turn could be supported by the decision to conjure and the attempt to do so becoming highly intellectual (9/2 in F #3's next six lines), with only the final line 'in thy likenesse thou appeare to us' becoming emotional (0/2)
- and even though Mercutio fails to conjure Romeo, while his description of Romeo sulking and wishing still remains intellectual (9/3, the first five lines of F #4), the fact of the onrush (which most modern texts destroy

First Folio

15/ Mercutio

1 This cannot anger him,+ t'would anger him
To raise a spirit in his Mistresse circle,
Of some strange nature, letting it [ ] stand
Till she had laid it,x and conjured it downe,
That were some spight.

2 My invocation is faire and honest,+ [&] in his Mistris name,x
{2 sections I conjure onely but to raise up him.
3 are reversed} Romeo,+ Humours,+ Madman,+ Passion,+ Lover,+
Appeare thou in the likenesse of a sigh,+
Speake but one rime, and I am satisfied: x
Cry [me] but ay me+,[Provant], but Love and [day],
Speake to my goship Venus one faire word,
One Nickname for her purblind Sonne and [her],
Young [Abraham] Cupid+ he that shot so [true],
When King Cophetua lov'd the begger Maid,+
He heareth not, he stirreth not, he moveth not,
The Ape is dead, [ ] I must conjure him,
I conjure thee by Rosalines bright eyes,
By her High forehead,x and her Scarlet lip,
By her Fine foote, Straight leg, and Quivering thigh,
And the Demeanes, that there Adjacent lie,
That in thy likenesse thou appeare to us. +

4 Now will he sit under a Medler tree,
And wish his Mistresse were that kind of Fruite,x
As Maids call Medlers+ when they laugh alone,

---

[5] Q2-4/Ff ='Abraham', some modern texts = 'Adam' (because of a contemporary reference to the legendary archery of Adam Bell), also Q1/some modern texts set 'trim' (for the same reason)

[6] Q2-4 and all modern texts add the word 'and' (maintaining pentameter)

10 O, Romeo, that she were, O that she were
An open[-arse], [ ] thou a Δpop'rin Δpear* !†

11 Romeo, good night, I'll to my Δtruckle-bed,
This Δfield-bed is to cold for me to sleep*. †

12 Come, shall we go?

by resetting F #4 as at least four separate rational sentences) suggests a Mercutio hastening to call it a night

• the final two and half line farewell starts passionately (2/1, the first two lines), though the final suggestion to leave ('Come shall we go?') is both unembellished and monosyllabic, perhaps indicating that tiredness has hit at last

O+ Romeo+ that she were, O that she were
An open [ ], or thou a Poprin Peare,+
Romeo+ goodnight, Ile to my Truckle bed,
This Field-bed is to cold for me to sleepe,
Come+ shall we go?

16/ Frier Lawrence **Holy S Francis, what a change is heere?** 2.3.65 - 80

Background: Having been told of Romeo's new found love for Juliet (see speech #26 below), and his insistence 'That thou consent to marrie us to day', Frier Lawrence is rightfully somewhat skeptical.

Style: as part of a two-handed scene

Where: somewhere in the fields close to his cell **To Whom:** Romeo

# of Lines: 16 **Probable Timing: 0.50 minutes**

Modern Text

16/ Frier Lawrence

1 Holy [Saint] Francis, what a change is here*!

2 Is Rosaline, that thou didst Δlove so dear*,
So soon* forsaken? †

3 Young men's Δlove then lies
Not truly* in their hearts, but in their eyes.

4 Jesu Maria, what a deal* of brine
Hath wash'd thy sallow cheeks* for Rosaline!

5 How much salt water thrown* away in waste*,
To season Δlove, that of it doth not taste* !

6 The Δsun nor yet thy sighs* from heaven clears*,
Thy old groans* yet ringing[7] in my ancient* ears*;
Lo here upon thy cheek* the stain* doth sit
Of an old tear* that is not wash'd off yet.

7 If e'er thou wast thyself* and these woes thine,
Thou and these woes were all for Rosaline.

8 And art thou chang'd? †

9 Pronounce this sentence then:
Women may fall, when there's no strength in men.

In addition to the obvious passion, most modern texts seem to present quite an emphatic Frier too (exclamation points ending mt. #1, #4, and #5 instead of F's question marks, and a colon ending the first line of mt's #9 instead of F's comma), whereas F seems to suggest a man who, while occasionally exasperated (the enormously emotional - and humourous? - F #5, 1/7 in just our lines), is one who attempts to deal with Romeo rationally as well.

• in no way does this rationality dismiss the Frier's sense of mocking humour, as the passionate (3/3) surround lines forming F #2 suggest
". Is Rosaline that thou didst Love so deare/So soone forsaken ? young mens Love then lies/Not truely in their hearts, but in their eyes ."

• and while the speech ending maxim seems quite serious in its unembellishment
". And art thou chang'd ? pronounce this sentence then,/Women may fall, when there's no strength in men ."
the fact that it is also made up of (two) surround phrases suggests that the Frier may be having some quiet fun too

• in the opening surprise and the first questioning/mocking of Romeo's tears for Rosaline, the speech starts passionately (8/7 in the eight lines F #1-4)

• then comes the enormous emotional release as the Frier reaches the climax to his mocking of Romeo's earlier mooning over Rosaline (F #5, 1/7)

• then the Frier becomes much more controlled, with the mock, if still there rather than a rebuke, first vastly reduced in terms of release (1/1, F #6), and then he finishes without any release at all (F #7, 0/0)

First Folio

16/ Frier Lawrence

1 Holy [S] Francis, what a change is heere?+

2 Is Rosaline+ that thou didst Love so deare+
So soone forsaken? young mens Love then lies
Not truely in their hearts, but in their eyes.

3 Jesu Maria+ what a deale of brine
Hath washt thy sallow cheekes for Rosaline? +

4 How much salt water throwne away in wast,
To season Love+ that of it doth not tast. +

5 The Sun nor yet thy sighes, $_x$ from heaven cleares,
Thy old grones yet ringingin my auncient eares: $_x$
Lo here upon thy cheeke the staine doth sit, $_x$
Of an old teare that is not washt off yet.

6 If ere thou wast thy selfe, $_x$ and these woes thine,
Thou and these woes, $_x$ were all for Rosaline.

7 And art thou chang'd?+ pronounce this sentence then,+
Women may fall, when there's no strength in men .

[7] Q2-3/F1 and some modern texts = 'yet ringing', Q4/F2/some modern texts = 'yet ring' (thus preserving pentameter), Q1 and some modern texts = 'ring yet' (again preserving pentameter)

17/ Mercutio **Here comes Romeo, without his Roe, like a dryed Hering.** 2.4.36 - 45

Background: Romeo's absence has extended from the night before (see the background to speech #15 above) through much of the morning, but at last, just before noon, he joins Mercutio and Benvolio, eliciting the following.

Style: as part of a three-handed scene

Where: a public street **To Whom:** Benvolio, as Romeo joins them

# of Lines: 8 **Probable Timing: 0.30 minutes**

Modern Text

17/ Mercutio

1 {ψ} Here comes Romeo,{w}ithout his △roe, like a dried* △herring: *
◊ O flesh, flesh, how art thou fishified!

2 Now is he for the numbers
that Petrarch flowed in. †

3 Laura to his Lady, was a kitchen wench
(marry₊ she had a better Love to berhyme₊ her), Dido
a dowdy₊, Cleopatra a △gipsy₊, Helen₊ and Hero hildings and
△harlots, Thisby* a grey eye₊ or so, but not to the purpose.

4 Signior Romeo, △*bon* °*jour*! there's a French salutation to
your French slop. †

5 You gave us the [ ] counterfeit* fairly₊ last
night.

The speech is highly factual throughout (18/4 in just eight lines), suggesting a Mercutio with a very agile brain who can restrict himself to intellectual games when he chooses – a far cry from the end of the 'Queene Mab' speech, #14, above.

- despite the vulgarity of F #2, being set as a separate sentence (unlike most modern texts) and being unembellished, Mercutio's comment does seem to suggest that Romeo's physical presence is quite changed

- and the first surround phrase ' . Now is he for the numbers that Petrarch flowed in : ' suggests that Romeo's appearance is somewhat poetic, while the last, ' : you gave us the counterfeit fairely last night . ' contains the only emotional moment in the speech, perhaps pointing to a Mercutio as unwilling to lose a friend as Benvolio seemed to be (speech #13 above) especially since the emotion comes at the end of a slightly onrushed sentence F #) rather than being set as a separate tease, as modern texts would have it

First Folio

17/ Mercutio

1 {ψ} Here comes Romeo,{w}ithout his Roe, like a dryed Hering.

2 O flesh, flesh, how art thou fishified?+

3 Now is he for the numbers
that Petrarch flowed in: Laura to his Lady, was a kitchen
wench,+marrie she had a better Love to berime her: ₓ Dido
a dowdie, Cleopatra a Gipsie, Hellen and Hero,ₓ hildings and
Harlots:ₓ Thisbie a gray eie or so, but not to the purpose.

4 Signior Romeo, Bonjour,+ there's a French salutation to your
French slop: you gave us the [the] counterfait fairely last
night.

#'S 18 - 20: FAMILY AND FRIENDS ABOUT JULIET

18/ Nurse **Faith I can tell her age unto an houre.** between 1.3.11 – 62

Background: Juliet's age is discussed by Capulet's wife (her blood mother) and the Nurse (her milk mother). Interestingly, the Nurse lays claim to more accurate dating than Juliet's mother.

Style: as part of a three-handed scene

Where: inside or in the grounds of the Capulet residence **To Whom:** Juliet's mother and Juliet

# of Lines: 38 **Probable Timing: 1.55 minutes**

Modern Text

18/ Nurse

1 Faith, I can tell her age unto an hour*.

2 I'll lay fourteen* of my teeth -
And yet, to my teen* be it spoken, I have but four*,
She's* not fourteen*.

3 {*O}f all days* in the year*,
Come Lammas-°Eve at night shall she be fourteen*, ◊
Susan and she - God rest all Christian souls* ! -
Were of an age.

4 Well, Susan is with God,
She was too good for me.

5 But as I said,
On Lammas-°Δeve at night shall she be fourteen*,
That shall she, marry*, I remember it well.

6 'Tis since the Δearthquake now eleven years*,
And she was wean'd - I never shall forget it -
Of all the days* of the year*, upon that day;
For I had then laid Δworm°wood to my Δdug,
Sitting in the Δsun under the Δdove-house wall. †

7 My Δlord and you were then at Mantua -
Nay I do* bear* a brain* - ◊ but as I said,
When it did taste* the Δworm*wood on the nipple
Of my Δdug* and felt it bitter, pretty fool*,
To see it tetchy* and fall out [wi'th]' Δdug* ! †

8 Shake quoth the Δdove-house; 'twas no need*, I trow,
To bid me* trudge. †

9 And since that time it is [ ] eleven years*,
For then she could stand [high-°lone], nay, by'th'rood*,

Apart from the first two sentences (possibly), Q1-4/Ff sets this speech in prose, in which she continues even beyond the key moment when Capulet's Wife as Old Lady turns the scene into verse - when she begins to discuss marriage: thus the marked contrast between the Nurse's earthy stream of consciousness view of life and Juliet's childlike vision both shown in the ease of prose, compared to the verse uttering of the 'Old Lady's' (Juliet's mother) more dutiful adult expectations, no matter how romantically stated, could not be more sharply and theatrically expressed: unfortunately, most modern texts reset the speech as verse.

- thus, if, as the source texts suggest, the speech is in prose. then this shaded passage is probably set in irregular verse (7/9/8/ syllables), and could denote something special for the Nurse, undue attention to Juliet perhaps, or gathering style and energy in preparation for the long story about to begin

- most modern texts not only create a more formal (verse speaking) Nurse, they add at least fourteen extra pieces of punctuation (marked + in the F text), thus slowing the speed of her flow, especially in F #8

- overall the speech is passionate veering to emotion (32/41), yet the start is marked by a huge swing between the opening emotion and the (quickly unsuccessful) attempt at intellectual control, while the end is marked by the sudden appearance of determined surround phrases

- in asserting Juliet's correct age the Nurse starts emotionally (0/6, F #1-2), but she offers the proof of 'Lammas Eve' (F #3-6) somewhat more intellectually (8/4), and the further affirmation (Juliet being 'wean'd' on the day of the 'Earth-quake') becomes passionate (F #7, 7/7), with a lovely self congratulatory moment ending the sentence ('nay I doe beare a braine')

First Folio

18/ Nurse

1 Faith+ I can tell her age unto an houre.

2 Ile lay fourteene of my teeth,
And yet+ to my teene[8] be it spoken,
I have but foure, shee's not fourteene.

3 {*O}f all daies in the yeare+ come
Lammas Eve at night shall she be fourteene.

4 Susan & she,
God rest all Christian soules,+ were of an age.

5 Well+ Susan
is with God, she was too good for me.

6 But as I said, on La-
mas Eve at night shall she be fourteene, that shall she+ ma-
rie, I remember it well.

7 'Tis since the Earth-quake now
eleven yeares, and she was wean'd+ I never shall forget it,
of all the daies of the yeare, upon that day:x for I had then
laid Worme-wood to my Dug+ sitting in the Sunne under
the Dovehouse wall, my Lord and you were then at
Mantua, nay I doe beare a braine.

8 But as I said, when it
did tast the Worme-wood on the nipple of my Dugge,
and felt it bitter, pretty foole, to see it teachie, xand fall out
[with the] Dugge, Shake quoth the Dove-house,+ 'twas no
neede+ I trow+ to bid mee trudge: and since that time it is
[a eleven] yeares, for then she could stand [alone],nay +bi'th'

{ctd. over}

[8] Q2-4/F1 and most modern texts = 'teene', F2 presents a rather nice gloss = 'teeth'

She could have run*, and waddled* all about;
For even the day before, she broke her brow,
And then my Husband - God be with his soul*!,
A was a merry* man - took* up the △child . †
10 "Yea," quoth he*, "dost* thou fall upon thy face?
Thou wilt fall backward* when thou hast more wit,
Wilt thou not, Jule?" ◊ and by my holi*dam,
The pretty wretch left* crying, & said, ["Ay*"] . †
11 To see now how a △jest shall come about !
12 I warrant, and I [should] live a thousand years*,
I never should forget it: "Wilt thou not [Jule?]" quoth he;
And, pretty fool*, it stinted, and said, ["Ay* "].
13 {ψ} I cannot choose* but laugh
To think* it should leave crying and say, ["Ay* "] . †
14 And yet I warrant it had upon it brow
A bump* as big as a young △cock'rels stone -
A perilous knock - and it cried* bitterly.
15 "Yea," quoth my husband, "fall'st upon thy face ?
Thou wilt fall backward when thou comest* to age,
Wilt thou not, Jule? "
16 It stinted and said, ["Ay*"] .
17 Peace, I have done . †
18 God mark* thee too his grace ! †
19 Thou wast the prettiest △babe that e'er I nurs'd. †
20 And I might live to see thee married once,
I have my wish.

• the build-up to the Earth-quake ('the Worme-wood on the nipple of my Dugge') is passionate (the first four lines of F #8, 5/5), then comes a moment of emotion at the recollection of Juliet being able to 'runne' even at her early age, and the new recollection of her husband, becomes passionate once more (4/5, F #8's final four and a half lines), with the memory of the naughty joke

" ? thou wilt fall backeward when thou hast more wit, wilt thou
not Jule ? "

highlighted by being set as the first surround phrase of the speech, after twenty-four lines

• and both passion and surround phrases continue as she offers various repetitions of both joke and circumstances (4/8 and six surround phrases, the ten lines of F #9-12) - a fixation on happier days when her husband was alive and Juliet a needy child dependent upon her care perhaps, . . .

• . . . especially since this is followed by F #13, the first unembellished (and short) sentence, the calm yet determined recollection

" . It stinted: and said I . "

heightened by also being set as two surround phrases

• an unembellished monosyllabic surround phrase also marks the Nurse's final agreement to keep quiet

" . Peace I have done : "

finishing with a passionate summation of Juliet's beauty as a child (2/1, F #14)

roode+ she could have runne, & wadled all about: x for even the day before+ she broke her brow, & then my Husband+ God be with his soule,+ a was a merrie man, tooke up the Child, yea+ quoth hee, doest thou fall upon thy face? thou wilt fall backeward when thou hast more wit, wilt thou not+ Jule?

9 And by my holy-dam, the pretty wretch lefte crying, & said [I]: to see now how a Jest shall come about.+

10 I warrant, & I [shall] live a thousand yeares, I never should forget it: wilt thou not+ [Julet] quoth he?x andx pretty foolex it stinted, and said+ [I].

11 {ψ} I cannot chuse but laugh,x to thinke it should leave crying,x & say + [I]: and yet I warrant it had upon it brow,x a bumpe as big as a young Cockrels stone?x A perilous knock, and it cryed bitterly.

12 Yea+ quoth my husband, fall'st upon thy face,+ thou wilt fall back -ward when thou commest to age: x wilt thou not +Jule?

13 It stinted: x and said + [I].

14 Peace+ I have done: God marke thee too his grace+ thou wast the prettiest Babe that ere I nurst, and I might live to see thee married once, I have my wish.

19/ {Mother as} Old Lady **Marry that marry is the very theame** between 1.3.63 - 104

Background: At the end of the Nurse's recollections she utters the wish 'and I might live to see thee married once, I have my wish', allowing Juliet's mother to jump in with the following, the reason for calling Juliet to her in the first place. (One note: throughout the play, and seeming to depend upon her function/staus within the scene, four different prefixes are set for Juliet's mother – 'Old Lady', 'Capulet's Lady', 'Mother', and 'Lady'. Thus here the prefix 'Old Lady'may be a key indicator as to how Shakespeare regards her in this scene.)

Style: essentially one on one dialogue as part of a three-handed scene

Where: inside or in the grounds of the Capulet residence **To Whom:** Juliet in front of the Nurse

# of Lines: 28 **Probable Timing: 1.30 minutes**

Modern Text

19/ {Mother as} Old Lady

1 Marry, that "marry" is the very theme*
I came to talk* of. †
2 Tell me, daughter Juliet,
How stands your disposition to be Δmarried?

3 Well, think* of marriage now; younger* [than] you,
Here* in Verona, Δladies of esteem*,
Are made already Δmothers ◊ by my count. †

4 I was your Δmother, much upon these years*
That you are now a Δmaid*. †

5 Thus then in brief*:
The valiant Paris seeks* you for his love.

6 Verona's Δsummer hath not such a flower.

7 What say you? can you love the Δgentleman?

8 This night you shall behold him at our Δfeast;
Read o'er the volume of young Paris' face,
And find delight, writ there with Δbeauty's* pen;
Examine every [married] lineament*,
And see how one another lends content;
And what obscur'd in this fair* volume lies
Find written in the Δmargent of his eyes. †

9 This precious Δbook* of Δlove, this unbound Δlover,
To Δbeautify* him, only* lacks a Δcover.

10 The fish lives in the Δsea, and 'tis much pride
For fair* without, the fair* within to hide. †

11 That Δbook* in many's* eyes doth share the glory*,
That in Δgold clasps*, Δlocks* in the Δgolden story*;
So shall you share all that he doth possess*,
By having him, making yourself* no less*.

Though Juliet's mother seems quite rational in most modern texts, F's combination of two ungrammatical fast link commas (connecting what modern texts set as mt. #1-2 and mt. #4-5) and the onrush of F #6 and #7 (reset as mt. #7-9 and mt. #10-11 respectively) suggest she is having some difficulty in getting her ideas across – especially when she has to resort to the formality of a fourteen line sonnet to instruct Juliet to examine Paris closely at the forthcoming Feast (starting with F #6's 'Read ore the volume of young Paris face.').

- thus the 'very theame' (the first half of the not quite rational F #1) is handled emotionally (0/2, the opening line and a half), followed immediately by an intellectual demand of Juliet as to what she thinks about being 'Married' (F #1's last line and a half, 2/0)

- the instruction to 'thinke of marriage now' and her own example releases her passions (6/7 in six lines, F #2-3)

- the reason for this line of questioning is made abundantly clear by the suddenly inserted surround phrase ' : The valiant Paris seekes you for his love . ' that ends F #3

- the two short sentences dwelling on Paris and demanding an answer are both intellectual (2/0, F #4-5), as are the opening four lines of the onrushed F #6 telling Juliet to take a good look at Paris at the Capulet feast to be held that night (3/1) - it being spoken as a sonnet, beginning with F #6's second line

- and then after the instruction 'Examine every severall liniament,' Old Lady becomes very quiet with the only unembellished lines of the speech 'And see how one another lends content:' and whether this is gentle counseling or ice-cold instruction is up to each actress to decide (perhaps Juliet's non-response has disturbed her)

- the next eight lines (the four ending F #6 and the first four of F#7, until the final couplet of the sonnet, from 'And what obscur'd . . . through to 'Lockes in the Golden storie:') become highly passionate (11/7) , though whether through being carried away with her own thoughts and images or a very determined attempt to force Juliet to consider marriage is again up to each actress to decide

- the flourish of persuasion ending the sonnet is emotional (0/3, F #7's last two lines), while F #8's prosaic demand for an answer is passionate once more (2/1, F #8-9)

First Folio

19/ {Mother as} Old Lady

1 Marry+ that marry is the very theame
I came to talke of, tell me+ daughter Juliet,
How stands your disposition to be Married?

2 Well+ thinke of marriage now, +yonger [then] you+
Heere in Verona, Ladies of esteeme,
Are made already Mothers.

3 By my count+
I was your Mother, much upon these yeares
That you are now a Maide, thus then in briefe:
The valiant Paris seekes you for his love.

4 Veronas Summer hath not such a flower.

5 What say you,+ can you love the Gentleman?

6 This night you shall behold him at our Feast,+
Read ore the volume of young Paris face,
And find delight, writ there with Beauties pen: x
Examine every [severall] liniament,
And see how one another lends content: x
And what obscur'd in this faire volume lies, x
Find written in the Margent of his eyes,
This precious Booke of Love, this unbound Lover,
To Beautifie him, onely lacks a Cover.

7 The fish lives in the Sea, and 'tis much pride
For faire without, the faire within to hide:
That Booke in manies eyes doth share the glorie,
That in Gold claspes, Lockes in the Golden storie: x
So shall you share all that he doth possesse,
By having him, making your selfe no lesse.

{ctd. over}

12 Speak* briefly, can you like of Paris' love?

13 {ψ} {T}he County* stays*.

• the bluntness of the Old Lady's informing Juliet that Paris awaits her is emphasised by the shortness both of sentence and spelling

8 Speake briefly, can you like of Paris love?

9 {ψ} {T}he Countie staies.

20/ Nurse **Mistris, what Mistris? Juliet? Fast I warrant her she.** 4.5.1 - 13

Background: Early in the morning of the wedding to Paris, the nurse has come to ready Juliet for the ceremony, unaware of the Frier's sleep 'like Death' potion that Juliet has taken to save her from the bigamous marriage and betrayal of Romeo.

Style: solo

Where: Juliet's chamber **To Whom:** self, audience, and the sleeping Juliet

# of Lines: 13 **Probable Timing: 0.45 minutes**

Modern Text

20/ Nurse

1 Mistress*! what Δmistress*!
2 Juliet!
3 Fast, I warrant her, she.
4 Why, Δlamb* ! why, Δlady ! fie, you slug-a-bed* !
5 Why, Δlove, I say ! ◊ madam ! sweet heart ! why, Δbride !
6 What, not a word?
7 You take your pennyworths* now; ◊
Sleep* for a week*, for the next night, I warrant,
The County* Paris hath set up his rest,
That you shall rest but little. †
8 God forgive me ! †
9 Marry* and Δamen ! †
10 How sound is she asleep* !
11 I [needs must] wake her. †
12 Madam, Madam, Madam. †
13 [Ay], let the County* take you in your bed,
He'll* fright you up, ifaith*.
14 Will it not be?
15 What, dress'd*, and in your clothes, and down* again*?
16 I must needs wake you. †
17 Lady, Δlady, Δlady?

F sets no exclamation marks (!), but rather has the Nurse call to Juliet with gentle (sometimes oratorical) questions – the gentleness is hardly surprising since, thanks to the forthcoming marriage, this is presumably the last time the Nurse will be called upon to do such a task, indeed it may be the last she'll ever be alone with Juliet. Most modern texts replace at least six of the question marks and three commas with exclamation points (often setting more than thirteen of them), suggesting it is a much more robust speech than originally conceived.

• the speech is essentially factually/intellectually driven (16/8 overall), the few emotional moments coming in three clusters - two rather risqué jokes about love-making, 'Sleepe for a weeke', as a prelude to what Paris probably intends that night, ending with 'Heele fright you up yfaith.', and the final last two word surprise at finding Juliet already 'drest, and in your clothes, and downe againe?'

• the opening of the speech moves much faster than most modern texts suggest, for they add or intensify eighteen pieces of punctuation (shown as + in the F text) in the first five lines of the speech

• charmingly (or exasperatedly perhaps), the fact of Juliet staying asleep is handled via four short unembellished sentences 'Fast I warrant her she.'; 'What not a word?'; 'You take your peniworths now.'; 'Will it not be?'

First Folio

20/ Nurse

1 Mistris, + what Mistris? +
2 Juliet? +
3 Fast + I warrant her +she.
4 Why + Lambe, + why + Lady? + fie +you sluggabed. +
5 Why + Love + I say? +
6 Madam, + sweet heart: + why + Bride? +
7 What + not a word?
8 You take your peniworths now.
9 Sleepe for a weeke, for the next night + I warrant +
The Countie Paris hath set up his rest,
That you shall rest but little, God forgive me: +
Marrie and Amen: + how sound is she a sleepe? +
10 I [must needs] wake her: Madam, Madam, Madam,
[I], let the Countie take you in your bed,
Heele fright you up + yfaith.
11 Will it not be?
12 What + drest, and in your clothes, and downe againe?
13 I must needs wake you: Lady, Lady, Lady?

#'S 21 - 26: ROMEO AND JULIET, THE LOVING BEGINNING

21/ Romeo **He jeasts at Scarres that never felt a wound,** between 2.2.1 - 32

Background: Following the first meeting with Juliet, and the kissing of her mouth, twice, Romeo attempts to elude his friends. Accidentally coming close to the upper-level balcony guarding Juliet's bedroom (though he doesn't realise it yet), he has been forced to hide from the unwarranted, and incredibly raunchy, intrusion of Mercutio and the somewhat embarrassed and concerned Benvolio (see speech #15 above). The following opens with Romeo's immediate response to their exit.

Style: solo

Where: outside, close to the balcony leading to Juliet's bedroom **To Whom:** self, the audience, and Juliet on the balcony (but not so that she can hear)

# of Lines: 32 **Probable Timing: 1.35 minutes**

Modern Text

21/ Romeo

1 He jests* at Δscars* that never felt a wound. †
2 But soft, what light through yonder window breaks?
3 It is the Δeast, and Juliet is the Δsun*. †
4 Arise, fair* Δsun, and kill the envious Δmoon*,
Who is already sick* and pale with grief*
That thou, her Δmaid, art far more fair* [than] she. †
5 Be not her Δmaid, since she is envious;
Her Vestal livery is but sick* and green*,
And none but fools* do wear* it; cast it off. †
6 It is my Δlady, O, it is my Δlove! †
7 O that she knew she were! †
8 She speaks*, yet she says* nothing; what of that?
9 Her eye discourses, I will answer* it. †
10 I am too bold, 'tis not to me she speaks*. †
11 Two of the fairest stars* in all the Δheaven,
Having some business*, do entreat her eyes
To twinkle* in their Δspheres till they return*.
12 What if her eyes were there, they in her head? †
13 The brightness* of her cheek* would shame those stars*,
As daylight doth a Δlamp*; her [eyes] in heaven
Would through the airy* Δregion stream* so bright
That Δbirds would sing and think* it were not night. †
14 See how she leans* her cheek* upon her hand!
15 O that I were a Δglove upon that hand,
That I might touch that cheek*!
xxxxxxxxxxxxxxxxxxxxxxxxxxxxxxxxxxxxxxxxxxxxxxxxxxxxxx
16 She speaks*!

F's often onrushed seven sentences and the very long penultimate line of F #2 present the pattern of a love-struck young man far more effectively than the seventeen sentences and much more regular setting of mt. #6-7 that most modern texts offer.

• the opening onrush of F #1, connecting the two lines via a fast-link and highly ungrammatical comma seems to suggest that, with the light suddenly appearing, Romeo may be afraid that his somewhat passionate denigration of Mercutio and Benvolio (1/2, F #1's first line) might have led to his being discovered, especially since the second unembellished line is obviously very quiet

• once he realises the light comes from Juliet's room (and he perhaps sees her) so F #2's first four lines are passionate (6/5) while the end of the sentence, with the exception of the extra long line discussed immediately below, is highly emotional (2/6) - as are F #3's first two surround phrase lines pointing to his desire/yet inability to act

". Her eye discourses, I will answere it : /I am too bold 'tis not to
me she speakes : "

• the strongly factual F and Q sixteen syllable line 'It is my Lady, O it is my Love, O that she knew she were,' (4/0) suggests an enormous release as he declares his love, at least to himself: most modern texts reset it as shown, reducing the outburst to a regular line followed by a short one of six syllables, implying a pause that was never originally intended

• while still emotional, his eight line dwelling on her eyes as 'Two of the fairest starres in all the Heaven', allows emotion to roar in (5/11, the last three lines of F #3 plus F #4's first five lines), especially after the wonderfully unembellished F #4 start to his fanciful flight of imagination 'What if her eyes were there,' (i.e. in the Heavens) 'they in her head,'

• the desire to touch her and hear her speak 'againe' releases even more emotion in him (2/8, the last line of F #4; all of F #5; and the extremely short #6, itself a wonderful give away as to his besottedness, and the first line of F #7)

First Folio

21/ Romeo

1 He jeasts at Scarres that never felt a wound,
But soft, what light through yonder window breakes?
2 It is the East, and Juliet is the Sunne,
Arise+ faire Sun+ and kill the envious Moone,
Who is already sicke and pale with griefe,x
That thou+ her Maid +art far more faire [then] she:
Be not her Maid+ since she is envious,+
Her Vestal livery is but sicke and greene,
And none but fooles do weare it,+ cast it off:
It is my Lady, O+ it is my Love,+O that she knew she were, +
She speakes, yet she sayes nothing,+ what of that?
3 Her eye discourses, I will answere it:
I am too bold+ 'tis not to me she speakes:
Two of the fairest starres in all the Heaven,
Having some businesse+ do entreat her eyes,x
To twinckle in their Spheres till they returne.
4 What if her eyes were there, they in her head,+
The brightnesse of her cheeke would shame those starres,
As day-light doth a Lampe,+ her [eye] in heaven,x
Would through the ayrie Region streame so bright,x
That Birds would sing,x and thinke it were not night:
See how she leanes her cheeke upon her hand.+
5 O that I were a Glove upon that hand,
That I might touch that cheeke. +
xxxxxxxxxxxxxxxxxxxxxxxxxxxxxxxxxxxxxxxxxxxxxxxxxxxxxx
6 She speakes. +

{ctd. over}

17 O*, speak* again*, bright ^Δ^angel*, for thou art
As glorious to this night, being o'er my head,
As is a winged messenger of heaven
Unto the white upturned wond'ring eyes
Of mortals* that fall back* to gaze on him,
When he bestrides the lazy* puffing ^Δ^clouds*,
And sails* upon the bosom* of the air*.

• quite charmingly, the praise of her glory as a 'bright Angell' becomes wonderfully quiet and unembellished for three lines (as if the image is almost too much for him to speak), until the final three line description of 'mortalls' that gaze on her as a 'winged messenger of heaven' releases his emotions very fully once more (1/6)

7 Oh+ speake againe+ bright Angell, for thou art
As glorious to this night+ being ore my head,
As is a winged messenger of heaven
Unto the white upturned wondring eyes
Of mortalls that fall backe to gaze on him,
When he bestrides the lazie puffing Cloudes,
And sailes upon the bosome of the ayre.

22/ Juliet **O Romeo, Romeo, wherefore art thou Romeo?** between 2.2.33 - 49

Background: Thinking she is alone, Juliet reveals that she has been as moved by the first meeting with Romeo as he.

Style: solo

Where: on the balcony leading to her bedroom **To Whom:** self and the audience, not knowing Romeo can hear everything she says

# of Lines: 15 **Probable Timing: 0.50 minutes**

Modern Text

22/ Juliet

1 O Romeo, Romeo, wherefore art thou Romeo?
2 Deny, thy Δfather and refuse thy name;
Or, if thou wilt not, be but sworn* my Δlove,
And I'll no longer be a Capulet.
xxxxxxxxxxxxxxxxxxxxxxxxxxxxxxxxxxxxxxxx
3 'Tis but thy name that is my Δenemy ;
Thou art thyself *, though not a [Montague] . †
4 What's [Montague] ? †
5 It is nor hand nor foot*,
Nor arm*, nor face, [nor any other part]
Belonging to a man.
6 O, be some other name ! †
7 [What's] ? in a [name?] †
8 That which we call a Δrose
By any other word would smell as sweet*,
So Romeo would, were he not Romeo call'd,
Retain* that dear* perfection which he owes
Without that title . †
9 Romeo, doff* thy name,
And for thy name, which is no part of thee,
Take all myself *.

While the first two sentences match in structure, F's onrush (modern texts resetting F #3 as four sentences and F #4 as three) suggests that at the end of F/mt. #2 Juliet suddenly finds a clever verbal way to get out of the dilemma, and the excitement of the discovery causes her to lose some control – and this would seem to be supported by F's peculiar verbal ending to F#3 (mt. #5), the preference for most modern texts being to set the second quarto version of the text as shown.

- the depth of the dilemma is established straightaway by the opening short intellectual F #1 (3/0) and the first improbable solution is emphasised by being set as a surround phrase ' . Denie thy Father and refuse thy name : '

- while the solution is also expressed as a surround phrase ' . 'Tis but thy name that is my Enemy : '

- up to this point the speech is almost totally intellectual (7/1 F #1-2 and the first line of F #3), and then, with her onrushed expanding on their way out of the problem 'Thou art thy selfe, though not a Mountague', Juliet becomes emotionally passionate (3/3, the three and a half lines ending F #3), even more so if 'Mountague' is regarded as being long-spelled

- after the unembellished opening of F #4, 'What? in a names' - perhaps reinforcing the solution (F only phrasing), she becomes passionate as she equates Romeo with 'perfection' (4/3 F #4's next three and a half lines), ending with a final emotional two line offer concluding with 'Take all my selfe.' (0/2)

First Folio

22/ Juliet

1 O Romeo, Romeo, wherefore art thou Romeo?
2 Denie thy Father and refuse thy name: x
Or+ if thou wilt not, be but sworne my Love,
And Ile no longer be a Capulet.
xxxxxxxxxxxxxxxxxxxxxxxxxxxxxxxxxxxxxxxx
3 'Tis but thy name that is my Enemy : x
Thou art thy selfe, though not a [Mountague],
What's [Mountague]? it is nor hand nor foote,
Nor arme, nor face, [9] [O+ be some other name
Belonging to a man].
4 [What]? in a [names] [10] that which we call a Rose, x
By any other word would smell as sweete,
So Romeo would, were he not Romeo cal'd,
Retaine that deare perfection which he owes, x
Without that title + Romeo, [11] doffe thy name,
And for thy name+ which is no part of thee,
Take all my selfe.

---

[9] this is the text as set in Q2-4/Ff: however, most modern texts i) add a phrase from Q1, 'nor any other part', and then follow it with ii) 'Belonging to a man', iii) thus placing 'O be some other name' last: the two lines thus read, 'Nor arme, nor face, nor any other part/Belonging to a man. O be some other name.'

[10] Q2-4/F2/most modern texts = 'What's in a name?' (adding Q1's question mark), F1 = 'What? in a names'

[11] F1-3 = 'Without that title Romeo, doffe thy name,': F4/ modern texts strengthen her request, setting major punctuation before 'Romeo', viz. 'Without that title; Romeo, doffe thy name,' (Q2 = ', Romeo, doffe thy name')

23/ Juliet **Thou knowest the maske of night is on my face,** 2.2.85 - 106

Background: Having heard Juliet's closest secrets (speech #22 immediately above), Romeo has sprung from his hiding place declaring his love, giving Juliet a great shock, since initially she can't see him and has no idea who is being so passionate. Once she discovers who it is, and that he is here because it is 'Love that first did promp me to enquire', she unequivocally confesses her (somewhat mixed) feelings.

Style: as part of a two-handed scene

Where: on her balcony **To Whom:** Romeo, below

# of Lines: 22 **Probable Timing: 1.10 minutes**

Modern Text

23/ Juliet

1 Thou knowest the mask* of night is on my face,
Else would a △maiden blush bepaint my cheek*
For that which thou hast heard me speak* to-night. †

2 Fain* would I dwell on form*, fain*, fain* deny*
What I have spoke, but farewell △compliment! †

3 Dost* thou △love [me]?

4 I know thou wilt say, ["Ay"],
And I will take thy word; yet, if thou swear'st,
Thou mayest* prove false: at △lovers' perjuries
They say Jove [laughs]. †

5 O* gentle Romeo,
If thou dost △love, pronounce it faithfully;
Or if thou thinkest I am too quickly won*,
I'll frown* and be perverse, and say thee nay,
So thou wilt woo*, △but else not for the world.

6 In truth, fair* [Montague], I am too fond:
And therefore thou mayest* think* my [havior]* light,
But trust me, △gentleman, I'll prove more true,
[Than] those that have [more cunning] to be strange. †

7 I should have been* more strange, I must confess*,
But that thou over heard'st, ere I was ware,
My true-△[love] passion; therefore pardon me,
And not impute this yielding* to light △love,
Which the dark* night hath so discovered.

Unlike the previous passionate speech #22 (13/10 overall) when Juliet was alone and emotions rarely took over, now that she is with Romeo though the speech again seems passionate overall (11/18) her emotions almost swamp her, at least as the speech starts.

- hardly surprisingly, Juliet's initial confession starts emotionally (1/7, F #4's first four lines), but an intellectual determination to speak her mind floods F #1's last line (2/0)

- following F #2's unembellished opening fears that Romeo 'maiest prove false', her explanation that 'Jove laught' at 'Lovers perjuries' is intellectual (4/1, the two and a half lines between F #2's first two colons), while the suggestion that she would play the courting game of nay-saying if it would better his opinion of her becomes emotional once more (1/3, F #2's last three lines)

- F#3's confession of being 'too fond' remains quietly emotional in the first six lines (2/4), though the denial that hers is a 'light Love' becomes adamantly passionate (2/2 in the last three lines)

- the few unembellished passages very clearly, carefully, and vulnerably point to her concerns: first as to her fears about possible betrayal (opening F #2), heightened further by being monosyllabic
  "I know thou wilt say I,/And I will take thy word, yet if thou swear'st,
  /Thou maiest prove false :"
  and then the occasional equally telling unembellished phrases referring to the depth of her own love are 'I am too fond'; 'Ile prove more true'; 'I should have beene more strange . . . /But that thou over heard'st ere I was ware'; and 'therefore pardon me'

- and the two surround phrases also point to the strength of her love, the end of F #2 emphasising that she doesn't want to play courting denial games
  " : But else not for the world . "
  and the opening of F #3
  " . In truth faire Mountague I am too fond : "

First Folio

23/ Juliet

1 Thou knowest the maske of night is on my face,
Else would a Maiden blush bepaint my cheeke, x
For that which thou hast heard me speake to night,
Faine would I dwell on forme, faine, faine, x denie
What I have spoke, but farewell Complement, +
Doest thou Love [ ]?

2 I know thou wilt say+ [I],
And I will take thy word,+ yet +if thou swear'st,
Thou maiest prove false: at Lovers perjuries
They say Jove [laught], oh gentle Romeo,
If thou dost Love, pronounce it faithfully: x
Or if thou thinkest I am too quickly wonne,
Ile frowne and be perverse, and say thee nay,
So thou wilt wooe: x But else not for the world.

3 In truth+ faire [Mountague]+ I am too fond:
And therefore thou maiest thinke my [behaviour] light,
But trust me+ Gentleman, Ile prove more true,
[Then] those that have [coying] to be strange,
I should have beene more strange, I must confesse,
But that thou over heard'st+ ere I was ware+
My true [Loves] passion,+ therefore pardon me,
And not impute this yeelding to light Love,
Which the darke night hath so discovered.

24/ Juliet **Three words deare Romeo,** between 2.2.142 - 154

Background: The exchange of love vows completed, they are interrupted by the nurse in the house calling for Juliet. This speech starts after Juliet returns having briefly exited, presumably to placate the Nurse (unsuccessfully, it seems, since the Nurse interrupts the following at least twice).

Style: as part of a two-handed scene **Where:** on her balcony **To Whom:** Romeo, below

# of Lines: 11 **Probable Timing: 0.40 minutes**

Modern Text

24/ Juliet

1 Three words, dear* Romeo, and good ° night indeed. †
2 If that thy bent of △love be △honorable*,
Thy purpose marriage, send me word to-morrow,
By one that I'll procure to come to thee,
Where and what time thou wilt perform* the [rite],
And all my △fortunes at thy foot* I'll lay,
And follow thee my △lord throughout the world.

[Within: Madam]

3 I come, anon. †
4 But if thou meanest not well,
I do beseech thee* -

[Within: Madam]

By and by, I come -
To cease thy strife, and leave me to my grief*. †
5 To-morrow will I send.

xxxxxxxxxxxxxxxxxxxxxxxxxxxxxxxxxxxxxxxxxxxxxxxxxxxxxxxxxxxxxxxxxxxxxxxxxxxxxxxx

6 A thousand times good night.

Considering the sometimes excessive releases elsewhere in the play, not just for Juliet but for all the characters, this is a remarkably contained speech (just 5/6 in eleven lines), suggesting that Juliet is taking great care in voicing the idea of marriage.

• thus the few releases underscore the tenor of the speech, pointing to

a/ first where her heart is so evidently on her sleeve 'deare Romeo' (1/2)

b/ then to the question of whether he means it, 'If that thy bent of Love be Honourable' (2/1)

c/ then to the idea of marriage itself, for if he will 'performe the right' (0/1)- right' being a lovely double meaning word somewhat diminished by most modern texts' correcting it to the more obvious and simplistic 'rite') - then 'all my Fortunes at thy foote Ile lay/And follow thee my Lord' (2/1)

d/ finally requesting that if he does not mean well, he should leave her to her 'griefe' (0/1)

First Folio

24/ Juliet

1 Three words+ deare Romeo,→
And goodnight indeed,
If that thy bent of Love be Honourable,
Thy purpose marriage, send me word to morrow,
By one that Ile procure to come to thee,
Where and what time thou wilt performe the [right],
And all my Fortunes at thy foote Ile lay,
And follow thee my Lord throughout the world.

[Within: Madam]

2 I come, anon: but if thou meanest not well,
I do beseech theee → +

[Within: Madam]

(x By and by+ I come - x)
To cease thy strife, and leave me to my griefe,
To morrow will I send.

xxxxxxxxxxxxxxxxxxxxxxxxxxxxxxxxxxxxxxxxxxxxxxxxxxxxxxxxxxxxxxxxxxxxxxxxxxxxxxxx

3 A thousand times goodnight.

25/ Frier Lawrence **The gray ey'd morne smiles on the frowning night,** 2.3.1 - 30

Background: This is the first speech of the character in the play. As such it explains much about his character and abilities.

Style: solo

Where: somewhere in the fields close to his cell **To Whom:** direct audience address

# of Lines: 30 **Probable Timing: 1.30 minutes**

Modern Text

25/ Frier Lawrence

1 The gray-ey'd morn* smiles on the frowning night,
Check'ring the Δeastern* Δclouds* with streaks of light,
And fleckled darkness* like a drunkard reels*
From forth day's* path, and Titan's [fiery] wheels*. †

2 Now ere the Δsun advance his burning eye,
The day to cheer* and night's dank* dew to dry,
I must up-°fill this Δosier Δcage of ours
With baleful* weeds* and precious-Δjuiced flowers . †

3 The earth that's Δnature's mother, is her Δtomb*,
What is her burying grave, that is her womb*;
And from her womb* children of divers kind
We sucking on her natural* bosom* find :
Many for many virtues excellent,
None but for some, and yet all different.

4 O, mickle is the powerful* grace that lies
In Δplants, Δherbs*, stones, and their true qualities;
For nought so vile, that on the earth doth live
But to the earth some special* good doth give ; ◊
Nor ought so good, but strain'd from that fair* use,
Revolts from true birth, stumbling on abuse . †

5 Virtue itself * turns* vice, being misapplied,
And vice [sometime's] by action dignified.

ENTER ROMEO

6 Within the infant rind of this weak* flower
Poison* hath residence and medicine power ;
For this, being smelt, with that part cheers* each part,
Being tasted, [stays] all senses with the heart.

7 Two such opposed Δkings encamp* them still
In man as well as Δherbs*, grace and rude will ;
And where the worser is predominant,
Full soon* the Δcanker death eats* up that Δplant.

For a man whose intervention affects the lives of everyone in the play, this opening speech is surprisingly free of pure intellect (15/29), veering as it does between passion and emotion, with the only possible intellectual moment occurring early on as he describes his work as a herbalist.

- the Frier's rich opening description of the morning is emotional (3/6, F #1's first four lines) while the next four lines outlining his morning task turns passionate (4/4)

- however, the further description of the power of the opposites he has just identified – see the equivalent of mt. #3 (the 'balefull weedes' versus 'precious Juiced flowers') becomes very mixed, full of quick switches - perhaps his natural enthusiasm for his work has got the better of him
  a/ the two lines of the 'earth' being a 'Tombe' are passionate (2/2)
  b/ whereas describing the different plants ('children') found 'sucking on her naturall bosome' turns emotional (0/3)
  c/ while the final summation
  " : Many for many vertues excellent : /None but for some, and yet all different ."
  is doubly emphasised by being both unembellished and made up of surround phrases, as if he were now passing on a very serious message

- coming out of this F #2's 'plant' maxim is still mixed, with its passion (2/3) surrounding yet another moment of serious calm, save for the key word 'speciall'
  "For nought so vile, that on the earth doth live, /But to the earth some 'speciall' good doth give."
  and this maxim expanded into the human realm turns emotional (F #3, 0/3), yet still contains similar serious moments - especially concerning good turning ill, and evil being given false dignity

- the practical example of both good and evil being found at one and the same time in 'this weake flower' continues emotionally (F #4, 0/4), the danger being paramount perhaps

- however, F #5's further expansion of this example of good and evil being inextricably intertwined in the world of man turns very passionate (4/4)

First Folio

25/ Frier Lawrence

1 The gray ey'd morne smiles on the frowning night,
Checkring the Easterne Cloudes with streaks of light : $_x$
And fleckled darknesse like a drunkard reeles, $_x$
From forth daies path, and Titans [burning] wheeles :
Now ere the Sun advance his burning eye,
The day to cheere, $_x$ and nights danke dew to dry,
I must upfill this Osier Cage of ours, $_x$
With balefull weedes, $_x$ and precious Juiced flowers,
The earth that's Natures mother, is her Tombe,
What is her burying grave+ that is her wombe : +
And from her wombe children of divers kind
We sucking on her naturall bosome find :
Many for many vertues excellent : $_x$
None but for some, and yet all different.

2 O+ mickle is the powerfull grace that lies
In Plants, Hearbs, stones, and their true qualities : $_x$
For nought so vile, that on the earth doth live, $_x$
But to the earth some speciall good doth give.

3 Nor ought so good, but strain'd from that faire use,
Revolts from true birth, stumbling on abuse,
Vertue it selfe turnes vice+ being misapplied,
And vice [sometime] by action dignified.

ENTER ROMEO

4 Within the infant rin'd of this weake flower, $_x$
Poyson hath residence, $_x$ and medicine power : $_x$
For this+ being smelt, with that part cheares each part,
Being tasted+ [slayes] all sences with the heart.

5 Two such opposed Kings encampe them still, $_x$
In man as well as Hearbes, grace and rude will : $_x$
And where the worser is predominant,
Full soone the Canker death eates up that Plant.

26/ Romeo **{I have not graced my} bed to night** between 2.3.42 - 64

Background: Immediately on leaving Juliet, Romeo has rushed to Frier Lawrence for help in marrying Juliet, but before he can get the words out, since he admits that he 'hath not been in bed to night' but 'the sweeter rest was mine', the Frier exclaims 'god pardon sin: wast thou with Rosaline', which triggers the following.

Style: as part of a two-handed scene

Where: the fields close to the Frier's cell **To Whom:** Frier Lawrence

# of Lines: 17 **Probable Timing: 0.55 minutes**

Modern Text

26/ Romeo

1 {I have not graced my} bed to night {-}
{ψ} the sweeter rest was mine.

2 With Rosaline ? my ghostly Δfather, ◊ no;
I have forgot that name, and that name's woe.

3 I have been* feasting with mine enemy$_*$,
Where on a sudden one hath wounded me
That's by me wounded; both our remedies
Within thy help* and holy physic* lies. †

4 I bear* no hatred, blessed man: for lo*
My intercession likewise steads my foe.

5 Then plainly know my heart's dear* Δlove is set,
On the fair* daughter of rich Capulet. †

6 As mine on hers, so hers is set on mine,
And all combin'd, save what thou must combine
By holy marriage. †

7 When and where and how
We met, we woo'd*, and made exchange of vow,
I'll tell thee as we pass*, but this I pray,
That thou consent to marry$_*$ us to-day.

The speech is a wonderful mix of self-control (the unembellished F #1, F #3, and parts of F #5); determination (the surround phrases); pussy-footing around; and finally the actual request for the Frier to marry Juliet and himself (F #4 and #5); an onrush in which the surround phrases are contained (however, most modern texts create far more control than originally set, with F #4 being split in two, and F #5 in three); and emotion (4/8 overall).

- while the unbembellished opening control (F #1-3) is interrupted by facts (the short F #2, 2/0), F #4's explanation of feasting 'with mine enemie' leading to the request for the Frier's 'helpe and holy phisicke' becomes purely emotional (0/5), the last three and a half lines of the request being set as surround phrases

- then, hardly surprisingly, the confession that he loves Juliet is passionate (2/2, F #5's opening two lines)

- but what is surprising is that the next three lines explaining that the feelings between he and Juliet are reciprocal and all that now is required is marriage, plus the final line and a half requesting the marriage, is unembellished, thus matching Juliet's careful control when she broached the subject of marriage with him earlier (speech #24 above)

- two lovely extra personal touches can be seen in, first, the two emotional surround phrases formed in part by the semicolon ' : As mine on hers, so hers is set on mine ; /And all combin'd, save what thou must combine/By holy marriage : ', and then in the extra breath thoughts (marked ,$_x$) as the onrushed 'when and where,$_x$ and how,$_x$/We met . . .' hopefully puts off any possible questions from the Frier - also heightened by being set within another surround phrase

First Folio

26/ Romeo

1 {I have not graced my} bed to night {-}
{ψ} the sweeter rest was mine.

2 With Rosaline, + my ghostly Father?

3 No,
I have forgot that name, and that names woe.

4 I have beene feasting with mine enemie,
Where on a sudden one hath wounded me,$_x$
That's by me wounded:$_x$ both our remedies
Within thy helpe and holy phisicke lies:
I beare no hatred, blessed man: for loe
My intercession likewise steads my foe.

5 Then plainly know my hearts deare Love is set,
On the faire daughter of rich Capulet:
As mine on hers, so hers is set on mine; $_x$
And all combin'd, save what thou must combine
By holy marriage: when and where,$_x$ and how,$_x$
We met, we wooed, and made exchange of vow:$_x$
Ile tell thee as we passe, but this I pray,
That thou consent to marrie us to day.

#'s 27 - 30: Romeo And Juliet, Awaiting The Nurse

27/ Juliet **The clocke strook nine, when I did send the Nurse,** 2.5.1 - 19

Background: Juliet is waiting for the nurse to return from her meeting with Romeo. Unfortunately, though the Nurse left at nine, she didn't meet Romeo until, as Mercutio brazenly put it, 'when the bawdy hand of the Dyall' was 'upon the pricke of noone', so she is very, very late.

Style: solo

Where: presumably outside, in the grounds of the Capulet residence **To Whom:** self, and direct audience address

# of Lines: 19 **Probable Timing: 1.00 minutes**

Modern Text

27/ Juliet

1 The clock* struck* nine, when I did send the Nurse ;
In half* an hour* she promised to return*. †

2 Perchance she cannot meet* him - that's not so. †

3 O*, she is lame ! †

4 Love's [△heralds*] should be thoughts,
Which ten times faster glides [than] the △sun's* beams*,
Driving back* shadows* over low'ring hills*; ◊
Therefore do nimble-△pinion'd △doves draw Love,
And therefore hath the wind-swift Cupid wings. †

5 Now is the △sun upon the highmost hill
Of this day's* journey, and from nine till twelve
[Is] three long hours*, yet she is not come.

6 Had she affections and warm* youthful* blood,
She would be as swift in motion as a ball ;
My words would bandy her to my sweet* △love,
And his to me. †

7 But old folks* - △many feign* as they were dead,
Unwieldy*, slow, heavy, and pale as lead.

ENTER NURSE

8 O God, she comes ! †

9 O honey* △nurse what news*?

10 Hast thou met with him? †

11 Send thy man away.

Since she has been waiting three hours for the Nurse's return (which was scheduled for two and half hours ago), the fact that the first three lines are highly emotional (1/6) and end in a surround phrase pushing aside thoughts of doom (' : that's not so : ') is hardly surprising.

- the attempt to justify the Nurse's lateness ('Oh she is lame, . . . ') at least adds some intellectual control to the speech (3/6)
- intellect gains more headway as she dwells on classical love images (4/0, F #2's first two lines), but the untroubled mood doesn't seem to last for F #2's last three lines, ending with the monosyllabic unembellished 'yet she is not come', becomes much less exuberant (1/1)
- and this quietness (an attempt not to give in to emotion? or a quiet pout perhaps?) continues through the mildly emotional F #3 denigration of 'old folkes' (1/5 in six lines)
- however, the enormity of her images' attack are underscored both by
  a/ the pauses inherent before voicing the melodramatic exaggeration contained in the two unusual short lines 'And his to me, but old folkes,/Many faine as they were dead' (7/7 syllables, the impact reduced by most modern texts resetting the passage as just one short line followed by one of regular length, 4/10 syllables)
  b/ and by the two unembellished lines that if the Nurse were young and had 'affections', 'She would be as swift in motion as a ball,' and the less than flattering description as Juliet finds her to be 'Unwieldie, slow, heavy and pale as lead.'
- yet when the Nurse enters all control momentarily disappears with F #4's excited intellect of 'O God she comes, . . .' (3/1), only to be followed by F #5's two short unembellished surround phrases that end the speech

First Folio

27/ Juliet

1 The clocke strook nine, when I did send the Nurse,
In halfe an houre she promised to returne,
Perchance she cannot meete him : x that's not so:
Oh+ she is lame, + Loves [Herauld] should be thoughts,
Which ten times faster glides [then] the Sunnes beames,
Driving backe shadowes over lowring hils.

2 Therefore do nimble Pinion'd Doves draw Love,
And therefore hath the wind-swift Cupid wings:
Now is the Sun upon the highmost hill
Of this daies journey, and from nine till twelve, x
[I] three long houres, yet she is not come.

3 Had she affections and warme youthfull blood,
She would be as swift in motion as a ball,+
My words would bandy her to my sweete Love,
And his to me, but old folkes,
Many faine as they were dead,
Unwieldie, slow, heavy, and pale as lead.

ENTER NURSE

4 O God+ she comes, + O hony Nurse what newes?

5 Hast thou met with him? send thy man away.

28/ Juliet **Gallop apace, you fiery footed steedes,** 3.2.1 - 35

Background: The marriage has taken place, and Juliet is waiting for the Nurse to bring the corded ladder 'by which your Love/Must climbe a birds nest Soone when it is darke'. Unfortunately, Juliet does not yet know that, since their marriage, in a street brawl Romeo has killed her cousin Tybalt in response for Tybalt's killing Romeo's friend Mercutio.

Style: solo

Where: presumably outside in the grounds of the Capulet residence **To Whom:** self, and direct audience address

# of Lines: 35 **Probable Timing: 1.45 minutes**

Modern Text

28/ Juliet

1 Gallop apace, you fiery-footed steeds*,
Towards [Phœbus'] lodging ; such a Δwaggoner*
As Phaeton would whip you to the west,
And bring in Δcloudy* night immediately.

2 Spread* thy close Δcurtain*, Δlove-performing night,
That [th'] runaways* eyes may wink*, and Romeo
Leap* to these arms* untalk'd of and unseen*! †

3 Lovers can see to do* their Δamorous [rites*]
[ ] By their own* Δbeauties, or, if Δlove be blind,
It best agrees with night. †

4 Come, civil* night,
Thou sober-suited* Δmatron all in black*,
And learn* me how to lose* a winning match,
Play'd* for a pair* of stainless* Δmaidenhoods. †

5 Hood my unmann'd* blood, baiting* in my Δcheeks*,
With thy Δblack* mantle ; till strange Δlove [grown] bold,
Think* true Δlove acted simple modesty*. †

6 Come night, come Romeo, come thou day in night,
For thou wilt lie upon the wings of night,
Whiter [than] new Δsnow upon a Δraven's back*. †

7 Come, gentle night, come, loving, black*Δbrow'd night, ◊
Give me my Romeo, and, when [hee][12] shall die,
Take him and cut him out in little stars*,
And he will make the Δface of heaven so fine
That all the world will be in Love with night,
And pay no worship to the Δgarish Δsun.

8 O, I have bought the Δmansion of a Δlove,
But not possess'd it, and though I am sold,
Not yet enjoy'd. †

Not surprisingly, as Juliet's hormone-driven adolescent imagination becomes fixated on the physical side of love she and Romeo are shortly going to share, so an almost uncontrollable onrush takes over, especially F #2 and #4 (which most modern texts make far more tidy and respectable by splitting F #2 into five sentences plus the first line of a sixth, and F #4 into five). To get the best out of the F speech, it is suggested that readers first work from the sentence structure of the modern text to separate/clarify what each of the rational stepping stones contain, and then turn to F'slayout to see what the onrush can add.

• thus it's lovely to see the two first surround phrases focusing in on love, viz. ' : or if Love be blind,/It best agrees with night : ' and, on the final exhortation for night to appear to facilitate their love-making, ' : Come gentle night, come loving blackebrow'd night . ' while the last pair demands a quick answer from the Nurse who has brought the rope ladder by which it has been planned that Romeo will come to Juliet's bedroom that night, ' : Now Nurse, what newes ? what hast thou there ? '

• the first instructions to the sun-god's horses to get to the west as quickly as possible so that night can make an early appearance is intellectual (6/2, F #1 and the first line of F #2)

• however, as the onrushed F #2 develops, the imagined result of night coming early, that 'Romeo/Leape to these armes', is highly emotional (1/5 in just two lines)

• quite naturally, the realisation that Lovers don't need light to 'doe their Amorous rights' is passionate (3/3, the equivalent of what has been set as mt. #3), while the ensuing five line plea for night to come turns emotional once more (4/9, the equivalent of mt. #4 and the first line and a half of mt. #5)

• however, she manages to regain some intellectual control instructing night how she should regard love and her renewed pleas for Romeo and night to arrive (5/3, the last five and a half lines of F #2)

• the instruction for night to cut Romeo into 'little starres' is firmly intellectual (5/1, F #3), which turns into a mixture of passion and sudden unembellishment (as if she is totally benumbed by some of her discoveries

First Folio

28/ Juliet

1 Gallop apace, you fiery footed steedes,
Towards [Phæbus] lodging,+ such a Wagoner
As Phaeton would whip you to the west,
And bring in Cloudie night immediately.

2 Spred thy close Curtaine+ Love-performing night,
That [ ] run-awayes eyes may wincke, and Romeo
Leape to these armes,x untalkt of and unseene, +
Lovers can see to doe their Amorous [rights],x
[And] by their owne Beauties : x or if Love be blind,
It best agrees with night : come+ civill night,
Thou sober suted Matron all in blacke,
And learne me how to loose a winning match,
Plaid for a paire of stainlesse Maidenhoods,
Hood my unman'd blood+ bayting in my Cheekes,
With thy Blacke mantle,+ till strange Love [grow] bold,
Thinke true Love acted simple modestie :
Come night, come Romeo, come thou day in night,
For thou wilt lie upon the wings of night+
Whiter [then] new Snow upon a Ravens backe :
Come+ gentle night, come +loving +blackebrow'd night.

3 Give me my Romeo, and+ when [I] shall die,
Take him and cut him out in little starres,
And he will make the Face of heaven so fine,x
That all the world will be in Love with night,
And pay no worship to the Garish Sun.

4 O+ I have bought the Mansion of a Love,
But not possest it, and though I am sold,
Not yet enjoy'd, so tedious is this day,x

{ctd. over}

---

12 despite the fact that only Q4 prints 'hee' (in place of 'I') some modern texts follow suit

9 So tedious is this day
As is the night before some △festival*
To an impatient child that hath new robes
And may not wear* them . †
10 O, here comes my △nurse,

ENTER NURSE WITH CORDS

And she brings news*; and every tongue that speaks
But Romeo's name speaks* heavenly eloquence . †
11 Now, △nurse, what news*? †
12 What hast thou there? ◊ the △cords
That Romeo bid thee fetch?

perhaps) as she realises her dilemma (3/2, F #4's first five lines) – the self-enforced quietness including

"But not possest it, and though I am sold/Not yet enjoy'd, so tedious is

this day, /As is the night before . . ., /To an impatient child that hath new robes . . ."

- the arrival of the Nurse, hopefully with the cords, continues the passion (3/3, the last three and a half lines of F #4)

- with no reply from the Nurse, Juliet turns intellectual for the last line (2/0)

As is the night before some Festivall, x
To an impatient child that hath new robes
And may not weare them, O+ here comes my Nurse: x

ENTER NURSE WITH CORDS

And she brings newes+ and every tongue that speaks
But Romeos, x name, x speakes heavenly eloquence:
Now x Nurse, what newes? what hast thou there?
The Cords that Romeo bid thee fetch?

29/ Juliet **What storme is this that blowes so contrarie?** between 3.2.64 - 85

Background: In her grief, for Tybalt was 'the best Friend' she had, the Nurse has not made it clear who is dead. As a result, Juliet has believed that it was Romeo who has died until the Nurse's comment 'O Tybalt . . . /That ever I should live to see thee dead' which thus triggers the following.

Style: as part of a two-handed scene

Where: either in Juliet's chambers or the grounds of the Capulet's residence **To Whom:** the Nurse

# of Lines: 17 **Probable Timing: 0.55 minutes**

Modern Text

29/ Juliet

1 What storm* is this that blows* so contrary*?
2 Did Romeo's* hand shed Tybalt's blood?
It did, it did, alas the day, it did.
3 {ψ} O Δserpent heart, hid with a flow'ring face ! [14]
4 Did ever Δdragon keep* so fair* a Δcave?
5 Beautiful* Δtyrant ! fiend Δangelical* !
[ ] Dove-feather'd Δraven, Δwolvish-ravening Δlamb*!
Despised substance of Δdivinest show !
Just opposite to what thou justly seem'st,
A [damned] Δsaint, an Δhonorable* Δvillain* ! †
6 O Δnature ! what had'st thou to do* in hell
When thou did'st bower the spirit of a fiend
In mortal* paradise of such sweet flesh? †
7 Was ever book* containing such vile matter
So fairly* bound?
8 O that deceit should dwell
In such a gorgeous Δpalace* !

Given the appalling news of Tybalt's death at the hands of her new husband Romeo, and of Romeo's banishment, it is hardly surprising that F's orthography shows little or no consistency from one moment to the next.

- thus F #1's short immediate response is emotional (0/2), while F #2-3's demand for confirmation is a combination of intellect (3/0) and an unembellished monosyllabic line as Juliet realises the truth 'It did, it did, alas the day, it did.'
- the list of her tormented love-hate descriptions of Romeo are deeply passionate (8/5, F #4 and the first four lines of F #5), the strain she's undergoing heightened both by F #5's onrush, opening with a surround phrase, and by the needed pauses implicit in the following two short lines (five to seven/five or six syllables) - the impact of which is removed by most modern texts that combine them as one longer line
- the nakedly unembellished quiet line, 'Just opposite to what thou justly seem'st', suggests that she can hardly voice the fear that she's deceived herself as to Romeo's goodness
- the attempt to reconcile/identify the opposites of a '[damned] Saint' and 'Honourable Villaine' pull her apart in just a line and a half as she springs back to passion (4/2)
- F #5's final four lines of berating nature becomes emotional (0/4), while the final, still unresolved, assessment turns slightly passionate once more (F #6, 1/1)

First Folio

29/ Juliet

1 What storme is this that blowes so contrarie?
2 Did Rom'os hand shed Tybalts blood +
It did, it did, alas the day, it did.
3 {ψ} O Serpent heart, hid with a flowring face. +
4 Did ever Dragon keepe so faire a Cave?
5 Beautifull Tyrant, + fiend Angelicall: +
[Ravenous] Dove-feather'd Raven,
Wolvish-ravening Lambe, [13] +
Dispised substance of Divinest show: +
Just opposite to what thou justly seem'st,
A [dimne] Saint, an Honourable Villaine: +
O Nature ! what had'st thou to doe in hell,x
When thou did'st bower the spirit of a fiend
In mortall paradise of such sweet flesh?
Was ever booke containing such vile matter
So fairely bound?
6 O that deceit should dwell
In such a gorgeous Pallace.

---

[13] Q2-3/Ff print the text as shown (8/6 syllables) where the diametrically opposed images once more momentarily take Juliet's breath away: Q4 = 'Ravenous dove, feathred Raven/Wolvish ravening Lamb': most modern texts print the two lines as one and omit the first word 'Ravenous' (thus maintaining pentameter)

30/ Juliet **Blister'd be thy tongue/For such a wish,** between 3.2.90 - 127

Background: In her grief, the Nurse has uttered the wish 'Shame come to Romeo'. The following is Juliet's response.

Style: as part of a two-handed scene

Where: in Juliet's chambers or the grounds of the Capulet's residence **To Whom:** the Nurse

# of Lines: 36 **Probable Timing: 1.45 minutes**

Modern Text

30/ Juliet

1 Blister'd be thy tongue
For such a wish ! he was not born* to shame :
Upon his brow shame is asham'd to sit;
For 'tis a throne* where Δhonor* may be Δcrown'd
Sole Δmonarch of the universal* earth. †
2 O what a beast was I to chide [at] him!

3 Ah, poor* my Δlord, what tongue shall smooth thy name,
When I, thy three hours* wife, have mangled it ?
4 But wherefore, Δvillain*, didst thou kill my Δcousin*?
5 That Δvillain* Δcousin* would have kill'd* my husband . †
6 Back*, foolish tears*, back* to your native spring,
Your tributary* drops belong to woe,
Which you mistaking, offer up to joy . †
7 My husband lives that [Tybalt] would have slain*,
And [Tybalt's] dead that would have slain* my husband .†
8 All this is comfort, wherefore weep* I then?
9 Some [word] there was, worser [than] Tybalt's death,
That murdered me ; I would forget it fain*,
But ΔO*, it presses to my memory
Like damned guilty deeds* to sinners' minds :
"Tybalt is dead, and Romeo banished ." †
10 That "banished", that one word "banished",
Hath slain* ten thousand [Tybalts] . †
11 [Tybalt's] death
Was woe enough if it had ended there;
Or if sour* woe delights in fellowship,
And needly will be rank'd with other griefs*,
Why followed not, when she said, ["Tybalt's] dead,"
Thy Δfather or thy Δmother, nay, or both,
Which modern* lamentation might have moved*?

The occasional return to unembellished moments suggest just how deeply affected Juliet is, once more being almost incapable of speech at key moments dealing with either herself or Romeo.

- as with the opening
  "Blister'd be thy tongue/For such a wish . . . :/Upon his brow shame is asham'd to sit ;"
  the latter heightened by being set as an emotional surround phrase, and with the following self-recrimination, also heightened as a surround phrase
  " : O what a beast was I to chide him ? "
- the further self-recrimination is also very quiet
  "Your tributarie drops belong to woe,/Which you mistaking offer up to joy :"
  as is the realisation of Romeo's ultimate fate
  "That banished, that one word banished,"
- however, most of the surround phrases concentrate on Tybalt and her relationship with him, and how she can resolve the dilemma, as with
  " . That Villaine Cozin would have kill'd my husband : "
  " : All this is comfort, wherefore weepe I then ? "
  " : That banished, that one word banished,/Hath slaine ten thousand Tibalts : Tibalts death/Was woe inough if it had ended there : "
- the speech starts with a mix of unembellished realisations and passion (6/8, F #1-3), however, the fairly rational grammatical structure with which she starts begins to disappear as the realisation that Tybalt would otherwise have killed Romeo hits home
- the onrushed F #4 plumping for Romeo (which most modern texts split into four sentences, mt. #5-8) becomes more emotional (4/8)
- but as Juliet begins to face up to the inevitability of Romeo's banishment, the onrush continues (F #5 being split into three by most modern texts), she initially becomes emotional (1/3, F #5's first four lines), and then, in following up with the idea that if only everything had ended just with Tybalt's death the outcome would be acceptable, turns intellectual (4/1, the next three lines,) only to end passionately as she suggests that even the death of her parents would be acceptable rather than Romeo's banishment (3/3, F #5's last six lines)
- the final realisation that Romeo's banishment is the equivalent of everyone else being dead is bleakly intellectual (7/3, F #6's first four lines) followed by the frighteningly unembellished lines

First Folio

30/ Juliet

1 Blister'd be thy tongue
For such a wish,+ he was not borne to shame:
Upon his brow shame is asham'd to sit;
For 'tis a throane where Honour may be Crown'd
Sole Monarch of the universall earth:
O what a beast was I to chide [ ] him?+

2 Ah+ poore my Lord, what tongue shall smooth thy name,
When I+ thy three houres wife +have mangled it. +
3 But wherefore+ Villaine+ did'st thou kill my Cozin?
4 That Villaine Cozin would have kil'd my husband:
Backe+ foolish teares, backe to your native spring,
Your tributarie drops belong to woe,
Which you mistaking+ offer up to joy:
My husband lives that [Tibalt] would have slaine,
And [Tibalt] dead that would have slaine my husband:
All this is comfort, wherefore weepe I then?
5 Some [words] there was+ worser [then] Tybalts death+
That murdered me,+ I would forget it feine,
But oh, it presses to my memory,x
Like damned guilty deedes to sinners minds,+
Tybalt is dead+ and Romeo banished:
That banished, that one word banished,
Hath slaine ten thousand [Tibalts]: [Tibalts] death
Was woe inough if it had ended there: x
Or if sower woe delights in fellowship,
And needly will be rankt with other griefes,
Why followed not+ when she said + [Tibalts] dead,
Thy Father or thy Mother, nay+ or both,
Which moderne lamentation might have mov'd. +

12 But [with] a rear*ward following Tybalt's death
"Romeo is banished," to speak* that word,
Is △father, △mother, Tybalt, Romeo, Juliet,
All slain*, all dead: "Romeo is banished !" †
13 There is no end, no limit, measure, bound,
In that word's death, no words can that woe sound.
14 Where is my △father and my △mother, △nurse?

"There is no end, no limit, measure, bound,/In that words death, no words can that woe sound."

• and she then takes charge of the situation (growing up perhaps), for her speech-ending request for information from the Nurse is totally intellectual (F #7, 3/0)

6 But [which] a rere-ward following Tybalts death
Romeo is banished+ to speake that word,
Is Father, Mother, Tybalt, Romeo, Juliet,
All slaine, all dead: Romeo is banished, +
There is no end, no limit, measure, bound,
In that words death, no words can that woe sound.
7 Where is my Father and my Mother, x Nurse?

#'s 31 - 35: Romeo And Juliet, The Tragedy

31/ Frier Lawrence **Hold thy desperate hand :** 3.3.108 - 158

Background: Distraught at the news of banishment, which means he can never see Juliet again, Romeo has attempted to kill himself with his dagger. The Nurse physically stops him, and Lawrence attempts to reason with him once more.

Style: as part of a three-handed scene

Where: Frier Lawrence's cell **To Whom:** Romeo, in front of the Nurse

# of Lines: 51 **Probable Timing: 2.30** minutes

Modern Text

31/ Frier Lawrence

1 Hold thy desperate hand ! †
2 Art thou a man? †
3 Thy form* cries out thou art;
Thy tears* are womanish, thy wild acts denote
The unreasonable △fury* of a beast.
4 Unseemly* woman, in a seeming man,
And ill beseeming beast in seeming both,
Thou hast amaz'd me !
5 By my holy order,
I thought thy disposition better temper'd.
6 Hast thou slain* Tybalt ? †
7 Wilt thou slay thyself *, ◊
And slay thy △lady that in thy life [lives],
By doing damned hate upon thyself *?
8 Why railest* thou on thy birth? the heaven and earth?
Since birth, and heaven and earth, all three do meet*
In thee at once, which thou at once would'st lose*.

The speech starts out extraordinarily carefully (just 5/9 in the first eighteen lines), as if the Frier were taking every effort possible to get Romeo to understand his situation, and not simply berate him.

• this is borne out both by F #1's three surround phrases in the first two lines (the first two of which are unembellished), and the unembellished lines that follow, the first dealing with Romeo's very humanity contending that his tears seem to suggest that he is a woman in a man's body

"And ill beseeming beast in seeming both,/Thou hast amaz'd me. By my holy order,/I thought thy disposition better temper'd."

• the Frier takes (deliberate?) unembellished care in arguing that Romeo should not rail on heaven or earth or his birth since all three meet

" In thee at once, which thou at once would'st loose./ Fie, fie, thou [sham'st] thy shape, thy love, thy wit,/ . . . /And usest none in that true use indeed,"

• and, after eighteen lines of laying in the various concepts he wants Romeo to acknowledge, the Frier becomes more excited in his releases, and far more deliberate than those offered by his modern counterpart, for, whereas in F he takes two sentences to establish his next points (F #7-8), most modern texts set their own version of an onrush by combining them as one (mt. #10)

First Folio

31/ Frier Lawrence

1 Hold thy desperate hand: +
Art thou a man? thy forme cries out thou art: x
Thy teares are womanish, thy wild acts denote
The unreasonable Furie of a beast.
2 Unseemely woman, in a seeming man,
And ill beseeming beast in seeming both,
Thou hast amaz'd me. +
3 By my holy order,
I thought thy disposition better temper'd.
4 Hast thou slaine Tybalt ? wilt thou slay thy selfe?
5 And slay thy Lady, x that in thy life [lies],[14]
By doing damned hate upon thy selfe?
6 Why rayl'st thou on thy birth? the heaven and earth?
Since birth, and heaven and earth, all three do meete
In thee at once, which thou at once would'st loose.

{ctd. over}

[14] Q2-4/F1-3 = 'lies', F4 and most modern texts = 'lives', Q1 = 'And slay thy Lady too, that lives in thee'

9 Fie, fie, thou shamest * thy shape, thy love, thy wit,
Which like a Δusurer abound'st in all,
And usest none in that true use indeed
Which should bedeck* thy shape, thy love, thy wit . †

10 Thy Δnoble shape is but a form* of wax*,
Digressing from the Δvalor* of a man ;
Thy dear* Δlove sworn* but hollow perjury*,
Killing that Δlove which thou hast vow'd to cherish ; ◊
Thy wit, that Δornament, to shape and Δlove,
Mishapen in the conduct of them both,
Like powder in a skilless* Δsoldier's* flask*,
Is set a fire by thine own* ignorance,
And thou dismemb'red with thine own* defense.

11 What, rouse* thee, man! thy Juliet is alive,
For whose dear* sake thou wast but lately dead : ◊
There art thou happy.

12 Tybalt would kill thee,
But thou [slewest] * Tybalt : there art thou happy*.

13 The law that threat'ned death [becomes] thy Friend,
And [turns] it to exile : there art thou happy.

14 A pack* [of blessings lights] upon thy back*,
Happiness* Δcourts thee in her best array,
But like a [mishaved] and sullen wench,
Thou [pouts upon] thy Δfortune and thy Δlove . †

15 Take heed, take heed, for such die miserable.

16 Go* get thee to thy Δlove as was decreed,
Ascend her Δchamber, hence and comfort her . †

17 But look* thou stay not till the watch be set,
For then thou canst not pass* to Mantua,
Where thou shalt live till we can find* a time
To blaze your marriage, reconcile your Δfriends,
Beg pardon of [the] Prince, and call thee back*
With twenty hundred thousand times more joy
[Than] thou went'st forth in lamentation.

18 Go* before, Δnurse ; commend me to thy Δlady,
And bid her hasten all the house to bed,
Which heavy sorrow makes them apt unto.

19 Romeo is coming*.

• building on Romeo's behaviour to date, he passionately denigrates Romeo's supposed 'Noble shape' and 'deare Love' (4/5, the last four lines of F #7); Romeo's 'wit' is treated almost equally cavalierly (3/5, F #8), while F #9's short instruction to 'rowse thee man' is equally passionate (1/2)

• and then the initial attempt to persuade Romeo that, with the fortunate outcome of the duel (Tybalt's death) and the Law exiling him instead of demanding his death, he should be 'happy' is as equally carefully handled as the opening eighteen lines (just 2/0 in four lines, F #10-12)

• but, whether because of Romeo's lack of reply or a conviction that he must say more, the Frier begins to become passionate as he elaborates on the 'packe of blessings' that now 'light upon thy backe' (F #13's first four lines, 3/3)

• however, with the unembellished warning of F #13's serious last line surround phrase ' : Take heed, take heed, for such die miserable . ' he becomes very careful again,

• the onrushed finale (F #14-15 being reworked into four sentences by most modern texts) is a mixture of intellect, as he gives instructions to both Romeo and the Nurse to go to Juliet (4/2, F #14's first two lines and the first of F #15), and passion, as he plans that Romeo must go to Mantua until they will 'call him backe' (3/4, F #14's lines three to seven)

• and in the onrush there are also two moments of unexpected calm, the first in describing/dreaming the manner of Romeo's return

"With twenty hundred thousand times more joy/Then thou went'st forth in lamentation ."

the quietness perhaps suggesting that the Frier is painting a mood to entice Romeo, and that he doesn't want to break it by speaking over-enthusiastically, and the second in the final instructions to the Nurse to go to Juliet

"And bid her hasten all the house to bed,/Which heavy sorrow makes them apt unto ."

which may be spoken as a quiet aside either to give the Nurse similar courage as he has just given Romeo or so as not to disturb Romeo from the mood the Frier has managed to instill in him

7 Fie, fie, thou sham'st thy shape, thy love, thy wit,
Which like a Usurer abound'st in all : x
And usest none in that true use indeed, x
Which should bedecke thy shape, thy love, thy wit :
Thy Noble shape, x is but a forme of waxe,
Digressing from the Valour of a man,+
Thy deare Love sworne but hollow perjurie,
Killing that Love which thou hast vow'd to cherish.

8 Thy wit, that Ornament, to shape and Love,
Mishapen in the conduct of them both : x
Like powder in a skillesse Souldiers flaske,
Is set a fire by thine owne ignorance,
And thou dismembred with thine owne defence.

9 What, rowse thee+ man,+ thy Juliet is alive,
For whose deare sake thou wast but lately dead.

10 There art thou happy.

11 Tybalt would kill thee,
But thou [slew'st] Tybalt,+ there art thou happie.

12 The law that threatned death [became] thy Friend,
And [turn'd] it to exile,+ there art thou happy.

13 A packe [or blessing light] upon thy backe,
Happinesse Courts thee in her best array,
But like a [mishaped] and sullen wench,
Thou [puttest up] thy Fortune and thy Love :
Take heed, take heed, for such die miserable.

14 Goe get thee to thy Love as was decreed,
Ascend her Chamber, hence and comfort her :
But looke thou stay not till the watch be set,
For then thou canst not passe to Mantua,
Where thou shalt live till we can finde a time
To blaze your marriage, reconcile your Friends,
Beg pardon of [thy] Prince, and call thee backe, x
With twenty hundred thousand times more joy
[Then] thou went'st forth in lamentation.

15 Goe before+ Nurse, +commend me to thy Lady,
And bid her hasten all the house to bed,
Which heavy sorrow makes them apt unto.

16 Romeo is comming.

32/ Frier Lawrence Hold then : goe home be merrie, give consent, 4.1.89 – 120

Background: Frier Lawrence's response to Juliet's plea for help in avoiding the bigamous marriage to Paris being forced on her by her parents.

Style: as part of as two-handed scene

Where: Frier Lawrence's cell **To Whom:** Juliet

# of Lines: 32 **Probable Timing: 1.35 minutes**

Modern Text

32/ Frier Lawrence

1 Hold then. †
2 Go* home be merry*, give consent
To marry* Paris. †
3 Wednesday* is to-morrow;
To-morrow night look* that thou lie alone,
Let not [the] Δnurse lie with thee in thy Δchamber.†
4 Take thou this Δvial*, being then in bed,
And this distilling liquor drink* thou off,
When presently through all thy veins* shall run
A cold and drowsy* humor*; for no pulse
Shall keep* his native progress*, but surcease;
No warmth, no breath shall testify* thou livest;
The Δroses in thy lips and cheeks* shall fade
To [paly] ashes, [thy] eyes windows* fall,
Like death when he [shuts] up the day of life;
Each part, depriv'd of supple government,
Shall, stiff * and stark* and cold, appear* like death,
And in this borrowed likeness* of shrunk* death
Thou shalt continue two and forty hours*,
And then awake, as from a pleasant sleep*.
5 Now when the Δbridegroom* in the morning comes
To rouse* thee from thy bed, there art thou dead.†
6 Then, as the manner of our country is,
In thy best Δrobes, uncover'd on the Δbier*,
[ ]
Thou shalt be borne to that same ancient vault
Where all the kindred of the Capulets lie. †
7 In the mean* time, against thou shalt awake,
Shall Romeo by my Δletters know our drift,

F's onrush (F #1 is split into five sentences and F #2 into four by most modern texts) suggests that Juliet's threat of suicide seems to have disturbed F's Frier far more than his modern counterpart. Indeed as with his dealings with Romeo (speech #31 above) emotion outweighed all else (25/34), here too emotion dominates (13/24 overall), suggesting a great deal of difficulty for him in attempting to maintain self-control.

- the opening two word monosyllabic unembellished surround phrase suggests just how very determined the Frier is to take control, after which he seems to settle into his task of persuading Juliet that there is a less drastic way to solve their dilemma, for the only other surround phrase
  " : for no pulse/Shall keepe his native progresse, but surcease : "
  seems deliberately used to reinforce the wonders of the potion he is passing on to her

- the initial instructions to go home and agree to marry Paris and ensure the Nurse doesn't spend the night with her are handled quickly and factually (3/2, F #1's first four lines)

- however, the instruction to 'drinke thou off' the 'distilling liquor' and the explanation of how it will work becomes almost completely emotional (the next five lines, 1/6) – perhaps the excitement of having an answer is getting to him - while further details of how she will 'appeare like death' to the uninstructed are more carefully but still passionately laid out (1/2, the next four lines), but he cannot stay so controlled, and the final explanation of how she will be 'stiffe and starke' for 'two and forty houres' becomes highly emotional once more (0/7, F #1's last five lines)

- in describing the result once the 'Bridegroome' comes (Juliet's being 'borne to buriall in thy kindreds grave'), the Frier initially becomes passionate (4/5, F #2's first seven lines), and then, in painting the picture of Romeo's return, his intellect tries to take over (4/2, F #2's last four lines)

- following F #3's opening unembellished, very careful, and unequivocal
  "And this shall free thee from this present shame,"
  which seems designed to impress upon her that this plan will work, the speech ending caveat will work only if she is brave enough to go through with taking the potion is fully emotional once more (0/2, F #3's last two lines)

First Folio

32/ Frier Lawrence

1 Hold then: goe home be merrie, give consent,$_x$
To marrie Paris: wensday is to morrow,+
To morrow night looke that thou lie alone,
Let not [thy] Nurse lie with thee in thy Chamber:
Take thou this Violl+ being then in bed,
And this distilling liquor drinke thou off,
When presently through all thy veines shall run,$_x$
A cold and drowsie humour: $_x$ for no pulse
Shall keepe his native progresse, but surcease: $_x$
No warmth, no breath shall testifie thou livest,+
The Roses in thy lips and cheekes shall fade
To [many] ashes, [the] eyes windowes fall+
Like death when he [shut] up the day of life: $_x$
Each part+ depriv'd of supple government,
Shall+ stiffe and starke,$_x$ and cold +appeare like death,
And in this borrowed likenesse of shrunke death
Thou shalt continue two and forty houres,
And then awake, as from a pleasant sleepe.
2 Now when the Bridegroome in the morning comes,$_x$
To rowse thee from thy bed, there art thou dead:
Then+ as the manner of our country is,
In thy best Robes+ uncover'd on the Beere,
[Be borne to buriall in thy kindreds grave:] [15]
Thou shalt be borne to that same ancient vault,$_x$
Where all the kindred of the Capulets lie,
In the meane time+ against thou shalt awake,
Shall Romeo by my Letters know our drift,

{ctd. over}

[15] most modern texts omit this Q2-4/Ff line, regarding it as merely a corruption of the one previous

And hither shall he come,[16] [and he and I
Will watch thy waking,] and that very night
Shall Romeo bear* thee hence to Mantua.
8 And this shall free thee from this present shame,
If no inconstant toy, nor womanish fear*,
Abate thy valor* in the acting it.

And hither shall he come,
[ ]
and that very night
Shall Romeo beare thee hence to Mantua.
3 And this shall free thee from this present shame,
If no inconstant toy+ nor womanish feare,
Abate thy valour in the acting it.

33/ Juliet **Farewell: /God knowes when we shall meete againe.** 4.3.14 – 58

Background: It is the eve of Juliet's bigamous marriage to Paris. Before her mother leaves Juliet has managed to get her agreement to allow the nurse to help with the wedding preparations instead of sleeping (in part as protectress) in the same room as Juliet as the Nurse normally does. Now Juliet has to steel herself to take Lawrence's sleep 'like Death' potion (see speech #32 immediately above), an action about which she has great doubts.

Style: solo

Where: her bed-chamber **To Whom:** self, and audience

# of Lines: 44 **Probable Timing: 2.10** minutes

Modern Text

33/ Juliet

1 Farewell ! †
2 God knows* when we shall meet* again*.
3 I have a faint cold fear* thrills through my veins*,
That almost freezes up the heat* of [life] . †
4 I'll call them back* again* to comfort me.
5 Nurse ! †
6 What should she do here?
7 My dismal* Δscene* I needs must act alone . †
8 Come, Δvial* . †
9 What if this mixture do not work* at all?
10 Shall I be married then to-morrow morning?
11 No, no, this [17] shall forbid it.
12 Lie thou there . †

Despite the emotional crises that Juliet's too vivid imagination creates for her during the course of the speech, F's orthography suggests that she eventually manages to conquer her fears and take control of herself when it is finally needed.

- the momentary hesitation offered by the F only split line opening (2/8 syllables) is apposite, for Juliet truly is saying 'good-bye' to everyone, and the potential pause very neatly allows her a moment of (sad?) silent recognition

- the surround phrases point to her sense of loneliness, and, eventually, fear
  " : Ile call them backe againe to comfort me . "
  " ? My dismall Sceane, I needs must act alone : /Come Viall, what if this mixture do not worke at all? /Shall I be married then to morrow morning ? "
  " ? There's a fearefull point : /Shall I not then be stifled in the Vault ? "
  " : stay Tybalt, stay ; /Romeo, Romeo, Romeo, here's drinke : I drinke to thee . "

- after finally divorcing herself from needing the Nurse with 'Nurse, what should she do here?', the remaining unembellished lines underscore her intertwined double concern of the mixture not working, and her therefore having to marry Paris, viz.

First Folio

33/ Juliet

1 Farewell: + →
God knowes when we shall meete againe.
2 I have a faint cold feare thrills through my veines,
That almost freezes up the heate of [fire]:
Ile call them backe againe to comfort me.
3 Nurse, what should she do here?
4 My dismall Sceane,ₓ I needs must act alone:
Come+ Viall, what if this mixture do not worke at all?
5 Shall I be married then to morrow morning?
6 No, no, this shall forbid it.
7 Lie thou there,

[16] Ff omit a line set by Q2 and most modern texts, viz. 'an he and I/Will watch thy waking': (Q3-4 set essentially the same material, printing 'and' for the first 'an', and 'walking' for 'waking')
[17] Q1 adds the word 'Knife'; most modern texts do not print the word, but instead insert a stage direction that Juliet produces a dagger and puts it down

13 What if it be a poison* which the Δfriar*
Subtilly hath minist'red to have me dead,
Lest* in this marriage he should be dishonor'd*,
Because he married me before to Romeo?

14 I fear* it is, and yet me-thinks* it should not,
For he hath still been* tried a holy man.

15 How if, when I am laid into the Δtomb*,
I wake before the time that Romeo
Come to redeem* me? ◊ there's a fearful* point ! †

16 Shall I not then be stifled in the Δvault,
To whose foul* mouth no healthsome air* breathes* in,
And there die strangled ere my Romeo comes?

17 Or if I live, is it not very like,
The horrible conceit of death and night,
Together with the terror of the place -
As in a Δvault*, an ancient receptacle,
Where for [this] many hundred years* the bones
Of all my buried Δancestors* are pack'd,
Where bloody Tybalt, yet but green* in earth,
Lies fest'ring in his shroud*, where, as they say,
At some hours* in the night, Δspirits resort -
Alack*, alack*, is it not like that I,
So early waking - what with loathsome smells*,
And shrieks* like Δmandrakes' torn* out of the earth,
That living mortals*, hearing them, run mad - ◊
O, if I [wake], shall I not be distraught,
Environed* with all these hideous* fears*,
And madly play with my forefathers' joints*,
And pluck* the mangled Tybalt from his shroud*, ◊
And in this rage, with some great kinsman's bone
As with a club, dash out [a] desperate brains* ?

18 O, look* ! methinks I see my Δcousin's* Δghost
Seeking out Romeo, that did spit his body
Upon [a] Δrapier's point. †

19 Stay, Tybalt, stay ! †

20 Romeo, Romeo, Romeo ! †

21 Here's drink* - I drink* to thee

.

" Shall I be married then to morrow morning? /No, no, this shall forbid it. Lie thou there,'

and of suspecting that it might be 'a poyson which the Frier'

"Subtilly hath ministred to have me dead,/Least in this marriage he should be dishonour'd,/Because he married me before . . ."

and then, almost as if she were claustrophobic

"Or if I live, is it not very like,/The horrible conceit of death and night,/ Together with the terror of the place,"

• not surprisingly the speech opens very emotionally (0/8, F #1-2) as the 'farewell' and the thrill of 'feare' are both faced, to be followed by a mixture of unembellished lines, broken up by momentary emotion (F #4, 2/4; F #8, 3/0) and intellect (F #7, 2/1) as her loneliness and the possibility of 'poyson' manifest themselves (F #3-8)

• then, as she faces the fear of waking and being 'stifled in the Vault' before 'my Romeo comes', her passions come to the fore (4/5, the six lines of F #9-10)

• after the fascinatingthree line unembellished 'terror of the place' opening F #11 come six lines of passion (4/6) at the realisation that she will be awake among 'all my buried Auncestors' who have lain there 'these many hundred yeeres', including 'bloody Tybalt . . . festring in his shrow'd', and the 'Spirits'

• thus her ever-growing fears of the 'smels', the 'shrikes like Mandrakes torne out of the earth', and of her 'madly' playing with 'my forefathers joynts' and eventually dashing out 'my desperate braines' leads to enormous emotional swamping (2/10 in just ten lines, the four ending F #11, and F #12-13)

• and though this leads to a vision of Tybalt 'seeking out Romeo', yet, surprisingly, the vision and her command that he should not hurt Romeo are handled intellectually (7/4, F #14), as if perhaps she now has found the courage to take the 'drinke' of the Frier's potion, whether 'poyson' or not, almost offering herself as a deliberate sacrifice in order to 'stay' Tybalt from his intended conquest

What if it be a poyson which the Frier
Subtilly hath ministred to have me dead,
Least in this marriage he should be dishonour'd,
Because he married me before to Romeo?

8 I feare it is, and yet me thinkes it should not,
For he hath still beene tried a holy man.

9 How,$_x$ if + when I am laid into the Tombe,
I wake before the time that Romeo
Come to redeeme me?

10 There's a fearefull point: +
Shall I not then be stifled in the Vault?$_x$
To whose foule mouth no healthsome ayre breaths in,
And there die strangled ere my Romeo comes. +

11 Or if I live, is it not very like,
The horrible conceit of death and night,
Together with the terror of the place,
As in a Vaulte, an ancient receptacle,
Where for [these] many hundred yeeres the bones
Of all my buried Auncestors are packt,
Where bloody Tybalt, yet but greene in earth,
Lies festring in his shrow'd, where+ as they say,
At some houres in the night, Spirits resort: $_x$
Alacke, alacke, is it not like that I+
So early waking, what with loathsome smels,
And shrikes like Mandrakes torne out of the earth,
That living mortalls+ hearing them, run mad.

12 O+ if I [walke], shall I not be distraught,
Invironed with all these hidious feares,
And madly play with my forefathers joynts?$_x$
And plucke the mangled Tybalt from his shrow'd?$_x$

13 And in this rage, with some great kinsmans bone,$_x$
As ($_x$with a club$_x$) dash out [my] desperate braines. +

14 O+ looke, + me thinks I see my Cozins Ghost,$_x$
Seeking out Romeo+ that did spit his body
Upon [my] Rapiers point: stay+ Tybalt, stay; +
Romeo, Romeo, Romeo, here's drinke: $_x$ I drinke to thee.

34/ Romeo **No matter : Get thee gone,** 5.1.32 - 57

Background: Instead of happy news, Romeo's man has brought him seemingly incontrovertible yet inaccurate news of Juliet's death. Having left Verona before the Frier Lawrence-Juliet potion plot was formed, and since a letter from Lawrence which should have reached Romeo before his man arrived has been unavoidably delayed, Romeo believes the news, and makes plans accordingly.

Style: initially to one man, and then solo

Where: a street in Mantua **To Whom:** self, and direct audience address

# of Lines: 26 **Probable Timing: 1.15 minutes**

Modern Text

34/ Romeo

1 No matter, Δget thee gone,
And hire* those Δhorses; I'll* be with thee straight.

2 Well, Juliet, I will lie with thee to night. †

3 Lets see for means*. †

4 O mischief *, thou art swift,
To enter in the thoughts of desperate men ! †

5 I do remember an Δapothecary* -
And here°abouts [a] dwells - which late I noted
In tatt'red weeds, with overwhelming brows*,
Culling of Δsimples, meagre* were his looks*,
Sharp* misery* had worn* him to the bones;
And in his needy* shop a Δtortoise hung,
An Δalligator* stuff'd*, and other skins
Of ill-°shap'd* fishes, and about his shelves
A beggarly* account of empty* boxes,
Green* earthen pots, Δbladders, and musty* seeds*,
Remnants of packthread*, and old cakes of Δroses
Were thinly scattered, to make up a show*.

6 Noting this penury, to my°self* I said,
"An' if a man did need a poison* now,
Whose sale is present death in Mantua,
Here lives a Δcaitiff * wretch would sell it him."

7 O, this same thought did but fore°run my need,
And this same needy* man must sell it me.

8 As I remember, this should be the house. †

9 Being [holiday*], the beggar's shop is shut.

10 What ho, ◊ apothecary*?

Despite the onrush of F #2, which most modern texts reset as four separate and more rational sentences, there seems to be a great growth in Romeo's ability to control himself, with the speech displaying two very different states of determination, the final sense of icy control markedly different from the opening surround phrase mix.

- Romeo's determination can be seen from the outset, the first five passionate lines (4/3) of coming to terms with the facts and deciding what to do about them being entirely composed of five surround phrases, the passion intermingled with three ice-cold unembellished instructions and determinations, from the opening dismissal of his servant's concern ' . No matter : ' and 'Ile be with thee straight.', to the reassuring of his (believed-to-be) dead wife 'I will lie with thee to night', the last two heightened even further by being monosyllabic

- the recollection and description of the 'Appothecarie' and his 'needie shop' turns highly emotional (6/12, F #2's last twelve lines)

- F #3's recollection of his original thought that here was a 'Caitiffe' would sell him a 'poyson' even though the punishment for so doing is 'present death' is also emotional and intellectual (2/3 in just four lines)

- the finish shows an entirely different form of determination, for the last five lines (F #4-7) attempting to raise the 'Appothecarie' who 'must sell' him the poison are totally unembellished, suggesting that he has either discovered an amazing sense of self-control or is being quiet in an effort not to draw attention to himself and his potentially illegal act

First Folio

34/ Romeo

1 No matter : x Get thee gone,
And hyre those Horses,+ Ile be with thee straight.

2 Well+ Juliet, I will lie with thee to night:
Lets see for meanes: O mischiefe+ thou art swift,
To enter in the thoughts of desperate men:
I do remember an Appothecarie,
And here abouts [ ] dwells, which late I noted
In tattred weeds, with overwhelming browes,
Culling of Simples, meager were his lookes,
Sharpe miserie had worne him to the bones: x
And in his needie shop a Tortoyrs hung,
An Allegater stuft, and other skins
Of ill shap'd fishes, and about his shelves, x
A beggerly account of emptie boxes,
Greene earthen pots, Bladders, and mustie seedes,
Remnants of packthred, and old cakes of Roses
Were thinly scattered, to make up a shew.

3 Noting this penury, to my selfe I said,
An if a man did need a poyson now,
Whose sale is present death in Mantua,
Here lives a Caitiffe wretch would sell it him.

4 O+ this same thought did but fore-run my need,
And this same needie man must sell it me.

5 As I remember, this should be the house,
Being [holy day], the beggers shop is shut.

6 What ho?

7 Appothecarie?

35/ Romeo **O give me thy hand,/One, writ with me in sowre misfortunes booke.** 5.3.81 - 120

Background: Unknown to Romeo, the grieving Paris has come to the Capulet tomb to mourn for Juliet whom he believes should have been his wife. As speech #34 above establishes, Romeo has come to open the tomb to take his last farewell of Juliet before killing himself. Inevitably the two clash, with Romeo only knowing he is being challenged and threatened with arrest, but not knowing by whom. In the ensuing duel Romeo fatally wounds Paris, whose dying request is 'Open the Tomb, lay me with Juliet'. This is Romeo's response.

Style: as part of a two-handed scene

Where: in front of the Capulet Monument **To Whom:** the County Paris

# of Lines: 40 **Probable Timing: 2.00 minutes**

Modern Text

35/ Romeo

1 O, give me thy hand,
One writ with me in sour* misfortune's book* !
2 I'll bury* thee in a triumphant grave.
3 A Δgrave ? †
4 O no, a Δlanthorn*, slaught'red Δyouth;
For here lies Juliet, and her beauty* makes
This Δvault a feasting presence full of light.
5 Death, lie thou there, by a dead man interr'd*. [18]
6 How oft when men are at the point of death
Have they been* merry*, Δwhich their Δkeepers call
A lightning before death !
7 O* how may I
Call this a lightning?
8 O my Δlove, my Δwife,
Death, that hath suck'd the honey of thy breath,
Hath had no power yet upon thy Δbeauty*:
Thou [art] not conquer'd, Δbeauty's* ensign* yet
Is Δcrimson* in thy lips and in thy cheeks*,
And Δdeath's pale flag is not advanced there.
9 Tybalt, liest* thou there in thy bloody* sheet?
10 O, what more favor* can I do to thee,
[Than] with that hand that cut thy youth in twain*,
To sunder his that was [thine] enemy*?
11 Forgive me, Δcousin* !
12 Ah, dear* Juliet,
Why art thou yet so fair*?

[18] some modern texts have Romeo place Paris' body in the tomb

The shaded section shown in the F text is as set in all of the possible source texts (Q2-3/and four F's), yet most modern texts follow Q4 and omit it, arguing the text is merely a cumbersome first draft of what appears more tidily in the remainder of the speech. F's onrushed #14 (reset as six rational sentences in most modern texts) is sufficient testimony to Romeo's state of mind at this moment, and the repeated text adds nothing to the action. Thus, while shown, the shaded text will not be discussed in the commentary below.

- in acknowledging Paris, F #1's extra breath thought (marked , x) without the sentence ending exclamation mark added by most modern texts suggests that the F Romeo is reflective and nowhere near as vehement as his modern counterpart, especially when followed by the calm unembellished short F #2
- however, as Romeo opens/reaches the mouth of the tomb, the gentle emotional calm of the first three lines (0/2) completely changes as he acknowledges (supposedly) dead Juliet's beauty, with F #3's sudden driving intellectual recognition (6/1) presumably difficult to speak, at least at first, for the opening line is composed of three emotional (semicolon formed) surround phrases
  ". A Grave ; O no, a Lanthorne ; slaughtred Youth : "
- the placing of the body of his noble victim close to Juliet (as requested) seems very carefully (courteously?) handled via the unembellished short F #4
- then, contemplating his own imminent self-administered death, Romeo becomes passionate (2/2, F #5-6), which is heightened by the two surround phrases of F #5 and the short F #6
- but as he focuses on Juliet and wonders at her still-lasting beauty (the first three lines of F #7), he becomes intellectual again (3/0), though the realisation ' : Thou art not conquer'd : ' seems to take his breath away, being doubly highlighted as an unembellished surround phrase – which quickly turns to passion as he comments on death's inability to make any inroads on either her 'lips' or 'cheekes' (3/3, F #7's last three lines)
- the five lines of apology to Tybalt are emotional (1/5, F #8-10)

First Folio

35/ Romeo

1 O+ give me thy hand,
One, x writ with me in sowre misfortunes booke. +
2 Ile burie thee in a triumphant grave.
3 A Grave; + O no, a Lanthorne; x slaughtred Youth: x
For here lies Juliet, and her beautie makes
This Vault a feasting presence full of light.
4 Death+ lie thou there, by a dead man inter'd.
5 How oft when men are at the point of death, x
Have they beene merrie? x Which their Keepers call
A lightning before death? +
6 Oh how may I
Call this a lightning?
7 O my Love, my Wife,
Death+ that hath suckt the honey of thy breath,
Hath had no power yet upon thy Beautie:
Thou [are] not conquer'd: x Beauties ensigne yet
Is Crymson in thy lips, x and in thy cheekes,
And Deaths pale flag is not advanced there.
8 Tybalt, ly'st thou there in thy bloody sheet?
9 O+ what more favour can I do to thee,
[Then] with that hand that cut thy youth in twaine,
To sunder his that was [thy] enemie?
10 Forgive me+ Cozen. +
11 Ah+ deare Juliet: x
Why art thou yet so faire?

{ctd. over}

13 [ ]Shall I believe*,
That unsubstantial* ΔDeath is amorous, ◊ And that the lean* abhorred Δmonster keeps*
Thee here in dark* to be his Δparamour?
14 For fear* of that, I still will stay with thee,
And never from this Δpalace* of dim* night
Depart again*. †
[ ]
15 Here, here will I remain*
With Δworms* that are thy chambermaids*; O here
Will I set up my everlasting rest,
And shake the yoke of inauspicious stars*
From this world-wearied flesh. †
16 Eyes, look* your last:
Arms*, take your last embrace ! †
17 And lips, O you
The doors* of breath, seal* with a righteous kiss*
A dateless* bargain* to engrossing* death !
18 Come, bitter conduct, come, unsavory* guide !
Thou desperate Δpilot, now at once run on
The dashing Δrocks thy Δsea-°sick* weary* Δbark*! †
19 Here's* to my Δlove !
20 O true Δapothecary* ! †
21 Thy drugs are quick*.
22 Thus with a kiss* I die.

• turning once more to Juliet, his third (passionate, F #11, 1/2) wondering as to her still visible beauty is underscored by being set as two surround phrases, ' . Ah deare Juliet : /Why art thou yet so faire ? '

• expanding on the fanciful notion that his own death will serve to keep the 'amorous . . . abhorred Monster' (death itself) from making Juliet its 'Paramour' it's not surprising that Romeo becomes highly emotional (3/10 in the five and half lines from F #12 through to the shaded section within F #13)

• in resolving to remain, the three consecutive surround phrases are testament to his passionate determination (3/4, the first four lines following the shaded section)
" ; here, here will I remaine,/With Wormes that are thy Chambermaides : O here/Will I set up my everlasting rest : /And shake the yoke of inauspicious starres/From this world-wearied flesh : "

• and in preparing for the final farewell, the surround phrases continue
" : Eyes looke your last : /Armes take your last embrace : "
and, hardly surprisingly, the invitation to 'lips' as well as 'Eyes;' and 'Armes' to take their last farewell becomes emotional (3/7, the next three and a half lines)

• however, as he readies himself to take the poison ('Come bitter conduct') Romeo becomes passionate (5/4, the three and a half lines to the end of F #15), and the surround phrase determination is continued with F #15's last phrase, the toast to Juliet ' : Heere's to my Love . '

• the surround phrases continue, underscoring his reaction to the speed of the drug in the short passionate F #16 (1/2)
" . O true Apothecary : /Thy drugs are quicke . "

• having taken them, his determination to kiss Juliet before dying is emotional (0/1, F #17)

12 [I will believe],
Shall I beleeve: that unsubstantiall death is amorous?
And that the leane abhorred Monster keepes
Thee here in darke to be his Paramour?
13 For feare of that, I still will stay with thee,
And never from this Pallace of dym night
Depart againe: come lie thou in my armes,
Heere's to thy health, where ere thou tumblest in,
O true Appothecarie!
Thy drugs are quicke.
Thus with a kisse I die.
14 Depart againe; here, here will I remaine, x
With Wormes that are thy Chambermaides: x O here
Will I set up my everlasting rest: x
And shake the yoke of inauspicious starres
From this world-wearied flesh: Eyes x looke your last:
Armes+ take your last embrace: +
And lips, O you
15 The doores of breath, seale with a righteous kisse
A datelesse bargaine to ingrossing death: +
Come+ bitter conduct, come+ unsavoury guide, +
Thou desperate Pilot, now at once run on
The dashing Rocks, x thy Sea-sicke wearie Barke: +
Heere's to my Love. +
16 O true Appothecary: +
Thy drugs are quicke.
17 Thus with a kisse I die.

#'s 36 - 37: Final Words

36/ Frier Lawrence **I am the greatest, able to doe least,** between 5.3.223 - 269

Background: The full tragedy has unfolded. Romeo has killed himself by drinking poison; Juliet, awaking just as the Frier arrives, finds Romeo dead and refusing to be helped or consoled by Lawrence, has stabbed herself to death with Romeo's dagger; and Romeo's mother, even prior to his return from Mantua, has died with grief. All the adults involved in the lives and deaths of Romeo and Juliet have gathered at the Monument, and the Prince, who has lost a second nephew when Paris died, is trying to sort out just how these events occurred. Lawrence attempts to explain, taking full responsibility for the tragedies.

Style: general address

Where: at the opened Capulet Monument **To Whom:** the Prince, Juliet's two Capulet parents, Romeo's Mountague father, members of the watch, and the pages to both Romeo and Paris, in front of the dead bodies of Romeo, Juliet, Paris, and the already shrouded Tybalt

# of Lines: 42 **Probable Timing: 2.00** minutes

Modern Text

36/ Frier Lawrence

1 I am the greatest, able to do* least,
Yet most suspected, as the time and place
Doth make against me, of this direful* [murder];
And here* I stand both to impeach and purge
Myself * condemned and myself * excus'd.

2 Romeo, there dead, was husband to that Juliet,
And she, there dead, [that] Romeo's faithful* wife,
I married them, and their stol'n* marriage day
Was Tybalt's Δdooms-day*, whose untimely death
Banish'd the new-made Δbridegroom* from this Δcity*,
For whom, and not for Tybalt, Juliet pin'd*.

3 You, to remove that siege of Δgrief * from her,
Betroth'd, and would have married her perforce
To County* Paris.

4 Then comes she to me,
And with wild* looks* bid me devise some [mean*]
To rid her from this second Δmarriage,
Or in my Δcell there would she kill herself *.

5 Then gave I her (so Δtutor'd by my Δart)
A sleeping Δpotion, which so took* effect
As I intended, for it wrought on her
The form* of death.

6 Mean* time, I writ to Romeo,
That he should hither come, as this dire* night,
To help* to take her from her borrowed grave,
Being the time the Δpotion's force should cease.

- the emotion of F #1's self-implication (0/5) is heightened in the final line by the extra breath-thought (marked), as if the Frier needs the extra moment to underscore that he is attempting to acknowledge his guilt but free himself from any sense of wrong-doing

- the intellectual statement of the (horror of the?) bare facts (9/5, F #2) is underscored by the four surround phrases that end F #2, the first two created in part by the emotional semicolon
  " : I married them ; and their stolne marriage day/Was Tybalts Doomesday : whose untimely death/Banish'd the new-made Bridegroome from this Citie : /For whom (and not for Tybalt) Juliet pinde . "

- while the catalyst that caused this latest tragedy is also intellectual (F #3, 3/1), the key fact is stated without any embellishment
  "You . . ./Betroth'd, and would have married her perforce'
  though whether the quiet is an attempt to lay the blame nakedly on the Capulets or simply because he can hardly voice the moment is up to each actor to explore

- not surprisingly, describing Juliet's coming to him and threatening to kill herself is emotional (F #4, 2/4), and his solution (giving her the potion and writing to Romeo) is reported passionately (5/5, the seven lines of F #5-6)

- once more the deus ex machina facts of his letter going astray through no fault of his or Frier John (who had been delayed by plague) is intellectually handled (4/1, F #7), though the final nail in the coffin
  " ; and yesternight/Return'd my Letter backe . "
  is underscored by being set as an emotional (i.e. semicoloned) surround phrase, and it seems that his intellectual self-control is now beginning to waver, for . . .

First Folio

36/ Frier Lawrence

1 I am the greatest, able to doe least,
Yet most suspected+ as the time and place
Doth make against me+ of this direfull [murther] : x
And heere I stand both to impeach and purge
My selfe condemned,x and my selfe excus'd.

2 Romeo+ there dead, was husband to that Juliet,
And she+ there dead, [that's] Romeos faithfull wife: x
I married them; x and their stolne marriage day
Was Tybalts Doomesday: x whose untimely death
Banish'd the new-made Bridegroome from this Citie:x
For whom (xand not for Tybaltx) Juliet pinde.

3 You, to remove that siege of Greefe from her,
Betroth'd, and would have married her perforce
To Countie Paris.

4 Then comes she to me,
And (xwith wilde lookesx) bid me devise some [meanes]
To rid her from this second Marriage,
Or in my Cell there would she kill her selfe.

5 Then gave I her (so Tutor'd by my Art)
A sleeping Potion, which so tooke effect
As I intended, for it wrought on her
The forme of death.

6 Meane time, I writ to Romeo,
That he should hither come, as this dyre night,
To helpe to take her from her borrowed grave,
Being the time the Potions force should cease.

{ctd. over}

7 But he which bore my $^{\Delta}$letter, Friar John,
Was stayed$_{*}$ by accident, and yesternight
Return'd my $^{\Delta}$letter back*.

8 Then all alone,
At the prefixed hour* of her waking,
Came I to take her from her $^{\Delta}$kindred's vault,
Meaning to keep* her closely at my $^{\Delta}$cell,
Till I conveniently could send to Romeo.

9 But when I came, some $^{\Delta}$minute ere the time
Of her [awakening], here* untimely lay
The $^{\Delta}$noble Paris and true Romeo dead.

10 She* wakes, and I entreated* her come forth*
And bear* this work* of $^{\Delta}$heaven with patience. †

11 But then, a noise* did scare* me from the $^{\Delta}$tomb*,
And she, too desperate, would not go with me,
But as it seems*, did violence on herself*.

12 All this I know, and to the $^{\Delta}$marriage
Her $^{\Delta}$nurse is privy; and if aught in this
Miscarried by my fault, let my old life
Be sacrific'd, some hour* before [his] time,
Unto the rigor* of severest $^{\Delta}$law.

• . . . his intended presence at Juliet's waking is described somewhat passionately (3/2, the four and a half lines of F #8), and his F #9 report of finding the bodies of Romeo and Paris attempts to maintain the intellectual control of his earlier presentation of essentially factual details (4/1, in three lines)

• however, then emotions flood in as he describes Juliet's waking, his failure to persuade her to leave, his own cowardice, and her presumed suicide (2/9 in just the five lines of F #10)

• though his offering proof of his story via the Nurse is factual (2/0, the first line of F #11), the final offer to die if he did anything wrong is, naturally, emotional (1/3, the last three lines of the speech)

• and, as the shaded text shows, the F offer shows far more loss of control than does the resetting by most modern texts (F #11's first three irregular lines, as the completely regular opening four lines of mt. #11), the longer lines of F (fourteen/eleven/fourteen syllables) suggest a character who can no longer maintain complete control in a supposedly formal/quasi judicial situation but instead finds his thoughts running away with him, a final capper to the ever-growing sense of discomfort and loss of control first seen in F #7: by regularising the passage modern texts have not only removed this moment of strain as he offers his life as recompense, but also diminished the last act denoting his almost complete mental collapse

7 But he which bore my Letter, Frier John,
Was stay'd by accident; $_x$ and yesternight
Return'd my Letter backe.

8 Then all alone,
At the prefixed houre of her waking,
Came I to take her from her Kindreds vault,
Meaning to keepe her closely at my Cell,
Till I conveniently could send to Romeo.

9 But when I came ($_x$some Minute ere the time
Of her [awaking]$_x$) heere untimely lay
The Noble Paris,$_x$ and true Romeo dead.

10 Shee wakes, and I intreated her come foorth,$_x$
And beare this worke of Heaven,$_x$ with patience:
But then, a noyse did scarre me from the Tombe,
And she ($_x$too desperate$_x$) would not go with me,
But ($_x$as it seemes$_x$) did violence on her selfe.

11 All this I know, and to the Marriage her Nurse is privy: $_x$
And if ought in this miscarried by my fault,
Let my old life be sacrific'd, some houre before [the] time,
Unto the rigour of severest Law.

37/ Prince **Seale up the mouth of outrage for a while,** three parts of 5.3: 216 - 221 + 291 - 295 + 305 - 310

Background: The final words of the play, preceded by a single line and then another sentence from an earlier part of the scene (sentences #1-2 as the speech now stands). Two notes: 'your hate' refers to both houses, Capulet and Mountague, alike; the loss of a 'brace of Kinsmen' refers to his now dead nephews Mercutio and Paris.

Style: general address

Where: at the opened Capulet Monument **To Whom:** Juliet's two Capulet parents, Romeo's Mountague father, Frier Lawrence, members of the watch, and the pages to both Romeo and Paris, in front of the dead bodies of Romeo, Juliet, Paris, and the already shrouded Tybalt

# of Lines: 17 **Probable Timing: 0.55 minutes**

Modern Text

37/ Prince

1 Seal* up the mouth of outrage for a while,
Till we can clear* these ambiguities,
And know their spring, their head, their true descent,
And then will I be general* of your woes,
And lead you even to death. †

2 Mean* time forbear*,
And let mischance be slave to patience. †

3 Where be these Δenemies?

4 Capulet! †

5 Montague! †

6 See what a scourge is laid* upon your hate,
That Δheaven finds means* to kill your joys* with Δlove. †

7 And I, for winking at your discords too
Have lost a brace of Δkinsmen. †

8 All are punish'd.

9 A [gloomy] peace this morning with it brings,
The Δsun*, for sorrow, will not show* his head. †

10 Go hence to have more talk* of these sad things;
Some shall be pardon'd, and some punished: ◊
For never was a Δstory* of more Δwoe*
[Than] this of Juliet and her Romeo.

• that the Prince is having difficulty maintaining self-control can be seen in
a/ the emotional opening (F #1, 1/5)
b/ the ungrammatical fast link connection via the question mark in line five jumping from shared grief to the instruction for 'patience' (where most modern texts create mt. #2)
c/ the onrush of F #2 (split into five sentences by most modern texts) where he speaks of the losses both families and he have suffered

• however, while F #2 is onrushed it is at least intellectually based (6/3) suggesting that the Prince is struggling hard to present the facts as best as he can

• the constant return to unembellished moments
'And know their spring, their head, their true descent,'
'And let mischance be slave to patience'
'A glooming peace this morning with it brings,'
'And I, for winking at your discords too,'
'Some shall be pardon'd, and some punished.'
suggest an exhausted man constantly needing a moment (either of rest, or to calm himself) before he can continue

• this lack of energy, still tinged with emotion, most affects F #3's 'glooming' assessment of the forthcoming day (1/3 in four lines)

• though the Prince manages to gather enough mental energy to make the final intellectual summation of the overall tragedy (F #4, 4/0)

First Folio

37/ Prince

1 Seale up the mouth of outrage for a while,
Till we can cleare these ambiguities,
And know their spring, their head, their true descent,
And then will I be generall of your woes,
And lead you even to death? meane time forbeare,
And let mischance be slave to patience,
Where be these Enemies?

2 Capulet,+ Montague, +
See what a scourge is laide upon your hate,
That Heaven finds meanes to kill your joyes with Love;
And I, for winking at your discords too,x
Have lost a brace of Kinsmen: All are punish'd.

3 A [glooming] peace this morning with it brings,
The Sunne+ for sorrow+ will not shew his head;
Go hence,x to have more talke of these sad things,+
Some shall be pardon'd, and some punished.

4 For never was a Storie of more Wo,x
[Then] this of Juliet,x and her Romeo.

JULIUS CÆSAR

SPEECHES IN ORDER

SPEECHES IN ORDER			TIME	PAGE
#'s 1: Cassius, The Individual				
1/	**Cassius**	For my part, I have walk'd about the streets,	1.30	97
#'s 2 - 4: Cassius & Brutus, The Initial Temptation				
2/	**Cassius**	I know that vertue to be in you Brutus,	2.00	98
3/	**Cassius**	Why man, he doth bestride the narrow world	1.30	100
4/	**Brutus**	That you do love me, I am nothing jealous:	0.45	101
#'s 5 - 6: Cassius & Brutus, The Decision Taken				
5/	**Brutus**	It must be by his death: and for my part,	1.15	102
6/	**Brutus**	Our course will seeme too bloody, Caius Cassius,	1.30	103
#'s 7 - 8: Cassius & Brutus As Things Fall Apart				
7/	**Brutus**	You wrong'd your selfe to write in such a case.	0.55	104
8/	**Cassius**	A Friend should beare his Friends infirmities;	0.55	105
#'s 9 - 12: A Cæsar For All Seasons				
9/	**Caska**	I can as well bee hang'd as tell the manner of it:	1.45	106
10/	**Calphurnia**	What mean you Cæsar?	1.10	108
11/	**Decius**	This Dreame is all amisse interpreted,	1.10	109
12/	**Cæsar**	I must prevent thee Cymber:	1.30	110
#'s 13 - 17: Antony's Response				
13/	**Antony**	O mighty Cæsar !/Dost thou lye so lowe?	0.50	111
14/	**Antony**	O pardon me, thou bleeding peece of Earth:	1.10	112
15/	**Antony**	Friends, Romans, Countrymen, lend me your ears:	1.45	113
16/	**Antony**	If you have teares, prepare to shed them now.	1.30	115
17/	**Antony**	This is a slight unmeritable man,	1.15	116
#'s 18 - 19: Others Affected By Events				
18/	**Murellus**	Wherefore rejoyce?/What Conquest brings he home?	1.10	117
19/	**Caska**	Are not you mov'd, when all the sway of Earth	1.30	118
#'s 20 - 23: Portia's Dilemma				
20/	**Portia**	Nor for yours neither. Y'have ungently Brutus	1.00	119
21/	**Portia**	Brutus is wise, and were he not in health,	1.00	120
22/	**Portia**	Within the Bond of Marriage, tell me Brutus,	1.00	121
23/	**Portia**	I prythee Boy, run to the Senate-house,	1.15	121

SPEECHES BY GENDER

		Speech #(s)
SPEECHES FOR WOMEN (5)		
Calphurnia	**Traditional & Today:** middle-aged woman and older	#10
Portia	**Traditional & Today:** middle-aged woman, sometimes younger	#20, #21, #22, #23
SPEECHES FOR EITHER GENDER (4)		
Caska	**Traditional:** male, any age, often late middle-aged or older **Today:** any age, any gender	#9, #19
Decius	**Traditional:** male, any age **Today:** any age, any gender	#11
Murellus	**Traditional:** older male **Today:** any age, any gender	#18
SPEECHES FOR MEN (14)		
Cassius	**Traditional:** early middle-aged man and older **Today:** male, any age	#1, #2, #3, #8
Brutus	**Traditional:** early middle-aged man and older **Today:** male, any age	#4, #5, #6, #7
Caæsar	**Traditional:** older male **Today:** middle-aged male and older	#12
Antony	**Traditional & Today:** younger man	#13, #14, #15, #16, #17

JULIUS CÆSAR

1: Cassius, The Individual

1/ Cassius **For my part, I have walk'd about the streets,** between 1.3.44 - 78

Background: Cassius has begun his plan to ensnare Brutus to lead a coup against Cæsar. That very night a huge and terrifying storm has hit Rome, delighting Cassius, as he explains to one of his eventual co-conspirators. The following is a very good key to his character, so different from the cautious, rational Brutus.

Style: as part of a two-handed scene

Where: a street in Rome **To Whom:** Caska

# of Lines: 30 **Probable Timing: 1.30 minutes**

Modern Text

1/ Cassius

1 For my part, I have walk'd about the streets,
Submitting me unto the perilous* Δnight;
And thus unbraced, [Casca], as you see,
Have bar'd my Δbosom* to the Δthunder-stone;
And when the cross* blue* Δlightning seem'd to open
The Δbreast$_*$ of Δheaven, I did present myself*
Even in the aim*, and very flash of it.

xxxxxxxxxxxxxxxxxxxxxxxxxxxxxxxxxxxxxxxxxxxxxxxxxxxxxxxxxxxxxxxxxxxxxxxx

2 You are dull, [Casca] ; and those sparks* of Life
That should be in a Roman you do* want,
Or else you use not.

3 You look* pale, and gaze,
And put on fear*, and cast yourself* in wonder,
To see the strange impatience of the Δheavens;
But if you would consider the true cause
Why all these Δfires, why all these gliding Δghosts,
Why Δbirds and Δbeasts from quality$_*$ and kind*,
Why Δold men, Δfools*, and Δchildren calculate,
Why all these things change from their Δordinance
Their Δnatures, and preformed Δfaculties,
To monstrous quality$_*$ - why, you shall find*,
That Δheaven hath infus'd them with these Δspirits,
To make them Δinstruments of fear* and warning
Unto some monstrous Δstate.

4 Now could I, [Casca], name to thee a man,
Most like this dreadful* Δnight,
That Δthunders, Δlightens, opens Δgraves, and roars*
As doth the Δlion* in the Capitol* -

F's orthography posits a very wild, almost unstable, character.

- F suggests that Cassius starts his opening brag more than somewhat erratically
  a/ the deceptively quiet unembellished monosyllabic first line
  b/ quickly giving way to a second passionate line (1/1) the 'perillous Night', enhanced by ending with an (emotional) semicolon
  c/ which in turn leads to an intellectual three and a half line description of baring his 'Bosome to the Thunder-stone' (6/3)
  d/ to be followed by an emotional flourish as he describes presenting himself in 'the ayme' (0/2)
  e/ only to finish F #1 as he opened it, with an unembellished phrase

  the whole suggesting rapid switches between his own inner dialogue and talking to Caska

- and this lack of control is even more marked in F #2's passionate 'You are dull, Caska' (3/2) and the first three emotional lines of F #3's rebuke of Caska's 'feare' of the storm - the emotion could range from enjoyment to genuine scorn, the lack of control further emphasised by . . .

- . . . F setting five irregular lines (five/twelve/eight/nine/seven syllables), the pauses surrounding the shorter lines suggesting self-absorption as he plays with the unfortunate Caska, the one longer line reminiscent of a moment of humiliating tongue-lashing: unfortunately, most modern texts set the passage as five almost regular lines (save for the last) as shown, and in so doing may have removed Cassius' wilder character traits

- following yet another unembellished line,
  "But if you would consider the true cause,$_x$/Why"
  the challenge heightened by the first of five extra breath-thoughts scattered throughout F #3 (marked , $_x$), all suggesting a closer attention to details for both himself and Caska than offered by most modern texts

- the speech becomes highly intellectual (21/8 the next thirteen lines, F #3 line five to the first four lines of F #4) as he suggests that the strange events should be read as signs that Cæsar (without actually naming him) has become as 'fearefull' as this 'dreadfull Night'

First Folio

1/ Cassius

1 For my part, I have walk'd about the streets,
Submitting me unto the perillous Night;
And thus unbraced, [Caska], as you see,
Have bar'd my Bosome to the Thunder-stone: $_x$
And when the crosse blew Lightning seem'd to open
The Brest of Heaven, I did present my selfe
Even in the ayme, and very flash of it.

xxxxxxxxxxxxxxxxxxxxxxxxxxxxxxxxxxxxxxxxxxxxxxxxxxxxxxxxxxxxxxxxxxxxxxxx

2 You are dull, [Caska]: $_x$
And those sparkes of Life,$_x$ that should be in a Roman, $_x$
You doe want, or else you use not.

3 You looke pale, and gaze, and put on feare,
And cast your selfe in wonder,
To see the strange impatience of the Heavens: $_x$
But if you would consider the true cause, $_x$
Why all these Fires, why all these gliding Ghosts,
Why Birds and Beasts,$_x$ from qualitie and kinde,
Why Old men, Fooles, and Children calculate,
Why all these things change from their Ordinance,$_x$
Their Natures, and pre-formed Faculties,
To monstrous qualitie; $_x$ why$^+$ you shall finde,
That Heaven hath infus'd them with these Spirits,
To make them Instruments of feare,$_x$ and warning, $_x$
Unto some monstrous State.

4 Now could I ($_x$[Caska]$_x$) name to thee a man,
Most like this dreadfull Night,
That Thunders, Lightens, opens Graves, and roares, $_x$
As doth the Lyon in the Capitoll: $_x$

{ctd. over}

A man no mightier [than] thyself*, or me,
In personal* action, yet prodigious grown*,
And fearful*, as these strange eruptions are.

• and in the last three lines of the speech, as the 'man' (not Cæsar by name) is more than hinted at, Cassius becomes totally emotional (0/4), the allusion to ' : A man no mightier then thy selfe, or me, /In personall action ; ' strengthened even more by being set as an emotional (via the semicolon) surround phrase

A man no mightier [then] thy selfe, or me,
In personall action; $_x$ yet prodigious growne,
And fearefull, as these strange eruptions are.

#'s 2 - 4: Cassius & Brutus, The Initial Temptation

2/ Cassius **I know that vertue to be in you Brutus,** 1.2.90 - 131

Background: This is Brutus' response to Cassius' initial overtures; his very much to the point question 'Into what dangers, would you/Lead me Cassius?'; plus his comment that the first set of flourishes and shouts from the Capitol makes him 'feare, the People choose Cæsar/For their King' gives Cassius the needed opening to begin exploring the more serious, possibly even treasonous, matter at hand.

Style: as part of a two-handed scene

Where: a street in Rome **To Whom:** Brutus

# of Lines: 42 **Probable Timing: 2.00 minutes**

Modern Text

2/ Cassius

1 I know that virtue to be in you, Brutus,
As well as I do know your outward favor*.

2 Well, Δhonor is the subject of my Δstory :
I cannot tell, what you and other men
Think* of this life; Δbut for my single self*,
I had as lief* not be as live to be
In awe of such a Δthing as I myself*.

3 I was born* free as Cæsar, so were you ;
We both have fed as well, and we can both
Endure the Δwinter's cold, as well as he*; ◊
For once, upon a Δraw* and Δgusty$_*$ day,
The troubled [Tiber] chafing with her Δshores,
Cæsar said* to me, "Dar'st thou, Cassius, now
Leap* in with me into this angry Δflood,
And swim to yonder Δpoint?"

4 Upon the word,
Accoutred as I was, I plunged in,
And bad him follow; so indeed he did.

5 The Δtorrent roar'd, and we did buffet it
With lusty Δsinews*, throwing it aside
And stemming it with hearts of Δcontroversy$_*$; ◊

Most modern texts alter undo two important clues by altering F's sentence pattern into a supposedly more rational structure. With F setting F #3 and #4 as separate sentences, the importance of each - F #3's statement that he (and presumably Brutus) should be regarded as Cæsar's equal, and F #4's setting up the first story of Cæsar's weakness - are highlighted as separate facts in and of themselves. Most modern texts jam the two sentences together as shown, reducing the power of each to a more general rant – which in fact comes later. But F's onrushed last sentence (#9) suggests that it is only now that Cassius seems to rant. Modern texts split F #9 in two setting up a much more rational finish for Cassius than originally set.

• the speech starts quite firmly, with the intellect (3/1) of the first three lines culminating in F #2's opening surround phrase reassuring Brutus that " . Well, Honor is the subject of my Story : "

• but his attempt to control himself as the 'Story' starts, 'I cannot tell, what you and other men', rapidly disappears, first into emotion (2/4 in F #2's remaining three lines) as he continues his self-definition, and then into passion as he begins to compare himself with Cæsar (2/2 the three lines of F #3)

• Cassius' first steps towards proving his contention, F #4's challenge to swim the 'troubled Tyber', are determinedly strongly intellectual (8/4), and then very quiet as he describes how he leapt in first, the totally unembellished F #5 ending via the surround phrase ' : so indeed he did . ' possibly underscoring how fixed this incident is in his memory, or how carefully he is attempting to ensnare Brutus in his honour-serving tale

First Folio

2/ Cassius

1 I know that vertue to be in you+ Brutus,
As well as I do know your outward favour.

2 Well, Honor is the subject of my Story :
I cannot tell, what you and other men
Thinke of this life : $_x$ But for my single selfe,
I had as liefe not be, $_x$ as live to be
In awe of such a Thing, $_x$ as I my selfe.

3 I was borne free as Cæsar, so were you,+
We both have fed as well, and we can both
Endure the Winters cold, as well as hee.

4 For once, upon a Rawe and Gustie day,
The troubled [Tyber], $_x$ chafing with her Shores,
Cæsar saide to me, Dar'st thou+ Cassius+ now
Leape in with me into this angry Flood,
And swim to yonder Point?

5 Upon the word,
Accoutred as I was, I plunged in,
And bad him follow : $_x$ so indeed he did.

6 The Torrent roar'd, and we did buffet it
With lusty Sinewes, throwing it aside, $_x$
And stemming it with hearts of Controversie.

But ere we could arrive the Δpoint propos'd,
Cæsar cried*, "Help* me, Cassius, or I sink* !"
6 I, as Æneas, our great Δancestor,
Did from the Δflames of Troy upon his shoulder
The old [Anchises] bear*, so from the waves of [Tiber]
Did I the tired Cæsar. †
7 And this Δman
Is now become a Δgod, and Cassius is
A wretched Δcreature, and must bend his body
If Cæsar carelessly$_*$ but nod on him.
8 He had a Δfever* when he was in Spain*,
And when the Δfit was on him, I did mark*
How he did shake - Δ'tis true, this Δgod did shake ;
His Δcoward lips* did from their color* fly*,
And that same Δeye, whose bend doth awe the Δworld,
Did lose* his Δlustre; I did hear* him groan*;
[Ay], and that Δtongue of his that bad the Romans
Mark* him, and write his Δspeeches in their Δbooks*,
Alas, it cried, "Give me some drink*, Titinius,"
As a sick* Δgirl*. †
9 Ye Δgods, it doth amaze me
A man of such a feeble temper should
So get the start of the Δmajestic* world
And bear* the Δpalm* alone.

• the first detailing of the actual swim (as 'the 'Torrent roar'd') starts factually (F #6, 3/1), and extra breath-thoughts seen first in F #2 (marked ,$_x$) start to appear more frequently , as if Cassius is taking great care to underscore the smallest of points in order to enhance his case

• Cæsar's weakness (F #7 and the first three and a half lines of F #8) and Cassius rescue of him are recalled passionately (10/7)

• however, the resultant denigration of Cæsar having 'now become a God' is totally intellectual (6/0 the last three and a half lines of F#8), presumably to ensure that personal feelings do not get in the way of Brutus' receiving the full force of Cassius' judgment

• but the passions come sweeping back in as Cassius adds in a second example of Cæsar's lack of backbone, the 'Feaver when he was in Spaine': the first outlining of it (9/7 in just the first five and a half lines of F #9) is momentarily interrupted by an emotional monosyllabic surround phrase adding his own amazed description ' : I did heare him grone : ' and then the passions flow uninterrupted (11/8) through the last seven lines ending the speech as Cassius once more describes Cæsar's behaviour 'as a sicke Girle' and then expresses his amazement that Cæsar should hold 'the Majesticke world' by himself 'alone'

7 But ere we could arrive the Point propos'd,
Cæsar cride, Helpe me+ Cassius, or I sinke. +
8 I ($_x$as Æneas, our great Ancestor,
Did from the Flames of Troy,$_x$ upon his shoulder
The old [Anchyses] beare$_x$) so, $_x$from the waves of [Tyber]
Did I the tyred Cæsar: And this Man,$_x$
Is now become a God, and Cassius is
A wretched Creature, and must bend his body,$_x$
If Cæsar carelesly but nod on him.
9 He had a Feaver when he was in Spaine,
And when the Fit was on him, I did marke
How he did shake: $_x$ Tis true, this God did shake,+
His Coward lippes did from their colour flye,
And that same Eye, whose bend doth awe the World,
Did loose his Lustre: $_x$ I did heare him grone: $_x$
[I], and that Tongue of his,$_x$ that bad the Romans
Marke him, and write his Speeches in their Bookes,
Alas, it cried, Give me some drinke+ Titinius,
As a sicke Girle: Ye Gods, it doth amaze me,$_x$
A man of such a feeble temper should
So get the start of the Majesticke world,$_x$
And beare the Palme alone.

3/ Cassius **Why man, he doth bestride the narrow world** 1.2.135 - 161

Background: Brutus does not directly respond to Cassius' initial anti-Cæsar diatribe, but instead seems disturbed by the fact that the further shouting from the Capitol could well signify 'these applauses are/For some new honors, that are heap'd on Cæsar'. Cassius immediately takes advantage of this to press home his argument even further.

Style: as part of a two-handed scene

Where: a street in Rome **To Whom:** Brutus

# of Lines: 27 **Probable Timing: 1.30 minutes**

Modern Text

3/ Cassius

1 Why, man, he doth bestride the narrow world
Like a Colossus, and we petty men
Walk* under his huge legs*, and peep* about
To find* our selves dishonorable* Δgraves.

2 Men at some ° time are Δmasters of their Δfates; ◊
The fault, dear* Brutus, is not in our Δstars*,
But in our Δselves, that we are underlings.

3 Brutus and Cæsar : Δwhat should be in that "Cæsar"?

4 Why should that name be sounded more [than] yours?†

5 Write them together, Δyours is as fair* a Δname;
Sound them, it doth become the mouth as ° well ;
Weigh them, it is as heavy ; Δconjure with 'em,
"Brutus" will start a Δspirit as soon* as "Cæsar" . †

6 Now in the names of all the Δgods at once,
Upon what meat* doth this our Cæsar feed*,
That he is grown* so great?

7 Age, thou art sham'd !

8 Rome, thou hast lost the breed of Δnoble Δbloods !

9 When went there by an Δage since the great Δflood
But it was fam'd with more [than] with one man?

10 When could they say, till now, that talk'd of Rome,
That her wide Δwalks[1]* encompass'd, but one man?

11 Now it is Rome indeed and Δroom* enough
When there is in it but one only* man.

12 O! you and I have heard our Δfathers say
There was a Brutus once that would have brook'd
Th'eternal* Δdevil* to keep* his Δstate in Rome
As easily as a Δking.

In this, the immediate follow-up to speech #2 above, Cassius seems to employ different tactics in his attempt to win Brutus. Now when he diminishes Cæsar, he initially makes a great use of quiet unembellished lines to drive his points home (F #1-8), and then, from F #8 on, he uses at least seven extra breath-thoughts (marked , $_x$) to ensure even the smallest of points are inescapably understood.

- the unembellished lines start with the very first Cæsar denigrating line "Why man, he doth bestride the narrow world"

- then come the personal Brutus-flattering surround-phrase implications from the top of F #4 through to F #5,
  "Brutus and Cæsar : What should be in that Cæsar ?/ Why should that name be sounded more then yours : /Write them together : Yours,is as faire a Name :/Sound them, it doth become the mouth [aswell] : /Weigh them, it is as heavy : "
  which in turn are expanded into F #6's extension of Cæsar's power affecting the Roman world at large 'Age, thou art sham'd .', to be supported by F #8's 'But it was fam'd with more [then] with one man?'

- in portraying himself and Brutus as nothings in comparison to Cæsar, the speech opens emotionally (2/5, F #1)

- then F #2's maxim that all men at some time are 'Masters of their Fates' is cleverly extended into F #5's repeated surround phrases, suggesting equality between Brutus and Cæsar - also adding the dangerous question of how 'in the names of all the Gods' has Cæsar grown so powerful, all of which is strongly intellectual (14/6, the eleven and a half lines of F #2-5)

- and once the maxim is extended to judging Rome's current shame, so the intellect of the argument is pushed just as hard (14/6 in the last eleven lines of the speech), the extra breath-thoughts underscoring the smallest of points he needs Brutus to acknowledge

- the only time anything breaks through the relentless intellectual drive is F #10's passionately ironic dismissal (2/2) of Rome being diminished 'When there is in it but one onely man'

First Folio

3/ Cassius

1 Why+ man, he doth bestride the narrow world
Like a Colossus, and we petty men
Walke under his huge legges, and peepe about
To finde our selves dishonourable Graves.

2 Men at sometime,$_x$ are Masters of their Fates.

3 The fault ($_x$deere Brutus$_x$) is not in our Starres,
But in our Selves, that we are underlings.

4 Brutus and Cæsar: What should be in that Cæsar?

5 Why should that name be sounded more [then] yours:
Write them together: $_x$ Yours,$_x$ is as faire a Name: $_x$
Sound them, it doth become the mouth aswell: $_x$
Weigh them, it is as heavy: $_x$ Conjure with 'em,
Brutus will start a Spirit as soone as Cæsar,
Now in the names of all the Gods at once,
Upon what meate doth this our Cæsar feede,
That he is growne so great?

6 Age, thou art sham'd. +

7 Rome, thou hast lost the breed of Noble Bloods. +

8 When went there by an Age,$_x$ since the great Flood,$_x$
But it was fam'd with more [then] with one man?

9 When could they say ($_x$till now$_x$) that talk'd of Rome,
That her wide Walkes incompast but one man?

10 Now it is Rome indeed,$_x$ and Roome enough
When there is in it but one onely man.

11 O! you and I,$_x$ have heard our Fathers say,$_x$
There was a Brutus once,$_x$ that would have brook'd
Th'eternall Divell to keepe his State in Rome,$_x$
As easily as a King.

[1] Ff = 'Walkes', some modern texts replace this with 'walls'

4/ Brutus **That you do love me, I am nothing jealous:** 1.2.162 - 175

Background: The following is Brutus' careful, but still not yet committed, response to Cassius' anti-Cæsar overtures (speeches #2-3 above).

Style: as part of a two-handed scene

Where: a street in Rome **To Whom:** Cassius

# of Lines: 14 **Probable Timing: 0.45 minutes**

Modern Text

4/ Brutus

1 That you do love me, I am nothing jealous;
What you would work* me to*, I have some aim*. †
2 How I have thought of this, and of these times,
I shall recount hereafter*.
3 For this present,
I would [not (so with] love I might entreat you)
Be any further mov'd*. †
4 What you have said,
I will consider ; what you have to say
I will with patience hear* and find* a time
Both meet* to hear* and answer such high things.
5 Till then, my ^noble ^friend, chew upon this:
Brutus had rather be a ^villager
[Than] to repute himself* a ^son* of Rome
Under these hard ^conditions as this time
Is like to lay upon us.

The question of Brutus' honour and how soon he reacts to temptation is the stuff of academic commentary, and F's orthography may be able to add pertinent information. In the shaded section F's opening parenthesis makes it abundantly clear that Brutus is already tempted and might be 'so' 'moov'd' at a later date by this same argument, though not just now - the placing of 'so' outside the bracket being the key: most modern texts set the 'so' inside the bracket, and unfortunately this seems to turn Brutus' reply into a much more morally correct lack of interest in any argument so far presented.

- that Brutus is taking great care in how much he commits to from the outset can be seen not only in F #1 being completely set as (three) surround phrases, but also in the fact that the first line of the first two sentences are unembellished as well

- however, it does seem that his feelings are stirred by the proposition, for F #1 is totally emotional (0/3), and though he seems to re-establish control via F #2's opening calm, following the all-telling surround phrase ' : What you have said,/I will consider : ', F #2's last two and a half lines are also emotional (0/4)

- but when he does finally commit himself, he does so fully, with F #3 opening via the unequivocal surround phrase ' . Till then my Noble Friend, chew upon this : ', the whole of the ensuing self-definition spoken highly intellectually (6/2)

First Folio

4/ Brutus

1 That you do love me, I am nothing jealous: x
What you would worke me too, I have some ayme:
How I have thought of this, and of these times+
I shall recount heereafter.
2 For this present,
I would [not so (with] love I might intreat you)
Be any further moov'd: What you have said,
I will consider: x what you have to say
I will with patience heare, x and finde a time
Both meete to heare, x and answer such high things.
3 Till then, my Noble Friend, chew upon this:
Brutus had rather be a Villager, x
[Then] to repute himselfe a Sonne of Rome
Under these hard Conditions, x as this time
Is like to lay upon us.

#'S 5 - 6: CASSIUS & BRUTUS, THE DECISION TAKEN

5/ Brutus **It must be by his death: and for my part,** 2.1.10 - 34

Background: Cassius has followed up the arguments of speeches #2-3 by sending Brutus several messages in different handwritings purporting to be from different concerned citizens, all urging Brutus to action, leading Brutus to explore the inevitable.

Style: solo

Where: the garden of Brutus' home **To Whom:** self, and audience

# of Lines: 25 **Probable Timing: 1.15 minutes**

Modern Text

5/ Brutus

1 It must be by his death; and for my part,
I know no personal* cause to spurn* at him,
But for the general*.
2 He would be crown'd:
How that might change his nature, there's the question.
3 It is the bright day that brings forth the Δadder,
And that craves wary* walking. †
4 Crown* him that,
And then I grant* we put a Δsting in him
That at his will he may do* danger with.
5 Th'abuse of Δgreatness* is when it disjoins*
Remorse from Δpower; Δand to speak* truth of Cæsar,
I have not known* when his Δaffections sway'd
More [than] his Δreason.
6 But 'tis a common proof*
That Δlowliness* is young Δambition's Δladder,
Whereto the Δclimber-upward turns* his Δface;
But when he once attains* the upmost Δround,
He then unto the Δladder turns* his Δback*,
Looks* in the Δclouds, scorning the base degrees
By which he did ascend. †
7 So Cæsar may;
Then lest* he may, prevent.
8 And since the Δquarrel*
Will bear* no color* for the thing he is,
Fashion it thus: that what he is, augmented,
Would run* to these and these extremities;
And therefore think* him as a Δserpent's egg*,
Which, hatch'd, would as his kind* grow mischievous,
And kill him in the shell!

That Brutus is racking his brains to solve the dilemma of moving against his one time mentor can be seen in the concentrated thought patterns F's surround phrases denote, with F's first four sentences opening with at least one, and the last two sentences ending the same way. (This is a tremendous rarity, with virtually no parallel throughout the canon.)

- the unequivocal opening ' . It must be by his death : ' couldn't be any bleaker, expressed as it is via a monosyllabic unembellished surround phrase, and it seems the inevitability of Cæsar's death has an emotional effect on him for the rest of F #1 (0/3)

- the same kind of bleak unembellished surround phrase realisation opens F #2, only the key words 'nature' and 'question' breaking the monosyllabic pattern
  " . He would be crown'd:/How that might change his nature, there's the question ? "

- amazingly, F #3 starts the same way, with just one very important key word, 'Adder', breaking the line's monosyllabic and unembellished pattern
  " . It is the bright day, that brings forth the Adder,/And that craves warie walking : "

- but the opening of F#4
  " . Th'abuse of Greatnesse, is, when it dis-joynes/Remorse from Power : "
though still surround-phrase heightened, now shows more release and becomes polysyllabic as more abstract fears are explored: indeed, in equating Cæsar as the 'Adder' and expanding on the dangerous 'Sting' Cæsar could now execute – though he has never yet let 'his Affections' sway his 'Reason' - Brutus' argument becomes highly passionate (8/7 in just seven lines to the end of F #4), as if he cannot prevent his thoughts from bursting forth

- yet as he finally establishes his 'common proofe' focusing on 'Ambitions Ladder' he becomes intellectual (5/1, F #5's first two and a half lines), only turning passionate with the corollary that the higher one climbs the more likely one is to turn his back on those below [2] (4/4 the next three and a half lines), leading him to the firm surround phrase understanding of what might happen to Cæsar, and what he, Brutus must do about it
  " : so Cæsar may ; /Then least he may, prevent . "

- which leads to great emotion (2/6, F #7) as Brutus realises what action he must take ' ; And kill him in the shell . ', the surround phrase strength of the conclusion supported by the other, in part emotional, surround phrase in the sentence, thus stressing the only reason by which Cæsar's death can be justified, viz. ' ; that what he is, augmented,/Would runne to these, and these extremities :)'

First Folio

5/ Brutus

1 It must be by his death: $_x$ and for my part,
I know no personall cause, $_x$ to spurne at him,
But for the generall.
2 He would be crown'd:
How that might change his nature, there's the question? $_x$
3 It is the bright day, $_x$ that brings forth the Adder,
And that craves warie walking: Crowne him that,
And then I graunt we put a Sting in him, $_x$
That at his will he may doe danger with.
4 Th'abuse of Greatnesse, $_x$ is, $_x$ when it dis-joynes
Remorse from Power: $_x$ And to speake truth of Cæsar,
I have not knowne, $_x$ when his Affections sway'd
More [then] his Reason.
5 But 'tis a common proofe, $_x$
That Lowlynesse is young Ambitions Ladder,
Whereto the Climber upward turnes his Face: $_x$
But when he once attaines the upmost Round,
He then unto the Ladder turnes his Backe,
Lookes in the Clouds, scorning the base degrees
By which he did ascend: so Cæsar may;
Then least he may, prevent.
6 And since the Quarrell
Will beare no colour, $_x$ for the thing he is,
Fashion it thus; $_x$ that what he is, augmented,
Would runne to these, $_x$ and these extremities: $_x$
And therefore thinke him as a Serpents egge,
Which+ hatch'd, would as his kinde grow mischievous; $_x$
And kill him in the shell. +

[2] a direct reference to the central Elizabethan tenet of society being organised as a chain or ladder of being with the notion that the higher up one is paced the more obligations there are to protect and nurse those below

6/ Brutus **Our course will seeme too bloody, Caius Cassius,** between 2.1.162 - 189

Background: As the anti-Cæsar plotting develops, the question has arisen 'Shall no man else be toucht'. Cassius has argued that when Cæsar dies Antony will prove 'A shrew'd contriver', therefore 'Let Antony and Cæsar fall together. Brutus disagrees.

Style: as part of a group address

Where: the garden of Brutus' home **To Whom:** Cassius, Trebonius, Decius, Caska, Cinna, Metellus Cymber

# of Lines: 27 **Probable Timing: 1.30 minutes**

Modern Text

6/ Brutus

1 Our course will seem* too bloody, Caius Cassius,
To cut the Δhead off, and then hack* the Δlimbs*-
Like wrath in death and Δenvy afterwards;
For Antony is but a Δlimb* of Cæsar.

2 Let's be Δsacrificers, but not Δbutchers, Caius. †

3 We all stand up against the spirit of Cæsar,
And in the Δspirit of men, there is no blood;
O that we then could come by Cæsar's Δspirit,
And not dismember Cæsar!

4 But, alas,
Cæsar must bleed for it!

5 And, gentle Δfriends,
Let's kill him Δboldly, but not Δwrathfully;
Let's carve him as a Δdish fit for the Δgods,
Not hew him as a Δcarcass* fit for Δhounds;
And let our Δhearts, as subtle Δmasters do,
Stir* up their Δservants to an act* of Δrage,
And after seem* to chide 'em.

6 This shall make
Our purpose Δnecessary, and not Δenvious; ◊
Which so appearing to the common eyes,
We shall be call'd Δpurgers, not Δmurderers.

7 And for Mark* Antony, think* not of him;
For he can do no more [than] Cæsar's Δarm*
When Cæsar's head is off.

8 Alas, good Cassius, do not think* of him. †

9 If he love Cæsar, all that he can do
Is to himself*; take thought, and die* for Cæsar,
And that were much he should: for he is given
To sports, to wildness*, and much company.

Though highly intellectual for most of the speech (40/15 overall), the emotion accompanying F #1's almost vehement refusal to consider killing Antony (8/4) and the passions urging exactly the same at the end of the speech (8/7, F #7-8) suggest not only how much Brutus is striving to ensure their actions will not 'seeme too bloody' but also how persistent Cassius is in his wish for Antony to die.

- Brutus' pain at having to kill Cæsar is doubly highlighted by the short F #3, the only unembellished section in the twenty-seven line speech
  ". But (alas)/Cæsar must bleed for it ."

- Brutus' double wish to make their actions seem 'Necessary' and his (incorrectly, as it turns out) dismissal of Antony's political worth are highlighted by the surround phrases, especially the six consecutive ones (shown in the last example below) that end the speech
  ". Let's be Sacrificers, but not Butchers Caius : "
  ". And gentle Friends,/Let's kill him Boldly, but not Wrathfully : "
  ": For Antony is but a Limbe of Cæsar . "
  ". And for Marke Antony, thinke not of him : /For he can do no more then Cæsars Arme,/When Cæsars head is off . /Alas, good Cassius, do not thinke of him : /If he love Cæsar, all that he can do/Is to himselfe ; take thought, and dye for Cæsar,/And that were much he should : for he is given/To sports, to wildenesse, and much company . "

- and F's slightly ungrammatical sentence structure underscores how hard Brutus is working

a/ F #2's onrush shows slightly less control in the let us not be 'Butchers' plea, compared to most modern texts which reset the text slightly more rationally as two separate sentences

b/ Brutus' argument that they must make their purpose 'Necessary, not Envious' (F #5) so they will appear 'Purgerers, not Murderers' (#6) is given far more weight by being set as two separate sentences than by being jammed together as one by most modern texts

c/ F #8's onrush shows some loss of control in the overly worked repeated dismissal of Antony, set as a more rational two sentence approach by most modern texts

- as noted above, apart from the opening emotions accompanying F #1 (8/4) and the passions closing the speech (8/7, F #7-8), all focusing on sparing Antony, the remainder of the argument is extraordinarily intellectual (24/4, F 2-6)

First Folio

6/ Brutus

1 Our course will seeme too bloody, Caius Cassius,
To cut the Head off, and then hacke the Limbes x
Like wrath in death, x and Envy afterwards: x
For Antony is but a Limbe of Cæsar.

2 Let's be Sacrificers, but not Butchers+ Caius:
We all stand up against the spirit of Cæsar,
And in the Spirit of men, there is no blood: x
O that we then could come by Cæsars Spirit,
And not dismember Cæsar!

3 But (xalasx)
Cæsar must bleed for it. +

4 And+ gentle Friends,
Let's kill him Boldly, but not Wrathfully: x
Let's carve him, x as a Dish fit for the Gods,
Not hew him as a Carkasse fit for Hounds: x
And let our Hearts, as subtle Masters do,
Stirre up their Servants to an acte of Rage,
And after seeme to chide 'em.

5 This shall make
Our purpose Necessary, and not Envious.

6 Which so appearing to the common eyes,
We shall be call'd Purgers, not Murderers.

7 And for Marke Antony, thinke not of him: x
For he can do no more [then] Cæsars Arme, x
When Cæsars head is off.

8 Alas, good Cassius, do not thinke of him:
If he love Cæsar, all that he can do
Is to himselfe; take thought, and dye for Cæsar,
And that were much he should: for he is given
To sports, to wildenesse, and much company.

#'s 7 - 8: Cassius & Brutus As Things Fall Apart

7/ Brutus **You wrong'd your selfe to write in such a case.** between 4.3.6 - 28

Background: In his funeral oration Antony has succeeded in turning the crowd against the conspirators (speeches #15-16 below) who have fled from Rome. Octavius, Cæsar's nephew, has been welcomed into Rome, and a tripartite leadership agreement to restore order and defeat the conspirators has been arranged between himself, Antony, and the insignificant Lepidus (see speech #17). In the mean time the conspirators are attempting to levy support, money, and men to withstand the inevitable tripartite-led war against them. In so doing Cassius is prepared to support his men who cut corners to get what they want, including one Lucius Pella accused of bribery, even writing letters of support on their behalf, which leads 'honourable' Brutus to speak as follows.

Style: as part of a two-handed scene

Where: Brutus' battlefield tent **To Whom:** Cassius

# of Lines: 18 **Probable Timing: 0.55 minutes**

Modern Text

7/ Brutus

1 You wrong'd yourself* to write in such a case.

2 Let me tell you, Cassius, you yourself*
Are much condemn'd to have an itching △palm*,
To sell and △mart your △offices for △gold
To △undeservers.

3 The name of Cassius △honors this corruption,
And △chastisement doth therefore hide his head.

4 Remember March, the △ides of March remember :
Did not great Julius bleed* for △justice' sake?

5 What △villain* touch'd his body, that did stab
And not for △justice?

6 What? ◊ shall one of △us,
That struck* the △foremost* man of all this △world
But for supporting △robbers, shall we now
Contaminate our fingers with base △bribes?
And sell the mighty space of our large △honors
For so much trash as may be grasped thus?

7 I had rather be a △dog*, and bay the △moon*,
[Than] such a Roman.

F's orthography shows how well Brutus is able to control his emotions and stay highly factually/intellectual focused in his 'Chasticement' of Cassius, almost until the end of the speech.

- the fact that there are no surround phrases and just one piece of major punctuation suggests that this highly intellectual speech (until the last sentence) comes springing forth without premeditation, making its lack of emotional release even more remarkable
- with such a springing forth, the lack of released emotion (22/6 the first sixteen lines of the speech) provides great witness to how much Btutus wishes to let the facts speak for themselves rather than let his heart do the work for him
- however, the sudden passion of the final sentence (F #8, 3/2) suggests just how much of a strain this causes him, especially since the outburst has been preceded by three extra breath-thoughts (marked, $_x$) that appear in the middle of F #7 as the appalling thought of 'shall we now/Contaminate our fingers, $_x$ with base Bribes', thus undoing all the hopes of speech #6 above, is voiced: the extra breaths suggest that Brutus is either taking great care to get the final points across and/or is almost speechless at the points he must now utter
- that the speech opens with a short, one line, monosyllabic sentence shows with what a tight rein Brutus is holding himself in check
- the few occasions of emotion that do break through deal in concepts of honour and its besmirching, with the moment of Cæsar's death, 'Did not great Julius bleede for Justice sake' being matched against the rumours of Cassius accepting bribes 'your selfe/Are much condemn'd to have an itching Palme' and against any 'Villaine' that touch'd Cæsar's body for anything other than 'Justice'

First Folio

7/ Brutus

1 You wrong'd your selfe to write in such a case.

2 Let me tell you⁺ Cassius, you your selfe
Are much condemn'd to have an itching Palme,
To sell, $_x$ and Mart your Offices for Gold
To Undeservers.

3 The name of Cassius Honors this corruption,
And Chasticement doth therefore hide his head.

4 Remember March, the Ides of March remember:
Did not great Julius bleede for Justice sake?

5 What Villaine touch'd his body, that did stab, $_x$
And not for Justice?

6 What?

7 Shall one of Us,
That strucke the Formost man of all this World, $_x$
But for supporting Robbers: $_x$ shall we now, $_x$
Contaminate our fingers, $_x$ with base Bribes?
And sell the mighty space of our large Honors
For so much trash, $_x$ as may be grasped thus?

8 I had rather be a Dogge, and bay the Moone,
[Then] such a Roman.

8/ Cassius **A Friend should beare his Friends infirmities;** between 4.3.86 - 107

Background: Despite Brutus' attack (speech #7 immediately above), Cassius goes off on an emotional tangent, preceding the following with 'Brutus hath riv'd my hart'.

Style: as part of a two-handed scene

Where: Brutus' battlefield tent **To Whom:** Brutus

# of Lines: 17 **Probable Timing: 0.55 minutes**

Modern Text

8/ Cassius

1 A Δfriend should bear* his Δfriend's infirmities;
But Brutus makes mine greater [than] they are.

2 Come Antony, and young* Octavius, come,
Revenge your selves alone on Cassius,
For Cassius is a-weary of the Δworld ;
Hated by one he loves, brav'd by his Δbrother,
Check'd like a bondman, all his faults observ'd,
Set in a Δnote-book*, learn'd, and conn'd* by rote*,
To cast into my Δteeth

3 O, I could weep*
My Δspirit from mine eyes !

4 There is a Δdagger,
And here* my naked Δbreast; Δwithin, a Δheart
Dearer* [than] Pluto's Δmine, Δricher [than]Δgold:
If that thou be'st* a Roman, take it forth*.

5 I, that denied* thee Δgold, will give my Δheart:
Strike as thou didst at Cæsar ; for I know,
When thou didst hate him worst, [thou] lov'dst *him better
[Than] ever thou lov'dst* Cassius.

Given Cassius' reputation as a hot-head, this is a remarkable attempt to keep himself under control, perhaps an attempt to match Brutus' rebuke that forces this response (speech #7 above). However, the surround phrases opening and closing the speech and the sudden non-intellectual outbursts clearly show both how much Cassius has to do to keep himself under control and where he fails to do so.

• not surprisingly despite F #1's intellectual orthography (3/1) the two surround phrases opening the speech have an emotional underpinning, linked as they are by the only semicolon in the speech

" . A Friend should beare his Friends infirmities ; /But Brutus makes mine greater then they are . "

• the melodramatic imagery of F #2's opening three line invitation for their enemies to take revenge on Cassius alone is offset by being completely intellectual (5/0) – perhaps this is a genuine realisation, not an emotional bleat

• the extension why (supposedly being hated by Brutus) undoes this by spinning into passion (3/2, ending F #2), which leads to the one short passionate sentence (F #3, 1/1) 'O I could weepe/My Spirit from mine eyes.' - both showing the emotional battle Cassius is struggling to contain

• which leads to intellectual determination (13/5 F #4-5) highlighted by the five consecutive surround phrases forming F #4 and the line and a half opening F #5

" . There is a Dagger,/And heere my naked Breast : Within, a Heart/Deerer then Pluto's Mine, Richer then Gold : /If that thou bee'st a Roman, take it foorth . /I that deny'd thee Gold, will give my Heart : /Strike as thou did'st at Cæsar : "

• this determination again removes the potential for melodrama, but not completely, for the end of each of the last two sentences betrays his control, with the one line outburst ending F #4, 'If thou bee'st a Roman, take it' (i.e. Cassius' dagger) 'foorth', slipping into passion and the two and a half line notion ending F #5, of Brutus loving Cæsar more than he ever did Cassius, becoming emotional (2/4 all told)

First Folio

8/ Cassius

1 A Friend should beare his Friends infirmities;
But Brutus makes mine greater [then] they are.

2 Come Antony, and yong Octavius+ come,
Revenge your selves alone on Cassius,
For Cassius is a-weary of the World: x
Hated by one he loves, brav'd by his Brother,
Check'd like a bondman, all his faults observ'd,
Set in a Note-booke, learn'd, and con'd by roate+
To cast into my Teeth.

3 O+ I could weepe
My Spirit from mine eyes. +

4 There is a Dagger,
And heere my naked Breast: x Within, a Heart
Deerer [then] Pluto's Mine, Richer [then] Gold:
If that thou bee'st a Roman, take it foorth.

5 I+ that deny'd thee Gold, will give my Heart:
Strike as thou did'st at Cæsar: x for I know,
When thou did'st hate him worst, [ÿ] loved'st him better
[Then] ever thou loved'st Cassius.

#'s 9 - 12: A Cæsar For All Seasons

9/ Caska **I can as well bee hang'd as tell the manner of it** between 1.2.235 - 287

Background: While Cæsar was being offered the Crowne, he collapsed. Caska, who was present, reports to Brutus and Cassius, who were not, what took place.

Style: as part of a three-handed scene

Where: a street in Rome **To Whom:** Brutus and Cassius

# of Lines: 36 **Probable Timing: 1.45 minutes**

Modern Text

9/ Caska

1 I can as well be* hang'd as tell the manner of
it: △it was mere* △foolery*, I did not mark* it.

2 I saw*
Mark* Antony, offer him a △crown* - yet 'twas not a
△crown* neither*, 'twas one of these △coronets - and as I
told you, he* put it by once; but for all that, to my thinking, he would fain* have had it.

3 Then he* offered it to
him again*; then he* put it by again*; but to my thinking, he was very loath to lay his fingers off it.

4 And then
he offered it the third time; he* put it the third time by,
and still as he* refus'd it, the rabblement hooted*, and
clapp'd their chopp'd* hands, and threw up* their sweaty*
△night-caps*, and utter'd* such a deal* of stinking
breath because Cæsar refus'd the △crown*, that it had,
almost, chok'd* Cæsar, for he* swounded*, and fell
down* at it; △and for mine own* part, I durst not laugh,
for fear* of opening my △lips* and receiving* the bad
△air*.

5 If the tag-rag* people did not
clap him and hiss* him, according as he pleas'd, and dis-
pleas'd them, as they use to do* the △players in the △thea-
tre, I am no true man.

6 Marry, before he fell down*, when he perceiv'd
the common △herd* was glad he refus'd the △crown*, he
pluck'd me ope his △doublet, and offer'd them his △throat
to cut. †

7 And I had been* a man of any △occupation, if I
would not have taken him at a word, I would I might
go* to △hell among the △rogues. †

8 And so he* fell.

Compared to the somewhat storm-omen shaken character seen later (speech #19), here F's orthography offers a man quite confident of himself, his views - one with passionate and/or emotional opinions about those lower than himself on the social ladder (the 'rabblement' of F #4; 'tag-ragge people' of F #5; and the 'Wenches' of F #8).

- the kernel of the information Caska passes on regarding Cæsar's ambition is shown in the surround phrases, especially F #1-3, for, despite initially dismissing what he saw
  " . I can as well bee hang'd as tell the manner of it: It was meere Foolerie, I did not marke it . "
  soon he is very definitive in describing what happened, when talking of the 'Coronet' (rather than a 'Crowne') Antony offered Cæsar
  " : and as I told you, hee put it by once: but for all that, to my thinking, he would faine have had it. Then hee offered it to him againe: then hee put it by againe: but to my thinking, he was very loath to lay his fingers off it. And then he offered it the third time ; "
  the last two surround phrases heightened even more by being unembellished too (perhaps he doesn't wish the most acute of his comments to be overheard by anyone other than Brutus and Cassius)

- and though terse, he is equally definitive in mentioning the fate of two well known anti-Cæsar Senators
  " . I could tell you more newes too: Murrellus and Flavius, for pulling Scarffes off Cæsars Images, are put to silence . "

- Caska opens passionately as he tries to dismiss recent events (2/3, F #1), which continue as he begins to describe the startling facts he starts intellectually (5/5, F #2's first two lines defining whether 'Crown' or 'Coronet') was offered, but becomes highly emotional about the second offer (0/6, F #2's last two lines and the first of F #3)

- and after the carefully unembellished comment as to Cæsar's reaction and the third offer, following the only semicolon of the speech, Caska's emotions swoop back in as he describes the crowd's reaction to Cæsar's third rejection (1/6, the next three and a half lines)

- the suggestion that their 'stinking breath . . . (almost) choak'd Cæsar' builds on the emotional mould by moving towards passion (3/5 in just one and half lines) presumably anticipating Caska's being

First Folio

9/ Caska

1 I can as well bee hang'd as tell the manner of
it: It was meere Foolerie, I did not marke it.

2 I sawe
Marke Antony+ offer him a Crowne, yet 'twas not a
Crowne neyther, 'twas one of these Coronets: ₓ and as I
told you, hee put it by once: ₓ but for all that, to my thinking, he would faine have had it.

3 Then hee offered it to
him againe: ₓ then hee put it by againe: ₓ but to my thinking, he was very loath to lay his fingers off it.

4 And then
he offered it the third time; hee put it the third time by,
and still as hee refus'd it, the rabblement howted, and
clapp'd their chopt hands, and threw uppe their sweatie
Night-cappes, and uttered such a deale of stinking
breath, ₓ because Cæsar refus'd the Crowne, that it had
(ₓalmostₓ) choaked Cæsar: ₓ for hee swoonded, and fell
downe at it: ₓ And for mine owne part, I durst not laugh,
for feare of opening my Lippes, ₓ and receyving the bad
Ayre.

5 If the tag-ragge people did not
clap him, ₓ and hisse him, according as he pleas'd, and dis-
pleas'd them, as they use to doe the Players in the Theatre, I am no true man.

6 Marry, before he fell downe, when he perceiv'd
the common Heard was glad he refus'd the Crowne, he
pluckt me ope his Doublet, and offer'd them his Throat
to cut: and I had beene a man of any Occupation, if I
would not have taken him at a word, I would I might
goe to Hell among the Rogues, and so hee fell.

9 When
he came to himself* again*, he* said, Δif he* had done or
said anything amiss*, he desir'd their Δworships to think*
it was his infirmity*.
10 Three or four* Δwenches, where I
stood, cried*, "Alas*, good Δsoul* !" and forgave him with
all their hearts. †
11 But there's no heed to be taken of them;
if Cæsar had stabb'd* their Δmothers, they would have done
no less*.

---

12 I could tell you more
news* too. †
13 [Murellus] and Flavius, for pulling Δscarfs*
off Cæsar's Δimages, are put to silence.
14 Fare you well.
15 There was more Δfoolery* yet, if I could remember it.

afraid to laugh, which he then reports emotionally (3/7, the three lines ending F #4) – the whole summed up by yet another (amazed? delighted?) surround phrase

" : for hee swoonded, and fell downe at it : "

• the further reaction of the 'tag-ragge people', clapping Cæsar as they would the 'Players in the Theatre' releases Caska's passions once more (F #5, 2/3), while his reaction to Cæsar's offering 'them his Throat to cut' is both intellectual and emotional (F #6, 7/4)

• though Caska's emotions momentarily cloud his reporting of Cæsar's apology to the crowd for his apparent 'infirmitie' (F #7, 2/6), his passions take over again in describing the reaction of 'Three or foure Wenches' (F #8, 6/5)

• that Caska suddenly switches to intellect in handling the surprising news of the deaths of Murrellus and Flavius (F #9, 5/2), followed by the very short monosyllabic unembellished 'Fare you well.' (F #10) and the careful intellectual reference to more 'Foolerie' (F #11, 1/0) suggests a rather circumspect finish – perhaps once more he is taking great care not to be overheard by any passer-by

7 When
he came to himselfe againe, hee said, If hee had done,$_{x}$ or
said anything amisse, he desir'd their Worships to thinke
it was his infirmitie.
8 Three or foure Wenches + where I
stood, cryed, Alasse+ good Soule,+ and forgave him with
all their hearts: But there's no heed to be taken of them;
if Cæsar had stab'd their Mothers, they would have done
no lesse.

---

9 I could tell you more
newes too: [Murrellus] and Flavius, for pulling Scarffes
off Cæsars Images, are put to silence.
10 Fare you well.
11 There was more Foolerie yet, if I could remember it.

10/ Calphurnia **What mean you Cæsar?** between 2.2.8 - 54

Background: Despite the prophetic nature of both the unusually ferocious storm (see speech #1 above) and his wife's nightmares 'Thrice hath Calphurnia in her sleepe cryed out,/Helpe, ho, they murther Cæsar', Cæsar is still considering going to the Senate as planned. The following is his wife's attempt to dissuade him.

Style: as part of a two-handed scene

Where: Cæsar's home **To Whom:** Cæsar

# of Lines: 23 **Probable Timing: 1.10 minutes**

Modern Text

10/ Calphurnia

1 What mean you, Cæsar?
2 Think you to walk forth?
3 You shall not stir* out of your house to-day.
4 {ψ} I never stood on Δceremonies,
Yet now they fright me. †
5 There is one within,
Besides the things that we have heard and seen*,
Recounts most horrid sights seen* by the Δwatch.
6 A Δlionness* hath whelped in the streets,
And Δgraves have yawn'd and yielded* up their dead;
Fierce fiery Δwarriors* fight upon the Δclouds
In Δrankes and Δsquadrons and right form* of Δwar*,
Which drizzled* blood upon the Capitol*;
The noise of Δbattle* hurtled in the Δair*;
Horses* [did] neigh, and dying men did groan*,
And Δghosts did shriek* and squeal* about the streets.
7 O Cæsar, these things are beyond all use,
And I do fear* them.
8 When Δbeggars* die*, there are no Δcomets seen;
The Δheavens themselves blaze forth the death of Δprinces. †
9 Do not go forth to day, Δcall it my fear*
That keeps* you in the house, and not your own*.
10 We'll* send Mark Antony to the Senate-°house,
And he shall say, you are not well today. †
11 Let me, upon my knee, prevail* in this.

- there are so few releases in the first three and a half lines of the speech (2/1) it seems as if Calphurnia is either so shocked by the possibility of Cæsar leaving the 'house to day' and/or is trying hard not to upset her husband that she is speaking very carefully, especially when the first three sentences are less than two lines long in total: what she has to say has to be said simply and directly without any unnecessary words or emotions
- indeed F #4's surround phrase start '. I never stood on Ceremonies /Yet now they fright me : ' seems to suggest that she is going to be able to present her argument with a great deal of care
- but she cannot keep control, for as soon as she details all the frightening and supernatural omens that have been seen she becomes highly passionate (13/14, F #4's final two and a half lines plus the eight lines of F #5)
- two extra breath-thoughts (marked ,$_{x}$) are found in the middle of F #5, as if she needs them to continue, which in turn leads to the surround phrase marking the one item indelibly (and, as it turns out prophetically) burnt in her mind ' : The noise of Battell hurtled in the Ayre : '
- while F #6's summation of her fear maintains the passion (1/1)
- but then, a sign of her inner strength, she does regain some control, for the two line maxim opening F #7 is strongly intellectual (4/2) – but this doesn't last, for she spills without any punctuation into the monosyllabic unembellished plea 'Do not go forth to day', followed by an emotional suggestion that he blame it on her fear and 'not your owne' (1/3)
- and her final factual act seems to be a series of uncontrolled grabbing at straws, for even though F #8's first line ('Wee'l send Mark Antony to the Senate house') is intellectual, it is then followed by an unembellished one line expansion (perhaps not to anger Cæsar at the suggestion that he should send a message that he is 'not well to day'), finishing with an emotional act (kneeling) and emotional plea ('Let me . . . prevaile in this')

First Folio

10/ Calphurnia

1 What mean you+ Cæsar?
2 Think you to walk forth?
3 You shall not stirre out of your house to day.
4 {ψ} I never stood on Ceremonies,
Yet now they fright me: There is one within,
Besides the things that we have heard and seene,
Recounts most horrid sights seene by the Watch.
5 A Lionnesse hath whelped in the streets,
And Graves have yawn'd,$_{x}$ and yeelded up their dead;
Fierce fiery Warriours fight upon the Clouds
In Rankes and Squadrons,$_{x}$ and right forme of Warre+
Which drizel'd blood upon the Capitoll: $_{x}$
The noise of Battell hurtled in the Ayre: $_{x}$
Horsses [do] neigh, and dying men did grone,
And Ghosts did shrieke and squeale about the streets.
6 O Cæsar, these things are beyond all use,
And I do feare them.
7 When Beggers dye, there are no Comets seen,+
The Heavens themselves blaze forth the death of Princes
Do not go forth to day: $_{x}$ Call it my feare,$_{x}$
That keepes you in the house, and not your owne.
8 Wee'l send Mark Antony to the Senate house,
And he shall say, you are not well to day:
Let me+ upon my knee, prevaile in this.

11/ Decius **This Dreame is all amisse interpreted,** between 2.2.83 - 104

Background: During the anti-Cæsar plotting the subject of Cæsar's basing his actions on prophecy was raised, fearing that, should the circumstances not seem favourable, Cæsar might not attend the Senate the day the assassination is planned. Decius then suggested that there was no need to worry, for Decius knows how to handle the problem should it arise. Here it has, and he does.

Style: as part of a three-handed scene

Where: Cæsar's home **To Whom:** Cæsar and Calphurnia, and perhaps a servant

# of Lines: 22 **Probable Timing: 1.10 minutes**

Modern Text

11/ Decius

1 This Δdream* is all amiss* interpreted,
It was a vision fair* and fortunate. †
2 Your Δstatue spouting blood in many pipes,
In which so many smiling Romans bath'd,
Signifies that from you great Rome shall suck*
Reviving blood, and that great men shall press*
For Δtinctures, Δstains*, Δrelics*, and Δcognizance*.
3 This by Calphurnia's Δdream* is signified.
4 And { you shall say I have} well expounded it {,}
{ψ} When you have heard what I can say;
And know it now: the Senate have concluded
To give this day a Δcrown* to mighty Cæsar.
5 If you shall send them word you will not come,
Their minds* may change.
6 Besides, it were a mock*
Apt to be render'd, for some one to say,
"Break* up the Senate till another time,
When Cæsar's wife shall meet* with better Δdreams*."
7 If Cæsar hide himself*, shall they not whisper,
"Lo* Cæsar is afraid*?"
8 Pardon me, Cæsar, for my dear* dear* love
To your proceeding bids me tell you this;
And reason to my love is liable.

• F #1's onrush suggests that there is far more urgency to interpret the 'Dreame' the way the conspirators wish for the F Decius than for his modern counterpart, especially since the first two lines open emotionally (1/3), and require the first of four extra breath-thoughts (marked , x)

• and though he continues onrushed, at the same time he begins to evince control, the reinterpretation that 'from you great Rome shall sucke/Reviving blood' becoming intellectual (9/5, F #1's last five lines and the short F #2)

• indeed F #3's unembellished tempting-tease of what he is about to say
"And { you shall say I have} well expounded it {,}/When you have heard what I can say: /And know it now,"
suggests that the easy calm of his seductive powers are now at their very best, with the follow up of announcement that
"the Senate have concluded/To give this day a Crowne, to mighty Cæsar."
being splendidly factual (3/1)

• and having shown his ability to stay calm, as Decius begins to ridicule Cæsar's possible refusal with what people will say, wait till 'Cæsar's wife shall meete with better Dreames' (heightened by being set as a surround phrase) or, worse, 'Loe Cæsar is affraid', he becomes passionately emotional (6/10, the seven lines F #4-6 and the first line of F #7) – though whether this is genuine or mere manipulation (of which he boasts he is a master, especially as far as Cæsar is concerned, in a previous scene with the conspirators) is up to each actor to decide

• certainly he is very careful in excusing himself from any possible insult to either Cæsar or Calphurnia, for after the emotional explanation that it is 'my deere deere love' the final
"bids me tell you this : /And reason to my love is liable . "
is unembellished, and ends with a determined surround phrase, only the second in the speech

First Folio

11/ Decius

1 This Dreame is all amisse interpreted,
It was a vision, x faire and fortunate:
Your Statue spouting blood in many pipes,
In which so many smiling Romans bath'd,
Signifies, x that from you great Rome shall sucke
Reviving blood, and that great men shall presse
For Tinctures, Staines, Reliques, and Cognisance.
2 This by Calphurnia's Dreame is signified.
3 And { you shall say I have} well expounded it {,}
{ψ} When you have heard what I can say : x
And know it now,+ the Senate have concluded
To give this day, x a Crowne to mighty Cæsar.
4 If you shall send them word you will not come,
Their mindes may change.
5 Besides, it were a mocke
Apt to be render'd, for some one to say,
Breake up the Senate, x till another time: x
When Cæsars wife shall meete with better Dreames.
6 If Cæsar hide himselfe, shall they not whisper+
Loe Cæsar is affraid?
7 Pardon me+ Cæsar, for my deere deere love
To your proceeding, x bids me tell you this: x
And reason to my love is liable.

12/ Cæsar **I must prevent thee Cymber:** between 3.1.35 - 74

Background: In the Senate, Cymber, by appealing for clemency for his brother, is allowing for his putative supporters, that is the other conspirators, to legitimately draw near to Cæsar without arousing suspicion. The following is Cæsar's interruption following Cymber's initial greeting, even before the appeal can be made.

Style: one on one address for the benefit of a much larger group

Where: the Senate **To Whom:** Cymber, and all the assembled Senators, including the conspirators

# of Lines: 28 **Probable Timing: 1.30 minutes**

Modern Text

12/ Cæsar

1 I must prevent thee, [Cimber] . †
2 These couchings and these lowly courtesies
Might fire the blood of ordinary men,
And turn* pre°ordinance, and first Δdecree
Into the [law] of Δchildren.
3 Be not fond
To think* that Cæsar bears* such Δrebel* blood
That will be thaw'd from the true quality
With that which melteth Δfools* - I mean* sweet words,
Low-crooked-curtsies, and base Δspaniel* fawning. †
4 Thy Δbrother by decree is banished;
If thou dost* bend, and pray, and fawn* for him,
I spurn* thee like a Δcur* out of my way . †
5 Know, Cæsar doth not wrong, nor without cause
Will he be satisfied.

6 {ψ} I am constant as the Δnorthern* Δstar*,
Of whose true-fix'd and resting quality
There is no fellow in the Δfirmament.
7 The Δskies are painted with unnumb'red* sparks*,
They are all Δfire, and every one doth shine;
But, there's but one in all doth hold his place.
8 So in the Δworld: Δ'tis furnish'd well with Δmen,
And Δmen are Δflesh and Δblood, and apprehensive;
Yet in the number I do know but Δone
That unassailable* holds on his Δrank*,
Unshak'd of Δmotion ; and that I am he,
Let me a little show* it, even in this -
That I was constant [Cimber] should be banish'd,
And constant do remain* to keep* him so.

9 Hence !†
10 Wilt thou lift up Olympus?

The speech opens and closes with surround phrases all of which suggest Cæsar's unwavering belief in his own strength and powers, but while the opening ' . I must prevent thee Cymber : " is quite straightforward, the speech becomes disturbing, growing to the final amazing double surround phrase megalomaniac statement , '. Hence : Wilt thou lift up Olympus ? '

- the unembellished lines initially point to an incredible sense of calm as Cæsar publicly voices his sense of his own uniqueness that places him above the abilities of 'ordinary men': the first refers to Cymber's humbling himself before him "These couchings, and these lowly courtesies/Might fire the blood of ordinary men," leading to the statement that his blood cannot 'be thaw'd from true quality', for he is 'constant' like the 'Northerne Starre' "Of whose true fixt, and resting quality,/There is no fellow"
- but the calm is not sustained, for almost from the start three of the multiple extra breath-thoughts (marked ,$_{x}$) make their appearance, suggesting that Cæsar needs these extra breaths to control himself and/or give the appearance of being in control
- then, the more definitive later references to his own constancy are heightened by being set as surround phrases
" : But, there's but one in all doth hold his place . "
" : and that I am he,/Let me a little shew it, even in this : "
- while the double surround phrase dismissal of ordinary men is even stronger,
" . So, in the World ; 'Tis furnish'd well with Men,/And Men are Flesh and Blood, and apprehensive ; "
intensified as it is by two emotional semicolons
- Cæsar opens the speech with a sense of intellectual control (4/1, F #1), but both the scolding ('be not fond') and the first step of grandiose self comparison to the 'Northerne Starre' become passionate (9/12, F #2-3)
- and while the further self-definition (essentially that there-is-one-beyond-all-men) is highly intellectual (8/2 the first four and a half lines of F #5 - though the emotional undertow of the two semicoloned surround phrases should not be disregarded), and then, following the unembellished the statement/confession/admission/brag that 'I am he', the remainder of the sentence turns emotional (1/4)
- that his belief in the final megalomaniac comparison of himself to 'Olympus' is genuine can be seen in that the surround phrases are entirely factual (F #6, 2/0)

First Folio

12/ Cæsar

1 I must prevent thee+ [Cymber]:
These couchings,$_{x}$ and these lowly courtesies
Might fire the blood of ordinary men,
And turne pre-Ordinance, and first Decree,$_{x}$
Into the [lane] of Children.
2 Be not fond,$_{x}$
To thinke that Cæsar beares such Rebell blood
That will be thaw'd from the true quality
With that which melteth Fooles, I meane sweet words,
Low-crooked-curtsies, and base Spaniell fawning:
Thy Brother by decree is banished: $_{x}$
If thou doest bend, and pray, and fawne for him,
I spurne thee like a Curre out of my way:
Know, Cæsar doth not wrong, nor without cause
Will he be satisfied.

3 {ψ} I am constant as the Northerne Starre,
Of whose true fixt,$_{x}$ and resting quality,$_{x}$
There is no fellow in the Firmament.
4 The Skies are painted with unnumbered sparkes,
They are all Fire, and every one doth shine: $_{x}$
But, there's but one in all doth hold his place.
5 So,$_{x}$ in the World; + 'Tis furnish'd well with Men,
And Men are Flesh and Blood, and apprehensive;
Yet in the number,$_{x}$ I do know but One
That unassayleable holds on his Ranke,
Unshak'd of Motion: $_{x}$ and that I am he,
Let me a little shew it, even in this: $_{x}$
That I was constant [Cymber] should be banish'd,
And constant do remaine to keepe him so.

6 Hence: + Wilt thou lift up Olympus?

#'S 13 - 17: ANTONY'S RESPONSE

13/ Antony **O mighty Cæsar ! Dost thou lye so lowe?** 3.1.148 - 163

Background: Promised that he can meet the conspirators and 'Depart untouch'd', Antony has arrived at the Senate. Despite Brutus' greeting of 'Welcome Mark Antony', his first words are to Cæsar's freshly stabbed corpse, and only then to the conspirators.

Style: mixed address

Where: the Senate **To Whom:** initially to the dead Cæsar, and then to the conspirators

# of Lines: 16 **Probable Timing: 0.50 minutes**

Modern Text

13/ Antony

1 O mighty Cæsar ! ◊ dost thou lie* so low*?
2 Are all thy △conquests, △glories, △triumphs*, △spoils*,
Shrunk* to this little △measure?
3 Fare thee well !
4 I know not, △gentlemen, what you intend,
Who else must be let blood, who else is rank*;
If I myself*, there is no hour* so fit
As Cæsar's death's hour*, nor no △instrument
Of half* that worth as those your △swords, made rich
With the most △noble blood of all this △world.
5 I do beseech ye*, if you bear* me hard,
Now, whil'st your purpled hands do reek* and smoke*,
Fulfill your pleasure.
6 Live a thousand years*,
I shall not find* myself* so apt to die*,◊
No place will please me so, no mean* of death,
As here* by Cæsar, and by you cut off,
The △choice and △master △spirits of this △age.

The shorter F sentences opening and closing the speech suggest that Antony is working very hard to maintain control and to not let his thoughts or emotions run away with him. However, the fact that the first four sentences, three of which are five words or less, all show a different pattern suggesting that he is in difficulty from the outset.

- the varying flood of thoughts shows no consistency, with the acknowledgement of Cæsar's body being purely factual (F #1, 1/0); the realisation that Cæsar is no longer triumphant emotional (F #2, 0/2); the supposition that death has shrunk all of Cæsar's glories passionate (F #3, 5/3); and then F #4's first 'farewell' is totally unembellished

- and after a careful intellectually/emotionally held-in-check skirting of 'who else is ranke' (1/1, the first two lines of F #5), Antony finally succumbs to emotion as he voices that if he is to die, now is the best time (5/13, the next nine lines, from F #5's last four lines through to the opening line of F #8)

- and as he gets to the crux of his request (F #5), so the only surround phrases of the speech appear

  " : If I my selfe, there is no houre so fit/As Cæsars deaths houre ; nor no Instrument/Of halfe that worth, as those your Swords ; made rich/With the most Noble blood of all this World . "

  the emotion even further heightened by all three phrases being linked by the only emotional semicolons in the speech

- yet at the very last minute Antony manages to regain superb intellectual (ironic?) control, in his last line 'praise' of the conspirators as 'The Choice and Master Spirits of this Age.' (4/0)

First Folio

13/ Antony

1 O mighty Cæsar !
2 Dost thou lye so lowe?
3 Are all thy Conquests, Glories, Triumphes, Spoiles,
Shrunke to this little Measure?
4 Fare thee well. +
5 I know not+ Gentlemen+what you intend,
Who else must be let blood, who else is ranke: x
If I my selfe, there is no houre so fit
As Cæsars deaths houre; x nor no Instrument
Of halfe that worth, x as those your Swords; x made rich
With the most Noble blood of all this World.
6 I do beseech yee, if you beare me hard,
Now, whil'st your purpled hands do reeke and smoake,
Fulfill your pleasure.
7 Live a thousand yeeres,
I shall not finde my selfe so apt to dye.
8 No place will please me so, no meane of death,
As heere by Cæsar, and by you cut off,
The Choice and Master Spirits of this Age.

14/ Antony **O pardon me, thou bleeding peece of Earth:** 3.1.254 - 275

Background: Left alone with the body, Antony is at last free to give vent to his true feelings.

Style: solo

Where: the Senate **To Whom:** to the dead body, self and audience

# of Lines: 22 **Probable Timing: 1.10 minutes**

Modern Text

14/ Antony

1 O pardon me, thou bleeding piece* of ^Δ^earth:
That I am meek* and gentle with these ^Δ^butchers!

2 Thou art the ^Δ^ruins* of the ^Δ^noblest man
That ever lived in the ^Δ^tide of ^Δ^times.

3 Woe to the hand that shed this costly ^Δ^blood !

4 Over thy wounds now do I ^Δ^prophesy*,
(Which like dumb* mouths* do ope their ^Δ^ruby lips,
To beg* the voice* and utterance of my ^Δ^tongue)
A ^Δ^curse shall light upon the limbs* of men;
Domestic* ^Δ^fury and fierce ^Δ^civil* strife
Shall cumber all the parts of Italy;
Blood and destruction shall be so in use,
And dreadful* ^Δ^objects so familiar,
That ^Δ^mothers shall but smile when they behold
Their ^Δ^infants quartered with the hands of ^Δ^war*;
All pity* chok'd* with custom* of fell deeds,
And Cæsar's ^Δ^spirit, ranging for ^Δ^revenge,
With Ate by his side come hot from ^Δ^hell,
Shall in these ^Δ^confines with a ^Δ^monarch's* voice*
Cry "^Δ^Havoc ! *" and let slip the ^Δ^dogs* of war*,
That this foul* deed*, shall smell above the earth
With ^Δ^carrion men, groaning for ^Δ^burial*.

Though the sentence structure of the two texts is identical, the addition of exclamation marks by most modern texts make Antony's growth towards his vow more predictable and far more vehement than F #1-3 suggest.

- though Antony's first address, now at last alone, to his dead mentor opens passionately (F #1, 2/2) and is formed by the only surround phrases in the speech, it is not followed up by a sentence ending exclamation mark, the lack suggesting Antony's initial outburst may be over

- indeed it seems that Antony gains self-control both in the praise for dead Cæsar as well as in the first swearing against 'the hand that shed this costly Blood' (5/1, F #2-3): the whole is deadly for its intellectual ferocity, especially when compared to what most modern texts suggest - for once again this section does not end with an emotional releasing exclamation mark as in most modern texts

- not surprisingly, the sight of Cæsar's wounds, with his description of them as 'dumbe mouthes', and the start of his 'Curse' release Antony's passion (4/5, F #4's first four lines), which is sustained (3/2 in the two lines between the semicolon and the next colon) as he springs, via the only semicolon in the speech, to prophesying the two things that would terrify an Elizabethan audience, 'Domesticke Fury, and fierce Civill strife'

- the impact of this is not lost on him, for the first of at least six extra breath thoughts (marked , $_x$) make their first appearance, suggesting that he needs the extra breaths to handle the frightening thoughts of what is to come, followed by the only unembellished line in the section, 'Blood and destruction shall be so in use,', unequivocally spelling out the inevitable result, but so quietly in comparison to what surrounds it, it seems as if Antony has difficulty in just saying the words

- and the remainder of the onrushed sentence now struggles between the polar opposites of intellect and emotion, with the horrific images of 'Mothers' smiling at their slaughtered children handled intellectually (4/2); the neutering of pity, emotionally (0/3 in just one line); 'Cæsar's Spirit ranging for Revenge', intellectually (7/2 in three lines); and the final cry of 'havocke' and letting 'slip the Dogges of Warre', passionately emotional (4/6, F #3's last three lines)

First Folio

14/ Antony

1 O pardon me, thou bleeding peece of Earth:
That I am meeke and gentle with these Butchers.+

2 Thou art the Ruines of the Noblest man
That ever lived in the Tide of Times.

3 Woe to the hand that shed this costly Blood. +

4 Over thy wounds, $_x$ now do I Prophesie,
(Which like dumbe mouthes do ope their Ruby lips,
To begge the voyce and utterance of my Tongue)
A Curse shall light upon the limbes of men;
Domesticke Fury, $_x$ and fierce Civill strife, $_x$
Shall cumber all the parts of Italy: $_x$
Blood and destruction shall be so in use,
And dreadfull Objects so familiar,
That Mothers shall but smile, $_x$ when they behold
Their Infants quartered with the hands of Warre: $_x$
All pitty choak'd with custome of fell deeds,
And Cæsars Spirit+ ranging for Revenge,
With Ate by his side, $_x$ come hot from Hell,
Shall in these Confines, $_x$ with a Monarkes voyce, $_x$
Cry havocke,+ and let slip the Dogges of Warre,
That this foule deede, shall smell above the earth
With Carrion men, groaning for Buriall.

15/ Antony **Friends, Romans, Countrymen, lend me your ears:** 3.2.73 – 107

16/ Antony **If you have teares, prepare to shed them now.** 3.2.169 - 197

Background: Unwisely as it proves, Brutus, over Cassius objections, has given Antony permission not only to participate in the funeral orations for Cæsar, but to present Cæsar's body to the general populace too. Young though he may be, and despite his protestations of being a poor orator ('I am no Orator, as Brutus is;/But . . . a plaine blunt man'), he succeeds in turning the people against the conspirators. The following are just two examples from the longer scene: speech #15 is the famous opening; speech #16 prepares the people for the sight of Cæsar's mutilated body.

Style: public open air address in front of a large group

Where: the steps of the Capitol **To Whom:** the common people

Speech 15: # of Lines: 35 **Probable Timing: 1.45 minutes**

Speech 16: # of Lines: 29 **Probable Timing: 1.30 minutes**

Modern Text

15/ Antony

1 Friends, Romans, Δcountrymen, lend me your ears! †
2 I come to bury Cæsar, not to praise him. †
3 The evil* that men do, lives after them,
The good is oft interred* with their bones;
So let it be with Cæsar.
4 The Δnoble Brutus,
Hath told you Cæsar was Δambitious;
If it were so, it was a grievous* Δfault,
And grievously* hath Cæsar answer'd it.
5 Here*, under leave of Brutus, and the rest
(For Brutus is an Δhonorable* man,
So are they all, all Δhonorable* men),
Come I to speak* in Cæsar's Δfuneral*.
6 He was my Δfriend, faithful* and just to me;
But Brutus says*, he was Δambitious,
And Brutus is an Δhonorable* man.
7 He hath brought many Δcaptives home to Rome,
Whose Δransoms*, did the general* Δcoffers fill;
Did this in Cæsar seem* Δambitious?
8 When that the poor* have cried*, Cæsar hath wept;
Ambition should be made of sterner stuff*:
Yet Brutus says*, he was Δambitious,
And Brutus is an Δhonorable* man.
9 You all did see that on the Lupercal*,
I thrice presented him a Δkingly Δcrown*,
Which he did thrice refuse.

Two questions often raised are 'just how politically shrewd is Antony?' and 'how deliberate and preplanned is his manipulation of the crowd?' In this speech F's orthography suggests that while the argument Antony wishes to make is probably predetermined, at times personal emotion seems to break through – though whether the end of the speech is preplanned or a genuine moment of loss of control is up to each actor to decide.

- while most of the surround phrases seem to underscore a specific point Antony wishes to drive into the Crowd's collective consciousness, the two that start the speech

  ". Friends, Romans, Countrymen, lend me your ears : /I come to bury Cæsar, not to praise him : "

  seem to be necessary simply to quieten down the crowd, while the only two formed in part by emotional semicolons

  "; all Honourable men)/Come I to speake in Cæsars Funerall . /He was my Friend, faithfull, and just to me ; "

  seem to reflect Antony's difficulty in handling the death of Cæsar rather than designed to advance any particular argument (though whether this is a public ploy to gain sympathy or genuine pain is up to each actor to decide)

- most of the remaining surround phrases hammer away at the two themes Antony keeps returning to, Brutus being (by implication not really) 'Noble' and Cæsar being (by implication not really) 'Ambitious'

  ". The Noble Brutus,/Hath told you Cæsar was Ambitious : "

  ": Did this in Cæsar seeme Ambitious ? /When that the poore have cry'de, Cæsar hath wept : "

  ": And Brutus is an Honourable man . "

  ". Yet Brutus sayes, he was Ambitious : /And sure he is an Honourable man ."

  while the last in the speech presents the key concept by which he hopes to sway the crowd

  ". O Judgement ! thou [are] fled to brutish Beasts,/And Men have lost their Reason . "

First Folio

15/ Antony

1 Friends, Romans, Countrymen, lend me your ears:
I come to bury Cæsar, not to praise him:
The evill that men do, lives after them,
The good is oft enterred with their bones,+
So let it be with Cæsar.
2 The Noble Brutus,
Hath told you Cæsar was Ambitious: x
If it were so, it was a greevous Fault,
And greevously hath Cæsar answer'd it.
3 Heere, under leave of Brutus, and the rest
(For Brutus is an Honourable man,
So are they all; x all Honourable men)+
Come I to speake in Cæsars Funerall.
4 He was my Friend, faithfull, x and just to me;
But Brutus sayes, he was Ambitious,
And Brutus is an Honourable man.
5 He hath brought many Captives home to Rome,
Whose Ransomes, did the generall Coffers fill: x
Did this in Cæsar seeme Ambitious?
6 When that the poore have cry'de, Cæsar hath wept; x
Ambition should be made of sterner stuffe,+
Yet Brutus sayes, he was Ambitious: x
And Brutus is an Honourable man.
7 You all did see, x that on the Lupercall,
I thrice presented him a Kingly Crowne,
Which he did thrice refuse.

{ctd. over}

10 Was this Δambition?

11 Yet Brutus says*, he was Δambitious,
And sure he is an Δhonorable* man.

12 I speak* not to disprove* what Brutus spoke,
But here* I am to speak* what I do know. †

13 You all did love him once, not without cause ;
What cause with-holds you then, to mourn* for him?

14 O Δjudgment*! thou [art] fled to brutish Δbeasts,
And Δmen have lost their Δreason.

15 Bear* with me,
My heart is in the Δcoffin there with Cæsar,
And I must pause* till it come back* to me.

- the opening to quieten the crowd and set up the theme of 'Noble Brutus/Cæsar . . . Ambitious' starts intellectually (8/2, F #1 and the first line and a half of F #2), while the suggestion that if Cæsar was ambitious he has 'greevously . . . answer'd it' and the explanation that he, Antony, is speaking now with the permission of the 'Honourable men' is very passionate (8/7 in the six lines made up of the last two lines of F #2 and all of F #3)

- as Antony begins to put forward the clever juxtaposition of Brutus saying Cæsar was Ambitious with the direct evidence (the 'Ransomes' of 'Captives' used to fill the 'generall Coffers') that Cæsar was anything but, he manages to keep much of his feelings in check (11/5, the six lines of F #4-5), though the two line direct reference to Cæsar's response to the crying poor, that ambition should be made of 'sterner stuffe', becomes highly emotional for just a moment (1/3, the first two lines of F #6)

- returning to the theme of the 'Honourable Brutus' saying Cæsar 'was Ambitious' and then clearly demonstrating that Cæsar was not, Antony gets his emotions back under control once more (11/6, the last two lines of F #6 through to F #9 - seven lines in all), the intellect heightened by the demanding (and tactic-revealing) three word F #8, 'Was this Ambition?'

- whether another public ploy to gain sympathy or genuinely upset, the last three sentences show no consistency, F #10's suggestion/question 'What cause with-holds you then, to mourne for him?' is highly emotional (1/5); the short statement that 'Judgement' is now lost is highlyintellectual (4/1, F #11); and the final admission 'My heart is in the Coffin there with Cæsar,' (2/3, F #12) is passionate

8 Was this Ambition?

9 Yet Brutus sayes, he was Ambitious: x
And sure he is an Honourable man.

10 I speake not to disproove what Brutus spoke,
But heere I am, x to speake what I do know;
You all did love him once, not without cause, +
What cause with-holds you then, to mourne for him?

11 O Judgement! thou [are] fled to brutish Beasts,
And Men have lost their Reason.

12 Beare with me,
My heart is in the Coffin there with Cæsar,
And I must pawse, x till it come backe to me.

Modern Text

16/ Antony

1 If you have tears*, prepare to shed them now.
2 You all do know this Δmantle . †
3 I remember
The first time ever Cæsar put it on;
'Twas on a Δsummer's Δevening, in his Δtent,
That day he overcame the [Nervii].
4 Look*, in this place ran Cassius' Δdagger through,
See what a rent the envious [Casca] made,
Through this the well*-beloved Brutus stabb'd,
And as he pluck'd his cursed Δsteel* away,
Mark* how the blood of Cæsar followed it,
As rushing out of doors* to be resolv'd
If Brutus so unkindly* knock'd or no;
For Brutus, as you know, was Cæsar's Δangel.
5 Judge, O you Δgods, how dearly* Cæsar lov'd him ! †
6 This was the most unkindest cut of all; ◊
For when the Δnoble Cæsar saw him stab,
Ingratitude, more strong [than] Δtraitors' arms*,
Quite vanquish'd him. †
7 Then burst his Δmighty heart,
And in his Δmantle muffling up his face,
Even at the Δbase of Pompey's* Δstatue
(Which all the while ran blood) great Cæsar fell.
8 O, what a fall was there, my Δcountrymen !
9 Then I, and you, and all of us fell down*,
Whilst bloody Δtreason flourish'd over us.
10 O now you weep*, and I perceive you feel*
The dint of pity*. †
11 These are gracious drops*.
12 Kind* Δsouls*, what weep* you when you but behold
Our Cæsar's Δvesture wounded?
13 Look* you here*,[3]
Here* is Δhimself*, marr'd as you see with Δtraitors .

Whatever personal emotion Antony was undergoing during the opening of the scene (previous speech, #15), here F's orthography suggests that Antony has a much better grip on himself, with just four extra breath-thoughts (marked ,$_x$), especially the ones relating to the stab wounds (the 'rents') in Cæsar's cloak (the 'mantle'), in F #3 and F #5 suggesting moments where his personal feelings might just break through without the tiniest need for self-control.

• the fact that F #1 is emotional is beyond doubt (0/1), though whether this is genuine or a ploy is again up to each actor to decide

• in displaying the highly emotionally charged blood-stained cloak of Cæsar and the first rents the conspirator's daggers made, the slightly onrushed F #2 (split into two by most modern texts) is totally factual (6/0, F#2, and 3/1, F #3's, first two lines) - though how Antony knows which rent was made by which conspirator is highly suspect since he was drawn away from the actual murder by Trebonius as part of the conspirators' plans: nevertheless, the stakes are even further increased with the description of these first rents being set as surround phrases

• but as Antony turns to the rent supposedly made by Brutus, his passions come to the fore (4/4, F #3's next five lines), and then, whether deliberate or no, he intellectually intensifies the attack on Brutus via the three surround phrases

" : For Brutus, as you know, was Cæsars Angel. /Judge, O you Gods, how deerely Cæsar lov'd him : /This was the most unkindest cut of all . "

the last line heightened by being unembellished, as if the quietness of the utterance were all that was needed to move the crowd

• and having (presumably) hushed the crowd Antony's intellect kicks in as he first describes this as the blow that 'burst his Mighty heart' (F #5) , going on (F #6-7) to superbly manipulatively reason that 'Then I, and you, and all of us fell downe' (11/3 overall)

• and then the emotional F #8 recognition (1/4) of having worked the crowd to where he wants them is highlighted by being set as two surround phrases

" . O now you weepe, and I perceive you feele/The dint of pitty: These are gracious droppes ."

• while the final revelation of the body itself is (triumphantly? personally upsetting?) passionate (5/7, the last three lines of F #9-10)

First Folio

16/ Antony

1 If you have teares, prepare to shed them now.
2 You all do know this Mantle, I remember
The first time ever Cæsar put it on,+
'Twas on a Summers Evening+ in his Tent,
That day he overcame the [Nervy].
3 Looke, in this place ran Cassius Dagger through: $_x$
See what a rent the envious [Caska] made: $_x$
Through this,$_x$ the wel-beloved Brutus stabb'd,
And as he pluck'd his cursed Steele away: $_x$
Marke how the blood of Cæsar followed it,
As rushing out of doores,$_x$ to be resolv'd
If Brutus so unkindely knock'd,$_x$ or no: $_x$
For Brutus, as you know, was Cæsars Angel.
4 Judge, O you Gods, how deerely Cæsar lov'd him: +
This was the most unkindest cut of all.
5 For when the Noble Cæsar saw him stab,
Ingratitude, more strong [then] Traitors armes,
Quite vanquish'd him: then burst his Mighty heart,
And in his Mantle,$_x$ muffling up his face,
Even at the Base of Pompeyes Statue
(Which all the while ran blood) great Cæsar fell.
6 O+ what a fall was there, my Countrymen?+
7 Then I, and you, and all of us fell downe,
Whil'st bloody Treason flourish'd over us.
8 O now you weepe, and I perceive you feele
The dint of pitty: These are gracious droppes.
9 Kinde Soules, what weepe you,$_x$ when you but behold
Our Cæsars Vesture wounded?
10 Looke you heere,
Heere is Himselfe, marr'd as you see with Traitors.

---

[3] this is the point at which most modern texts have Antony remove the cloak masking Cæsar's body

17/ Antony **This is a slight unmeritable man,** between 4.1.12 - 40

Background: The following occurs following the first on-stage meeting of the tripartite leadership (established to restore order and defeat the conspirators). With Lepidus having left, Antony is exceedingly candid with Octavius about his feelings for their partner.

Style: as part of a two handed scene

Where: unspecified, a meeting room at the Senate **To Whom:** Octavius

# of Lines: 26 **Probable Timing: 1.15 minutes**

Modern Text

17/ Antony

1 This is a slight unmeritable man,
Meet to be sent on △errands; is it fit,
The three-fold △world divided, he should stand
One of the three to share it?

2 And though we lay these △honors* on this man
To ease our selves of divers sland'rous loads,
He shall but bear* them as the △ass* bears* △gold,
To groan* and sweat* under the △business*,
Either led or driven, as we point the way;
And having brought our △treasure where we will,
Then take we down* his △load, and turn* him off
(Like to the empty △ass*) to shake his ears*
And graze in △commons.

3 {ψ} {You say he* is} a tried, and valiant △soldier*.

4 So is my △horse, Octavius, and for that
I do appoint him store of △provender.

5 It is a △creature that I teach to fight,
To wind*, to stop, to run directly on,
His corporal* △motion govern'd by my △spirit;
And in some taste is Lepidus but so:
He must be taught, and train'd, and bid go forth;
A barren-spirited △fellow; one that feeds
On △objects, △arts and △imitations, ◊
Which, out of use, and stal'd* by other men,
Begin his fashion.

6 Do not talk* of him
But as a property.

At first it seems that Antony's dislike of Lepidus can be held in check, for though F #1 opens with a surround phrase, unembellished till the very last scornful dismissive image, the sentence is only mildly intellectual (2/0 in four lines), but then F's orthography shows how disturbed Antony becomes (with a man unworthy to stand within Cæsar's shadow perhaps) before he manages to re-establish control.

- on the one hand the unembellished phrases suggest that Antony can deny without too much problem Lepidus' worthiness to share in the 'three-fold World'
  "is it fit/ . . . he should stand/One of the three to share it?"
  he being only fit to be
  "Either led or driven, as we point the way"
  "To ease our selves of divers sland'rous loads"
  "He must be taught, and train'd, and bid go forth"

- yet F #2's images dismissing Lepidus as an 'Asse' are scathing, and not only are they passionate (8/10) but four of at least six extra breath-thoughts scattered through the speech (marked , $_x$) make their appearance here, suggesting either that Antony is trying to rein himself in and needs the extra breaths to do so, or, the exact opposite, that he is being overly-abusive in making the most of even the tiniest points of ridicule

- F #3's challenge to Octavius as to Lepidus' reputation is the final moment of passion (1/2), its shortness suggesting a last attack before establishing self-control

- and even though the dismissive comparisons continue, Antony dwelling at length on comparing Lepidus to a horse that needs training, his intellect takes over (11/2, the nine lines of F #4-5), and the scorn is emphasised by the surround phrases ending F #5
  " : He must be taught, and train'd, and bid go forth : /A barren spirited Fellow ; one that feeds/On Objects, Arts and Imitations ."
  a scorn even further heightened by the fact that the surround phrases are preceded by two more of the extra breath-thoughts and linked by the only emotional semicolon in the speech

- and the ending of the speech is not only emotional (0/2, F #6-7) it is also ungrammatical, with most modern texts adding the non-syntactical F #6 to the previous sentence: as set it seems that Antony most definitely needs a pause (however ungrammatical) before continuing

First Folio

17/ Antony

1 This is a slight unmeritable man,
Meet to be sent on Errands: $_x$ is it fit+
The three-fold World divided, he should stand
One of the three to share it?

2 And though we lay these Honours on this man, $_x$
To ease our selves of divers sland'rous loads,
He shall but beare them, $_x$ as the Asse beares Gold,
To groane and swet under the Businesse,
Either led or driven, as we point the way: $_x$
And having brought our Treasure, $_x$ where we will,
Then take we downe his Load, and turne him off
(Like to the empty Asse) to shake his eares, $_x$
And graze in Commons.

3 {ψ} {You say hee is} a tried, and valiant Souldier.

4 So is my Horse+ Octavius, and for that
I do appoint him store of Provender.

5 It is a Creature that I teach to fight,
To winde, to stop, to run directly on: $_x$
His corporall Motion, $_x$ govern'd by my Spirit,+
And in some taste, $_x$ is Lepidus but so:
He must be taught, and train'd, and bid go forth: $_x$
A barren spirited Fellow; one that feeds
On Objects, Arts and Imitations.

6 Which+ out of use, and stal'de by other men+
Begin his fashion.

7 Do not talke of him, $_x$
But as a property.

#'s 18 - 19: Others Affected By Events

18/ Murellus **Wherefore rejoyce?/What Conquest brings he home?** 1.1.32 - 55

Background: At the top of the play, Cæsar has returned to Rome in triumph after defeating Pompey. The citizens have been given a holiday, to the disgust of two pro-Pompey supporters Flavius and Murellus who in their anguish not only remove laurel wreaths of victory from Cæsar's statuary (for which they are later executed), but, as here, berate the general citizenry in the midst of their celebrations.

Style: general address to a large group, initially via one man

Where: a public street **To Whom:** initially the Cobbler, in front of Flavius, and a large group of holidaying citizens

# of Lines: 23 **Probable Timing: 1.10 minutes**

Modern Text

18/ Murellus

1 Wherefore rejoice*?
2 What Δconquest brings he home?
3 What Δtributaries follow him to Rome,
To grace in Δcaptive bonds his Δchariot-Δwheels*?
4 You Δblocks*, you stones, you worse [than] senseless* things! †
5 O you hard hearts, you cruel* men of Rome,
Knew you not Pompey? †
6 Many a time and oft
Have you climb'd up to Δwalls* and Δbattlements,
To Δtow'rs* and Δwindows*, ◊ yea, to Δchimney-tops,
Your Δinfants in your Δarms*, and there have sate
The livelong day, with patient expectation,
To see great Pompey pass* the streets of Rome;
And when you saw his Δchariot but appear*,
Have you not made an Δuniversal* shout,
That [Tiber] trembled underneath her banks*
To hear* the replication of your sounds
Made in her Δconcave Δshores?
7 And do you now put on your best attire*?
8 And do you now cull out a Δholiday*?
9 And do you now strew Δflowers in his way,
That comes in Δtriumph over Pompey's* blood?
10 Be gone! †
11 Run* to your houses, fall upon your knees,
Pray to the Δgods to intermit the plague
That needs must light on this Δingratitude.

The opening of two short sentences suggests a Murellus almost at a loss for words, while the peculiar and very ungrammatical setting of F #4 through to the opening of F #6 points to a reckless character, one not in full control of himself or his rhetoric: most modern texts set the much more grammatical three sentences as shown, establishing a sense of self-control that hardly matches his offstage foolhardiness in desecrating Cæsar's images by removing the scarves that adorned them. The shading illustrates the enormous punctuation differences.

• despite this, it seems that Murellus can contain his feelings, for the first three sentences of rebuke are highly factual (6/2)

• but as the insults intensify (comparing the crowd to 'worse than senslesse things' – one of the most appalling denigrations to Elizabethans who prided their sense of humanity above all things), so not only does the lack of grammar referred to above kick in, Murellus also becomes highly passionate (7/6 in just the four and a half lines of F #4-5)

• though he almost regains self-control in F #6's opening description of how the people used to sit in wait for their previous hero, Pompey, 'The live-long day, with patient expectation' (5/2, the first three and a half lines) Murellus' passions quickly take over once again at the memory how they received Pompey 'with 'an Universall shout' (5/4, F #6's remaining five lines)

• the ensuing three sentences as to how they now respond to Cæsar (F #7 putting on their 'best attyre', #8's calling it a 'Holiday', and #9's strewing 'Flowers in his way') are also passionate (4/3), the shortness of F #7-8 suggest that, as with the opening, Murellus ia once more almost at a loss for words

• fascinatingly, by the start of F #10's final instruction "Be gone,/Runne to your houses, fall upon your knees,' - with the two unembellished phrases surrounding the emotional command to 'Runne' - it seems his energy is almost dissipated, and the final interdiction to 'Pray' becomes bleakly intellectual (2/0, the last two lines of the speech)

First Folio

18/ Murellus

1 Wherefore rejoyce?→[4]
2 What Conquest brings he home?
3 What Tributaries follow him to Rome,
To grace in Captive bonds his Chariot Wheeles?
4 You Blockes, you stones, you worse [then] senslesse things:[+]
O you hard hearts, you cruell men of Rome,
Knew you not Pompey[+] many a time and oft? x
5 Have you climb'd up to Walles and Battlements,
To Towres and Windowes?
6 Yea, to Chimney tops,
Your Infants in your Armes, and there have sate
The live-long day, with patient expectation,
To see great Pompey passe the streets of Rome: x
And when you saw his Chariot but appeare,
Have you not made an Universall shout,
That [Tyber] trembled underneath her bankes
To heare the replication of your sounds, x
Made in her Concave Shores?
7 And do you now put on your best attyre?
8 And do you now cull out a Holyday?
9 And do you now strew Flowers in his way,
That comes in Triumph over Pompeyes blood?
10 Be gone,[+]
Runne to your houses, fall upon your knees,
Pray to the Gods to intermit the plague
That needs must light on this Ingratitude.

---

[4] the potential gap between this and the next short line (printed as one iambic line in most modern texts) offers Murellus the chance to wait for a reply from the crowd before continuing

19/ Caska **Are not you mov'd, when all the sway of Earth** between 1.3.3 - 32

Background: The storm that so energises Cassius (speech #1 above) has the opposite effect on Caska.

Style: as part of a two-handed scene

Where: a street in Rome **To Whom:** Cicero, a fellow senator

# of Lines: 29 **Probable Timing: 1.30 minutes**

Modern Text

19/ Caska

1 Are not you mov'd, when all the sway of Δearth
Shakes like a thing unfirm*?
2 O Cicero,
I have seen* Δtempests when the scolding Δwinds
Have riv'd the knotty Δoaks*, and I have seen*
Th'ambitious Δocean swell, and rage, and foam*,
To be exalted with the threat'ning Δclouds;
But never till to-°Δnight, never till now,
Did I go* through a Δtempest °dropping ° fire.
3 Either* there is a Δcivil* strife in Δheaven,
Or else the Δworld, too sawcy with the Δgods,
Incenses them to send destruction.

---

4 A common slave - you know him well by sight -
Held up his left Δhand, which did flame and burn*
Like twenty Δtorches join'd*; and yet his Δhand,
Not sensible of fire, remain'd unscorch'd.
5 Besides - I ha'not since put up my Δsword -
Against the Capitol* I met a Δlion*,
Who glaz'd upon me, and went surly by,
Without annoying me.
6 And there were drawn*
Upon a heap* a hundred ghastly Δwomen,
Transformed with their fear*, who swore they saw
Men, all in fire, walk* up and down* the streets*.
7 And yesterday the Δbird of Δnight did sit
Even at Δnoon*-day upon the Δmarket-place,
Hooting* and shrieking*.
8 When these Δprodigies
Do* so conjointly* meet, let not men say,
"These are their Δreasons, they are Δnatural*";
For I believe* they are portentous things
Unto the Δclimate* that they point upon.

Though obviously disturbed by the night's events, F's orthography suggests that Caska can report what he saw and conduct himself fairly rationally, at least at the top of the speech. However, as the speech develops, a deceptive calmness intrudes, especially when describing the more bizarre events witnessed (particularly F #4-5), and handling the final images and their implications leads to a sudden need for many extra breath-thoughts (marked , $_x$) as if the events were almost too frightening to contemplate and the extra breaths are needed to establish some form of self-control and/or to ensure that not the smallest of details escapes his colleague Cicero.

- though F #1 starts out relatively calmly (1/1), Caska needs an extra breath-thought almost immediately - before describing the earth as 'a thing unfirme'
- and F #2 continues passionately as he equates the night's 'Tempest-dropping-fire' to nothing he has ever seen before (6/5)
- initially the realisation that either there is 'a Civill strife in Heaven' or the 'Gods' are about to destroy the world is handled intellectually (F #3, 4/2), but then finishes with a bleak unembellished line (the first of several) as the latter thought hits home
- the unembellished lines point not only to how carefully he expresses his overall fear, that the 'Gods', having lost patience with the 'World', make use of the 'heavens'
  "Incenses them to send destruction."
  but also how equally carefully he starts to voice the night's amazing happenings, starting with the apparent bursting into flame of the left hand of
  "A common slave, you know him well by sight,/ . . . /Not sensible of fire, remain'd unscorch'd."
  and continuing with his own meeting of a 'Lyon' in the 'Capitoll'
  "Who glaz'd upon me, and went surly by,/Without annoying me."
- yet these unembellished passages are still surrounded by passion (F #4-5, 6/4)
- as the details pile one on top of another, and become more intense with the fears of a 'hundred gastly Women', not only do Caska's emotions break through (F #6, 1/6), the extra breath-thoughts noted above begin to sweep in (two in F #6, four in F #7, and two in the final F #8)
- 'the Bird of Night' in F #7, where most of these extra breath-thoughts appear, refers to the owl, which, according to Elizabethan belief, when seen/heard hooting during the day, signifies the death of princes and leaders – as such both F #7 (4/3) and F #8's summary of all these events as 'portentous things' (4/5) are highly passionate (8/8 overall in the remaining seven lines)

First Folio

19/ Caska

1 Are not you mov'd, when all the sway of Earth
Shakes,$_x$ like a thing unfirme?
2 O Cicero,
I have seene Tempests,$_x$ when the scolding Winds
Have riv'd the knottie Oakes, and I have seene
Th'ambitious Ocean swell, and rage, and foame,
To be exalted with the threatning Clouds: $_x$
But never till to Night, never till now,
Did I goe through a Tempest-dropping-fire.
3 Eyther there is a Civill strife in Heaven,
Or else the World, too sawcie with the Gods,
Incenses them to send destruction.

---

4 A common slave, you know him well by sight,
Held up his left Hand, which did flame and burne
Like twentie Torches joyn'd; and yet his Hand,
Not sensible of fire, remain'd unscorch'd.
5 Besides, I ha'not since put up my Sword,
Against the Capitoll I met a Lyon,
Who glaz'd upon me, and went surly by,
Without annoying me.
6 And there were drawne
Upon a heape,$_x$ a hundred gastly Women,
Transformed with their feare, who swore,$_x$ they saw
Men, all in fire, walke up and downe the streetes.
7 And yesterday,$_x$ the Bird of Night did sit,$_x$
Even at Noone-day,$_x$ upon the Market place,
Howting,$_x$ and shreeking.
8 When these Prodigies
Doe so conjoyntly meet, let not men say,
These are their Reasons, they are Naturall: $_x$
For I beleeve,$_x$ they are portentous things
Unto the Clymate,$_x$ that they point upon.

#'s 20 - 23: Portia's Dilemma

20/ Portia	**Nor for yours neither. Y'have ungently Brutus**	2.1.236 - 256
21/ Portia	**Brutus is wise, and were he not in health,**	between 2.1.258 - 278
22/ Portia	**Within the Bond of Marriage, tell me Brutus,**	between 2.1.280 - 302

Background: Already disturbed at Brutus' apparent withdrawal from their hitherto exemplary marriage of equals, and by his sudden lack of sleep and disinterest in food, or her, his unwell wife Portia is further disturbed by so many men having visited him late at night, who, despite the dark, seem to have taken great pains to muffle themselves from public view. The following are her attempts to get him to share with her all his thoughts as he once did - as such each speech seems self-explanatory.

Speech #21 is her opening, triggered by his attempt to side-track her with 'It is not for your health, thus to commit/Your weake condition, to the raw cold morning'.

Speech #22 is triggered by his attempt to avoid a detailed answer to her final direct request of speech #21 (sentence #6) with a simple 'I am not well in health, and that is all'.

Speech #23 is her demand for complete knowledge of what is disturbing him made full and manifest.

Style: as part of a two-handed scene

Where: in the garden of Brutus' and Portia's home **To Whom:** Brutus

Speech 20: # of Lines: 20	**Probable Timing: 1.00 minutes**
Speech 21: # of Lines: 20	**Probable Timing: 1.00 minutes**
Speech 22: # of Lines: 19	**Probable Timing: 1.00 minutes**

Modern Text

20/ Portia

1 Nor for yours neither.
2 Y'have ungently, Brutus,
Stole from my bed; and yesternight at Δsupper
You suddenly* arose and walk'd about,
Musing and sighing, with your arms* across*;
And when I ask'd you what the matter was,
You star'd upon me with ungentle looks*.
3 I urg'd you further; then you scratch'd your head,
And too impatiently stamp'd with your foot*. †
4 Yet I insisted, yet you answer'd not,
But with an angry wafter of your hand
Gave sign* for me to leave you. †
5 So I did,
Fearing to strengthen that impatience
Which seem'd too much enkindled*; and withal*
Hoping it was but an effect of Δhumor*,
Which sometime hath his hour* with every man.
6 It will not let you eat*, nor talk*, nor sleep*;
And could it work* so much upon your shape
As it hath much prevail'd* on your {condition},
I should not know you Brutus.

For most of the time Portia's attempt to get a response from Brutus by simply stating the facts is handled very carefully, as the large numbers of unembellished lines show - though, as the speech develops, the imbalance of emotional releases quickly shows how difficult she is finding it to maintain self-control.

• the unembellished lines first dismiss Brutus' concerns for her health
"Nor for yours neither."
but then swiftly turn to recalling his recent disturbing and unusual actions
"Y'have ungently . . . /Stole from my bed: and yesternight . . . /You sodainly arose, and walk'd about,/Musing, and sighing, . . . /And when I ask'd you what the matter was,/You star'd upon me, ...
not only does she equally carefully describe how she pressured him for a response
"I urg'd you further, then you scratch'd your head,/And too impatiently stampt . . . /Yet I insisted, yet you answer'd not,/But with an angry wafter of your hand"
she also expresses her own responses in exactly the same way
"Fearing to strengthen that impatience/Which seem'd too much inkindled ;"
as if she were still taking care not to 'strengthen that impatience' even now

• the first indication of his strange behaviour is expressed via a surround phrase
" . Y'have ungently Brutus/Stole from my bed : "
while the overall summation is via an even more impassioned monosyllabic surround phrase, formed in part by the (emotional) semicolon
" . It will not let you eate, nor talke, nor sleepe ; "

First Folio

20/ Portia

1 Nor for yours neither.
2 Y'have ungently+ Brutus+
Stole from my bed: x and yesternight at Supper
You sodainly arose,x and walk'd about,
Musing,x and sighing, with your armes a-crosse: x
And when I ask'd you what the matter was,
You star'd upon me,x with ungentle lookes.
3 I urg'd you further,+ then you scratch'd your head,
And too impatiently stampt with your foote:
Yet I insisted, yet you answer'd not,
But with an angry wafter of your hand
Gave signe for me to leave you: So I did,
Fearing to strengthen that impatience
Which seem'd too much inkindled; and withall,x
Hoping it was but an effect of Humor,
Which sometime hath his houre with every man.
4 It will not let you eate, nor talke, nor sleepe;
And could it worke so much upon your shape,x
As it hath much prevayl'd on your {condition},
I should not know you Brutus.

{ctd. over}

7 Dear* my Δlord,
Make me acquainted with your cause of grief*.

• despite Portia's unembellished care, and the speech's intellectual opening (2/0, the first two lines of the speech), after the unembellished (shock?) of his sudden walking about, she becomes emotional as she recalls asking 'what the matter was' (0/3, F #2's last three lines)

• F #3's complete catalogue of disturbing events is still emotional, but much more carefully/only occasionally released (2/4, in nine lines)

• but then her emotion gets the better of her as she sums up the effect his actions have on both of them (F #4) and in her F #5's asking to be 'acquainted with your cause of greefe' (2/7 overall in the speech's last five lines)

5 Deare my Lord,
Make me acquainted with your cause of greefe.

Modern Text

21/ Portia

1 Brutus is wise, and were he not in health,
He would embrace the means* to come by it.

2 Is Brutus sick*? ◊ and is it Δphysical*
To walk* unbraced and suck* up the humors*
Of the dank* Δmorning?
3 What, is Brutus sick*?
4 And will he steal* out of his wholsome bed
To dare the vile contagion of the Δnight,
And tempt the Δrheumy* and unpurged Δair*
To add* unto hi{s} sickness*?
5 No, my Brutus,
You have some sick* Δoffense within your mind*,
Which, by the Δright and Δvirtue of my place,
I ought to know of; Δand upon my knees
I charm* you, by my once commended Δbeauty,
By all your vows* of Δlove, and that great Δvow
Which did incorporate and make us one,
That you unfold to me, yourself*, your half*
Why you are heavy ; and what men to-night
Have had resort to you ; for here* have been*
Some six* or seven, who did hide their faces
Even from darkness*.

As the scene develops Portia's ability to keep herself calm begins to dissipate, as this speech clearly shows, though she does try to establish some sense of control by bringing her considerable intellect into play.

• as with the earlier speech that opens this scene (#20 above), in challenging Brutus yet again Portia opens very carefully (0/1, F #1), starting straightaway with the first of only two unembellished lines found in the speech
"Brutus is wise, and were he not in health,"
this opening care further heightened by being monosyllabic

• then, as she challenges his plea of sickness more directly than at any earlier time in the scene, she first becomes quite emotional (3/6, F #2-3), but finishes quite passionately (6/8, F #4-5 and the first two lines of F #6, just five and a half lines overall) as she denies his plea, finally accusing him of having 'some sicke Offence within your minde'

• but, as befits the daughter of a Roman Senator famous for his skills in both debate and oratory, as she begins to demand to know 'by the Right and Vertue of my place' (as Brutus' wife and partner) just what is going on, her sense of control kicks in, her intellect coming to the fore (6/2 for the next five lines)

• sadly, this does not last, for, as she baldly states her request 'That you unfold to me, your selfe', so emotions take over fully (0/6 the remaining four and half lines of the speech) and as she defines herself as 'your halfe' and what she wants to know, the only two surround phrases of the speech present themselves
" ; your halfe/Why you are heavy : and what men to night/Have had resort to you : "
the first underscored by being started via the emotional semicolon (the only one in the speech), the latter further heightened by being only the second unembellished line in the speech

First Folio

21/ Portia

1 Brutus is wise, and were he not in health,
He would embrace the meanes to come by it.

2 Is Brutus sicke?
3 And is it Physicall
To walke unbraced,x and sucke up the humours
Of the danke Morning?
4 What, is Brutus sicke?
5 And will he steale out of his wholsome bed
To dare the vile contagion of the Night?
And tempt the Rhewmy,x and unpurged Ayre,x
To adde unto hi{s} sicknesse?
6 No+ my Brutus,
You have some sicke Offence within your minde,
Which+ by the Right and Vertue of my place+
I ought to know of: x And upon my knees,x
I charme you, by my once commended Beauty,
By all your vowes of Love, and that great Vow
Which did incorporate and make us one,
That you unfold to me, your selfe; x your halfe
Why you are heavy : x and what men to night
Have had resort to you : x for heere have beene
Some sixe or seven, who did hide their faces
Even from darknesse.

Modern Text

22/ Portia

1 Within the Δbond of Δmarriage, tell me, Brutus,
Is it excepted I should know no Δsecrets
That appertain* to you?
2 Am I your Δself*,
But, as it were, in sort, or limitation. †
3 To keep* with you at Δmeals*, comfort your Δbed,
And talk* to you sometimes?
4 Dwell I but in the Δsuburbs
Of your good pleasure?
5 If it be no more,
Portia is Brutus' Δharlot, not his Δwife.
6 I grant* I am a Δwoman; but withal*,
A Δwoman that Lord Brutus took* to Δwife. †
7 I grant* I am a Δwoman; but withal*,
A Δwoman well reputed, Cato's Δdaughter.
8 Think* you I am no stronger [than] my Δsex,
Being so Δfather'd and so Δhusbanded?
9 Tell me your Δcounsels, I will not disclose 'em. †
10 I have made strong proof* of my Δconstancy*,
Giving myself* a voluntary wound
Here*, in the Δthigh; Δcan I bear* that with patience,
And not my Δhusband's Δsecrets?

F's three separate slight onrushes (F #2, #5, and #7) show where, despite her intellect and logic, Portia's control slips, as do the three extra breath-thoughts (marked , x) found in the first four lines of the speech. And though F #5 is formed of five consecutive surround phrases, underscoring the strength of her determination, the fact that four of the five are in part formed by the (only) two emotional semicolons in the speech it seems that even here she has to struggle not to let her emotions get the better of her.

- the speech's opening argument based on the 'Bond of Marriage' is strongly intellectual (4/1, F #1), though it seems Brutus' lack of reply breaks this pattern, for the next question (whether she plays only a limited role in his life) is highly passionate (3/4, the three lines of F #2) - but this break is only momentary, for, despite the very strong imagery that follows, starting with a long (thirteen syllable line) and ending with her suggestion she is merely his 'Harlot, not his Wife', she manages to re-establish intellectual control (4/0, F #3-4)

- and it seems his lack of reply causes this pattern to break yet again, for the demanding and repetitive five consecutive surround phrase sequence forming F #5 swings back to intellectual passion yet again (9/5 in just four lines)

- though F #6's direct challenge as to her worth ('no stronger than my Sex') swings back to intellectual control (3/1), the demand seems a little difficult for her, for two extra breath-thoughts split the two line sentence into four thoughts rather than most modern texts two

- and the intellectual strength of F #7's surround phrases opening ' . Tell me your Counsels, I will not disclose 'em : ' (0/1) and the speech's final challenge " . Can I beare that with patience,/And not my Husbands Secrets ? " (3/1) only serve to illustrate how hard she is still trying to maintain self-control - even though the 'strong proofe of my Constancie' is offered passionately yet again (2/3)

First Folio

22/ Portia

1 Within the Bond of Marriage, tell me+ Brutus,
Is it excepted, x I should know no Secrets
That appertaine to you?
2 Am I your Selfe,
But+ as it were+ in sort, x or limitation? x
To keepe with you at Meales, comfort your Bed,
And talke to you sometimes?
3 Dwell I but in the Suburbs
Of your good pleasure?
4 If it be no more,
Portia is Brutus Harlot, not his Wife.
5 I graunt I am a Woman; but withall,
A Woman that Lord Brutus tooke to Wife:
I graunt I am a Woman; but withall,
A Woman well reputed: x Cato's Daughter.
6 Thinke you, x I am no stronger [then] my Sex+
Being so Father'd, x and so Husbanded?
7 Tell me your Counsels, I will not disclose 'em:
I have made strong proofe of my Constancie,
Giving my selfe a voluntary wound
Heere, in the Thigh: x Can I beare that with patience,
And not my Husbands Secrets?

23/ Portia **I prythee Boy, run to the Senate-house,** between 2.4.1 - 46

Background: On the day of the intended assassination Portia fears that something terrible is about to happen, without knowing what. The following opens the scene, and presumably both her fears and her health create in her the inability to shake off or clarify the vagueness of the requests she is making of Brutus' young servant Lucius.

Style: as part of a two-handed scene

Where: a street in Rome **To Whom:** Lucius, Brutus' young servant

# of Lines: 24 **Probable Timing: 1.15 minutes**

Modern Text

23/ Portia

1 I prithee*, Δboy, run to the Senate-house;
Stay not to answer me, but get thee gone.
2 Why dost* thou stay?

Portia's inability to decide on a single course of action could well be highlighted by the surround phrase, ' . I have a mans minde, but a womans might : ' - a dreadful tug of opposites - while the several onrushes (F#3, split into four by most modern texts, and the final F #12, split into three) show where her inability to maintain logical disciplined self-control is at its height.

First Folio

23/ Portia

1 I prythee+ Boy, run to the Senate-house,+
Stay not to answer me, but get thee gone.
2 Why doest thou stay?

{ctd. over}

3 I would have had thee there and here* again*
Ere I can tell thee what thou shouldst do there. † -
4 O Δconstancy⁎, be strong upon my side,
Set a huge Δmountain* 'tween* my Δheart and Δtongue !†
5 I have a man's mind*, but a woman's might. †
6 How hard it is for women to keep* counsel* !
7 Art thou here* yet?
8 {ψ} Bring me word, Δboy, if thy Δlord look well,
For he went sickly forth; and take good note
What Cæsar doth, what Δsuitors⁎ press* to him.
9 Hark*, Δboy, what noise* is that?
10 I heard a bustling⁎ Δrumor, like a Δfray,
And the wind* brings it from the Capitol*.
11 I must go in. †
12 Ay* me!
13 How weak* a thing
The heart of woman is !
14 O Brutus,
The Δheavens speed* thee in thine enterprise* !
15 Sure the Δboy heard me. †
16 Brutus hath a suit*
That Cæsar will not grant.
17 – O, I grow faint. † –
18 Run, Lucius, and commend me to my Δlord,
Say I am merry. †
19 Come to me again*,
And bring me word what he doth say to thee.

• as when with Brutus (speeches #20-22 above), this speech also starts carefully, with one and a half unembellished lines being opened by a first-line factual order (2/1), and interrupted by one emotional one (0/1) as she voices her inability to tell Brutus' boy 'what thou should'st do'

• thus it's not surprising that the request for 'Constancie' should be so strongly passionate (4/2, in just lines three and four of F #3), but then her emotions quickly sweep in just as strongly (0/4 in F #3's last two lines and the very short F #4) as she voices the perceived weakness of her 'womans might'

• then she immediately swings back again to a form of self-control as she finally is able to tell Lucius what she wants him to do (4/1, F #5), a control which is immediately undone by her response to noises only she can hear (4/4, the three lines of F #6-7)

• even F's setting of F #8 as two short lines could well be a further indication of Portia's confusion, especially since it and the short sentence once more expressing how 'weake/The heart of woman is?' that follow are emotional (0/2)

• her good wishes for Brutus' success is very passionate (2/2 in F #10's line and a half)

• but once more she has to dig deep into what mental reserves she has left, for not only is F #11 and the opening of F #12 composed of four successive surround phrases

"．Sure the Boy heard me : Brutus hath a suite/That Cæsar will not grant. O, I grow faint: /Run Lucius, and commend me to my Lord,/Say I am merry ; "

she is also very intellectual (5/1), all pointing to a desperate attempt to take control

• though she cannot keep it till the end, for while the final surround phrase command 'Come to me againe' starts passionately (1/1), she finishes with an unembellished monosyllabic last line

"And bring me word what he doth say to thee."

as if she simply has no energy left

3 I would have had thee there and heere agen
Ere I can tell thee what thou should'st do there:
O Constancie, be strong upon my side,
Set a huge Mountaine 'tweene my Heart and Tongue: +
I have a mans minde, but a womans might:
How hard it is for women to keepe counsell. +
4 Art thou heere yet?
5 {ψ} Bring me word+ Boy, if thy Lord look well,
For he went sickly forth: x and take good note
What Cæsar doth, what Sutors presse to him.
6 Hearke+ Boy, what noyse is that?
7 I heard a bussling Rumor+ like a Fray,
And the winde brings it from the Capitoll.
8 I must go in: + →
Aye me!
9 How weake a thing
The heart of woman is?+
10 O Brutus,
The Heavens speede thee in thine enterprize. +
11 Sure the Boy heard me: Brutus hath a suite
That Cæsar will not grant.
12 O, I grow faint:
Run+ Lucius, and commend me to my Lord,
Say I am merry; Come to me againe,
And bring me word what he doth say to thee.

SPEECHES IN ORDER		TIME	PAGE
HAMLET			
#'s 1 - 5: Hamlet, His Father, & Claudius			
1/ Hamlet	Oh that this too too solid Flesh, would melt,	1.30	125
2/ King	'Tis sweet and commendable	1.35	126
3/ Hamlet	Angels and Ministers of Grace defend us :	1.00	128
4/ Ghost	But soft, me thinkes I [scent] the Mornings Ayre ;	1.40	129
5/ Hamlet	Oh all you host of Heaven! Oh Earth ; what els?	1.00	131
#'s 6 - 8: Hamlet And Thoughts Of Revenge			
6/ Hamlet	I so, God buy'ye : Now I am alone.	2.50	132
7/ King	Oh my offence is ranke, it smels to heaven,	2.00	134
8/ Hamlet	Now might I do it pat, now he is praying,	1.10	136
#'s 9 - 12: Hamlet & Ophelia			
9/ Polonius	Tis told me {Hamlet} hath very oft of late	1.35	137
10/ Ophelia	Alas my Lord, I have beene so affrighted.	1.10	139
11/ Hamlet	Get thee to a Nunnerie.	1.10	140
12/ Ophelia	O what a Noble minde is heere o're-throwne?	0.40	141
#'s 13 - 16: Hamlet And Self Definition			
13/ Hamlet	To be, or not to be, that is the Question :	1.45	142
14/ Hamlet	I will tell you why {you were sent for;} . . .	0.55	144
15/ Hamlet	I do not well understand that.	0.50	145
16/ Hamlet	Alas poore Yorick, I knew him Horatio,	1.10	146
#'s 17 - 18: Hamlet & The Players			
17/ Polonius	My Lord, I have Newes to tell you.	0.30	147
18/ Hamlet	Speake the Speech I pray you, as I pronounc'd	2.00	148
#'s 19: Polonius & Laertes			
19/ Polonius	Yet heere Laertes? Aboord, aboord for shame,	1.30	149
#'s 20 - 25: The Decline And Death Of Ophelia & Laertes			
20/ Ophelia	***How should I your true love know from another one ?***	0.50	151
21/ Ophelia	Ile make an end ont.	0.45	152
22/ Queen	One woe doth tread upon anothers heele,	1.00	153
23/ Clown	Is she to bee buried in Christian buriall,	1.00	154
24/ Priest	Her Obsequies have bin as farre inlarg'd,	0.40	155
25/ Laertes	I am justly kill'd with mine owne Treacherie.	0.40	156

SPEECHES BY GENDER		Speech #(s)
SPEECHES FOR WOMEN (5)		
Ophelia	**Traditional & Today:** young woman	#10, #12, #20, #21
Queene	**Traditional & Today:** woman old enough to have an adult son	#22
SPEECHES FOR EITHER GENDER (1)		
Priest	**Traditional:** middle-aged man and older **Today:** any age, any gender	#24
SPEECHES FOR MEN (19)		
Hamlet	**Traditional & Today:** young man	#1, #3, #5, #6, #8, #11, #13, #14, #15, #16, #18
King	**Traditional & Today:** younger middle aged man or older	#2, #7
Ghost	**Traditional & Today:** middle aged man or older	#4
Polonius	**Traditional & Today:** older male	#9, #17, #19
Clown	**Traditional:** early middle-aged man and older **Today:** male, any age	#23
Laertes	**Traditional & Today:** young man	#25

HAMLET

#'s 1 - 5: Hamlet, His Father, & Claudius

1/ Hamlet **Oh that this too too solid Flesh, would melt,** 1.2.129 - 159

Background: Hamlet's father has died, murdered by his brother, Hamlet's uncle Claudius. Claudius, to secure his claim to the Danish throne, has married Gertrude, Hamlet's mother, thus displacing Hamlet who by rights should be king. The death and marriage (an act in some Elizabethan eyes very akin to incest) took place two months ago, and Claudius has just publicly reprimanded Hamlet for still appearing in mourning clothes for his father (see speech #2 below). In addition, while Hamlet's contemporary Laertes has been given permission to leave the court to go to Paris, Hamlet's bid to return to his studies at the university of Wittenberg (at the time one of the finest philosophy universities the world has ever known) has been publicly blocked, in part by the wishes of his mother. Finally, for the first time in the play, he is alone.

Style: solo

Where: the great hall of the castle at Elsinore **To Whom:** audience and self

# of Lines: 31 **Probable Timing:** 1.30 minutes

Modern Text

1/ Hamlet

1 O* that this too too [sallied] △flesh, would melt,
Thaw, and resolve itself* into a △dew!
Or that the Everlasting had not fix'd
His △canon* 'gainst self*-slaughter !

2 O God, [ ] God!

3 How weary, stale, flat, and unprofitable
[Seem]* to me all the uses of this world!

4 Fie on't,◊ [ah fie!] 'tis an unweeded △garden
That grows* to △seed, △things rank and gross* in △nature
Possess* it merely*.

5 That it should come to this !
But two months dead, △nay, not so much, not two . †

6 So excellent a △king, that was to this
[Hyperion,] to a △satyr*, so loving to my △mother
That he might not [beteem] the winds* of heaven
Visit her face too roughly.

7 Heaven and △earth,
Must I remember ? †

8 Why, she [should] hang on him,
As if increase* of △appetite had grown*
By what it fed on, and yet within a month - ◊
Let me not think* on't ! †

9 Frailty, thy name is woman ! -

10 A little △month, or ere those shoes* were old
With which she followed my poor* △father's body,
Like Niobe, all tears* - ◊ why, she, even she - ◊

The surprising switches and sudden lack of releases support the idea of a thinker under strain, F's orthography – especially the staccato F #9 – #14 suggestive of mental swamping (reduced by the modern texts' resetting the text as mt. #10 - 11, suggesting both passionate thinking as well as the bi-polar condition somewhat akin to the thought processes of a manic-depressive.

- tracing the unembellished moments throughout the speech clearly illustrates the three disruptions from which Hamlet's pain and (self-) questioning stems

  "How weary, stale, flat, and unprofitable/[Seemes] to me all the uses of this world?/Fie on't?",

  first the pain of the death of his father

  "That it should come to this : /But two months dead"

  and (including the following part phrases) the way his mother was with his father

  "Must I remember: why she would hang on him'

  then, the fact that the attraction of Claudius has proven too much for her

  " ; and yet within a month?" "Why she, even she." "She married. O most wicked speed"

  and finally that Hamlet finds himself powerless to do anything

  "for I must hold my tongue."

- both the short sentences (all with explosive sentence ending punctuation)

  "O God, O God!"; "Fie on't?"; "Why she, even she?"; "O Heaven!' and "Within a Moneth?"

  and surround phrases show why, where, and just how deeply the pain is embedded, especially the six phrases that run in sequence from F #5 into F #6

  " . Oh fie, fie, 'tis an unweeded Garden/That growes to Seed : Things rank,and grosse in Nature/Possesse it meerely . That it should come to this :/But two months dead : Nay, not so much ; not two,/So excellent a King, that was to this/Hiperion to a Satyre : "

First Folio

1/ Hamlet

1 Oh that this too too [solid] Flesh, would melt,
Thaw, and resolve it selfe into a Dew : +
Or that the Everlasting had not fixt
His Cannon 'gainst Selfe-slaughter. +

2 O God, [O] God!

3 How weary, stale, flat, and unprofitable
[Seemes] to me all the uses of this world? +

4 Fie on't?

5 [Oh fie,+ fie+], 'tis an unweeded Garden
That growes to Seed :x Things rank,x and grosse in Nature
Possesse it meerely.

6 That it should come to this : +
But two months dead :x Nay, not so much ; x not two,
So excellent a King, that was to this
[Hiperion] to a Satyre :x so loving to my Mother,
That he might not [beteene] the windes of heaven
Visit her face too roughly.

7 Heaven and Earth+
Must I remember : why+ she [would] hang on him,
As if encrease of Appetite had growne
By what it fed on ; x and yet within a month?

8 Let me not thinke on't : + Frailty, thy name is woman. +

9 A little Month, or ere those shooes were old,x
With which she followed my poore Fathers body+
Like Niobe, all teares.

{ctd. over}

O [God], ◊ a beast that wants discourse of $^{\Delta}$reason
Would have mourn'd longer - married with [my] $^{\Delta}$uncle*,
My $^{\Delta}$father's $^{\Delta}$brother : but no more like my $^{\Delta}$father,
[Than] I to Hercules.
11 Within a $^{\Delta}$month* , ◊
Ere yet the salt of most unrighteous $^{\Delta}$tears*
Had left the flushing [in] her galled* eyes,
She married ◊ - O most wicked speed : to post
With such dexterity to $^{\Delta}$incestuous sheets ! †
12 It is not, nor it cannot come to good, ◊
But break* my heart, for I must hold my tongue.

" . Heaven and Earth/Must I remember : . . . ; and yet within a month ?/Let me not thinke on't : Frailty, thy name is woman . "
" : but no more like my Father,/Then I to Hercules . "
" . O most wicked speed, to post/With such dexterity to Incestuous sheets : /It is not, nor it cannot come to good ."

• as befits a one-time student of philosophy (Wittenberg being one of the most noted Philosophy universities in the western world), the speech starts off strongly intellectually (F #1-2, 8/3) as he establishes his wish for death

• and after the virtually unembellished admission of his deep discontent is made (F #3, 0/1), as the circumstances causing his grief are listed one after the other (F #5-#9) not surprisingly he becomes quite passionate (9/8)

• then as he focuses more on his mother, Gertrude (the 'she' of F #10), so he first becomes unembellished, a dangerous calm perhaps – especially considering the determinedly intellectual dismissal both of her (essentially as a 'Beast' that lacks 'Reason') and her hasty marriage to (in Hamlet's eyes) the vastly inferior brother (Claudius) of her late husband (7/1, F #11-12)

• and then, perhaps surprisingly, as he cannot seem to let go of the 'wicked' speed of her 'Incestuous' behaviour, he is more controlled than might be expected (3/4, F #13-16, the last six and half lines of the speech) – though somewhat passionate the partial internalisation of feelings perhaps could be seen as a foreshadowing of the dangers to come, both to himself and his mother

10 Why+ she, even she.
11 (xO [Heaven]! x
12 A beast that wants discourse of Reason
Would have mourn'd longerx) married with [mine] Unkle,
My Fathers Brother : but no more like my Father,
[Then] I to Hercules.
13 Within a Moneth?
14 Ere yet the salt of most unrighteous Teares
Had left the flushing [of] her gauled eyes,
She married.
15 O most wicked speed,+ to post
With such dexterity to Incestuous sheets : +
It is not, nor it cannot come to good.
16 But breake my heart, for I must hold my tongue.

2/ King **'Tis sweet and commendable** 1.2.87 - 117

Background: This is Claudius' public reprimand of Hamlet's continuing to publicly mourn for his father, even to the extent of still wearing mourning clothes, two months after his father's death - all against his mother's wishes.

Style: one on one address for a larger group to hear

Where: the great hall of the castle at Elsinore **To Whom:** Hamlet, in front of his mother Gertrude, Polonius and his children Laertes and Ophelia, and 'lords attendant'

# of Lines: 32 **Probable Timing: 1.35 minutes**

Modern Text

2/ King
1 'Tis sweet and commendable in your $^{\Delta}$nature Hamlet,
To give these mourning duties to your $^{\Delta}$father. †
2 But you must know, your $^{\Delta}$father lost a $^{\Delta}$father,
That $^{\Delta}$father lost, lost his, and the $^{\Delta}$survivor bound
In filial* $^{\Delta}$obligation, for some term*
To do obsequious $^{\Delta}$sorrow.
3 But to persever
In obstinate $^{\Delta}$condolement is a course

• F's opening of two short lines (7/6 syllables) allows Claudius a moment before starting to speak, and another before starting the third line (perhaps as if he were deliberately drawing the attention of everyone in the room before starting and continuing, or as if he were taking great care to control himself): most modern texts follow Q2 in setting these two short Ff lines as one thirteen syllable line as if he starts with an outburst

• as Claudius begins by expounding a general maxim as to the inevitability of death, he seems to be taking care not to let his feelings get away with him (9/2, F #1)

• but as he begins to show how much Hamlet has stepped over the line in 'obstinate Condolement' his passions start to flow (5/4, F #2 and F #3's first three and a half lines)

First Folio

2/ King
1 'Tis sweet and commendable →
In your Nature Hamlet+
To give these mourning duties to your Father :
But you must know, your Father lost a Father,
That Father lost, lost his, and the Surviver bound
In filiall Obligation, for some terme
To do obsequious Sorrow.
2 But to persever
In obstinate Condolement,x is a course

Of impious stubbornness*, ◊ 'tis unmanly grief*,
It shows* a will most incorrect to △heaven,
A △heart unfortified, [or] △mind* impatient,
An △understanding simple, and unschool'd:
For what we know must be, and is as common
As any the most vulgar thing to sense,
Why should we in our peevish △opposition
Take it to heart?
4 Fie*, 'tis a fault to △heaven,
A fault against the △dead, a fault to △nature,
To △reason most absurd, whose common △theme*
Is death of △fathers, and who still hath cried,
From the first △corse* till he that died* to-day,
"This must be so."
5 We pray you throw to earth
This unprevailing* woe, and think* of us
As of a △father, △for let the world take note
You are the most immediate to our △throne,
And with no less* △nobility of △love
[Than]that which dearest △father bears* his △son*
Do I impart towards you.
6 For your intent
In going back* to △school* in Wittenberg,
It is most retrograde to our desire,
And we beseech you bend you to remain*
Here* in the cheer* and comfort of our eye,
Our chiefest* △courtier, △cousin*, and our △son*.

• yet the stinging rebuke 'For,x what we know must be, and is as common/As any the most vulgar thing to sence,' is icy calm in its two line lack of embellishment, as if the velvet glove was off at last, with the extra breath-thought (marked ,x) allowing Claudius a slight pause (for effect?) before the slap is so effectively administered

• and then, quite brilliantly in the political sense, the reason why this should be known, it being a fault to 'Heaven', 'Dead', Nature', and 'Reason', is advanced intellectually (8/4, F #3's last line and a half and all of F #4)

• F #5's plea to Hamlet to give up his 'woe' and think of Claudius 'As of a Father' is doubly emotional (1/2, and ending with the only emotional semicolon of the speech) – though whether this is genuine or an act of calculated public rhetoric is up to each actor to decide

• while the ensuing 'good news' public announcement that Hamlet is 'most immediate to our Throne', offset by the bad news refusal to let Hamlet return to 'Wittenberg', seems well under intellectual control (8/5 – the last four lines of F #5 and the first two and a half of F #6), the announcement of Hamlet as Claudius' successor is broken up by two more extra breath-thoughts - whether this is another deliberate use to enhance the announcement or because Claudius is somewhat disturbed at having to make such a public statement is again up to each actor to decide

• interestingly, while the last three line wrap-up of 'we beseech you . . . to remain' starts out emotionally (0/4), the final flourish of how Hamlet should consider himself as 'Courtier Cosin, and our Sonne' is strongly intellectual (3/2, the last line of the speech) – though underneath the apparent honesty the extra breath-thought (,x) preceding 'bend you to remain' smacks much of the iron fist hidden within the velvet glove

Of impious stubbornnesse.
3 'Tis unmanly greefe,
It shewes a will most incorrect to Heaven,
A Heart unfortified, [a] Minde impatient,
An Understanding simple, and unschool'd:
For,x what we know must be, and is as common
As any the most vulgar thing to sence,
Why should we in our peevish Opposition
Take it to heart?
4 Fye, 'tis a fault to Heaven,
A fault against the Dead, a fault to Nature,
To Reason most absurd, whose common Theame
Is death of Fathers, and who still hath cried,
From the first Coarse,x till he that dyed to day,
This must be so.
5 We pray you throw to earth
This unprevayling woe, and thinke of us
As of a Father; x For let the world take note,x
You are the most immediate to our Throne,
And with no lesse Nobility of Love,x
[Then] that which deerest Father beares his Sonne,x
Do I impart towards you.
6 For your intent
In going backe to Schoole in Wittenberg,
It is most retrograde to our desire: x
And we beseech you,x bend you to remaine
Heere in the cheere and comfort of our eye,
Our cheefest Courtier+ Cosin, and our Sonne.

3/ Hamlet **Angels and Ministers of Grace defend us :** 1.4.39 - 57

Background: Faring no better than the soldiers in questioning the Ghost, Horatio has brought Hamlet to the battlements to see what effect his presence might have.

Style: one on one as part of a four-handed scene

Where: on the battlements of Elsinore castle **To Whom:** the Ghost, in front of Horatio and the soldier Marcellus

# of Lines: 19 **Probable Timing: 1.00 minutes**

Modern Text

3/ Hamlet

1 Angels and Δministers of Δgrace defend us! †

2 Be thou a Δspirit of health, or Δgoblin damn'd,
Bring with thee airs* from Δheaven, or blasts from Δhell,
Be thy [intents] wicked, or charitable,
Thou com'st in such a questionable shape
That I will speak* to thee.

3 I'll call thee Hamlet,
King, Δfather, Δroyal* Dane. †

4 Oh, [ ], answer me ! †

5 Let me not burst in Δignorance, but tell
Why thy Δcanoniz'd bones Δhearsed in death,
Have burst their cerements*; why the Δsepulchre*,
Wherein we saw thee quietly [interr'd],
Hath op'd his ponderous and Δmarble jaws*
To cast thee up again* .

6 What may this mean*,
That thou, dead Δcorse*, again* in complete* steel*
Revisits thus the glimpses of the Δmoon*,
Making Δnight hideous*, Δand we fools* of Δnature
So horridly to shake our disposition
With thoughts beyond [the] reaches of our Δsouls*? ◊

7 Say why is this? wherefore? what should we do*?

Hamlet's strength of mind and purpose can be seen in that despite facing an apparition he still is able to maintain solid intellectual discipline, at least for the first two sentences of the speech (16/6, F #1-2) - and even in the last feverish questioning his passions rather than rampant emotions take over (6/9, F #3)[1].

- considering the potential fear shown by others who have faced it, his steadfastness and courage is even more remarkable, as shown in the quiet of the calm unembellished lines, not only when challenging the Ghost
  "Be thy events wicked or charitable,/Thou com'st in such a questionable shape"
  but also realising the possible results of any intercourse with it
  "So horridly to shake our disposition/With thoughts beyond thee"
  and especially when demanding point blank an explanation
  "Say, why is this? wherefore?"
- the few surround phrases define the key moments of Hamlet's struggle, from the opening ' . Angels and Ministers of Grace defend us : ' through to
  " . Ile call thee Hamlet,/King, Father, Royall Dane : Oh, [oh], answer me,/Let me not burst in Ignorance ; "
  and the highly disturbed broken off questioning any basic belief which
  " ; reaches of our Soules,/Say, why is this ? wherefore ? what should we doe ? "
- the only moment emotion breaks through is at the top of F #3 as he repeats his demand that the Ghost tell him 'What may this meane?' (1/5, F #3's first one and half lines), though this quickly turns to intellectual passion once the specifics of time and place are stated (5/3 the next four lines)
- and then he reveals his strength once again, for the final line reiterating his demand for information is almost completely calm and unembellished (0/1)

First Folio

3/ Hamlet

1 Angels and Ministers of Grace defend us :
Be thou a Spirit of health, or Goblin damn'd,
Bring with thee ayres from Heaven, or blasts from Hell,
Be thy [events] wicked+ or charitable,
Thou com'st in such a questionable shape
That I will speake to thee.

2 Ile call thee Hamlet,
King, Father, Royall Dane : Oh, [oh],[2] answer me, +
Let me not burst in Ignorance ;x but tell
Why thy Canoniz'd bones Hearsed in death,
Have burst their cerments,+ why the Sepulcher+
Wherein we saw thee quietly [enurn'd],
Hath op'd his ponderous and Marble jawes,x
To cast thee up againe?x

3 What may this meane?+
That thou+ dead Coarse+ againe in compleat steele,x
Revisits thus the glimpses of the Moone,
Making Night hidious?x And we fooles of Nature
So horridly to shake our disposition,x
With thoughts beyond [thee;x] reaches of our Soules,
\+
Say,x why is this? wherefore? what should we doe?

---

[1] thanks to the Elizabethan/early Jacobean orthography which allows a capital letter to follow a period, question mark , or exclamation mark without necessarily indicating that it is the start of a new sentence, what is shown here as a single sentence could just as easily be treated as different sentences

[2] Q2 and some modern texts = 'O' (a ten syllable line), Ff = 'Oh, Oh' (creating eleven syllables)

4/ Ghost **But soft, me thinkes I [scent] the Mornings Ayre ;** 1.5.58 - 91

Background: The Ghost has succeeded in separating Hamlet from his fellows, and convinced Hamlet that it really is the ghost of his father. Before the break of day, at which time he must disappear back into the 'sulphurous and tormenting flames', the Ghost has much to tell his son. He has already imparted the hitherto only suspected news that 'The Serpent that did sting thy Father's life,/Now weares his Crowne', and that, in addition, Claudius 'Won to his shamefull Lust/The will of my most seeming vertuous Queene', claiming that Gertrude though seeming the epitome of 'Vertue' in fact has shown herself as the embodiment of 'Lust'. Sensing the dawn, the Ghost must now sketch in the final details, including what he wants Hamlet to do.

Style: as part of a two-handed scene

Where: on the battlements of Elsinore castle **To Whom:** Hamlet

# of Lines: 34 **Probable Timing: 1.40 minutes**

Modern Text

4/ Ghost

1 But soft, methinks* I [scent* the △morning] △air*,
Brief* let me be. †
2 Sleeping within mine △orchard,
My custom* always* in the afternoon*,
Upon my secure hour* thy △uncle stole,
With juice* of cursed [hebona] in a △vial*,
And in the △porches of △mine ears* did pour*
The leprous* △distillment*, whose effect
Holds such an enmity [wi'th] blood* of △man
That swift as △quicksilver it courses through
The natural* △gates and [△alleys] of the △body,
And with a sudden* vigor* it doth posset
And curd, like [△eager*] droppings into △milk*,
The thin and wholesome* blood. †
3 So did it mine,
And a most instant △tetter [bark'd] about,
Most △lazar-like, with vile and loathsome crust,
All my smooth △body.
4 Thus was I, sleeping, by a △brother's hand
Of △life, of △crown*, [of] △queen*, at once dispatch'd,
Cut off even in the △blossoms* of my △sin*,
Unhous'led*, disappointed, unanel'd*,
No reck'ning* made, but sent to my account
With all my imperfections on my head. †
5 O*, horrible, O*, horrible, most horrible ! †
6 If thou hast nature in thee, bear* it not;
Let not the △royal* △bed of Denmark* be
A △couch for △luxury and damned △incest.

The fact that eleven of the sixteen pieces of major punctuation are semicolons points to just what an emotional state the Ghost is now in (modern texts turn seven into commas, two into periods, one into an exclamation mark, setting only one of F's semicolons as such.

- the passionate urgency of the first three lines (scenting the 'Mornings Ayre', 4/6) are heightened by being set as three surround phrases, themselves further heightened by use of semicolons
- and the Ghost's passions continue as Hamlet is told how 'thy Uncle . . . in mine eares did poure/The leaperous Distilment;' (5/6, the next three and a half lines), though its 'effect' coursing through his Body becomes intellectual (5/2, the next three lines set between the two semicolons), at least momentarily
- the greater details of the 'Distilment's' curdling like eager 'droppings into Milke' become emotional (2/4, the two and a half lines to the next colon), which leads to one of the few unembellished passages in the speech, the incredibly bleak ' : so did it mine ; ', its iciness made even more powerful by being both a surround phrase and monosyllabic as well
- this bleakness leads to a purely intellectual description of what happened to his body (3/0, F #1's last two and a half lines)
- while the summation of what he lost ('Life', 'Crowne' and 'Queene') seems to be still primarily intellectual (4/2, F #2's first two lines), the semicolon ending the passage leads to a passionate one line acknowledgement of how he died as a Sinner since, as the three unembellished lines immediately following bleakly explain, he had not made confession
- the recollection of dying as a sinner moves the Ghost to two surround phrases, the first of pain, the second, the emotional start to urging Hamlet to revenge " : Oh horrible, Oh horrible, most horrible : /If thou hast nature in thee beare it not ; "
- the terse two line explanation as to why Hamlet should avenge the Ghost's death (for 'the Royall Bed of Denmarke') is strongly intellectual (6/2, F #2's last two lines), yet the warning for Hamlet to beware of both damaging his mind and to avoid harming his mother - even though she has been a willing party to the incest and thus destruction of the house of Denmark's reputation - is passionate (4/4, F #3), heightened by opening with two emotional surround phrases

First Folio

4/ Ghost

1 But soft, me thinkes I [sent the Mornings] Ayre ; x
Briefe let me be : Sleeping within mine Orchard,
My custome alwayes in the afternoone ; x
Upon my secure hower thy Uncle stole+
With juyce of cursed [Hebenon] in a Violl,
And in the Porches of △mine eares did poure
The leaperous Distilment ; x whose effect
Holds such an enmity [with] bloud of Man, x
That swift as Quick-silver, x it courses through
The naturall Gates and [Allies] of the Body ; x
And with a sodaine vigour it doth posset
And curd, like [Aygre] droppings into Milke,
The thin and wholsome blood : so did it mine ; x
And a most instant Tetter [bak'd] about,
Most Lazar-like, with vile and loathsome crust,
All my smooth Body.
2 Thus was I, sleeping, by a Brothers hand, x
Of Life, of Crowne, [and] Queene+ at once dispatcht ;
Cut off even in the Blossomes of my Sinne,
Unhouzzled, disappointed, unnaneld,
No reckoning made, but sent to my account
With all my imperfections on my head ;
Oh+ horrible, Oh+ horrible, most horrible : +
If thou hast nature in thee+ beare it not ;
Let not the Royall Bed of Denmarke be
A Couch for Luxury and damned Incest.

{ctd. over}

7 But howsoever thou [pursues] this △act,
Taint not thy mind, nor let thy △soul* contrive
Against thy △mother [aught] . †
8 Leave her to heaven,
And to those △thorns* that in her bosom* lodge
To prick* and sting her.
9 Fare thee well at once ! †
10 The △glow-worm* shows* the △matin* to be near*,
And gins to pale his uneffectual* △fire . †
11 Adieu*, adieu*, [adieu]! remember me.

• the final sentence's surround phrases ' . Fare thee well at once ; ' and ' . Adue, adue, Hamlet : remember me . ' all unembellished save for Hamlet's name, could well indicate that the Ghost is fighting with his last strength (especially with the seemingly short spelling of 'adue') to ensure his message is not lost on Hamlet as he is forced to disappear by the approach of morning

3 But howsoever thou [pursuest] this Act,
Taint not thy mind ;ₓ nor let thy Soule contrive
Against thy Mother [ought] ; leave her to heaven,
And to those Thornes that in her bosome lodge,ₓ
To pricke and sting her.
4 Fare thee well at once ; +
The Glow-worme showes the Matine to be neere,
And gins to pale his uneffectuall Fire :
Adue, adue, [ ] Hamlet :+ remember me.

5/ Hamlet **Oh all you host of Heaven! Oh Earth ; what els?** 1.5.92 - 112

Background: The Ghost has left, leaving Hamlet alone for the second time in the play.

Style: solo

Where: on the battlements of Elsinore castle **To Whom:** self, and direct audience address

# of Lines: 20 **Probable Timing: 1.00 minutes**

Modern Text

5/ Hamlet

1 O* all you host of Δheaven!
2 O* Δearth! †
3 What else*!
4 And shall I couple Δhell?
5 O* fie, hold, [hold,] my heart,
And you, my sinews*, grow not instant Δold,
But bear* me stiffly* up. †
6 Remember thee!
7 [Ay], thou poor* Δghost, [whiles] memory holds a seat*
In this distracted Δglobe. †
8 Remember thee!
9 Yea, from the Δtable of my Δmemory
I'll wipe away all trivial* fond Δrecords,
All saws* of Δbooks*, all forms*, all pressures* past
That youth and observation copied*, there,
And thy Δcommandment all alone shall live
Within the Δbook* and Δvolume of my Δbrain*,
Unmix'd with baser matter. †
10 Yes, [ ] by Δheaven! †
11 O* most pernicious woman!
12 O* Δvillain*, Δvillain*, smiling, damned Δvillain*!
13 My Δtables - [ ]; meet it is I set it down* [3]
That one may smile, and smile, and be a Δvillain*! †
14 At least I'm sure it may be so in Denmark*. †
15 So Δuncle* there you are. †
16 Now to my word:
It is, "Adieu*, Δadieu*! Δremember me." †
17 I have sworn't.

The impact of the scene creates a gigantic brainstorm within Hamlet, and F's orthography shows where, how, and why, for within the twenty passionate lines of the speech (28/23 overall) there are eighteen surround phrases, six (logical) colons, ten (emotional) semicolons, and two rare (for an Elizabethan/early Jacobean text) exclamation marks.

- the three moments of mental clarity, where intellect dominates and he manages to gain some small measure of self-control, are those where Hamlet assures the departed Ghost that he will be remembered, F #5 (3/2); that his 'Commandment all alone shall live/Within the Booke and Volume of my Braine . . .' (5/2); and the last line of the speech ending with 'I have sworn't' ((3/0), heightened by being only one of two very short unembellished monosyllabic surround phrases in the speech – after all the passion let loose throughout the speech, finally no more need be said

- until the end of the speech nearly all of the semicoloned surround phrases reflect his almost losing himself in the shock of what he has just learned, viz. F #2's " . Oh Earth ; what els ? ", F #4's " hold my heart ; /And you my sinnewes, grow not instant Old ; /But beare me stiffely up : ", and F #6's " ; yes, yes, by Heaven : "

- the most released moment in the speech is the double condemnation of both his mother ('most pernicious woman!') and Claudius (the thrice repeated 'Villaine') – /4 in just ten words, the end of F #6 and the short F #7

- then, as he tries to find a concrete way of setting down all the Ghost has told him, all mental control seems to disappear, for F sets the vastly onrushed and totally ungrammatical #8 (split into five rational sentences by most modern texts, thus diminishing the moment when Hamlet finally breaks), the whole formed by seven consecutive surround phrases shifting rapidly between the need for a permanent record of how ('My Tables'); the sidebar explanations as to why, especially in Denmark; the final knowledge of his Unckle's hand in his father's death; Hamlet's promise to keep his word; the farewell to the Ghost; and the swearing to action

- and this final sentence is marked by the first four lines of passion (5/4) suddenly turning to a final line of intellectual farewell and icy resolve to action, all set with seven pieces of heavy punctuation, five of which are semicolons – a veritable brainstorm indeed

First Folio

5/ Hamlet

1 Oh all you host of Heaven!
2 Oh Earth ; +what els? +
3 And shall I couple Hell?
4 Oh fie :x hold+ [ ] my heart ; x
And you+ my sinnewes, grow not instant Old ; x
But beare me stiffely up : Remember thee? +
5 [I], thou poore Ghost, [while] memory holds a seate
In this distracted Globe : Remember thee? +
6 Yea, from the Table of my Memory,x
Ile wipe away all triviall fond Records,
All sawes of Bookes, all formes, all presures past,x
That youth and observation coppied there ; x
And thy Commandment all alone shall live
Within the Booke and Volume of my Braine,
Unmixt with baser matter ; yes, [yes], by Heaven : +
Oh most pernicious woman!
7 Oh Villaine, Villaine, smiling+ damned Villaine!
8 My Tables, [my Tables] ; meet it is I set it downe,x
That one may smile, and smile+ and be a Villaine ; +
At least I'm sure it may be so in Denmarke ;
So Unckle there you are : now to my word ; +
It is ; x Adue, Adue, + Remember me : I have sworn't.

[3] most modern texts follow Q2 and split the 13 syllable F line into a short line followed by a regular line of pentameter (3/10 syllables): the F length allows for the moment to run away with Hamlet, the Q2 setting allows him to regain self-control: the same resetting takes place with the last line of this sentence: this also applies to the last line of the F speech where modern restructuring sets a 13 syllable Ff line as two short lines (6/7 syllables)

#'S 6 - 8: HAMLET AND THOUGHTS OF REVENGE

6/ Hamlet **I so, God buy'ye : Now I am alone.** 2.2.549 -605

Background: Already on edge from the ghost's intervention, and suspicious of having two not particularly close friends (Rosincrance and Guildensterne) join him with effusive greetings, Hamlet has quickly deciphered that Claudius and Gertrude have begun to set spies upon him. Further unbalanced by such a blatant act, and having savagely stripped the truth from them (see speech #14 below), Hamlet is further disturbed when an 'old Friend', the leader of a troop of players due to play at the castle, seems to slip so easily into a genuine mood of disturbed active revenge when re-enacting a speech describing Hecuba's laments for her recently and unjustly slaughtered husband Priam. The following occurs when Hamlet is left alone once more.

Style: solo

Where: the Lobby of the Castle **To Whom:** self and audience

# of Lines: 57 **Probable Timing: 2.50** minutes

Modern Text

6/ Hamlet

1 Ay* so, God buy [to you]. †
2 Now I am alone.
3 O*, what a Δrogue and Δpeasant* slave am I!
4 Is it not monstrous that this Δplayer here*,
But in a Δfiction*, in a dream* of Δpassion,
Could force his soul* so to his whole conceit
That from her working all his visage [wann'd],
Tears* in his eyes, distraction in's Δaspect,
A broken voice*, and his whole Δfunction suiting
With Δforms* to his Δconceit?
5 And all for nothing?
6 For Hecuba!
7 What's Hecuba to him, or he to Hecuba,
That he should weep* for her?
8 What would he do*
Had he the Δmotive and the Δcue for passion
That I have?
9 He would drown* the Δstage with tears*,
And cleave the general* ear* with horrid speech,
Make mad the guilty, and appall* the free,
Confound the ignorant, and amaze indeed
The very [facultes] of Δeyes and Δears*.
10 Yet I,
A dull and muddy-mettled* Δrascal*, peak*
Like John a-dreams*, unpregnant of my cause,
And can say nothing; Δno, not for a Δking,
Upon whose property and most dear* life,
A damn'd defeat* was made.

With the surprising lack of major punctuation and therefore surround phrases, it would seem that, unlike speech #5 above, this speech sets up stream of consciousness realisations rather than a series of rational step by step discoveries – and this applies even after sentence F#21, mt #20, when Hamlet begins to explore what to do next, which suggests that his first ideas are simply ideas released in their first flush, warts and all, not yet plans fully formulated.

- in acknowledging his isolation and, in his own eyes, his diminished status the speech starts with two emphatically short intellectual sentences (4/1, F #1-2), the first heightened by being set as two surround phrases
- his first reaction to the First Player's ability 'in a dreame of Passion,/Could force his soule to his whole conceit' is passionate (3/4 F #3's first three lines), then hushed for the first unembellished line in the speech
  "That from her working, all his visage [warm'd];"
  heightened by ending with an emotional semicolon
- then the wonder of how it was done, and for someone who meant nothing to the Player, becomes strongly intellectual (9/5, the remainder of F #3 through to F #7, seven and a half lines in all)
- it's as if the just finished performance of the Player has caused Hamlet to re-assess both himself and his own actions, for F #8's imagined end-result of how the Player would behave if he had Hamlet's 'Motive and the Cue for passion', is a mixture of emotion (3/6) and quiet unembellished wonder
  "Make mad the guilty, and . . . /Confound the ignorant, and amaze indeed,"
- which leads to his continuing denial of his own self-worth, his self-assessment as a 'muddy-metled Rascall' being passionate (4/5, F #9)
- his inescapable short sentence demand of himself 'Am I a Coward?" (1/0), is anwered with more emotion within the passion (6/10 in just three and half lines) by F #11's imagined (?) insults that have been/will be piled upon him

First Folio

6/ Hamlet

1 I so, God buy'[ye]: Now I am alone.
2 Oh+ what a Rogue and Pesant slave am I? +
3 Is it not monstrous that this Player heere,
But in a Fixion, in a dreame of Passion,
Could force his soule so to his whole conceit,x
That from her working,x all his visage [warm'd]; x
Teares in his eyes, distraction in's Aspect,
A broken voyce, and his whole Function suiting
With Formes,x to his Conceit?
4 And all for nothing?
5 For Hecuba? +
6 What's Hecuba to him, or he to Hecuba,
That he should weepe for her?
7 What would he doe,x
Had he the Motive and the Cue for passion
That I have?
8 He would drowne the Stage with teares,
And cleave the generall eare with horrid speech: x
Make mad the guilty, and apale the free,
Confound the ignorant, and amaze indeed,x
The very [faculty] of Eyes and Eares.
9 Yet I,
A dull and muddy-metled Rascall, peake
Like John a-dreames, unpregnant of my cause,
And can say nothing: x No, not for a King,
Upon whose property,x and most deere life,
A damn'd defeate was made.

11 Am I a Δcoward?
12 Who calls* me Δvillain*, breaks* my pate across*,
Plucks* off my Δbeard and blows* it in my face,
Tweaks* me by'th'Δnose, gives me the Δlie* i'th'Δthroat*
As deep* as to the Δlungs?
13 Who does me this?
14 Ha, ◊ ['swounds], I should take it ; for it cannot be
But I am Δpigeon-Δliver'd, and lack* Δgall
To make Δoppression bitter, or ere this
I should Δhave fatted all the Δregion Δkites
With this Δslave's Δoffal* . †
15 Bloody*, [ ] Δbawdy villain* !
Remorseless*, Δtreacherous, Δlecherous*, kindless* villain*.
[ ]
[ ]
16 [Why] ◊ what an Δass* am I?
17 [ ] This is most brave,
That I, the Δson* of [a dear* father murdered],
Prompted to my Δrevenge by Δheaven and Δhell,
Must like a Δwhore unpack* my heart with words,
And fall a -Δcursing like a very Δdrab,
A [stallion]?
18 Fie* upon't, Δfoh !
19 About, my [Δbrains*] !
20 [Hum] - I have heard
That guilty Δcreatures sitting at a Δplay
Have by the very cunning of the Δscene*
Been* struck* so to the soul*, that presently
They have proclaim'd their Δmalefactions: ◊
For Δ[murder], though it have no tongue, will speak*
With most miraculous* Δorgan.
21 I'll have these Δplayers
Play something like the murder of my Δfather
Before mine Δuncle*.
22 I'll observe his looks*,
I'll tent him to the quick* . †
23 If ['a do] blench,
I know my course.
24 The Δspirit that I have seen*
May be [a] Δdev'l*, and the Δdev'l* hath power
T'assume a pleasing shape, yea, and perhaps,

• the realisation that he would accept all the insults is bleakly unembellished
"Who does me this? / Ha? Why I should take it : "
the inescapable inevitabilty of the quiet realisation underscored by being set as two short sentences (F #12-13) followed by one of the few surround phrases in the speech

• Hamlet's proof of his being 'Pigeon-Liver'd' and lacking 'Gall' by the fact of not having yet (violently) dealt with his uncle is once more strongly (and thus perhaps as a result, frighteningly) intellectual (8/3 in F #14's five lines between the two colons)

• then the thought of scattering 'this Slaves Offall' (i.e. his uncle's) leads to a very passionate outburst, (4/4 in just the two lines comprising F #14's last line and a half plus the short F #15)

• F seems to suggest, admittedly highly ungrammatically, that before the outburst he does try to rein himself in via the syntactically incorrect colon after F #14's 'bloudy' – but the pause for control doesn't work and the spew leading to the cry for 'Vengeance' is released nevertheless: unfortunately, most modern texts follow Q2 and simply set a comma instead, allowing the flow into the outburst to continue unchecked

• then, when all seems, lost a self-deprecating sense of humour seems to save him, for via the two short sentences F #16-17 and the longer F #18, pouring scorn on himself for 'a Cursing like a very Drab', he, perhaps unconsciously, re-establishes a mental control (10/3) not seen in the previous eight sentences

• this results in a final passionate and presumably conscious attempt to stop himself from unnecessary dwelling on things past, in two short sentences (F #19-20, 2/2 in just six words), F #19's determination heightened by being composed of two short surround phrases ' . Fye upon't : Foh. About my Braine.'

• interestingly, here F allows this to spring out of his previous sentence unchecked, and the following sentence of rediscovered memory starts as a leap into the new idea by setting a thirteen syllable line (in all F sets just two longer overwrought lines, 11/13 syllables, though whether this is a matter of losing control or sheer excitement is up to each actor to decide): Q2 sets an even more overwrought opening (17 or 18/8 syllables)

'And fall a cursing like a very drab: a stallyon, fie upon't, foh./About my braines; hum, I have heard'

most modern texts set up three shorter lines as shown (7/8/10 syllables and add 'Hum'), totally altering the tenor of the moment, establishing pauses where none originally existed thus slowing down both the attempt at control and removing the leap into the new idea by restructuring the shaded passage as shown

• the belief that 'guilty Creatures sitting at a Play' can be 'strooke so to the soule' that they eventually confess their crimes hits him first intellectually (the idea, 3/1, F #21's first two lines) then emotionally (the confession, 1/3, F #21's last two lines), and then passionately (the idea that murder will out, 2/2, F #22)

10 Am I a Coward?
11 Who calles me Villaine? x breakes my pate a-crosse?x
Pluckes off my Beard,x and blowes it in my face? x
Tweakes me by'th'Nose?x gives me the Lye i'th'Throate,x
As deepe as to the Lungs?
12 Who does me this?
13 Ha?
14 [Why]+ I should take it : x for it cannot be,x
But I am Pigeon-Liver'd, and lacke Gall
To make Oppression bitter, or ere this,x
I should Δhave fatted all the Region Kites
With this Slaves Offall, bloudy : x [a] Bawdy villaine,+
Remorselesse, Treacherous, Letcherous, kindles villaine!x
15 Oh Vengeance!
16 [Who?]
17 What an Asse am I?
18 [I sure], this is most brave,
That I, the Sonne of [the Deere murthered],
Prompted to my Revenge by Heaven,x and Hell,
Must (xlike a Whorex) unpacke my heart with words,
And fall a Cursing like a very Drab,
A [Scullion]?
19 Fye upon't : x Foh. +
20 About+ my [Braine]. +
21 [ ] I have heard,x that guilty Creatures sitting at a Play, x
Have by the very cunning of the Scœne,x
Bene strooke so to the soule, that presently
They have proclaim'd their Malefactions.
22 For [Murther], though it have no tongue, will speake
With most myraculous Organ.
23 Ile have these Players,x
Play something like the murder of my Father,x
Before mine Unkle.
24 Ile observe his lookes,
Ile tent him to the quicke : If [he but] blench+
I know my course.
25 The Spirit that I have seene
May be [the] Divell, and the Divel hath power
T'assume a pleasing shape, yea+ and perhaps+

{ctd. over}

Out of my △weakness* and my △melancholy*,
As he is very potent with such △spirits,
Abuses me to damn* me.
25 I'll have grounds
More △relative [than] this - △the △play's the thing
Wherein I'll catch the △conscience of the △king.

• with the idea of having the Players play 'something like the murder of my father', he returns to intellect once more (perhaps at last he has found the answer as to how to "out" Claudius) and emotion floods back as the idea of closely examining his uncle for any sign of guilt is expressed (F #24, 2/1) the decision heightened by being set as two surround phrases

• the fear that the Ghost of his father may in fact be the 'Divell' and thus that he may be falling into a trap becomes passionate once more (6/5, F #25)

• yet, after all Hamlet has been through in this speech, his intellectual strength (and greatness?) returns in the final emotionall-controlled (5/0, F #26) double surround phrase resolve
" . Ile have grounds/More Relative then this : The Play's the thing,/Wherein Ile catch the Conscience of the King . "
it seems he is at last determined to act

Out of my Weaknesse,ₓ and my Melancholly,
As he is very potent with such Spirits,
Abuses me to damne me.
26 Ile have grounds
More Relative [then] this : ₓ The Play's the thing,ₓ
Wherein Ile catch the Conscience of the King.

7/ King **Oh my offence is ranke, it smels to heaven,** 3.2.36 - 72

Background: The bulk of the palace audience attending the players performance only know that for some reason Claudius became upset and stopped the show of 'The Murther of Gonzago' (more familiarly known by critics and scholars as 'The Mousetrap') . However, only he and Hamlet know how close the play came to mirroring how Claudius killed Hamlet's father (by pouring poison in his ear). Alone, Claudius, unsuccessfully, attempts to pray for forgiveness.

Style: solo

Where: a small alcove somewhere off the lobby of the castle **To Whom:** self, audience, and god

# of Lines: 39 **Probable Timing: 2.00 minutes**

Modern Text

7/ King
1 O* my offense* is rank*, it smells₊ to heaven,
It hath the primal* eldest curse upon't,
A △brother's [murder].
2 Pray can I not,
Though inclination be as sharp* as will. †
3 My stronger guilt, defeats my strong intent,
And like a man to double business* bound,
I stand in pause where I shall first begin,
And both neglect. †
4 What if this cursed hand
Were thicker [than] itself* with △brother's blood,
Is there not △rain enough in the sweet △heavens
To wash it white as △snow?
5 Whereto serves mercy,
But to confront the visage of △offense*?

In comparison to his earlier confident and usually in-control brow-beating of Hamlet (speech #2 above), the orthography of this speech shows a Claudius experiencing a very troubling process of self-exploration.

• the basis of Claudius' struggle can be seen in the very few surround phrases set for him, from F #2's
" . Pray can I not,/Though inclination be as sharpe as will : "
to the ironic mimicking of his own prayer
" . Forgive me my foule Murther : "
especially since he still possesses the rewards for which he murdered
" . My Crowne, mine owne Ambition, and my Queene : /May one be pardon'd, and retaine th'offence ? "
which leads to the hopeless realisation that
" . Oh limed soule, that strugling to be free,/Art more ingag'd : Helpe Angels, make assay : "

First Folio

7/ King
1 Oh my offence is ranke, it smels to heaven,
It hath the primall eldest curse upon't,
A Brothers [murther].
2 Pray can I not,
Though inclination be as sharpe as will:
My stronger guilt, defeats my strong intent,
And like a man to double businesse bound,
I stand in pause where I shall first begin,
And both neglect; what if this cursed hand
Were thicker [then] it selfe with Brothers blood,
Is there not Raine enough in the sweet Heavens
To wash it white as Snow?
3 Whereto serves mercy,
But to confront the visage of Offence?

6 And what's in Δprayer but this two-fold force,
To be forestalled ere we come to fall,
Or pardon'd being down*? ◊ then I'll look* up . †
7 My fault is past, ◊ Δbut, ΔO*, what form* of Δprayer
Can serve my turn*?
8 "Forgive me my foul* Δ[murder]"? †
9 That cannot be, since I am still posses'd
Of those effects for which I did the Δ[murder] : ◊
My Δcrown*, mine own* Δambition, and my Δqueen* . †
10 May one be pardon'd and retain* th'offense*?
11 In the corrupted currents of this world
Offense's gilded hand may shove by Δjustice,
And oft 'tis seen*, the wicked prize itself*
Buys* out the Δlaw, but 'tis not so above :
There is no shuffling, there the Δaction lies*
In his true Δnature, and we ourselves compell'd
Even to the teeth and forehead of our faults,
To give in evidence.
12 What then?
13 What rests?
14 Try what Δrepentance can.
15 What can it not?
16 Yet what can it, when one cannot repent?
17 O* wretched state!
18 O* bosom* black* as death!
19 O* limed soul*, that struggling* to be free,
Art more engag'd* ! †
20 Help*, Δangels ! †
21 Make assay,
Bow, stubborn* knees, and heart, with strings of Δsteel*,
Be soft as sinews* of the new-born* Δbabe ! †
22 All may be well.
23 My words fly* up, my thoughts remain below :
Words without thoughts never to Δheaven go.

- the depth of his struggle can be seen from the start in the mixture of emotion and unembellished lines (1/5, F #1 and the first five lines of F #2), the quiet, especially of F #2, pointing to the concentrated calm with which Claudius is examining his political and spiritual state
  "Pray can I not,/. . . / My stronger guilt, defeats my strong intent,/ . . . //I stand in pause where I shall first begin,/And both neglect;"
- however, and hardly surprisingly, the key questions, whether the heavens pardon him and 'Whereto serves mercy', become more intellectual (5/3, the remainder of F #2 and F #3, four lines in all)
- but the corollaries as to what constitutes 'Prayer' and 'what forme of Prayer/ Can serve my turne?' become emotional once more (2/5, F #4-6)
- then with the irony? despair? as Claudius voices the possible prayer (F #7), the reason why it cannot work (F #8), and the realisation that while in the human world the corrupt may win out 'tis not so above' he turns to passion (the first five and a half lines of F #9, 4/4)
- but then Claudius becomes bleakly focused, a lengthy quiet unembellished passage – save for the fascinatingly capitalised 'Repenteance' (F #9's last two lines through to F #14) marking when he realises he will eventually have to speak against himself
  "and we our selves compell'd/Even to the teeth and forehead of our faults,/To give in evidence. What then? What rests?/Try what Repentance can. What can it not?/Yet what can it, when one cannot repent?"
  the one released word of the passage being an intellectualisation of the key concept of 'Repentance', something Claudius has not hitherto explored
- then it seems that Claudius finally breaks down, for his self summation beginning with 'Oh wretched state!' (the two short sentences F #15-16, heightened by both ending in the rare - for Elizabethan texts - exclamation mark, and the opening surround phrase of F #17) is totally emotional (0/6)
- his subsequent surround phrase appeal ' : Helpe Angels, make assay : ' and the determined command to his 'knees' and 'heart' to 'bow' becomes passionate once more (4/5, the last three lines of F #17)
- the unembellished hope for success 'All may be well' (the end of F #17) is quickly diminished by an equally quiet realisation of failure (in the middle of F #18) 'my thoughts remain below/Words without thoughts' – this final acknowledgement surrounded by a moment of intellect and emotion (1/1)

4 And what's in Prayer,ₓ but this two-fold force,
To be fore-stalled ere we come to fall,
Or pardon'd being downe?
5 Then Ile looke up,
My fault is past.
6 But+ oh, what forme of Prayer
Can serve my turne?
7 Forgive me my foule [Murther] :
That cannot be, since I am still possest
Of those effects for which I did the [Murther].
8 My Crowne, mine owne Ambition, and my Queene :
May one be pardon'd,ₓ and retaine th'offence?
9 In the corrupted currants of this world,ₓ
Offences gilded hand may shove by Justice,
And oft 'tis seene, the wicked prize it selfe
Buyes out the Law ; ₓ but 'tis not so above,+
There is no shuffling, there the Action lyes
In his true Nature, and we our selves compell'd
Even to the teeth and forehead of our faults,
To give in evidence.
10 What then?
11 What rests?
12 Try what Repentance can.
13 What can it not?
14 Yet what can it, when one cannot repent?
15 Oh wretched state!
16 Oh bosome,ₓ blacke as death!
17 Oh limed soule, that strugling to be free,
Art more ingag'd : Helpe+ Angels, make assay : ₓ
Bow+ stubborne knees, and heart+ with strings of Steele,
Be soft as sinewes of the new-borne Babe,
All may be well.
18 My words flye up, my thoughts remain below,+
Words without thoughts,ₓ never to Heaven go.

8/ Hamlet **Now might I do it pat, now he is praying,** 3.2.73 - 96

Background: Hamlet comes across Claudius as Claudius attempts to pray - unattended, defenceless, and vulnerable. This seems a wonderful moment to take revenge - or is it?

Style: solo

Where: a small alcove somewhere off the lobby of the castle **To Whom:** self and audience, so that the praying Claudius does not hear

# of Lines: 22 **Probable Timing: 1.10 minutes**

Modern Text

8/ Hamlet

1 Now might I do it pat, now [a] is [a-praying];
And now I'll do't*. †[4]
2 And so [a] goes to Δheaven,
And so am I reveng'd. †
3 That would be scann'd:
A Δvillain* kills* my Δfather, and for that
I, his [sole] Δson*, do this same Δvillain* send
To heaven.
4 [Why], this is hire* and Δsalary*, not Δrevenge.
5 ['A] took* my Δfather grossly*, full of bread,
With all his Δcrimes broad blown*, as [flush] as May,
And how his Δaudit stands who knows* save Δheaven? †
6 But in our circumstance and course of thought
'Tis heavy* with him. †
7 And am I then reveng'd,
To take him in the purging of his Δsoul*,
When he is fit and season'd for his passage?
8 No!
9 Up, Δsword, and know thou a more horrid hent:
When he is drunk* asleep*: or in his Δrage,
Or in th'incestuous pleasure of his bed,
At gaming, [a-swearing], or about some act*
That has no relish* of Δsalvation in't -
Then trip him, that his heels* may kick* at Δheaven,
And that his Δsoul* may be as damn'd and black*
As Δhell, whereto it goes.
10 My Δmother stays*,
This Δphysic* but prolongs thy sickly days*.

Though most modern texts show a rational Hamlet at the start only becoming more disturbed by the end of the speech as he decides not to kill Claudius at this particular moment, F's Hamlet is nowhere near as controlled as the onrushed F #1 and #3 show (each split into three by most modern texts).

- throughout, the quiet of the unembellished lines points to the dilemma of Hamlet killing a man at prayer, from the opening
  "Now might I do it pat, now [he] is [praying],/ . . . /And so am I reveng'd : that would be scann'd,"
- the remaining quiet lines serve to deepen Hamlet's dilemma, for Claudius, if killed when at prayer, would be in a state of grace, something not granted to Hamlet's father: therefore (in the following the first 'him' refers to his father, the second to Claudius)
  "But in our circumstance and course of thought/'Tis heavie with him : and am I then reveng'd,/To take him . . . /When he is fit and season'd for his passage?"
  so Hamlet has no other choice but to accept that his 'Sword' must wait until
  "know thou a more horrid hent"
  such as when Claudius is
  " in th'incestuous pleasure of his bed,/At gaming, swearing,"
- the opening onrushed recognition of the dilemma is a mixture of the very quiet (fear of being overheard perhaps?) and passion (5/5, F #1), while the dismissal of such a killing as 'Sallery, not Revenge' becomes a sudden very passionate release (2/2 in just the eight words of the short F #2)
- the onrushed recognition that Claudius killed his father 'With all his Crimes broad blowne' continues the passion (5/4, F #3's first three lines), and then the implications of taking Claudius when saved, as it were, is quiet and circumspect (3/3 from F #3's last four lines through the first three and a half lines of F #5)
- then, for the only time in the speech, Hamlet's emotions begin to colour his envisaging taking Claudius in an act 'That ha's no rellish of Salvation in't' (4/6, F #5's last four lines)
- finally, in resolving to leave Claudius till later and go face his mother, Hamlet's passions return once more (2/3, F #6's line and half)

First Folio

8/ Hamlet

1 Now might I do it pat, now [he] is [praying],+
And now Ile doo't, and so Δhe goes to Heaven,
And so am I reveng'd: that would be scann'd,
A Villaine killes my Father, and for that
I+ his [soule] Sonne, do this same Villaine send
To heaven.
2 [Oh]+ this is hyre and Sallery, not Revenge.
3 [He] tooke my Father grossely, full of bread,
With all his Crimes broad blowne, as [fresh] as May,
And how his Audit stands,x who knowes,x save Heaven:
But in our circumstance and course of thought
'Tis heavie with him: and am I then reveng'd,
To take him in the purging of his Soule,
When he is fit and season'd for his passage?
4 No. +
5 Up+ Sword, and know thou a more horrid hent+
When he is drunke asleepe: or in his Rage,
Or in th'incestuous pleasure of his bed,
At gaming, [swearing], or about some acte
That ha's no rellish of Salvation in't,
Then trip him, that his heeles may kicke at Heaven,
And that his Soule may be as damn'd and blacke
As Hell, whereto it goes.
6 My Mother stayes,
This Physicke but prolongs thy sickly dayes.

---

[4] most modern texts add the stage direction that Hamlet now draws his sword

#'s 9 - 12: Hamlet & Ophelia

9/ Polonius **Tis told me {Hamlet} hath very oft of late** between 1.3.91 - 135

Background: Ophelia's older brother Laertes has already warned Ophelia to be careful of Hamlet's attentions towards her, 'weigh with what losse your honour may sustaine,/If with too credent eare you list his Songs;/Or lose your Heart; or your chast Treasure open/To his umastered importunity./Feare it Ophelia, feare it my deare Sister'. And now her father Polonius starts in on the same theme, though much more bluntly.

Style: as part of a two-handed scene

Where: Polonius' chambers **To Whom:** his daughter Ophelia

# of Lines: 32 **Probable Timing: 1.35 minutes**

Modern Text

9/ Polonius

1 Tis told me {Hamlet} hath very oft of late
Given private time to you, and you yourself*
Have of your audience been* most free and bounteous.

2 If it be so - as so 'tis put on me,
And that in way of caution - I must tell you,
You do* not understand yourself* so clearly*
As it behooves* my Δdaughter and your Δhonor*.

3 {ψ} Think* yourself* a Δbaby,
That you have ta'en his tenders for true pay,
Which are not [sterling].

4 Tender yourself* more dearly,
Or (not to crack the wind* of the poor* Δphrase,
[Running] it thus) you'll* tender me a fool*.

5 I do* know
When the Δblood* burns*, how Δprodigal* the Δsoul*
[Lends] the tongue vows*. †

6 These blazes, Δdaughter,
Giving more light [than] heat*, extinct in both,
Even in their promise, as it is a-making,
You must not take for fire.

7 [From] this time [ ]
Be somewhat scanter of your Δmaiden presence,
Set your entreatments at a higher rate
[Than] a command to [parle].

8 For Lord Hamlet,
Believe* so much in him, that he is young,
And with a larger tether may he walk*,
[Than] may be given you .

F's orthography suggests that though Polonius tries to maintain the quiet control expected of the King's counselor, though at times the situation is just too much for him, especially when his honour and that of his daughter are concerned; and within the calm come sudden bursts of emotion and passion that might take both of them by surprise.

- given the circumstances Polonius broaches the awkward subject very carefully, the quietness (1/2 in the first four and half lines) underscored by being completely set as determined surround phrases: however, the fact that all four are formed in part by (emotional) semicolons might suggest that the calm appearance is not maintained without some internal strife.

- emotional surround phrases of warning crop up throughout the speech,
  " . Tender your selfe more dearly ; "
  " : these blazes, Daughter,/Giving more light then heate ; extinct in both,/ Even in their promise, as it is a making ; /You must not take for fire . [For] this time Daughter,/Be somewhat scanter of your Maiden presence; Set your entreatments at a higher rate,/Then a command to parley . "
  " . In few, Ophelia,/Doe not beleeve his vowes ; for they are Broakers,/Not of the eye, which their Investments show : "
  " : Looke too't, I charge you ; come your wayes . "

- the quiet of the unembellished phrases shows how he needs to control himself when informing her how he feels about what she has done and what he expects of her (some of which are intensified by being surround phrases)
  "you have tane his tenders for true pay,/Which are not [starling]."
  "these blazes, . . ./Giving more light . . . ; extinct in both/Even in their promise, as it is a making ; /You must not take for fire,"
  "Set your entreatments at a higher rate,/Then a command to parley ."
  with Hamlet's words dismissed as 'implorators of unholy Sutes'
  "Breathing like sanctified and pious bonds,/The better to beguile."
  " This is for all : /I would not, . . . , from this time forth, /Have you so slander any moment leisure,/ . . . / . . . I charge you ; "

First Folio

9/ Polonius

1 Tis told me {Hamlet} hath very oft of late
Given private time to you ; x and you your selfe
Have of your audience beene most free and bounteous.

2 If it be so, as so tis put on me ; x
And that in way of caution : x I must tell you,
You doe not understand your selfe so cleerely,x
As it behoves my Daughter and your Honour.

3 {ψ} Thinke your selfe a Baby,
That you have tane his tenders for true pay,
Which are not [starling].

4 Tender your selfe more dearly ;x
Or+ not to crack the winde of the poore Phrase,
[Roaming] it thus, you'l tender me a foole.

5 I doe know
When the Bloud burnes, how Prodigall the Soule
[Gives] the tongue vowes : these blazes, Daughter,
Giving more light [then] heate ; x extinct in both,
Even in their promise, as it is a making ; x
You must not take for fire.

6 [For] this time Daughter,x
Be somewhat scanter of your Maiden presence ; x
Set your entreatments at a higher rate,x
[Then] a command to [parley].

7 For Lord Hamlet,
Beleeve so much in him, that he is young,
And with a larger tether may he walke,
[Then] may be given you.

{ctd. over}

9 In few, Ophelia,
Do* not believe* his vows*, for they are △brokers*,
Not of [that dye], which their △investments show,
But mere* implorators of unholy △suits,
Breathing like sanctified and pious bonds,
The better to beguile.
10 This is for all:
I would not, in plain* terms*, from this time forth
Have you so slander any moment leisure
As to give words or talk* with the Lord Hamlet. †
11 Look* to't*, I charge you. †
12 Come your ways*.

• following the careful opening (see above), Polonius' self-control seems to snap at the mention of her 'Honour' and how it reflects on him, leading to calling her a 'Baby' (3/6, the last two and a half lines of F #2, and the first line of F #3), and the emotion continues during the warnings to 'Tender herself more dearly' because he knows what happens 'When the Bloud burnes' (5/11, F #4-5)

• however, he manages to re-assert self-control when ordering Ophelia to 'Be somewhat scanter of your Maiden presence', starting intellectually (2/0, F #6's first line and a half), and ending the sentence very quietly (forcing himself?) without any embellishment at all (F #6's last two lines)

• the warning that Hamlet can operate with more freedom than her and thus she mustn't trust his vows is passionate (F #7-8, 6/7 overall),

• however, the urgent opening of F #8, 'Doe not beleeve his vowes', is highly emotional (0/3), as is the sentence with his final orders (2/6, F #9), some of the emotion coming in two clusters – 'plaine termes' and 'looke too't' as if vocally he is about to snap once more

8 In few, Ophelia,
Doe not beleeve his vowes; x for they are Broakers,
Not of [the eye], which their Investments show: x
But meere implorators of unholy Sutes,
Breathing like sanctified and pious bonds,
The better to beguile.
9 This is for all:
I would not, in plaine tearmes, from this time forth, x
Have you so slander any moment leisure, x
As to give words or talke with the Lord Hamlet:
Looke too't, I charge you; come your wayes.

10/ Ophelia **Alas my Lord, I have beene so affrighted.** between 2.1.72 - 97

Background: Despite her father's warnings, and even if she followed them to the letter, Ophelia is powerless to prevent Hamlet approaching her - which he has just done, in what seems to be a very strange manner. [5]

Style: as part of a two-handed scene

Where: Polonius' chambers **To Whom:** her father Polonius

# of Lines: 23 **Probable Timing: 1.10 minutes**

Modern Text

10/ Ophelia

1 [O] my Lord, [my lord,] I have been* so affrighted !

2 {ψ} {A}s I was sewing in my [closet],
Lord Hamlet, with his doublet all unbrac'd,
No hat upon his head, his stockings fouled$_*$,
Ungart'red, and down°- gyved* to his ᐞankle*,
Pale as his shirt, his knees knocking each other,
And with a look* so piteous* in purport
As if he had been loosed out of hell
To speak* of horrors. {ψ}

3 He took* me by the wrist, and held me hard,
Then goes he to the length of all his arm*,
And with his other hand thus o'er his brow,
He falls$_*$ to such perusal* of my face
As ['a] would draw it.

4 Long stay'd$_*$ he so. †

5 At last, a little shaking of mine ᐞarm*,
And thrice his head thus waving up and down*,
He rais'd a sigh so piteous* and profound
That it did seem* to shatter all his bulk*
And end his being.

6 That done, he lets me go*,
And with his head over his [shoulder] turn'd,
He seem'd to find* his way without his eyes,
For out [a'doors*] he went without their [helps]*,
And to the last bended their light on me.

While the speech is emotional overall (5/17), not surprising given the circumstances, F's orthography shows that though whatever intellectual control she may possess at the beginning of the speech quickly disappears (essentially after the first five lines), she still does not go overboard in any melodramatic way – for even when the unembellished lines evaporate after the first appearance of Hamlet has been described (F #2), the remaining twelve emotional releases are scattered throughout the last fourteen lines of the speech without any sudden unexpected outbursts.

- after the first short disturbed sentence establishing her fear (F #1, 1/1) for a moment Ophelia becomes somewhat quieter (2/0 for F #2's first line and a half) in establishing Hamlet's unscheduled arrival in her 'Chamber), followed by an unembellished passage, occasionally broken by emotion (1/4), as she describes his appearance

  "with his doublet all unbrac'd,/No hat upon his head, his stockings foul'd,/ Ungartred, . . . /Pale as his shirt, his knees knocking each other,/ . . . /As if he had been loosed out of hell,"

  and whether the quiet means she has managed some degree of control or that she is so frightened by what occurred that she can hardly speak about it is up to each actor to explore

- but as she describes how Hamlet held her and examined her face 'As he would draw it' her memories seem to become a little more intense, for though she continues to contain most of her emotions (0/3 in F #3's four and half lines) the effort in so doing seems to cost more, for the sentence opens with two emotional (semicoloned) surround phrases

  " . He tooke me by the wrist, and held me hard ; /Then goes he to the length of all his arme ; "

- the opening of F #4, how long he stayed with her and the peculiar 'waving' of his head', also seems difficult for her, for it too opens with two surround phrases

  " . Long staid he so,/At last, a little shaking of mine Arme : /And thrice his head thus waving up and downe ; "

- and as she completes the story (F #4-5) the emotions flow just a little more (1/9 in nine lines), the final moment also singled out by an emotional surround phrase

  " ; And to the last,$_x$ bended their light on me . "

  these last details heightened by the extra breath-thought (marked,$_x$), which suggests that Ophelia is not only moved by how Hamlet behaved, but also by the fact that everything he did focused on her to the very last moment

First Folio

10/ Ophelia

1 [Alas] my Lord, [ ] I have beene so affrighted. +

2 {ψ} {A}s I was sowing in my [Chamber],
Lord Hamlet + with his doublet all unbrac'd,
No hat upon his head, his stockings foul'd,
Ungartred, and downe gived to his Anckle,
Pale as his shirt, his knees knocking each other,
And with a looke so pitious in purport,$_x$
As if he had been loosed out of hell,$_x$
To speake of horrors. {ψ}

3 He tooke me by the wrist, and held me hard; $_x$
Then goes he to the length of all his arme; $_x$
And with his other hand thus o're his brow,
He fals to such perusall of my face,$_x$
As [he] would draw it.

4 Long staid he so,
At last, a little shaking of mine Arme: $_x$
And thrice his head thus waving up and downe; $_x$
He rais'd a sigh,$_x$ so pittious and profound,$_x$
That it did seeme to shatter all his bulke,$_x$
And end his being.

5 That done, he lets me goe,
And with his head over his [shoulders] turn'd,
He seem'd to finde his way without his eyes,
For out [adores] he went without their [helpe]; $_x$
And to the last,$_x$ bended their light on me.

---

[5] this speech opens one of two interesting possibilities: what Ophelia is describing is essentially the second step of the nine stages of chivalric wooing (a somewhat archaic practice by Shakespeare's day): in it, the young man was supposed to dress slovenly to show how much the throes of love took away any time for the niceties of sartorial splendour (see also Rosalind, speech #15, Comedies, As You Like It): so the question here is whether Hamlet went overboard in his 'dis-attire', or whether Ophelia is too naive to recognise the wooing process for what it actually is

11/ Hamlet **Get thee to a Nunnerie.** between 3.1.120 - 149

12/ Ophelia **O what a Noble minde is heere o're-throwne?** 3.1.150 - 161

Background: Not content with sending Rosincrance and Guildensterne to spy on Hamlet, to prove that spurned love for Ophelia is the cause of Hamlet's madness, Polonius and Claudius have ordered Ophelia to lay in wait for Hamlet and give him back all the gifts he sent to her, while they spy on the whole transaction. Unfortunately they have underestimated Hamlet's current depth of psychic disturbance plus his loathing of obvious deceit, and the plan goes very awry, as the following two speeches show .

Speech #11 is the start of the intense build-up of Hamlet's verbal attack.

Speech #12 is Ophelia's bewildered response once he has left (note how none of the descriptions in the first part of line #2 actually match sequentially the nouns in the second part of the line).

Style: speech #11 as part of a two-handed scene, with two others spying on the proceedings; speech #12, solo

Where: the lobby in the castle at Elsinore **To Whom:** speech #11 to Ophelia, #12 to self and audience

Speech 11: # of Lines: 23 **Probable Timing: 1.10 minutes**

Speech 12: # of Lines: 12 **Probable Timing: 0.40 minutes**

Modern Text

11/ Hamlet

1 Get thee to a $^{\Delta}$nunn'ry$_{*}$◊ , why wouldst thou
be a breeder of $^{\Delta}$sinners?
2 I am myself* indifferent honest,
but yet I could accuse me of such things that it were better my $^{\Delta}$mother had not borne me: ◊ I am very proud*, revengeful*, $^{\Delta}$ambitious, with more offenses* at my beck* [than] I have thoughts to put them in, imagination to give them shape, or time to act* them in.
3 What should such
$^{\Delta}$fellows* as I do, crawling between* [$^{\Delta}$earth and $^{\Delta}$heaven] ?
4 We are arrant $^{\Delta}$knaves [ ], believe* none of us.
5 Go* thy
ways* to a $^{\Delta}$nunn'ry*.
6 If thou dost* $^{\Delta}$marry, I'll give thee this $^{\Delta}$plague
for thy $^{\Delta}$dowry$_{*}$: ◊ be thou as chaste$_{*}$ as $^{\Delta}$ice, as pure as $^{\Delta}$snow, thou shalt not escape $^{\Delta}$calumny.
7 Get thee to a $^{\Delta}$nunn'ry* ◊,
[ ], $^{\Delta}$farewell.

While often played as a sustained attack on Ophelia, sometimes quite physically (see the Branagh film for example), F's orthography seems to suggest that much of Hamlet's focus is inward, releasing his own self disgust, and disgust with the actions of his mother and uncle. Since most of his words to Ophelia start or finish with the word 'Nunnery' the question of what the term means to him is of key importance, for if a 'convent' it would seem he is trying to save her, if a 'brothel', as some commentators suggest, then he is condemning her from the very start.

- F #1's opening intellectual challenge (2/0) is heightened by being set as two short sentences
- and though the start of his self-denigration is very emotional (2/6, F #3-4), as he extends his own sins to cover every one else and repeats his instruction to 'Goe thy wayes to a Nunnery.' he becomes very passionate (5/5, F #5-7)
- yet Hamlet seems to regains his opening self-control (11/3, the six lines F #8-13), though the content of what he is about to say about marriage is extraordinarily harsh (presumably coloured by his bleak view of what he regards as his mother's treachery towards the memory of his just deceased father)

First Folio

11/ Hamlet

1 Get thee to a Nunnerie. [6]
2 Why would'st thou
be a breeder of Sinners?
3 I am my selfe indifferent honest,
but yet I could accuse me of such things,$_{x}$ that it were better my Mother had not borne me.
4 I am very prowd, revengefull, Ambitious, with more offences at my becke,$_{x}$ [then] I have thoughts to put them in,$^{+}$ imagination,$_{x}$ to give them shape, or time to acte them in.
5 What should such
Fellowes as I do, crawling betweene [Heaven and Earth].$^{+}$
6 We are arrant Knaves [all], beleeve none of us.
7 Goe thy
wayes to a Nunnery.
8 If thou doest Marry, Ile give thee this Plague
for thy Dowrie.
9 Be thou as chast as Ice, as pure as Snow,
thou shalt not escape Calumny.
10 Get thee to a Nunnery.
11 [Go], Farewell.

[6] *The Oxford Textual Companion* (op. cit.) points out the phrase 'to a Nunnery go' appears seven times in Q1, twice in Q2 and three times in F1 (page 406, footnote 3.1.140)

8 Or if thou wilt needs Δmarry, marry a fool,
for Δwise men know well enough, what monsters you
make of them.
9 To a Δnunn'ry*, go, and quickly too.
10 God [hath] given you one [face], and you make [your selves]
another. †
You [jig*] you amble, and you lisp*, and nick-name
God's creatures and make your Δwantonness*, your Δignorance.
11 Go to*, I'll no more on't, it hath made me mad.
12 I say we will have no more [Δmarriage].
13 Those that are
married already (all but one) shall live, the rest shall keep
as they are.
14 To a Δnunnery, go.

- as he begins to attack women in general and Ophelia in particular, the attack is intensified by the few surround phrases (F #12)
  " . Or if thou wilt needs Marry, marry a fool : for Wise men know well enough, what monsters you make of them ."
  and especially the opening to F #14
  " . God has given you one [face], and you make your selfe another : "
- with this (no matter how pained) misogynist attack, Hamlet's emotions break through again (2/4, F #14-15)
- and then it seems that a new idea (of revenge), no matter how strange, has hit, which causes him to go very quiet
  "I say, we will have no more Marriages. Those that are married already, all but one shall live, the rest shall keep as they are."
  for, as expressed in F #16-17, the notion of revenge is almost unembellished (1/0 ,with just the key word 'Marriage' capitalised) – presumably the one who shall not live being Claudius
- the final command to leave is once more deliberate (1/0)

12 Or if thou wilt needs Marry, marry a fool: x
for Wise men know well enough, what monsters you
make of them.
13 To a Nunnery+ go, and quickly too.
14 God [has] given you one [pace], and you make [your selfe]an -
other: you [gidge], x you amble, and you lispe, and nick
name Gods creatures, x and make your Wantonnesse, your
Ignorance.
15 Go too, Ile no more on't, it hath made me mad.
16 I say, x we will have no more [Marriages].
17 Those that are
married already,+ all but one+ shall live, the rest shall keep
as they are.
18 To a Nunnery, go.

Modern Text

12/ Ophelia

1 O, what a Δnoble mind* is here* o'erthrown*!
2 The Δcourtier's, Δsoldier's, Δscholar's*, Δeye, tongue, sword,
Th'[expectation] and Δrose of the fair* Δstate,
The glass* of Δfashion and the mold* of Δform*,
Th'observ'd of all Δobservers, quite, quite down* !
3 [And] I, of Δladies most deject and wretched,
That suck'd the Δhoney* of his Δmusic* Δvows*,
Now see that Δnoble and most Δsovereign* Δreason,
Like sweet Δbells* jangled out of [time], and harsh ;
That unmatch'd Δform* and Δfeature of blown* youth
Blasted with ecstasy*.
4 O*, woe is me
T'have seen* what I have seen*, see what I see !

Compared to the emotional pattern of speech #10 above, (5/17 in twenty-three lines), it seems that Hamlet's attack has taken her to the edge, for here she releases far more passion than ever before (20/17 in just twelve lines).

- in spight of the attack, Ophelia's first (emotional, not surprisingly) thought is for Hamlet (F #1, 1/3)
- and even the intellectual start to F #2 (3/1) is still about him – though the intellect is more than somewhat disturbed since the pairings of 'Courtiers' with 'Eye', 'Soldiers' with 'tongue', and 'Schollers' with 'sword' don't match
- indeed the intellect turns to passion as she continues to bemoan what has happened to Hamlet (5/5, F #2's last three lines)
- even though describing herself as 'deject and wretched', her switch to self-focus reverts to intellect (10/5, F #3), but her intellectual stamina gives out at the last moment, for the opening of F #4's 'woe is me' is initially emotional (0/3), only to finish with an unembellished monosyllabic surround phrase ' : see what I see . ', as if all energy had finally been leached out of her

First Folio

12/ Ophelia

1 O+ what a Noble minde is heere o're-throwne? +
2 The Courtiers, Soldiers, Schollers: Eye, tongue, sword,
Th'[expectansie] and Rose of the faire State,
The glasse of Fashion, x and the mould of Forme,
Th'observ'd of all Observers, quite, quite downe. +
3 [Have] I+ of Ladies most deject and wretched,
That suck'd the Honie of his Musicke Vowes: x
Now see that Noble, x and most Soveraigne Reason,
Like sweet Bels jangled out of [tune], and harsh,+
That unmatch'd Forme and Feature of blowne youth, x
Blasted with extasie.
4 Oh+ woe is me, x
T'have seene what I have seene: x see what I see. +

#'S 13 - 16: HAMLET AND SELF DEFINITION

13/ Hamlet **To be, or not to be, that is the Question :** 3.1.55 - 89

Background: Arguably the most famous of all Shakespeare speeches, these are Hamlet's first words following his previous soliloquy where he is triggered to action by the impromptu performance of the first player (see Hamlet's comments in speech #6 above). In the see-saw battle in Hamlet's mind, just as that speech started with questioning and ended with planned action, so this speech reverts to philosophical questioning once more.

Style: solo

Where: the lobby of the castle of Elsinore **To Whom:** self and the audience

# of Lines: 35 **Probable Timing: 1.45 minutes**

Modern Text

13/ Hamlet

1 To be, or not to be, that is the Δquestion:
Whether 'tis Δnobler in the mind* to suffer
The Δslings and Δarrows* of outrageous* Δfortune,
Or to take Δarms* against a Δsea of troubles,
And by opposing, end them. †
2 To die*, to sleep* -
No more, and by a sleep*, to say we end
The Δheart-ache* and the thousand Δnatural* shocks*
That Δflesh is heir* to*; ◊ Δ'tis a consummation
Devoutly to be wish'd.
3 To die*, to sleep -
To sleep*, perchance to Δdream* - Δay*, there's the rub,
For in that sleep* of death what dreams* may come,
When we have shuffled* off this mortal* coil*,
Must give us pause*; ◊ Δthere's the respect
That makes Δcalamity of so long life:
For who would bear* the Δwhips and Δscorns* of time,
[Th 'Δoppressor's] wrong, the [proud] man's Δcontumely,
The pangs of [despis'd] Δlove, the Δlaw's* delay,
The insolence of Δoffice, and the Δspurns*
That patient merit of [th'unworthy] takes,
When he himself* might his Δquietus make
With a bare Δbodkin; ◊ Δwho would [ ] Δfardles bear*,
To grunt and sweat under a weary life,
But that the dread of something after death,

In comparing the sentence structure of the two texts, it seems that F (with its slightly onrushed F #1, and, in comparison to the modern texts, the shorter F #2-5) shows a character in the process of discovery and understanding, whereas the very long mt. #3 shows a character more in a state of release.

- thus the four surround phrases, three starting sentences, all seem to set up (as might be expected from a good philosophy student) a basic question about life and death from which the next explorations spring
  " . To be, or not to be, that is the Question : "
  " : to dye to sleepe/No more ; "
  " . To dye, to sleep,/To sleepe, perchance to Dreame ; "
  " . There's the respect/That makes Calamity of so long life : "
- and, quite fascinatingly, the few unembellished lines seem to focus on either the blessings of 'sleepe' (enhanced by being set as a very short and, according to most modern texts, ungrammatical sentence)
  " 'Tis a consummation/Devoutly to be wish'd . "
  or the rather ugly burdens ('Fardles') that life offers
  "To grunt and sweat under a weary life,/But that the dread of something after death,"
- Hamlet's first posing of the 'To be, or not to be' question is intellectual (7/3, F #1's first four and a half lines), then he interrupts himself with an emotional surround phrase ' : to dye, to sleepe /No more ; ' (0/2) - here some modern texts add a dash separating 'to sleepe' and 'No more' thus totally changing the meaning, for F/Q2's 'sleepe/No more' seems to mean just that, no more sleep, whereas the modern readjustment seems to suggest that Hamlet stops himself halfway through with the command 'no more')
- then comes a surge of passion as he considers the 'Heart-ake' of humanity (3/4, F #1's last two lines) – which in turn leads to an ungrammatical and unembellished devout wish (F #2) from which springs an enormous emotional response to the consideration of 'what dreames may come,/When we have shuffel'd off this mortall coile' (1/9, F #3)

First Folio

13/ Hamlet

1 To be, or not to be, that is the Question:
Whether 'tis Nobler in the minde to suffer
The Slings and Arrowes of outragious Fortune,
Or to take Armes against a Sea of troubles,
And by opposing end them: to dye, to sleepe
No more; x and by a sleepe, to say we end
The Heart-ake, x and the thousand Naturall shockes
That Flesh is heyre too? x
2 'Tis a consummation
Devoutly to be wish'd.
3 To dye x to sleep,
To sleepe, perchance to Dreame; x I, there's the rub,
For in that sleepe of death, x what dreames may come,
When we have shufflel'd off this mortall coile,
Must give us pawse.
4 There's the respect
That makes Calamity of so long life:
For who would beare the Whips and Scornes of time,
[The Oppressors] [7] wrong, the [poore] mans Contumely,
The pangs of [dispriz'd] Love, the Lawes delay,
The insolence of Office, and the Spurnes
That patient merit of [the unworthy] [8] takes,
When he himselfe might his *Quietus* make
With a bare Bodkin?
5 Who would [these] Fardles beare+
To grunt and sweat under a weary life,
But that the dread of something after death,

---

[7] Q2 = 'Th'oppressors' (thus maintaining the line at 10 syllables), F = 'The Oppressors'

[8] Q2 = 'th'unworthy' (thus maintaining the line at 10 syllables), Ff = 'the unworthy'

The undiscovered △country*, from whose △bourn*
No △traveller returns*, △puzzles* the will,
And makes us rather bear* those ills* we have,
[Than] fly* to others that we know not of?

4 Thus △conscience does make △cowards of us all,
And thus the △native hue* of △resolution
Is sicklied o'er, with the pale cast of △thought,
And enterprises* of great [pitch] and moment
With this regard their △currents* turn* [awry],
And lose* the name of △action. -

5 Soft you now,
The fair* Ophelia?

6 Nymph*, in thy △orisons*
Be all my sins* rememb'red.

• though the next set of information is not set as a new sentence in most modern texts, F #4 shows him exploring a new tangent, the 'Calamity of so long life', and returning to intellect (11/5), while the answer, set as a new F passionate sentence (F #5, 5/7), itself implies a brand new discovery - the new sentence a mixture of unembellishment surrounded by passion: however, most modern texts, in carrying on the text as mt. #3, seem to suggest that the information is merely a continuation of what is already known

• the conclusion that 'Conscience does make Cowards of us all' as an explanation that everyone, not just himself, loses 'the name of Action' is, once more, intellectual (F #6, 7/4) which would suggest that Hamlet has managed to re-establish some form of self-control – but this quickly disappears, for the appearance of Ophelia brings his passions to the fore (2/3, the very short F #7-8, the shortness perhaps suggesting that the sight of her drives away any need for large-scale word-play or excessive verbiage – through delight at seeing her perhaps?, which in turn would make her rejection of him even more painful)

The undiscovered Countrey, from whose Borne
No Traveller returnes, Puzels the will,
And makes us rather beare those illes we have,
[Then] flye to others that we know not of. +

6 Thus Conscience does make Cowards of us all,
And thus the Native hew of Resolution
Is sicklied o're, with the pale cast of Thought,
And enterprizes of great [pith] and moment,x
With this regard their Currants turne [away],
And loose the name of Action.

7 Soft you now,
The faire Ophelia?

8 Nimph, in thy Orizons
Be all my sinnes remembred.

14/ Hamlet **I will tell you why {you were sent for;} so shall my anticipation** 2.2.293 - 310

Background: In stripping Rosincrance and Guildensterne of any pretence of friendship and thus revealing them to be spies for Claudius and Gertrude, Hamlet eventually does make an attempt to explain his current disaffection (with the strange punctuation of the First Folio revealing just how difficult it is for him to put coherent thoughts together, at least for now).

Style: as part of a three-handed scene

Where: the lobby of the castle **To Whom:** Rosincrance and Guildensterne

# of Lines: 18 **Probable Timing: 0.55 minutes**

Modern Text

14/ Hamlet

1 I will tell you why {you were sent for ;} so shall my anticipation prevent your discovery, [and] your secrecy* to the King and Queen* moult no feather . †

2 I have of late - but wherefore I know not - lost all my mirth, forgone all custom* of exercise ; and indeed it goes so [heavily] with my disposition, that this goodly frame, the Δearth, seems* to me a sterile* Δpromontory ; this most excellent Δcanopy, the Δair*, look you, this brave o'er°hanging [firmament], this Δmajestical* Δroof* fretted with golden fire, why, it [appeareth nothing] to me* [but] a foul* and pestilent congregation of vapors*.

3 What a piece of work* is a man, how Δnoble in Δreason, how infinite in [faculties,] in form* and moving, how express* and admirable in Δaction, how like an Δangel in apprehension, how like a Δgod! the beauty of the world ; the Δparagon* of Δanimals ; and yet to me what is this Δquintessence of Δdust?

4 Man delights not me - [ ] nor [Δwomen] neither, though by your smiling you seem* to say so.

The hallmark of this speech as set in F is that Hamlet is having difficulty in expressing himself, as evidenced by the punctuation and phrasing going awry - as if his feigned 'madness' has led him almost to a momentary loss of reason: this pattern is repeated more and more, especially in F, until the meeting with Osricke: as seen here, most modern texts tend to repunctuate for rationality, and in so doing probably lose one of the most important character developments and struggles that Hamlet faces throughout the middle and later sequences of the play.

- the enormously quiet opening is very unusual (the first five lines mainly unembellished, 2/2, save for the cluster of both capitals and one long spelling referring to his uncle and mother by their formal titles 'King' and 'Queene') - a quiet which could suggest either a deliberately deceptive calm as he breaks to Rosincrance and Guildensterne his knowledge of their spying on him, or a character desperately trying to prevent himself from snapping under the strain of yet another act of betrayal

- however, once he begins to explain how he regards 'this goodly frame the Earth', first his passion breaks through in listing its supposed beauty (6/5 the three and half lines to 'golden fire:') only to then finish emotionally as he describes its appearance to him as 'foule and pestilent' (0/3, F #1's last two lines)

- while F #2's listing of the supposed beauty of man is deeply intellectual (9/3, F #2), its staggeringly ungrammatical punctuation and its opening with six successive surround phrases point to a mind undergoing tremendous strain

- and though in terms of release F #3 seems to regain some control, the three surround phrases formed by the two emotional semicolons underscore the strain beneath the extraordinarily bleak words

First Folio

14/ Hamlet

1 I will tell you why {you were sent for ;} so shall my anticipation prevent your discovery+ [of] your secricie to the King and Queene :$_x$ moult no feather, I have of late, but wherefore I know not, lost all my mirth, forgone all custome of exercise ; and indeed,$_x$ it goes so [heavenly] with my disposition ;$_x$ that this goodly frame+ the Earth, seemes to me a sterrill Promontory ; this most excellent Canopy+ the Ayre, look you, this brave ore-hanging,[ ] this Majesticall Roofe,$_x$ fretted with golden fire :$_x$ why, it [appeares no other thing] to mee,$_x$ [then] a foule and pestilent congregation of vapours.

2 What a piece of worke is a man!$_x$ how Noble in Reason? $_x$ how infinite in [faculty?$_x$] in forme and moving+ how expresse and admirable?$_x$ in Action, how like an Angel?$_x$ in apprehension, how like a God? + the beauty of the world,+ the Parragon of Animals ; and yet to me,$_x$ what is this Quintessence of Dust?

3 Man delights not me ;$_x$ [no], nor [Woman] neither ;$_x$ though by your smiling you seeme to say so.

15/ Hamlet **I do not well understand that. Will you play/upon this Pipe?** between 3.2.250 - 373

Background: Following the confusion stemming from Claudius' abrupt closing down of 'The Murther of Gozago' (see background to speech #7), Guildensterne has revealed himself to be much move closely allied with Claudius and Gertrude than Hamlet realised. He has delivered news of the 'King' being 'in his retyrement, marvellous distemper'd', and that the 'Queene your Mother, in most great affliction of spirit, hath sent me to you' since Hamlet's 'behavior hath stroke her into amazement'. Hamlet thus demands of Guildensterne an explanation of himself, to which Guildensterne has replied 'O my Lord, if my Dutie be too bold, my love is too unmannerly'. This response Hamlet promptly deflates - a musical instrument, a recorder, just having been brought into the room.

Style: one on one in front of a larger group

Where: wherever 'The Muder of Gonzago/The Mousetrap' has been played

To Whom: Guildensterne, in front of Rosincrance, Horatio, and some (or all) of the Players

# of Lines: 16 **Probable Timing: 0.50 minutes**

Modern Text

15/ Hamlet

1 I do not well understand that.

2 Will you play upon this Δpipe?

3 I pray you.

4 I do beseech you.

5 'Tis as easy* as lying. †

6 ΔGovern* these Δventages* with your finger and [thumbs*], give it breath with your mouth, and it will discourse most [eloquent] Δmusic*.

7 Look* you, these are the stops*.

8 Why, look* you now, how unworthy a thing you make of me! †

9 You would play upon me*, you would seem* to know my stops, you would pluck out the heart of my Δmystery*, you would sound me* from my lowest *note to the top of my Δcompass*; and there is much Δmusic*, excellent Δvoice, in this little Δorgan*, yet cannot you make it [speak].

10 [S'blood] do you think*, [ ] I am easier to be* play'd* on, [than] a Δpipe?

11 Call me what Δinstrument you will, though you can fret me, [yet] you cannot play upon me.

12 God bless* you, Δsir.

F's orthography clearly shows how Hamlet's quiet self-control eventually disappears - whether as a deliberate ploy, or because he is genuinely angry at the treachery of his so-called friends, is up to each actor to explore.

- Hamlet opens his challenge to Claudius' spies deceptively quietly (1/0, the first four short sentences - in themselves sufficient warning to his listeners that something is very wrong), and the opening unembellished surround phrase of F #5, the naked attack of ' . 'Tis as easie as lying ; '
- then, having essentially accused Rosincrance and Guildensterne of 'lying', his emotions break through as he goes through the motions of explaining to them how to play the recorder (2/4, the remainder of F #5)
- now that the emotions have broken through, they continue (0/3, F #7's first two and half lines) as he becomes even more direct in his attack, starting the 'how unworthy a thing you make of me' passage with five consecutive surround phrases, the last four of which are heightened by being linked in part by the emotional semicolons
  " . Why looke you now, how unworthy a thing you make of me : you would play upon mee ; you would seeme to know my stops : you would pluck out the heart of my Mysterie ; you would sound mee from my lowest Note, to the top of my Compasse : "
- then his scorn? anger? turns to passion as he lays into them for their desire to 'pluck out the heart of my Mysterie' (6/4, the last four lines of F #7)
- and as the speech ends, the passion intensifies as Hamlet finally demands an answer from them (F #8-9) and then challenges the entry of Polonius (3/2, F #8-10) in that these last three sentences are all short and directly to the point

First Folio

15/ Hamlet

1 I do not well understand that.

2 Will you play upon this Pipe?

3 I pray you.

4 I do beseech you.

5 'Tis as easie as lying: governe these Ventiges with your finger and [thumbe], give it breath with your mouth, and it will discourse most [excellent] Musicke.

6 Looke you, these are the stoppes.

7 Why+ looke you now, how unworthy a thing you make of me: you would play upon mee;x you would seeme to know my stops: x you would pluck out the heart of my Mysterie; x you would sound mee from my lowest Note,x to the top of my Compasse: x and there is much Musicke, excellent Voice, in this little Organe, yet cannot you make it [ ].

8 [Why] do you thinke, [that] I am easier to bee plaid on, [then] a Pipe?

9 Call me what Instrument you will, though you can fret me, [ ] you cannot play upon me.

10 God blesse you+ Sir.

16/ Hamlet **Alas poore Yorick, I knew him Horatio,** between 5.1.184 - 216

Background: Despite all the odds Hamlet has escaped the murderous trap Claudius' set for him in England (and in so doing has caused the deaths of Rosincrance and Guildensterne in his place). Upon returning to Elsinore he has once more teamed up with Horatio, and on their way to the castle they have been side-tracked into talking with a very loquacious Grave-Digger/Clowne. The Grave-Digger has produced the scull of 'a whoreson mad Fellowe' who 'pou'rd a Flaggon of Rhennish on my head once, and pronounced it to be 'Yoricks Scull, the Kings Jester', a man Hamlet knew well, which leads him to the following exploration of time and death.

Style: as part of a three-handed scene

Where: a grave-yard **To Whom:** the scull and Horatio, in front of the Grave-Digger

# of Lines: 22 **Probable Timing: 1.10 minutes**

Modern Text

16/ Hamlet

1 Alas, poor* Yorick ! †
2 I knew him Ho-
ratio, a fellow of infinite Δjest, of most excellent fancy . †
3 He
hath [bore] me on his back* a thousand times, [Δand now
how abhorr'd* in my Δimagination it is!] my gorge rises at it
•
4 Here*
hung those lips* that I have kiss'd. I know not how oft.
5 Where be your Δgibes now, ◊ your Δgambols*, ◊ your
Δsongs, ◊ your flashes of Δmerriment, that were wont to
set the Δtable on a Δroar*?
6 [Not] one now to mock your own
[grinning] - ◊ quite chop-fall'n*.
7 Now get you to my Δlady's*
Δchamber, and tell her, let her paint an inch thick*, to this
favor* she must come; ◊ Δmake her laugh at that. †
8 To what base uses we may return* ! {ψ}
9 Why may not Δimagination trace the Δnoble dust of A-
lexander, till Δhe find it stopping a bunghole.
[ ]
10 Alexander died, Alexander was buried, Alexander re-
turneth into dust, the dust is earth, of earth we make

As the final sequence highlights (F #14-15), F's orthography suggests that underneath the apparent light hearted words and ideas runs an under-currant of something personally quite disturbing.

- Hamlet's fixation on the physical reminder of death is underscored both by the three surround phrase passages that open the speech (F #1), and the final almost unembellished monosyllabic phrase of F #1 'my gorge rises at it'
- his understanding of the transience of life is marked by the two surround phrases that make up F #10
  " . Make her laugh at that : /To what base uses we may returne . "
  and the four that open F #13, the doggerel about the once great Alexander now being nothing more than dust
- F #1's first and third surround phrases are strongly factual (5/2), but Hamlet's lack of self-control might be seen in the intervening emotional phrase that splits the other two (0/2)
- as he begins to examine Yorick's scull more closely, his emotions take over again (0/2, F #2), at least momentarily, for in the long mordant/black humour teasing shaded section (which could be anywhere between one and seven sentences long) his mental control returns (9/3, the four lines from F #3 up to and including the first line of F #9)
- yet, almost immediately after F #8's punning climax 'Quite Chopfalne?' he turns once more to emotion at the thought of death visiting 'my Ladies Chamber' (0/3 the rest of F #9-10) - though whether this is a reference to women in general or his mother in particular is up to each actor to explore
- as befits a philosopher, his move to explore the 'Noble dust of Alexander' becomes intellectual once more (7/2, F #11-12 and the

First Folio

16/ Hamlet

1 Alas+ poore Yorick,+ I knew him Ho-
ratio, a fellow of infinite Jest : x of most excellent fancy, he
hath [borne] me on his backe a thousand times :x [And
how abhorred my Imagination is,]+ my gorge rises at it.
2 Heere
hung those lipps,x that I have kist I know not how oft.
3 Where be your Jibes now?
4 Your Gambals?
5 Your
Songs?
6 Your flashes of Merriment+ that were wont to
set the Table on a Rore?
7 [No] one now to mock your own
[Jeering?]
8 Quite chopfalne? x
9 Now get you to my Ladies
Chamber, and tell her, let her paint an inch thicke, to this
favour she must come.
10 Make her laugh at that : -
To what base uses we may returne {ψ}. +
11 Why may not Imagination trace the Noble dust of A-
lexander, till Δhe find it stopping a bunghole.
12 {A}s thus.
13 Alexander died : x Alexander was buried :x Alexander re-
turneth into dust ; x the dust is earth ;x of earth we make

Δloam*, and why of that Δloam* whereto he was converted might they not stop* a Δbeer*-barrel*?

11 [Imperious] Caesar, dead and turn'd to clay,
Might stop a hole to keep* the wind* away.

12 O* that that earth which kept the world in awe
Should patch a Δwall t'expel* the winter's flaw !

first three and half lines of F #13), the only emotion coming as he considers what a degrading end might be the fate of such a noble dust ('stopp a Beere-barrell' (1/3)

- and though the final doggerel as to the possible fate of Cæsar is irreverent, it is still emotional (2/5, F #14-15), perhaps suggesting that under the light hearted words Hamlet is still disturbed at the thought of death

Lome, and why of that Lome ($_x$whereto he was conver-ted$_x$) might they not stopp a Beere-barrell?

14[9] [Imperiall] Caesar, dead and turn'd to clay,
Might stop a hole to keepe the winde away.

15 Oh,$_x$ that that earth,$_x$ which kept the world in awe,$_x$
Should patch a Wall,$_x$ t'expell the winters flaw. +

#'s 17 - 18: Hamlet & The Players

17/ Polonius **My Lord, I have Newes to tell you.** between 2.2.390 - 402

Background: A short speech from Polonius, hoping to drag Hamlet out of his gloom with news that he knows Hamlet will enjoy, the arrival of the Players - little knowing that Hamlet has already heard it, though not in such a convoluted manner as Polonius now presents it. One note: this could be a spur-of-the-moment flight of fancy, or a reading of a play-bill.

Style: as part of a four-handed scene **Where:** in the lobby of the castle

To Whom: Hamlet, in front of Rosincrance and Guildensterne

# of Lines: 9 **Probable Timing: 0.30 minutes**

Modern Text

17/ Polonius

1 My Δlord, I have Δnews* to tell you.

2 The Δactors are come hither, my Δlord.

3 The best Δactors in the world, either for Δtrage-dy$_*$, Δcomedy$_*$, Δhistory$_*$, Δpastoral*, *[Δpastoral]*-Δcomical*,-Δhistorical*-Δpastoral*, Δtragical*-Δhistorical*, Δtragical*-Δcomical*-Δhistorical*-Δpastoral*, Δscene [individible], or Δpoem unlimited; ◊ Seneca cannot be too heavy, nor Plautus too light. †

4 For the law of Δwrit, and the Δliberty: ◊ Δthese are the only* men.

This is one of the few occasions where F sets more sentences than most modern texts, the effect of mt. #3 being split into two allows the F Polonius a wonderful theatrical/oratorical flourish not permitted to his modern counterpart.

- the first announcements both of the arrival of the 'Actors' (F #1-2) and (presumably) the first reading of their handbill (F #3's first line and a half) open strongly intellectually(9/2)
- though it seems the excitement becomes almost too much for him, for F #3's next two line listing of the genres they are capable of playing is both extraordinarily passionate (10/10) and couched in surround phrases
- for whatever reason (reactions from Hamlet, and Rosincrance and Guildensterne perhaps) Polonius returns to intellect for the final lines of the playbill (5/0, F #3's last two phrases and F #4)
- the last short sentence is emotional (F #5, 0/1) - though whether this is still the playbill or Polonius adding his own comment (inevitably trying to have the last word) is up to each actor to decide

First Folio

17/ Polonius

1 My Lord, I have Newes to tell you.

2 The Actors are come hither+ my Lord.

3 The best Actors in the world, either for Trage-die, Comedie, Historie, Pastorall: $_x$ [Pastoricall] - Comicall-
Historicall-Pastorall: $_x$ Tragicall-Historicall: $_x$ Tragicall-Comicall-Historicall-Pastorall: $_x$ Scene [indivible], or Poem unlimited.

4 Seneca[10] cannot be too heavy, nor Plautus
too light, for the law of Writ, and the Liberty.

5 These are the onely men.

---

[9] though Qq/Ff simply set the following passage as verse, most modern texts suggest the four lines should be set as a song or doggerel

[10] Q2 = 'Sceneca' (which some modern texts suggest is a pun on 'scene'), Ff = 'Seneca'

18/ Hamlet **Speake the Speech I pray you, as I pronounc'd** 3.2.1 - 45

Background: Just before the playing of the requested 'The Murther of Gonzago' (with 'some dosen or sixteene lines' added by Hamlet for Claudius' benefit), Hamlet seems to feel the need to instruct the actors in their business (or as the scholars suggest, Shakespeare felt the need to remind *his* own actors of *their* craft which some of them seem to have neglected).

Style: general address to a small group

Where: somewhere near the great hall of the castle **To Whom:** the first player and his colleagues (an unspecified number)

# of Lines: 40 **Probable Timing: 2.00 minutes**

Modern Text

18/ Hamlet

1 Speak* the △speech, I pray you, as I pronounc'd
it to you, trippingly on the △tongue, △but if you mouth it,
as many of your △players do, I had as live the △town-△crier*
had spoke my △lines. †
2 Nor do not saw the △air* too much [with]
your hand, thus, but use all gently, for in the very △torrent,
△tempest, and, as I may say, the △whirl*wind* of [your]
△passion, you must acquire and beget a △temperance that
may give it △smoothness*.
3 O, it offends me* to the △soul* to
[hear] a robustious △peri°wig*-pated △fellow tear* a △passi-
on to tatters, to very$_*$ rags*, to split the ears* of the
△groundlings, who for the most part are capable* of
nothing but inexplicable dumb* shows* & noise. †
4 I [would]
have such a △fellow whipt for o'erdoing Termagant, it
out-Herod's Herod, ◊ pray you avoid it.
5 Be not too tame neither*, but let your own*
△discretion be your △tutor.
6 Suit* the △action to the △word,
the △word to the △action, with this special* observance, △that
you [o'erstep] not the modesty$_*$ of △nature: for any
thing so [o'er]-done, is [from] the purpose of △playing, whose
end, both at the first and now, was and is, to hold as 'twere$_*$
the △mirror* up to △nature: to show* △virtue her own*
△feature, △scorn* her own △image, and the very$_*$ △age and
△body$_*$ of the △time his form* and pressure.
7 Now this
over-done, or come tardy$_*$ off, though it [makes] the unskil-
ful* laugh, cannot but make the △judicious △grieve*; the
censure of the which △one must in your allowance o'er-
weigh$_*$ a whole △theater of △others.

The speech is essentially composed of two parts, Hamlet's instructions to the actors and his seemingly irrelevant digressions into his own reflections upon and reactions to what he regards as 'bad acting' - and while commentators offer several contemporary explanations as to why, to satisfy an audience there still must be a theatrical reason to justify these distractions. F's orthography shows that while the instructions are mainly intellectual, the sidebars are either emotional or passionate – the need to release seeming to be very important, perhaps suggesting his distress with all the bad real-life acting going on around him (Claudius, Rosincrance, Guildensterne, and even Ophelia).

- the importance of the forthcoming event is underscored by there being virtually no unembellished lines throughout the forty-one lines of advice and reminiscence until the very last words, F #10's 'Go make you readie.'

- the short F #3, 'Pray you avoid it.', is the other interesting exception, for both it and the very few surround phrases seem to go beyond just advice to the players, but reveal Hamlet's need for outward signs of honourable behaviour from all around him
  ". Nor do not saw the Ayre too much [ ] your hand thus, but use all gently ;"
  ": I could have such a Fellow whipt for o're-doing Termagant : it out-Herod's Herod."
  ": that's Villanous, & shewes a most pittifull Ambition in the Foole that uses it."

- the opening advice of 'Speake the Speech' is strongly intellectual (F #1, 15/6) only to be broken by strong emotion as he becomes sidetracked into expressing at length what 'offends mee to the Soule' (5/9, F #2's first four and a half lines), while the thought of whipping the 'Fellow' that offends him becomes totally intellectual (4/0 in F #2's last two surround phrase line and a half)

First Folio

18/ Hamlet

1 Speake the Speech+ I pray you, as I pronounc'd
it to you+ trippingly on the Tongue: $_x$ But if you mouth it,
as many of your Players do, I had as live the Town-Cryer
had spoke my Lines: Nor do not saw the Ayre too much [ ]
your hand+ thus, but use all gently; $_x$ for in the verie Torrent,
Tempest, and ($_x$as I may say$_x$) the Whirle-winde of [ ]
Passion, you must acquire and beget a Temperance that
may give it Smoothnesse.
2 O+ it offends mee to the Soule,$_x$ to
[see] a robustious Pery-wig-pated Fellow teare a Passion to tatters, to verie ragges, to split the eares of the
Groundlings: $_x$ who ($_x$for the most part$_x$) are capeable of
nothing,$_x$ but inexplicable dumbe shewes,$_x$ & noise: I [could]
have such a Fellow whipt for o're-doing Termagant: $_x$ it
out-Herod's Herod.
3 Pray you avoid it.
4 Be not too tame neyther: $_x$ but let your owne
Discretion be your Tutor.
5 Sute the Action to the Word,
the Word to the Action, with this speciall observance: $_x$That
you [ore-stop] not the modestie of Nature; + for any
thing so [over-done], is [frö] the purpose of Playing, whose
end+ both at the first and now, was and is, to hold as 'twer
the Mirrour up to Nature; + to shew Vertue her owne
Feature, Scorne her owne Image, and the verie Age and
Bodie of the Time,$_x$ his forme and pressure.
6 Now,$_x$ this
over-done, or come tardie off, though it [make] the unskil-
full laugh, cannot but make the Judicious greeve; The
censure of the which One,$_x$ must in your allowance o're-
way a whole Theater of Others.

8 O*, there be* Δplayers that
I have seen* Δplay - and heard others praise, and that highly - not to speak* it profanely*, that, neither* having the accent of Christians nor the [gait*] of Christian, Δpagan, [nor man], have so strutted and bellowed that I have thought some of Nature's Δjourney°men had made men, and not made them well, they imitated Δhumanity so abominably*.

9 {ψ} And let those that
play your Δclowns* speak* no more [than] is set down* for them, ◊ for there be of them, that will themselves laugh, to set on some quantity* of barren Δspectators to laugh too, though in the mean* time some necessary Δquestion of the Δplay be [than] to be considered. †

10 That's villainous*, and
shows* a most pitiful* Δambition in the Δfool* that uses it.

11 Go make you ready*.

• after the quiet imploring of the short F #3, as Hamlet returns to his series of instructions his passions return (F #4, 2/2) which he quickly reins in, re-establishing intellectual control (21/9, F #5-6) for the remainder of his instructions

• but once more, as he breaks off into describing bad actors whose performances have offended him, his intellect gives way, this time to passion (8/9, F #7)

• commentators acknowledge that F #8-9 is a contemporary reference to the 'Clownes' of his own company improvising too much, so it's hardly surprising that this moment is first emotional (1/3, F #8) then with the intellectual elaboration (3/1, F #9's first three and a half lines), quickly turning to passion in his final surround phrase denunciation (3/3, F #9's last line and half)

• and after all the verbiage and side-tracks, as the time grows near for the performance which Hamlet hopes will reveal all, at last Hamlet becomes quiet (the unembellished F #10)

7 Oh, there bee Players that
I have seene Play, and heard others praise, and that highly (x not to speake it prophanely x) that+ neyther having the accent of Christians, x nor the [gate] of Christian, Pagan, [or Norman], have so strutted and bellowed, x that I have thought some of Natures Jouerney-men had made men, and not made them well, they imitated Humanity so abhominably.

8 {ψ} And let those that
play your Clownes, x speake no more [then] is set downe for them.

9 For there be of them, that will themselves laugh, to set on some quantitie of barren Spectators to laugh too, though in the meane time, x some necessary Question of the Play be [then] to be considered: that's Villanous, & shewes a most pittifull Ambition in the Foole that uses it.

10 Go make you readie.

#'s 19: Polonius & Laertes

19/ Polonius **Yet heere Laertes? Aboord, aboord for shame,** 1.2.55 - 81

Background: This is Polonius' first major speech in the play - his previous appearance having been in a formal situation. This domestic advice is both self-explanatory and sheds light on the personal values he claims to hold, which don't always stand up in public (considering his later treatment of his daughter).

Style: as part of a three-handed scene

Where: somewhere in or close to Polonius' chambers **To Whom:** Laertes, in front of Ophelia

# of Lines: 27 **Probable Timing: 1.30 minutes**

Modern Text

19/ Polonius

1 Yet here*, Laertes?
2 Aboard*, aboard*, for shame! †
3 The wind* sits in the shoulder of your sail*,
And you are stay'd* for [ ]. †
4 There - my blessing with [thee !]
And these few Δprecepts in thy memory
See thou Δcharacter.
5 Give thy thoughts no tongue,
Nor any unproportion'd thought his Δact. †
6 Be thou familiar, but by no means* vulgar. †

• as befits a father giving his blessing/advice to his only son, much of the information (more than fifteen of the twenty-seven lines) is given extra weight by being spoken via surround phrases, many of them highlighted either by (emotional) semicolons, starting with " : my blessing with [you] ; /And these few Precepts in thy memory,/See thou Character . "
" ; be thou familiar ; but by no means vulgar : "
and/or by being set within a lengthy sequence
" . Beware/Of entrance to a quarrell : but being in/Bear't that th'opposed may beware of thee . /Give every man thine eare ; but few thy voyce : /Take each mans censure ; but reserve thy judgement : /Costly thy habit as thy purse can buy/But not exprest in fancie ; rich, not gawdie : /For the Apparell oft proclaimes the man."

First Folio

19/ Polonius

1 Yet heere+ Laertes?
2 Aboord, aboord+ for shame,+
The winde sits in the shoulder of your saile,
And you are staid for there: x my blessing with [you];+
And these few Precepts in thy memory, x
See thou Character.
3 Give thy thoughts no tongue,
Nor any unproportion'd thought his Act:
Be thou familiar; x but by no meanes vulgar:

{ctd. over}

7 [Those] friends thou hast, and their adoption tried*,
Grapple them to thy △soul*, with hoops* of steel*,
But do* not dull thy palm* with entertainment
Of each [new-hatch'd], unfledg'd △comrade.
8 Beware
Of entrance to a quarrel*, but being in,
Bear't that th'opposed may beware of thee.
9 Give every man thine ear*, but few thy voice*,
Take each man's censure, but reserve thy judgment*.†
10 Costly thy habit as thy purse can buy,
But not express'd* in fancy*, rich, not gaudy*,
For the △apparel* oft proclaims* the man, ◊
And they in France of the best rank* and station
Are of a most select and generous chief* in that.
11 Neither a borrower, nor a lender be,
For loan* oft loses both itself* and friend,
And borrowing [dulleth] th'edge] of △husbandry.
12 This above all: to thine own* self* be true,
And it must follow, as the △night the △day,
Thou canst not then be false to any man.
13 Farewell, my △blessing season this in thee!

" . Neither a borrower, nor a lender be ; /For lone oft loses both it selfe and friend : /And borrowing duls the edge of Husbandry. /This above all ; to thine owne selfe be true : "
finishing with
"Farewell : my Blessing season this in thee . "

- beneath this heavy weight the unembellished phrases show where Polonius becomes quiet (imparting the personal philosophies he holds most dear perhaps)
"Give thy thoughts no tongue," and "Take each mans censure"
and, if having unsuccessfully avoided a quarrel,
" : but being in/Bear't that th'opposed may beware of thee . "
this sense of honour enhanced by being set as a surround phrase, the sense of proportion being applied to the clothing Laertes should wear, once more heightened as surround phrases
" : Costly thy habit as thy purse can buy /But not exprest in fancie ; rich, not gawdie : "

- the opening chiding of his son (whether teasing or serious) opens emotionally (1/5, the first two and a half lines), then becomes intellectual as he prepares to offer both 'blessing' and 'these few Precepts' (2/0, F #2's last two lines)

- the initial advice concerning his 'thoughts' and 'friends' is both passionate and emotional (4/7, F #3), and then Polonius becomes both quiet and emotional in outlining the way Laertes should behave in public, be it in a quarrel, treating criticism and advice, or manner of dress (1/6, F #4-5)

- and in finishing, leading to the all important ' . This above all ; to thine owne selfe be true : ' the quietness continues with only a few intellectual and emotional releases, (just 5/5, the nine lines F #6-9)

- and considering the emotional flashes throughout the speech the fact that the last three lines show no such release is quite fascinating

[The] friends thou hast, and their adoption tride,
Grapple them to thy Soule, with hoopes of Steele : x
But doe not dull thy palme,x with entertainment
Of each [unhatch't], unfledg'd Comrade.
4 Beware
Of entrance to a quarrell :x but being in+
Bear't that th'opposed may beware of thee.
5 Give every man thine eare ;x but few thy voyce : x
Take each mans censure ;x but reserve thy judgement :
Costly thy habit as thy purse can buy +
But not exprest in fancie ;x rich, not gawdie :x
For the Apparell oft proclaimes the man.
6 And they in France of the best ranck and station,x
Are of a most select and generous cheff in that.
7 Neither a borrower, nor a lender be ;x
For lone oft loses both it selfe and friend :x
And borrowing [duls the edge] of Husbandry.
8 This above all ;x to thine owne selfe be true :x
And it must follow, as the Night the Day,
Thou canst not then be false to any man.
9 Farewell :x my Blessing season this in thee.+

#'S 20 - 25: THE DECLINE AND DEATH OF OPHELIA & LAERTES

20/ Ophelia ***How should I your true love know from another one ?*** between 4.5.23 - 55

21/ Ophelia **Ile make an end ont.** between 4.5.57 - 74

Background: Following her father Polonius' enforcing of her break-up with Hamlet, with unexpectedly violent verbal results (speeches #11-12), and then Polonius' slaying, Ophelia's wits have turned. Asking to speak to Gertrude, Ophelia breaks into what at first appears to be mere doggerel and song. However, the content contains clear references not only to the obvious fact of how deeply her father's loss has affected her but also to the possibility that despite the warnings of her father and brother she and Hamlet have been more than good friends. Two notes: first, the two speeches can be combined as one; second, the famous speech where she hands flowers and herbs of remembrance to all listed below as well as her brother Laertes is not included here, since it involves such specific interaction with four different characters.

Style: as part of (eventually) a four-handed scene

Where: unspecified in the palace, perhaps the Queene's chambers **To Whom:** speech #20: initially Gertrude, in front of Claudius and Horatio; speech #21: Gertrude, Claudius, Horatio & Laertes

Speech 20: # of Lines: 16 **Probable Timing: 0.50 minutes**

Speech 21: # of Lines: 14 **Probable Timing: 0.45 minutes**

Modern Text

20/ Ophelia

1 "How should I your true-love know
From another one ? †

2 By his Δcockle hat and staff*,
And his Δsandal shoon*. "

3 Nay, pray you mark*.

4 "He is dead and gone, Δlady,
He is dead and gone,
At his head a grass*-green* Δturf*,
At his heels* a stone . "

5 Pray you mark*.

6 "White his Δshroud* as the Δmountain* Δsnow -◊
Larded with sweet flowers,
Which bewept to the grave did not go
With true-love showers*. "

7 Lord, we* know what we are, but
know not what we may be.

8 God be at your Δtable !

The reason for the bolding of F #1 and #3 is that the setting of this part of Ophelia's song is in the reversed heartbeat patterns associated with magic – suggesting that these particular lines are extremely powerful for her, not surprising since they are the first public references to Hamlet's supposed love for her (F #1) and the death of her father.

• it may just be that in the so-called madness she is trying to tell her listeners what has happened between Hamlet and herself, for the only surround phrase, F #9's
" . When they aske you what it meanes, say you this : "
precedes the possible loss of virginity song

• at certain moments it seems the recollections are almost too much for her, for she becomes very quiet with the unembellished
"How should I your true love know from another one?"
"he is dead and gone"
"Larded with sweet flowers/Which bewept to the grave did not go, /With true-love showres."
"but know not what we may be."
"Then up he rose, & don'd his clothes, & dupt the chamber dore,"
and finally, perhaps referring to a loss of virginity (whether just the 'Maid' in the song, or her own is up to each actress to decide)
"never, departed more."

• the singing, possibly about Hamlet rather than her father's death, starts out passionately (2/2, F #1) but, perhaps because her listeners

First Folio

20/ Ophelia

1 ***How should I your true love know from another one ?***
By his Cockle hat and staffe, and his Sandal shoone .

2 Nay+ pray you marke.

3 ***He is dead and gone+ Lady, he is dead and gone,***
At his head a grasse-greene Turfe, at his heeles a stone .

4 Pray you marke.

5 [11] *White his Shrow'd as the Mountaine Snow .*

6 *Larded with sweet flowers +*
Which bewept to the grave did not go,ₓ
With true-love showres.

7 Lord, wee know what we are, but
know not what we may be.

8 God be at your Table. +

{ctd. over}

[11] though all the songs and poems Ophelia quotes throughout this and the following scene are set in the italicised font used for songs and poetry, this is only one of two in this scene where Ff's setting is laid out in a poetic format (the other being the next but one, starting 'By gis, and by S. Charity'): all the songs/poems are set poetically in the next scene, perhaps suggesting in this first sequence it takes her a while to discover her full (poetic/singing) voice: Q2 throughout does not set any of the material in a poetic format or special font, but simply adds a stage direction to indicate when she sings: also, the first song is the only one set in the magic/ ritual pattern (seven syllable reversed heart-beat, trochaic) found in *Macbeth* and *A Midsommer Nights Dreame,* perhaps suggesting the content of this first song has special import for Ophelia

9 When they ask* you what it means*, say you this :

10 "Tomorrow is [Saint] Valentines day,
All in the morning betime,
And I a $^{\Delta}$maid at your $^{\Delta}$window,
To be your Valentine .

11 Then up he rose and donn'd$_*$ his clothes,
And dupp'd$_*$ the chamber-door*,
Let in the $^{\Delta}$maid, that out a $^{\Delta}$maid
Never departed more . "

cannot grasp what she is trying to tell them, Ophelia becomes emotional in F #2's short and very direct plea/order 'Nay pray you marke.' and the subsequent (F #3) lines about her father (2/5)

• even though it seems that now all present listen to her for F #4's second short 'Pray you marke.' and the subsequent F #5 still remain passionate (3/3): however, save for 'showres' the ensuing F #6 is totally unembellished, so it looks as if Ophelia has now managed to control herself, especially when the apparent summary and farewell (F #7-8) is handled so well (1/1)

• but then comes the emotional surround phrase opening F #9 (0/2), and it seems that she attaches great importance to the final information she tries to impart, for three of the final four lines are strongly intellectual (8/0) with F #11's final line, the lover (Hamlet?) letting in the about to be deflowered maid, being unembellished

9 {W}hen they aske you what it meanes, say you this :

10 *Tomorrow is [S]. Valentines day, all in the morning betime,*
And I a Maid at your Window, to be your Valentine .

11 *Then up he rose,$_x$ & don'd his clothes, & dupt the chamber dore,*
Let in the Maid, that out a Maid,$_x$ never departed more .

Modern Text

21/ Ophelia

1 {ψ}I'll make an end on't.

2 "By $^{\Delta}$Gis, and by [Saint] Charity,
Alack*, and fie for shame ! †

3 Young* men will$_*$ do t*, if they come to t*,
By Cock* they are to* blame .

4 Quoth she 'Before you tumbled me,
You promis'd me to $^{\Delta}$wed' - "
[He answers]
" 'So would I ['a'] done, by yonder $^{\Delta}$sun*,
And thou hadst not come to my bed . ' "

5 We must be* patient,
but I cannot choose but weep* to think* they should
lay him i'th'cold ground . †

6 My brother shall know* of it,
and so I thank* you for your good counsel*.

7 Come, my
$^{\Delta}$coach ! †

8 Goodnight $^{\Delta}$ladies, $^{\Delta}$goodnight . †

9 Sweet $^{\Delta}$ladies,
Goodnight, goodnight.

• the three unembellished phrases point to the heart of her troubles, from the determined opening
"Ile make an end ont."
"Quoth she before you tumbled me,'
and the final recognition of why the male lover will now have nothing to do with the woman he has seduced
"And thou hadst not come to my bed."

• while the appearance of the surround phrases occuring only at the end of the speech seems to suggest that she might be trying to keep up appearances, from the first reassurance that she still has a family (who will probably take revenge)
" : My brother shall knowe of it,/and so I thanke you for your good counsell. "
and the final ensuing over-effusive farewells (which could range from genuine to sardonic)
" . Come, my Coach : Goodnight Ladies : Goodnight sweet Ladies : Goodnight, goodnight."

• after the quiet F #1, F #2's first verse of the song, the general blaming-of-men, is passionate (3/4), while the second verse (the rejection of the woman after the loss of her virginity) seems somewhat more awkward, with the passion (2/1) framed by two unembellished lines – as if it were difficult to admit

• then suddenly the emotions flood through at F #4's thought of her father laid 'i'th cold ground' (1/6), which springs somewhat ungrammatically via the colon into the sudden mentioning of her brother – an onrush/surprise connection not normally set by most modern texts which usually split F #4 into two

• yet she seems to make a remarkable recovery, for the final farewells are totally intellectual (6/0), yet the self-control may be illusory, for the whole is set within an onrush which most modern texts rework as three separate sentences

First Folio

21/ Ophelia

1 {ψ}Ile make an end ont.

2 *By gis, and by [S]. Charity,*
Alacke, and fie for shame : +
Yong men wil doo't, if they come too't,
By Cocke they are too blame .

3 *Quoth she before you tumbled me,*
You promis'd me to Wed :
[ ]
So would I [ha] done+ by yonder Sunne,
And thou hadst not come to my bed .

4 We must bee patient,
but I cannot choose but weepe,$_x$ to thinke they should
lay him i'th'cold ground : My brother shall knowe of it,
and so I thanke you for your good counsell.

5 Come, my
Coach : + Goodnight Ladies :$_x$ Goodnight+ sweet Ladies :
Goodnight, goodnight.

22/ Queen **One woe doth tread upon anothers heele,** between 4.7.163 - 183

Background: Laertes' anger towards Hamlet for the death of his father, Hamlet's dallying (as Laertes sees it) with Laertes' sister Ophelia, and his witnessing Ophelia's last public act of madness, the herb and flower-giving, has grown exponentially. Claudius is using it to plan a second attempt on Hamlet's life when Gertrude interrupts with the following sad news.

Style: as part of a three-handed scene

Where: unspecified in the palace, perhaps Claudius' private chambers **To Whom:** Laertes, in front of Claudius

# of Lines: 20 **Probable Timing: 1.00 minutes**

Modern Text

22/ Queen

1 One woe doth tread upon another's heel*,
So fast [they] follow. †
2 Your △sister's drown'd, Laertes.
3 There is a △willow grows* [askant the] △brook*,
That shows* his [hoary$_*$] leaves in the glassy$_*$ stream*,
There with fantastic* △garlands did she [make]
Of △crow-flowers, △nettles, △daisies*, and long △purples
That liberal* △shepherds* give a grosser name,
But our cold △maids do* △dead △men's △fingers call them. †
4 There on the pendant boughs* her △coronet weeds
Clamb'ring to hang, an envious sliver broke,
When down* the weedy Trophies and herself*
Fell in the weeping △brook*. †
5 Her clothes* spread$_*$ wide,
And △mermaid-like awhile they bore her up,
Which time she chanted* snatches of old [lauds],
As one incapable of her own* distress*,
Or like a creature △native and indued
Unto that △element. †
6 But long it could not be
Till that her garments, heavy with [their] drink*,
Pull'd$_*$ the poor* wretch from her melodious [lay]
To muddy death.

While most modern texts present a somewhat rational Gertrude, telling Laertes the news of his sister's death in six essentially rational sentences, F shows her self-control to be much more difficult, mt. #1 and 2 originally set as the slightly onrushed F #1 (the lead-in to and the quick juxtaposition of the news of Ophelia's drowning), with the details, spread over mt. #6, jammed together in the one long seventeen and a half line F #2.

- all that really need be said can be found in the two surround phrases that open the speech, F #1
  ". One woe doth tread upon anothers heele,/So fast [they'l] follow: your Sister's drown'd Laertes ."
  the first emotional (0/1), the information of the second strictly factual (2/0)

- at first the only two other surround phrases seem unnecessary
  "; But our cold Maids doe Dead Mens Fingers call them : /There on the pendant boughes, her Coronet weeds/Clambring to hang ; "
  yet the semicolons (suggesting great emotion) and the second phrase, beginning to explain how Ophelia came to fall in the water, point to the extreme strain Gertrude is under, with the first phrase perhaps an attempt to put off (or ready herself) having to speak about the actual drowning

- in establishing the what and where of the new 'woe' the speech starts passionately (4/4 the first four lines), while the details of the 'Garlands' of flowers Ophelia was weaving are handled much more factually (10/5, F #2's lines three to six, to the second colon)

- in describing Ophelia's 'Clambring' on to the 'pendant boughes' and falling into the 'weeping Brooke', Gertrude becomes passionate once more (3/4, F #2's lines seven to ten) while the remainder of the speech, right up to the point of 'muddy death', is gently emotional (2/5, the last seven lines), the only intellectual digression being when Gertrude elaborates the earlier 'Mermaid-like' image of Ophelia as seeming to belong to the water 'like a creature Native, and indued/Unto that Element'

First Folio

22/ Queen

1 One woe doth tread upon anothers heele,
So fast [they'l] follow: your Sister's drown'd+ Laertes.
2 There is a Willow growes [aslant a] Brooke,
That shewes his [hore] leaves in the glassie streame:$_x$
There with fantasticke Garlands did she [come],$_x$
Of Crow-flowers, Nettles, Daysies, and long Purples,$_x$
That liberall Shepheards give a grosser name; $_x$
But our cold Maids doe Dead Mens Fingers call them:
There on the pendant boughes,$_x$ her Coronet weeds
Clambring to hang; $_x$ an envious sliver broke,
When downe the weedy Trophies,$_x$ and her selfe,$_x$
Fell in the weeping Brooke, her cloathes spred wide,
And Mermaid-like,$_x$ a while they bore her up,
Which time she chaunted snatches of old [tunes],
As one incapable of her owne distresse,
Or like a creature Native,$_x$ and indued
Unto that Element: but long it could not be,$_x$
Till that her garments, heavy with [her] drinke,
Pul'd the poore wretch from her melodious [buy],$_x$
To muddy death.

23/ Clown **Is she to bee buried in Christian buriall,** between 5.1.1 - 29

Background: Despite the suspicion that Ophelia committed suicide and therefore should not be accorded a Christian burial (see speech #24 immediately below), she is to be buried in sanctified ground, to the surprise of the Gravediggers.

Style: as part of a two-handed scene

Where: a grave-yard **To Whom:** his fellow Grave-Digger/Clowne

# of Lines: 19 **Probable Timing: 1.00 minutes**

Modern Text

23/ Clown

1 Is she to be* buried in Christian burial* [when she]
willfully* seeks* her own* salvation?

2 How can that be, unless* she drowned herself* in
her own* defense?

3 It must be se offendendo, it cannot be* else. †
4 For here*
lies the point: Δif I drown* myself* wittingly, it argues an Δact, and an Δact hath three branches - ◊ it is [to]
Δact, to do*, and to perform*; argal*, she drown'd herself*
wittingly.

5 Give me leave. †
6 Here* lies the water; good. †
7 Here* stands the man; good. †
8 If the man go* to this wa-
ter and drown* himself*, it is, will he, nill he, he goes,
mark* you that?
9 But if the water come to him & drown*
him, he* drowns* not himself*; ◊ argal*, he* that is
not guilty of his own* death shortens not his own* life.

10 Will you ha' the truth on't. †
11 If this had not
been* a Δgentlewoman, Δshe* should have been* buried
out ['a] Christian Δburial*.

12 {ψT}he more pity* that
great folk* should have count'nance* in this world to
drown* or hang themselves, more [than]their even Christian.

It seems that the Clown becomes very emotional when debating (whether this particular situation is pleasurable or the class-struggle unfairness of an upper class suicide being allowed a Christian burial has riled him is up to each actor to explore), for in the long sequence of sixteen consecutive surround phrases (F #3-6) suggesting that he is pushing his argument quite relentlessly, no fewer than eight of the twelve pieces of major punctuation are emotional semicolons.

- in questioning the idea of 'Christian buriall' even before the intense debate manifests itself, the speech starts emotionally (1/7, F #1-2)
- the moment the assertion that it was suicide ('Se offendendo') is spoken aloud, the Clowne becomes passionate (4/4, F #3), but the heightened surround phrase elaboration as to why it must be considered suicide (F #5-7) turns very emotional (1/14)
- after the proof is finished comes a very careful monosyllabic unembellished surround phrase ' . Will you ha the truth on't : ' (perhaps pointing to the underlying political awareness beneath the Clowne's more usually accepted mask of fun and humour), which springs into a second passionate release (4/4, F #8's remaining two lines) as the key social class distinction is voiced
- which in turn leads to a final emotional class struggle denunciation of the privileges 'great folke' seem to have when compared to other Christians (0/4, F #9)

First Folio

23/ Clown

1 Is she to bee buried in Christian buriall,x [that]
wilfully seekes her owne salvation?

2 How can that be, unlesse she drowned her selfe in
her owne defence?

3 It must be *Se offendendo*, it cannot bee else: for heere
lies the point; x If I drowne my selfe wittingly, it argues an Act: x and an Act hath three branches.
4 It is [an] Act+
to doe+ and to performe; argall+ she drown'd her selfe
wittingly.

5 Give me leave; heere lies the water; good:
heere stands the man; good: If the man goe to this water and drowne himselfe; x it is+ will he+ nill he, he goes;x
marke you that?
6 But if the water come to him & drowne
him; x hee drownes not himselfe.
7 Argall, hee that is
not guilty of his owne death,x shortens not his owne life.

8 Will you ha the truth on't: If this had not
beene a Gentlewoman, Δshee should have beene buried
out [of] Christian Buriall.

9 {ψT}he more pitty that
great folke should have countenance in this world to
drowne or hang themselves, more [then] their even Christian.

24/ Priest **Her Obsequies have bin as farre inlarg'd,** between 5.1.226 - 238

Background: At the King's command, Ophelia is being buried in holy ground. The event is being handled before a tiny group of mourners with as little ceremony as possible, offending her brother mightily, who has demanded twice 'What Cerimony else?'. The following is the Priest's unequivocal reply.

Style: initially to one man, for the benefit of the small group present

Where: a grave-yard **To Whom:** Laertes, in front of the King and Queene, some 'Lords attendant', with Hamlet and Horatio watching unobserved

# of Lines: 12 **Probable Timing: 0.40 minutes**

Modern Text

24/ Priest

1 Her Δobsequies have been* as far* enlarg'd*
As we have [warranty]. †
2 Her death was doubtful*,
And but that great Δcommand, o'ersways* the order,
She should in ground unsanctified [been] lodg'd
Till the last Δtrumpet; ◊ for charitable [prayers],
Shards*, Δflints, and Δpebbles* should be thrown* on her. †
3 Yet here* she is allowed her Δvirgin [crants],
Her Δmaiden strewments, and the bringing home
Of Δbell and Δburial*.
4 {To do more }
We should profane* the service of the dead
To sing [a] Δrequiem and such rest to her
As to peace-parted Δsouls*.

F's orthography points not only to just how disturbed the priest is, but also where he gains and loses self-control.

- his outlining of the facts of what has occurred so far, including political interference, starts passionately (3/2, F #1)
- and the Priest becomes even more passionate in the explanation of what really should be the treatment for Ophelia, as for any suicide, (2/3 in F #2's first line and a half)
  " . For charitable [praier],/Shardes, Flints, and Peebles, should be throwne on her : "
- and then he seems to gain a good degree of self-control as he explains what rights have been granted her thanks to political interference (5/2, the remainder of F #2)
- but then in his protest that to do even more would 'prophane the service of the dead' it seems that self-control begins to crack, for this final sentence is passionate – though not overly so (2/2) , perhaps suggesting that he is being quite circumspect in this protest (attempting to save his own skin)

First Folio

24/ Priest

1 Her Obsequies have bin as farre inlarg'd,x
As we have [warrantis], her death was doubtfull,
And but that great Command, o're-swaies the order,
She should in ground unsanctified [have] lodg'd,x
Till the last Trumpet.
2 For charitable [praier],
Shardes, Flints, and Peebles,x should be throwne on her:
Yet heere she is allowed her Virgin [Rites],
Her Maiden strewments, and the bringing home
Of Bell and Buriall.
3 {To do more }
We should prophane the service of the dead,x
To sing [sage] Requiem,x and such rest to her
As to peace-parted Soules.

25/ Laertes **I am justly kill'd with mine owne Treacherie.** between 5.2.307 - 331

Background: In the supposed exhibition-only duel at the end of the play Laertes, at the urgings of Claudius, has prepared his unbarbed foil with poison. Claudius has further poisoned a loving-cup, planning that if Hamlet isn't scratched by Laertes' foil at least he will drink the poison. But everything goes awry, with Gertrude drinking the poison, and though Hamlet is fatally scratched, in the ensuing scuffle his and Laertes foils are switched and Laertes is mortally wounded too. The following is Laertes' dying confession.

Style: one on one address in front of, and perhaps for the benefit of, a larger group

Where: the great hall of the palace **To Whom:** Hamlet, in front of Claudius, the dead Gertrude, Horatio, Osricke, with 'lords' and 'other attendants'

# of Lines: 12 **Probable Timing: 0.40 minutes**

Modern Text

25/ Laertes

1 I am justly kill'd with mine own* Δtreachery*.
2 Hamlet, thou art slain* . †
3 No Δmed'cine[12]* in the world can do thee good; ◊
In thee there is not half* an [hour's*] life. †
4 The Δtreacherous Δinstrument is in thy hand,
Unbated and envenom'd. †
5 The foul* practice*
Hath turn'd itself* on me.
6 Lo* here* I lie*,
Never to rise again*. †
7 Thy Δmother's poison'd*. †
8 I can no more - the King, the King's to* blame.
9 Exchange forgiveness* with me, Δnoble Hamlet. †
10 Mine and my Δfather's death come not upon thee,
Nor thine on me !

While most modern texts allow Laertes a dignified and rational final confession by setting the speech as ten sentences, F's five onrushed sentences and over-punctuated orthography in F #3-4 shows a character much more under the influence of the poison (painfully? struggling to fight the effects?) as well as his urgency to ensure Hamlet understands and forgives all before both of them die.

- of the nine consecutive surround phrases from F #3 to the end of the speech,
  a/ the first seven of F #3-4 show first the strain and importance to Laertes in explaining all the facts hitherto unknown to Hamlet
  b/ while the final two (F #5) encompass Laertes' request for Hamlet's forgiveness for Laertes' part in his death, and Laertes' act of forgiveness for Hamlet's part in the deaths of his father and sister, Polonius and Ophelia

- that the structure of F #2 and the opening of F #3 are very different from those of most modern texts have important human implications: again the modern texts seem to concentrate on rationality, while F seems more concerned with Hamlet's (and thus Laertes') fate
  a/ the onrush of F #2 suggests the emphasis is to be on the fact there is no possible remedy for Hamlet, whereas most modern texts place equal (and more rational) weight on both being 'slain' and 'No med'cine'
  b/ F's next sentence, F#3, opens with the inescapable fact that for Hamlet 'In thee, there is not half an houre of life;', enhanced by the semicolon ending the surround phrase, whereas in the modern texts this is folded into mt. #3's lack of 'med'cine', with the next new sentence (mt. #4) placing emphasis on 'The treacherous instrument'

- the speech opens passionately (2/3, F #1-2); the circumstances of Hamlet's imminent death are emotional (2/4, the onrushed F #3); the presentation of Laertes' own death (perhaps as proof of his own honesty) and the blaming of Claudius for the Queene's death is passionate (4/6, the onrushed F #4)

- and the dignity that modern texts seem to need throughout the speech is finally shown in the final F moment, where the request for mutual acts of forgiveness are offered intellectually (3/1, the slightly onrushed F #5) – a lovely suggestion of Laertes achieving self control at the last moment

First Folio

25/ Laertes

1 I am justly kill'd with mine owne Treacherie.
2 Hamlet, thou art slaine,
No Medicine in the world can do thee good.
3 In thee,x there is not halfe an [houre of] life;
The Treacherous Instrument is in thy hand,
Unbated and envenom'd: the foule practise: x
Hath turn'd it selfe on me.
4 Loe,x heere I lye,
Never to rise againe: Thy Mothers poyson'd:
I can no more, the King, the King's too blame.
5 Exchange forgivenesse with me, Noble Hamlet;
Mine and my Fathers death come not upon thee,
Nor thine on me. +

[12] Q2 = 'medcin', thus maintaining a ten syllable line, Ff = 'Medicine'

SPEECHES IN ORDER		TIME	PAGE
TROYLUS & CRESSIDA			
#'s 1 - 8: The Pangs Of Love			
1/ Troylus	Oh Pandarus! I tell thee Pandarus;	0.50	159
2/ Pandarus	Harke they are comming from the field,	2.30	160
3/ Cressida	Words, vowes, gifts, teares, & loves full sacrifice,	0.45	163
4/ Pandarus	Come, come, what neede you blush?	0.55	164
5/ Cressida	Boldnesse comes to mee now, and brings mee	1.00	166
6/ Cressida	Prophet may you be:/If I be false, or swerve a haire	0.45	167
7/ Cressida	O you immortall gods! I will not goe.	0.45	168
8/ Troylus	This she? no, this is Diomids Cressida:	2.00	169
#'s 9 - 12: The Greeks' Problem, Especially With Achilles			
9/ Ulysses	Agamemnon./Thou great Commander, . . .	3.45	171
10/ Ulysses	Thank the heavens L. thou art of sweet composure;	1.15	174
11/ Achilles	What meane these fellowes? know they not . . .	1.15	175
12/ Ulysses	Time hath (my Lord) a wallet at his backe,	2.10	177
#'s 13 - 15: Thersites			
13/ Thersites	A wonder./Ajax goes up and downe the field	1.00	179
14/ Thersites	Prythee be silent boy, I profit not by thy talke,	0.40	180
15/ Thersites	With too much bloud, and too little Brain, these	0.55	181
#'s 16 - 18: Single Combat			
16/ Æneas	Trumpet blow loud,	1.30	182
17/ Hector	Thou art great Lord, my Fathers sisters Sonne;	1.00	184
18/ Nestor	I have (thou gallant Troyan) seene thee oft	0.55	185
#'s 19 - 21: Cassandra and the Finality of War			
19/ Cassandra	Cry Troyans cry; lend me ten thousand eyes,	0.40	186
20/ Cassandra	O farewell, deere Hector:/Looke how thou diest;	0.35	187
21/ Troylus	Hector is slaine.	1.30	188

SPEECHES BY GENDER		Speech #(s)
SPEECHES FOR WOMEN (6)		
Cressida	**Traditional & Today:** young teenage woman	#3, #5, #6, #7
Cassandra	**Traditional & Today:** young to middle-aged woman	#19, #20
SPEECHES FOR EITHER GENDER (0)		
SPEECHES FOR MEN (15)		
Troylus	**Traditional & Today:** young, perhaps teenage, male	#1, #8, #21
Pandarus	**Traditional:** older man **Today:** male, old enough to have an adolescent niece	#2, #4
Ulysses	**Traditional:** capable military male, middle-aged or older **Today:** male, any age	#9, #10, #12
Achilles	**Traditional & Today:** male , any age capable of military action	#11
Thersites	**Traditional & Today:** male, any age, often cast as a twisted form of a jester, though commentator might be a better description	#13, #14, #15
Æneas	**Traditional:** capable military male, middle-aged or older **Today:** male, any age	#16
Hector	**Traditional & Today:** young married man	#17
Nestor	**Traditional & Today:** older male commander	#18

TROYLUS & CRESSIDA

#'s 1 - 8: The Pangs of love

1/ Troylus **Oh Pandarus! I tell thee Pandarus ;** 1.1.48 - 63

Background: The young soldier Troylus is head over heels in love with Cressida, so much so that he is almost prepared not to join in the daily battle with the Greeks; to make matters worse, he is getting little sympathy from her uncle Pandarus.

Style: as part of a two-handed scene

Where: somewhere in Troy close to the gates and the battle **To Whom:** Pandarus

# of Lines: 16 **Probable Timing: 0.50 minutes**

Modern Text

1/ Troylus
1 O* Pandarus!
2 I tell thee, Pandarus -
When I do* tell thee there my hopes lie* drown'd,
Reply not in how many Δfathoms* deep*
They lie* indrench'd.
3 I tell thee I am mad
In Cressid's love; ◊ thou answer'st she is Δfair*,
Pourest* in the open Δulcer of my heart
Her Δeyes, her Δhair*, her Δcheek*, her [gait], her Δvoice;
Handlest in thy discourse,◊ O, that her Δhand,
In whose comparison all whites are Δink*
Writing their own* reproach; to whose soft seizure
The Δcygnet's* Δdown* is harsh, and spirit of Δsense
Hard as the palm* of Δploughman: ◊ this thou tell'st$_*$ me,
As true thou tell'st$_*$ me, when I say I love her,
But saying thus, instead of Δoil* and Δ balm*,
Thou lay'st$_*$ in every gash that love hath given me
The Δknife that made it.

While Troylus' words of love are more than sufficient indication of the depth of his passion, F's more broken up text, both in the extra sentences F #3-6 (set as one long onrush by most modern texts) and in the ungrammatical punctuation towards the end of F #4 shows how both the thoughts and the expression of his love are somewhat less than rational.

- from the very start, in telling Pandarus 'my hopes lye drown'd', Troylus seems agitated, with the two word passionate F #1 (1/1) ending with a rare (for an original Shakespeare printing) exclamation mark and the emotional F #2 (2/5) being composed entirely of three surround phrases, the first two heightened even further by being linked by an (emotional) semicolon

- however, in explaining the root of the problem, 'I am mad in Cressids love', and how Pandarus is not helping by continuing to talk about her, Troylus seems to regain intellectual control (8/4, F #3-4) – but F's peculiar punctuation suggests that this may only mask how deeply he is still disturbed: most modern texts attempt to clarify the text by setting major punctuation after 'voice' and removing F's period (and Q's colon) after 'discourse', as shown, although this rational rewrite doesn't really match Troylus' passion as originally expressed - especially when considering the broken nature of the rest of his comments

- after the broken end to F #4's, as Troylus' focuses on Cressida's hand he starts passionately (via the first two lines of the new F only #5, 2/2), but the struggle to stay on even keel seems difficult for him to manage, for he seesaws back to intellect (4/2, F #5's last two lines) with the moment of transition marked by the second emotional semicolon of the speech

- certainly the final sentence continues to show this struggle, for the calm start
  " This thou tel'st me ; /As true thou tel'st me, when I say I love her : "
  (its unembellishment doubly weighted by being monosyllabic and made up of two surround phrases) is quickly replaced by a passionate cluster (3/2) as he clarifies just what pain Pandarus has caused him – though, interestingly, the lead in 'Thou lai'st in every gash that love hath given me' is once more unembellished, as if Troylus can hardly give it voice

First Folio

1/ Troylus
1 Oh Pandarus!
2 I tell thee+ Pandarus; $_x$
When I doe tell thee,$_x$ there my hopes lye drown'd:$_x$
Reply not in how many Fadomes deepe
They lye indrench'd.
3 I tell thee,$_x$ I am mad
In Cressids love.
4 Thou answer'st she is Faire,
Powr'st in the open Ulcer of my heart,$_x$
Her Eyes, her Haire, her Cheeke, her [Gate], her Voice,+
Handlest in thy discourse.
5 O+ that her Hand+
($_x$In whose comparison,$_x$ all whites are Inke$_x$)
Writing their owne reproach; to whose soft seizure,$_x$
The Cignets Downe is harsh, and spirit of Sense
Hard as the palme of Plough-man.
6 This thou tel'st me;$_x$
As true thou tel'st me, when I say I love her: $_x$
But saying thus, instead of Oyle and Balme,
Thou lai'st in every gash that love hath given me,$_x$
The Knife that made it.

2/ Pandarus **Harke they are comming from the field,** between 1.2.177 - 246

Background: Pandarus is wooing Cressida on Troylus' behalf, by showing her (how unworthy are) the many other young Trojan men returning from battle, setting her up before Troylus finally appears.

Style: as part of a two-handed scene with possibly one other present

Where: outdoors, somewhere near the gates of Troy **To Whom:** Cressida, with perhaps her man Alexander still present

# of Lines: 49 **Probable Timing: 2.30 minutes**

Modern Text

2/ Pandarus

1 Hark*, they are coming* from the field. †
2 Shall* we
stand up here, and see them as they pass* toward [Ilion]? †
3 Good Δniece*, do, sweet Δniece* Cressida.
4 Here*, here*, here's an excellent place, here* we
may see most bravely. †
5 I'll tell* you them all by their names
as they pass* by, but mark* [Troilus] above the rest.
6 That's Æneas; is not that a brave man? †
7 He's* one of
the flowers of Troy, I can [tell] you. †
8 But mark* [Troilus]; you
shall* see anon.
9 That's Antenor. †
10 He has a [shrewd] wit, I can tell
you, and he's* a man good enough. †
11 He's* one o'th soun-
dest [judgments*] in Troy, whosoever, and a proper man of
person. †
12 When comes [Troilus]?
13 I'll show* you [Troilus]
anon. †
14 If he* see me, you shall see him [ ] nod at me.
15 You shall see.
16 That's Hector, that, that, look* you, that there's a
fellow!
17 Go* thy way, Hector! †
18 There's a brave man, Δniece*. †
19 O brave Hector! ◊ look* how he* looks*! †

The fact that F sets thirty-three short sentences, which most modern texts rework into at least sixty-four, suggests that Pandarus' wonderful state of expectation is onrushed, and that often he is in much less personal control than his modern counterpart. Even a first reading only observing the sentence structure of the two speeches should reveal a different energy state between the two characters. In addition F's orthography brings up a very interesting point, that sometimes the sight of three of the four brothers (Hector, Paris, and Troylus – though not Hellenus) leaches all vocal energy out of Pandarus, as if just for a moment something about each of them causes him to become very quiet (whether this leads to a series of personal introspective comments, or is simply being quiet when talking to Cressida is up to each actor to decide).

- in suggesting that he and Cressida find an advantageous place to watch the men return from war, Pandarus begins passionately (F #1, 4/5), and in finding the best place and advising to 'marke Troylus' when he passes he becomes extremely emotional (1/6, in just the three lines of F #2)
- Pandarus' noting the passing of both Æneas (F #3) and Antenor (F #4) and his subsequent urging of Cressida to 'marke Troylus above the rest' is passionate (7/7, the seven and a half lines of F #3-5)
- F #6's very short monosyllabic 'You shall see.' is the first of several unembellished lines scattered through the speech, its quietness - whether directed towards Cressida or more for Pandarus' own benefit - suggests that Pandarus is very taken with Troylus . . .
- . . . as well as with certain other men, for after his initial passionate excitement of seeing Hector (F #7-9, 4/6) the final comments about Troylus' older brother are set up via two more unembellished surround phrases capped off with an unembellished monosyllabic short sentence
  "? there's a countenance; ist not a brave man? Is a not?"

First Folio

2/ Pandarus

1 Harke+ they are comming from the field, shal we
stand up here+ and see them,x as they passe toward [Illium],+
good Neece+ do, sweet Neece Cressida.
2 Heere, heere, here's an excellent place, heere we
may see most bravely, Ile tel you them all by their names,x
as they passe by, but marke [Troylus] above the rest.
3 That's Æneas,+ is not that a brave man,+ hee's one of
the flowers of Troy+ I can [ ] you, but marke [Troylus]+ you
shal see anon.
4 That's Antenor, he has a [shrow'd] wit+ I can tell
you, and hee's a man good inough, hee's one o'th soun-
dest judgement in Troy+ whosoever, and a proper man of
person: when comes [Troylus]?
5 Ile shew you [Troylus] anon,
if hee see me, you shall see him [him[1]] nod at me.
6 You shall see.
7 That's Hector, that, that, looke you, that there's a
fellow. +
8 Goe thy way+ Hector,+ there's a brave man+ Neece,
O brave Hector!

[1] F2/Q and most modern texts = 'him', F1 = 'him him'

20 There's a countenance ! †
21 Is't not a brave man?
22 Is a not?
23 It does* a man's heart good, . †
24 Look* you what hacks are on his △helmet . †
25 Look* you yonder, do you see?
26 Look* you there? ◊ there's no jesting ; [there's] laying on, take't⁎ off who will, as they say . †
27 There be hacks!
28 By God's lid, it does* one's heart good.
29 Yonder comes Paris, yonder comes Paris . †
30 Look* ye* yonder, △niece*; is't not a gallant man too⁎, is't not?
31 Why, this is brave now . †
32 Who said he came hurt home to-day?
33 He's* not hurt . †
34 Why, this will do [Helen's] heart good now, ha?
35 Would I could see [Troilus] now ! †
36 You shall [see] Troilus anon.
37 That's [Helenus] . †
38 I marvel* where [Troilus] is . †
39 That's Helenus . †
40 I think* he went not forth to day . †
41 That's [Helenus].
42 {ψ} Yes, he'll* fight indifferent, well . †
43 I marvel* where [Troilus] is . †
44 Hark*, do you not hear* the people cry⁎ "[Troilus]" ?

- and then Pandarus greets the signs of Hector's success in battle (the hacks on his helmet) with a mixture of emotion (F #11-14, 2/5) and a rather strange moment of unembellishment
  'There's no jesting, laying on, tak't off who will as they say, there be hacks.'
  (perhaps Pandarus is concerned for Hector's wellbeing)

- Pandarus greets the arrival of Paris (F #15-17) with the same mixture of passion and unembellished monosyllabic surround phrases ('Why this is brave now : who said he came hurt home to day ? '), the latter suggesting perhaps Pandarus' moment of relief for both Paris and his lover, the Greek Helen (the woman over whom the war is being fought)

- his F #18 need to see Troylus (notice not Cassandra's need) is expressed intellectually (2/0) – a rarity in this speech

- and even the arrival of Troylus' younger brother cannot sway Pandarus from his need to see Troylus, and though F #19-23 reads as passionate (14/14 overall),
  a/ F #19's fast-link jumps back and forth between the two men (expressed as five separate sentences in most modern texts, mt. #37-41) are passionate (4/4)
  b/ F #20's jump from Hellenus fighting 'indifferent, well' [2] to the possible arrival of Troylus is emotional (2/6)
  c/ F #21's curt dismissal of 'Hellenus is a Priest.' followed by the short F #22, highlighted by the exclamation mark (a rarity for a first Elizabethan printing) announcing the arrival, at last, of Troylus, is handled passionately (2/2)

- the intellect continues through F #23's two surround phrases
  " Ther's a man Neece, hem ; Brave Troylus the Prince of Chivalrie . "
  Pandarus' emotional undercurrent underscored by the semicolon linking the two phrases

- and as Pandarus points out how Troylus' 'Sword is bloodied, and his helme more hackt then Hectors', the excitement continues, with F #24 becoming passionate (5/7) and opening with two surround phrases

9 Looke how hee lookes?+ there's a countenance ; + ist not a brave man?
10 Is a not?
11 It dooes a mans heart good, looke you what hacks are on his Helmet, looke you yonder, do you see?
12 Looke you there?
13 There's no jesting+ , laying on, tak't off who will+ as they say, there be hacks. +
14 By Gods lid+ it dooes ones heart good.
15 Yonder comes Paris, yonder comes Paris : looke yee yonder+ Neece,+ ist not a gallant man to, ist not?
16 Why+ this is brave now : who said he came hurt home to day?
17 Hee's not hurt, why+ this will do [Hellens] heart good now, ha?
18 Would I could see [Troylus] now,+ you shall [ ] Troylus anon.
19 That's [Hellenus], I marvell where [Troylus] is, that's Helenus, I thinke he went not forth to day : that's [Hellenus].
20 {ψ} Yes+ heele fight indifferent, well, I marvell where [Troylus] is ; harke, do you not heare the people crie [Troylus]?

{ctd. over}

---

[2] most modern texts follow F2 and set 'indifferent well': Q/F1 add a comma 'indifferent, well', suggesting the 'well' could be read as an extra dismissal of Helenus' reputation

45 [Helenus] is a △priest.

46 'Tis Troi-
lus!

47 There's* a man, △niece* ! †

48 Hem ! †

49 Brave [Troilus] the △prince
of △chivalry* !

50 Mark* him, [note] him . †

51 [O] brave [Troilus] ! †

52 Look*
well upon him, △niece* . †

53 Look* you how his △sword is bloo-
died*, and his △helm* more hack'd [than] Hector's, and how
he looks*, and how he goes !

54 O admirable youth! he [never]
saw three and twenty.

55 Go thy way, [Troilus] , go thy way ! †

56 Had I a sister were a △grace, or a daughter a △goddess*, he*
should take his choice.

57 O admirable man!

58 Paris?

59 Paris
is dirt* to him, and I warrant Helen, to change, would
give [an eye] to boot.

60 {ψ} Here* [comes] more.

61 Asses, fools*, dolts ! chaff* and bran, chaff* and
bran ! porridge* after meat !

62 I could live and die* [in the eyes]
of [Troilus] .

63 Ne'er look*, ne'er look*, the Eagles are gone*,
△crows* and △daws*, △crows* and △daws* ! †

64 I had rather be
such a man as [Troilus] [than]Agamemnon and all Greece.

- for a third time Pandarus becomes quiet in expounding a young man's grace, for, save for the name 'Troylus', F #25 and #27-8 are unembellished, interrupted by F #26's passionate hint (3/2) to Cressida that Troylus could make a choice of any of Pandarus' female relatives (if he had any) were they a 'Grace' or a 'Goddesse'

- to finish his urging, despite his earlier praise (F #15-17), Pandarus now somewhat more calmly dismisses Paris as 'durt' in comparison to Troylus (F #29, 1/1)

- in comparison with Troylus', Pandarus now becomes emotional in his dismissal of the other men who now appear (1/5, F #30-31) - the final comment being a wonderful emotional surround phrase ' ; porredge after meat .'

- the final urging of Troylus above all others (F #32 and #33's first line and half) is passionate (6/8), again involving an emotional surround phrase as he commands Cressida not to look at the other men ' . Ne're looke, ne're looke ; '

- while the admission that he himself would rather be Troylus than even the Greek leader Agamemnon is surprisingly intellectual (3/1) – a moment of personal truth perhaps

21 [Hellenus] is a Priest.

22 'Tis Troy-
lus!

23 Ther's a man+ Neece,+ hem ; Brave [Troylus]+ the
Prince of Chivalrie. +

24 Marke him, [not] him : brave [Troylus] : + looke
well upon him+ Neece, looke you how his Sword is blou-
died, and his Helme more hackt [then] Hectors, and how
he lookes, and how he goes. +

25 O admirable youth! he [ne're]
saw three and twenty.

26 Go thy way+ [Troylus], go thy way,+
had I a sister were a Grace, or a daughter a Goddesse, hee
should take his choice.

27 O admirable man!

28 Paris?

29 Paris
is durt to him, and I warrant,x Helen+ to change, would
give [money] to boot.

30 {ψ} Heere [come] more.

31 Asses, fooles, dolts,+ chaffe and bran, chaffe and
bran ; + porredge after meat. +

32 I could live and dye [i'th'eyes]
of [Troylus] .

33 Ne're looke, ne're looke ; x the Eagles are gon,
Crowes and Dawes, Crowes and Dawes : + I had rather be
such a man as [Troylus],x [then] Agamemnon,x and all Greece.

3/ Cressida **Words, vowes, gifts, teares, & loves full sacrifice,** 1.2.282 - 295

Background: Though young, Cressida shows her understanding of the world in general, and especially its sexual machinations – indeed just before this speech she has had a wit-duel with her uncle on this subject. Now he's gone she reveals her innermost thoughts to the audience

Style: initially with possibly one other present, and then solo

Where: outdoors, somewhere near the gates of Troy **To Whom:** perhaps her man Alexander is still present at the top of the speech, and then to audience and self

# of Lines: 14 **Probable Timing: 0.45 minutes**

Modern Text

3/ Cressida

1 Words, vows*, gifts, tears*, and love's full sacrifice,
He offers in another's enterprise. †

2 But more in [Troilus] thousand fold I see
[Than] in the glass* of Pandar's praise may be;
Yet hold I off.

3 Women are △angels, wooing:
Things won are done, joy's* soul* lies* in the doing*. †

4 That she belov'd, knows* nought that knows* not this:
Men prize the thing ungain'd more [than] it is.

5 That she was never yet that ever knew
Love got so sweet, as when desire did sue. †

6 Therefore this maxim* out of love I teach:
"Achievement*, is command; ungain'd, beseech"; ◊
[Then] though my heart's [△content] firm* love doth bear*,
Nothing of that shall from mine eyes appear*.

In what is a very adult assessment and some would argue cynical view of love, it is not surprising that Cressida is essentially emotional (4/16 overall), the calm of the unembellished lines and the determined assessments of the surround phrases pointing to the depth of her understanding. Yet the onrush of F #1-2, and the reworking of F #3 (longer than the mt. equivalent) and F #4 (shorter) suggest that she is not quite as calm as the words and orthography alone would indicate.

- thus it's fascinating that the only intellectual moment concerns her obvious admiration of Troylus (F #1's last two and a half lines), and that the most released emotional moment is in her expression of the dilemma of 'joyes soule lyes in the dooing' versus what every woman 'knowes' - that men do not prize what is easily won (0/6 in the second and third lines of F #2)

- the surround phrases underscore the very clear thoughts that currently drive Cressida not to accept Pandarus' surface blandishments, and why
  "; Yet hold I off."
  ". Women are Angels wooing,/Things won are done, joyes soule lyes in the dooing : /That she belov'd, knowes nought, that knowes not this ; /Men prize the thing ungain'd, more then it is."
  ". Therefore this maxime out of love I teach ; /Atchievement, is command; ungain'd, beseech."

- while the calm of the unembellished lines demonstrates a surprisingly clear understanding of manipulations in the name of love for one so young, first dismissing Pandarus because
  "He offers in anothers enterprise:"
then neatly and effortlessly skewering the superficiality of men's desires
  "Men prize the thing ungain'd, more then it is./That she was never yet, that ever knew/Love got so sweet, as when desire did sue:"

First Folio

3/ Cressida

1 Words, vowes, gifts, teares, & loves full sacrifice,
He offers in anothers enterprise:
But more in [Troylus] thousand fold I see,ₓ
[Then] in the glasse of Pandar's praise may be;
Yet hold I off.

2 Women are Angels⁺ wooing,⁺
Things won are done, joyes soule lyes in the dooing:
That she belov'd, knowes nought,ₓ that knowes not this;⁺
Men prize the thing ungain'd,ₓ more [then] it is.

3 That she was never yet,ₓ that ever knew
Love got so sweet, as when desire did sue:
Therefore this maxime out of love I teach; ₓ
"Atchievement, is command; *ungain'd, beseech*.

4 [That] though my hearts [Contents] firme love doth beare,
Nothing of that shall from mine eyes appeare.

4/ Pandarus **Come, come, what neede you blush?** between 3.2.40 – 59

Background: Pandarus has finally brought the would-be lovers together, who seem somewhat awkwardly hesitant, at least in his eyes.

Style: as part of a three-handed scene

Where: just outside where Cressida lives **To Whom:** Cressida and then Troylus

# of Lines: 17 **Probable Timing: 0.55 minutes**

Modern Text

4/ Pandarus[3]

1 Come, come, what need* you blush?
2 Shame's a baby*. †
3 Here she is now, swear* the oaths* now
to her that you have sworn* to me.
4 What, are you gone a-
gain*? †
5 You must be watch'd ere you be made tame, must
you? †
6 Come your ways*, come your ways*; and you draw
backward, we'll* put you i'th fills*. †
7 Why do* you not speak
to her?
8 Come, draw this curtain*, & let's see your picture.
9 Alas* the day, how loath you are to offend day light! †
10 And
'twere dark* you'ld close sooner.
11 So, so, rub on and kiss*
the mistress*. †
12 How now, a kiss* in fee-farm*? †
13 Build there,
^Δ^carpenter, the air* is sweet*.

F #s onrushed sentences (nine overall versus nineteen set by most modern texts) coupled with the wording of F's eleven surround phrases and the overall emotional quality of the speech (7/25) suggest a character very excited not just by what he has arranged but more especially by the action that eventually unfolds before him (thus it would seem that voyeur might not be too strong a description for him).

- at first the surround phrases completely forming F #2 seem to suggest that there's going to be no action, as does the last monosyllabic surround phrase of F #3, ' : why doe you not speak to her ? ", and the first two surround phrases of F #5, ' . Alasse the day, how loath you are to offend day light? and 'twere darke you'ld close sooner : '
- all of his encouragement to counterbalance this lack of action has been completely emotional (0/12 the first eight and half lines up to and including the first line and a half of F #5)
- finally Troylus and Cressida get together, with the next set of surround phrases that immediately follow heightening Pandarus' pleasure

" : So, so, rub on, and kisse the mistresse ; how now, a kisse in fee-farme ? build there Carpenter, the ayre is sweete . "

with the observation being highly emotional (2/6 in just two lines)

First Folio

4/ Pandarus

1 Come, come, what neede you blush?
2 Shames a babie; here she is now, sweare the oathes now
to her,+ that you have sworne to me.
3 What+ are you gone a-
gaine,+ you must be watcht ere you be made tame, must
you? come your wayes, come your wayes,+ and you draw
backward+ weele put you i'th fils: why doe you not speak
to her?
4 Come+ draw this curtaine, & let's see your picture.
5 Alasse the day, how loath you are to offend day light? + and
'twere darke you'ld close sooner: So, so, rub on,x and kisse
the mistresse; how now, a kisse in fee-farme? build there+
Carpenter, the ayre is sweete.

---

[3] most modern texts provide a series of directions as the speech continues, as follows

{to Cressida} Come, come, what neede you blush?
Shames a babie; **{To Troylus}** here she is now, sweare the oathes now
to her, that you have sworne to me.
{To Cressida} What are you gone a-
gaine, you must be watcht ere you be made tame, must
you? come your wayes, come your wayes, and you draw
backward weele put you i'th fils: **{To Troylus}** why doe you not speak
to her?
{He unveils her} Come draw this curtaine, & let's see your picture.
Alasse the day, how loath you are to offend day light? and
'twere darke you'ld close sooner: **{To Troylus}** So, so, rub on, and kisse
the mistresse; **{They kisse}** how now, a kisse in fee-farme? build there
Carpenter, the ayre is sweete.

14 Nay, you shall fight your hearts out ere I part you - ◊ the Δfalcon*, as the Δtercel*, for all the Δducks i'th' Δriver. †

15 Go too, go too.

16 Words pay no debts, give her deeds*; but she'll* bereave you [a'th'] deeds too, if she* call your activity in question. † [4]

17 What, billing again*? †

18 Here's "ΔIn witness* whereof the Δparties interchangeably" -

19 Come in, come in, I'll go get a fire.

• the unembellished F #6 suggests that they may be aware that Pandarus is watching, and he is aware that they are aware, which could explain his very quiet monosyllabic 'Nay, you shall fight your hearts out ere I part you.', whether it is said to them (quietly so as not to alarm them) or just to himself (quietly so he won't disturb them and they will continue)

• the six surround phrases of F #7-8 continue to show that they haven't stopped and that he hasn't stopped enjoying himself, the (amazed? amused?) intellect of F #7 (4/2) quickly turning to emotion as he encourages Troylus to stop talking and 'give her deedes' instead (1/5, F #8)

• the final short sentence, directly to them, is unembellished, perhaps again suggesting that he is being very quiet so as not to disturb the magic of the moment for them, and the magic of the moment for him

6 Nay, you shall fight your hearts out ere I part you.

7 The Faulcon, as the Tercell, for all the Ducks ith River: go too, go too.

8 Words pay no debts;x give her deedes: x but sheele bereave you ['oth'] deeds too, if shee call your activity in question: what+ billing againe? here's in witnesse whereof the Parties interchangeably.

9 Come in, come in, Ile go get a fire? +

---

[4] most modern texts suggest (no matter how many times they have done so before) they now kiss again

5/ Cressida **Boldnesse comes to mee now, and brings mee** between 3.2.113 - 133

Background: Cressida finally confesses to Troylus how she has felt about him - though whether she is behaving genuinely or behaving archly is up to each actress and production to decide.

Style: as part of a three-handed scene

Where: just outside where Cressida lives **To Whom:** to Troylus in front of her uncle Pandarus

# of Lines: 20 **Probable Timing: 1.00 minutes**

Modern Text

5/ Cressida

1 Boldness* comes to me* now, and brings me* heart .†

2 Prince [Troilus] , I have lov'd you night and day
ΔFor many weary months*.

3 Hard to seem* won ; but I was won, my Δlord,
With the first glance that ever - pardon me,
If I confess* much, you will play the tyrant . †

4 I love you now, but [till not now] so much
But I might master* it . †

5 In°faith I lie*,
My thoughts were like unbridled* children [grown]
Too head-strong for their mother . †

6 See, we fools*!

7 Why have I blabb'd. ? †

8 Who shall be true to us,
When we are so unsecret to ourselves*?

9 But though I lov'd you well, I wooed* you not,
And yet, good faith, I wish'd myself* a man,
Or that we women had men's privilege*
Of speaking first.

10 Sweet, bid me hold my tongue,
For in this rapture I shall surely speak*
The thing I shall repent . †

11 See, see, your silence,
[Cunning] in dumbness*, from my weakness* draws*
My soul* of counsel* [ ] !

12 Stop my mouth.

Cressida's emotionality (3/20 overall) and the fact that the first twelve lines of the speech are all made up of surround phrases, together with F/Q's transition from #1's prose to #2's verse (see below) reinforces the idea of a lady not at all sure of herself, and working very hard to get her thoughts across, at least at the beginning of the speech. However, the large number of unembellished lines among the surround phrases, and continuing thereafter, suggests that what she does have to say she often says with quiet dignity (whether out of embarrassment or quiet conviction is for each actor to explore).

- the opening line is highly emotional (0/3) and though Q/F set the slightly onrushed F #1 as prose, thus adding to the idea of it being an awkward start for Cressida, most modern texts set their more rational equivalent mt. #1-2 as verse, as shown, thus removing the transition when she finally summons up enough strength to move into the heightened awareness that verse usually suggests

- then, in the second line of F #2/mt. #3, most modern texts create an awkwardness not shown in F: F allows Cressida a certain dignity in setting an emotional (via the semicolon), but clear, quiet, unembellished explanation acknowledging her forwardness at falling in love 'With the first glance ; that ever pardon me,': most modern texts repunctuate this to 'With the first glance that ever - pardon me,' setting up a much more fumbling apology, undermining the independent young woman that was seen in speech #3 above

- other unembellished lines offer further examples of her dignity under pressure, 'I love you now, but not till now so much . . . '; and the three consecutive lines
 "Why have I blab'd : who shall be true to us/When we are so unsecret to our selves?/But though I lov'd you well, I woed you not,"
together with the monosyllabic opening to F #4 'Sweet, bid me hold my tongue,' and her final request, 'Stop my mouth.'

- the most emotional moment in an already emotional speech comes in F #4's last two lines when she chides both him for his silence and herself for giving too much away 'see, see, your silence/[Cunning] in dumbnesse, from my weaknesse drawes/My soule of counsell from me.' (0/6), while the only time capitals are seen is in her early formal address to him as 'Prince Troylus', the second line of F #10, and the end of F #2's line one, referring to him as her 'Lord'

First Folio

5/ Cressida

1 Boldnesse comes to mee now, and brings mee
heart : Prince [Troylus], I have lov'd you night and day,ₓ for
many weary moneths.

2 Hard to seeme won : ₓ but I was won+ my Lord+
With the first glance ; ₓ that ever+ pardon me,
If I confesse much+ you will play the tyrant :
I love you now, but [not till now] so much
But I might maister it ; infaith I lye :
My thoughts were like unbrideled children [grow]
Too head-strong for their mother : see+ we fooles,+
Why have I blab'd : + who shall be true to us+
When we are so unsecret to our selves?

3 But though I lov'd you well, I woed you not,
And yet+ good faith+ I wisht my selfe a man ; ₓ
Or that we women had mens priviledge
Of speaking first.

4 Sweet, bid me hold my tongue,
For in this rapture I shall surely speake
The thing I shall repent : see, see, your silence+
[Comming] in dumbnesse, from my weakenesse drawes
My soule of counsell [from me] . +

5 Stop my mouth.

6/ Cressida **Prophet may you be: /If I be false, or swerve a haire from truth,** 3.3.183 - 196

Background: Troylus has sworn eternal constancy in his love for her, which Cressida now attempts to out-vie - the last line being ironically prophetic given later events between she and the Greek soldier Diomedes.

Style: as part of a three-handed scene

Where: just outside where Cressida lives **To Whom:** to Troylus in front of her uncle Pandarus

# of Lines: 14 **Probable Timing: 0.45 minutes**

Modern Text

6/ Cressida

1 Prophet may you be ! †

2 If I be false, or swerve a hair* from truth,
When time is old and hath forgot itself*,
When water-drops have worn* the Δstones of Troy,
And blind* oblivion swallow'd Δcities up,
And mighty₊ Δstates characterless* are grated
To dusty₊ nothing, yet let memory,
From false to false among false Δmaids in love,
Upbraid my falsehood ! †

3 When [th'have] said as false
As Δair*, as Δwater, [ ] Δwind*, [or] sandy₊ earth,
As* Δfox* to Δlamb*, [or] Δwolf* to Δheifers Δcalf*,
Pard to the Δhind*, or Δstep-dame to her Δson*,
Yea, let them say, to stick* the heart of falsehood,
"As false as Cressid."

F's onrush notwithstanding, the fact that this is the first of her speeches selected where intellect (17) matches emotions (15), together with nine pieces of major punctuation in just thirteen lines, suggests that now Cressida is in full verbal flight – though since seven of the nine pieces of major punctuation are semicolons, it may be that her emotions are still quite close to the surface and that she may not be able to maintain self-discipline throughout . . .

- especially since the speech opens with an unembellished phrase, followed by two emotional lines setting up her vow that if she prove 'false, or swerve a haire from truth' (0/2), and continues with three more surround phrases of wonderfully passionate (4/3) youthful exaggeration as to how long she should be condemned
  " : When water drops have worne the Stones of Troy ; /And blinde oblivion swallow'd Cities up ; /And mightie States characterlesse are grated/To dustie nothing ; "

- then come two virtually unembellished lines of (perhaps) quiet determination as she suggests that she should be the yardstick by which all 'false Maids' (the capital 'Maids' being the only released word in the passage) be judged

- and then the passion flows virtually unchecked (12/10 in just five lines) as she suggests that she should replace all other traditional measures by which falsehood has hitherto been judged

First Folio

6/ Cressida

1 Prophet may you be : +
If I be false, or swerve a haire from truth,
When time is old and hath forgot it selfe : x
When water drops have worne the Stones of Troy ; x
And blinde oblivion swallow'd Cities up ; x
And mightie States characterlesse are grated
To dustie nothing ; x yet let memory,
From false to false,x among false Maids in love,
Upbraid my falsehood,+ when [they'ave] said as false,x
As Aire, as Water, [as] Winde, [as] sandie earth ; x
As Foxe to Lambe ; x [as] Wolfe to Heifers Calfe ; x
Pard to the Hinde, or Stepdame to her Sonne ; x
Yea, let them say, to sticke the heart of falsehood,
As false as Cressid.

7/ Cressida **O you immortall gods! I will not goe.** between 4.4.85-108

Background: The exchange of Cressida (to go to join her father in the Greek camp) in return for the captured Trojan Antenor has been arranged, and is to take place immediately, the very night that she and Troylus have become lovers. The task of collecting her has been delegated by Paris and the Greek Diomedes to a Trojan commander, Æneas, who in turn has left it to Pandarus to tell her she must go. The following is her immediate reply.

Style: perhaps part of a four-handed scene, though a two-handed scene is more likely

Where: just outside where Cressida lives **To Whom:** to her uncle Pandarus with (perhaps) Troylus and Æneas in nearby attendance

# of Lines: 14 **Probable Timing: 0.45 minutes**

Modern Text

7/ Cressida

1 O you immortal* gods!
2 I will not go*.

3 I will not, Δuncle*. †
4 I have forgot my Δfather,
I know no touch of consanguinity*;
No kin, no love, no blood*, no soul*, so near* me
As the sweet [Troilus] : O you gods divine! †
5 Make Cressid's name the very crown* of falsehood*,
If ever she leave [Troilus] ! †
6 Time, force and death,
Do to this body what [extremes] you can;
But the strong base and building of my love
Is as the very Δcenter of the earth,
Drawing all things to it.
7 [I'll] go* in and weep*{,}

Tear* my bright [hair], and scratch my praised cheeks*,
Crack* my clear* voice* with sobs, and break* my heart,
With sounding [Troilus] .
8 I will not go* from Troy.

Not surprisingly given the news that she must leave Troylus immediately, overall the speech seems highly emotional (8/18 in just fourteen lines) yet apart from the first two incredibly short sentences of protest (0/2) and the protest that she knows 'no bloud, no soule, so neere me,' (0/3), Cressida manages to contain her emotions and maintain a great deal of self control in the first half of the speech (7/2, the other eight and a half lines, including the incredibly quiet denial of her father 'I know no touch of consanguinitie').

- the already passionate opening is enhanced by the rare (for an original Shakespeare printing) exclamation mark (F #1)

- her determination not leave Troy and Troylus is enhanced by the three surround phrases that open F #3
  ". I will not Unckle : I have forgot my Father : /I know no touch of consanguinitie : "
  while the pain of having to break her promise not to leave Troylus
  " : O you gods divine ! /Make Cressids name the very crowne of falshood! /If ever she leave Troylus : time, force and death,/Do to this body what extremitie you can ; "
  is similarly intensified, and highlighted even more by the surround phrases, two more exclamation marks, and an emotional semicolon, with the last two heightened even further by being unembellished (save for the name of Troylus)

- and then, save for the all-important 'Center', come three more unembellished lines proclaiming the strength of her love (it seems she is determined that all who hear her should be impressed by her intense calmness) to end F #3

- but then, with the dreadful tug of 'I will . . weepe' versus 'I will teare my bright [heire] and scratch my praised cheekes' versus 'I will not goe from Troy.', her emotions finally get the better of her (2/11 the speech's last three and a half lines, F #4-5)

First Folio

7/ Cressida

1 O you immortall gods!
2 I will not goe.

3 I will not+ Unckle: I have forgot my Father: x
I know no touch of consanguinitie: x
No kin, no love, no bloud, no soule, so neere me, x
As the sweet [Troylus]: O you gods divine!
Make Cressids name the very crowne of falshood! x
If ever she leave [Troylus]: time, force and death,
Do to this body what [extremitie] you can;
But the strong base and building of my love, x
Is as the very Center of the earth,
Drawing all things to it.
4 [I will] goe in and weepe{,}

Teare my bright [heire], and scratch my praised cheekes,
Cracke my cleere voyce with sobs, and breake my heart+
With sounding [Troylus].
5 I will not goe from Troy.

8/ Troylus **This she? no, this is Diomids Cressida :** between 5.2.137 - 187

Background: The love-sick Troylus has been given safe passage by the Greek Ulysses to see Cressida, now living with her father in the Greek camp. To his horror, despite her earlier protestations of unswerving faithfulness to him (speech #6 above) he finds her not simply flirting with the Greek Diomedes, but presenting him with the very gift Troylus had given her to symbolise their unity. Once the new lovers have exited, Ulysses tries to get Troylus to leave, initially without much success.

Style: as part of a two-handed scene, with a third person watching unobserved

Where: the Greek camp **To Whom:** Ulysses, with the hidden Thersites watching

# of Lines: 39 **Probable Timing: 2.00 minutes**

Modern Text

8/ Troylus

1 This she? no, this is [Diomed's]Cressida . †

2 If beauty* have a soul*, this is not she ;
If souls* guide vows*, if vows* are [sanctimonies],
If sanctimony* be the gods' delight,
If there be rule in unity* itself*,
This is not she . †

3 O madness* of discourse, ◊
That cause sets up with and against [it°self*] ! †

4 [Bi-fold] authority* : where reason can revolt
Without perdition, and loss* assume all reason
Without revolt.

5 This is, and is not, Cressid ! †

6 Within my soul* there doth conduce a fight
Of this strange nature, that a thing inseparate*
Divides more wider [than] the sky* and earth,
And yet the spacious breadth* of this division
Admits no Δorifex for a point as subtle
As [Ariadne's] broken woof* to enter . †

7 Instance, O instance, strong as Pluto's* gates,
Cressid is mine, tied with the bonds of heaven ;
Instance, O instance, strong as heaven itself*,
The bonds of heaven are slipp'd*, dissolv'd, and loos'd,
And with another knot five-finger-tied,
The fractions of her faith, orts of her love,
The fragments, scraps, the bits, and greasy* relics*
Of her o'er-eaten faith, are [given] to Diomed.

8 Hark*, Greek : as much [as] I do* [Cressid] love,
So much by weight hate I her Diomed . †

9 That Sleeve is mine that he'll* bear* [on] his Δhelm*.†

Given the circumstances of Cressida's apparent infidelity, it's not surprising that F sets Troylus' grief as seven onrushed essentially passionate sentences (29/33 overall): most modern texts rework the speech as a much more dignified sixteen sentences of rational distancing and explanation.

- the coloned surround phrases first underscore his denial of what he has seen
  " : no, this is Diomids Cressida : /If beautie have a soule, this is not she : "
  " : If there be rule in unitie it selfe,/This is not she : . . . /That cause sets up, with, and against [thy selfe]/[By foule] authoritie : "
  " . This is, and is not Cressid : "
  " . Let all untruths stand by thy stained name,/And theyle seeme glorious . "
  " . My curteous Lord adew : /Farewell revolted faire : and, Diomed,/ Stand fast, and weare a Castle on thy head."

  and then add determination to what he plans to do with the love token he originally gave Cressida which she in turn has just given Diomedes
  " . Harke Greek : " " : Were it a Caske compos'd by Vulcans skill,/My Sword should bite it : "

- the semicoloned surround phrases focus on Cressida and their supposed love
  " : If soules guide vowes ; if vowes are sanctimonie ; /If sanctimonie be the gods delight : "
  " : Cressid is mine, tied with the bonds of heaven ; /Instance, O instance, strong as heaven it selfe : "
  " : as much as I doe Cressida love ; "
  " ; [than] shall my prompted sword,/Falling on Diomed . "

- the exclamation mark created surround phrases (unusual in Shakespeare first printings) all deal with moments where Troylus must release his tension
  " : O madnesse of discourse ! ", " . Instance, O instance ! "
  " . O Cressid ! O false Cressid ! false, false, false : "

- the only intellectual moment comes in the two surround phrase line of denial opening the speech, while the next eight lines of dense logic, attempting to keep matters as an abstract exercise, become emotional in their complexity (1/9, the remainder of F #1 and all of F #2)

- by F #3, when he finally comes back to his own circumstances, after voicing the dilemma 'This is, and is not Cressid' (1/1 the opening line and a half), he becomes very quiet in acknowledging the struggle within, with four and a half unembellished lines (save for the word 'Orifex' here meaning narrow opening),

First Folio

8/ Troylus

1 This she? no, this is [Diomids] Cressida :
If beautie have a soule, this is not she : $_{x}$
If soules guide vowes ; if vowes are sanctimonie ; $_{x}$
If sanctimonie be the gods delight : $_{x}$
If there be rule in unitie it selfe,
This is not she : O madnesse of discourse!

2 That cause sets up,$_{x}$ with,$_{x}$ and against [thy selfe]+
[By foule] authoritie : where reason can revolt
Without perdition, and losse assume all reason,$_{x}$
Without revolt.

3 This is, and is not+ Cressid :
Within my soule,$_{x}$ there doth conduce a fight
Of this strange nature, that a thing inseperate,$_{x}$
Divides more wider [then] the skie and earth : $_{x}$
And yet the spacious bredth of this division,$_{x}$
Admits no Orifex for a point as subtle,$_{x}$
As [Ariachnes] broken woofe to enter :
Instance, O instance!$_{x}$ strong as Plutoes gates :$_{x}$
Cressid is mine, tied with the bonds of heaven ;
Instance, O instance, strong as heaven it selfe :$_{x}$
The bonds of heaven are slipt, dissolv'd+ and loos'd,
And with another knot five finger tied,
The fractions of her faith, orts of her love :$_{x}$
The fragments, scraps, the bits, and greazie reliques,$_{x}$
Of her ore-eaten faith, are [bound] to Diomed.

4 Harke+ Greek : as much [ ] I doe [ΔCressida] love ;$_{x}$
So much by weight,$_{x}$ hate I her Diomed,
That Sleeve is mine,$_{x}$ that heele beare [in]his Helme :

{ctd. over}

10 Were it a △casque* compos'd by Vulcan's skill,
My △sword should bite it . †
11 Not the dreadful* spout
Which △shipmen do* the △hurricano call,
Constring'd in mass* by the almighty [sun],
Shall dizzy‚ with more clamor* Neptune's ear*,
In his descent, [than] shall my prompted sword,
Falling on Diomed.

12 O Cressid!
13 O false Cressid*! false, false, false ! †
14 Let all untruths stand by thy stained name,
And they'll* seem* glorious.

15 {ψ} {M}y courteous‚ △lord, adieu*. †
16 Farewell, revolted fair* ! and, Diomed,
Stand fast, and wear* a △castle on thy head !

• and, after three passionate lines of confused classical imagery suggesting nothing can break the thread he imagines keeps him and Cressida inextricably bound, the quietness returns for three and a half unembellished lines as he realises Cressid has broken this heavenly thread and replaced it with 'fragments, scraps', but this quietness cannot last, for the final description of this new thread as 'greazie reliques/Of her ore-eaten faith' is slightly emotional (1/2, F #3's last line and a half)

• then passion breaks loose unchecked as Troylus vows to reclaim his love token ('That Sleeve') given to Cressida who in turn has given it to Diomedes (13/13 in F #4's first eight and a half lines), though the final description of his 'prompted sword,/ Falling on Diomed.' becomes very quiet once again (1/0, F #4's last line and a half)

• and even though his determination is swamped by his anguish with 'false Cressid', his passions remain during his calling her out (2/2, F #5-6) and the peculiarly mixed F #7 (3/3) which jams together both his farewell to Ulysses and still anguished goodbyes to the betrayers Cressida and Diomedes

Were it a Caske compos'd by Vulcans skill,
My Sword should bite it : Not the dreadfull spout,ₓ
Which Shipmen doe the Hurricano call,
Constring'd in masse by the almighty [Fenne],
Shall dizzie with more clamour Neptunes eare+
In his discent ; ₓ [then] shall my prompted sword,
Falling on Diomed.

5 O Cressid!
6 O false Cressid! false, false, false : +
Let all untruths stand by thy stained name,
And theyle seeme glorious.

7 {ψ} {M}y curteous Lord+ adew :
Farewell+ revolted faire : + and, Diomed,
Stand fast, and weare a Castle on thy head. +

#'s 9 - 12: The Greeks' Problem, Especially With Achilles

9/ Ulysses **Agamemnon./ Thou great Commander, Nerve, and Bone of Greece,** between 1.3.54 - 137

Background: The Trojan war has been a stalemate for far too long. Ulysses initially sets up what can only be described as a philosophically cosmic background to the problem, and then goes straight to the pragmatic facts - not only will one of the key Greek commanders Achilles not fight [5], he and his close companion Patroclus are undermining morale.

Style: initially one on one for the benefit of all present

Where: the Greek camp **To Whom:** the commanders Agamemnon, Nestor, Diomedes, Menelaus, with others

# of Lines: 78 **Probable Timing: 3.45 minutes**

Modern Text

9/ Ulysses

1 Agamemnon, ◊
Thou great Δcommander, [Δnerves] and Δbone of Greece,
Heart of our Δnumbers, soul* and only* [sprite]
In whom the tempers and the minds* of all
Should be shut up, Δhear* what Ulysses speaks*. †

2 Besides th'applause and approbation
The which, most mighty for thy place and sway,
And thou most reverend for thy stretch'd-out life,
I give to both your speeches, which were such,
As Agamemnon and the hand [6] of Greece
Should hold up high in Δbrass*, and such again*
As venerable Nestor, hatch'd in Δsilver,
Should with a bond of air* strong as the Δaxle-tree
[On which the Δheaven rides], knit all Greeks* ears*
To his experienc'd tongue, yet let it please both,
Thou Δgreat, and Δwise, to hear* Ulysses speak*.

3 Troy, yet upon his [bases], had been* down*
And the great Hector's sword had lack'd a Δmaster,
But for these instances.

4 The specialty of Δrule hath been* neglected,
And look* how many Grecian Δtents do stand
Hollow upon this Δplain*, so many hollow Δfactions.

5 When that the Δgeneral* is not like the Δhive
To whom the Δforagers* shall all repair*,
What Δhoney* is expected?

In a very long speech, the very few surround phrases establish how carefully Ulysses advances his controversial viewpoint.

" : yet let it please both/(Thou Great, and Wise) to heare Ulysses speake . "
" . The specialty of Rule hath beene neglected ; "
" . Take but Degree away, un-tune that string,/And hearke what Discord followes : each thing meetes/In meere oppugnancie . "
" . Great Agamemnon : /This Chaos, when Degree is suffocate,/Followes the choaking : "
" . The Generall's disdain'd/By him one step below ; he, by the next,/That next, by him beneath : "

summing up everything equally carefully by the last two short sentences

"And 'tis this Feaver that keepes Troy on foote,/Not her owne sinewes. To end a tale of length, /Troy in our weaknesse [lives], not in her strength."

though his emotions give him away at this last moment (2/6, F #16-17)

- that Ulysses has to be/is being careful can be seen in the way he starts the speech, F #1's single word centering attention on the Greek leader, skillfully placing his worth ahead of the also to be reckoned with Nestor

- that Ulysses knows he is faced with a very tricky task could well be seen in the inconsistency opening F #2, with the first line and half publicly acknowledging Agamemnon's greatness being intellectual (5/0), the next line and a half of further praise being emotional (0/2) and the post-colon request to be heard being passionate (2/2) – all this variety in just four lines, and this pattern of swinging between intellect and especially passion is consistently repeated throughout the speech

- this lack of control continues: F's onrush via the fast-link comma (where most modern texts set mt. #2) suggests that Ulysses, concerned that Agamemnon is being seduced by 'the applause and approbation' he is hearing, is sufficiently disturbed to break grammatical niceties to make this point, unlike his modern counterpart who makes the transition with syntactic elegance

First Folio

9/ Ulysses

1 Agamemnon.

2 Thou great Commander, [Nerve],x and Bone of Greece,
Heart of our Numbers, soule,x and onely [spirit],x
In whom the tempers,x and the mindes of all
Should be shut up :x Heare what Ulysses speakes,
Besides the applause and approbation
The which+ most mighty for thy place and sway,
And thou most reverend for thy stretcht-out life,
I give to both your speeches : x which were such,
As Agamemnon and the hand of Greece
Should hold up high in Brasse : and such againe
As venerable Nestor (xhatch'd in Silverx)
Should with a bond of ayre,x strong as the Axletree
In which the [Heavens ride], knit all Greekes eares
To his experienc'd tongue : x yet let it please both+
(xThou Great, and Wisex) to heare Ulysses speake.

3 Troy+ yet upon his [basis]+ had bene downe,x
And the great Hectors sword had lack'd a Master+
But for these instances.

4 The specialty of Rule hath beene neglected ; x
And looke how many Grecian Tents do stand
Hollow upon this Plaine, so many hollow Factions.

5 When that the Generall is not like the Hive,x
To whom the Forragers shall all repaire,
What Hony is expected?

{ctd. over}

[5] in all fairness, one of the main reasons for (the Greek) Achilles' not fighting is that he is in love with one of the (Trojan) daughters of Priam, king of Troy, the enemy they are currently fighting

[6] though most modern texts agree with Ff/Q and set 'and the hand', one gloss = 'and every hand'

6 Degree being vizarded,
Th'unworthiest shows* as fairly* in the Δmask*.
7 The Heavens themselves, the Δplanets, and this Δcenter
Observe degree, priority, and place,
Insisture, course, proportion, season, form*,
Office, and custom*, in all line of Δorder;
And therefore is the glorious Δplanet Sol
In noble eminence enthron'd and spher'd*
Amidst the other; whose med'cinable eye
Corrects the [influence of evil* Δplanets],
And posts* like the Δcommandment of a Δking,
Sans check*, to good and bad.
8 But when the Δplanets
In evil* mixture to disorder wander,
What Δplagues and what portents, what mutiny!
What raging of the Δsea, shaking of Δearth!
Commotion in the Δwinds*! Δfrights, changes, horrors,
Divert, and crack*, rend and deracinate
The unity, and married calm* of States
Quite from their fixure!
9 O, when Δdegree is shak'd,
Which is the Δladder to all high designs*,
The enterprise* is sick*.
10 How could Δcommunities,
Degrees in Δschools*, and Δbrother-hoods in Δcities,
Peaceful* Δcommerce from dividable shores,
The [primogenity] and due of Δbirth*,
Prerogative of Δage, Δcrowns*, Δsceptres, Δlaurels*,
(But by Δdegree) stand in Δauthentic* place?
11 Take but Δdegree away, un-tune that string,
And hark* what Δdiscord follows*. †
12 Each thing [melts*]
In mere* oppugnancy*: ◊ the bounded Δwaters
Should lift their bosoms* higher [than] the Δshores,
And make a sop* of all this solid Δglobe;
Strength should be Δlord of imbecility,
And the rude Δson* should strike his Δfather dead;
Force should be right, or rather, right and wrong
(Between* whose endless* jar* Δjustice resides)
Should[lose their] names, and so should Δjustice too!

• having broken the rules to approach this rather ticklish point that could offend not only Agamemnon and Nestor but the sycophants advising them, Ulysses explanation becomes a very careful unembellished three and a half lines
"Besides the applause and approbation/The which most mighty for thy place and sway,/And thou most reverend for thy stretcht-out life,/I give to both your speeches:"

• after which it seems that Ulysses feels that either he has carefully negotiated these tricky waters, or that he needs to add his own praise to both men, for F #2's remaining highly fulsome seven and a half lines somewhat intellectual (11/7) – suggesting the F Ulysses is now confident of his own abilities, and, after sixteen and a half lines of preamble, turns to the key troubling matter at hand – chaos amongst the military leadership

• the three sentences F #3-5, unequivocally suggesting that without the current disputes between various Greek factions Troy would have been defeated long ago, remains in the same vein (11/8), but the short F #6's warning, that when leadership becomes clouded 'th'unworthiest' can hold sway, turns emotional (1/3)

• Ulysses then regains his mental control to drive his worry home by drawing one of the most powerful parallels for an Elizabethan - pointing to how the heavens should operate, by observing 'degree, priority, and place,/Insisture, course, proportion, season' - and initially the discussion of adhering to order becomes strongly intellectual once more (10/6, F #7)

• yet again, as soon as Ulysses voices the negative aspects of ignoring order, his intellectual control becomes subsumed in passion (F #8-9, 9/7)

• but in returning his listeners to social order, arguing that 'Communities', 'Schooles', 'Cities', and 'Commerce' can only '(. . . by Degree) stand in Authentique place?', Ulysses manages to allow his intellect to rise to the fore (F #10, 12/6) - only to lose it once more in the first totally surround phrase sentence suggesting that without degree, 'each thing meetes /In meere oppugnancie.' (F #11, 2/4)

• Ulysses continues the image via another powerful Elizabethan parallel, the world of nature (here the 'bounded Waters', 6/3, F #12's first four and half lines), to eventually suggest that if strength were all then 'the rude Sonne should strike his Father dead'; though he starts intellectually once more as he follows this through to its dreadful conclusion - that everything 'Must make perforce a universall prey,/And last, eate up himselfe.' – he becomes passionate again (10/10, F #12's last three lines and all F #13)

• as Ulysses brings this heady extended argument back to how it affects Agamemnon, F #14 offers a fine series of (careful?) debating pauses with four line irregular F passage (6/5/10/5 syllables): however, as he begins his final summation, most modern texts remove these key 'debating pauses' by restructuring the passage to two overly-long lines (11/15 syllables) as shown

6 Degree being vizarded,
Th'unworthiest shewes as fairely in the Maske.
7 The Heavens themselves, the Planets, and this Center,x
Observe degree, priority, and place,
Insisture,[7] course, proportion, season, forme,
Office, and custome, in all line of Order: x
And therefore is the glorious Planet Sol
In noble eminence,x enthron'd and sphear'd
Amid'st the other,+ whose med'cinable eye
Corrects the [ill Aspects of Planets evill],
And postes like the Command'ment of a King,
Sans checke, to good and bad.
8 But when the Planets
In evill mixture to disorder wander,
What Plagues,x and what portents, what mutiny? +
What raging of the Sea? x shaking of Earth? +
Commotion in the Windes?+ Frights, changes, horrors,
Divert, and cracke, rend and deracinate
The unity, and married calme of States
Quite from their fixure?+
9 O, when Degree is shak'd,
(xWhich is the Ladder to all high designesx)
The enterprize is sicke.
10 How could Communities,
Degrees in Schooles, and Brother-hoods in Cities,
Peacefull Commerce from dividable shores,
The primogenitive,x and due of Byrth,
Prerogative of Age, Crownes, Scepters, Lawrels,
(But by Degree) stand in Authentique place?
11 Take but Degree away, un-tune that string,
And hearke what Discord followes: each thing [meetes]
In meere oppugnancie.
12 The bounded Waters,x
Should lift their bosomes higher [then] the Shores,
And make a soppe of all this solid Globe: x
Strength should be Lord of imbecility,
And the rude Sonne should strike his Father dead: x
Force should be right, or rather, right and wrong,x
(Betweene whose endlesse jarre,x Justice recides)
Should [loose her] names, and so should Justice too. +

[7] much has been written about this unusual word, and while most commentators accept Q/Ff's 'Insisture', one text sets 'Infixture' - see *The Arden Shakespeare Troilus and Cressida,* op. cit., p. 127, footnote to line 87

13 Then every thing includes itself* in △power,
Power into △will, △will into △appetite,
And △appetite, an universal* △wolf*,
(So doubly seconded with △will, and △power),
Must make peforce an universal* prey,
And last, eat* up himself*.
14 Great Agamemnon,
This △chaos, when △degree is suffocate, follows* the choking*,
And this neglection of △degree [it is]
That by a pace goes backward [with] a purpose
It hath to climb*.
15 The △general's* disdain'd
By him one step below, he, by the next,
That next by him beneath ; so every step,
Exampled by the first pace that is sick*
Of his △superior*, grows* to an envious △fever*
Of pale, and bloodless* △emulation : ◊
And 'tis this △fever* that keeps* Troy on foot*,
Not her own* sinews*.
16 To end a tale of length,
Troy in our weakness* [stands], not in her strength.

• Ulysses' cannot maintain self-control during the summation only lasts for F #14's first three lines (3/2)

• the two surround phrases by which he brings head-on 'Chaos' (one of the most terrifying Elizabethan images) for Agamemnon's consideration, ' . Great Agamemnon : /This Chaos, when Degree is suffocate,/ Followes the choaking : ' seem to plunge Ulysses into passion as he points to the inevitable results of the 'neglection of Degree' (2/2 the two and half lines ending F #14 and the two lines opening F #15) and the last emotional surround phrases of the speech essentially points to the kernel of their current problem

" . The Generall's disdain'd/By him one step below ; he, by the next,/
That next, by him beneath : "

• stating the final unpalatable conclusion, Ulysses gives way to his emotions far more than anywhere else in the speech (5/11, F #15's last three and a half lines, plus F #16-17)

13 Then everything includes it selfe in Power,
Power into Will, Will into Appetite,
And Appetite (x an universall Wolfe,
+So doubly seconded with Will, and Power)+
Must make peforce an universall prey,
And last, eate up himselfe.
14 Great Agamemnon : x
This Chaos, when Degree is suffocate,
Followes the choaking : x
And this neglection of Degree, x [is it]
That by a pace goes backward [in] a purpose
It hath to climbe.
15 The Generall's disdain'd
By him one step below ; x he, by the next,
That next, x by him beneath : x so every step+
Exampled by the first pace that is sicke
Of his Superiour, growes to an envious Feaver
Of pale, and bloodlesse Emulation.
16 And 'tis this Feaver that keepes Troy on foote,
Not her owne sinewes.
17 To end a tale of length,
Troy in our weaknesse [lives], not in her strength.

10/ Ulysses **Thank the heavens L. thou art of sweet composure ;** between 2.3.240 - 264

Background: In an attempt to stir Achilles to action, Ulysses has come up with a plan for all the generals to cease persuading Achilles to fight. Rather, not only will they ignore him, but will also praise at every opportunity one of his main rivals, the very brave but extremely stupid ('beef-witted' as Thersites terms him) Ajax. Here, as an essential precursor to the plot, Ulysses, with the help of his fellow generals, succeeds in fostering in Ajax even more anti-Achilles feelings than he had had before.

Style: one on one for the benefit of all present

Where: the Greek camp **To Whom:** Ajax, in front of Agamemnon, Nestor, and Diomedes

# of Lines: 24 **Probable Timing: 1.15 minutes**

Modern Text

10/ Ulysses

1 Thank the heavens,[Lord], thou art of sweet composure .†
2 Praise him that [gat] thee, she that gave thee suck* ;
[Fam'd] be thy Δtutor, and thy parts of nature
Thrice fam'd beyond, beyond all erudition ;
But he that disciplin'd [thine] arms* to fight,
Let Mars divide* Δeternity in twain*,
And give him half*; and for thy vigor*,
Bull-bearing Milo his addition yield*
To sinewy* Ajax . †
3 I will not praise thy wisdom*,
Which like a bourn*, a pale, a shore, confines
Thy spacious and dilated parts . †
4 Here's Nestor,
Instructed by the Δantiquary times ;
He must, he is, he cannot but be wise.
5 But pardon, Δfather Nestor, were your days*
As green* as Ajax', and your brain* so temper'd,
You should not have the eminence of him,
But be as Ajax.
6 There is no tarrying here, the Δhart Achilles
Keeps* thicket . †
7 Please it our [great] Δgeneral*
To call together all his state of war* . †
8 Fresh Δkings are come [8] to Troy ; to-morrow
We must with all our main* of power stand fast ;
And here's a Δlord - come Δknights from Δeast to Δwest,
And cull their flower*, Ajax shall cope the best.

F's three sentence onrush suggests that Ulysses is on a roll and not working so hard as his modern counterpart, whose eight sentences present a far more careful, logical approach. However, F's Ulysses' skillful use of the surround phrases together with the build up to a large scale passionate/intellectual release in the last sentence shows that despite not working so logically as his modern counterpart, he can still skillfully apply his rhetorical cunning as and when needed.

- F #1's flattery starts beautifully contained (just 2/2 in the first five lines), with the opening skillfully designed to win any listener, let alone the none too bright Ajax, with the first two lines of surround phrases
  "Thank the heavens [Lord] thou art of sweet composure ; /Praise him that [got] thee, she that gave thee sucke : "
  heightened in being linked by the emotional semicolon (as well as being almost unembellished), followed by two purely unembellished lines
  " : [Fame] be thy Tutor, and thy parts of nature/Thrice fam'd beyond, beyond all erudition ; "
  suggesting to Ajax an honesty and integrity which isn't really there
- this seductive quietness then turns to passion as Ulysses gives thanks that Ajax has been granted the warring-skills of Mars and the immense strength of Milo (a renowned Crotonan athlete) (4/5 the next three and a half lines finishing with the surround phrase ' : his addition yeelde/To sinnowie Ajax ; ')
- Ulysses' suggestion that he cannot praise Ajax enough is emotional (0/2, the next two lines), and is then beautifully capped by the emotionally started two surround phrases ending F #1 suggesting that, while Nestor is the wisest among those present (the second surround phrase deftly offered with an unembellished calm as if to stress Nestor's wisdom), even Nestor in his prime (F #2's corollary) could not compare with Ajax - all this offered passionately once more (6/3 overall)
- and then the onrushed F #3 (10/4) provides the intellectual coup de grace, jamming together the notion that Achilles, who should be fighting, is a coward, with the urging that Agamemnon can finally call his 'state of warre' because, with Ajax being available to 'cope the best', at last the Trojans can face with confidence the battle due tomorrow with the 'Fresh Kings' come to oppose them – the whole beautifully onrushed, presumably to prevent Ajax from being able to voice a word of protest or question

First Folio

10/ Ulysses

1 Thank the heavens+ L. + thou art of sweet composure ;
Praise him that [got] thee, she that gave thee sucke : x
[Fame] be thy Tutor, and thy parts of nature
Thrice fam'd beyond, beyond all erudition ;
But he that disciplin'd [thy] armes to fight,
Let Mars devide Eternity in twaine,
And give him halfe,+ and for thy vigour,
Bull-bearing Milo : x his addition yeelde
To sinnowie Ajax : I will not praise thy wisdome,
Which like a bourne, a pale, a shore+ confines
Thy spacious and dilated parts ; here's Nestor+
Instructed by the Antiquary times : x
He must, he is, he cannot but be wise.
2 But pardon+ Father Nestor, were your dayes
As greene as Ajax, and your braine so temper'd,
You should not have the eminence of him,
But be as Ajax.
3 There is no tarrying here, the Hart Achilles
Keepes thicket : please it our [ ] Generall, x
To call together all his state of warre,
Fresh Kings are come to Troy ; to morrow
We must with all our maine of power stand fast : x
And here's a Lord, come Knights from East to West,
And cull their flowre, Ajax shall cope the best.

[8] Q/Ff set a short nine syllable line, one modern text adds 'today', presumably both for clarity and to bolster the meter

11/ Achilles **What meane these fellowes? know they not Achilles?** 3.3.70 - 94

Background: The Greek commander Ajax has been fooled into joining the anti-Achilles faction (he seriously, they more lightheartedly but with a very serious purpose underneath - see speech #9 above). Now the commanders, with Ajax, deliberately walk by Achilles' tent barely giving Achilles the time of day, leaving Ulysses to follow a little later once Achilles realises something is wrong, as he now does. Achilles offers the following to his close companion Patroclus.

Style: as part of a two-handed scene

Where: outside Achilles' tent **To Whom:** Patroclus

# of Lines: 24 **Probable Timing: 1.15 minutes**

Modern Text

11/ Achilles

1 What mean* these fellows*? †
2 Know they not Achilles?
3 {ψ}They pass* by strangely. †
4 They were us'd to bend,
To send their smiles before them {*,}
To come as humbly as they [use] to creep*
To holy Altars.
5 What, am I poor* of late?
6 'Tis certain*, greatness*, once fall'n* out with fortune,
Must fall out with men too. †
7 What the declin'd is,
He shall as soon* read* in the eyes of others,
As feel* in his own* fall; for men, like butterflies,
Show* not their mealy* wings but to the △summer,
And not a man, for being simply man,
Hath any honor*, but [honor*] for those honors*
That are without him, as place, riches, and favor*
Prizes of accident, as oft as merit,
Which when they fall, as being slippery standers,
The love that lean'd on them as slippery too,
[Do th'one] pluck* down* another, and together
Die* in the fall.
8 But 'tis not so with me,
Fortune and I are friends. †
9 I do* enjoy
At ample point, all that I did possess*,
Save these men's looks*, who do me thinks* find* out
Something not worth in me such rich beholding
As they have often given.

In a very emotional speech (5/25), the fact that Achilles is working very hard to understand why he is suddenly out of favour is underscored by the first fourteen lines being composed almost entirely of eleven surround phrases and one short sentence, with the fifteen syllable line ending F #2 suggesting an explosion - most modern texts reduce this by setting up a much more controlled response (10/5 syllables as shown), establishing a pause where none originally existed.

- the first self-doubts come from the realisation that Agamemnon, Nestor and Ajax who have just passed him by with scant greetings ' ; they were us'd to bend/To send their smiles before them /To come as humbly as . . .' - the unembellished quiet adding enormous (startled ? horrified?) depth to the realisation, especially when set within the emotional F #1-2 (2/4)

- the only exception to the intense surround phrase start is the two line passage of climactic realisation that results from his previous seven surround phrase self-questioning ' : what the declin'd is,/He shall as soone as reade in the eyes of others,/As feele in his owne fall :' - climactic in that this marks an 0/7 three and half line passage opening F #4

- then comes a moment of intellect, the surround phrase pointing to a logical maxim to justify his not venturing himself on any worthless task
  " : for men like butter-flies,/Shew not their mealie wings, but to the Summer : "

- but this may not satisfy Achilles, for, as he explores honour coming upon people by happenchance, the next three surround phrases are emotionally created (via the semicolons) and emotional in release too (0/4)
  " : And not a man for being simply man, /Hath any honour ; but honour'd for those honours/That are without him ; as place, riches, and favour, /Prizes of accident, as oft as merit : "

- then he becomes very quiet (perhaps he is disturbed by these and the ensuing thoughts of quick abandonment) 'Which when they fall, as being slippery standers ; /The love that leand on them as slippery too,' – the unembellished realisation enhanced by being set as yet two more emotional surround phrases – with the final inevitable conclusion of downfall becoming emotional once more (0/3, F #4's last two lines)

First Folio

11/ Achilles

1 What meane these fellowes? know they not Achilles?
2 {ψ}They passe by strangely: they were us'd to bend+
To send their smiles before them {Ψ}: x
To come as humbly as they [us'd] to creepe to holy Altars.
3 What+ am I poore of late?
4 'Tis certaine, greatnesse+ once falne out with fortune,
Must fall out with men too: what the declin'd is,
He shall as soone reade in the eyes of others,
As feele in his owne fall: x for men+ like butter-flies,
Shew not their mealie wings, x but to the Summer: x
And not a man+ for being simply man,
Hath any honour; x but [honour'd] for those honours
That are without him; x as place, riches, and favour, x
Prizes of accident, as oft as merit: x
Which when they fall, as being slippery standers; x
The love that leand on them as slippery too,
[Doth one] plucke downe another, and together
Dye in the fall.
5 But 'tis not so with me; x
Fortune and I are friends, I doe enjoy
At ample point, all that I did possesse,
Save these mens lookes: x who do me thinkes finde out
Something not worth in me such rich beholding, x
As they have often given.

{ctd. over}

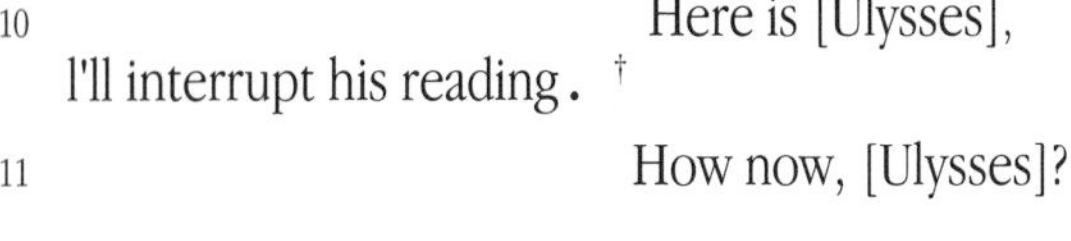

10 Here is [Ulysses],
I'll interrupt his reading. †
11 How now, [Ulysses]?

• the denial that this could possibly happen to him seems very important and emphatic, being set as an emotional unembellished monosyllabic surround phrase ' . But 'tis not so with me ; ', while the subsequent explanation as to why becomes emotional again (0/5, F #5's last four lines)

• and in an interesting (and determined?) turnaround, Achilles' resolve to do something about the problem (question Ulysses) becomes intellectual (2/0), the decision heightened by being set as two surround phrases - yet the short spelling of Ulysses as 'Ulisses'(twice) suggests that Achilles' start may not be quite as confident as he would wish

6 Here is [Ulisses],
lle interrupt his reading: how now+ [Ulisses]?

12/ Ulysses **Time hath (my Lord) a wallet at his backe,** 3.3.145 - 190

Background: Following the commanders ploy of virtually ignoring Achilles (see the background to speeches #10-11 above), Ulysses walks by, as planned. Achilles confides in him, in the end asking 'What are my deedes forgot?', which allows Ulysses the opening he needs.

Style: as part of a three-handed scene

Where: outside Achilles' tent **To Whom:** Achilles, with Patroclus silently listening

# of Lines: 45 **Probable Timing: 2.10 minutes**

Modern Text

12/ Ulysses

1 Time hath, my Δlord, a wallet at his back*,
Wherein he puts alms* for oblivion,
A great-siz'd monster of ingratitudes. †
2 Those scraps are good deeds* past, which are devour'd
As fast as they are made, forgot as soon*
As done: perseverance, dear* my Δlord,
Keeps* honor bright; to have done, is to hang
Quite out of fashion, like a rusty* [mail]
In monumental* mock'ry*. †
3 Take the instant way,
For honor* travels in a [strait] so narrow,
Where one but goes abreast. †
4 Keep* then the [path],
For emulation hath a thousand Δsons*,
That one by one pursue. †
5 If you give way,
Or hedge aside from the direct forth right,
Like to an ent'red Δtide*, they all rush by
And leave you hindmost;
Or like a gallant Δhorse fall'n* in first rank*,
Lie* there for pavement to the abject [rear],
Ore-run and trampled on. †
6 Then what they do* in present,
Though less* [than] yours in past, must o'er-top yours;
For ΔTime is like a fashionable Δhost*
That slightly shakes his parting Δguest by th'hand,
And with his arms* out-stretch'd as he would fly*,
Grasps* in the comer*. †
7 The welcome ever smiles,
And [farewell] goes out sighing. †

Amazingly, for what modern texts set as such a rational twelve sentence speech, F shows the normally phlegmatic Ulysses in an extraordinarily onrushed situation (F #1 being split into nine separate modern sentences, F #2 into three). As a matter of pure editorial conjecture, just as commentators have suggested that Prospero's final Epilogue might be Shakespeare's very personal farewell to the theatre, the highly emotional onrush of this speech (8/33 overall) might reveal a very personal Shakespearean reaction to the fleeting quality of fame. Whatever the reason for the onrush, it is suggested that readers work through the modern texts first to find the stepping stones of the speech and only then turn to exploring F's onrush and the possible reasons for it.

- the surround phrases are so cleverly designed to move Achilles out of his current inaction, each driving home the penalties for remaining too long out of the public eye: the following is not necessarily in chronological order: first, there are always the emulators
  " ; if you give way,/Or hedge aside from the direct forth right ; /Like to an entred Tyde, they all rush by, /And leave you hindmost : "
  for time essentially is
  " . A great siz'd monster of ingratitudes : "
  " ; And with his armes out-stretcht, as he would flye,/Graspes in the commer : the welcome ever smiles,/And [farewels] goes out sighing :"
  and as a consequence
  " : then what they doe in present,/Though lesse then yours in past, must ore-top yours : "
- as a result of which Ulysses very cleverly reminds Achilles that
  " : O let not vertue seeke/Remuneration for the thing it was : "
  since
  " : One touch of nature makes the whole world kin : "
  " . The present eye praises the present object :"
  " ; Since things in motion begin [to] catch the eye, /[than] what [not stirs]: "

First Folio

12/ Ulysses

1 Time hath (x my Lord x) a wallet at his backe,
Wherein he puts almes for oblivion : x
A great siz'd monster of ingratitudes :
Those scraps are good deedes past,
Which are devour'd as fast as they are made,
Forgot as soone as done : perseverance, deere my Lord,
Keepes honor bright,+ to have done, is to hang
Quite out of fashion, like a rustie [male], x
In monumentall mockrie : take the instant way,
For honour travels in a [straight] so narrow,
Where one but goes a breast, keepe then the paths+
For emulation hath a thousand Sonnes,
That one by one pursue ; if you give way,
Or hedge aside from the direct forth right ; x
Like to an entred Tyde, they all rush by, x
And leave you hindmost : x
Or like a gallant Horse falne in first ranke,
Lye there for pavement to the abject, x [neere]+
Ore-run and trampled on : then what they doe in present,
Though lesse [then] yours in past, must ore-top yours : x
For time is like a fashionable Hoste, x
That slightly shakes his parting Guest by th'hand ; x
And with his armes out-stretcht, x as he would flye,
Graspes in the commer : the welcome ever smiles,
And [farewels] goes out sighing : [O] let not vertue seeke

{ctd. over}

8 [ ] Let not virtue seek*
Remuneration for the thing it was:
For beauty$_*$, wit,
High birth, vigor of bone, desert in service,
Love, friendship, charity, are subjects all
To envious and calumniating ΔTime. †
9 One touch of nature makes the whole world kin,
That all with one consent praise new-born* gawds*,
Though they are made and moulded of things past,
And [give] to dust, that is a little$_*$ gilt*,
More laud [than] gilt* o'erdusted.
10 The present eye praises the present object. †
11 Then marvel* not, thou great and complete* man,
That all the Greeks* begin to worship Ajax;
Since things in motion [sooner] catch the eye
[Than]what [stirs not]. †
12 The cry went [once] on thee,
And still it might, and yet it may again*,
If thou wouldst not entomb* thyself* alive,
And case thy reputation in thy Δtent,
Whose glorious deeds* but in these fields of late
Made emulous missions 'mongst the gods themselves,
And drave great Mars to faction.

• the seriousness of what Ulysses has to offer is underscored, first, by an unusually long passage of unembellished lines explaining why virtue should not seek

"Remuneration for the thing it was : for beautie, wit,/High birth, vigor of bone, desert in service,/Love, friendship, charity, are subjects all/To envious and calumniating time :/One touch of nature makes the whole world kin:"

and then by two key passages of irregular line length, shaded as shown: the first (F lines four to six, 6/10/13 syllables) pushes the idea of 'perseverance' hard via the long last line: the second (F line twenty-seven, 14 syllables) driving home the start of the idea just quoted above, i.e. not striving for 'Remuneration'

• initially Ulysses seems to attempt to ensnare Achilles by quiet argument driven home by surround phrases, for the first sixteen lines show only sporadic releases (4/11) – sporadic perhaps, but nearly always emotional

• it is not until the image of the past valiant being trampled on 'like a gallant Horse falne in first ranke' that the argument become a little more emotional (4/11 in nine lines – up to the unembellished 'Remuneration' passage'); and after the unembellishment F #1's last four lines describing the tributes paid to 'new borne gaudes' are also emotional (0/4)

• then in F #2, as Ulysses begins to turn what has been an argument in general terms to deal with Achilles' current situation, the first three lines become passionate as he advises Achilles not to wonder 'That all the Greekes begin to worship Ajax ;' (2/3),

• then he so cleverly turns the knife of serious unembellished quietness once again, advising Achilles 'Since things in motion [begin to] catch the eye, /[than] what [not stirs] : the cry went [out] on thee,/And still it might,', before finishing with the urging that it is such a shame that Achilles 'entombes' himself in his tent, especially since his 'glorious deedes' once 'drave great Mars to faction'

• this last temptation is carefully passionate (2/4, F #2's last six lines – the caution presumably deliberate so as not to break the spell his calm urging has worked upon the worried Achilles), the carefulness enhanced by the two extra breath-thoughts (marked , $_x$) that suddenly appear two and half lines from the finish, the additional tiny phrases ('Whose glorious deedes,$_x$ but in these fields of late,$_x$') adding two tiny extra seduction moments in pushing home the idea of Achilles' one time greatness

Remuneration for the thing it was : for beautie, wit,
High birth, vigor of bone, desert in service,
Love, friendship, charity, are subjects all
To envious and calumniating time :
One touch of nature makes the whole world kin : $_x$
That all with one consent praise new borne gaudes,
Though they are made and moulded of things past,
And [goe] to dust, that is a litle guilt,
More laud [then] guilt oredusted.
2 The present eye praises the present object :
Then marvell not+ thou great and compleat man,
That all the Greekes begin to worship Ajax ;
Since things in motion [begin to] catch the eye,$_x$
[Then] what [not stirs] : the cry went [out] on thee,
And still it might, and yet it may againe,
If thou would'st not entombe thy selfe alive,
And case thy reputation in thy Tent ; $_x$
Whose glorious deedes,$_x$ but in these fields of late,$_x$
Made emulous missions 'mongst the gods themselves,
And drave great Mars to faction.

#'S 13 - 15: THERSITES [9]

13/ Thersites	**A wonder./Ajax goes up and downe the field, asking for**	between 3.3.242 - 265
14/ Thersites	**Prythee be silent boy, I profit not by thy talke,**	between 5.1.14 - 36
15/ Thersites	**With too much bloud, and too little Brain, these**	5.1.48 - 66

Background: As found in Homer's Iliad this very bitter character was accounted an officer, and eventually killed by Achilles who, like everyone else, grew tired of his attacks. Here, in the following three speeches, is Shakespeare's version heard in all his insulting and wondrously foul-mouthed glory.

Speech #13, Thersites brings news to Achilles that the generals have selected Ajax and not Achilles for the following day's honour of single combat with the Trojan Hector.

Speech #14, Thersites pulls no punches as he names Patroclus to his face as Achilles' male whore.

Speech #15, alone, Thersites sums up the whole Greek command.

Style: speeches #13 - 14, three-handed scene; speech #15, solo

Where: various places in the Greek camp **To Whom:** speech #13, Achilles in front of Patroclus; speech #14, Patroclus in front of Achilles; speech #15, direct audience address

Speech 13: # of Lines: 20	**Probable Timing: 1.00 minutes**
Speech 14: # of Lines: 11	**Probable Timing: 0.40 minutes**
Speech 15: # of Lines: 18	**Probable Timing: 0.55 minutes**

Modern Text

13/ Thersites

1 A wonder !

2 Ajax goes up and down* the field, asking for
himself*.

3 He* must fight singly to-morrow with Hector,
and is so prophetically proud of an heroical* cudgelling
that he raves in saying nothing.

4 Why, [a] stalks* up and down* like a Δpeacock - a
stride and a stand ; ruminates like an hostess* that hath
no Δarithmetic* but her brain* to set down* her reckoning ; bites his lip with a politic* regard, as who should
say, "There were wit in [this] head and 'twould* out" - and
so there is ; but it lies* as coldly in him as fire in a flint,
which will not show* without knocking.

5 The man's undone
for ever, for if Hector break* not his neck* i'th'combat, he'll* break't himself* in vainglory*.

Compared to his much more intellect-emotion balanced face to face quarrel with Patroclus, speech #14 below (14/15 overall), here, in his audience- direct mocking of Ajax, Thersites is very emotional (9/28).

- Thersites starts deceptively quietly, though the shortness of the unembellished F #1 should suggest something is about to break –
- - and break it does, but slowly, for F #2-3's start to the put down of Ajax, simply setting up the facts of Ajax talking to himself in public, is mildly emotional (1/4 in four lines) and then the extended F #4's wonderfully wicked descriptions of Ajax's 'Peacock/hostesse'-like behaviour suddenly explodes emotionally (2/9 in six and a half lines), reinforced by three surround phrases, two of them formed in part by an (emotional) semicolon
- following Thersites' unembellished surround phrase suggestion 'The mans undone for ever ; ' (again deceptively quiet, calm in his own certainty perhaps), the idea of Ajax's neck being broken either by his opponent Hector or by Ajax's owne 'vaine-glory' allows his emotion to sweep in once more (1/5 in just over one line)

First Folio

13/ Thersites

1 A wonder. +

2 Ajax goes up and downe the field, asking for
himselfe.

3 Hee must fight singly to morrow with Hector,
and is so prophetically proud of an heroicall cudgelling, $_x$
that he raves in saying nothing.

4 Why+ [he] stalkes up and downe like a Peacock, a
stride and a stand : $_x$ ruminates like an hostesse, + that hath
no Arithmatique but her braine to set downe her reckoning : $_x$ bites his lip with a politique regard, as who should
say, there were wit in [his] head and twoo'd out ; $_x$ and
so there is : $_x$ but it lyes as coldly in him, $_x$ as fire in a flint,
which will not shew without knocking.

5 The mans undone
for ever ; $_x$ for if Hector breake not his necke i'th'combat, heele break't himselfe in vaine-glory.

{ctd. over}

[9] by the time of this play, Will Kemp, the very popular low comic-type Clown had left the company, : the roles that were to replace his "line" (written for Robert Armin) would eventually become those of the reflective all-licensed Fool (someone allowed to mock anyone in society no matter how high their rank): in between, there are two extraordinarily bitter and sardonic characters seeming to bridge the two lines, both being created in approximately the same period of writing: Lavache from *All's Well That Ends Well*, in many ways the junior of the two, is extremely sardonic about women and love, while in this play, Thersites is truly the bitterest misanthrope Shakespeare ever created - for Timon, also created fairly close to these characters, at least has both redeeming qualities and on-stage reasons for the blackness that descends upon him and all who meet him in the second part of his play

6 He knows*
not me*. †
7 I said, "Good morrow Ajax"; $^{\Delta}$and he replies*, "Thanks* Agamemnon."
8 What think* you of this man
that takes me for the $^{\Delta}$general*?
9 He's* grown* a very
land-fish, languageless*, a monster. †
10 A plague of o-
pinion ! a man may wear* it on both sides, like a leather $^{\Delta}$jerkin.

• the fact that in his bemusement Ajax mistook Thersites for the general Agamemnon is spoken of with (delighted?) passion (F #6, 3/4), enhanced by F #6 being set as three surround phrases (two of which are emotional)

" , He knowes not mee : I said, good morrow Ajax ; And he replyes, thankes Agamemnon . "

• and Thersites' emotion continues to be released with his final questioning of the audience as to 'What thinke you of this man, . . . ', as well as the final summation, again starting with the surround phrase heightening Thersites' own assessment of Ajax ' . Hee's growne a very land-fish, languagelesse, a monster : ' (2/6, F #7-8)

6 He knowes
not mee : I said, good morrow Ajax ; And he replyes, thankes Agamemnon.
7 What thinke you of this man,$_{x}$
that takes me for the Generall?
8 Hee's growne a very
land-fish, languagelesse, a monster : a plague of o-
pinion,+ a man may weare it on both sides+ like a leather Jerkin.

Modern Text

14/ Thersites

1 Prythee be silent, boy, I profit not by thy talk*. †
2 Thou art [said] to be Achilles' male $^{\Delta}$varlot{, ψ}
his masculine $^{\Delta}$whore.
3 Now the rotten diseases
of the $^{\Delta}$south, [the] guts-griping, $^{\Delta}$ruptures, $^{\Delta}$catarrhs*, $^{\Delta}$loads* of a gravel* i'th'back*, $^{\Delta}$lethargies, cold $^{\Delta}$palsies, [10] [raw* eyes*, dirt* rotten $^{\Delta}$livers, [wheezing] lungs, bladders full of imposthurne*, $^{\Delta}$sciaticas* lime-kills ith'palm*, incurable bone-ache*, and the rivell'd* fee simple of the tetter] take and take again* such preposterous* discoveries !
4 {ψ} {T}hou idle
immaterial* skein* of [$^{\Delta}$sleave]- silk*; thou green* $^{\Delta}$sarcenet flap for a sore eye, thou tassle* of a $^{\Delta}$prodigal's purse, thou {.}†
5 Ah, how the poore world is pest'red with such water-flies, diminutives of $^{\Delta}$nature !
6 Finch-$^{\Delta}$egg* !

Compared to his audience- direct mocking of Ajax, where Thersites was very emotional (9/28, speech #13 above), here in his face to face quarrel with Patroclus, he is much more passionate (14/15 overall), the bracketed and shaded Q only text, usually set by most modern texts, adding to the list of horrors and insults piled upon 'Achilles male Varlot'.

• the speech remains passionate almost throughout, with intellect slightly dominating emotion in F #1, #2, and #4

• however, once the insults of F #3 based on images of slightness and vanity begin ('Sley'd silke' – or 'sleave' silk as most modern would have it – being a form of silk that can be broken down into smaller components, and 'Sarcenet' being an inferior form of silk used for linings rather than show in the best of clothing), not only does emotion dominate for a moment (3/6, the first two and half lines), the power of both the opening of the insult

" . Thou idle, immateriall skiene of [Sleyd] silke ;"

and the sentence ending summation

" . Ah how the poore world is pestred with such water-flies,diminutives of Nature ."

are intensified by being set as the only surround phrases in the speech, the first even further heightened by being formed in part by the only emotional semicolon of the piece

First Folio

14/ Thersites

1 Prythee be silent+ boy, I profit not by thy talke,
thou art [thought] to be Achilles male Varlot{, ψ}
his masculine Whore.
2 Now the rotten diseases
of the South, [ ] guts-griping+ Ruptures, Catarres, Loades of a gravell i'th'backe, Lethargies, cold Palsies, [and the like], take and take againe,$_{x}$ such prepostrous discoveries. +
3 {ψ} {T}hou idle,$_{x}$
immateriall skiene of [Sleyd] silke ; thou greene Sarcenet flap for a sore eye, thou tassell of a Prodigals purse+ thou : Ah+ how the poore world is pestred with such water-flies, diminutives of Nature. +
4 Finch Egge.

[10] within the following (Q based) shaded passage any reference to capital letters ($^{\Delta}$) or spelling variations (*) is in comparison with the quarto text, viz.
"durt rotte livers, [whissing] lungs, bladders full of imposturen. Sciaticæ's lime kills ith' palme, incurable bone-ach, and the riveled fee simple of the tetter,"

Modern Text

15/ Thersites

1 With too much blood*, and too little Δbrain, these
two may run mad, but, if with too much brain* and too
little blood they do, I'll be a curer of madmen.

2 Here's*
Agamemnon, an honest fellow enough, and one that loves
Δquails*, but he has not so much Δbrain* as ear*-wax; and
the goodly transformation of Jupiter there, his Δbrother,
the Δbull, the primitive* Δstatue and oblique memorial* of
Δcuckolds, a thrifty shoeing-horn* in a chain*, [ ]
at his Δbrother's leg* - to what [form] but that he is, should*
wit larded with malice, and malice forced with wit, turn*
him to* ? †

3 To an Δass*, were nothing, he* is both Δass* and
Δox*; to an Δox*, were nothing, he* is both Δox* and Δass*. †

4 To be a Δdog*, a Δmule, a Δcat, a [Δfitchook], a Δtoad*, a Δli-
zard, an Δowl*, a Δputtock*, or a Δherring without a Δroe,
I would not care; but to be Menelaus, I would conspire
against Δdestiny.

5 Ask* me not what I would be if I were
not Thersites, for I care not to be* the louse* of a Δlazar,
so I were not Menelaus.

Thersites' contempt knows neither bounds nor rank, for after dismissing both Achilles and Patroclus (F #1) he then goes on to insult two of the Princes, and while at least his passionate (3/4) contempt for the General Agamemnon is somewhat tempered by grudging respect, the all-over-the-place pulling apart of Agamemnon's brother Menelaus (over whose wayward wife the war is being fought) shows no such respect.

- though starting with a surround phrase, Thersites' F #1 dismissal of Achilles and Patroclus as being essentially brainless is an easy (resigned?) mixture of intellect, emotion (1/2), and unembellishment

- F #2's opening two line passionate dismissal of Agamemnon is much more energetic (3/4), and then the first two line extension to Agammemnon's brother, the start of what turns into a lengthy diatribe (dismissing him as a 'primative Statue'), opens intellectually (4/1)

- then in expanding the contempt to (correctly) describe Menelaus as a Cuckold getting his status from the power of his brother, Thersites' emotions get the better of him (2/6, the next three and a half lines)

- F #2 ends with the intellectual surround phrase ' : but to be Menelaus, I would conspire against Destiny . ' (2/0), the build up to this first of two unequivocal conclusions, listing anything Thersites would rather be, is amazingly passionate (16/12 in just four lines, including four surround phrases)

- F #3's summation, essentially an even more vehement restatement of the end of F #2, is equally passionate (3/3), its passion extra weighted by being set as two surround phrases

First Folio

15/ Thersites

1 With too much bloud, and too little Brain, these
two may run mad : x but+ if with too much braine,x and too
little blood,x they do, Ile be a curer of madmen.

2 Heere's
Agamemnon, an honest fellow enough, and one that loves
Quailes, but he has not so much Braine as eare-wax; and
the goodly transformation of Jupiter there+ his Brother,
the Bull, the primative Statue,x and oblique memoriall of
Cuckolds, a thrifty shooing-horne in a chaine, [hanging]
at his Brothers legge, to what [for me] but that he is, shold
wit larded with malice, and malice forced with wit, turne
him too :+ to an Asse+ were nothing ;x hee is both Asse and
Oxe ; to an Oxe+ were nothing, hee is both Oxe and Asse :
to be a Dogge ;x a Mule, a Cat, a [Fitchew], a Toade, a Li-
zard, an Owle, a Puttocke, or a Herring without a Roe,
I would not care :x but to be Menelaus, I would conspire
against Destiny.

3 Aske me not what I would be,x if I were
not Thersites : x for I care not to bee the lowse of a Lazar,
so I were not Menelaus.

#'S 16 - 18: SINGLE COMBAT (IN CONTRAST TO CASSANDRA'S VISIONS AND THE FINAL SLAYING OF HECTOR)

16/ Æneas **Trumpet blow loud,** 1.3.256 - 283

Background: On behalf of the Trojan Hector, Æneas has come to issue the Greeks a challenge to single combat, based on the subtle insult that Hectors' wife is lovelier than even the beautiful Grecian Helen (taken from her husband the Grecian commander Menelaus by the Trojan Paris), thus suggesting that whomever the Greeks choose will have to fight over the reputation of a woman no longer in their possession.

Style: public address in the open air

Where: the Greek camp **To Whom:** the commanders Agamemnon, Nestor, Diomedes, and Menelaus, with others

# of Lines: 28 **Probable Timing: 1.30 minutes**

Modern Text

16/ Æneas

1 Trumpet, blow loud,
Send thy Δbrass* voice* through all these lazy$_*$ Δtents,
And every Greek* of mettle, let him know,
What Troy means* fairly* shall be spoke aloud*.

[The Trumpets sound]

2 We have, great Agamemnon, here* in Troy,
A Prince called$_*$ Hector - Priam is his Δfather -
Who in this dull and long-continued* Truce
Is [resty] grown*.
3 He bad me take a Δtrumpet,
And to this purpose speak*: Δkings, Δprinces, Δlords! †
4 If there be one [among] the fair'st* of Greece,
That holds his Δhonor higher [than] his ease,
That seeks his praise more [than] he fears* his peril*,
That knows* his Δvalor*, and knows* not his fear*,
That loves his Δmistress$_*$ more [than] in confession
With truant vows* to her own* lips he loves,
And dare avow her Δbeauty and her Δworth
In other arms* [than] hers - to him this Δchallenge !
5 Hector, in view of Troyans and of Greeks*,
Shall make it good, or do his best to do it.
6 He hath a Δlady, wiser, fairer, truer,
[Than] ever Greek* did [couple] in his arms*,
And will to-morrow with his Δtrumpet call,
Midway between* your Δtents, and walls* of Troy,
To rouse* a Grecian that is true in love.
7 If any come, Hector shall$_*$ honor* him;
If none, he'll* say in Troy when he retires*,

In what is essentially a public address, it is not surprising that the speech is highly passionate (36/29 in just twenty-eight lines) - oratory is all. And the two slight onrushes (F#3 and #6) suggesting an enthusiastic man in full rhetorical flow, are also to be expected (though by splitting each in two most modern texts suggest slightly more control than originally shown). What may be surprising, especially in this play where there are very few such examples, are the extra breath-thoughts (marked , $_x$) that suddenly appear in F #3-4's listing of the honour-belief-system Hector is looking for in an opponent.

- the surround phrases set up the basic message that Æneas has come to deliver to the Greeks from the Trojan Hector
  " : Who in this dull and long-continew'd Truce/Is [rusty] growne . He bad me take a Trumpet,/And to this purpose speake : "
  wishing to find someone to fight
  " : to him this Challenge . " " . If any come, Hector shal honour him : "
  " : Even so much ."
- the opening exhortation for the trumpet to sound to gain the attention of 'every Greeke of mettle' is passionate (4/6)
- then, having caught the attention of the Greeks, the descriptions both of 'a Prince calld Hector' (F #2) and of those whom Hector has bid Æneas address (F#3's first two and a half lines) is splendidly intellectual (12/5)
- the delineating of Hector's searching for an opponent 'That holds his Honor higher then his ease' is, for the only time in the speech, slightly more emotional than intellectual (6/9, F #3's last eight lines)
- Æneas' suggestion that Hector is prepared to prove by combat that 'He hath a Lady, wiser, fairer, truer/Then ever Greeke did compasse in his armes.' is, hardly surprisingly, passionate (F #4-5, 8/6)
- while the final flourish/courteous insult becomes intellectual once more (6/3)

First Folio

16/ Æneas

1 Trumpet+ blow loud,
Send thy Brasse voyce through all these lazie Tents,
And every Greeke of mettle, let him know,
What Troy meanes fairely,$_x$ shall be spoke alowd.

[The Trumpets sound]

2 We have+ great Agamemnon+ heere in Troy,
A Prince calld Hector, Priam is his Father: $_x$
Who in this dull and long-continew'd Truce
Is [rusty] growne
3 He bad me take a Trumpet,
And to this purpose speake: Kings, Princes, Lords,+
If there be one [among'st] the fayr'st of Greece,
That holds his Honor higher [then] his ease,
That seekes his praise,$_x$ more [then] he feares his perill,
That knowes his Valour, and knowes not his feare,
That loves his Mistris more [then] in confession,$_x$
($_x$With truant vowes to her owne lips he loves,$_x$)
And dare avow her Beauty,$_x$ and her Worth,$_x$
In other armes [then] hers: $_x$ to him this Challenge. +
4 Hector, in view of Troyans,$_x$ and of Greekes,
Shall make it good, or do his best to do it.
5 He hath a Lady, wiser, fairer, truer,
[Then] ever Greeke did [compasse] in his armes,
And will to morrow with his Trumpet call,
Midway betweene your Tents, and walles of Troy,
To rowze a Grecian that is true in love.
6 If any come, Hector shal honour him: $_x$
If none, hee'l say in Troy when he retyres,

The Grecian △dames are sunburnt, and not worth
The splinter of a △lance. †
8 Even so much.

The Grecian Dames are sun-burnt, and not worth
The splinter of a Lance: Even so much.

17/ Hector **Thou art great Lord, my Fathers sisters Sonne ;** 4.5120 - 138

Background: Through a combination of circumstances (see speeches #9-10 and #13 above) Ajax and not Achilles was chosen for the honour of the single-combat-but-not-to-the-death challenge with Hector. After the first skirmish Ajax is more than willing to continue to the fight. However, as Hector reminds him, as they are related (historically Hector was his uncle) Hector would rather not continue.

Style: one on one address in front of a larger group

Where: the Greek camp **To Whom:** Ajax, with, in the background ', all of Troy' - including Paris, Æneas, Helenus and Attendants, and, of the Greek party, Agamemnon, Achilles, Patroclus, Menelaus, Ulysses, Nestor, and 'others'

# of Lines: 19 **Probable Timing: 1.00 minutes**

Modern Text

17/ Hector

1 Thou art great ^Δ^lord, my ^Δ^father's sister's ^Δ^son*,
A cousin*- °german to great Priam's seed*;
The obligation of our blood* forbids
A gory* emulation 'twixt us twain*. †

2 Were thy commixtion Greek* and [Troyan*] so
That thou couldst say, "This hand is Grecian all,
And this is [Troyan*] ; the sinews* of this ^Δ^leg*
All Greek*, and this all Troy ; my ^Δ^mother's blood*
Runs on the dexter cheek*, and this sinister
Bounds in my father's" : by Jove multipotent,
Thou shouldst not bear* from me a Greekish member
Wherein my sword had not impressure made
Of our rank* feud ; but the just gods gainsay
That any drop thou borrowd'st from thy mother,
My sacred ^Δ^aunt, should by my mortal* ^Δ^sword
Be drained !

3 Let me embrace thee, Ajax . † [11]

4 By him that thunders, thou hast lusty* ^Δ^arms* ! †

5 Hector would have them fall upon him thus.

6 Cousin*, all honor to thee !

The opening of this post-fight speech is presented somewhat more rationally by most modern texts, which split the surround phrase riddled onrushed F #1 in two. However, as set, F's opening and the overall passion of the speech (18/16 throughout) could well represent the patterns of someone moderately winded by the armed combat and genuinely delighted to have crossed swords honourably with a fine soldier whom has him term a 'cousen'.

- the opening public-acknowledgement surround phrases attest to his pleasure
  " . Thou art great Lord, my Fathers sisters Sonne ; /A cousen german to great Priams seede : "
  and the mixture of styles, the first intellectual (3/1) and the second emotional (1/2) serve to illustrate the conflicting tugs within him - hardly surprising since he is giving due praise to an enemy who is also a relative

- thus the next two line suggestion that, since they come from common blood, no blood should be spilled is emotional (0/2)

- in eventually (and fancifully, as a joke perhaps?) suggesting that if different body parts of Ajax could be identified as either Greek or Trojan, Hector would not allow him to leave with any Greek members intact, Hector at least begins intellectually (4/1, F #1's lines five to half way through line seven)

- however, the surround phrase ' : the sinewes of this Legge,/All Greeke, and this all Troy : ' turns the notion up a notch, for the next six lines become passionate (6/7)

- and then, for whatever reason (courtesy? or that the non too bright Ajax takes him seriously?) the unembellished section 'but the just gods gainsay, /That any drop thou borrowd'st from thy mother,' leads to a gentle sentence ending avowal that he will not spill Ajax's blood (2/1, F #1's last three lines)

- and in offering to embrace Ajax, the totally surround phrase passionate F #2 (2/1) and the short emotional F #3 (0/1) reinforce all that Hector has said to date

First Folio

17/ Hector

1 Thou art great Lord, my Fathers sisters Sonne ; x
A cousen german to great Priams seede : x
The obligation of our bloud forbids
A gorie emulation 'twixt us twaine : x
Were thy commixion, x Greeke and [Troian] so, x
That thou could'st say, this hand is Grecian all,
And this is [Troian] : x the sinewes of this Legge, x
All Greeke, and this all Troy : x my Mothers bloud
Runs on the dexter cheeke, and this sinister
Bounds in my fathers : by Jove multipotent,
Thou should'st not beare from me a Greekish
member
Wherein my sword had not impressure made
Of our ranke feud : x but the just gods gainsay, x
That any drop thou borrowd'st from thy mother,
My sacred Aunt, should by my mortall Sword
Be drained. +

2 Let me embrace thee+ Ajax :
By him that thunders, thou hast lustie Armes ; +
Hector would have them fall upon him thus.

3 Cozen, all honor to thee. +

[11] some modern texts suggest they embrace, or at the very least Hector touches Ajax's arm

18/ Nestor **I have (thou gallant Troyan) seene thee oft** 4.5.183 - 200

Background: Following the single combat between Ajax and Hector, the Greek Nestor praises the Trojan Hector.

Style: one on one address in front of as larger group

Where: the Greek camp **To Whom:** Hector, in front of 'all of Troy' - including Paris, Æneas, Helenus and Attendants, and, of the Greek party, Agamemnon, Ajax, Achilles, Patroclus, Menelaus, Ulysses, and 'others'

# of Lines: 18 **Probable Timing: 0.55 minutes**

Modern Text

18/ Nestor

1 I have, thou gallant Troyan, seen* thee oft,
Laboring* for destiny, make cruel* way
Through ranks* of Greekish youth, and I have seen thee,
As hot as Perseus, spur* thy Phrygian Δsteed,
[Despising many] forfeits and subduements$_*$,
When thou hast hung thy advanced sword i'th'air*,
Not letting it decline, on the declined,
That I have said [to some] my standers by
"Lo* Jupiter is yonder, dealing life !"

2 And I have seen* thee pause and take thy breath,
When that a ring of Greeks* have hemm'd$_*$ thee in,
Like an Olympian wrestling.

3 This have I seen*,
But this thy countenance, still lock'd in steel*,
I never saw till now.

4 I knew thy Δgrandsire,
And once fought with him. †

5 He was a Δsoldier* good,
But, by great Mars, the Δcaptain* of us all,
Never like thee.

6 [O], let an old Δ man embrace thee,
And, worthy Δwarrior*, welcome to our Δtents.

Given Nestor's usual volubility, this is a somewhat restrained speech, though that is always a relative term with this character: what is surprising is that, with the relative lack of major punctuation, his usually rhetorical speechifying seems here to have been replaced by a more spontaneous and genuine series of compliments.

- after the opening emotional two and a half lines of praising Hector's soldiership (2/4), the passion of F #1's remaining fulsome praise (4/3) is highlighted by the next to the last line's single extra breath-thought (marked ,$_x$) allowing the final line
  ',$_x$ Loe Jupiter is yonder, dealing life.'
  to have that extra flourish so beloved of politicians of all stripes

- F #2's comparison to an 'Olympian wrestling' is equally passionate (2/2), but then emotion once more gets the better of him as he expresses delight in seeing Hector's face for the first time (F #3, 0/2)

- he becomes intellectual for the only time in the speech (F # 4-5, 6/3) both in the acknowledgement that he has never seen anyone who could match Hector's prowess, not even Hector's 'Grandsire' who was 'the Captaine of us all', and in his welcoming of Hector 'to our Tents' . . .

- . . . there is something quite fascinating in the opening of F #4 being set as an emotional surround phrase
  " . I knew thy Grandsire,/And once fought with him ; "
  (the only surround phrase in the speech) – perhaps the quality of Hector's abilities has truly startled him, or perhaps he is beginning to feel his age

First Folio

18/ Nestor

1 I have ($_x$thou gallant Troyan$_x$) seene thee oft+
Labouring for destiny, make cruell way
Through rankes of Greekish youth :$_x$ and I have seen thee+
As hot as Perseus, spurre thy Phrygian Steed,
[And seene thee scorning] forfeits and subduments,
When thou hast hung thy advanced sword i'th'ayre,
Not letting it decline, on the declined : $_x$
That I have said [unto] my standers by,$_x$
Loe Jupiter is yonder, dealing life. +

2 And I have seene thee pause,$_x$ and take thy breath,
When that a ring of Greekes have hem'd thee in,
Like an Olympian wrestling.

3 This have I seene,
But this thy countenance ($_x$still lockt in steele$_x$)
I never saw till now.

4 I knew thy Grandsire,
And once fought with him ; he was a Souldier good,
But+ by great Mars, the Captaine of us all,
Never like thee.

5 [ ] Let an oldman
embrace thee,
And ($_x$worthy Warriour$_x$) welcome to our Tents.

#'s 19 - 21: Cassandra and the Finality of War

19/ Cassandra **Cry Troyans cry ; lend me ten thousand eyes,** between 2.2.101 - 112

Background: Known as a prophetess, Cassandra, the only one of Priam's daughters shown in the play, bursts in on the family with her very dark visions.

Style: group address

Where: unspecified, but probably in the family's private chambers **To Whom:** her father Priam and her brothers Hector, Troylus, Paris, and Helenus

# of Lines: 11 **Probable Timing: 0.40 minutes**

Modern Text

19/ Cassandra

1 Cry, Troyans, cry ! lend me ten thousand eyes,
And I will fill them with ^Δ^prophetic* tears*.

2 Virgins, and ^Δ^boys*, mid-age & wrinkled [eld],
Soft infancy*, that nothing [canst] but cry,
Add* to my [clamors] ! †

3 Let us pay betimes
A moi'ty of that mass* of moan* to come.

4 Cry, Troyans, cry !, practice your eyes with tears*!
†

5 Troy must not be, nor goodly Ilion* stand . †

6 Our fire-brand ^Δ^brother Paris burns* us all.

7 Cry, Troyans, cry ! a Helen and a woe ! † [12]

8 Cry, cry ! †

9 Troy burns*, or else let Helen go*.

The rational nine sentence structure offered by most modern texts in no way reflects the onrush of F's four sentences or the fact that both F's opening and closing sentences, as well as the opening of F #2, are incredibly heightened by being formed by emotional (semicoloned) surround phrases (five in all).

- F #1's emotional surround phrase opening invocation ' . Cry Troyans cry ; ' eventually becomes passionate (2/2), though interestingly the bulk of the release doesn't occur until the end of the sentence - 'Propheticke teares', as if, at the very last, she cannot contain herself, and the release now turns to emotion, the surround phrases of the ensuing F #2 (1/4) spelling out who should mourn and how, ' . Virgins and Boyes ; . . . : let us pay betimes/A moity of that masse of moane to come . '

- but then, very surprisingly, Cassandra seems to take hold of herself, for despite the unrelenting appalling clarity of her images, the warning/prophecy of her next five lines (F #3 and the first of F #4) are strongly factual (6/2)

- placing Helen as the cause of Troy's forthcoming losses releases her emotions once more, for the two surround phrases forming this last sentence (F #4) are linked by an emotional semicolon

- which in turn leads to the final passionate plea/warning of the last line 'Troy burnes, or else let Helen goe.' (2/2 in just seven words)

First Folio

19/ Cassandra

1 Cry^+^ Troyans^+^ cry ; ^+^ lend me ten thousand eyes,
And I will fill them with Propheticke teares.

2 Virgins, and Boyes; ₓ mid-age & wrinkled [old],
Soft infancie, that nothing [can] but cry,
Adde to my [clamour] : ^+^ let us pay betimes
A moity of that masse of moane to come.

3 Cry^+^ Troyans^+^ cry,^+^ practise your eyes with teares,^+^
Troy must not be, nor goodly Illion stand,
Our fire-brand Brother Paris burnes us all.

4 Cry^+^ Troyans^+^ cry,^+^ a Helen and a woe ; ^+^
Cry, cry, ^+^ Troy burnes, or else let Helen goe.

[12] Q/Ff/most modern texts reshape it to read as a lament, 'a Helen and a woe', one modern text reshapes it read 'ah Helen, and ah woe'

20/ Cassandra **O farewell, deere Hector:/ Looke how thou diest ;** between 5.3.80 - 90

Background: Having foreseen Hector's death, Cassandra has begged her father Priam, in front of Hector, his wife Andromache, and Troylus, 'hold him fast:/He is thy crutch: now if thou loose thy stay,/Thou on him leaning, and all Troy on thee,/Fall all together'. This is supported by Andromache's own dreams, and those of Hector's mother. Hecuba. Nevertheless Hector insists he 'must not breake my faith' and, backed by Troylus, begs permission to go to the day's battle as planned. Andromache leaves silently, but not Cassandra.

Style: one on one in front of a small family group

Where: unspecified, but probably in the family's private chambers **To Whom:** Hector, in front of Priam and Troylus

# of Lines: 10 **Probable Timing: 0.35 minutes**

Modern Text

20/ Cassandra

1 O, farewell, dear* Hector. †
2 Look* how thou diest, look* how thy eye turns* pale. †
3 Look* how thy wounds [do] bleed* at many vents. †
4 Hark* how Troy roars*, how Hecuba cries out,
How poor* Andromache shrills⁎ her [dolors]* forth. †
5 Behold, [destruction], frenzy⁎, and amazement,
Like witless* △antics*, one another meet*,
And all cry, Hector ! †
6 Hector's dead ! †
7 O Hector !

8 Farewell; [yet], soft: Hector, I take my leave. †
9 Thou dost thyself* and all our Troy deceive.

The relentless onrushed build of F #1, especially the opening of seven consecutive surround phrases in the first five lines, suggests a character who, once started, cannot prevent herself from uttering the prophecy that she sees. Modern texts' splitting F #1 into six separate sentences suggests a far more rational character who knowingly (even deliberately?) builds the picture of catastrophe logically, step by step. This is a great shame, for both in this and the previous speech it seems that while the F opening of her visions is emotional or passionate, eventually she regains self-control to drive the point home intellectually before she leaves (do the visions come despite herself, and when they are finished only then can she regain self control?).

- her gruesome description of Hector's death is highly emotional (1/6, F #1's first three lines), the emotion intensified by the four surround phrases - especially the second and third - formed in part by the emotional semicolon
- the two line vision of the reaction of both the city of Troy and his wife and mother is passionate (3/4) again heightened by three more semicolon surround phrases
- then it seems as if she is quietened by what she sees, for the next set of images 'Behold [distraction], frenzie, and amazement,' is unembellished
- the ensuing chaos that will result when all these abstracts meet 'Like witlesse Antickes' is very emotional (1/3)
- and the last three lines of the speech, triggered in her imagination by everyone crying 'Hectors dead', becomes profoundly intellectual (6/1), as if she cannot escape the inevitability of the image - the bleak vision intensified by ending with five surround phrases, the last, essentially blaming Hector for what is about to come, heightened further by the emotional semicolon

First Folio

20/ Cassandra

1 O+ farewell, deere Hector:
Looke how thou diest; x looke how thy eye turnes pale:
Looke how thy wounds [doth] bleede at many vents:
Harke how Troy roares; x how Hecuba cries out; x
How poore Andromache shrils her [dolour] forth;
Behold+ [distraction], frenzie, and amazement,
Like witlesse Antickes x one another meete,
And all cry+ Hector,+ Hectors dead: + O Hector!

2 Farewell: x yes, soft: Hector+ I take my leave;
Thou do'st thy selfe, x and all our Troy deceive.

21/ Troylus **Hector is slaine.** between 5.10.2 - 31

Background: Hector has been surrounded while unarmed, and, under orders from Achilles, mercilessly slaughtered by a group of Achilles' followers known as the Myrmidons. His body has then been dragged over the battlefield tied to the tail of Achilles' horse. Troylus gives the news to a group of Greek commanders who had believed they were victorious in the day's battle.

Style: address to a small group

Where: somewhere on the battlefield **To Whom:** Æneas, Anthenor, Paris, and Deiphobus

# of Lines: 27 **Probable Timing: 1.30 minutes**

Modern Text

21/ Troylus

1 Hector is slain*.

2 He's* dead, and at the [murderer's] △horse's tail*,
In beastly sort, dragg'd x through the shameful* △field . †

3 Frown* on, you heavens, effect your rage with speed*!†

4 Sit, gods, upon your thrones*, and smile at Troy ! [13]

5 I say at once, let your brief* plagues be mercy,
And linger not our sure destructions on !

6 I do* not speak* of flight, of fear* of death,
But dare all imminence that gods and men
Address* their dangers in.

7 Hector is gone . †

8 Who shall tell Priam so, or Hecuba?

9 Let him that will a screech-°owl* aye be call'd,
Go* in to Troy, and say there, "Hector's dead !" †

10 There is a word will Priam turn* to stone,
Make wells x and Niobes of the maids* and wives,
[Cold] statues of the youth, and in a word,
Scare* Troy out of itself*.

11 But march away,
Hector is dead ; there is no more to say.

12 Stay yet . †

13 You vile abominable* △tents,
Thus proudly [pitched] upon our Phrygian plains*,
Let Titan rise as early as he dare,
I'll through and through you ! &,thou great siz'd coward,
No space of △earth shall sunder our two hates. †

F's orthography highlights in three different ways just where and how Troylus struggles in trying to come to terms with the implications of Hector's unwelcome death, and then in trying to take control of the situation. The onrush of F #2 (split into four by most modern texts), F #5-6 (each split in two), F #8 (split into three), and F #9 (split in two) show where Troylus loses self-control, even if only momentarily. The surround phrases that suddenly appear in great numbers between F #5-7 underscore the enormity of Troylus' realisations of what Hector's death is going to mean. And the extra breath-thoughts (marked , x), especially towards the end of F #8 and in F #9, show where he has difficulty in continuing to speak without a small extra breath to gain much sought for self-control.

- essentially F #1's naked short sentence opening says it all; thus the ensuing surround phrases could well suggest a stunned Troylus attempting to come to terms with the enormity resulting from the unchivalric death of his unarmed brother at the hands not of Achilles but of the whole troop of Myrmidons that follow him
  - ". Hee's dead : ", " : Sit gods upon your throanes, and smile at Troy. "
  - ". Hector is gone : /Who shall tell Priam so ? or Hecuba ? "
  - " : There is a word will Priam turne to stone ; /Make wels, and Niobes of the maides and wives ; /[Coole] statues of the youth : and in a word,/ Scarre Troy out of it selfe . But march away,/Hector is dead : there is no more to say ."

  while those from F #8 on deal with Troylus' new resolve
  - ". Stay yet : you vile abhominable Tents,/Thus proudly [pight] upon our Phrygian plaines : /Let Titan rise as early as he dare,/Ile through, and through you ; & thou great siz'd coward : "
  - ". Strike a free march to Troy, with comfort goe : /Hope of revenge, shall hide our inward woe."
- announcing Hector's death starts emotionally (3/6, F #1-2), with the ungrammatical fast-link switch from the death to exhorting the heavens to 'effect your rage with speed' (the middle of F #2) underscoring his distress – while F #3's elaboration of the same point is so quiet (save for the key request that the plagues to be visited upon Troy should be 'briefe') that it seems Troylus is extraordinarily determined to face whatever should come . . .

First Folio

21/ Troylus

1 Hector is slaine.

2 Hee's dead : x and at the [murtherers] Horses taile,
In beastly sort, drag'd through the shamefull Field
Frowne on+ you heavens, effect your rage with speede :+
Sit+ gods+ upon your throanes, and smile at Troy. +

3 I say at once, let your briefe plagues be mercy,
And linger not our sure destructions on. +

4 I doe not speake of flight, of feare, x of death,
But dare all imminence that gods and men, x
Addresse their dangers in.

5 Hector is gone :
Who shall tell Priam so? x or Hecuba?

6 Let him that will a screechoule aye be call'd,
Goe in to Troy, and say there, Hector's dead : +
There is a word will Priam turne to stone ; x
Make wels, x and Niobes of the maides and wives; x
[Coole] statues of the youth : x and in a word,
Scarre Troy out of it selfe.

7 But march away,
Hector is dead : x there is no more to say.

8 Stay yet : you vile abhominable Tents,
Thus proudly [pight] upon our Phrygian plaines : x
Let Titan rise as early as he dare,
Ile through, x and through you ;+ &+ thou great siz'd coward :
No space of Earth shall sunder our two hates,

[13] Q/Ff = 'smile at Troy', one gloss = 'smite all Troy'

14 I'll haunt thee like a wicked conscience still,
That mouldeth goblins swift as frenzy's$_{*}$ thoughts.
15 Strike a free march. [†]
16 To Troy with comfort go*;
Hope of revenge shall hide our inward woe.

• . . . for though his F #4 defiant assertion that he is asking for this not out of fear is initially emotional (0/3, the first line), he then becomes very quiet in his unembellished determined statement that he does so to dare 'gods and men'

• his intellectual understanding of what needs to be done (informing his parents - F #5, 2/0) is quickly lost in the passion and surround phrases as he imagines what their (and Troy's) response will be (5/6, F #6)

• but then he seems to take control of both himself and the situation, for F #7's two surround phrase order to march away is once more unembellished, and the the two line vehement address to the Grecian 'Tents/Thus proudly pight upon our Phrygian plaines' is passionate (2/2), and the remaining seven lines of the speech show very little release (3/1): the fact of virtually no emotional release and the extra breath thoughts suggest that Troylus has found a way to turn his pain into vows and action – though the onrush of both F #8-9 suggests that this outward appearance of calm does not come without continual struggle

Ile haunt thee,$_{x}$ like a wicked conscience still,
That mouldeth goblins swift as frensies thoughts.
9 Strike a free march[+] to Troy,$_{x}$ with comfort goe: $_{x}$
Hope of revenge,$_{x}$ shall hide our inward woe.

OTHELLO

SPEECHES IN ORDER

SPEECHES IN ORDER		TIME	PAGE
#'s 1 - 5: The Unexpected Marriage			
1/ Iago	Sir, y'are rob'd, for shame put on your Gowne,	0.25	191
2/ Brabantio	Oh thou foule Theefe	1.00	192
3a/ Othello	Most Potent, Grave, and Reveren'd Signiors,	1.00	193
b/ Othello	Her father love'd me, oft invited me;	2.00	194
4/ Desdemona	My Noble Father,/I do perceive heere a divided dutie	0.35	196
5/ Desdemona	Nor would I {at home} recide,	0.55	197
#'s 6 - 11: Iago's Discomfort, And Planning Revenge			
6/ Iago	But you'l not heare me.	1.35	198
7/ Iago	O Sir content you.	1.30	200
8/ Iago	{Love} is meerly a Lust of the blood,	1.15	201
9/ Iago	Thus do I ever make my Foole, my purse:	1.10	202
10/ Iago	He takes her by the palme: I, well said, whisper.	0.40	204
11/ Iago	That Cassio loves her, I do well beleev't:	1.30	205
#'s 12 - 15: The Plan In Action, Cassio & Desdemona			
12/ Iago	And what's he then, /That saies I play the Villaine?	1.30	206
13/ Æmilia	Goodmorrow (good Lieutenant) I am sorrie	0.40	208
14/ Desdemona	Do not doubt Cassio/But I will have my Lord, and you	0.50	209
15/ Desdemona	How now my Lord?/I have bin talking with a Suitor	1.45	210
#'s 16 - 19: The Plan In Action, Iago & Othello			
16/ Othello	Avant, be gone: Thou hast set me on the Racke:	1.10	211
17/ Iago	I see you are eaten up with Passion:	0.55	213
18/ Othello	O that the Slave had forty thousand lives:	0.55	214
19/ Othello	That's a fault: That Handkerchiefe	1.10	215
#'s 20 - 29: The Plan's Tragic Consequences			
20/ Bianca	'Save you (Friend Cassio.)	0.40	216
21/ Bianca	What did you meane by that same Handkerchiefe,	0.30	217
22/ Æmilia	Alas (Iago) my Lord hath so bewhor'd her,	1.15	217
23/ Desdemona	I prythee do {go meet him}. Something sure	0.45	219
24/ Othello	What would you with her, Sir?	0.45	220
25/ Rodorigo	I do not finde /That thou deal'st justly with me.	1.00	221
26/ Æmilia	Marry, I would not doe such a thing for a joynt Ring,	1.30	222
27/ Othello	It is the Cause, it is the Cause (my Soule)	1.10	224
28/ Æmilia	Oh Heaven! oh heavenly Powres!	0.50	225
29/ Othello	Soft you; a word or two before you goe:	1.00	226

SPEECHES BY GENDER

		Speech #(s)
SPEECHES FOR WOMEN (11)		
Æmilia	**Traditional & Today:** young woman, younger than her sister Adrianna	#13, #22, #26, #28
Desdemona	**Traditional & Today:** middle-aged woman, or younger	#4, #5, #14, #15, #23
Bianca	**Traditional & Today:** an attractive young woman of the town	#20, #21
SPEECHES FOR EITHER GENDER (1)		
Brabantio	**Traditional:** older male with adult daughter **Today:** any gender	#2
SPEECHES FOR MEN (17)		
Iago	**Traditional & Today:** early middle-aged (and older) military man	#1, #6, #7, #8, #9,#10, #11, #12, #17
Othello	**Traditional & Today:** early middle-aged military man	#3a, #3b, #16, #18, #19, #24, #27, #29
Rodorigo	**Traditional:** younger male **Today:** any age, usually middle-aged or younger	#25

OTHELLO

#'S 1 - 5: THE UNEXPECTED MARRIAGE

1/ Iago **Sir, y'are rob'd, for shame put on your Gowne,** 1.1.86 - 92

2/ Brabantio **Oh thou foule Theefe,/Where hast thou stow'd my Daughter?** 1.2.62 - 81

Background: Othello, an older man of colour (a 'Moore'), and a foreigner, is one of Venice's leading (mercenary) generals. He has secretly married young Desdemona, the only daughter of Brabantio, a leading white Senator, much to the dismay of a not very bright man-about-town Rodorigo. Iago, Othello's sergeant, has been handsomely paid by Rodorigo to woo Desdemona on Rodorigo's behalf. In speech #1 Iago abruptly and callously informs Brabantio of the secret marriage knowing this will enrage him to move against Othello (this is an attempt by Iago not only to destroy Othello whom he hates - see speeches #9, 11, and 12, below - but to keep flowing the money and jewels from Rodorigo to Desdemona, gifts which Iago has kept for himself). In speech #2 Brabantio and his followers encounter Othello and his men in the street on their way to the Senate.

Style: speech #1 as part of a three-handed scene; speech #2 one on one in front of a larger group for all to hear

Where: speech #1 outside Brabantio's home; speech #2 in a street in Venice **To Whom:** speech #1 Brabantio in front of Rodorigo; speech #2 Othello, in front of Othello's men including Cassio and Iago, and Rodorigo plus members of Brabantio's household

Speech 1: # of Lines: 7 **Probable Timing: 0.25 minutes**

Speech 2: # of Lines: 20 **Probable Timing: 1.00 minutes**

Modern Text

1/ Iago

1 [Zounds] sir, y'are robb'd, ! †
2 For shame put on your ᐞgown*;
Your heart is burst, you have lost half* your soul*;
Even now, now,[1] very now, an old black* ᐞram
Is tupping your white ᐞewe.
3 Arise, arise !
Awake the snorting ᐞcitizens* with the ᐞbell,
Or else the devil* will make a ᐞgrandsire of you.
4 Arise I say !

Fascinatingly, with Iago presumably on the stage floor and Brabantio 'above', with most of the releases of the speech coming at the end of each line, especially in F #1, it seems that Shakespeare (unconsciously?) has written the speech pattern of a man calling out urgently over a distance.

- the slightly onrushed F #1 allows Iago's game-playing deliberate trouble-creating opening a greater impetus, and, though emotion slightly dominates intellect (3/4) the capitalised words are placed in key positions emphatically at the end of lines

- F #2 becomes more factual (3/2) as if having got Brabantio's attention, Iago can now feed his mind full of horrors, while the surprisingly unembellished F #3 could well suggest 'Arise I say.' is spoken for his own pleasure (or for Rodorigo – to get him ready for the next stage of the plot?) rather than directly to Desdemona's father

First Folio

1/ Iago

1 [ ], Sir, y'are rob'd,+ for shame put on your Gowne,+
Your heart is burst, you have lost halfe your soule+
Even now, now, very now, an old blacke Ram
Is tupping your white Ewe.
2 Arise, arise,+
Awake the snorting Cittizens with the Bell,
Or else the devill will make a Grand-sire of you.
3 Arise I say. +

---

[1] Qq/F3/some modern texts do not set the second 'now' which F1 - 2 have added

Modern Text

2/ Brabantio

1 O* thou foul* thief*, where hast thou stow'd my Δdaughter?
2 Damn'd as thou art, thou hast enchanted* her,
For I'll refer* me to all things of sense,
If she in Δchains* of Δmagic* were not bound,
Whether a Δmaid so tender, Δfair*, andΔ happy*,
So opposite to Δmarriage, that she shunn'd*
The wealthy curled [darlings] of our Δnation,
Would ever have, t'encur* a general* mock*,
Run from her Δguardage to the sooty* bosom*
Of such a thing as thou - to fear*, not to delight!
3 Judge me the world, if 'tis not gross* in sense,
That thou hast practic'd* on her with foul* Δcharms*,
Abus'd her delicate Δyouth with Δdrugs or Δminerals
That weakens Δmotion.
4 I'll have't disputed on,
'Tis probable, and palpable to thinking. †
5 I therefore apprehend and do attach thee
For an abuser of the Δworld, a practicer*
Of Δarts inhibited, and out of warrant. †
6 Lay hold upon him, if he do resist
Subdue him, at his peril*.

- the opening split line gives Brabantio a moment to gather himself together before starting F #1's passionate attack on Othello (2/3), and, as with Iago above, the key words in this first sentence are capitalised at the end of the lines

- having made his meaning abundantly clear, Brabantio's intellect begins to come into play as he accuses Othello of ensnaring Desdemona in 'Chaines of Magick', (8/5, F #2's first six lines), at least initially, but then, in finishing the sentence with an out and out racial smear, Brabantio's emotions come to the fore (1/5, F #2's last three lines) – perhaps giving himself away in his attitude towards race-relations with the first surround phrase in the speech, suggesting that without 'Magick' Desdemona's response to Othello would have been ' : to feare, not to delight ? '

- and this emotion continues as Brabantio repeats the charge that Othello has 'practis'd on her with foule Charmes' (F #3's first two lines, 1/3), but then becomes factually driven as he elaborates the charges, suggesting that Othello used 'Drugs or Minerals' (4/0, F #3's last two lines)

- then, despite Brabantio's attempts to rein himself in and recover some semblance of public dignity and despite the two and a half unembellished lines deciding to take the matter to a judicial hearing ('Ile have't disputed on'), the cost of maintaining such public calm is enormous, for
  - a/ unlike most modern texts which split the final passage into three separate sentences, F sets a single onrush jamming together the notion of judicial action, the arrest, and the command to his own forces to lay hold of Othello
  - b/ the emotional semicolons only now make their appearance in this onrushed F #4, suggesting that even the unembellished surround phrase idea of 'Ile have't disputed on,/'Tis probable, and palpable to thinking ; ' is not as calm as might first appear

- thus F #4's relative lack of release (0/0 for the idea of a hearing; 2/0 for the formal arrest; 0/1 for the 'Lay hold upon him . . . at his perill.') suggests an enforced calm struggling to control emotion rather than a relaxed or easy self-control

First Folio

2/ Brabantio

1 Oh thou foule Theefe, →
Where hast thou stow'd my Daughter?
2 Damn'd as thou art, thou hast enchaunted her+
For Ile referre me to all things of sense,
(xIf she in Chaines of Magick were not boundx)
Whether a Maid,x so tender, Faire, and Happie,
So opposite to Marriage, that she shun'd
The wealthy curled [Deareling] of our Nation,
Would ever have (xt'encurre a generall mockex)
Run from her Guardage to the sootie bosome,x
Of such a thing as thou :x to feare, not to delight? +
3 Judge me the world, if 'tis not grosse in sense,
That thou hast practis'd on her with foule Charmes,
Abus'd her delicate Youth,x with Drugs or Minerals,x
That weakens Motion.
4 Ile have't disputed on,
'Tis probable, and palpable to thinking ;
I therefore apprehend and do attach thee,x
For an abuser of the World, a practiser
Of Arts inhibited, and out of warrant ;
Lay hold upon him, if he do resist
Subdue him, at his perill.

3a/ Othello **Most Potent, Grave, and Reveren'd Signiors,** 1.3.76 – 94
3b/ Othello **Her father lov'd me, oft invited me;** 1.3.128 - 170

Background: Othello has been summoned to the Senate, and, though possibly not the first choice, called upon to lead the Venetian forces to the island of Cyprus to protect it from a Turkish invasion already en route. Before he can embark, Brabantio has insisted the Duke hear his charge against Othello for practicing witchcraft upon his daughter. The following is Othello's reply, which can be explored as two separate speeches, or joined together as one.

Style: general address to a large group

Where: the Senate chamber **To Whom:** the Duke, Brabantio, & the Senators at large

Speech 3a: # of Lines: 20 **Probable Timing: 1.00 minutes**
Speech 3b: # of Lines: 43 **Probable Timing: 2.00 minutes**

Modern Text

3a/ Othello

1 Most △potent, △grave, and △reverend △signiors,
My very △noble and approv'd good △masters:
That I have ta'en away this old man's △daughter,
It is most true; true I have married her;
The very, head and front of my offending,
Hath this extent, no more.
2 Rude am I in my speech,
And little bless'd with the soft phrase of △peace;
For since these △arms* of mine, had seven years* pith
Till now some nine △moons* wasted, they have us'd
Their dearest* action, in the △tented △field;
And little of this great world can I speak*
More [than] pertains* to [△feat of △broil*] and battle*,
And therefore little shall I grace my cause
In speaking for myself*.
3 Yet (by your gracious* patience)
I will a round unvarnish'd △tale deliver
Of my whole course of △love - ◊ what △drugs*, what △charms*,
What △conjuration, and what mighty △magic*
(For such proceeding I am charg'd withal*)
I won his △daughter.

• Othello's (deliberate?) attempt to intellectually catch the Duke and the Senate's attention both by his opening courteous salutations and free admission that he has 'tane away this old mans Daughter' (7/0, F #1's first three lines) is intensified by F #1's last four lines being set as four surround phrases, all in part linked by emotional semicolons

> " ; That I have tane away this old mans Daughter,/It is most true : true I have married her ; /The verie head, and front of my offending,/Hath this extent ; no more . "

the dignity and care of the last three lines nakedly announcing that he and Desdemona are in fact married further heightened by being unembellished

• the probable truth of F #2's opening apology for his bluntness is underscored by also being set as a surround phrase, '. Rude am I, in my speech,/And little bless'd with the soft phrase of Peace ; ", the careful intellect (1/0) subtly underscored by the phrase being formed in part by yet another emotional semicolon

• but then, as he attempts to explain why 'little shall I grace my cause,/In speaking for my selfe.', emotions join intellect in suddenly flooding his words (7/9, F #2's remaining six and a half lines)

• and though he regains self-control in asking permission to deliver a 'round un-varnish'd Tale' (F #3, 2/0), F's subsequent orthography seems to suggest that Brabantio's accusations have disturbed him, for

a/ F sets two short lines (6/4 syllables) split by a very ungrammatical period starting the new F #4, a strong indication that Othello needs a careful break before voicing the life-threatening charge laid against him of using 'Drugges', 'Charmes', 'Conjuration', and 'Magicke' (most modern texts remove both indicators by removing the period and setting the two short lines as a single line of normal length, as shown)

b/ despite the momentary self-control of F #3, then his passions flood in once more (5/4, F #4)

First Folio

3a/ Othello

1 Most Potent, Grave, and Reveren'd Signiors,
My very Noble,x and approv'd good Masters; +
That I have tane away this old mans Daughter,
It is most true:x true I have married her;
The verie head,x and front of my offending,
Hath this extent;x no more.
2 Rude am I,x in my speech,
And little bless'd with the soft phrase of Peace;
For since these Armes of mine, had seven yeares pith,x
Till now,x some nine Moones wasted, they have us'd
Their deerest action, in the Tented Field:x
And little of this great world can I speake,x
More [then] pertaines to [Feats of Broiles],x and Battaile,
And therefore little shall I grace my cause,x
In speaking for my selfe.
3 Yet,x (by your gratious patience)
I will a round un-varnish'd Tale deliver,x
Of my whole course of Love.[2] →
4 What Drugges, what Charmes,
What Conjuration, and what mighty Magicke,x
(For such proceeding I am charg'd withall)
I won his Daughter.

---

[2] Ff set a split line suggesting a minute hesitation (perhaps there is a reaction from all around him) before Othello continues: Qq/most modern texts set one full line: F1 also shows a faint mark which F2 - 4 have interpreted as a period: Q1 sets a comma, most modern texts set a dash

Modern Text

3b/ Othello

1 Her △father lov'd me, oft invited me;
Still question'd me the △story* of my life
From year* to year* - the [△battles*], △sieges, [△fortunes],
That I have pass'd*.
2 I ran it through, even from my boyish days*,
To th'very moment that he bad me tell it; ◊
Wherein I spoke of most disastrous chances:
Of moving △accidents by △flood and △field,
Of hair*-breadth scapes i'th'imminent deadly breach,
Of being taken by the △insolent △foe
And sold to slavery, ◊ of my redemption thence,
And portance in my [△travel's] history*; ◊
Wherein of △antres* vast and △deserts* idle,
Rough △quarries, △rocks, [and] △hills, whose [heads] touch heaven,
It was my hint to speak* - ◊ △such was my △process* -
And of the Cannibals* that each [other] eat*,
The [Anthropophagi], and men whose heads
[Do grow] beneath their shoulders.
3 These things to hear*
Would Desdemona seriously incline;
But still the house △affairs* would draw her [thence],
Which ever as she could with haste dispatch,
She'ld come again*, and with a greedy* ear*
Devour* up my discourse.
4 Which I observing,
Took* once a pliant hour*, and found good means*
To draw from her a prayer of earnest heart,
That I would all my △pilgrimage dilate,
Whereof by parcels she had something heard,
But not [intentively]. †
5 I did consent,
And often did beguile her of her tears*,
When I did speak* of some distressful* stroke
That my youth suffer'd. †
6 My △story* being done,
She gave me for my pains* a world of [sighs];
She swore, in faith 'twas strange, 'twas passing strange;
'Twas pitiful*, 'twas wondrous pitiful*.

F's orthography suggests a wonderful transition between the initial recounting of the details of his relationship with Brabantio and thus Desdemona, and what happens to him once he begins to recount how he and Desdemona came to fall in love.

- the surround phrases point out the bare bones of how Othello and Desdemona came together
  " . Her Father lov'd me, oft invited me : /Still question'd me the Storie of my life,/From yeare to yeare : the Battaile, Sieges, Fortune,/ That I have past . "
  and thus
  " . Wherein I spoke of most disastrous chances : / . . . ; /Of being taken by the Insolent Foe, /And sold to slavery ."
  " . These things to heare,/Would Desdemona seriously incline : /But still the house Affaires would draw her [hence] : "
  so, at her request, he found another time to tell her everything
  " : My Storie being done,/She gave me for my paines a world of kisses : /She swore in faith 'twas strange : 'twas passing strange,/'Twas pittifull : 'twas wondrous pittifull . "
- while the final surround phrases directly challenge Brabantio and the Senate as a whole, ' . Here comes the Ladie : Let her witnesse it . '
- though Othello starts intellectually in opening the speech by describing Brabantio's questioning (thus unwittingly playing a key role in Desdemona's becoming attracted to Othello), there is some emotion too (F #1, 5/3)
- then he becomes very quiet, with three consecutive unembellished lines establishing both the time frame involved and the 'disasterous chances' that he was to cover (all of F #2 and F#3's first line), but then, in recalling the wondrous events he talked of, his intellect takes over almost completely (14/6, F #3-6)
- but his pattern changes as soon as he begins to describe Desdemona's reaction, first with a passionate recounting of how she didn't have time to hear everything at once (2/2, F #7's first two lines) and then turning to an almost completely emotional recalling of their time together when he told her of every event, no matter how 'distressefull' (1/10, F #7's last two and a half lines, and the first eight of F #8)
- in describing her kisses and words once 'My Storie being done', not surprisingly comes passion (2/3, F #8's last three and a half lines), which he quickly brings under control as he describes the very clear hints Desdemona gave that he should openly 'wooe' her (3/1, F #9-10)

First Folio

3b/ Othello

1 Her Father lov'd me, oft invited me : x
Still question'd me the Storie of my life, x
From yeare to yeare : x the [Battaile], Sieges, [Fortune],
That I have past.
2 I ran it through, even from my boyish daies,
T{o t}h'very moment that he bad me tell it.
3 Wherein I spoke of most disastrous chances:
Of moving Accidents by Flood and Field,
Of haire-breadth scapes i'th'imminent deadly breach; x
Of being taken by the Insolent Foe, x
And sold to slavery.
4 Of my redemption thence,
And portance in my [Travellours] historie.
5 Wherein of Antars vast, x and Desarts idle,
Rough Quarries, Rocks, [ ] Hills, whose [head] touch heaven,
It was my hint to speake.
6 Such was my Processe,
And of the Canibals that each [others] eate,
The [Antropophague]+ and men whose heads
[Grew] beneath their shoulders.
7 These things to heare, x
Would Desdemona seriously incline : x
But still the house Affaires would draw her [hence] : x
Which ever as she could with haste dispatch,
She'l'd come againe, and with a greedie eare
Devoure up my discourse.
8 Which I observing,
Tooke once a pliant houre, and found good meanes
To draw from her a prayer of earnest heart,
That I would all my Pilgrimage dilate,
Whereof by parcels she had something heard,
But not [instinctively]: I did consent,
And often did beguile her of her teares,
When I did speake of some distressefull stroke
That my youth suffer'd: My Storie being done,
She gave me for my paines a world of [kisses] : x
She swore+ in faith 'twas strange : x 'twas passing strange,+
'Twas pittifull : x 'twas wondrous pittifull.

7 She wish'd she had not heard it, yet she wish'd
That Δheaven had made her such a man.
8 She thank'd me,
And bad me, if I had a Δfriend that lov'd her,
I should but teach him how to tell my Δstory,
And that would woo* her.
9 Upon this hint I spake :
She lov'd me for the dangers I had pass'd*,
And I lov'd her that she did pity* them.
10 This only* is the witchcraft I have us'd.
11 Here comes the Δlady*; Δlet her witness* it.

• he then becomes very quiet as he describes as simply as possible that he did as asked, and their ensuing love for each other, (F #11, 0/1), its calm almost unembellished statement broken only by the one word 'pitty' (offered as the reason he loved her)

• not surprisingly, the denial of the charge of 'witch-craft' is handled very directly by one short (slightly emotional) sentence (F #12, 0/1)

• and in welcoming the arrival of Desdemona, he takes full control of the situation, F #13 being short and composed of two surround phrases - the first (of welcome) intellectual (1/0), the second (suggesting that she can bear 'witnesse' to what he has said) passionate (1/1)

9 She wish'd she had not heard it, yet she wish'd
That Heaven had made her such a man.
10 She thank'd me,
And bad me, if I had a Friend that lov'd her,
I should but teach him how to tell my Story,
And that would wooe her.
11 Upon this hint I spake,+
She lov'd me for the dangers I had past,
And I lov'd her,$_{x}$ that she did pitty them.
12 This onely is the witch-craft I have us'd.
13 Here comes the Ladie :$_{x}$ Let her witnesse it.

4/ Desdemona **My Noble Father,/I do perceive heere a divided dutie.** 1.3.180 - 189

5/ Desdemona **Nor [ ] [would I] {at home} recide,** between 1.3.241 - 259

Background: Othello has taken the unusual step of asking that Desdemona, his new wife (Brabantio's daughter), be allowed to give witness in and to the Senate on the charges of witchcraft brought by Brabantio against Othello. In speech #4, her first in the play, she responds to a very loaded question from her father, 'Do you perceive in all this Noble Companie,/Where you most owe obedience'. Speech #5 is a plea to the Duke to be allowed to accompany Othello to the war in Cyprus, triggered by the initial suggestion from the Duke that while Othello is away she reside 'at her Fathers', a suggestion immediately rejected by both Brabantio and Othello.

Style: one on one address in front of a larger group

Where: the Senate chamber **To Whom:** the Duke, in front of Othello, Brabantio, and the Senators at large

Speech 4: # of Lines: 10 **Probable Timing: 0.35 minutes**

Speech 5: # of Lines: 18 **Probable Timing: 0.55 minutes**

Modern Text

4/ Desdemona

1 My Δnoble Δfather,
I do perceive here* a divided duty*: ◊
To you I am bound for life, and education;
My life and education both do learn* me
How to respect you; ◊ Δyou are the Δlord of duty;
I am hitherto your Δdaughter.
2 But here's* my Δhusband;
And so much duty* as my Δmother show'd*
To you, preferring you before her Δfather,
So much I challenge, that I may profess*
Due to the Moor*, my lord.

That Desdemona is very carefully arguing her case logical step by logical step, rather than just emitting a generalised emotive blurt, can be seen in

a/ the fact that F sets four sentences rather than most modern texts' two

b/ only two lines (two and three of F #4) are not set as short sentences or surround phrases, which suggests that she is attempting to ensure that every point is clearly understood

c/ in terms of release, despite the difficulty of the situation intellect is slightly more predominant than emotion (9/6 overall)

- the logical surround phrases (the two of F #2 and the last finishing the speech) cleverly and carefully delineate that, while respecting her father and what she owes him, by family precedent (when her mother chose Brabantio – by implication over her family's wishes) her duty is to her husband Othello and not to her father and thus quite splendidly, the only emotional surround phrase refers to Othello
  ". But heere's my Husband ;"

- the only slightly emotional sentence is F #2 (0/1), suggesting that while she respects her father and is bound to him for much, that's as far as her 'duty' to him goes

First Folio

4/ Desdemona

1 My Noble Father,
I do perceive heere a divided dutie.
2 To you I am bound for life, and education: $_x$
My life and education both do learne me, $_x$
How to respect you.
3 You are the Lord of duty, +
I am hitherto your Daughter.
4 But heere's my Husband;
And so much dutie, $_x$ as my Mother shew'd
To you, preferring you before her Father: $_x$
So much I challenge, that I may professe
Due to the Moore $_x$ my Lord.

Modern Text

5/ Desdemona

1 Nor [I, I would not] {at home} reside,
To put my Δfather in impatient thoughts
By being in his eye.

2 Most Δgracious Duke,
To my unfolding, lend [a gracious] ear*,
And let me find* a Δcharter in your voice
T'assist my simpleness*.

3 That I [did] love the Moor* to live with him,
My down*right violence, and storm* of Δfortunes,
May trumpet to the world.

4 My heart's subdu'd
Even to the very quality of my Lord. †

5 I saw Othello's visage in his mind,
And to his Δhonors* and his valiant parts
Did I my soul* and Δfortunes consecrate.

6 So that, dear* Δlords, if I be left behind,
A Δmoth of Δpeace, and he go to the Δwar*,
The Δrites for [which] I love him are bereft me,
And I a heavy$_*$ interim shall support
By his dear* absence.

7 Let me go with him.

- the foundation for Desdemona's love is shown by the only emotional semicolon in the speech which connects the surround phrase ' . My heart's subdu'd/Even to the very quality of my Lord ; ' to the key statement that follows, 'I saw Othello's visage in his mind,'

- F #1's denial of the Duke's suggestion (that she stay at her father's while Othello takes up duty in Cyprus) is carefully expressed (1/0)

- yet she becomes very passionate (for the first time since she came onstage) in her plea to be heard (in what is going to be a virtually unprecedented request – to be allowed to go to war with Othello (F #2, 3/3)

- and this passion continues as she begins to explain why, starting with an unequivocal statement of her love for Othello (F #3, 2/3)

- starting with the surround phrase discussed above, her explanation of why she loves him and the statement that she has consecrated her 'soule and Fortunes' to him, while still passionate, become slightly more intellectual (4/2, F #4) and her statement that she doesn't want to be left behind as a 'Moth of Peace' is even more so (5/3, F #5), the final explanation

  " : And I a heavie interim shall support/By his deere absence . "

  heightened by being set as the only logical surround phrase in the speech

- finally, Desdemona's self-controlled dignity (remarkable for one so young, and important for the rest of the play) is clearly seen in F #6's extraordinarily simple and unequivocal summation/request, ' . Let me go with him.' – a dignity triply enhanced by being set as a short sentence which is monosyllabic and unembellished

First Folio

5/ Desdemona

1 Nor [ ] [would I] {at home} recide,
To put my Father in impatient thoughts
By being in his eye.

2 Most Gracious Duke,
To my unfolding, lend [your prosperous] eare,
And let me finde a Charter in your voice
T'assist my simplenesse.

3 That I [ ] love the Moore,$_x$ to live with him,
My downe-right violence, and storme of Fortunes+
May trumpet to the world.

4 My heart's subdu'd
Even to the very quality of my Lord;
I saw Othello's visage in his mind,
And to his Honours and his valiant parts,$_x$
Did I my soule and Fortunes consecrate.

5 So that ($_x$deere Lords$_x$) if I be left behind+
A Moth of Peace+ and he go to the Warre,
The Rites for [why] I love him,$_x$ are bereft me:$_x$
And I a heavie interim shall support
By his deere absence.

6 Let me go with him.

#'S 6 - 11: IAGO'S DISCOMFORT, AND PLANNING REVENGE

6/ Iago **But you'l not heare me. /Three Great-ones of the Cittie,** between 1.1.4 – 39
7/ Iago **O Sir content you. /I follow him, to serve my turne upon him.** 1.1.41 - 65

Background: Iago has been handsomely paid by Rodorigo to woo Desdemona on Rodorigo's behalf, unsuccessfully as it turns out, since she has just secretly married Othello, Iagos' military superior and commanding officer. Unknown to Rodorigo, Iago has been pocketing Rodorigo's gifts (money and jewels) to Desdemona, and, in order to keep the bounty flowing, it's essential for Iago to prove to Rodorigo that he hates Othello (not a difficult task, for he really does). Speech #6 deals with the situation at hand and speech #7 allows Iago to expand on his personal philosophy.

Style: as part of a two-handed scene

Where: a street near the home of Desdemona's father **To Whom:** Rodorigo

Speech 6: # of Lines: 32 **Probable Timing: 1.35 minutes**

Speech 7: # of Lines: 27 **Probable Timing: 1.30 minutes**

Modern Text

6/ Iago

1 [S'blood,] Δbut you'll$_*$ not hear* me.

2 Three Δgreat-ones of the Δcity*,
In personal suit* to make me his Δlieutenant,
Off-capp'd to him ; and by the faith of man,
I know my price, I am worth no worse* a place.

3 But he (as loving his own* pride and purposes)
Evades them with a bombast* Δcircumstance
Horribly stuff'd with Δepithets* of war*,
[And in conclusion]
Nonsuits* my Δmediators; ◊ for "ΔCertes", says$_*$ he,
"I have already chose my Δofficer."

4 And what was he ?

5 Forsooth, a great Δarithmetician*,
One Michael* Cassio, a Florentine
(A Δfellow almost damn'd in a fair* Δwife),
That never set a Δsquadron in the Δfield,
Nor the division* of a Δbattle* knows*
More [than] a Δspinster - ◊ unless* the Δbookish Δtheoric*,
Wherein the [Δtoged] Δconsuls can propose
As Δmasterly as he.

6 Mere* prattle$_*$, without practice,
Is all his Δsoldiership*.

F's orthography reveals two fascinating patterns about the way Iago functions, in that he can maintain tremendous intellectual control over what would seem to be emotional situations but, at the same time, certain strains appear while he is so doing. One note: it's important that though this speech seems to be a diatribe against the unfairness of Cassio's appointment, what Iago is also trying to do is convince Rodorigo that he can be trusted to woo the just married Desdemona on Rodorigo's behalf : how much of the following is genuine and how much for effect is up to each actor to decide.

- the only moment intellect plays a part in the opening litany of complaint comes as Iago explains that not even 'Three Great-ones of the Cittie' could get Othello to appoint him as his Lieutenant (3/2, F #2's first two lines): the rest of F #1-3's condemnation of Othello and praise of himself is strongly emotional (2/7), with the need for three extra breath-thoughts (marked ,$_x$) also pointing to Iago's need to get every sarcastic and painful detail across to the gullible Rodorigo

- yet Iago, like a good soldier, seems capable of making a very careful assessment of the situation before him, for he becomes highly intellectual (17/7 in just nine and a half lines, the last line of F #3 to F #7) in detailing his failure to get the post and, more particularly, with the appointment of Cassio ('a great Arithmetician' referring to Cassio being a man versed in the important new art of military gunnery rather than in Iago's first-hand battle-experienced traditional field knowledge)

- nevertheless, despite the analysis, the seething emotional underpinnings are enough for the F Iago to lose metrical control as Othello's choice of 'Officer' is first mentioned (the shaded passage ending F #4, as shown, fourteen/nine or ten syllables), and the scorn about that choice (F #7) is heightened by being set as two surround phrases

First Folio

6/ Iago

1 [ ] But you'l not heare me.

2 Three Great-ones of the Cittie,
($_x$In personal suite to make me his Lieutenant$_x$)+
Off-capt to him :$_x$ and by the faith of man+
I know my price, I am worth no worsse a place.

3 But he (as loving his owne pride,$_x$ and purposes)
Evades them,$_x$ with a bumbast Circumstance,$_x$
Horribly stufft with Epithites of warre,
[∞]
Non-suites my Mediators.

4 For certes, saies he,
I have already chose my Officer.

5 And what was he ? [3]

6 For-sooth, a great Arithmatician,
One Michaell Cassio, a Florentine,$_x$
(A Fellow almost damn'd in a faire Wife)+
That never set a Squadron in the Field,
Nor the devision of a Battaile knowes
More [then] a Spinster.

7 Unlesse the Bookish Theoricke :$_x$
Wherein the [Tongued] Consuls can propose
As Masterly as he.

8 Meere pratle ($_x$without practise$_x$)
Is all his Souldiership.

---

[3] though Q1/Ff set this as a fourteen syllable line revealing the depth of Iago's inner emotions, some modern texts set up two lines with a pause (10/4), as shown

7 But he, Δsir, had th'election;
And I, of whom his eyes* had seen* the proof*
At Rhodes, at [Cyprus], and on [other] grounds
[Christian] and Δheathen, must be [belee'd] and calm'd
By Δdebitor, and Δcreditor - ◊ this Δcounter-caster,
He (in good time!) must his Δlieutenant be,
And I ([God] bless* the mark*!) his [Worship's*] Δancient*.
8 [But], there's no remedy*.
9 'Tis the curse* of Δservice;
Preferment goes by letter and affection,
[Not by the] old gradation, where each second
Stood Δheir* to'th'first.
10 Now, Δsir, be judge yourself *
Whether I in any just term* am Δaffin'd
To love the Moor*.

"Unlesse the Bookish Theoricke : /Wherein the [Tongued] Consuls can propose/As Masterly as he ."

• thus it's not surprising that Iago becomes momentarily emotional in F #8's direct dismissal of Cassio's soldiership as 'Meere pratle' (1/2)

• then comes F #9's intellectual recovery (6/2) as he speaks to the fact that the 'proofe' of his own worth was put aside by the interference of unspecified others ('Debitor' and 'Creditor') - though an emotional undercurrent can be seen from the outset with the opening emotional (semicoloned) surround phrase attack on Othello's choice of Cassio " . But he (Sir) had th'election ; "

• and then, as he finally acknowledges that all that is left for him is to be 'his Mooreships Auntient' (as the Arden suggests, perhaps the modern equivalent would be the lower rank of 'regimental sergeant major), so his passions break through in full (9/9, F #10-13) as he attempts to prove to Rodorigo how much he hates the Moore and is thus worthy to be the intermediary between Rodorigo and Desdemona

9 But he (xSirx) had th'election;
And I (xof whom his eies had seene the proofe
At Rhodes, at [Ciprus], and on [others] grounds
[Christen'd] and Heathen,x) must be [be-leed]x and calm'd
By Debitor, and Creditor.
10 This Counter-caster,
He (in good time+) must his Lieutenant be,
And I ([ ]blesse the marke+) his [Mooreships] Auntient.
11 [Why], there's no remedie. → [4]
12 'Tis the cursse of Service;
Preferment goes by letter,x and affection,
[And not by] old gradation, where each second
Stood Heire to'th'first.
13 Now+ Sir, be judge your selfe,x
Whether I in any just terme am Affin'd
To love the Moore? x

[4] Q1/Ff set up two short (6 syllable) lines, suggesting tiny need-to-breathe pauses for Iago: most modern texts join the two lines together

Modern Text

7/ Iago

1 O, $^{\Delta}$sir, content you ; ◊
I follow him to serve my turn* upon him.
2 We cannot [be all] $^{\Delta}$masters, nor all $^{\Delta}$masters
Cannot be truly* follow'd.
3 You shall mark*
Many a duteous* and knee-crooking knave
That (doting on his own* obsequious bondage)
Wears* out his time, much like his $^{\Delta}$master's $^{\Delta}$ass*,
For naught but $^{\Delta}$provender, & when he's old,$^{\Delta}$ cashier'd*.
4 Whip me such honest knaves.
5 Others there are
Who, trimm'd* in $^{\Delta}$forms* and visages of $^{\Delta}$duty$_{*}$,
Keep* yet their hearts attending on themselves,
And throwing but shows* of $^{\Delta}$service on their $^{\Delta}$lords,
Do* well thrive by them; ◊ and when they have lin'd their $^{\Delta}$coats*,
Do* themselves $^{\Delta}$homage .
6 [Those] $^{\Delta}$fellows* have some soul*,
And such a one do I profess* myself*.
7 For, $^{\Delta}$sir,
It is as sure as you are Rodorigo,
Were I the Moor*, I would not be Iago . †
8 In following him, I follow but myself*; ◊
Heaven is my $^{\Delta}$judge, not I for love and duty$_{*}$,
But seeming so, for my peculiar end;
For when my outward $^{\Delta}$action doth demonstrate
The native act, and figure of my heart
In $^{\Delta}$complement extern*, 'tis not long after
But I will wear* my heart upon my sleeve
For $^{\Delta}$[Doves]* to peck* at : I am not what I am.

In following immediately on from speech #6 above, the passion that ended the last three sentences there infuses this speech throughout (21/24 overall), with F's orthography suggesting some very interesting cracks in Iago's self-control.

- the whole tenor of the speech seems to stem from F #5's one unembellished short sentence as Iago, having described any honest servant as a 'knee-crooking knave' - the equivalent of their 'Masters Asse' - finally dismisses them with
  "Whip me such honest knaves."

- this is counterbalanced/expanded on the only logical surround phrase in the speech, explaining that that in serving Othello, Iago is in fact putting his own interests above all,
  ": In following him, I follow but my selfe ."

- that this conviction is so deep set it that knocks him off balance can be seen as he describes himself as his own self-serving master - so F #7-8 set four short lines (five/six/five/six syllables)

- it's also possible that the small pauses therein not only indicate that Iago is taking great care to exert self-control as he explains his philosophy very precisely, but they might also show that he is pausing just to see how Rodorigo is reacting to such an out and out statement of practiced deceit

- interestingly, the lead into this is via the first of only two emotional surround phrases, F #4's
  ". You shall marke/Many a dutious and knee-crooking knave ;"

- the two emotional moments underscore
  a/ Iago's metrically irregular admiration of 'These Fellowes' (F #8, 1/4)
  b/ the final lead up to the second emotional surround phrase of self definition, ' ; I am not what I am .', its enormity further heightened by being both monosyllabic and unembellished too

- and, in what must be remembered throughout the rest of the play, the only intellectual moment in the speech marks the moment when Iago swears that 'Heaven is my Judge' that all he does is not 'for love and dutie' but for 'my peculiar end' (3/1, F #10's first four and half lines)

First Folio

7/ Iago

1 O^{+} Sir^{+} content you .
2 I follow him,$_{x}$ to serve my turne upon him.
3 We cannot [all be] Masters, nor all Masters
Cannot be truely follow'd.
4 You shall marke
Many a dutious and knee-crooking knave ;$_{x}$
That (doting on his owne obsequious bondage)
Weares out his time, much like his Masters Asse,
For naught but Provender, & when he's old^{+} Casheer'd.
5 Whip me such honest knaves.
6 Others there are
Who trym'd in Formes, and visages of Dutie,
Keepe yet their hearts attending on themselves,
And throwing but showes of Service on their Lords^{+}
Doe well thrive by them.
7 And when they have lin'd their Coates
Doe themselves Homage.
8 [These] Fellowes have some soule,
And such a one do I professe my selfe.
9 For ($_{x}$Sir$_{x}$)
It is as sure as you are Rodorigo,
Were I the Moore, I would not be Iago:
In following him, I follow but my selfe.
10 Heaven is my Judge, not I for love and dutie,
But seeming so, for my peculiar end :$_{x}$
For when my outward Action doth demonstrate
The native act, and figure of my heart
In Complement externe, 'tis not long after
But I will weare my heart upon my sleeve
For [Dawes] to pecke at ; $^{+}$ I am not what I am.

8/ Iago **{Love} is meerly a Lust of the blood,** 1.3.334 - 361

Background: Following Desdemona's public defence of marrying Othello against her father's wishes, and her successful plea to be allowed to leave Venice and accompany him to the expected war in Cyprus, Rodorigo is inconsolable ('I will incontinently drowne my selfe'). For his own pocket's sake, Iago once more has to persuade Rodorigo to stay the course and keep providing money in the attempt to win Desdemona, even though she is currently married. This is how he begins.

Style: as part of a two-handed scene

Where: the Senate chamber **To Whom:** Rodorigo

# of Lines: 26 **Probable Timing: 1.15 minutes**

Modern Text

8/ Iago

1 {Love} is merely* a △lust of the blood and a permission of the will.

2 Come, be a man ! †

3 Drown* thyself*? ◊ drown △cats, and blind △puppies !

4 I [profess]* me thy △friend, and I confess* me knit to thy deserving with △cables of perdurable toughness*.

5 I could never better stead* thee [than] now.

6 Put △money in thy purse; follow thou [these] △wars*; defeat* thy favor* with an usurp'd △beard.

7 I say put △money in thy purse.

8 It cannot be [that Desdemona should long] continue her love [unto] the Moor* ◊ - put △money in thy purse - nor he [ ] to her.

9 It was a violent △commencement [], and thou shalt see an answerable △sequestration - put but △money in thy purse.

10 These Moors* are changeable in their wills* - fill thy purse with △money.

11 The △food that to him now is as luscious* as △locusts, shall°be to him shortly as [acerb] as △coloquintida.

12 She must change for youth; when she is sated with his body, she will find the [error] of her choice.

13 [She must have change, she must;] △therefore put △money in thy purse.

- the shortness of most of the sentences suggests that Iago is working very hard to keep his meal ticket on his side, especially the three that open the speech

- even though the opening seems passionate (F #1-3, 3/3), Iago quickly, efficiently, and brilliantly uses three different styles to grab Rodorigo's attention, F #1's passionate equating of 'Love' with 'Lust' (1/1); F #2's emotional refusal to let Rodorigo drown himself (0/2); and F #3's intellectual dismissal of drowning as being only fit for animals (2/0) - the bewildering switches in attack guaranteed to keep Rodorigo off balance

- there are two repetitions within the speech, first the constant reminder about money and second the stylistic/rhetorical tactic - for many of the surround phrases start a new idea/sentence, as if Iago is determined to grab Rodorigo's attention (and deflect his suicidal intentions) with the opening moment of each new point
  - ". Come, be a man : drowne thy selfe ? " (F #2)
  - ". Put Money in thy purse : " (F #6 and F #9)
  - ". These Moores are changeable in their wils : fill thy purse with Money." (F #11)
  - ". She must change for youth : " (F #13)
  - ". Make all the Money thou canst : " (F #16)
  - " : therefore make Money : a pox of drowning [thy selfe], it is cleane out of the way . " (F #16)

- once Iago quickly dismisses Rodorigo's notion of drowning himself (F #1-3 as described above), he reassures him with
  ".I could never better steed thee then now."
the unembellished quality of the short F #5 presumably designed to add a quiet calm to the upset would-be wooer: and this calm quite brilliantly stands out as reassurance by being sandwiched between two very passionate sentences (Iago's F #4's professing to be bound to Rodorigo, 2/2, and F #6's succinct advice as to how Rodorigo may succeed – with money and disguising himself to go to the wars, 3/3)

- once the money idea has been broached Iago becomes tantalisingly intellectual (12/3) as he dangles before Rodorigo images of Desdemona soon becoming dissatisfied with Othello, all intermingled with the repetition of getting more money (F#7-12)

First Folio

8/ Iago

1 {Love} is meerly a Lust of the blood, and a permission of the will.

2 Come, be a man: + drowne thy selfe?

3 Drown Cats, and blind Puppies. +

4 I [have profest] me thy Friend, and I confesse me knit to thy deserving, x with Cables of perdurable toughnesse.

5 I could never better steed thee [then] now.

6 Put Money in thy purse: x follow thou [the] Warres, + defeate thy favour, x with an usurp'd Beard.

7 I say put Money in thy purse.

8 It cannot be [long that Desdemona should] continue her love [to] the Moore.

9 Put Money in thy purse: nor he [his] to her.

10 It was a violent Commencement [in her], and thou shalt see an answerable Sequestration, put but Money in thy purse.

11 These Moores are changeable in their wils: x fill thy purse with Money.

12 The Food that to him now is as lushious as Locusts, shalbe to him shortly, x as [bitter] as Coloquintida.

13 She must change for youth: x when she is sated with his body + she will find the [errors] of her choice.

14 [ ] Therefore, x put Money in thy purse.

{ctd. over}

14 If thou wilt needs damn* thyself*, do
it a more delicate way [than] drowning.
15 Make all the Δmo-
ney thou canst. †
16 If Δsanctimony* and a frail* vow be-
twixt an erring Δbarbarian, and [a] super-subtle Venetian
be not too hard for my wits and all the Δtribe of hell,
thou shalt enjoy her; therefore make Δmoney. †
17 A pox of drow-
ning [ ], it is clean* out of the way.
18 Seek* thou ra-
ther to be hang'd in Δcompassing thy joy [than] to be
drown'd and go without her.

- yet again Iago resorts to unembellished calm to get across another key (sexual) image of Desdemona becoming available soon, F #13's
  "She must change for youth : when she is sated with his body she will find the errors of her choice ."
- now that Rodorigo can dream upon possible conquest, Iago's intellect again comes to the fore, still cleverly mixing 'thou shalt enjoy her' with the inevitable refrain of the need for more money (8/1, F #14, and the first four lines of F #16) and brilliantly counterbalancing these ideas with the emotional condemnation of the earlier notion of Rodorigo drowning himself (0/4, F #15 and the last line of F #16)
- and having thoroughly won him over, Iago finishes with a fine flourish, a wonderful mixture of passionate sexual imagery to start with (1/1, the first phrase of F #17) and, in ending, a quiet unembellished reminder if Rodorigo does drown himself he will 'go without her'

15 If thou wilt needs damne thy selfe, do
it a more delicate way [then] drowning.
16 Make all the Mo-
ney thou canst: If Sanctimonie,$_x$ and a fraile vow,$_x$ betwixt an erring Barbarian, and [ ] super-subtle Venetian
be not too hard for my wits,$_x$ and all the Tribe of hell,
thou shalt enjoy her:$_x$ therefore make Money: a pox
of drowning [thy selfe], it is cleane out of the way.
17 Seeke thou ra-
ther to be hang'd in Compassing thy joy,$_x$ [then] to be
drown'd,$_x$ and go without her.

9/ Iago **Thus do I ever make my Foole, my purse :** 1.3.383 - 404

Background: Iago's attempt to persuade Rodorigo to stay the course and keep giving Iago money to attempt to win Desdemona, even though she is currently married to Othello (see speech #8 immediately above) has succeeded beyond his wildest dreams, for to raise the necessary money Rodorigo has exited with the vow 'I'll sell all my Land'. Now, in the first of three great soliloquies, Iago explains to the audience all his dreams and plans.

Style: solo

Where: the Senate chamber **To Whom:** direct audience address and self

# of Lines: 22 **Probable Timing: 1.10 minutes**

Modern Text

9/ Iago

1 Thus do I ever make my Δfool*, my purse;
For I mine own* gain'd knowledge should profane*
If I would time expend with such [a] Δsnipe
But for my Δsport and Δprofit. †
2 I hate the Moor*,
And it is thought abroad that 'twixt my sheets
[ ] Ha's done my Δoffice.
3 I know not if't be true,
[Yet] I, for mere* suspicion* in that kind*,
Will do, as if for Δsurety.
4 He holds me well,
The better shall my purpose work* on him. †
5 Cassio's a proper man. †

The excitement and tiny moments of sudden lack of control can be seen in the occasional irregularities F's that orthography presents, such as

a/ the short third line (nine syllables with the lack of the word 'a')
b/ the wonderful 's' assonance so created with 'such Snipe
c/ what most modern texts regard as a highly ungrammatical mid-section sentence structure (F #3 onwards) and have tried to restructure rationally, failing to realise that F's mixture of onrush (F #3, and #7-8) and very short sentences (F #4-6) perfectly express Iago's intellectual struggle/dilemma in trying to find some way to work his revenge.

- the key building blocks in Iago's journey of initially frustrated planning are marked by the surround phrases
  ". Thus do I ever make my Foole my purse : "
  ". He holds me well,/The better shall my purpose worke on him : /Cassio's a proper man : "
  ": He hath a person, and a smooth dispose/To be suspected : fram'd to make women false . "

First Folio

9/ Iago

1 Thus do I ever make my Foole, my purse:$_x$
For I mine owne gain'd knowledge should prophane
If I would time expend with such [ ] Snipe,$_x$
But for my Sport,$_x$ and Profit: I hate the Moore,
And it is thought abroad,$_x$ that 'twixt my sheets
[She] ha's done my Office.
2 I know not if't be true,
[But] I, for meere suspition in that kinde,
Will do, as if for Surety.
3 He holds me well,
The better shall my purpose worke on him:
Cassio's a proper man: Let me see now,+

6 Let me see now :
To get [this] Δplace and to plume up my will
[A] double Δknavery ◊- Δhow? ◊ Δhow? ◊-Δ[let me] see ◊-
After some time, to abuse Othello's [ear]
That he is too familiar with his wife . †

7 He hath a person and a smooth dispose
To be suspected - fram'd to make women false.

8 The Moor* is of a free and open Δnature,
That thinks* men honest that but seem* to be so,
And will as tenderly be lead by th'Δnose
As Δasses are . †

9 I have't . †

10 It is engend'red . †

11 Hell and Δnight,
Must bring this monstrous Δbirth to the worlds light.

": I have't : it is engendred : Hell, and Night,/Must bring this monstrous Birth, to the worlds light . "

- the driving need for a solution is underscored by the two unembellishments
  - a/ first of searching 'How? How? Let's see.', the quiet desperation heightened by being both monosyllabic and set as three short sentences (though not by most modern texts)
  - b/ and then the final discovery ' : I have't : it is engendred : ', again heightened by being set as surround phrases

- Iago opens passionately (6/4, F #1), combining in one swift swoop his use of the foolish Rodorigo for financial gain, his hatred of Othello, and his suspicions of his wife's (Æmilia) possible infidelity, but rapidly becomes emotional at the need for revenge whether the infidelity occurred or no (1/4, F #2 and the first line and a half of F #3)

- however, after the emotion, the plan to pull down Cassio and take his place becomes totally intellectual (3/0) - marking a very different form of hatred from that Iago displays when discussing his other enemies

- after his unembellished quest for an answer (F #4-6), as he begins to form his plot the audacity of his passionate first line, to 'abuse Othello's eares' (1/1, F #7), drives him into a three line unembellished consideration of how perfectly Cassio will function as the fulcrum around which everything will revolve/evolve, for Iago can easily get Othello to believe of Cassio
  "That he is too familiar with his wife : /He hath a person, and a smooth dispose/To be suspected : fram'd to make women false."

- then the passion flows free as Iago outlines Othello's flaws that will allow him to believe whatever lies Iago feeds him (4/3, F #8's first three and a half lines), while the final two lines of realisation that he at least has the bare bones of the plot in place are totally intellectual (3/0)

To get [his] Place,$_{x}$ and to plume up my will
[In] double Knavery.

4 How?

5 How?

6 [Let's] see.

7 After some time, to abuse Othello's [eares],$_{x}$
That he is too familiar with his wife :
He hath a person,$_{x}$ and a smooth dispose
To be suspected :$_{x}$ fram'd to make women false.

8 The Moore is of a free,$_{x}$ and open Nature,
That thinkes men honest,$_{x}$ that but seeme to be so,
And will as tenderly be lead by'th'Nose
As Asses are :
I have't : it is engendred : Hell,$_{x}$ and Night,
Must bring this monstrous Birth,$_{x}$ to the worlds light.

10/ Iago **He takes her by the palme : I, well said, whisper.** 2.1.166 - 178

Background: Iago has feelings for Desdemona which, perhaps surprisingly, are 'not out of absolute Lust'. Since she, the hated and distrusted Cassio, and himself arrived at Cyprus before Othello, Iago has attempted (and failed) to amuse Desdemona with some traditional sexist witticisms, for which he has been firmly and publicly put down. To add to his dismay, in her nervousness while awaiting Othello's arrival, she has turned to Cassio for comfort – and he seems to be succeeding easily where Iago clumsily failed. The following is triggered by Cassio taking hold of Desdemona's hand.

Style: solo, away from a larger group not interested in overhearing what he has to say

Where: the harbour at Cyprus **To Whom:** direct audience address, away from the group containing Cypriot gentry, plus Desdemona and Cassio

# of Lines: 11 **Probable Timing: 0.40 minutes**

Modern Text

10/ Iago

1 He takes her by the palm*; [ay], well said, whisper.
2 [ ] As little a web as this will [ ] ensnare as great a Δfly as Cassio.
3 [Ay] smile upon her, do; I will [catch], thee in thine own* Δ[courtesies].
4 You say true, 'tis so indeed.
5 If such tricks as these strip you out of your Δlieutenantry*, it had been* better you had not kiss'd your three fingers so oft, which now again* you are most apt to play the Δsir, in.
6 Very good; well kiss'd ! [an] excellent [Δcourtesy*] ! †
7 'Tis so indeed.
8 Yet again*, your fingers [at] your lips*?
9 Would they were Δclyster*-pipes for your sake!
10 The Moor* ! †
11 I know his Δtrumpet.

This speech is often tossed off as pure malevolence, especially since Cassio is succeeding in entertaining Desdemona where Iago failed miserably. However, F's orthography suggests that this may be the moment when Iago begins to get an inkling of exactly how he can get his revenge.

- F #1, #3, and #6 are all composed of surround phrases, and all deal with Cassio's physical social intimacies with Desdemona (almost as if Iago were storing away what he sees for future use)

- the unembellished lines (some set as surround phrases)
  " : I, well said, whisper. With as little a web as this, will I ensnare . . . "
  "You say true, 'tis so indeed . " and " . Very good : well kiss'd . . . "
  " : 'tis so indeed . "
  could well mark moments when Iago realises how he can advance his plot to pull all his enemies down, the quiet denoting his concentration

- while the first glimpse of Cassio touching her is passionate (F #1, 1/1), the realisation that this is how he will catch Cassio is intellectual (2/0, F #2), which in turn leads to more passion as he observes Cassio now kissing her (3/3, F #3-5, punctuated by the unembellished F #4 mentioned above)

- and as Iago realises how 'excellent' this 'Curtsie' is – presumably for his own purposes – his self-control takes over (4/1, F #6, #8-9) – momentarily broken by F #7's emotional (joyous?) response to Cassio making kissing motions yet again (0/2)

First Folio

10/ Iago

1 He takes her by the palme :x [I], well said, whisper.
2 [With] as little a web as this,x will [I] ensnare as great a Fly as Cassio.
3 [I] smile upon her, do:x I will [give] thee in thine owne [Courtship].
4 You say true, 'tis so indeed.
5 If such tricks as these strip you out of your Lieutenantrie, it had beene better you had not kiss'd your three fingers so oft, which now againe you are most apt to play the Sir, in.
6 Very good:x well kiss'd,+ [and] excellent [Curtsie]:+ 'tis so indeed.
7 Yet againe, your fingers [to] your lippes?
8 Would they were Cluster[5]-pipes for your sake. +
9 The Moore I know his Trumpet.

[5] most modern texts set Q1/F2's 'clister-pipes' (an instrument for the administration of a vaginal douche): F1 = 'Cluster-pipes'

11/ Iago **That Cassio loves her, I do well beleev't :** 2.1.286 - 212

Background: The second great soliloquy (see speech #9 above), where, having seen Cassio and Desdemona be familiar in public (speech #10 above) as well as Othello's obviously besotted attentions towards her, the 'engendred' plot now has more form.

Style: solo

Where: the harbour at Cyprus **To Whom:** direct audience address and self

# of Lines: 27 **Probable Timing: 1.30 minutes**

Modern Text

11/ Iago

1 That Cassio loves her, I do well believ't*;
That she loves him, 'tis apt, and of great △credit*.

2 The Moor* (howbeit that I endure him not)
Is of a constant, △[noble, loving], △nature,
And I dare think* he'll* prove to Desdemona
A most dear* husband.

3 Now I do love her too,
Not out of absolute △lust (though peradventure
I stand [accountant*] for as great a sin),
But partly* led to diet* my △revenge,
For that I do suspect the [lustfull] △ Moor*
Hath leap'd into my △seat*; ◊ △the thought whereof
Doth (like a poisonous* △mineral*) gnaw my △inwards*;
And nothing can [nor] shall content my △soul*
Till I am even'd* with him, wife, for [wife]; ◊
Or failing* so, yet that I put the Moor*
At least into a △jealousy* so strong
That judgement cannot cure.

4 Which thing to do,
If this poor* △trash of Venice, whom I [trash]
For his quick* hunting, stand the putting on,
I'll have our Michael Cassio on the hip,
Abuse him to the Moor* in the [rank] garb*
(For I fear* Cassio with my △night-△cap* too),
Make the Moor* thank* me, love me, and reward me,
For making him egregiously an △ass*,
And practicing* upon his peace and quiet
Even to madness*.

While the speech is passionate tending towards emotion (25/33 overall, with very little variation throughout), F's sentence structure shows the speech falling into three parts, with two, the opening (F #1-2) and closing (F #6-7) regarded as grammatical by most modern texts. However, the third - F #3-5, where Iago is struggling very hard to equate his love for Desdemona, his hatred for Othello (which is eating away at him) and his determination to be 'eeven'd' with him or, failing that, put him into an incurable 'Jelouzie' - where each step is painfully given its own sentence, is regarded by most modern texts as ungrammatical, so, instead of matching F's stepping stone attempt at rationality, they jam the passage together as one much more emotive blurt.

- F #1's surround phrases underscore just how much, or how little, Iago has managed to establish, essentially

  ". That Cassio loves her, I do well beleev't :/That she loves him, 'tis apt, and of great Credite . "

- the only other surround phrases highlight the already singled out ungrammatical F #4 explosion at the thought of Othello having bedded Æmilia

  ". The thought whereof,/Doth (like a poysonous Minerall) gnaw my Inwardes : "

  and the final admission that though the plot is there it's still not complete

  ". 'Tis heere : but yet confus'd,/Knaveries plaine face, is never seene, till us'd . "

- the icy quiet of the one true unembellished section shows just how far Iago's loathing of Othello goes, to the extent of

  "And practising upon his peace, and quiet,"

  while the almost unembellished earlier passage points to his fixation on Desdemona (the only release being the all important, yet in part denied, factor of 'Lust')

  "Now I do love her too,/Not out of absolute Lust, (though peradventure/I stand accomptant for as great a sin)"

- in the sea of passion - F #6's jamming together of his admission of fearing 'Cassio with my Night-Cape too' with his dreams of a double revenge on Othello (line six to nine, 5/5) - there are two especially dominating sequences,

First Folio

11/ Iago

1 That Cassio loves her, I do well beleev't :$_x$
That she loves him, 'tis apt, and of great Credite.

2 The Moore (how beit[6] that I endure him not)
Is of a constant, [loving, Noble] + Nature,
And I dare thinke,$_x$ he'le prove to Desdemona
A most deere husband.

3 Now I do love her too,
Not out of absolute Lust,$_x$ (though peradventure
I stand [accomptant] for as great a sin) +
But partely led to dyet my Revenge,
For that I do suspect the [lustie] Moore
Hath leap'd into my Seate.

4 The thought whereof,$_x$
Doth (like a poysonous Minerall) gnaw my Inwardes :$_x$
And nothing can,$_x$ [or] shall content my Soule
Till I am eeven'd with him, wife, for [wift].

5 Or fayling so, yet that I put the Moore,$_x$
At least into a Jelouzie so strong
That judgement cannot cure.

6 Which thing to do,
If this poore Trash of Venice, whom I [trace]
For his quicke hunting, stand the putting on,
Ile have our Michael Cassio on the hip,
Abuse him to the Moore,$_x$ in the [right] garbe
(For I feare Cassio with my Night-Cape too)$_x$
Make the Moore thanke me, love me, and reward me,
For making him egregiously an Asse,
And practising upon his peace,$_x$ and quiet,$_x$
Even to madnesse.

{ctd. over}

[6] F1 = 'how beit', F2 = 'howbeit', Q1/most modern texts = 'howbe't', thus maintaining a ten syllable line

5 'Tis here*; but yet confus'd,
Knaveries plain* face is never seen* till us'd.

a/ F #4's syntactically appalling statement that the only thing to 'content my Soule' will be to be 'eeven'd' with Othello 'wife for wift' - the peculiar formation of the last word probably being compositorial error, though if spoken as set it releases the most wonderful spitting sound (3/5)
b/ F #7's two surround phrase summation/recognition that only by putting the plan into practice will the extent of his villainy become clear (0/3)

7 'Tis heere:$_x$ but yet confus'd,
Knaveries plaine face,$_x$ is never seene,$_x$ till us'd.

#'s 12 - 15: The Plan In Action, Cassio & Desdemona

12/ Iago **And what's he then,/That saies I play the Villaine?** 2.3.326 - 382

Background: The third great soliloquy (see speeches #9 and 11 above). Iago has managed to get Cassio drunk on duty. Cassio, enraged by a deliberate attack on him, planned by Iago and carried out by Rodorigo, has created such a stir that the alarm bells which should only be sounded in the event of an enemy attack have been rung, and, even worse, has wounded Montano, the local Governor of Cyprus. Othello has no choice but to release him from his position as Othello's Lieutenant - but this is only the first part of Iago's plan. He wants to pull down Othello and Desdemona too, and Cassio, in seeking Iago's advice, has created the opportunity for him to do so. Thus Iago has advised Cassio to ask Desdemona to intercede with Othello for Cassio's reinstatement, knowing that if she does Iago can use this to suggest to Othello she and Cassio are having an affair.

Style: solo

Where: the garrison in Cyprus **To Whom:** direct audience address and self

# of Lines: 30 **Probable Timing: 1.30 minutes**

Modern Text

12/ Iago

1 And what's he then, △that says* I play the △villain*,
When this advice* is free I give, and honest,
Probal* to thinking, and indeed the course
To win the Moor* again*?
2 For 'tis most easy*
Th'inclining* Desdemona to subdue
In any honest △suit*; ◊ she's fram'd as fruitful*
As the free △elements.
3 And then for her
To win the Moor*, [were't] to renounce his △baptism*,
All △seals* and △symbols* of redeemed sin,
His △soul* is so enfetter'd to her △love,
That she may make, unmake, do what the list,
Even as her △appetite shall play the △god
With his weak* △function.

That Iago is on a free-wheeling almost stream of consciousness roll can be seen in the fact that, as with some of his earlier diatribes with Rodorigo, there is virtually no heavy punctuation (just two colons), no surround phrases, and essentially just one unembellished moment. Indeed, the mood throughout seems to be one of celebration, self-congratulation, and audience teasing, for .

- . . . there are three separate occasions where F sets a pair of short lines (not matched by most modern texts), suggesting that Iago is taking a small pause to savor the moments of success - as with F #1's opening line (perhaps he cannot believe how successful he has been, or perhaps he is actually challenging the audience to answer his opening rhetorical question); as with the ending of F #1/start of F #2 (perhaps the thought of 'Th'inclyning Desdemona' quietens him for a moment); and as with the very end of the speech (perhaps the sight of the only-recently-beaten-by-Cassio Rodorigo gives him great satisfaction and/or amusement) . . .

- . . . and the quiet self-absorption of the only unembellished line, F #1's "When this advice is free I give, and honest,"

points to his delight in his chess-like cleverness in that, though his advice may indeed be 'the course/To win the Moore againe.', he will so manipulate matters that it will soon prove to be Cassio's downfall (and Othello's and Desdemona's too)

First Folio

12/ Iago

1 And what's he then, →
That saies I play the Villaine? $_x$
When this advise is free I give, and honest,
Proball to thinking, and indeed the course
To win the Moore againe.+ →
2 For 'tis most easie
Th'inclyning Desdemona to subdue
In any honest Suite.
3 She's fram'd as fruitefull
As the free Elements.
4 And then for her
To win the Moore, [were] to renownce his Baptisme,
All Seales,$_x$ and Simbols of redeemed sin:$_x$
His Soule is so enfetter'd to her Love,
That she may make, unmake, do what the list,
Even as her Appetite shall play the God,$_x$
With his weake Function.

4 How am I then a Δvillain*,
To Δcounsel* Cassio to this parallel * course,
Directly to his good?
5 Divinity* of hell ! †
6 When devils* will [their] blackest sins* put on,
They do suggest at first with heavenly shows*,
As I do now; ◊ Δfor whiles this honest Δfool*
Plies Desdemona to repair* his Δfortune,
And she for him pleads* strongly to the Moor*,
I'll pour* this pestilence into his ear*-
That she repeals* him, for her body's* Δlust;
And by how much she strives to do him good,
She shall undo her Δcredit* with the Moor*.
7 So will I turn* her virtue into pitch,
And out of her own* goodness* make the Net
That shall en[mesh]* them all.
8 How now, Rodorigo.

- in his first audience challenge Iago starts emotionally (2/4, F #1)

- but this is quickly replaced by passion as he dwells on the 'fruitefull' and 'inclyning' Desdemona (3/3, F #2-3)

- his F #4 picturing of how easily and how far Desdemona can twist Othello (with its finishing sexual double-entendres) becomes intellectual for the only time in the speech (9/5) , while his second challenge to the audience to prove he is a 'Villaine' is passionate (3/3, F #5)

- F #6 is a wonderfully elegant, convoluted (and emotional, 0/3) suggestion that while his pretence to help Cassio on the surface equals 'heavenly shewes', he is in fact operating as an agent of 'hell' and is planning the 'blackest sinnes': not surprisingly, F sets it as an individual sentence, as if Iago's delight in his own cleverness (the 'paralell course' of F #5) deserves a celebratory sentence all by itself whether grammatical or no (most modern texts reduce its impact by not setting it separately but placing it as the opening to their longer mt. #6 which merely explains what the plot is going to be)

- Iago's explanation of the fine details of the plot that he can now envisage in all its splendour starts passionately (4/4, F #7's first two and a half lines) as he predicts how his three targets will work upon each other (Cassio on Desdemona, Desdemona on Othello), then becomes emotional (4/8, F #7's last four lines and F #8) as he pictures just what 'pestilence' he will pour into Othello's 'eare' – all based on the idea of Desdemona being unfaithful

5 How am I then a Villaine,
To Counsell Cassio to this paralell course,
Directly to his good?
6 Divinitie of hell, +
When divels will [the] blackest sinnes put on,
They do suggest at first with heavenly shewes,
As I do now.
7 For whiles this honest Foole
Plies Desdemona,x to repaire his Fortune,
And she for him,x pleades strongly to the Moore,
Ile powre this pestilence into his eare :x
That she repeales him, for her bodies Lust +
And by how much she strives to do him good,
She shall undo her Credite with the Moore.
8 So will I turne her vertue into pitch,
And out of her owne goodnesse make the Net,x
That shall en-[mash] them all. →
9 How now+ Rodorigo.

13/ Æmilia **Goodmorrow (good Lieutenant) I am sorrie** between 3.1.41 - 55

Background: Following Iago's advice, Cassio has gone to Desdemona's companion Æmilia (Iago's wife) to ask for her help in getting him access to Desdemona. The following is her reply, her first major speech in the play.

Style: as part of a two-handed scene

Where: somewhere in the garrison **To Whom:** Cassio

# of Lines: 12 **Probable Timing: 0.40 minutes**

Modern Text

13/ Æmilia

1 Good°morrow, good △lieutenant . †
2 I am sorry*
For your displeasure ; but all will [soon] be well.
3 The △general* and his wife are talking of it,
And she speaks* for you stoutly.
4 The Moor* replies,
That he you hurt is of great △fame in Cyprus,
And great △affinity*; and that in wholesome* △wisdom*
He might not but refuse you.
5 But he protests he loves you,
And needs no other △suitor but his likings
[To take the safest occasion by the front]
To bring you in again*.

6 Pray you come in . †
7 I will bestow you where you shall have time
To speak* your bosom* freely.

In a speech where the metrical irregularity [7] suggests concern, the orthographic inconsistency Æmilia shows after F #1 suggests a woman who is finding it difficult, for whatever reason, to maintain self-control.

- F #1's opening intellectual surround phrases (1/0), including the unembellished
  " . . . I am sorrie/For your displeasure : but all will sure be well . "
  point to a very careful opening (considering Iago's suspicions about Æmilia and Cassio, even if they are not lovers it could well be that she is carrying a torch for him and doesn't want to give herself away) - but then come the inconsistencies
- the fact that Cassio is being talked about is emotional (1/2, F #2); the fact that the man he has hurt is of 'great Fame . . ./And great Affinitie' is intellectual (4/1, the first two lines of F #3); while the end to F #3, explaining Othello
  " : and that in wholsome Wisedome/He might not but refuse you . "
  is heightened by being set as a passionate surround phrase (1/1)
- then comes another unembellished phrase, F #4's opening 'But he protests he loves you', the quietness seeming to suggest a very careful (delicate) reassurance – whether because of Cassio's distress or a genuine belief is up to each actor to decide – yet the explanation is passionate once more (1/1)
- and so comes an extended unembellished passage to open F #5, 'Pray you come in : /I will bestow you where you shall have time . . . ", (and whether the quiet and the surround phrase start are a further reminder of Æmilia's fondness or simply genuine empathy is again up to each actor to decide)
- the speech's last line finishes emotionally (0/2)

First Folio

13/ Æmilia

1 Goodmorrow (ₓgood Lieutenantₓ) I am sorrie
For your displeasure : ₓ but all will [sure] be well.
2 The Generall and his wife are talking of it,
And she speakes for you stoutly.
3 The Moore replies,
That he you hurt is of great Fame in Cyprus,
And great Affinitie : ₓ and that in wholsome Wisedome
He might not but refuse you.
4 But he protests he loves you+
And needs no other Suitor,ₓ but his likings
[ ]
To bring you in againe.

5 Pray you come in :
I will bestow you where you shall have time
To speake your bosome freely.

[7] i.e. where the first nine lines can only be counted as regular pentameter if various poetic devices - compression, elision, feminine endings - are applied

14/ Desdemona **Do not doubt Cassio/But I will have my Lord, and you againe** between 3.3.5 - 28
15/ Desdemona **How now my Lord?/I have bin talking with a Suitor heere,** between 3.3.41 - 83

Background: As Cassio (and Iago) hoped, once Desdemona is asked to intercede to get Cassio reinstated as Othello's lieutenant, she goes at it whole-heartedly. Speech #14 is her promise to Cassio and speech #15 is her attempt so to do.

Style: speech #14 as part of a three-handed scene; speech #15 as part of a four-handed scene

Where: both unspecified, but somewhere in the garrison or its gardens at Cyprus **To Whom:** speech #14 Cassio, in front of Æmilia; speech #15, in front of Iago and Æmilia

Speech 14: # of Lines: 15 **Probable Timing: 0.50 minutes**
Speech 15: # of Lines: 36 **Probable Timing: 1.45 minutes**

Modern Text

14/ Desdemona

1 Do not doubt, Cassio,
But I will have my Δlord, and you again*
As friendly as you were.

2 You do love my Δlord;
You have known* him long, and be you well assur'd
He shall in strangeness* stand no farther off
[Than] in a politic* distance.

3 Do not doubt {ψ}; before [Emilia] here,
I give thee warrant of thy place.

4 Assure thee,
If I do vow a friendship, I'll perform* it
To the last Δarticle.

5 My Δlord shall never rest,
I'll watch him tame, and talk* him out of patience;
His Δbed shall seem* a Δschool*, his Δboard* a Δshrift,
I'll intermingle every thing he does,
With Cassio's suit*. †

6 Therefore be merry, Cassio,
For thy Δsolicitor shall rather die*
[Than] give thy cause away.

F's orthography beautifully reveals the two sides of Desdemona, her controlled dignity and her delightful exuberance, as well as how quickly she can move from one mood to another.

- the surround phrases highlight the very clear logic of what she is prepared to do for Cassio, and her rationale, from F #2's opening monosyllabic
  ' . You do love my Lord : "
  through to F #3's
  " . Do not doubt : before Æmilia here,/I give thee warrant of thy place . "
  to F #5's opening
  " . My Lord shall never rest,/Ile watch him tame, and talke him out of patience ; "
  - the emotional semicolon of the latter perhaps suggesting a youthful anticipation (joy? fun? mischief? delight?) of what may come
- F #1's opening reassurance to Cassio that he and Othello will soon be friends again is slightly passionate (2/1), which then turns to emotion in the F #2 promise that Othello shall only stand off from Cassio 'a politique distance' (1/3)
- in its virtually unembellished calm, F #3 shows great dignity, her determination enhanced by two surround phrases as she gives Cassio 'warrant of thy place' (1/0),
- and the calm determination is continued into F #4 (her unembellished statement ' Assure thee,/If I do vow a friendship,') with what she promises ('My Lord shall never rest,') becoming passionate (2/2, the last line of F #4 and the first line and a half of F #5)
- the promises having been made, the emotional semicolon releases a sudden onrushed flurry of intellectual and emotional verbiage (8/5, the speech's last four and a half lines) as she pictures just where (mainly, it seems, Othello's 'Bed') she shall plead for Cassio and the, to her, inevitable happy outcome

First Folio

14/ Desdemona

1 Do not doubt+ Cassio+
But I will have my Lord, and you againe
As friendly as you were.

2 You do love my Lord: x
You have knowne him long, and be you well assur'd
He shall in strangenesse stand no farther off,+
[Then] in a politique distance.

3 Do not doubt {ψ}: x before [Æmilia] here,
I give thee warrant of thy place.

4 Assure thee,
If I do vow a friendship, Ile performe it
To the last Article.

5 My Lord shall never rest,
Ile watch him tame, and talke him out of patience;
His Bed shall seeme a Schoole, his Boord a Shrift,
Ile intermingle every thing he do's
With Cassio's suite: Therefore be merry+ Cassio,
For thy Solicitor shall rather dye, x
[Then] give thy cause away.

Modern Text

15/ Desdemona

1 How now my Δlord?
2 I have been* talking with a Δsuitor here*,
A man that languishes in your displeasure{,}
{ψ} your Δlieutenant, Cassio. †
3 Good my Δlord,
If I have any grace or power to move you,
His present reconciliation take; ◊
For if he be not one that truly loves you,
That errs* in Δignorance and not in Δcunning,
I have no judgment* in an honest face.
4 I prithee* call him back*.
5 {ψ} He hath left part of his grief* with me*
To suffer with him.
6 Good Δlove, call him back* { }
{ψ}Shortly {.}
7 {ψ} Tonight, at Δsupper {.}
8 To morrow Δdinner then{.}
9 Why then tomorrow night, [or] Tuesday morn*;
On Tuesday noon*, or night; on We'n'sday Δmorn*.
10 I prithee* name the time, but let it not
Exceed three days*.
11 Ifaith*, he's* penitent:
And yet his Δtrespass*, in our common reason
(Save that they say the wars* must make example
Out of [their] best), is not almost a fault
T'incur* a private check*.
12 When shall he come?
13 Tell me, Othello.
14 I wonder in my Δsoul*
What you would ask* me, that I should deny,
Or stand so mamm'ring* on?
15 What?
16 Michael Cassio,
That came a-wooing* with you, and so many a time,
When I have spoke of you dispraisingly,

In may ways this is the only truly innocent private domestic scene between Desdemona and Othello, and thus her rapid changes of mood need not be dismissed as skittishness but rather represents the teasing that should be part of a happily married couple's relationship – especially when she herself describes herself as 'mam'ring on', F #14.

• the two unembellished passages show Desdemona's belief in her own powers to woo Othello to reinstate Cassio, hence her ease in starting

"If I have any grace, or power to move you,/His present reconciliation take ./For if he be not one, that truly loves you,"

the importance of F #12's asking 'When shall he come?' given extra weight by being set as a monosyllabic short question, moving on to comment – again with ease

"That came a woing with you ? and so many a time/(When I have spoke of you dispraisingly)/Hath tane your part, to have so much to do/To bring him in ? /[Trust me], I could do much"

• the very few surround phrases (suggesting that the speech is more a stream of consciousness than a carefully preplanned deliberate argument) all seem to emphasise her (innocent) wish to have Othello welcome Cassio back into their fold, almost childlike in reasoning, for she wants him soon, ' ; on Wensday Morne . ' (and emotionally, via the only semicolon in the speech, F #9) because ' . Infaith hee's penitent : '(not necessarily a valid reason for reinstatement, F #11); trying to explain it is really for Othello's benefit (almost a piece of chop-logic, F #18)

• the first four lines, setting up that she is talking on behalf of a 'Suitor' are (carefully?) factual (6/1, F #1 and the first three lines of F #2) and her calm statement as to her own worth and Cassio's love for Othello is totally unembellished – the opening thus being fairly well contained

• however, this (dignified?) self control soon disappears, for her avowal that in her opinion Cassio is guilty only of 'Ignorance' and not 'Cunning' then becomes passionate (2/2, F #3's last two lines) while the first request for his reinstatement (heightened by being set as three short sentence F #4-6) is emotional (1/5)

• whether conscious of her sudden over-energy or no, Desdemona returns to her intellect as, (teasingly?) assuming that Cassio will be reinstated, she asks Othello to define 'when' (6/3, F #7-9); then when Othello does not reply, her plea that it should be within the next 'three dayes', with the further explanation that 'hee's penitent' and of the 'best', turns emotional (1/8, F #10-11)

• with still no reply forthcoming, the repeated unembellished challenge 'When shall he come?' is followed by passion as she suggests that she couldn't refuse Othello anything were he to talk so much as she has done (2/2, F #13-14); and then comes the factual naming of Cassio (F #16, with the shortness and directness of the sentence perhaps suggesting that the idea of keeping him out of service is ridiculous)

• then comes the lengthy unembellished passage pointing to the very intimate way the three of them have been since the beginning of their relationship (for Cassio 'came a woing with you', F #16-17)

First Folio

15/ Desdemona

1 How now my Lord?
2 I have bin talking with a Suitor heere,
A man that languishes in your displeasure{,}
{ψ} your Lieutenant+ Cassio: Good my Lord,
If I have any grace,$_x$ or power to move you,
His present reconciliation take.
3 For if he be not one,$_x$ that truly loves you,
That erres in Ignorance,$_x$ and not in Cunning,
I have no judgement in an honest face.
4 I prythee call him backe.
5 {ψ} He hath left part of his greefe with mee
To suffer with him.
6 Good Love, call him backe { }
{ψ}Shortly{.}
7 {ψ} To night, at Supper{.}
8 To morrow Dinner then{.}
9 Why then to morrow night, [on] Tuesday morne,+
On Tuesday noone, or night; on Wensday Morne.
10 I prythee name the time, but let it not
Exceed three dayes.
11 Infaith+ hee's penitent:
And yet his Trespasse, in our common reason
($_x$Save that they say the warres must make example$_x$)
Out of [her] best, is not almost a fault
T'encurre a private checke.
12 When shall he come?
13 Tell me+ Othello.
14 I wonder in my Soule
What you would aske me, that I should deny,
Or stand so mam'ring on?
15 What?
16 Michael Cassio,
That came a woing with you?$_x$ and so many a time+
($_x$When I have spoke of you dispraisingly$_x$)

Hath ta'en your part - to have so much to do
To bring him in!
17 [By'r lady], I could do much - ◊
{ψ} This is not a △boon*;
'Tis as I should entreat* you wear* your △gloves,
Or feed* on nourishing dishes, or keep* you warm*,
Or sue to you to do a peculiar profit
To your own* person.
18 Nay, when I have a suit*
Wherein I mean* to touch your △love indeed,
It shall be full of poise* and [difficulty],
And fearful* to be granted.

• finally her emotions sweep in (3/11 in the last seven lines of the speech) as she explains that this is 'not a Boone' but for Othello's benefit (F #18) and that Othello should look out when she has a really weighty request to bring to him (F #19)

Hath tane your part, to have so much to do
To bring him in? +
17 [Trust me], I could do much.
18 {ψ} This is not a Boone: x
'Tis as I should entreate you weare your Gloves,
Or feede on nourishing dishes, or keepe you warme,
Or sue to you, x to do a peculiar profit
To your owne person.
19 Nay, when I have a suite
Wherein I meane to touch your Love indeed,
It shall be full of poize, x and [difficult waight],
And fearefull to be granted.

#'s 16 - 19: The Plan In Action, Iago & Othello

16/ Othello **Avant, be gone : Thou hast set me on the Racke :** between 3.3.335 - 357

Background: Following Desdemona's full blooded intercession for Cassio's reinstatement, Iago has begun to pour poisonous ideas into Othello's ears. There has been a series of insinuations, one suggesting that Cassio might have gone too far when he initially wooed Desdemona on Othello's behalf (a traditional chivalric approach, innocent in and of itself) - 'Did Michael Cassio/When he woo'd my Lady, know of your love?'; another about the nature of Venetian women, which as a foreigner Othelloe might not appreciate 'I may feare/Her will, recoyling to better judgement,/May fal to match you with her country formes,/And happily repent'; and another about Desdemona's boldness 'Shee that so young could give out such a Seeming/To seele her Fathers eyes up, close as Oake,/He thought 'twas witchcraft'. Thus when Othello questions 'Why did I marry?'. Iago knows he has succeeded, especially when greeted with the following.

Style: as part of a two-handed scene **Where:** somewhere in the garrison **To Whom:** Iago

# of Lines: 22 **Probable Timing: 1.10 minutes**

Modern Text

16/ Othello
1 Avaunt*, be gone! △thou hast set me on the △rack*.†
2 I swear* 'tis better to be much abus'd
[Than] but to know't a little.
3 What sense had I [of] her stol'n* hours* of △lust?
4 I saw't not, thought it not; it harm'd not me. †
5 I slept the next night well, [ ] was free, and merry*; ◊
I found not Cassio's kisses on her △lips*. †
6 He that is robb'd, not wanting what is stol'n*,
Let him not know't, and he's not robb'd at all.

Given the circumstances, the large number of surround phrases are not surprising – yet their pattern sets up an interesting proposition that while at the start Othello displays remarkable self control, as he comes to the realisation that the disgrace of Desdemona's infidelity might cost him his career, so control becomes much more difficult to maintain.

• that the opening self control is tricky from the outset but is nevertheless there can be seen in the mix of passionate and unembellished lines in F #1-4 – for following the passionate first line and a half of dismissal (2/2) comes
"'tis better to be much abus'd,/Then but to know't a little."
and in the short sentence (F #2) that immediately follows the (enforced?) quiet continues almost unbroken until the last five-word key phrase
"What sense had I, in her stolne houres of Lust?"

First Folio

16/ Othello
1 Avant, be gone: + Thou hast set me on the Racke:
I sweare 'tis better to be much abus'd, x
[Then] but to know't a little.
2 What sense had I, x [in] her stolne houres of Lust?
3 I saw't not, thought it not: x it harm'd not me:
I slept the next night well, [fed well], was free, and merrie.
4 I found not Cassio's kisses on her Lippes:
He that is robb'd, not wanting what is stolne,
Let him not know't, and he's not robb'd at all.

{ctd. over}

7 I had been* happy, if the general* ^Δ^camp*,
Pioneers* and all, had tasted her sweet ^Δ^body,
So I had nothing known*.
8 O* now, for ever
Farewell the ^Δ^tranquil* mind*! farewell ^Δ^content !
Farewell the plumed ^Δ^troops*, and the big* ^Δ^wars*,
That makes ^Δ^ambition, ^Δ^virtue!
9 O* farewell ! †
10 Farewell the neighing ^Δ^steed and the shrill ^Δ^trump*,
The ^Δ^spirit-stirring ^Δ^drum, th'^Δ^ear*-piercing ^Δ^fife,
The ^Δ^royal* ^Δ^banner, and all ^Δ^quality*,
Pride, ^Δ^pomp*, and ^Δ^circumstance of glorious ^Δ^war* !†
11 And O [ye] mortal* ^Δ^engines, whose [wide] throats*
Th'immortal* Jove's [great] ^Δ^clamors* counterfeit*,
Farewell ! †
12 Othello's ^Δ^occupation's gone.

• then, amazingly in terms of self control, four of the next five lines are also unembellished

"I saw't not, thought it not : it harm'd not me : /I slept the next night well, [fed well], was free, and merrie . / . . . He that is robb'd, not wanting what is stolne,/Let him not know't, and he's not robb'd at all ."

the one image that breaks this remarkable extended quiet utterance deals with another direct physical aspect of the supposed affair (2/1, F #4's first line)

" . I found not Cassio's kisses on her Lippes :"

• thus it seems that while Othello can discuss the theoretical implications of adultery as a general principle, whenever the images come close to his own situation, emotions break through - as with the next statement that he would have been 'happy' if he 'had nothing knowne' (2/4, F #5)

• to date the surround phrases have been logical, thus supporting the determination with which he is trying to maintain self-control (F #1- the first line of F #4, seven in all), but the four that contain F #6's first passionate words of farewell (to his 'Tranquill minde' and 'Content', his 'Troopes' and the 'bigge Warres', 6/6) are all formed with the emotional semicolon

• which leads to the onrushed F #7 (itself split into three by most modern texts), where, though his mind is still capable of great envisionings in his long list of what he is most likely to lose (summed up in the final surround phrase ' : Othellos Occupation's gone.'), his emotions are in full flow too (18/10 in F #7's seven and a half lines)

5 I had beene happy, if the generall Campe,
Pyoners and all, had tasted her sweet Body,
So I had nothing knowne.
6 Oh now, for ever
Farewell the Tranquill minde ; + farewell Content ; +
Farewell the plumed Troopes, and the bigge Warres,
That makes Ambition, Vertue!
7 Oh farewell ; +
Farewell the neighing Steed,x and the shrill Trumpe,
The Spirit-stirring Drum, th'Eare-piercing Fife,
The Royall Banner, and all Qualitie,
Pride, Pompe, and Circumstance of glorious Warre :
And O [you] mortall Engines, whose [rude] throates
Th'immortall Joves [dread] Clamours,x counterfet,
Farewell : Othello's Occupation's gone.

17/ Iago **I see you are eaten up with Passion :** between 3.3.391 - 408

Background: Having thoroughly thrown Othello into a series of appalling doubts, see-sawing between 'I thinke my Wife be honest, and thinke she is not' and demanding 'Ile have some proofe', Iago now applies the final coup-de-grace. The following is triggered by Othello's 'Would I were satisfied'.

Style: as part of a two-handed scene

Where: somewhere in the garrison **To Whom: Othello**

# of Lines: 17 **Probable Timing: 0.55 minutes**

Modern Text

17/ Iago

1 I see, [sir], you are eaten up with Δpassion;
I do repent me that I put it to you.
2 You would be satisfied?

3 And may; but how?
4 How satisfied, my Δlord?
Would you, the [super-visor] grossly* gape on?
Behold her topp'd*. [8]

5 It were a tedious difficulty, I think*,
To bring them to that Δprospect; Δdamn* them then,
If ever mortal* eyes [did] see them bolster*
More [than] their own*.
6 What then?
7 How then?
8 What shall I say?
9 Where's Δsatisfaction?
10 It is impossible you should see this,
Were they as prime as Δgoats*, as hot as Δmonkeys*,
As salt as Δwolves in pride, and Δfools* as gross*
As Δignorance, made drunk*.
11 But yet, I say,
If imputation and strong circumstances
Which lead* directly to the door* of Δtruth
Will give you satisfaction, you might have't.

Amazingly, the most powerful of the poisoned suspicions Iago is pouring into Othello's ears seems to be those heightened by being unembellished, as if their very calmness was the final ingredient necessary to overthrow Othello's sense of reason and self-control.

" : I do repent me, that I put it to you . /You would be satisfied ? / . And may : but how ? How satisfied, . . . /Would you . . . /Behold her top'd ."

" . What then ? How then ? What shall I say ? / . . . It is impossible you should see this, . . . "

" . But yet, I say,/If imputation, and strong circumstances,/ . . . /Will give you satisfaction, you might have't ."

- while the unembellished lines seem to be based on information/hints of information, the few surround phrases seem somewhat more manipulative, as in F #1, F #3, and the opening of F #6

- in a speech that is slightly more emotional than intellectual (10/13 overall) the only slightly intellectual moments (both 1/0) are remarkably skillfully evocative, as with the opening of F #1,
  " . I see [ ] you are eaten up with Passion : "
  and the short F #10
  "Where's Satisfaction?"

- the most emotional outburst comes as Iago suggests to Othello that it will be next to impossible to catch Cassio and Desdemona in the act (F #6, 2/5)

- and the most emotional moment comes as Iago elaborates this further in the most salacious terms, 'Were they as prime as Goates, as hot as Monkeyes', (5/5, the three and half lines of F #11)

First Folio

17/ Iago

1 I see+ [ ]+ you are eaten up with Passion :ₓ
I do repent me,ₓ that I put it to you.
2 You would be satisfied?

3 And may :ₓ but how?
4 How satisfied, my Lord?
5 Would you+ the [super-vision] grossely gape on?
Behold her top'd.

6 It were a tedious difficulty, I thinke,
To bring them to that Prospect :ₓ Damne them then,
If ever mortall eyes [do] see them boulster
More [then] their owne.
7 What then?
8 How then?
9 What shall I say?
10 Where's Satisfaction?
11 It is impossible you should see this,
Were they as prime as Goates, as hot as Monkeyes,
As salt as Wolves in pride, and Fooles as grosse
As Ignorance, made drunke.
12 But yet, I say,
If imputation,ₓ and strong circumstances,ₓ
Which leade directly to the doore of Truth,ₓ
Will give you satisfaction, you might have't.

[8] Qq/Ff all set a variation of 'top'd', one modern gloss suggests the more flagrant 'tupp'd'

18/ Othello **O that the Slave had forty thousand lives :** between 3.3.442 - 462

Background: Iago finally plays his trump card of proof. As his first gift, Othello had given Desdemona a very special family heirloom, a handkerchief reputed to possess magical powers. Desdemona accidentally dropped it (ironically while attending to him) and it was retrieved by Desdemona's companion, Iago's wife Æmilia. In all innocence she has passed it on to Iago, who has thrown it into Cassio's lodging so that he can legitimately tell Othello 'such a Handkerchiefe/ . . . did I to day/See Cassio wipe his Beard with'.

Style: as part of a two-handed scene

Where: somewhere in the garrison **To Whom:** Iago

# of Lines: 18 **Probable Timing: 0.55 minutes**

Modern Text

18/ Othello

1 O that the Δslave had forty thousand lives ! †
2 One is too poor*, too weak* for my revenge.
3 Now do I see 'tis true.
4 Look* here*, Iago,
All my fond love thus do I blow to Δheaven.
5 'Tis gone.
6 Arise, black* vengeance, from the hollow hell ! †
7 Yield* up, O Δlove, thy Δcrown* and hearted Δthrone
To tyrannous Δhate !
8 Swell, bosom*, with thy fraught,
For 'tis of Δaspics'* tongues !
9 {ψ} {My} mind* {will never} change.
10 {ψ} Like to the Pontic* Sea,
Whose Δicy* Δcurrent and compulsive course,
Nev'r [feels] retiring* ebb*, but keeps* due on
To the Propontic* and the Hellespont,
Even so my bloody thoughts, with violent pace
Shall nev'r look* back*, nev'r ebb* to humble Δlove,
Till that a capable* and wide Δrevenge
Swallow them up.
11 Now by yond Δmarble Δheaven,
In the due reverence of a Δsacred vow
I here* engage my words.

Given the circumstances, F's slight onrush in Othello's explosion about the extent of his desired revenge on Cassio (F #1) and in his first call on 'blacke vengeance' (F #5) (both of which most modern texts split into two slightly more rational sentences) as well as the overall passion (20/21), are only to be expected. What is both unexpected and ultimately quite frightening is that, though the speech starts passionately, the final act of what Othello is certain will be a 'Sacred vow' made in the eyes of 'Marble Heaven' is intellectual (3/1, F #9) – which makes all his future actions, emotional and passionate digressions not withstanding, backed by a firm moral and thus intellectual determination.

- the hint of the eventual control to come can be seen in the two short monosyllabic unembellished sentences with which Othello finally announces his belief in the supposed affair, F #2's 'Now do I see 'tis true.', and the renunciation of his blind (i.e. 'fond') love, F #4's terse ' 'Tis gone.'
- yet these bleak moments provide the only quietness amidst the evident turmoil still in his heart, soul, and mind, for they are part of a generally passionate opening (3/4, F #1-3) - the passion generated by his hatred for Cassio, for he opens with the only surround phrases in the speech focusing directly on Cassio
  ". O that the Slave had forty thousand lives : /One is too poore, too weake for my revenge . "
- and the passion only swells as Othello first calls on 'blacke vengeance' to arise from 'the hollow hell' (F #5), for his own bosom to swell with poison (F #6), and then (F #7 and the first three and half lines of F #8), asserts that his 'minde will never change' (12/11 in just seven and half lines)
- then he becomes emotional (2/4) in promising that his 'bloody thoughts' will 'nev'r looke backe' until 'wide Revenge/Swallow' Cassio and Desdemona up (F #8's last three and a half lines)
- in many ways the final sentence is the most frightening of all, not only for its content, in which Othello seems to regard any future actions of revenge as a religious act, but even more by the manner in which the vow is made, essentially intellectually (3/1), suggesting that this is not just an emotional blurt but evidence of something much more dangerous – a controlled and focused determination

First Folio

18/ Othello

1 O that the Slave had forty thousand lives : +
One is too poore, too weake for my revenge.
2 Now do I see 'tis true.
3 Looke heere+ Iago,
All my fond love thus do I blow to Heaven.
4 'Tis gone
.
5 Arise+ blacke vengeance, from the hollow hell, + [9]
Yeeld up (,O Love,) thy Crowne, and hearted Throne
To tyrannous Hate. +
6 Swell+ bosome+ with thy fraught,
For 'tis of Aspickes tongues. +
7 {ψ} {My} minde {will never} change.
8 {ψ} Like to the Ponticke Sea,
Whose Icie Current,x and compulsive course,
Nev'r [keepes] retyring ebbe+ but keepes due on
To the Proponticke,x and the Hellespont :x
Even so my bloody thoughts, with violent pace
Shall nev'r looke backe, nev'r ebbe to humble Love,
Till that a capeable,x and wide Revenge
Swallow them up.
9 Now by yond Marble Heaven,
In the due reverence of a Sacred vow,x
I heere engage my words.

[9] Qq and some commentators = 'thy hollow Cell', Ff/most modern texts = 'the hollow hell'

19/ Othello **That's a fault : That Handkerchiefe** between 3.4.55 - 76

Background: Not knowing what has happened to Othello's handkerchief (see background and speech #18 immediately above), Desdemona is horrified by its loss 'Beleeve me, I had rather have lost my purse/Full of Cruzadoes'. And now, with Othello asking for it, pushed to it by Iago's insinuations, Desdemona cannot produce it.

Style: as part of a three-handed scene

Where: somewhere in the garrison or its gardens **To Whom:** Desdemona, in front of Æmilia

# of Lines: 21 **Probable Timing: 1.10 minutes**

Modern Text

19/ Othello

1 That's a fault. †
2 That Δhandkerchief*
Did an [Egyptian] to my Δmother give;
She was a Δcharmer, and could almost read
The thoughts of people.
3 She told her, while she kept it,
'T'would make her Δamiable, and subdue my Δfather
Entirely* to her love; Δbut if she lost it,
Or made a Δgift* of it, my Δfather's eye
Should hold her loathed, and his Δspirits should hunt
After new Δfancies.
4 She, dying, gave it me,
And bid me, when my Δfate would have me Δwiv'd,
To give it her.
5 I did [so]; and take heed* on't,
Make it a Δdarling like your precious eye. †
6 To lose't* or give't away were such perdition
As nothing else could match.

---

7 'Tis true; Δthere's Δmagic* in the web of it. †
8 A Δsybil*, that had numb'red in the world
The Δsun to course two hundred compasses,
In her Δprophetic* fury* sew'd* the Δwork*;
The Δworms* were hallowed that did breed* the Δsilk*,
And it was dy'd* in Δmummy* which the Δskillful*
[Conserve] of Δmaidens' hearts.

---

9 {ψ} {T}herefore look to't* well.

In what is often played as an emotional outburst of anger and distrust, F's orthography shows the speech falling into three parts - a very surprising intellectual start as Othello describes the properties for good and bad of 'That Handkerchiefe'; an attempt to keep passion in check as he describes how he came to pass it on to Desdemona and how carefully she must guard it; and then an enormous and unexpected passionate outburst as he describes the 'Magicke in the web' - the gigantic switch from controlled opening to passionate ending suggesting the polar extremes of a man whose mind is beginning to turn thanks to Iago's poisoned words.

- in outlining the properties of 'That Handkerchiefe' Othello's intellectual start (12/2, F 1-2) and three surround phrase first sentence suggest a very detached approach, one more suited to a subordinate in the military chain of command rather than his once adored and still adoring wife.

- even F #3's in-part unembellished mention of his mother 'dying, gave it me' to pass on when 'Fate would have me Wiv'd' is startlingly free of emotion (2/0)

- but then, perhaps with the mention of being 'Wiv'd', it seems that his control begins to crack, for now come the only two emotional (semicoloned) surround phrases in the speech

  " . I did to ; and take heede on't/Make it a Darling, like your precious eye : "

  the emotion about to be released (1/2) caught back by the unembellished warning that if Desdemona lost it or gave it away

  "were such perdition,/As nothing else could match."

- and it seems as if Othello has regained control, for the opening explanation (admittedly overly firm surround phrase enhanced)

  " . 'Tis true : There's Magicke in the web of it : "

  is factual once more (4/2, F #5's first two and a half lines), but then matters start getting out of hand

- for no apparent reason the onrushed sentence detailing the almost mystical way the cloth was created, Othello suddenly becomes enormously passionate (7/9, the last five lines of the speech) – and whether this signifies just a loss of control, or mental breakdown, or a profound reverence for the sacred objects from his own cultural background is up to each actor to decide

First Folio

19/ Othello

1 That's a fault: That Handkerchiefe
Did an [Ægyptian] to my Mother give:$_{x}$
She was a Charmer, and could almost read
The thoughts of people.
2 She told her, while she kept it,
'T would make her Amiable, and subdue my Father
Intirely to her love:$_{x}$ But if she lost it,
Or made a Guift of it, my Fathers eye
Should hold her loathed, and his Spirits should hunt
After new Fancies.
3 She+ dying, gave it me,
And bid me ($_{x}$when my Fate would have me Wiv'd$_{x}$)
To give it her.
4 I did [to]; and take heede on't,
Make it a Darling,$_{x}$ like your precious eye:
To loose't,$_{x}$ or give't away,$_{x}$ were such perdition,$_{x}$
As nothing else could match.

---

5 'Tis true:$_{x}$ There's Magicke in the web of it:
A Sybill+ that had numbred in the world
The Sun to course,$_{x}$ two hundred compasses,
In her Prophetticke furie sow'd the Worke:$_{x}$
The Wormes were hallowed,$_{x}$ that did breede the Silke,
And it was dyde in Mummey,$_{x}$ which the Skilfull
[Conserv'd] of Maidens hearts.

---

6 {ψ} {T}herefore looke too't well.

#'s 20 - 29: The Plan's Tragic Consequences

20/ Bianca **'Save you (Friend Cassio.)** between 3.4.169 - 187

21/ Bianca **What did you meane by that same Handkerchiefe, you gave me** between 4.1.148 - 161

Background: Arriving in Cyprus, Cassio took up with the courtesan, Bianca, though since his firing and reinstatement he has taken care to see much less of her than before, hence speech #20. Iago can use this relationship to poison Othello's mind even further, especially since during speech #21 Bianca produces the missing magical handkerchiefe (see background to speech #18, and speech #19) in front of the hidden Othello, thus confirming Cassio's possession of it.

Style: speech #20, part of a two-handed scene; speech #21, part of a three-handed scene with a hidden observer

Where: in a Cyprus street **To Whom:** speech #20 Cassio; speech #21 Cassio in front of Iago, with the hidden Othello watching

Speech 20: # of Lines: 12 **Probable Timing: 0.40 minutes**

Speech 21: # of Lines: 9 **Probable Timing: 0.30 minutes**

Modern Text

20/ Bianca

1 'Save you , △friend Cassio !

2 {ψ} I was {coming} to your △lodging {ψ}.

3 What? keep* a week* away? ◊ △seven days* and △nights?

4 Eight°score eight hours*? ◊ and △lovers' absent hours*,
More tedious [than] the △dial*, eight°score times?

5 O* weary reck'ning !

6 {W}hence came this {handkerchief*}?

7 {You} found it in {your} △chamber . †

8 {You} like the work* well ; △ere it be demanded
(As like enough it will) {you} would have it copied* . †

9 Take it, and do't*, and leave {you} for this time {?}

10 This is some △token from a newer △friend ;
To the felt-△absence now I feel* a △cause . †

11 Is't come to this?
[ ]

12 {W}ho's is it?

- the speech opens quite factually (F #1-2, 3/0), perhaps suggesting a moment of care from a kept woman meeting her soldier/lover in a public space

- but then comes Bianca's emotional (seductive perhaps) reprimand for his staying away from her for a week (1/4, F #3-5), the approach heightened in being set as three short sentences – as if each were sufficient in and of itself to get some form of response, verbal or otherwise

- and as the implied sexual heat turns up a notch ('Lovers absent howres') so Bianca becomes passionate (2/3, F #6-7)

- however, once the 'handkerchiefe' is produced for her to copy her manner changes – becoming emotional both in release (2/4, F #8-9), and in the appearance of surround phrases, the first two linked by the only emotional semicolon in the speech
  "{You} found it in {your} Chamber,/{You} like the worke well ; Ere
  it be demanded/(As like enough it will) {you} would have it coppied : /Take it, and doo't, and leave {you} for this time {?} "
  - the firm challenging logic of the latter heightened by being monosyllabic

- then, as she challenges Cassio to tell her where it came from (suspecting 'a newer Friend'), her intellect sweeps in (4/1, F #10's first two lines) - the demand of the sentence intensified by being set as thee more logical surround phrases

- and after all the releases Bianca ends very quietly (dangerously so?)
  " ; Is't come to this ? Well, well. {Who's} is it?"
  - the unembellished calm doubly heightened by being monosyllabic and set either via a surround phrase (F #10) or as two very short sentences (F #11-12)

First Folio

20/ Bianca

1 'Save you ($_x$Friend Cassio.$_x$)+

2 {ψ} I was {coming} to your Lodging {ψ}.

3 What? keepe a weeke away?

4 Seven dayes,$_x$ and Nights?

5 Eight score eight houres? $_x$

6 And Lovers absent howres
More tedious [then] the Diall, eight score times?

7 Oh weary reck'ning. +

8 {W}hence came this {handkerchiefe}?

9 {You} found it in {your} Chamber,
{You} like the worke well ; Ere it be demanded
(As like enough it will) {you} would have it coppied :
Take it, and doo't, and leave {you} for this time {?}

10 This is some Token from a newer Friend,+
To the felt-Absence :$_x$ now I feele a Cause :
Is't come to this?

11 [Well, well.]

12 {W}ho's is it?

Modern Text

21/ Bianca

1 {ψ} What did you mean* by that same ^Δhandkerchief* you gave me even now?

2 I was a fine ^Δfool* to take it. †

3 I must take out the work*?

4 A likely piece of work*, that you should find* it in your ^Δchamber, and [not know] who left it there !

5 This is some ^Δminx's* token, and I must take out the work*?

6 There, give it [the] ^Δhobby*-horse. †

7 Wheresoever you had it, I'll take out no work* on't.

8 [An'] you'll* come to supper to night, you may; [an'] you will not, come when you are next prepar'd for.

Whereas the previous verse speech – suggesting some form of grace or heightened awareness – was passionate (12/12 overall), here Bianca's prose – suggesting much more commonplace and/or direct release – is emotional virtually throughout (5/11).

- the only surround phrases underscore her awareness of both self and situation, F #2's
  " I was a fine Foole to take it : I must take out the worke ? "
- in ending, the only unembellished lines in the speech place the decision whether or not to continue the relationship firmly in Cassio's hands for either he comes tonight for supper or
  "if you will not, come when you are next prepar'd for."
- in terms of release, most of her energy is expended in the opening challenge to him over the 'Handkerchiefe' (twelve releases in the first five lines, F #1-4, 4/8); there is slightly less release in giving it back to him (1/2, F #5's line and a half); and the final challenge to him to continue the relationship is very quiet (0/1, F #6) – F #6's (enforced?) calm perhaps suggesting how important this moment is for her

First Folio

21/ Bianca

1 {ψ} What did you meane by that same Handkerchiefe,ₓ you gave me even now?

2 I was a fine Foole to take it: I must take out the worke?

3 A likely piece of worke, that you should finde it in your Chamber, and [know not] who left it there.+

4 This is some Minxes token, & I must take out the worke?

5 There, give it [your] Hobbey-horse, wheresoever you had it, Ile take out no worke on't.

6 [If] you'le come to supper to night+ you may,+ [if] you will not, come when you are next prepar'd for.

22/ Æmilia **Alas (Iago) my Lord hath so bewhor'd her,** between 4.2.115 - 147

Background: Under the weight of supposed evidence, and his recall to Venice delivered by members of Brabantio's (and thus Desdemona's) family Othello has finally snapped, asking Desdemona directly 'Are you not a Strumpet?'. When she denies any 'foule unlawfull touch', in his pain Othello sarcastically apologises for mistaking her for Desdemona, since 'I tooke you for that cunning Whore of Venice./that married with Othello'. In her bewilderment she has turned to Æmilia and Iago for help. The following is Æmilia's reply to Iago's asking Desdemona 'What is the matter Lady?' .

Style: as part of a three-handed scene

Where: close to Othello's private chambers within the garrison **To Whom:** Iago, in front of Desdemona

# of Lines: 24 **Probable Timing: 1.15 minutes**

Modern Text

22/ Æmilia

1 Alas, Iago, my ^Δlord hath so bewhor'd her,
Thrown* such despite* and heavy terms* upon her
[As true hearts cannot bear*].

2 He call'd her whore. †

3 A ^Δbeggar *in his drink*
Could not have laid such terms* upon his ^Δcallet.

- the surround phrases highlight the main points that are disturbing her, first as to the indignities Othello has piled upon Desdemona
  ". He call'd her whore : a Begger in his drinke : /Could not have laid such termes upon his Callet . /Hath she forsooke so many Noble Matches ? /Her Father ? And her Country ? And her Friends ? /To be call'd Whore ? "

  and then as to the cowards who lied to Othello about her
  " : I will be hang'd else ."
  " . Oh fie upon [them] : "

First Folio

22/ Æmilia

1 Alas (ₓIagoₓ) my Lord hath so bewhor'd her,
Throwne such dispight,ₓ and heavy termes upon her
[That true hearts cannot beare it].

2 He call'd her whore: a Begger in his drinke:ₓ
Could not have laid such termes upon his Callet.

{ctd. over}

4 Hath she forsook* so many ^noble ^matches?
Her ^father? ^and her ^country? ^and her ^friends?
To be call'd ^whore?
5 Would it not make one weep*?

6 I will be hang'd, if some eternal* ^villain*,
Some busy* and insinuating ^rogue,
Some cogging, cozening ^slave, to get some ^office,
Have not devis'd this ^slander. †
7 I will be hang'd else.

8 Who keeps* her company*?
9 What ^place? ◊what ^time? ◊what ^form*? ◊what ^likelihood*?
10 The Moor's* abus'd by some [outrageous] ^knave,
Some base notorious ^knave, some scurvy ^fellow.
11 O* [^heaven], that such companions thou'd'st unfold,
And put in every honest hand a whip
To lash the ^rascals* naked through the world
Even from the ^east to th'^west !

12 O* fie upon [him] !
13 Some such ^squire he was
That turn'd your wit the seamy-side without,
And made you to suspect me with the Moor*.

- while the few unembellished moments are testimony to how, when matters really sting, instead of becoming emotionally upset Æmilia becomes determinedly self-controlled and focused, as with F #12's praying to heaven
  "that such companions thou'd'st unfold,/And put in every honest hand a whip,"
  and F #13's unflinchingly embarrassing (to him) self-defending comment to Iago, comparing Desdemona's supposed detractors to those
  "That turn'd your wit, the seamy-side without,/And made you suspect me . . . "
- not surprisingly, Æmilia starts out passionately (4/6, F #1-2)
- she then becomes strongly intellectual (13/4, F #3-5) as she piles fact upon fact to prove Desdemona's innocence (F #3) and then suggests that these 'Slanders' have been created by 'some eternall Villaine' so as to advance himself 'to get some Office' (F #5) – the one emotional moment is the short F #4 ('Would it not make one weepe?', 0/1) that interrupts the two longer sentences
- Æmilia's passionate demand (3/3, F #6-10) for someone to offer specific facts or even 'liklyhood' to prove her wrong (and Desdemona unchaste) is heightened by being set as five short sentences, three of which are further heightened by being monosyllabic – the pauses in the irregular (shaded) structure adding to her perplexed demands
- the (suddenly discovered?) thought that Othello has been 'abus'd by some most villanous Knave' is strongly intellectual (8/3, F #11-12), while the challenging rebuke to Iago that the situation is similar to that which 'turn'd your wit' and led him to suspect Æmilia of being unfaithful is passionate (2/2, F #13)

3 Hath she forsooke so many Noble Matches?
Her Father? And her Country? And her Friends?
To be call'd Whore?
4 Would it not make one weepe?

5 I will be hang'd, if some eternall Villaine,
Some busie and insinuating Rogue,
Some cogging, cozening Slave, to get some Office,
Have not devis'd this Slander: I will be hang'd else.

6 Who keepes her companie?
7 What Place?
8 What Time?
9 What Forme?
10 What liklyhood?
11 The Moore's abus'd by some [most villanous] [10] Knave,
Some base notorious Knave, some scurvy Fellow.
12 Oh [Heavens], that such companions thou'd'st unfold,
And put in every honest hand a whip
To lash the Rascalls naked through the world,ₓ
Even from the East to th'West. +

13 Oh fie upon [them]: + some such Squire he was
That turn'd your wit,+ the seamy-side without,
And made you to suspect me with the Moore.

[10] Ff/Q2 = 'some most villanous', Q1 and most modern texts = 'some outrageous', thus preserving the pentameter

23/ Desdemona **I prythee do {go meet him}. Something sure of State,** 3.4.140 - 154

Background: Finally Desdemona asks Iago to go to intercede with Othello on her behalf.

Style: as part of a three-handed scene

Where: close to Othello's private chambers within the garrison **To Whom:** Iago, in front of Æmilia

# of Lines: 14 **Probable Timing: 0.45 minutes**

Modern Text

23/ Desdemona

1 I prithee* do {go meet him}.
2 Something sure of Δstate,
Either from Venice, or some unhatch'd practice
Made demonstrable here* in Cyprus to him,
Hath puddled* his clear* Δspirit; and in such cases
Men's Δnatures wrangle with inferior* things,
Though great ones are [the] object.
3 'Tis even so;
For let our finger ache*, and it endues
Our other healthful* members, even to [that] sense
Of pain*.
4 Nay, we must think* men are not Δgods,
Nor of them look* for such [observances]
As fits the Δbridal*.
5 Beshrew me much, [Emilia],
I was (unhandsome Δwarrior as I am)
Arraigning his unkindness* with my soul*;
But now I find* I had subborn'd* the Δwitness*,
And he's Δindicted* falsely.

That the situation may be slowly becoming too much for Desdemona to maintain her previously displayed self-control at times of stress can be seen in that while her intellect predominates in searching for a political/military/ matters of state reason for Othello's sudden change of behaviour (5/3, F #1-3), emotion (2/6, F #4-5) and passion (4/4, F #6) swamp her once she believes she has found one.

- her determined attempt to maintain self-control might well be seen in the opening unembellished short sentence request for Iago to go to Othello (F #1)
- the immediate sense of relief when she believes that she has found an answer might be seen in the quiet of the even shorter unembellished F #3, ' 'Tis even so.'
- while the passionate blaming of her self for, as she now thinks, her faulty understanding of her own view of herself as not worthy as a 'Warrior', (4/4, F #6) is heightened by the only surround phrase in the speech
  " : But now I finde, I had suborn'd the Witnesse,/And he's Indited falsely . "
  - her self-denigration made even stronger by being the last words of the speech
- what might be somewhat unexpected is the F #4 emotion (0/3) with which she tries to justify Othello's taking out on her what she believes is a problem either from Venice or from his presence in Cyprus, as well as F #5's passion (2/3) with which she suggests it might be better if women realised first that men are not Gods (and therefore should not expect them to withstand serious distractions) and that they cannot always behave (with as much courtesy?) as they do when they are making love

First Folio

23/ Desdemona

1 I prythee do {go meet him}.
2 Something sure of State,
Either from Venice, or some unhatch'd practise
Made demonstrable heere in Cyprus,$_x$ to him,
Hath pudled his cleare Spirit :$_x$ and in such cases,$_x$
Mens Natures wrangle with inferiour things,
Though great ones are [their] object.
3 'Tis even so.
4 For let our finger ake, and it endues
Our other healthfull members, even to [a] sense
Of paine.
5 Nay, we must thinke men are not Gods,
Nor of them looke for such [observancie]
As fits the Bridall.
6 Beshrew me much, [Æmilia],
I was (unhandsome Warrior,$_x$ as I am)
Arraigning his unkindnesse with my soule :$_x$
But now I finde,$_x$ I had suborn'd the Witnesse,
And he's Indited falsely.

24/ Othello **What would you with her, Sir? /{that} you did wish, that I would make her turne :** between 4.1.250 - 263

Background: Lodovico, Desdemona's cousin, and Gratiano, her uncle, have arrived from Venice with orders for Othello's recall. Whether this is normal procedure since war with the Turks has been averted, and the situation calls for a diplomatic posting, or whether the recall is thanks to Brabantio's family's influence is up to each production to decide. What is appallingly difficult for Othello to accept is that Cassio is to take over the mission in his place. Already distracted to the extent of speaking his private thoughts in public, Othello has committed the unforgivable act of striking Desdemona in front of her relatives, and commanded her to leave - which she is about to do. Now he adds to the already tense situation by what might be described as a passive-aggressive response to her cousin's innocent request 'I do beseech your Lordship call her backe'.

Style: initially one on one address for the benefit of the small group watching

Where: the garrison at Cyprus **To Whom:** Lodovico, then Desdemona, in front of Iago, and, presumably, Desdemona's Uncle, Gratiano, together with 'attendants'

# of Lines: 14 **Probable Timing: 0.45 minutes**

Modern Text

24/ Othello

1 What would you with her, $^{\Delta}$sir?
{that} you did wish that I would make her turn*. †
2 Sir, she can turn*, and turn*; and yet go on
And turn* again*; ◊ $^{\Delta}$and she can weep*, $^{\Delta}$sir, weep*; ◊
And she's obedient, as you say, obedient; ◊
Very obedient. †
3 – Proceed you in your tears*. –
4 Concerning this, $^{\Delta}$sir, – $^{\Delta}$O* well-painted passion! –
I am commanded [here]. †
5 – Get you away;
I'll send for you anon.
6 – Sir, I obey the $^{\Delta}$mandate,
And will return* to Venice.
7 – Hence, avaunt! †
8 Cassio shall have my $^{\Delta}$place.
9 And, $^{\Delta}$sir, to night
I do entreat that we may sup together.
9 You are welcome, $^{\Delta}$sir, to Cyprus.
10 – Goats*, and $^{\Delta}$monkeys!

Considering the situation, it's amazing that Othello prevents his emotions from spilling over more than they do, especially given the very strong images and circumstances the speech puts him through. Instead, with just two exceptions (the opening and close of the speech), he seems to be exercising enormous mental control, though the seven short sentences and the twelve surround phrases testify as to how much of a strain this must be causing him.

- the mental control is only established after the opening explosion (F #1-2, 1/5 – the double-entendre attack on Desdemona, essentially pointing to her sexual activities with the repetition of 'she can turne'), but is lost again in F #10's closing expression of disgust at the sexual activities (and perhaps intelligence) of all present

- the unembellished lines throw his control into sharp relief, though the venom of what is being said and/or done is brought into more terrifying relief by being so icy calm, for some diminish Desdemona, as with the opening 'What would you with her,'; plus F #3's surround phrases and the surround phrase opening of F #4 '. And she's obedient : as you say obedient . /Very obedient : ', while others show how he takes out on Desdemona the order 'I am commanded home' with F #5's surround phrases ' ; get you away ; /Ile send for you anon . ' and F #7's incredibly short 'Hence, avaunt : '

- full intellectual control is put to purpose as he announces his acceptance of the 'Mandate' and 'returne to Venice' (6/1, F #6-9), as if he were trying to keep up public appearances – though at the last moment the final passionate outburst (F #10, 1/1) destroys whatever he has just managed to establish

First Folio

24/ Othello

1 What would you with her, Sir?
{that} you did wish, $_{x}$ that I would make her turne :
Sir, she can turne, and turne : $_{x}$ and yet go on
And turne againe.
2 And she can weepe, Sir, weepe.
3 And she's obedient : as you say+ obedient.
4 Very obedient : proceed you in your teares.
5 Concerning this+ Sir, ($_{x}$oh well-painted passion+)$_{x}$
I am commanded [home] : get you away : $_{x}$
Ile send for you anon.
6 Sir+ I obey the Mandate,
And will returne to Venice.
7 Hence, avaunt : +
Cassio shall have my Place.
8 And+ Sir, to night
I do entreat,+ that we may sup together.
9 You are welcome+ Sir+ to Cyprus.
10 Goates, and Monkeys. +

25/ Rodorigo **I do not finde/That thou deal'st justly with me.** between 4.2.173 - 203

Background: Iago's careful plans are not working out to his complete satisfaction. While Othello is in disgrace and the marriage effectively over, Rodorigo will never win Desdemona and the hated Cassio has been promoted. Now Rodorigo has finally woken up to what Iago has been doing with the money he has given him for gifts to Desdemona (in a nutshell, keeping it for himself), and is about to demand full reparation.

Style: as part of a two-handed scene

Where: unspecified, but probably somewhere in the garrison **To Whom:** Iago

# of Lines: 20 **Probable Timing: 1.00 minutes**

Modern Text

25/ Rodorigo

1 I do not find* that thou deal'st justly with me.

2 Every day thou daff'st* me with some device*, Iago, and rather, as it seems* to [me, thou] keep'st from me all convenience then suppliest me with the least ad vantage of hope. †

3 I will indeed no longer endure it; ◊ nor am I yet persuaded* to put up in peace what already I have foolishly suff'red.

4 {ψ} Your words and [△performance] are no kin together.

5 I have wasted myself* out of [ ] means*.

6 The △jewels you have had from me to deliver Desdemona would half* have corrupted a △votarist.

7 You have told me she hath receiv'd them, and return'd me expectations and comforts of sudden* respect, and [acquittance], but I find* none.

8 [By this hand, I say 'tis very] scurvy, and begin to find* myself* fopp'd* in it.

9 {ψ} I will make myself* known* to Desdemona.

10 If she will return* me my △jewels, I will give over my △suit and repent my unlawful* solicitation; ◊ if not, assure yourself* I will seek* satisfaction of you.

That there are relatively few releases (7/16 in nineteen lines) in what are very emotional circumstances suggests that the character is trying to control himself – a new stage of development for a man whose second scene was one of self-pitying half-hearted threats of committing suicide. However, the fact that he reverts to prose after just two awkward short lines of verse that open the speech suggests that the self-control may be causing him considerable strain.

- the few surround phrases point to a character who is standing up for himself for the first time in the play
  " : I will indeed no longer endure it . "
  " . [Nay] I think it is] scurvy: and begin to finde my selfe fopt in it . "

- his anger/disgust is explained in more detail via the unembellished
  "Your words and Performances are no kin together."
  " I have said nothing but what I protest intendment of doing."
  - a great indication of how determined he has now become, especially when the unembellished quality of most of the first two surround phrases listed above are added into the equation

- the fact that so much of his attack is expressed in very short sentences suggests that he has no time for social niceties and is determined not to waste words nor energy in driving his points home throughout
  "I do not finde/That thou deal'st justly with me ." (F #1)
  "I have wasted my selfe out of my meanes ." (F #5)
  "I will make my selfe knowne to Desdemona." (F #9)
  "If not, assure your selfe, I will seeke satisfaction of you ." (F #11)

- given what Rodorigo has to say, that he manages so much self-control, with virtually no releases for the first nine lines of the speech (F #1-4, 1/3), is a great tribute to his determination that, for the first time in the play, he will be the one to take charge of a conversation with Iago

- as long as he focuses on Iago's wrongdoings Rodorigo manages to stay in control, but as soon as he turns to his own concerns releases start coming thick and fast, with F #5's wasting 'my meanes' being emotional (0/2); F #6's statement that the 'Jewels' given to Iago should have 'corrupted' Desdemona is strongly factual (3/1, in just two lines); while the rebuke that, despite Iago's assurances to the contrary, he is getting no positive response from Desdemona and thinks Iago is fooling turns him emotional again (F #7-8, 0/3)

First Folio

25/ Rodorigo

1 I do not finde →
That thou deal'st justly with me.

2 Every day thou dafts me with some devise+ Iago, and rather, as it seemes to [me now], keep'st from me all convenience,$_x$ then suppliest me with the least advantage of hope: I will indeed no longer endure it.

3 Nor am I yet perswaded to put up in peace,+ what already I have foolishly suffred.

4 {ψ} Your words and [Performances] are no kin together.

5 I have wasted my selfe out of [my] meanes.

6 The Jewels you have had from me to deliver Desdemona,$_x$ would halfe have corrupted a Votarist.

7 You have told me she hath receiv'd them, and return'd me expectations and comforts of sodaine respect, and [acquaintance], but I finde none.

8 [Nay] I think it is] scurvy:$_x$ and begin to finde my selfe fopt in it.

9 {ψ} I will make my selfe knowne to Desdemona.

10 If she will returne me my Jewels, I will give over my Suit,$_x$ and repent my unlawfull solicitation.

11 If not, assure your selfe,$_x$ I will seeke satisfaction of you.

{ctd. over}

11 I {have}saidnothing but what I protest intendment of doing.

• then comes his only passionate moment in the speech, as he states that he will confront Desdemona and, if she will return his jewels, he will apologise for and cease his 'unlawfull solicitation' (F #9-10, 3/4)

• and his facing down of Iago concludes first with an emotional threat that if he doesn't get his jewels back 'I will seeke satisfaction of you' (F #11, 0/2) then with F #12's final icy quiet, unembellished, assurance that he will do exactly as he has promised

12 I {have}said nothing but what I protest intendment of doing.

26/ Æmilia **Marry, I would not doe such a thing for a joynt Ring,** between 4.3.72 - 103

Background: In the only 'women-alone' scene in the play, there has been a fairly frank discussion about sexuality. Having established that there are women who 'do abuse their husbands/In such grosse kinde', an emotionally disturbed Desdemona (haunted by thoughts of death, both her own and of a love-sick maid who once worked for her) has twice asked Æmilia 'Would'st thou do such a deed for al the world'. The following is Æmilia's reply.

Style: as part of a two handed scene

Where: Desdemona's bed-chamber **To Whom:** Desdemona

# of Lines: 27 **Probable Timing: 1.30 minutes**

Modern Text

26/ Æmilia

1 Marry, I would not do* such a thing for a joint*
Δring, [or] for measures of Δlawn*, nor for Δgowns*, [or [11]
Δpetticoats, nor Δcaps, nor any [such] Δexhibition; ◊ but for
[ ] the whole world - [ud's pity], who would not make
her husband a Δcuckold to make him a Δmonarch?

2 I should venture Δpurgatory for't.

3 {ψ} {T}he wrong is but a wrong i'th'world;
and having the world for your labor*, 'tis a wrong in
your own* world, and you might quickly make it right.

4 But I do think* it is their Δhusbands' faults
If Δwives do fall. †

5 Say, that they slack* their duties,
And pour* our Δtreasures into foreign* laps;
Or else break* out in peevish Δjealousies,
Throwing restraint upon us; Δor say they strike us,
Or scant our former having in despite*:
Why, we have galls*; and though we have some Δgrace,

Surprisingly, despite Iago's on-stage disparaging treatment of Æmilia both publicly (the verbal put-down about a scolding tongue in front of all on their arrival at Cyprus) and privately (the rather nasty sexual dig before she gives him the handkerchief that the 'thing' she has for him is a 'common thing'), the brevity with which she utters the very strong images of 'I should venture Purgatory for't.' (i.e that she would commit adultery if it would help Iago become 'a Monarch') seems to suggest that she still loves him – which makes even more surprising the (just realised?) speech-ending statement of equality for wives if husbands 'fail'.

• whether joking or no, in asserting that she would not commit adultery for 'any petty exhibition', Æmilia starts passionately (F #1, 5/4), though the notion of being rewarded for infidelity with the whole world is examined far more factually (F #2, 2/0), triply enhanced by the opening monosyllabic unembellished surround phrase ' . But for all the whole world : '

• and the thought of the world as reward starts the next sentence equally provocatively, suggesting that ' . The wrong is but a wrong 'i'th'world ; ' which, she goes on to explain, will be her own world if the adultery makes her husband king, the whole being expressed emotionally (F #4, 0/2)

First Folio

26/ Æmilia

1 Marry, I would not doe such a thing for a joynt
Ring, [nor] for measures of Lawne, nor for Gownes, [ ]
Petticoats, nor Caps, nor any [petty] exhibition.

2 But for
[all] the whole world : x [why], who would not make
her husband a Cuckold, x to make him a Monarch?

3 I should venture Purgatory for't.

4 {ψ} {T}he wrong is but a wrong i'th'world;
and having the world for your labour, 'tis a wrong in
your owne world, and you might quickly make it right.

5 But I do thinke it is their Husbands faults
If Wives do fall: (xSay, that they slacke their duties,
And powre our Treasures into forraigne laps;
Or else breake out in peevish Jealousies,
Throwing restraint upon us : x Or say they strike us,
Or scant our former having in despight)+
Why+ we have galles : x and though we have some Grace,

[11] Q1 and most modern texts = 'or', Ff/Q2 omit the word

Yet have we some ^Δrevenge.
6 Let ^Δhusbands know
Their wives have sense like them; ^Δthey see, and smell,
And have their ^Δpalates both for sweet and sour*,
As ^Δhusbands have.
7 What is it that they do
When they change us for others?
8 Is it ^Δsport?
9 I think* it is. †
10 And doth ^Δaffection breed it?
11 I think* it doth.
12 Is't ^Δfrailty that thus errs*?
13 It is so too.
14 And have not we ^Δaffections,
Desires for ^Δsport, and ^Δfrailty, as men have?
15 Then let them use us well; else let them know,
The ills* we do, their ills* instruct us so.

• the move into exploring the relationship between husbands and wives seems to be more serious, for the speech now becomes verse, and F #5's initial six line supposition, intensified by opening with the very strongly worded surround phrases 'But I do thinke it is their Husbands faults/If Wives do fall : (Say, that they slacke their duties,/And powre our Treasures into forraigne laps ; ' , is passionate (6/6) – whether this is just a general empathy with all wronged wives or stems from her own experiences is up to each actor to explore . . .

• . . . however, F #5's final surround phrase ': and though we have some Grace,/Yet have we some Revenge . '; plus that which opens F #6, 'Let Husbands know,/Their wives have sense like them : '; in addition to the intellectual quality of them both and the rest of F #6 (6/1 overall) tends to suggest that what triggers all this might well be highly personal

• then the final challenge to 'Husbands' becomes a mixture of passion in summing what men do (the two and half lines of F #8-11, 3/3), intellect in suggesting that women can react exactly the same way (F #13 3/0), and pure emotion in the final threat that women will follow men's example (0/2, F #14's last line)

• that this may well be the first time Æmilia has thought on this (or at least the first time she has voiced it) might be seen in F #7's unembellished question that triggers this explosion 'What is it that they do,/When they change us for others?' and in the equally quiet realisation of F #12 that men's 'Frailty' is responsible 'It is so too,', the realisation heightened by being set as such a short and monosyllabic sentence

Yet have we some Revenge.
6 Let Husbands know,$_x$
Their wives have sense like them :$_x$ They see, and smell,
And have their Palats both for sweet,$_x$ and sowre,
As Husbands have.
7 What is it that they do,$_x$
When they change us for others?
8 Is it Sport?
9 I thinke it is : and doth Affection breed it?
10 I thinke it doth.
11 Is't Frailty that thus erres?
12 It is so too.
13 And have not we Affections? $_x$
Desires for Sport ?$_x$ and Frailty, as men have?
14-* Then let them use us well :$_x$ else let them know,
The illes we do, their illes instruct us so.

27/ Othello **It is the Cause, it is the Cause (my Soule)** 5.2.1 - 22

Background: Othello has bidden Desdemona to go to bed, to dismiss Æmilia, and to wait alone for him to join her (a most unusual act, since a wife's companion normally keeps her company until the husband's return). Believing Cassio to be dead, Othello has now come to commit the final act, the killing of Desdemona - though whether he regards it as murder or religious sacrifice is open to question, for when she wakes he gives her time to pray and tells her 'I would not kill thy unprepared Spirit,/ . . . I would not kill thy Soule'. As he enters he discovers Desdemona asleep in the candlelight, which triggers the following.

Style: solo

Where: Desdemona's bed-chamber **To Whom:** to the sleeping Desdemona, himself, and the audience

# of Lines: 22 **Probable Timing: 1.10 minutes**

Modern Text

27/ Othello

1 It is the Δcause, it is the Δcause, my Δsoul*;
Let me not name it to you, you chaste Δstars*,
It is the Δcause.
2 Yet I'll not shed her blood,
Nor scar* that whiter skin of hers, [than] Δsnow,
And smooth as Δmonumental [Δalabaster] . †
3 Yet she must die*, else she'll* betray more men . †
4 Put out the Δlight, and then put out the Δlight :
If I quench thee, thou flaming Δminister,
I can again* thy former light restore,
Should I repent me; ◊ But once put out [thine] Δlight,
Thou [cunning] Δpattern* of excelling Δnature,
I know not where is that [Promethean] heat*
That can thy Δlight re-Δlume.
5 When I have pluck'd [the] Δrose,
I cannot give it vital* growth again*,
It [must needs] wither.
6 I'll smell thee on the Δtree ! [12]
8 [A]* Δbalmy breath, that dost almost persuade*
Justice to break* her Δsword !
9 One more, one more.† [13]
10 Be thus when thou art dead, and I will kill thee,
And love thee after.
11 [Once] more, and [this] the last.

- the unembellished lines seem to point to Othello's determination to make the act a religious murder performed with dignity out of love, for he will mutilate her
  " Yet Ile not shed her blood," (F #2)
  and yet still needs to kiss her, the importance of the following doubly weighted by being both monosyllabic and set as two surround phrases and one short sentence
  "One more, one more : /Be thus when thou art dead, and I will kill thee,/And
  love thee after. One more, and that's the last." (F #7-8)
  and then realises that his
  "sorrow's heavenly,/It strikes, where it doth love." (F #10)

- the struggle between love and perceived (murderous) duty is underscored by the few surround phrases, as when Othello follows up his description of her skin as 'Monumentall Alablaster' with the cold (to him) logic of
  " : Yet she must dye, else shee'l betray more men : "
  which is immediately followed by the recognition of the brightness she has brought to him (one probable interpretation of the second setting of 'Light')
  " : Put out the Light, and then put out the Light : "
  the importance of more than one kiss immediately shattered by the thought of her death, the already quoted unembellished F #7

- though Othello seems to start in strong intellectual control of both self and situation (F #1, 5/2), this is undermined by the ubalanced logic he advances - telling heaven any blame for his actions stems from the (beauty of?) the sleeping Desdemona

- then his control begins to disappear, the onrushed F #2 (in part split into three by most modern texts) jamming together the disparate thoughts that he won't mutilate her with her having to die, but despite this loss of clarity he manages to cling on to his intellect as emotions begin to rise (F #2, 6/5)

- then he becomes even more philosophical, exploring the troubling thought that if he does kill her, he will not be able to rekindle her 'light' even more intellectually (F #3, 6/2) – though, as he changes imagery to compare taking her

First Folio

27/ Othello

1 It is the Cause, it is the Cause (ₓmy Souleₓ)⁺
Let me not name it to you, you chaste Starres,
It is the Cause.
2 Yet Ile not shed her blood,
Nor scarre that whiter skin of hers, [then] Snow,
And smooth as Monumentall [Alablaster] :
Yet she must dye, else shee'l betray more men :
Put out the Light, and then put out the Light :
If I quench thee, thou flaming Minister,
I can againe thy former light restore,
Should I repent me.
3 But once put out [thy] Light,
Thou [cunning'st] Patterne of excelling Nature,
I know not where is that [Promethaen] heate
That can thy Light re-Lume. →
4 When I have pluck'd [thy] Rose,
I cannot give it vitall growth againe,
It [needs must] wither.
5 Ile smell thee on the Tree. ⁺
6 [Oh] Balmy breath, that dost almost perswade
Justice to breake her Sword. ⁺
7 One more, one more:
Be thus when thou art dead, and I will kill thee,
And love thee after.
8 [One] more, and [that's] the last.

---

[12] most modern texts add Q2's stage direction that he kisses her

[13] Q1/some modern texts = 'Justice her selfe to breake her sword once more', Ff = 'Justice to breake her Sword. One more, one more'

12 So sweet was ne'er so fatal*.
13 I must weep*,
But they are cruel* Δtears*. †
14 This sorrow's heavenly,
It strikes where it doth love.

life to the plucking of 'thy Rose', he becomes emotional (F #4, 1/2)

- the sensual imagery of Desdemona as a rose moves him to the passionate idea/exploration of smelling her breath as he kisses her (F #5-6, 3/3) – but after the first kisses he becomes very quiet, which he maintains as he kisses her twice more, the two and a half unembellished lines suggesting that he doesn't wish to wake her and/or that he has been struck almost dumb by the experience

- and the (sweetness of? the finality of?) the kisses moves him to tears as he emotionally ends the speech (F #9-10, 1/4)

9 So sweet,x was ne're so fatall.
10 I must weepe,
But they are cruell Teares: This sorrow's heavenly,
It strikes,x where it doth love.

28/ Æmilia **Oh Heaven! oh heavenly Powres! (Modern Text, 'O God! 'O heavenly God!)** between 5.2.118 - 234

Background: Othello has offered the evidence that he believes justifies his killing Desdemona, viz. 'Iago knows/That she with Cassio hath the Act of shame/A thousand times committed' and that 'she did gratifie his amorous workes/With that Recognizance and pledge of Love/Which I first gave her: I saw it in his hand:/It was a Handkerchiefe, an Antique Token/My Father gave my Mother'. To her horror, Æmilia realises the truth, which triggers the following (which results in Iago stabbing her to death).

Style: as part of a five-handed scene, to the whole group

Where: Desdemona's bed-chamber **To Whom:** Montano, Gratiano, Iago, in front of the body of Desdemona

# of Lines: 16 **Probable Timing: 0.50 minutes**

Modern Text

28/ Æmilia

1 O* [God]! ΔO* heavenly [God]!
2 'Twill out, 'twill out!
3 I peace?
4 [I'll be in speaking*, liberall* as the Δair];
Let Δheaven and Δmen and Δdevils*, let them all,
All, all, cry* shame against me, yet I'll speak*.
5 O* thou dull Moor*,
That Δhandkerchief* thou speak'st [on]
I found by Δfortune, and did give my Δhusband;
For often, with a solemn* earnestness*
(More [than] indeed belong'd to such a Δtrifle),
He begg'd of me, to steal't*.
6 She [gave] it Cassio?
7 No, alas, I found it,
And I did giv't my Δhusband.
8 By Δheaven, I do not {lie}, I do not, Δgentlemen. †
9 O* murd'rous Δcoxcomb*, what should such a Δfool*
Do with so good a [woman]?

The enormity of the scales having dropped from Æmilia's eyes is stressed not only by the passionate opening (6/6, F #1-4), nor the strong orthography, viz.

a/ the three short sentences that open the speech (F #1-3)
b/ F #1 set as two surround phrases created by the rare (for original Elizabethan/early Jacobean texts) exclamation marks
c/ the emotional (semicoloned) surround phrase that opens F #4
". No, I will speake as liberall as the North ;"
but also by the incredible monosyllabic short sentences plus unembellished calmness (F #2, 0/0) with which she realises that it is time for her to speak out, no matter what
"'Twill out, 'twill out. I peace?"

- after the opening passionate oath and determination to speak 'as liberall as the North', her first direct address to Othello about the 'Handkerchiefe' and her discovering it and giving it to Iago is equally passionate (4/3, F #5's first two and a half lines)

- but infroming those present that Iago had 'begg'd of me, to steale it' is emotional (1/3, F#5's last two and half lines), as if she were just realising the significance of what she has said

- the repetition that she found it and gave it to Iago (F #6-7) and the assertion she is not lying (F #8's first line) are totally intellectual (4/0) – perhaps suggesting that there is a stunned disbelief from all the men present at the revelation/accusation of what she has just said

- finally, in turning her attention back to Othello, her verbal onslaught becomes passionate once more (2/3, F #8's last line and a half)

First Folio

28/ Æmilia

1 Oh [Heaven]! oh heavenly [Powres]!
2 'Twill out, 'twill out. +
3 I peace?
4 [No, I will speake as liberall as the North]; x
Let Heaven,x and Men,x and Divels, let them all,
All, all, crie shame against me, yet Ile speake.
5 Oh thou dull Moore,
That Handkerchiefe thou speak'st [of]
I found by Fortune, and did give my Husband: x
For often, with a solemne earnestnesse,x
(More [then] indeed belong'd to such a Trifle)+
He begg'd of me, to steale't.
6 She [give] it Cassio?
7 No, alas+ I found it,
And I did giv't my Husband.
8 By Heaven+ I do not {lie}, I do not+ Gentlemen:
Oh murd'rous Coxcombe, what should such a Foole
Do with so good a [wife]?

29/ Othello **Soft you ; a word or two before you goe :** 5.2.338 - 356

Background: Othello's final speech before taking his own life.

Style: small group address

Where: Desdemona's bed-chamber **To Whom:** Lodovico, Cassio, Montano, Gratiano, Iago with arresting Officers, in front of the bodies of Desdemona and Æmilia

# of Lines: 20 **Probable Timing: 1.00 minutes**

Modern Text

29/ Othello

1 Soft you ; a word or two before you go*. †
2 I have done the Δstate some service, and they know't -
No more of that.
3 I pray you in your Δletters,
When you shall these unlucky$_{*}$ deeds relate,
Speak* of [them as they are]; ◊ nothing extenuate,
Nor set down* ought in malice.
4 Then must you speak*,
Of one that lov'd not wisely but too well ;
Of one not easily Δjealous*, but being wrought,
Perplexed in the extreme*; Δof one, whose hand
(Like the base [Indian]) threw a Δpearl* away
Richer [than] all his Δtribe ; Δof one whose subdu'd Δeyes,
Albeit unused to the melting mood*,
Drops tears* as fast as the Arabian Δtrees
Their Δ[medicinal] gum*.
5 Set you down* this;
And say besides, that in Aleppo once,
Where a malignant and a Δturban'd° ΔTurk*
Beat* a Venetian and traduc'd the Δstate,
I took* by th'throat the circumcised Δdog*,
And smote* him - thus.

Despite the apparent calm with which Othello asks for the assembled worthies to hear him (1/1, F #1), the fact that F #1 is composed of four surround phrases, the opening two linked by the only emotional semicolon of the speech, suggests that he has to work very hard to maintain the quiet dignity with which he wants his final words to be uttered and received.

- the other moments of strain appear just before he begins to tell them how they should 'Speake of me, as I am' (the end of F #2), with F setting what most modern texts regard as a completely ungrammatical one line F #3, which in turn leads to two short lines (seven/four syllables) ending F #3 and starting F #4, all of which suggests that Othello is forced to break conventional grammatical/rhetorical niceties (leading to tiny pauses) in his struggle to maintain his longed for self control: most modern texts combine F #2-3 as mt. #3, and join F's two short lines (ending F #3 and opening F #4) together as shown

- that Othello is slightly emotional throughout the opening (2/4, the first six and half lines) is to be expected, and the fact that, given the circumstances, there is relatively little release is a great tribute to his self-control (F #1 to the first one and half lines of F #4), which continues up to and including the description of how he would like to be remembered, the unembellished
 "Of one that lov'd not wisely, but too well"

- and as he begins to list the weaknesses through which he fell, his passion finally springs free (16/12 the last eleven and a half lines), the points he wants clearly understood first underscored by the surround phrases
 ". Then must you speake,/Of one that lov'd not wisely, but too well : /Of one, not easily Jealious, but being wrought,/Perplexed in the extreame : "

and then by the extra breath-thoughts (marked , $_{x}$) that suddenly appear, the two in F #4 ensuring that the tiniest of important details ('not easily Jealious' 'whose subdu'd Eyes') are not overlooked and the two in F #5 perhaps suggesting he were readying himself for the ritual act of suicide he is about commit

First Folio

29/ Othello

1 Soft you ; a word or two before you goe :
I have done the State some service, and they know't : $_{x}$
No more of that.
2 I pray you in your Letters,
When you shall these unluckie deeds relate,
Speake of [me, as I am].
3 Nothing extenuate,
Nor set downe ought in malice.
4 Then must you speake,
Of one that lov'd not wisely,$_{x}$ but too well : $_{x}$
Of one,$_{x}$ not easily Jealious, but being wrought,
Perplexed in the extreame : $_{x}$ Of one, whose hand
(Like the base [Judean]) threw a Pearle away
Richer [then] all his Tribe : Of one,$_{x}$ whose subdu'd Eyes,
Albeit un-used to the melting moode,
Drops teares as fast as the Arabian Trees
Their [Medicinable] gumme.
5 Set you downe this : $_{x}$
And say besides, that in Aleppo once,
Where a malignant,$_{x}$ and a Turbond-Turke
Beate a Venetian,$_{x}$ and traduc'd the State,
I tooke by th'throat the circumcised Dogge,
And smoate him, thus.

SPEECHES IN ORDER

SPEECHES IN ORDER		TIME	PAGE
MACBETH			
# 1: The Political Background			
1/ Captaine	Doubtfull it stood,/As two spent Swimmers, . . .	1.45	229
#'s 2 - 5: The Temptation Of Macbeth			
2/ Macbeth	Two Truths are told	1.00	230
3/ Lady	*They met me in the day of successe : and I have*	0.40	232
4/ Lady	Glamys thou art, and Cawdor, and shalt be	0.55	233
5/ Lady	The Raven himselfe is hoarse,	1.10	234
#'s 6 - 18: The Assassination, Dream & Fact, And Its Effects			
6/ King (or Banquo)	This Castle hath a pleasant seat,	0.35	235
7/ Macbeth	If it were done, when 'tis done, then 'twer well,	1.30	236
8/ Lady	Was the hope drunke,/Wherein you drest your selfe?	0.40	237
9/ Lady	What Beast was't/That made you breake this	1.15	238
10/ Macbeth	Goe bid thy Mistresse, when my drinke is ready,	1.40	239
11/ Lady	That which hath made thë drunk, hath made me bold:	0.45	241
12/ Lady	My Hands are of your colour: but I shame . . .	0.35	242
13/ Porter	Here's a knocking indeede: if a man were	1.00	243
14/ Porter	Drinke, Sir, is a great provoker of three things.	0.35	244
15/ Lenox	The Night ha's been unruly:	0.35	245
16/ Macduff	O horror, horror, horror,	0.50	246
17/ Old Man	Threescore and ten I can remember well,	1.00	247
18/ Banquo	Thou hast it now, King, Cawdor, Glamis, all,	0.35	248
#'s 19 - 23: Macbeth Steps In Too Far			
19/ Macbeth	Bring them before us./To be thus, is nothing, . . .	1.15	249
20/ Macbeth	I, in the Catalogue ye goe for men,	0.55	250
21/ Macbeth	We have scorch'd the Snake, not kill'd it:	0.50	251
22/ Lenox	My former Speeches,/Have but hit your Thoughts	1.15	252
23/ Malcome	What I beleeve, Ile waile;/What know, beleeve; . . .	1.10	254
#'s 24 - 27: The Bloody Finale			
24/ Rosse	I have words/That would be howl'd out	0.40	255
25/ Macduff	All my pretty ones?/Did you say All?	0.55	256
26/ Lady	Yet heere's a spot.	0.55	257
27/ Macbeth	She should have dy'de heereafter;	0.40	258

SPEECHES BY GENDER

		Speech #(s)
SPEECHES FOR WOMEN (8)		
Lady Macbeth	**Traditional & Today:** young woman and older	#3, #4, #5, #8, #9, #11, #12, #26
SPEECHES FOR EITHER GENDER (5)		
Captaine	**Traditional:** military male, any age **Today:** with the above proviso, any gender, any age	#1
Lenox	**Traditional:** older male **Today:** any age, any gender	#15, #22
Rosse	**Traditional:** older male **Today:** any age, any gender	#24
Old Man	**Traditional:** old male **Today:** older person, any gender	#17
SPEECHES FOR MEN (15)		
Macbeth	**Traditional & Today:** younger- middle-aged male and older	#2, #7, #10, #19, #20, #21, #27
King	**Traditional & Today:** older male (father of two young adult sons)	#6
Porter	**Traditional & Today:** male, any age	#13, #14
Macduff	**Traditional & Today:** younger middle-aged male and older	#16, #25
Banquo	**Traditional & Today:** younger middle-aged male and older	#6, #18
Malcome	**Traditional & Today:** a young man	#23

MACBETH

1: The Political Background

1/ Captaine **Doubtfull it stood,/As two spent Swimmers, that doe cling together,** between 1.2.7 - 42

Background: The injured Captain (called the 'Serjeant' by Malcome, and named as such in some modern texts) reports on the most recent battle in the civil war. One note, the Scottish rebels are being aided by foreign powers, hence the reference to 'Westerne Isles' (of Scotland) and 'the Norweyan Lord'.

Style: one on one address for the benefit of the group as a whole

Where: close to the battlefield **To Whom:** King Duncan, with his sons Malcome and Donalbaine, Lenox, and 'attendants'

# of Lines: 35 **Probable Timing: 1.45 minutes**

Modern Text

1/ Captaine

1 Doubtful* it stood,
As two spent Δswimmers that do* cling together
And choke* their Δart. †
2 The merciless* Macdonwald
(Worthy$_*$ to be a Δrebel*, for to that
The multiplying Δvillainies$_*$ of Δnature
Do* swarm* upon him) from the Western* Isles
Of Δkerns* and [Δgallowglasses] is supplied*,
And Fortune, on his damned [Δquarrel] smiling,
Show'd* like a Δrebel's* Δwhore. †
3 But all's too weak*;
For brave Macbeth (well he* deserves that Δname),
Disdaining* Fortune, with his brandish'd Δsteel*,
Which smok'd* with bloody execution,
(Like Valor's* Δminion)
Carv'd out his passage till he* fac'd the Δslave;
Which nev'r shook* hands, nor bad farewell$_*$ to him,
Till he unseam'd him from the Δnave toth'Δchops,
And fix'd his Δhead upon our Δbattlements.
4 As whence the Δsun* 'gins his reflection
Shipwracking Δstorms* and direful* Δthunders [break],
So from that Δspring whence comfort seem'd to come
Discomfort swells. †
5 Mark*, King of Scotland, mark*!
No sooner Δjustice had, with Δvalor* arm'd,
Compell'd these skipping Δkerns* to trust their heels*,
But the Norweyan Lord, surveying vantage,
With furbish'd Δarms* and new supplies* of men,
Began a fresh assault.

At times F's orthography makes the Captaine's pain very evident, as with

a/ at least eight extra breath-thoughts (marked , $_x$ and seen first in the second line of the speech and clustering at the opening of F #2), the tiny extra pauses suggesting that he needs to counteract the pain before continuing

b/ at the opening and closing of F #3, where the shaded text shows where F has set the Captaine five short lines, the pauses all pointing to moments of pain that threaten to swamp him as he struggles to finish his story: most modern editions reduce the five irregular lines to three of almost pure pentameter, thus reducing the last moments of his bravery

There is also much to suggest that the information is coming out in streams of consciousness rather than as a preplanned report, viz.

a/ the onrush (modern texts splitting F #1 and #3 into three and F #2 in two)

b/ the lack of unembellished lines

c/ the very few surround phrases

d/ the enormous number of releases throughout (50/34)

• the three surround phrases seem to signify an extra urgency where he needs even more energy to get past the pain, first when he describes the overall situation ' : but all's too weake : ' ; then the bravery of Macbeth and Banquo who regarded the new wave of enemy forces without fear ' : Or the Hare, the Lyon ; '; and finally his own injuries ' : but I am faint,/My Gashes cry for helpe.'

• the speech is essentially passionate throughout

• there is no single moment when emotion dominates the proceedings

• the only time intellect is paramount comes at the end of F #1 where the Captaine describes how Macbeth beheaded the rebel Macdonwald and 'fix'd his Head upon our Battlements'
(4/0, the last two and half lines of F #1)

First Folio

1/ Captaine

1 Doubtfull it stood,
As two spent Swimmers,$_x$ that doe cling together,$_x$
And choake their Art: The mercilesse Macdonwald
(Worthie to be a Rebell, for to that
The multiplying Villanies of Nature
Doe swarme upon him) from the Westerne Isles
Of Kernes and [Gallowgrosses] is supply'd,
And Fortune+ on his damned [Quarry] smiling,
Shew'd like a Rebells Whore: but all's too weake: $_x$
For brave Macbeth (well hee deserves that Name)+
Disdayning Fortune, with his brandisht Steele,
Which smoak'd with bloody execution+
(Like Valours Minion) carv'd out his passage,$_x$
Till hee fac'd the Slave: $_x$
Which nev'r shooke hands, nor bad farwell to him,
Till he unseam'd him from the Nave toth'Chops,
And fix'd his Head upon our Battlements.
2 As whence the Sunne 'gins his reflection,$_x$
Shipwracking Stormes,$_x$ and direfull Thunders [ ] : $_x$
So from that Spring,$_x$ whence comfort seem'd to come,$_x$
Discomfort swells: Marke+ King of Scotland, marke,+
No sooner Justice had, with Valour arm'd,
Compell'd these skipping Kernes to trust their heeles,
But the Norweyan Lord, surveying vantage,
With furbusht Armes,$_x$ and new supplyes of men,
Began a fresh assault.

{ctd. over}

6 {ψ} {This d}ismay'd
Our △captains*, Macbeth and [Banquo]? {,}
{ψ} As △sparrows*, △eagles; or the △hare, the △lion*.†

7 If I say sooth, I must report they were
As △cannons overcharg'd with double △cracks,
So they doubly redoubled strokes* upon the △foe. †

8 Except they meant to bathe in reeking △wounds,
Or memorize another Golgotha,
I cannot tell -
But I am faint, my △gashes cry for help*.

3 {ψ} {This d}ismay'd our Captaines, Macbeth and
[Banquoh?] {,} {ψ} as Sparrowes, Eagles;
Or the Hare, the Lyon:
If I say sooth, I must report they were
As Cannons over-charg'd with double Cracks,
So they doubly redoubled stroakes upon the Foe:
Except they meant to bathe in reeking Wounds,
Or memorize another Golgotha,
I cannot tell: ₓ but I am faint,
My Gashes cry for helpe.

#'s 2 - 5: The Temptation Of Macbeth

2/ Macbeth **Two Truths are told, /As happy Prologues to the swelling Act** between 1.3.127 - 147

Background: Macbeth and Banquo have been greeted by the three 'weyard Sisters' (more commonly referred to as 'witches'). While they prophesied to Banquo 'Thou shalt get Kings, though thou be none', Macbeth has been promised swifter and higher glories - that in addition to his current holding of the thaneship of Glamis he will become 'thane of Cawdor' and, better still, he 'shalt be King hereafter'. In theory, neither of these should happen, but news comes from the King that Macbeth, thanks to his bravery in battle, is indeed to add Cawdor to his holdings, the current Thane being executed for treason. This coming so soon after the prophecy starts Macbeth wondering about the greater prize.

Style: aside, away from a small group not attempting to overhear him

Where: a moor **To Whom:** direct audience address, and self

# of Lines: 20 **Probable Timing: 1.00 minutes**

Modern Text

2/ Macbeth

1 Two △truths are told,
As happy △prologues to the swelling △act
Of the △imperial * theme*.
2 - I thank* you, △gentlemen. † [1]
3 This supernatural* soliciting*
Cannot be ill; cannot be good.
4 If ill?
Why hath it given me earnest of success*,
Commencing in a △truth?
5 I am Thane of Cawdor.

Macbeth's steadfastness is revealed by the strong intellectual strands running throughout the speech – however, F's orthography points to moments where this steadfastness is severely challenged.

- the realisation that the first of the Weyward Sisters' prophecies is coming true starts intellectually (F #1, 5/2) then acknowledging the news-bearers and separating himself from them is done via a quick, passionate surround phrase (F #2's first phrase, 1/1)
- then his mind and emotions kick into overdrive as he begins to closely examine the prophecies' further implications, with the emotional remainder of F #2-3 (1/3) underscored by the drive of five successive surround phrases

First Folio

2/ Macbeth

1 Two Truths are told,
As happy Prologues to the swelling Act
Of the Imperiall Theame.
2 I thanke you⁺ Gentlemen:
This supernaturall solliciting
Cannot be ill; cannot be good.
3 If ill? why hath it given me earnest of successe,
Commencing in a Truth?
4 I am Thane of Cawdor.

[1] all modern texts indicate this is the only line said to those on-stage in an otherwise series of asides

6 If good, why do* I yield* to that suggestion,
Whose horrid Δimage doth unfix* my Δ[hair],
And make my seated Δheart knock at my Δribs*,
Against the use of Δnature?
7 Present Δfears*
Are less* [than] horrible Δimaginings:
My Δthought, whose Δ[murder] yet is but fantastical*,
Shakes so my single state of Δman, that Δfunction
Is smother'd in surmise, Δand nothing is
But what is not.
8 If Δchance will have me Δking, Δwhy Δchance may Δcrown*me
Without my stir*.
9 Come what come may,
Time and the Δhour* runs through the roughest Δday.

" . I thanke you Gentlemen : /This supernaturall solliciting/Cannot be
ill ; cannot be good . /If ill ? why hath it given me earnest of successe, /Commencing in a Truth ? "
- the dilemma of 'ill . . . good' marked by being linked with the only emotional semicolon in the speech

• to further mark this dilemma, F's irregular setting between F #2-3 (the shaded lines, eight/twelve or thirteen syllables) allows Macbeth a moment of reflection (the pause offered by the short line) before bursting into the exploration of how the news might not be 'ill': most modern texts remove these potential moments by restructuring the text to two almost normal lines, as shown

• he momentarily regains intellectual control as he confirms the second step of the prophecy 'I am Thane of Cawdor.' (F #4's short sentence, 2/0), but the fear that the prophecy is 'good' is passionate (F #5, 5/4)

• and it seems that he is resolved to withstand further temptation, for his understanding that even the thought of murder 'Shakes so my single state of Man' (F #6) and that 'Chance may Crowne me,/Without my stirre.' (F #7) is strongly intellectual (10/5) – yet this doesn't come without a struggle, for F's five short lines (the shaded passage, 8/9/8/6/6 syllables) point to Macbeth's self-absorbed difficulties in dealing with such enormities, and the extra breath-thoughts that suddenly appear (marked ,$_x$) point to the care with which he tries to establish his steadfastness

• the final couplet decision to let 'Time' decide the outcome points to his intellectual strength (2/1) being challenged a little emotionally

5 If good?$_x$ why doe I yeeld to that suggestion,
Whose horrid Image doth unfixe my [Heire],
And make my seated Heart knock at my Ribbes,
Against the use of Nature?
6 Present Feares
Are lesse [then] horrible Imaginings:
My Thought, whose [Murther] yet is but fantasticall,
Shakes so my single state of Man,
That Function is smother'd in surmise,
And nothing is,$_x$ but what is not.
7 If Chance will have me King,
Why Chance may Crowne me, $_x$
Without my stirre.
8 Come what come may,
Time,$_x$ and the Houre,$_x$ runs through the roughest Day.

3/ Lady ***They met me in the day of successe : and I have*** 1.5.1 - 14
4/ Lady **Glamys thou art, and Cawdor, and shalt be** 1.5.15 - 30
5/ Lady **The Raven himselfe is hoarse,** 1.5.42 - 58

Background: These are Lady Macbeth's (referred to in the first folio simply as 'Lady') first series of speeches in the play, all triggered by a letter from her husband telling her of the strange greetings and prophecies, including that of becoming King. Speech #3 deals with the letter itself (the italics being a conventional First Folio method of setting written documents); in speech #4 she unflinchingly faces what weaknesses must be overcome if Macbeth is to become king; in speech #5, following the news that both Macbeth and the current king, Duncan, will arrive at the castle that same day, she appeals to the darker supernatural powers for help. [2]

Style: all solo

Where: somewhere in the castle at Inverness, possibly her private chambers **To Whom:** self

Speech 3: # of Lines: 12 **Probable Timing: 0.40 minutes**
Speech 4: # of Lines: 17 **Probable Timing: 0.55 minutes**
Speech 5: # of Lines: 22 **Probable Timing: 1.10 minutes**

Modern Text

3/ Lady

1 "They met me in the day of success*; and I have
learn'd by the perfect'st report, they have more in them, [than]
mortal* knowledge .
2 When I burnt in desire to question them further,
they made themselves Δair*, into which they vanish'd .
3 Whiles I stood rapt in the wonder of it, came Δmissives from
the King, who all-hail'd me 'Thane of Cawdor,' by which Δ
title, before, these [weird*] Δsisters saluted me, and referr'd
me to the coming* on of time, with 'Hail*, King that shalt be!'
4 This
have I thought good to deliver thee, my dearest Δpartner of
Δgreatness*, that thou mightst not lose* the dues of
rejoicing* by being ignorant of what Δgreatness* is promis'd
thee .
5 Lay it to thy heart, and farewell ."

Her immediate response to the various stages of information the letter presents her suggests that she is reading it for the first time or is at last alone where she can read it aloud and react to it for the first time - and though the overall speech seems passionate (10/10 overall), each piece of news seems to bring a different stylistic response.

- given the circumstances, it's hardly surprising that she starts emotionally (F #1, 0/2), yet - a wonderful sign of her strength of mind throughout - she opens carefully, with two of the first four phrases being unembellished
  "and I have learn'd by the perfect'st report, they have more in them,"
  and the surround phrase that opens the reading of the letter
  ' . They met me in the day of successe ; '
  suggesting great concentration

- and she remains calm with the information that the Weyward Sisters just disappeared, for with the exception of the 'Ayre' they vanished into, this is also unembellished (F #2, 1/1)

- then her mind becomes very active as she processes how 'Missives from the King' confirmed the 'Thane of Cawdor' (6/0, F #3's first three lines) – at least until she reads the prophecy that Macbeth will be 'King', at which point the first emotion kicks in (1/2, F #3's last line)

- and so comes passion (3/4, F #4) as she reads Macbeth's confirmation that she is now and will in the future be 'my dearest Partner of Greatnesse'

- that the last sentence is unembellished is surprising, perhaps suggesting that the news and/or her immediate reaction to it has almost taken her breath away

First Folio

3/ Lady

1 *They met me in the day of successe:* [x] *and I have*
learn'd by the perfect'st report, they have more in them, [then]
mortall knowledge.
2 *When I burnt in desire to question them*
further, they made themselves Ayre, into which they vanish'd.
3 *Whiles I stood rapt in the wonder of it, came Missives from*
the King, who all hail'd me Thane of Cawdor, by which Title [x]
before, these [weyward] Sisters saluted me, and referr'd me to
the comming on of time, with haile[+] *King that shalt be* . [+]
4 *This*
have I thought good to deliver thee ([x]*my dearest Partner of*
Greatnesse[x]*) that thou might'st not loose the dues of rejoycing*
by being ignorant of what Greatnesse is promis'd thee .
5 *Lay*
it to thy heart, and farewell.

[2] there is a possibility that in speech #5 the 'murth'ring Ministers' do to her exactly what is asked, step by step, and that a metamorphosis takes place on-stage, with her finishing up as more, or less, than human - hence her rapid decline once royalty has been achieved, all her energies having been spent in ensuring that any obstacle to that goal is overcome, so the 'golden round' can be successfully attained

Modern Text

4/ Lady

1 [Glamis] thou art, and Cawdor, and shalt be
What thou art promis'd. †
2 Yet do* I fear* thy Δnature,
It is too full o'th'Δmilk* of [human]* kindness*
To catch the nearest* way.
3 Thou wouldst be great,
Art not without Δambition, but without
The illness* should attend it.
4 What thou wouldst highly,
That wouldst thou holily; wouldst not play false,
And yet wouldst wrongly win*.
5 Thou'ldst have, great [Glamis],
That which cries*, *"Thus thou must do*, if thou have it*;"
And that which rather thou dost fear* to do*
[Than] wishest should be undone.
6 High thee hither,
That I may pour* my Δspirits in thine Δear*,
And chastise with the valor* of my Δtongue
All that impedes* thee from the Δgolden Δround,
Which Δfate and Δmetaphysical* aid* doth seem*
To have thee crown'd withal*.

It is only after much husband-character-analysis and having found the approach 'To have thee crown'd withall', that her passions finally flow.

- the speech starts very carefully, the opening intellectual surround phrase

  " . Glamys thou art, and Cawdor, and shalt be/What thou art promis'd : "

  not simply summing up all that she knows to date but promising that the Weyward Sisters' prophecy will be fulfilled in full

- but her concerns that his nature is 'too full o'th'Milke of humane kindnesse' are very emotional (2/6, F #1's last two lines), which turns to passion as she so quickly assesses his fundamental flaw - that he want greatness but is not sufficiently ruthless to achieve it (F #2. 1/1)

- her further detailing of what she perceives as his weakness now becomes emotional (F #3-4, 1/6), and is immediately thrown into even greater relief with F #3's two surround phrases

  " . What thou would'st highly,/would'st thou holily : would'st not play false,/And yet would'st wrongly winne . "

- her F #4 understanding that her manipulative strength will lie in the fact that though he hears 'that which cryes,/Thus thou must doe, if thou have it ;' and fears it, he'd rather hear it 'Then wishest should be undone.' is underscored by
  - a/ the moment of realisation linking the two ideas, via the only emotional semicolon in the speech
  - b/ F #3's recognition of his weakness, marked by F's three irregular shaded lines (six/seven or eight/eight syllables) that suggest a pause before she begins to discover F #4's solution – a pause most modern texts remove by resetting the text as two almost pentameter lines (nine or ten/eleven), as shown

- at last, as she realises how she may manipulate him, passions spring forth (F #5, 7/8) as she envisages stirring him by pouring 'my Spirits in thine Eare'

First Folio

4/ Lady

1 [Glamys] thou art, and Cawdor, and shalt be
What thou art promis'd: yet doe I feare thy Nature,
It is too full o'th'Milke of [humane] kindnesse,x
To catch the neerest way.
2 Thou would'st be great,
Art not without Ambition, but without
The illnesse should attend it.
3 What thou would'st highly,
That would'st thou holily: x would'st not play false,
And yet would'st wrongly winne.
4 Thould'st have, great [Glamys], that which cryes,
Thus thou must doe, if thou have it;
And that which rather thou do'st feare to doe,x
[Then] wishest should be undone.
5 High thee hither,
That I may powre my Spirits in thine Eare,
And chastise with the valour of my Tongue
All that impeides thee from the Golden Round,
Which Fate and Metaphysicall ayde doth seeme
To have thee crown'd withall.

Modern Text

5/ Lady

1 The △raven himself* is hoarse
That croaks* the fatal* entrance of Duncan
Under my △battlements.
2 Come, you △spirits,
That tend on mortal* thoughts, unsex me here,
And fill me from the △crown* to the △toe top-full
Of direst △cruelty$_*$! †
3 Make thick my blood,
Stop up th'access* and passage to △remorse,
That no compunctious visitings of △nature
Shake my fell purpose, nor keep* peace between*
Th'effect, and [it] !
4 Come to my △woman's △breasts,
And take my △milk* for △gall, you [murd'ring] △ministers,
Whereever in your sightless* substances
You wait on △nature's △mischief* !
5 Come, thick △night,
And pall thee in the dunnest smoke* of △hell,
That my keen* △knife see not the △wound it makes,
Nor △heaven peep* through the △blanket of the dark*
To cry, hold, hold.

[Enter Macbeth]

6 Great [Glamis] !, worthy Cawdor !
Greater [than]both, by the all-hail* hereafter ! †

7 Thy △letters have transported me beyond
This ignorant present, and I feel* now
The future in the instant.

With only one major piece of punctuation and no surround phrases it would seem that once she starts, rather than controlling the event, her recognition of what happens to her and her need to complete the transformation is what drives the speech -though the onrush after Macbeth's arrival may suggest that she cannot yet control the new being she has become.

- whether real or symbolic, the opening recognition of the cry of the bird of foreboding (itself a fascinating contrast to the innocent and abundant 'temple-haunting martlet' that greeted Duncan and the royal party when they arrived) is voiced passionately (F #1, 3/3), while the first invitation to the 'Spirits/That tend on mortall thoughts' to 'unsex me' (4/2, F #2's first three lines) becomes more controlled

- but then the first of two onrushed moments in the speech mark what most modern texts regard as a slight loss of grammatical control (setting a more rational mt. #3), while the ensuing text turns passionate (2/3, the last four lines of F #2) - the two factors suggesting that perhaps the 'make thick my blood', and why, is a reaction to what is happening to her rather than an order to continue

- she seems to re-establish control of self and situation with F #3's 'Come to my Womans Brests' (7/3), and, to a lesser extent, in the double request for 'thick Night' to come, so she will not see 'the Wound' her knife makes, and 'Heaven' will not witness the attack on Duncan (F #4, 6/4)

- it may be more of a struggle for her to maintain such control than the modern texts suggest, for F has added four extra breath-thoughts (marked ,$_x$), two in F #2 and one each in F #3-4, suggesting that what follows is of great difficulty for her to endure (',$_x$ top-full/Of direst Crueltie'; ',$_x$ and passage to Remorse,'), or is very specific to her needs (',$_x$ in your sightlesse substances'; ',$_x$ To cry, hold, hold')

- though most modern texts separate the greeting (mt. #6) and her description of the effect that his letter has had on her (mt. #7), F jams both together, this onrush suggesting a slight loss of control once more as he appears - again, as with the end of mt. #2, the content of the onrush is passionate (3/2)

First Folio

5/ Lady

1 The Raven himselfe is hoarse,$_x$
That croakes the fatall entrance of Duncan
Under my Battlements.
2 Come+ you Spirits,
That tend on mortall thoughts, unsex me here,
And fill me from the Crowne to the Toe,$_x$ top-full
Of direst Crueltie: make thick my blood,
Stop up th'accesse,$_x$ and passage to Remorse,
That no compunctious visitings of Nature
Shake my fell purpose, nor keepe peace betweene
Th'effect, and [hit]. +
3 Come to my Womans Brests,
And take my Milke for Gall, you [murth'ring] Ministers,
Where-ever,$_x$ in your sightlesse substances,$_x$
You wait on Natures Mischiefe. +
4 Come+ thick Night,
And pall thee in the dunnest smoake of Hell,
That my keene Knife see not the Wound it makes,
Nor Heaven peepe through the Blanket of the darke,$_x$
To cry, hold, hold.

[Enter Macbeth]

5 Great [Glamys],+ worthy Cawdor,+
Greater [then] both, by the all-haile hereafter,+
Thy Letters have transported me beyond
This ignorant present, and I feele now
The future in the instant.

#'S 6 - 18: THE ASSASSINATION, DREAM & FACT, AND ITS EFFECTS

6/ King or Banquo **This Castle hath a pleasant seat,** 1.6.1- 10

Background: Duncan and his party train arrive at Macbeth's castle at Inverness, Macbeth having reached home beforehand. Since in F #1 the first sentence is spoken by the King, and the remainder by Banquo, either character could handle the speech.

Style: general address to a small group, and then to one woman for the group's benefit and hers

Where: at Inverness' castle gates **To Whom:** his sons Malcome and Donalbaine; the Thanes Banquo, Lenox, Macduff, Rosse and Angus, & attendants

# of Lines: 10 **Probable Timing: 0.35 minutes**

Modern Text

6/ King (or Banquo)

1 This Δcastle hath a pleasant seat, the Δair*
Nimbly and sweetly recommends itself*
Unto our gentle senses.

2 {ψ} This Δguest of Δsummer,
The Δtemple-haunting [Δmarlet], does approve,
By his loved [Δmansionry*], that the Δheaven's breath
Smells wooingly here; no Δjutty, frieze,
Buttress*, nor Δcoign* of Δvantage, but this Δbird
Hath made his pendant Δbed and procreant Δcradle. †

3 Where they [most] breed and haunt, I have observ'd
The air* is delicate.

With their new mt. #3, most modern texts set a logical and straightforward finish to the bird watching: F's continued F #2 establishes a much more human onrush of delight as to what he is sensing - as well as perhaps an almost self-mocking finish by an enthusiast who knows he has been caught out by others who don't necessarily share his passion.

- given the end of the war, and their arrival for R & R, it's hardly surprising that the speech opens slightly emotionally (1/2, F #1)
- the description of 'This Guest of Summer' is so dominantly factual (12/1, F #2's first five and a half lines, the equivalent of mt. #2) that it would seem his enthusiasm is running away with him and/or he is embarking on what amounts to a lecture
- the speech ends in a slightly emotional onrush (only the second piece of emotion throughout), ' : I have observ'd/The ayre is delicate . ', the change in style suggesting that the character is forcing himself to finish rather more abruptly than he originally intended (apologising? embarrassment? or perhaps self-mockery?)

First Folio

6/ King (or Banquo)

1 This Castle hath a pleasant seat,
The ayre nimbly and sweetly recommends it selfe
Unto our gentle sences.

2 {ψ} This Guest of Summer,
The Temple-haunting [Barlet]+ does approve,
By his loved [Mansonry], that the Heavens breath
Smells wooingly here: x no Jutty+ frieze+
Buttrice, nor Coigne of Vantage, but this Bird
Hath made his pendant Bed, x and procreant Cradle,
Where they [must] breed, x and haunt: x I have observ'd
The ayre is delicate.

7/ Macbeth **If it were done, when 'tis done, then 'twer well,** 1.7.1 - 28

Background: With his wife pushing him to assassinate Duncan, Macbeth explores all the possible reasons pro and con, realising there are none 'pro' except his own ambition.

Style: solo

Where: Inverness castle, somewhere close to the ongoing banquet **To Whom:** self, and audience

# of Lines: 28 **Probable Timing: 1.30 minutes**

Modern Text

7/ Macbeth

1 If it were done, when 'tis done, then 'twere* well
It were done quickly . †
2 If th'△assassination
Could trammel* up the △consequence, and catch
With his surcease, △success*; that but this blow
Might be the be-all, and the end-all - ◊ △here,
3 But △here*, upon this △bank* and [△shoal*] of time,
We'ld* jump* the life to come.
4 But in these △cases
We still have judgment* here*, that we but teach
Bloody △instructions, which, being taught, return*
To plague th'△inventor* . †
5 This even-handed △justice
Commends th'△ingredience of our poison'd* △chalice*
To our own* lips.
6 He's* here* in double trust:
First, as I am his △kinsman and his △subject,
Strong both against the △deed; △then, as his △host,
Who should against his △{murderer] shut the door*,
Not bear* the knife myself*.
7 Besides, this Duncan*
Hath born* his △faculties so meek*; hath been*
So clear* in his great △office, that his △virtues
Will plead* like △angels, △trumpet-tongu'd, against
The deep* damnation of his taking off;
And △pity*, like a naked △new-born* △ babe,
Striding the blast, or △heaven's △cherubin, hors'd
Upon the sightless* △couriers* of the △air*,
Shall blow the horrid deed in every eye,
That tears* shall drown* the wind*.
8 I have no △spur*
To prick* the sides of my intent, but only*
Vaulting Ambition, which ore-leaps* itself*,
And falls* on th'other - ◊

This is often played as quiet rational exploration, but F's orthography shows just how much of an intellectual/emotional roller-coaster Macbeth undergoes in trying to find a valid reason to justify his murderous intent.

- the quiet of the only two virtually monosyllabic and unembellished passages in the text underscore Macbeth's desire, and the quietness is made all the more noteworthy by forming the bulk of the first sentence in the speech
  " . If it were done, when 'tis done, then 'twer well, /It were done quickly : . . . : that but this blow/Might be the be all, and the end all . "
- however, the calm is only momentary, for the description of Duncan's death as an 'Assassination' (by all accounts a Shakespeare invented word) intellectually breaks the calm (4/2, the two lines between F #1's two colons)
- and while F #2's response to the idea that if the deed were all Macbeth would jump at it is surprisingly strongly emotional (2/6), the F #3 realisation that, by example, his killing of Duncan could easily lead to his own death becomes very passionate (7/6 in just five lines)
- fascinatingly, expressing two of society's reasons why he should not kill Duncan seems to greatly disturb Macbeth
  " . Hee's heere in double trust ; /First, as I am his Kinsman, and his Subject, /Strong both against the Deed : "
  " . Besides, this Duncane/Hath borne his Faculties so meeke ; "
  for both are expressed as emotional surround phrases
- the struggle between Macbeth's intellect and emotion/passion continues, for, not surprisingly, while the idea of breaking that trust ('Hee's heere in double trust') and the act of killing him ('Not beare the knife my selfe.') trigger his emotions (0/2 twice, in the opening and closing of F #4), what is sandwiched between is an intellectual assessment (6/1 in just three lines) that he has a chivalric double duty to protect Duncan
- as he voices Duncan's excellent qualities, which again should protect him, Macbeth is moved to passion (6/6, F #5's first four and half lines)
- the realisation that Duncan's death will generate such an outcry of 'Pitty' becomes slightly more intellectual (F #5's next three lines 7/5), with the fact that all will know of Macbeth's deed striking him with icy certainty via the unembellished
  "Shall blow the horrid deed in every eye."
  with the resultant 'teares' being known world-wide, since the deed 'shall drowne the winde', becomes emotional (0/3)
- as he realises that there is no reason to kill Duncan except for his own 'Vaulting Ambition' to become king, the emotion flows free (F #6, 2/6)

First Folio

7/ Macbeth

1 If it were done, when 'tis done, then 'twer well, x
It were done quickly: If th'Assassination
Could trammell up the Consequence, and catch
With his surcease, Successe: x that but this blow
Might be the be all, and the end all.
2 Heere,
But heere, upon this Banke and [Schoole] of time,
Wee'ld jumpe the life to come.
3 But in these Cases, x
We still have judgement heere, that we but teach
Bloody Instructions, which+ being taught, returne
To plague th'Inventer, This even-handed Justice
Commends th'Ingredience of our poyson'd Challice
To our owne lips.
4 Hee's heere in double trust; +
First, as I am his Kinsman, x and his Subject,
Strong both against the Deed: x Then, as his Host,
Who should against his [Murtherer] shut the doore,
Not beare the knife my selfe.
5 Besides, this Duncane
Hath borne his Faculties so meeke; hath bin
So cleere in his great Office, that his Vertues
Will pleade like Angels, Trumpet-tongu'd+ against
The deepe damnation of his taking off: x
And Pitty, like a naked New-borne-Babe,
Striding the blast, or Heavens Cherubin, hors'd
Upon the sightlesse Curriors of the Ayre,
Shall blow the horrid deed in every eye,
That teares shall drowne the winde.
6 I have no Spurre
To pricke the sides of my intent, but onely
Vaulting Ambition, which ore-leapes it selfe,
And falles on th'other.

8/ Lady **Was the hope drunke,/Wherein you drest your selfe?** 1.7.35 - 45

9/ Lady **What Beast was't/That made you breake this enterprize to me?** between 1.7.47 - 72

Background: Having realised there is no legitimate or honest reason for killing Duncan, Macbeth informs his wife 'we will proceed no further in this Businesse'. These two speeches comprise the bulk of her eventually successful rhetoric which keeps him to the proposed task in hand, for he eventually responds not just with the admiring 'Bring forth Men-Children onely', but 'I am settled, and bend up/Each corporall Agent to this terrible Feat'.

Style: as part of a two-handed scene **Where:** Inverness castle, somewhere close to the ongoing banquet

To Whom: Macbeth

Speech 8: # of Lines: 11 **Probable Timing: 0.40 minutes**

Speech 9: # of Lines: 26 **Probable Timing: 1.15 minutes**

Modern Text

8/ Lady

1 Was the hope drunk*
Wherein you dress'd$_*$ yourself*?
2 Hath it slept since?
3 And wakes it now to look* so green*, and pale,
At what it did so freely?
4 From this time
Such I account thy love.
5 Art thou afear'd*
To be the same in thine own* △act and △valor*
As thou art in desire?
6 Wouldst thou have that
Which thou esteem'st the △ornament of △life,
And live a △coward in thine own* esteem*,
Letting "I dare not" wait upon "I would",
Like the poor* △cat i'th'△adage*.

This comes from one of the trickiest sequences facing any actress in the whole of Shakespeare – for the temptation is to play it as an emotional attack from the outset, whereas F's opening establishes a struggle to maintain control, as if she were trying to avoid unnecessarily antagonising him, unless she has to.

• the opening sentence is emotional, the two released words ('drunke' and 'selfe') coming at the end of each phrase, suggesting a careful posing of a necessary question and a great care to maintain control (0/2, F #1)

• signs of her control succeeding can be seen in the unembellished, monosyllabic, and very short F #2 ('Hath it slept since?'), though while F #3 is as equally emotionally careful as F #1 (0/2), the two released words coming in the first phrase ('looke so greene') might indicate that self-control is becoming a little more difficult to maintain

• yet the calm of unembellishment is regained with the end of F #3 and the short F #4
" : At what it did so freely? From this time,/Such I account thy love."
though the extra breath-thoughts that now begin to occur (marked ,$_x$) suggest that this re-established control does not come without another struggle

• and then the releases start to flow, (8/7 overall in the last six and a half lines: however, the patterns shift quite interestingly, according to the question/tactic being used to gain any response from her husband - F #5's fear-based questioning is emotional (2/3); her challenging just how deep his desire is for the 'Ornament of Life' switches to intellect (2/0, F #6's first one and half lines); and then, whether deliberately as a rhetorical tactic or unconsciously, the final cowardice blow is passionate 4/4, (F #6's last three lines)

First Folio

8/ Lady

1 Was the hope drunke,$_x$
Wherein you drest your selfe?
2 Hath it slept since?
3 And wakes it now to looke so greene, and pale,
At what it did so freely?
4 From this time,$_x$
Such I account thy love.
5 Art thou affear'd
To be the same in thine owne Act,$_x$ and Valour,$_x$
As thou art in desire?
6 Would'st thou have that
Which thou esteem'st the Ornament of Life,
And live a Coward in thine owne Esteeme?$_x$
Letting I dare not,$_x$ wait upon I would,
Like the poore Cat i'th'Addage.

Modern Text

9/ Lady

1 What △beast was't {ψ}
That made you break* this enterprise* to me?

2 When you durst do it, then you were a man;
And to be more [than]what you were, you would
Be so much more the man.

3 Nor time, nor place,
Did then adhere, and yet you would make both:
They have made themselves, and that their fitness* now
Do's unmake you.

4 I have given △suck*, and know
How tender 'tis to love the △babe that milks* me;
I would, while it was smiling* in my △face,
Have pluck'd my △nipple from his △boneless* △gums*,
And dash'd the △brains* out, had I so sworn* as you
Have done to this.

5 {ψ} {S}crew your courage to the sticking place,
And we'll* not fail*. †

6 When Duncan is asleep*
(Whereto the rather shall his days* hard △journey
Soundly invite him), his two △chamberlains*
Will I with △wine, and △wassail* so convince,
That △memory*, the △warder of the △brain*,
Shall be a △fume, and the △receipt* of △reason
A △limbeck* only*. †

7 When in △swinish sleep*
Their drenched △natures lies* as in a △death,
What cannot you and I perform* upon
Th'unguarded Duncan? ◊ what not put upon
His spungy* △officers, who shall bear* the guilt
Of our great quell?

As with the previous speech, this comes from one of the trickiest sequences facing any actress in the whole of Shakespeare – for the temptation is to play it as an emotional attack from the outset, whereas F's opening establishes a struggle to maintain control, as if she were trying to avoid unnecessarily antagonising him, unless she has to.

- the speech opens very carefully, for after F #1's single striking capital release 'Beast' (building on her previous image of comparing Macbeth to the 'poore Cat i'th'Addage' and thus less than a man, an appallingly demeaning insult to any Elizabethan) and cunning emotional release 'enterprize' (suggesting that their acsending to the throne – by whatever means – is merely a business proposition)

- the care with which she is trying to win him by rational argument (and very strong images) rather than off-putting emotion can be clearly seen in F #2's and nearly all of F #3's next four and a half lines of apparently reasonable debate, which is couched in three very rare unembellished surround phrases (and, save for the one word 'adhere', monosyllabic too)
  " . When you durst do it, then you were a man : And to be more then what you were, you would/Be so much more the man . Nor time, nor place/Did then adhere, and yet you would make both : / . . . "

- this control does not last, for the end of F #3 (the time's 'fitnesse') first plunges her into passion as she proves her valour to shame him into action (7/7, F #4), and then, in attempting to forestall his fear of failure (0/2, F #5's opening surround phrase 'Screw your courage to the sticking place/And wee'le not fayle') she momentarily becomes emotional

- that the full planning of the details from the moment 'when Duncan is asleepe' and her belief 'What cannot you and I performe upon/Th'unguarded Duncan?' excites her can be seen in her sudden enormous onrushed release (16/9, F #5's last nine lines), though whether the passion stems from the idea itself or in trying to get Macbeth to see and grasp the possibilities is up to each actor to explore: this onrush is removed by most modern texts setting two more rational sentences - mt. #6 for why Duncan will sleep, mt. #7 what they can then do to him

- indeed most modern texts regard F's final sentence as ungrammatical: as set F seems to suggest that at the very last moment her control slips just a little, yet the immediacy of the circumstances and the urgency of her final F #6 extra sentence demand ' . What not put upon/His spungie Officers ? who shall beare the guilt/Of our great quell . ' is underscored
  a/ by being set as two surround phrases
  b/ by the question mark acting as a link (here functioning as the modern exclamation mark)
  c/ the slight emotion involved (1/2)
  much more so than by the new modern rationality

First Folio

9/ Lady

1 What Beast was't {ψ}
That made you breake this enterprize to me?

2 When you durst do it, then you were a man: [x]
And to be more [then] what you were, you would
Be so much more the man.

3 Nor time, nor place[+]
Did then adhere, and yet you would make both:
They have made themselves, and that their fitnesse now
Do's unmake you.

4 I have given Sucke, and know
How tender 'tis to love the Babe that milkes me,[+]
I would, while it was smyling in my Face,
Have pluckt my Nipple from his Bonelesse Gummes,
And dasht the Braines out, had I so sworne
As you have done to this.

5 {ψ} {S}crew your courage to the sticking place,
And wee'le not fayle: when Duncan is asleepe,[x]
(Whereto the rather shall his dayes hard Journey
Soundly invite him)[+] his two Chamberlaines
Will I with Wine, and Wassell,[x] so convince,
That Memorie, the Warder of the Braine,
Shall be a Fume, and the Receit of Reason
A Lymbeck onely: when in Swinish sleepe,[x]
Their drenched Natures lyes as in a Death,
What cannot you and I performe upon
Th'unguarded Duncan?

6 What not put upon
His spungie Officers?[x] who shall beare the guilt
Of our great quell. [+]

10/ Macbeth **Goe bid thy Mistresse, when my drinke is ready,** 2.1.31 - 64

Background: Macbeth now steels himself to do the deed. One note: just as a possible metamorphosis took place for Lady Macbeth (see footnote #2, referring to speech #5, page 232), here there is perhaps one for him here too - notice that after sentence #9, where he refuses to accept the (conscience-driven?) warning of the blood-stained dagger, he is suddenly able to sense and even hear the 'halfe World' of witches and their agents, a sense that grows stronger and leads to ever increasingly reckless and less-than-humanity driven behaviour as the play wears on.

Style: solo

Where: the castle at Inverness, probably the battlements **To Whom:** self, the 'imaginary' dagger, & the audience

# of Lines: 34 **Probable Timing: 1.40 minutes**

Modern Text

10/ Macbeth

1 Go* bid thy △mistress*, when my drink* is ready,
She strike upon the △bell.
2 Get thee to bed.

[Exit {Servant}]

3 Is this a △dagger, which I see before me,
The △handle toward my △hand?
4 Come, let me clutch thee:
I have thee not, and yet I see thee still.
5 Art thou not, fatal* △vision, sensible
To feeling as to sight? or art thou but
A △dagger of the △mind*, a false △creation,
Proceeding from the heat-oppressed △brain*?
6 I see thee yet, in form* as palpable
As this which now I draw.
7 Thou marshal'st* me the way that I was going,
And such an △instrument I was to use.
8 Mine △eyes are made the fools* o'th'other △senses,
Or else worth all the rest. †
9 I see thee still;
And on thy △blade, and △dudgeon, △gouts of △blood,
Which was not so before.
10 There's no such thing:
It is the bloody △business* which informs*
Thus to mine △eyes.
11 Now o'er the one half* △world
Nature seems* dead, and wicked △dreams* abuse
The △curtain'd sleep*; △witchcraft celebrates
Pale Hecat's* △off'rings; and wither'd △[murder],

The speech is remarkable in that Macbeth initially shows enormous self-control when faced with the 'fatall Vision' of the dagger, yet once he decides he knows from whence it comes and he gets side-tracked into the 'one halfe World' his control disappears until the bell (the signal from his wife) reminds him of the need for immediate action.

- for a simple Servant dismissal, Macbeth is surprisingly passionate (2/3, F #1), which he may suddenly realise for F #2's follow-up 'Get thee to bed.' is short, monosyllabic, and unembellished

- and this control is maintained at the sight of the 'Dagger' for the first questioning of what he sees is staunchly/steadfastly intellectual (F #3, 3/0), and the attempt to grasp it and his response to his inability to do so is very quiet
  ". Come, let me clutch thee : /I have thee not, and yet I see thee still . /Art thou not . . . , sensible/To feeling, as to sight ? "
  whether the unembellished calm is enforced or natural, given the circumstances his control is remarkable, especially considering the releases of the previous soliloquy – speech #7 above

- though emotion makes itself felt as he faces the possibility that the dagger stems from his own fevered brain he nevertheless still stays in intellectual control (4/2, F #5's last two lines) – until the dagger still remains visible and motions him towards Duncan's chamber when, for a moment, Macbeth's emotions get the better of him (1/2, F #6-7)

- even while not knowing what to believe he still maintains his reason (F #8, 6/1), though it takes two surround phrases - one emotional (semicolon created)
  ". Mine Eyes are made the fooles o'th'other Sences,/Or else worth all the rest : I see thee still ; "

- however, the passion of his surround phrase refusal to accept the dagger as real (F #9, 2/2)
  ". There's no such thing : /It is the bloody Businesse, which informes/ Thus to mine Eyes ."
  completely blows his self control, for presuming the vision is of his own creating and thus refusing any possibility of his conscience and/or divine intervention preventing him from destroying himself leads him into a sudden flurry of passion (12/8 in F #10's eight and a half lines) as he experiences for the very first time the

First Folio

10/ Macbeth

1 Goe bid thy Mistresse, when my drinke is ready,
She strike upon the Bell.
2 Get thee to bed.

[Exit{Servant}]

3 Is this a Dagger, which I see before me,
The Handle toward my Hand?
4 Come, let me clutch thee:
I have thee not, and yet I see thee still.
5 Art thou not+ fatall Vision, sensible
To feeling,$_x$ as to sight? or art thou but
A Dagger of the Minde, a false Creation,
Proceeding from the heat-oppressed Braine?
6 I see thee yet, in forme as palpable,$_x$
As this which now I draw.
7 Thou marshall'st me the way that I was going,
And such an Instrument I was to use.
8 Mine Eyes are made the fooles o'th'other Sences,
Or else worth all the rest: I see thee still;
And on thy Blade, and Dudgeon, Gouts of Blood,
Which was not so before.
9 There's no such thing:
It is the bloody Businesse,$_x$ which informes
Thus to mine Eyes.
10 Now o're the one halfe World
Nature seemes dead, and wicked Dreames abuse
The Curtain'd sleepe: $_x$ Witchcraft celebrates
Pale Heccats Offrings: $_x$ and wither'd [Murther],

{ctd. over}

Alarum'd by his △centinel*, the △wolf*,
Whose howl's* his △watch, thus with his stealthy pace,
With Tarquin's ravishing [strides], towards his design*
Moves like a △ghost.
12 Thou [sure*] and firm*-set △earth,
Hear* not my steps, which [way they] walk*, for fear*
Thy very stones prate of my whereabout,
And take the present horror from the time,
Which now suites⁎ with it.
13 Whiles I threat, he lives:
Words to the heat of deeds* too cold breath gives.

BELL RINGS

14 I go*, and it is done; the △bell invites me.
15 Hear* it not, Duncan, for it is a △knell,
That summons thee to △heaven or to △hell.

exhilarating half-world linking man and the supernatural, the key understanding highlighted by yet another surround phrase ' : Witchcraft celebrates/Pale Heccats Offrings : '

- the determination that no-one should hear him approach Duncan is very emotional initially (1/5, F #11's first two lines), while the notion/fear that everything will give him away suddenly causes him to go very quiet
  "Thy very stones prate of my where-about, /And take the present horror from the time,/Which now sutes with it."

- yet his strength enables him to go beyond his fear and he returns to determined surround phrase control as he realises he must act (F #12, 0/1) - the sentence is also unembellished save for the one key word 'deedes', ' . Whiles I threat, he lives : /Words to the heat of deedes too cold breath gives . '

- the final determination to go on is strongly intellectual once more (5/2, F #13-14); the understanding that all is ready and that if he just goes to Duncan everything will be achieved is also voiced via yet more surround phrases, F #13's ' . I goe, and it is done : the Bell invites me . '

Alarum'd by his Centinell, the Wolfe,
Whose howle's his Watch, thus with his stealthy pace,
With Tarquins ravishing [sides], towards his designe
Moves like a Ghost.
11 Thou [sowre] and firme-set Earth+
Heare not my steps, which [they may] walke, for feare
Thy very stones prate of my where-about,
And take the present horror from the time,
Which now sutes with it.
12 Whiles I threat, he lives:
Words to the heat of deedes too cold breath gives.

BELL RINGS

13 I goe, and it is done: ₓ the Bell invites me.
14 Heare it not, Duncan, for it is a Knell,
That summons thee to Heaven,ₓ or to Hell.

11/ Lady **That which hath made thë drunk, hath made me bold:** 2.2.1 - 13

Background: Lady Macbeth awaits her husband's return from killing Duncan, and lay the blame on 'his spungie Officers' by leaving the incriminating blood-stained daggers by their drug-induced sleeping hands.

Style: solo

Where: the castle at Inverness, probably the battlements **To Whom:** self and the audience

# of Lines: 14 **Probable Timing: 0.45 minutes**

Modern Text

11/ Lady

1 That which hath made [them] drunk hath made me bold;
What hath quench'd them, hath given me fire.
2 Hark* ! †
3 Peace ! †
4 It was the Δowl* that shriek'd, the fatal* Δbell-man,
Which gives the stern'st good-night.
5 He is about it :
The Δdoors* are open; and the surfeited, Δgrooms*
Do* mock their charge with Δsnores.
6 I have drugg'd their Δpossets,
That Δdeath and Δnature do* contend about them,
Whether they live or die*.

7 Alack, I am afraid they have awak'd,
And 'tis not done; th'attempt, and not the deed,
Confounds us. †
8 Hark* ! †
9 I laid* their Δdaggers ready,
He could not miss* 'em.
10 Had he not resembled
My Δfather as he slept, I had don't.

In the first two lines of this speech Macbeth's Lady tells us that she has been drinking, that she is 'bold' and has 'fire': following F's first line come six irregular ones (8 or 9/8/11/9 or 10/10/8 syllables) and these, plus F #2's onrush, suggest that she is finding it very difficult to keep an even balance: most modern texts remove both hints by restructuring the shaded passage to five lines as shown (10 or 11/11/11/10 or 11/12 syllables) and splitting F #2 into three.

- whatever the effects of the drink she starts very quietly (afraid others will overhear perhaps) but with great conviction, with F #1 being triply weighted as two unembellished and almost monosyllabic surround phrases

- her determination to stay in control continues, with four more consecutive surround phrases, but the calm is now swept aside by passion, the onrushed F #2 (2/3) dealing with her being startled by the owl-cry and F #3 (3/3) dealing with her envisioning Macbeth about to strike

- the passion continues, though without the extra intensity of surround phrases, as she dwells on how she has played her part by having drugged their drinks (F #4, 3/2)

- but (as the text suggests) a noise disturbs her and, as with the opening, she returns to five consecutive surround phrases, the fear of the first three heightened by being unembellished - as if she can barely voice the thoughts

  ". Alack, I am afraid they have awak'd,/And 'tis not done : th'attempt, and not the deed,/Confounds us : "

  while perhaps another noise triggers the emotion (1/3) of the two that follow

  " : hearke : I lay'd their Daggers ready,/He could not misse them . "

- thus the quiet intellect of her last statement that it's only Duncan's resemblance to her father that has prevented her from killing him herself (F #6, 1/0) is thrown into even more relief as something very key to her inner workings (is this why she didn't want heaven to see her activities, speech # 5 above?)

First Folio

11/ Lady

1 That which hath made [thë] drunk, x hath made me bold: x
What hath quench'd them, hath given me fire.
2 Hearke, + peace: + it was the Owle that shriek'd,
The fatall Bell-man, which gives the stern'st good-night.
3 He is about it, + the Doores are open: x
And the surfeted Groomes doe mock their charge
With Snores.
4 I have drugg'd their Possets,
That Death and Nature doe contend about them,
Whether they live, x or dye.

5 Alack, I am afraid they have awak'd,
And 'tis not done: x th'attempt, and not the deed,
Confounds us: hearke: + I lay'd their Daggers ready,
He could not misse 'em.
6 Had he not resembled
My Father as he slept, I had don't.

12/ Lady **My Hands are of your colour: but I shame/To weare a Heart so white.** 2.2.61 - 69

Background: Macbeth has killed Duncan. However, he has failed to incriminate the guards as planned (see speeches #9 and #11 above). The reasons? He heard a 'voyce cry, Sleep no more' which, together with his inability to 'say Amen' when the two guards 'did say God blesse us' after their laughing or crying 'Murther' in their sleep, has prevented him from further rational behaviour, to the extent of bringing the murder weapons back down with him. Thus his wife has had to take the daggers and place them besides the guards, which triggers the following as she returns.

Style: as part of a two-handed scene

Where: the castle at Inverness, probably the battlements **To Whom:** her husband

# of Lines: 10 **Probable Timing: 0.35 minutes**

Modern Text

12/ Lady

1 My $^{\Delta}$hands are of your color*; but I shame
To wear* a $^{\Delta}$heart so white.

[Knocke]

2 I hear* a knocking
At the $^{\Delta}$south entry. †
3 Retire* we to our $^{\Delta}$chamber. †
4 A little $^{\Delta}$water clears* us of this deed; ◊
How easy, is it then! †
5 Your $^{\Delta}$constancy,
Hath left you unattended.

[Knocke]

6 Hark*, more knocking.
7 Get on your $^{\Delta}$night-$^{\Delta}$gown*, least occasion call us,
And show* us to be $^{\Delta}$watchers. †
8 Be not lost
So poorly* in your thoughts.

The temptation in such a short speech with such driving circumstances is to play the overall excitement/emotion as one generalised urging. However, F's orthography suggests that the speech falls into three distinct parts, a passionate opening and closing (F #1-2, and F #5), and a central portion that is far more reasoned and controlled – suggesting an attempt at reasoning which doesn't necessarily succeed. One note: the pauses inherent the F only short lines ending F #2 and between F #3-4 (indicated as shaded text) show where she offers Macbeth a chance to respond and he doesn't – which could well explain her increasing sense of frustration as well as the need for her to switch tactics twice in a very short speech.

- the passion of F #1, showing him Duncan's blood (2/2), and of F #2, the attempt to quickly wash the blood off of both of them so that they can face whoever's knocking without fear of discovery (3/3), is heightened by being set as five consecutive surround phrases
- and though two more consecutive surround phrases and then a short sentence follow in her attempt to get him to comply (F #3-4, 1/1), she becomes very quiet - as if she were coaxing rather than scolding or verbally abusing him
- then, with no apparent response, her surround-phrase passion sweeps in once more as she attempts to move him to action (F #5, 3/2, all but the last phrase), while at the very last moment her emotion gets the better of her (0/1) as she orders/pleads with him via the surround phrase
  " : be not lost/So poorely in your thoughts . "

First Folio

12/ Lady

1 My Hands are of your colour: $_{x}$ but I shame
To weare a Heart so white.

[Knocke]

2 I heare a knocking at the South entry:
Retyre we to our Chamber:
A little Water cleares us of this deed.
3 How easie is it then? $^{+}$ your Constancie
Hath left you unattended.

[Knocke]

4 Hearke, more knocking.
5 Get on your Night-Gowne, least occasion call us,
And shew us to be Watchers: be not lost
So poorely in your thoughts.

13/ Porter **Here's a knocking indeede : if a man were** 2.3.1 - 21

Background: Macduff and Lenox have arrived to escort Duncan on his customary morning ride. It was their knocking that so disturbed the Macbeths (speech #12 immediately above). The Porter, in his only scene in the play, seems to be taking his own sweet time to let the visitors in.

Style: solo

Where: the courtyard of Inverness castle **To Whom:** self, those beyond the gate, and the audience

# of Lines: 19 **Probable Timing:** 1.00 minutes

Modern Text

13/ Porter

1 Here's a knocking indeed*! †
2 If a man were
Δporter of Hell Gate, he* should have old turning the
Δkey. **[Knock]**
3 Knock, Δknock, Δknock !
4 Who's there,
i'th'name of Belzebub?
5 Here's a Δfarmer, that hang'd
himself* on th'expectation of Δplenty*: †
6 Come in time ! †[3]
7 Have
Δnapkins enow about you, here you'll* sweat for't. **[Knock]**
8 Knock, knock !
9 Who's there, in th'other Δdevil's Δname?
10 Faith, here's an Δequivocator, that could swear* in both
the Δscales against either* Δscale, who committed Δtreason
enough for God's sake, yet could not equivocate to Δheaven. †
11 O*, come in, Δequivocator. **[Knock]**
12 Knock,
Δknock, Δknock !
13 Who's there?
14 'Faith, here's an English
Δtailor* come hither - for stealing out of a French Δhose.†
15 Come in, Δtailor*, here you may roast* your Δgoose. **[Knock]**
16 Knock, [knock], Δknock !
17 Never at quiet ! †
18 What are you? †

Quite fascinatingly, despite the entertainment value of the piece and the woken-very-early-in-the-morning-when-I-supposedly-have-a-hangover circumstances, the Porter remains in strong intellectual control throughout (34/11 overall) and there isn't a single section where passion or emotion gets the better of him, suggesting that no matter what his status and condition, he is a very centred and knowledgeable man. One note: for clarity this text will bold and bracket when F shows 'Knock' as a stage direction rather than spoken dialogue from the Porter (in the original setting, F distinguished the stage direction via an italicised font).

- with F #1's surround phrase opening ' . Here's a knocking indeede : ', it seems the knocking has got to the Porter right from the outset, especially since F #1 is regarded as an ungrammatical onrush by most modern texts, that usually split it in two
- however, he stays in wonderful intellectual control for the first four sentences (11/3 the opening six lines) – the one distinction between the F setting and modern texts is that F #4's onrush is split into three, thus the modern texts create a more rational hard working character than his F counterpart
- then comes F #5's very short, unembellished, monosyllabic sentence 'Knock, knock.' – the quiet perhaps suggesting that the knocking is getting to him again, a pattern to be repeated twice more with F #8-9 and #11
- and following F #6's intellectual challenge (2/0) the first tiny tinge of emotion creeps in as the Porter faces what many Elizabethans had just been taught to hate via a public and inflammatory political trial, an 'Equivocator' (F #7, 7/3) , and there's a tiny bit more as he faces down the imaginary thieving 'English Taylor' (F #10, 6/2)
- then, with F #12 and the opening of F #13 being voiced as four consecutive surround phrases

" . Never at quiet : What are you ? but this place is too cold for Hell . Ile Devill-Porter it no further : "

First Folio

13/ Porter

1 Here's a knocking indeede: + if a man were
Porter of Hell Gate, hee should have old turning the
Key. **[Knock]**
2 Knock, Knock, Knock. +
3 Who's there+
i'th'name of Belzebub?
4 Here's a Farmer, that hang'd
himselfe on th'expectation of Plentie: Come in time,+ have
Napkins enow about you, here you'le sweat for't. **[Knock]**
5 Knock, knock. +
6 Who's there+ in th'other Devils Name?
7 Faith+ here's an Equivocator, that could sweare in both
the Scales against eyther Scale, who committed Treason
enough for Gods sake, yet could not equivocate to Heaven: oh+ come in, Equivocator. **[Knock]**
8 Knock,
Knock, Knock. +
9 Who's there?
10 'Faith+ here's an English
Taylor come hither, for stealing out of a French Hose:
Come in+ Taylor, here you may rost your Goose. **[Knock]**
11 Knock, [ ] Knock. +
12 Never at quiet: + What are you? but this

{ctd. over}

[3] for Ff's obscure 'time' some commentators offer 'time-pleaser' or 'time-server'

19 But this
place is too cold for Δhell.
20 I'll Δdevil*-Δporter it no further. [†]
21 I had thought to have let in some of all Δprofessions, that go* the Δprimrose way to th'everlasting Δbonfire. **[Knock]**
22 Anon, anon ! [†]
23 I pray you remember the Δporter.

it appears that something in his imagination seems to disturb the Porter (or perhaps his unspecified reaction - mock-horror perhaps? - is a game being played with an unsuspecting audience member)

- but then he recovers control (4/1, the last three lines of the speech) for the summation before admitting those who have disturbed him

place is too cold for Hell.
13 Ile Devill-Porter it no further:
I had thought to have let in some of all Professions, that goe the Primrose way to th'everlasting Bonfire. **[Knock]**
14 Anon, anon,[+] I pray you remember the Porter.

14/ Porter **Drinke, Sir, is a great provoker of three things** between 2.3.25 - 36

Background: Having let Macduff and Lenox in, the Porter expands on his reason for taking so long to open the gates. This speech follows on from his first line 'Faith Sir, we were carousing till the second Cock/And'. . . .

Style: as part of a three-handed scene

Where: the courtyard of Inverness castle **To Whom:** Macduff and Lenox

# of Lines: 10 **Probable Timing: 0.35 minutes**

Modern Text

14/ Porter

1 {ψ} Drink*, Δsir, is a great provoker of three things {-}
{* -} Δnose-painting, Δsleep*, and Δurine.
2 Lechery*, Δsir, it provokes, and unprovokes: it provokes the desire, but it takes away the performance.
3 Therefore
much Δdrink* may be said to be an Δequivocator with Δlechery*: it makes him, and it mars* him; it sets him on, and it takes him off; it persuades* him, and dis-heartens him; makes him stand to*, and not stand [to]: in conclusion, equivocates him in a sleep*, and giving him the Δlie*, leaves him.

Though often played as an extended bawdy joke designed to get money from Macduffe and Lenox, there is sufficient evidence in the orthography to suggest post-drink-impotency may be a problem for the Porter.

- after the intellectual opening dealing with the more general debilitating effects of over-drinking (4/1, F #1) comes a virtually unembellished surround phrase (with the capitalised 'Sir' being the only release in F #2
  ". Lecherie, Sir, it provokes, and unprovokes : it provokes the desire, but it takes away the performance . "
  the quietness perhaps suggesting a confidential aside (or, if the 'joke' is to be played as such, a set-up for the punch lines to follow)

- after F #3's intellectual opening to the idea of 'Drinke' being an 'Equivocator with Lecherie' (3/1) come four consecutive emotional surround phrases (formed in part by three semicolons) setting up the inability to perform sexually after drink – with both phrases dealing with the inability to maintain tumescence heightened by being unembellished,
  ' : it makes him, and it marres him ; it sets him on, and it takes him off ; it perswades him, and dis-heartens him ; makes him stand too, and not stand too : '

- while the final result (falling asleep and creating more urine – another meaning of 'Lye') is spoken of emotionally (1/2, F #3's last line and two words)

First Folio

14/ Porter

1 {ψ} Drinke, Sir, is a great provoker of three things {-}
{* -} Nose-painting, Sleepe, and Urine. [4]
2 Lecherie, Sir, it provokes, and unprovokes: it provokes the desire, but it takes away the performance.
3 Therefore
much Drinke may be said to be an Equivocator with Lecherie: it makes him, and it marres him; it sets him on, and it takes him off; it perswades him, and dis-heartens him; makes him stand too, and not stand [too]: in conclusion, equivocates him in a sleepe, and giving him the Lye, leaves him.

---

[4] these two opening lines could be in verse: if so, it is the only time the Porter speaks verse in the play

15/ Lenox **The Night ha's been unruly:** 2.3.54 - 61

Background: Macduff has gone, as he thinks, to awaken Duncan. The audience and Macbeth are waiting for the inevitable cry of horror that must come when Macduff finds Duncan slaughtered (see speech #16 immediately below). As they wait, Lenox, in way of conversation, describes the chaotic, natural, and even supernatural, events that have occurred during the night. [5]

Style: as part of a two-handed scene

Where: the courtyard of Inverness castle **To Whom:** Macbeth

# of Lines: 10 **Probable Timing: 0.35 minutes**

Modern Text

15/ Lenox

1 The Δnight has been unruly . †
2 Where we lay,
Our Δchimneys were blown* down*, and (as they say)
Lamentings heard i'th'Δair* ; Δstrange Δscreams* of Δdeath,
And Δprophesying, with Δaccents terrible,
Of dire* Δcombustion, and confus'd Δevents
New hatch'd to Δ th' woeful* time.
3 The obscure Δbird
Clamor'd the livelong Δnight.
4 Some say, the Δearth
Was feverous, and did shake.

Given the disturbing background to the speech, the fact that it appears intellectual overall (12/5) seems surprising, until F's very irregular line structure, right from the opening surround phrase, is taken into account.

• F's ten lines are very irregular (7/9/10/4/11/10/7/10/7 or 8/3 syllables) yet they serve a remarkable dramatic purpose, the pauses so created (especially at the momentous 'Strange Schreemes of Death' four syllable line) marking where Lenox re-experiences the incidents as he tells the story of the momentously frightening night: modern texts have regularised the speech to eight lines of almost pure pentameter (10/10/10/11/10/10/10/11 or 12) but in so doing have created a totally different set of on-stage circumstances in the re-telling of the story - now there is almost a mood of evenness in the recollections as if he were reporting, not re-experiencing things: as Lenox is only given two lengthy speeches in the play, it would appear that here his character has been quite radically altered by the relineation of the modern texts

First Folio

15/ Lenox

1 The Night ha's been unruly:
Where we lay, our Chimneys were blowne downe,
And (as they say) lamentings heard i'th'Ayre;
Strange Schreemes of Death,
And Prophecying, with Accents terrible,
Of dyre Combustion, and confus'd Events, x
New hatch'd toth' wofull time.
2 The obscure Bird clamor'd the live-long Night.
3 Some say, the Earth was fevorous,
And did shake.

[5] the upsetting of nature when men do shameful deeds, especially the assassination of rulers, is a theme that occurs several times in Shakespeare - see speech #17 below, and Julius Cæsar

16/ Macduff **O horror, horror, horror,/Tongue nor Heart cannot conceive, nor name thee.** between 2.3.64 - 80

Background: Macduff has found Duncan stabbed to death, and this is his immediate response as he comes back onstage.

Style: initially as part of a three-handed scene, and then for anyone not yet awake

Where: the courtyard of Inverness castle **To Whom:** Macbeth and Lenox, and then all others sleeping in the castle

# of Lines: 16 **Probable Timing: 0.50 minutes**

Modern Text

16/ Macduff

1 O horror, horror, horror ! †
2 Tongue nor △heart
Cannot conceive nor name thee.

3 Confusion now hath made his △masterpiece! †
4 Most sacrilegious △[murder] hath broke ope
The Lord's anointed* △temple, and stole thence
The △life o'th'△building !

5 Approach* the △chamber, and destroy your sight
With a new Gorgon.
6 Do* not bid me speak*;
See, and then speak* yourselves. †
7 Awake, awake ! †

[Exeunt Macbeth and Lenox]

8 Ring the △alarum-△bell ! †
9 [Murder], and △treason ! †
10 Banquo and Donalbain* !
11 Malcolm*, awake !
Shake off this △downy* sleep*, △death's counterfeit,
And look* on △death itself* ! †
12 Up, up, and see
The great △doom's* △image ! †
13 Malcolm* ! Banquo !
As from your △graves rise up, and walk* like △sprites*,
To countenance this horror !
14 Ring the △bell.

F suggests that Macduffe manages to maintain great self-control in the opening (9/3, F #1-3), the main sign of stress seen in that F's opening allows him a pause either before or after his first line as he enters: surprisingly some modern texts restructure as shown, creating a much speedier start. In addition, when Macduffe finally does move into an onrushed call for support (F #4) most modern texts maintain the 'correct' separate sentences of the earlier part of the speech, thus setting fourteen sentences overall as opposed to the original five.

- amidst F #2's intellectualism (6/2), its opening surround phrase
  " . Confusion now hath made his Master-peece : "
  points to a horror even deeper than that of Duncan's death (the death of chivalry itself, and the entry into the world of the one thing Elizabethans feared above all, chaos, here described as 'Confusion')

- though he has been able to maintain intellectual discipline in speaking of the facts that have disturbed him, once F #3's factual urging to go see for themselves (2/0) is questioned, his emotions momentarily sweep through (1/3) in the first line and a half of F #4's repeated urging to 'See, and then speake your selves : '

- and though intellect somewhat dominates his emotions for the rest of the speech, (15/10, the remaining seven lines), Macduffe's compulsion to get others to see for themselves is driven by
  a/ the overall onrush of F #4 (reset by most modern texts as eight grammatical – though hardly human – sentences)
  b/ F #4 starting out as seven consecutive surround phrases
  " . Doe not bid me speake : /See, and then speake your selves : awake, awake, /Ring the Alarum Bell : Murther, and Treason,/Banquo, and Donalbaine : Malcolme awake, Shake off this Downey sleepe, Deaths counterfeit,/ And looke on Death it selfe : up, up, and see/The great Doomes Image : "

- some modern texts omit the last sentence (F #5), suggesting that it was intended as a stage direction, not dialogue

First Folio

16/ Macduff

1 O horror, horror, horror,+
Tongue nor Heart cannot conceive,x nor name thee.

2 Confusion now hath made his Master-peece : +
Most sacrilegious [Murther] hath broke ope
The Lords anoynted Temple, and stole thence
The Life o'th'Building. +

3 Approch the Chamber, and destroy your sight
With a new Gorgon.
4 Doe not bid me speake : x
See, and then speake your selves : awake, awake,+

[Exeunt Macbeth and Lenox]

Ring the Alarum Bell : + [Murther], and Treason,+
Banquo,x and Donalbaine : + Malcolme+ awake,+
Shake off this Downey sleepe, Deaths counterfeit,
And looke on Death it selfe : + up, up, and see
The great Doomes Image : + Malcolme,+ Banquo,+
As from your Graves rise up, and walke like Sprights,
To countenance this horror. +
5 Ring the Bell.

17/ Old Man **Threescore and ten I can remember well,** between 3.1.1 - 19

Background: As the old man reports, since Duncan's death more supernatural events have occurred, matching those spoken of by Lenox (see speech #15 above). This speech is made up from lines originally assigned both to the Old Man and to Rosse.

Style: as part of a two-handed scene

Where: unspecified, but possibly somewhere on a public road **To Whom:** Rosse

# of Lines: 20 **Probable Timing: 1.00 minutes**

Modern Text

17/ Old Man

1 Threescore and ten I can remember well,
Within the Δvolume of which Δtime I have seen*
Hours* dreadful*, and things strange; but this sore Δnight
Hath trifled former knowing.

2 {ψ} Thou seest the Δheavens, as troubled with man's Δact,
Threatens his bloody Δstage. †

3 By th'Δclock 'tis Δday,
And yet dark* Δnight strangles the [travelling] Δlamp*. †

4 Is't Δnight's predominance, or the Δday's* shame,
That Δdarkness* does the face of Δearth entomb*,
When living Δlight should kiss* it?

5 'Tis unnatural*,
Even like the deed that's done. †

6 On Tuesday last,
A Δfalcon*, tow'ring in her pride of place,
Was by a Δmousing* Δowl* hawk'd at, and kill'd.

7 {ψ}And Duncan's Δhorses (a thing most strange, and certain*)
Beauteous and swift, the Δminions of their Δrace,
Turn'd wild* in nature, broke their stalls, flung* out,
Contending 'gainst Δobedience, as they would make
ΔWar* with Δmankind*.

8 {T}hey {ate} each other ,

{ψ} To th'amazement of mine eyes that look'd upon't.

Throughout, the inner cracks in F's orthography point to just how much the strangeness of the 'Night' is affecting the Old man's recounting of events – each by themselves (the minor onrush of F #2-3, the information contained within the few surround phrases, the F only split line starting F #4, and the unembellished final horrific sentence) could be almost ignored, but when put together the upheaval in thisseventy-odd year old's world is clearly visible.

- the surround phrases of F #1-3 point to the unnaturalness of what has occurred,
  ": but this sore Night/Hath trifled former knowings . /Thou seest the Heavens, as troubled with mans Act,/Threatens his bloody Stage : by th'Clock 'tis Day,/And yet darke Night strangles the [travailing] Lampe :"
  ". 'Tis unnaturall, Even like the deed that's done : "
  and the onrush of the sentences, F #2's darkness at noon and F #3's first example of the overturning of the laws of nature, cause him so much disturbance that he waivers in his grammatical niceties (this clue is wiped out by most modern texts that divide them into three and two sentences respectively)

- and F #4's second example of overturned nature – Duncan's horses 'Contending 'gainst Obedience' - seem equally disturbing, for not only does the Old Man use two extra breath-thoughts (marked ,$_x$) to ensure that all of the details are heard, he also needs two short lines (five/seven syllables) to start – though most modern texts join the two together to create one longer twelve syllable line as shown

- the Old man opens passionately in declaring that this is the worst night he has experienced in his seventy years, (F #1, 3/3), he becomes strongly intellectual pointing to the 'Heavens . . troubled' as the cause (5/0, F #2's first two lines)

- but then passion takes over as he describes how the 'darke Night strangles' daylight (7/7, the four and half lines ending F #2 and the first line of F #3)

- in offering confirmation of the unnatural events, he becomes much more factual – though accompanied by some emotion – for both examples of animal revolt (the killing of the falcon and the disobedience of Duncan's horses) are intellectually handled (12/7)

- yet the final horror, of Duncan's horses eating each other, seems to strike the Old Man almost dumb, for F #5 is totally unembellished

First Folio

17/ Old Man

1 Threescore and ten I can remember well,
Within the Volume of which Time,$_x$ I have seene
Houres dreadfull, and things strange:$_x$ but this sore Night
Hath trifled former knowings.

2 {ψ} Thou seest the Heavens, as troubled with mans Act,
Threatens his bloody Stage: by th'Clock 'tis Day,
And yet darke Night strangles the [travailing] Lampe:
Is't Nights predominance, or the Dayes shame,
That Darknesse does the face of Earth intombe,
When living Light should kisse it?

3 'Tis unnaturall,
Even like the deed that's done: On Tuesday last,
A Faulcon+ towring in her pride of place,
Was by a Mowsing Owle hawkt at, and kill'd.

4 {ψ} And Duncans Horses,$_x$→
(A thing most strange, and certaine)
Beauteous,$_x$ and swift, the Minions of their Race,
Turn'd wilde in nature, broke their stalls, flong out,
Contending 'gainst Obedience, as they would
Make Warre with Mankinde.

5 {T}hey {ate} each other,

{ψ} To th'amazement of mine eyes that look'd upon't.

18/ Banquo **Thou hast it now, King, Cawdor, Glamis, all,** 3.1.1 - 10

Background: Earlier, when facing the same temptations as Macbeth, Banquo prayed for heavenly protection, 'Mercifull Powers, restraine in me the cursed thoughts/That Nature gives way to in repose'. It seems that he now believes Macbeth has taken a different route.

Style: solo

Where: the great hall of the palace at Scone, where Macbeth has been recently invested as King **To Whom:** self and audience

# of Lines: 10 **Probable Timing: 0.35 minutes**

Modern Text

18/ Banquo

1 Thou hast it now : King, Cawdor, Glamis, all,
As the [weird] $^{\triangle}$women promis'd, and I fear*
Thou play'dst most foully* for't : yet it was said*
It should not stand in thy $^{\triangle}$posterity,
But that myself* should be the $^{\triangle}$root* and $^{\triangle}$father
Of many $^{\triangle}$kings.
2 If there come truth from them -
As upon thee Macbeth, their $^{\triangle}$speeches shine -
Why, by the verities on thee made good,
May they not be my Oracles as well,
And set me up in hope ?
3 But hush, no more.

- though the first line and half of the speech open with a strong intellectual recognition of Macbeth's success (4/1, F #1's first line and half), the fact that the opening phrase is both monosyllabic and unembellished might well suggest that Banquo is being initially very careful in voicing his thoughts (the first moment of taking stock perhaps?) - as if he can hardly voice the thought or is scared of being overheard
- his 'feare' of Macbeth playing 'most fowly for't' and the thought that the prophecy suggested that Banquo himself would become 'Father/Of many Kings' releases his passion (4/5, F #1's last four lines) . . .
- . . . but he quickly regains intellectual control during his F #2 realisation if the prophecy came true for Macbeth it could also for him (3/0)
- and just as the speech opened with no embellishment, it closes the same way, with F #3's injunction that he should be quiet, though whether this is simply because others, including the Macbeths, have entered the room or a more deeper command to speak (or even think) these thoughts no more is a decision for each actor to make

First Folio

18/ Banquo

Thou hast it now,$_{x}$ King, Cawdor, Glamis, all,
As the [weyard] Women promis'd, and I feare
Thou playd'st most fowly for't : yet it was saide
It should not stand in thy Posterity,
But that my selfe should be the Roote,$_{x}$ and Father
Of many Kings.
2 If there come truth from them,
As upon thee Macbeth, their Speeches shine,
Why,$_{x}$ by the verities on thee made good,
May they not be my Oracles as well,
And set me up in hope. $^{+}$
3 But hush, no more.

#'S 19 - 23: MACBETH STEPS IN TOO FAR

19/ Macbeth	**Bring them before us./To be thus, is nothing, but to be safely thus:**	3.1.47 - 71
20/ Macbeth	**I, in the Catalogue ye goe for men,**	3.1.91 - 107

Background: So far Macbeth has gone along with the plans developed by his wife - killing Duncan and laying the blame on the guards, then arranging it so that both of Duncan's sons should fall under suspicion for the deed. Now he decides to go it alone, and is planning to kill his old friend Banquo together with his young son Fleance to ensure that the third part of the witches' prophecy - Banquo's children inheriting the throne ('Thou shalt get Kings, though thou be none') - does not come true. Thus he has summoned two murderers for a second meeting. Speech #19 deals with the reasons why he feels such an act is necessary, while in speech #20 he attempts to shame the two very hesitant and non-communicative murderers into agreeing to his plan.

Style: speech #19, solo; speech #20, as part of a three-handed scene

Where: the great hall of the palace at Scone **To Whom:** speech #19, self and direct audience address; speech #20, the two Murderers

Speech 19: # of Lines: 26 **Probable Timing: 1.15 minutes**

Speech 20: # of Lines: 17 **Probable Timing: 0.55 minutes**

Modern Text

19/ Macbeth

1 Bring them before us.
[Exit Servant]
2 To be thus, is nothing,
But to be safely thus. †
3 Our fears* in Banquo
Stick* deep*, and in his Δroyalty* of Δnature
Reigns* that which would be fear'd.
4 'Tis much he dares,
And to that dauntless* temper of his Δmind*,
He hath a Δwisdom*, that doth guide his Δvalor*
To act in safety*.
5 There is none but he
Whose being I do* fear*; and under him
My Δgenius is rebuk'd, as it is said
Mark Anthony's* was by Cæsar.
6 He chid the Δsisters
When first they put the Δname of Δking upon me,
And bad them speak* to him; ◊ Then Δprophet-like,
They hail'd* him Δfather to a Δline of Δkings.
7 Upon my Δhead they plac'd a fruitless* Δcrown*,
And put a barren Δsceptre in my Δgripe,
Thence to be wrench'd with an unlineal* Δhand,
No Δson* of mine succeeding. †
8 If't be so,
For Banquo's Δissue have I fil'd my Δmind*,

F's opening five irregular lines (5/12/7/11/8 syllables) seem to capture beautifully both Macbeth's need for privacy and his struggle in starting to voice his predicament and fears about his one time colleague: unfortunately, as the shading shows, most modern texts' four line restructuring (11/11/11/10) renders this most difficult of moments back into a poetic regularity not necessarily warranted by the on-stage action.

- that there are only two surround phrases, surprisingly few for such a complex speech, suggests that this is not a premeditated speech revealing already known information but one flowing journey of new discoveries: the two that there are go straight to the heart of the problem as Macbeth's perceives it, the first enhanced by opening an onrushed sentence and being unembellished too
  " . To be thus, is nothing, but to be safely thus : "
  the second enhanced by the last two words' sudden emotional realisation ('doe feare', 0/2)
  " . There is none but he,/Whose being I doe feare : "

- the full gamut of releases that the speech quickly develops shows a Macbeth under enormous strain - the unembellished first two lines of the speech suggesting an enormous amount of concentration, only to be broken by the sudden one line emotional flurry of 'Our feares in Banquo sticke deepe' (0/3) in turn controlled by the intellectual assessment why, Banquo's 'Royaltie of Nature' (2/1) which is then expanded/expounded passionately in F #3's ' 'Tis much he dares' (3/3)

- as with F #2, F #4's 'feare' of Banquo motif plunges Macbeth again into emotion (0/2, F #4's opening line), which he once more puts aside intellectually (4/0), as he realises, whether rightly or wrongly, that his very spirit and nature ('Genius') is rebuk'd by Banquo's being, and how the Weyward Sisters 'hayl'd' him not just as king but 'Father to a Line of Kings' (F #5 – 6, 7/2 overall) after Banquo chid them

First Folio

19/ Macbeth

1 Bring them before us.
[Exit Servant]
2 To be thus, is nothing, but to be safely thus:
Our feares in Banquo sticke deepe,
And in his Royaltie of Nature reignes that
Which would be fear'd.
3 'Tis much he dares,
And to that dauntlesse temper of his Minde,
He hath a Wisdome, that doth guide his Valour,x
To act in safetie.
4 There is none but he,x
Whose being I doe feare:x and under him,x
My Genius is rebuk'd, as it is said
Mark Anthonies was by Cæsar.
5 He chid the Sisters,x
When first they put the Name of King upon me,
And bad them speake to him.
6 Then Prophet-like,
They hayl'd him Father to a Line of Kings.
7 Upon my Head they plac'd a fruitlesse Crowne,
And put a barren Scepter in my Gripe,
Thence to be wrencht with an unlineall Hand,
No Sonne of mine succeeding: if't be so,
For Banquo's Issue have I fil'd my Minde,

{ctd. over}

For them the gracious Duncan have I [murder'd],
Put Δrancors* in the Δvessel* of my Δpeace
Only* for them, and mine eternal* Δjewel*
Given to the common Δenemy* of Δman,
To make them Δkings - the Δseeds* of Banquo Δkings !
9 Rather [than]so, come Δfate into the Δlist*,
And champion me to th'utterance !

• with the implication that his Kingship will be wrench'd from his grip 'with an unlineall Hand', the top of the onrushed F #7 becomes passionate (6/5, the first three and half lines)

• which leads to another intellectual realisation that 'if't be so' he has murdered Duncan essentially for 'Banquo's Issue' (4/1, the two and a half lines following F #7's only colon), while the even more horrific understanding that in so doing he has damned himself is at first passionate (4/5, the two lines dealing with the destruction of his 'Peace' and soul, i.e. 'mine eternall Jewell') with the last two line irony of Macbeth having given the devil his own soul so as to make 'the Seedes of Banquo Kings' hitting him intellectually (6/1) yet again

• but true to his fighting/soldier nature, he passionately seeks the help of 'Fate into the Lyst' (2/1) before the unembellished last line stating that he will, with Fate's help, see matters through till the very end

For them,$_x$ the gracious Duncan have I [murther'd],
Put Rancours in the Vessell of my Peace
Onely for them, and mine eternall Jewell
Given to the common Enemie of Man,
To make them Kings, the Seedes of Banquo Kings.+
8 Rather [then] so, come Fate into the Lyst,
And champion me to th'utterance. +

Modern Text

20/ Macbeth

1 [Ay], in the Δcatalogue ye go* for men,
As Δhounds and Δgreyhounds, Δmungrels, Δspaniels, Δcurs*,
Showghs*, Δwater-Δrugs, and Δdemi*-Δwolves are clipt
All by the Δname of Δdogs*; the valued file
Distinguishes the swift, the slow, the subtle,
The Δhouse-keeper, the Δhunter, every one,
According to the gift which bounteous Δnature
Hath in him clos'd; whereby he does receive
Particular addition, from the Δbill
That writes them all alike: and so of men.
2 Now, if you have a station in the file,
Not i'th' worst rank* of Δmanhood, say't,
And I will put that Δbusiness* in your Δbosoms*,
Whose execution takes your Δenemy* off,
Grapples you to the heart and love of us,
Who wear* our Δhealth but sickly in his Δlife,
Which in his Δdeath were perfect.

F #1's factual opening (13/5 in just three and half lines) is one of the most intellectual bludgeonings Shakespeare offers at the start of any speech in any play: then, presumably having caught the murderer's attention, comes a gradual wind-down, though whether it is deliberately rhetorical or simply springs from Macbeth's unconscious need is up to each actor to decide.

• the follow-up, explaining that each has a unique quality, while still intellectual, is nowhere near as relentless (3/0 in four lines) - and the further intellectual suggestion (between the last two colons of the sentence) that it is the differences that make each type of dog valuable is even less pushed (1/0 in two lines)

• and then, whether consciously or not, comes the brilliant icy calm of the unembellished line and a half ending F #1 and opening F #2
" : and so of men. /Now, if you have a station in the file,"
applying the same idea to them (inescapably putting in place the question he is about to jab them with, are-you-going-to-prove-yourselves-valuable-to-me?), the transition heightened by starting with the only surround phrase of the speech

• the ensuing three line demand that if they are then 'say't' and he will employ them is the only time Macbeth becomes passionate in the speech (4/3, F#2, lines two to four))

• and then as Macbeth regains intellectual control (3/1, the last three lines of the speech) and offers two very elusive 'bribes' (closeness to his 'heart'; and love'), F's semicolon underscoring even more the emotional demand that they answer: however, for syntactical reasons some modern texts set no punctuation at all and so destroy what is probably the speech's key moment

First Folio

20/ Macbeth

1 [I], in the Catalogue ye goe for men,
As Hounds,$_x$ and Greyhounds, Mungrels, Spaniels, Curres,
Showghes, Water-Rugs, and Demy-Wolves are clipt
All by the Name of Dogges: $_x$ the valued file
Distinguishes the swift, the slow, the subtle,
The House-keeper, the Hunter, every one+
According to the gift,$_x$ which bounteous Nature
Hath in him clos'd: $_x$ whereby he does receive
Particular addition, from the Bill,$_x$
That writes them all alike: and so of men.
2 Now, if you have a station in the file,
Not i'th' worst ranke of Manhood, say't,
And I will put that Businesse in your Bosomes,
Whose execution takes your Enemie off,
Grapples you to the heart; $_x$ and love of us,
Who weare our Health but sickly in his Life,
Which in his Death were perfect.

21/ Macbeth **We have scorch'd the Snake, not kill'd it:** 3.2.13 - 26

Background: For a while Macbeth has kept himself apart from his wife, not letting her in on any of his thoughts or plans. She finally confronts him, challenging him especially over his brooding, 'why doe you keepe alone?/Of sorryest Fancies your companions making,/Using those Thoughts, which should indeed have dy'd/With them they thinke on: things without all remedie/Should be without regard: what's done, is done', which triggers the not particlarly useful (to her) or logical reply. Her simple and firm rejection of this speech, 'You must leave this', leads to the even more obscure ending 'O, full of Scorpions is my Minde, deare Wife'- which could be added here as a possible start to the speech. (No wonder she eventually 'marvell'st' at final speech in the scene – not set here -, so full are they of the dark images associated with witchcraft and black magic.)

Style: both as part of a two-handed scene

Where: unspecified, but probably their private chambers at Scone **To Whom:** Lady Macbeth

# of Lines: 15 **Probable Timing: 0.50 minutes**

Modern Text

21/ Macbeth

1 We have [scotch'd] the Δsnake, not kill'd it;
She'll* close and be her self*, whilst* our poor* Δmalice*
Remains* in danger of her former Δtooth.

2 But let the frame of things disjoint*, both the Δworlds suffer,
Ere we will eat* our Δmeal* in fear*, and sleep*
In the affliction of these terrible Δdreams*
That shake us Δnightly. †

3 Better be with the dead,
Whom we, to gain* our peace, have sent to peace,
[Than] on the torture of the Δmind* to lie*
In restless* ecstasy*.

4 Duncan* is in his Δgrave;
After Δlife's fitful* Δfever, he sleeps* well. †

5 Treason has done his worst; nor Δsteel*, nor Δpoison*,
Malice* domestic*, foreign* Δlevy*, nothing,
Can touch him further.

As Macbeth utters the appalling thoughts of allowing the order of both the natural and the magical world to 'dis-joynt' (the start of F #2) and that life is 'fitful' and perhaps death is welcome (the link between F #2 and F #3), F emphasises the struggle within him by setting two sets of short lines (8/5 syllables and 6/6 syllables respectively) – the tiny pauses thus created allowing him moments to regain self-control: most modern texts reset both as single lines, longer than iambic pentameter (13 and 12 syllables respectively), thus substituting F's pause with an onrush instead.

- the depth of the problem shared by both Macbeth and his wife is intensified via the opening surround phrase ' . We have scorch'd the Snake, not kill'd it : ' and F #1's subsequent emotions (3/6)

- but after the passionate split-line avowal that he is prepared to let 'the frame of things dis-joynt' (1/1), F #2's fleshing out of the horrors he is now undergoing through lack of sleep he returns to emotions once more (5/9)

- while the strange passionate thoughts (F #3, 6/8) which seem to be created by his inability to sleep are also heightened with surround phrases
  ". Duncane is in his Grave : /After Lifes fitfull Fever, he sleepes well,/Treason ha's done his worst : "

First Folio

21/ Macbeth

1 We have [scorch'd] the Snake, not kill'd it: x
Shee'le close, x and be her selfe, whilest our poore Mallice
Remaines in danger of her former Tooth.

2 But let the frame of things dis-joynt,→
Both the Worlds suffer,
Ere we will eate our Meale in feare, and sleepe
In the affliction of these terrible Dreames, x
That shake us Nightly: Better be with the dead,
Whom we, to gayne our peace, have sent to peace,
[Then] on the torture of the Minde to lye
In restlesse extasie. →

3 Duncane is in his Grave: x
After Lifes fitfull Fever, he sleepes well,
Treason ha's done his worst: x nor Steele, nor Poyson,
Mallice domestique, forraine Levie, nothing,
Can touch him further.

22/ Lenox **My former Speeches,/Have but hit your Thoughts** 3.6.1 - 24

Background: With the unusual number of deaths of people close to or standing in Macbeth's way, and especially after his most peculiar behaviour at the celebratory feast (where, in facing down the supposed ghost of Banquo - which only Macbeth could see - Macbeth opened a great deal of conjecture about his complicity in Banquo's death), people are beginning to talk, as here.

Style: as part of a two-handed scene

Where: unspecified, but perhaps close to the palace at Scone **To Whom:** an un-named Lord

# of Lines: 24 **Probable Timing: 1.15 minutes**

Modern Text

22/ Lenox

1 My former Δspeeches have but hit your Δthoughts,
Which can interpret farther ; Δonly* I say
Things have been* strangely born*.
2 The gracious Duncan
Was pitied* of Macbeth ; marry, he was dead. †
3 And the right valiant Banquo walk'd too late,
Whom you may say (if't please you) [Fleance] kill'd,
For [Fleance] fled. †
4 Men must not walk* too late.
5 Who cannot want the thought, how monstrous
It was for Malcolm* and for [Donalbain*]
To kill their gracious Δfather?
6 Damned Δfact !,
7 How it did grieve* Macbeth !
8 Did he not straight
In pious rage the two delinquents tear*,
That were the Δslaves of drink* and thralls* of sleep*?
9 Was not that Δnobly done?
10 [Ay], and wisely too;
For 'twould have anger'd any heart alive
To hear* the men deny't.
11 So that, I say,
He has borne all things well, and I do think*
That had he Duncan's Δsons* under his Δkey
(As, and't please Δheaven he shall not) they should find*
What 'twere to kill a Δfather ; Δso should [Fleance].
12 But peace ! for from broad words, and 'cause he fail'd*
His presence at the Δtyrant's Δfeast, I hear*
Macduff* lives in disgrace.

This is one of the finest oblique double-speak speeches in Shakespeare, for while Lenox ensures that his words cannot be used against him should any of Macbeth's spies overhear, nevertheless his language and phrasing probes much of Macbeth's actions to date – demanding that his listener commit himself one way or another before he does so himself – and F's orthography shows just how very careful and clever he can be.

- F's short opening lines (5/5 syllables) allow Lenox a very careful start as he embarks on what could be interpreted as treasonous remarks: most modern texts set them as one full line of verse, as shown, removing the opening clue

- his determined care is also seen both his intellectual control as he starts by posing the facts in a rather provocative way F #1-2 (9/4), and in the four surround phrases by which the key points are made
  " : Onely I say/Things have bin strangely borne . The gracious Duncan /Was pittied of Macbeth : marry he was dead : "
  " : Men must not walke too late . "

- Lenox then becomes passionate in raising F #3's more dangerous question of the involvement of Duncan's sons in their father's murder (3/2) and in F #4's even more dangerous notion of attaching Macbeth's grief to the event (2/1)

- then intellectual control almost completely disappears as he describes Macbeth's tearing apart of Duncan's supposed murderers and suggests that it was wisely done (2/5, F #5-7), the irony of the wording heightened by being expressed as two surround phrases
  " . I, and wisely too : /For 'twould have anger'd any heart alive/To heare the men deny't . "

- as Lenox so cleverly at one and the same time raises doubts about Macbeth's integrity by praising him, he regains a degree of intellectual control (F #8, 7/3)

- finally, having made statements throughout the speech so far, Lenox finally turns to direct questioning - and as he does so full intellectual control is lost, replaced first by passion (F #9, 2/3) as he indirectly asks confirmation of Macduffe's whereabouts, and then byemotion as he asks more directly (F #10, 0/2)

First Folio

22/ Lenox

1 My former Speeches,$_{x}$→
Have but hit your Thoughts+
Which can interpret farther: $_{x}$ Onely I say
Things have bin strangely borne.
2 The gracious Duncan
Was pittied of Macbeth: $_{x}$ marry+ he was dead:
And the right valiant Banquo walk'd too late,
Whom you may say (if't please you) [Fleans] kill'd,
For [Fleans] fled: Men must not walke too late.
3 Who cannot want the thought, how monstrous
It was for Malcolme,$_{x}$ and for [Donalbane]
To kill their gracious Father?
4 Damned Fact,+
How it did greeve Macbeth?+
5 Did he not straight
In pious rage,$_{x}$ the two delinquents teare,
That were the Slaves of drinke,$_{x}$ and thralles of sleepe?
6 Was not that Nobly done?
7 [I], and wisely too: $_{x}$
For 'twould have anger'd any heart alive
To heare the men deny't.
8 So that+ I say,
He ha's borne all things well, and I do thinke,$_{x}$
That had he Duncans Sonnes under his Key,$_{x}$
(As, and't please Heaven he shall not) they should finde
What 'twere to kill a Father: $_{x}$ So should [Fleans].
9 But peace; + for from broad words, and cause he fayl'd
His presence at the Tyrants Feast, I heare
Macduffe lives in disgrace.

13 Sir, can you tell
Where he bestows* himself*?

• interestingly, the decision to do this seems to be difficult for him for the first phrase of F #9 is set as a very short, monosyllabic, emotional (via the only semicolon in the speech) surround phrase ' . But peace ; ' – though whether this is intended for his colleague because he has offended him or for himself to calm himself down is up to each actor to explore

10 Sir, can you tell
Where he bestowes himselfe?

23/ Malcome **What I beleeve, Ile waile ; /What know, beleeve ; and what I can redresse,** between 4.3.8 - 31

Background: Macduff has fled to England, not to save himself but in an attempt to bring Malcome, Duncan's oldest son (who was legitimately named king by his father before Macbeth began his murderous attacks) back to Scotland as the leader of a growing number of anti-Macbeth dissidents. However, Malcome has been tempted too often by agents of Macbeth to believe in Macduff's integrity without a great deal of questioning and challenges.

Style: as part of a two-handed scene

Where: somewhere in the English court **To Whom:** Macduff

# of Lines: 22 **Probable Timing: 1.10 minutes**

Modern Text

23/ Malcome

1 What I believe*, I'll wail*,
What know, believe*; and what I can redress*,
As I shall find* the time to friend, I will*.

2 What you have spoke, it may be so perchance.

3 This $^{\Delta}$tyrant, whose sole name blisters our tongues,
Was once thought honest; you have lov'd him well;
He hath not touch'd you yet.

4 I am young*, but something
You may [deserve] of him through me, and wisdom*
To offer up a weak*, poor*, innocent $^{\Delta}$lamb*
T'appease an angry $^{\Delta}$god.

5 A good and virtuous* $^{\Delta}$nature may recoil*
In an $^{\Delta}$imperial* charge.

6 But I shall crave your pardon;
That which you are, my thoughts cannot transpose:
Angels are bright still, though the brightest fell.

7 Though all things foul* would wear the brows of grace,
Yet $^{\Delta}$grace must still look* so.

8 Why in that rawness* left you $^{\Delta}$wife, and $^{\Delta}$child*,
Those precious $^{\Delta}$motives, those strong knots of $^{\Delta}$love,
Without leave-taking?

9 I pray you,
Let not my $^{\Delta}$jealousies be your $^{\Delta}$dishonors,
But mine own* $^{\Delta}$safeties. †

10 You may be rightly just,
What ever I shall think*.

Malcome starts out extraordinarily strongly (even vehemently), the emotional opening of his mistrust (0/5, F #1) made even stronger by being set as four consecutive surround phrases,
" . What I beleeve, Ile waile ; /What know, beleeve ; and what I can redresse,/As I shall finde the time to friend : I wil . "
- the first three even further enhanced by the extra emotional power of the first two semicolons.

- the drive continues with the short F #2 - suggesting Macduffe might be honest - with F #3's two more surround phrases challenging this assumption because when Macbeth was thought honest Macduffe loved him: in doing so, Malcome becomes very quiet since, save for the word 'Tyrant' (itself a wonderful indicator of his feelings about Macbeth) F #2-3 are unembellished - though whether Malcome is trying to control himself or is just freezing out Macduffe is up to each actor to explore

- F #4's extension that Macduffe may be thus tempted to deliver Malcome to Macbeth is emotional (2/4), in turn triggering passion (2/2) for his damning F #5 suggestion that anyone could prove treacherous 'In an Imperiall charge'

- that Malcome is torn can be seen in the ensuing three surround phrase F #6
" . But I shall crave your pardon : /That which you are, my thoughts cannot transpose ; /Angels are bright still, though the brightest fell . "
for not only does the apology/attack seem to be very carefully worded and voiced, in that the sentence is unembellished, it also seems to cause him strain, for the last two surround phrases are again linked by an emotional semicolon

- which leads to yet another emotional elaboration, F #7 suggesting in no uncertain terms that appearances (and therefore Macduffe) can be deceptive (1/2)

- Malcome then becomes slightly more intellectual for the rest of the speech both for the all-important question of why Macduffe so suddenly abandoned his family (F #8, 4/2) and for the F #9 apology for his doubts (3/2)

- after all the doubts, the possibility that Macduffe may be honest is heightened with the last words of the speech, the surround phrase
" : you may be rightly just,/What ever I shall thinke . "

First Folio

23/ Malcome

1 What I beleeve, Ile waile; $_{x}$
What know, beleeve; and what I can redresse,
As I shall finde the time to friend: $_{x}$ I wil.

2 What you have spoke, it may be so perchance.

3 This Tyrant, whose sole name blisters our tongues,
Was once thought honest: $_{x}$ you have lov'd him well,$^{+}$
He hath not touch'd you yet.

4 I am yong, but something
You may [discerne] of him through me, and wisedome
To offer up a weake, poore^{+} innocent Lambe
T'appease an angry God.

5 A good and vertuous Nature may recoyle
In an Imperiall charge.

6 But I shall crave your pardon: $_{x}$
That which you are, my thoughts cannot transpose; $^{+}$
Angels are bright still, though the brightest fell.

7 Though all things foule,$_{x}$ would wear the brows of grace^{+}
Yet Grace must still looke so.

8 Why in that rawnesse left you Wife, and Childe?$_{x}$
Those precious Motives, those strong knots of Love,
Without leave-taking. $^{+}$

9 I pray you,
Let not my Jealousies,$_{x}$ be your Dishonors,
But mine owne Safeties: you may be rightly just,
What ever I shall thinke.

#'S 24 - 27: THE BLOODY FINALE

24/ Rosse **I have words/That would be howl'd out in the desert ayre,** between 4.3.193 - 207

Background: Rosse has come to England on a double mission - to add his voice in bringing Malcome back to Scotland and to give the appalling news to Macduff of his family's slaughter. Having put the second task off for some time, Rosse finally begins to break the news.

Style: one on one address with a third person present

Where: somewhere in the English court **To Whom:** Macduff, in front of Malcome

# of Lines: 12 **Probable Timing: 0.40 minutes**

Modern Text

24/ Rosse

1 I have words
That would be howl'd out in the desert air*,
Where hearing should not latch them.

2 No mind* that's honest
But in it shares some woe, though the main* part
Pertains* to you alone.

3 Let not your ears* despise* my tongue for ever,
Which shall possess* them with the heaviest sound
That ever yet they heard.

4 Your Δcastle is surpris'd*; your Δwife, and Δbabes
Savagely slaughter'd. †

5 To relate the manner,
Were on the Δquarry of these [murder'd] deer*
To add* the death of you.

• that Rosse is attempting to keep himself in check can be seen in F #1's set-up to the bad news

"I have words/That would be howl'd out in the desert ayre, /Where hearing should
not latch them."

which is unembellished save for the one word 'ayre'

• that, understandably, he cannot stay unemotional can be seen in the next two sentences, both in F #2's suggesting that the news 'Pertaines to you alone' (0/3) and F #3's apology for what he is about to say (0/2)

• and then his style completely changes as he begins to report the horrors, becoming intellectual (F #4, 6/3) with the voicing of the dreadful

". Your Castle is surpriz'd : your Wife, and Babes/Savagely slaughter'd : "

heightened by being set as two successive surround phrases - whether as an attempt not to let himself be swamped by the information or to ensure that he can make the briefness of each point tell without unnecessary elaboration is up to each actor to explore

First Folio

24/ Rosse

1 I have words
That would be howl'd out in the desert ayre,
Where hearing should not latch them.

2 No minde that's honest
But in it shares some woe, though the maine part
Pertaines to you alone.

3 Let not your eares dispise my tongue for ever,
Which shall possesse them with the heaviest sound
That ever yet they heard.

4 Your Castle is surpriz'd: x your Wife, and Babes
Savagely slaughter'd: To relate the manner+
Were on the Quarry of these [murther'd] Deere
To adde the death of you.

25/ Macduff **All my pretty ones?/Did you say All?** between 4.3.216 - 234

Background: This is Macduff's immediate response to Rosse's appalling news (speech #24 immediately above).

Style: one on one address with a third person present

Where: somewhere in the English court **To Whom:** Rosse, in front of Malcome

# of Lines: 18 **Probable Timing: 0.55 minutes**

Modern Text

25/ Macduff

1 All my pretty ones?
2 Did you say Δall?
3 O* Δhell-Δkite!
4 All?
5 What, Δall my pretty Δchickens, and their Δdam*,
At one fell swoop*?
6 I shall {dispute it like a man};
But I must also feel* it as a man:
I cannot but remember such things were
That were most precious to me. †
7 Did heaven look* on,
And would not take their part?
8 Sinful* Macduff,
They were all strook* for thee! Δnaught that I am,
Not for their own* demerits, but for mine,
Fell slaughter on their souls*. †
9 Heaven rest them now.
10 O, I could play the woman with mine eyes,
And Δbraggart with my tongue!
11 But, gentle Δheavens,
Cut short all intermission. †
12 Front to Δfront,
Bring thou this Δfiend of Scotland and myself*;
Within my Δsword's length set him; if he scape
Heaven forgive him too.

Quite remarkably under such extraordinarily emotional circumstances, F's orthography suggests that Macduffe is attempting to control himself with a series of reasoned statements (the whole speech being more intellectual than emotional 17/10), with only minute shifts in F's orthography showing where self-control may be too much for him.

- the speech opens with a series of very short sentences (F #1-4) - further proof of his attempt to maintain self-control – each offering the very minimum that need be said, the four together part of an intellectual start (6/3, F #1-5)

- after the virtually unembellished bulk of F #6 (0/1, the first three and a half lines), the realisation that they were killed for him is the only emotional passage in the speech (3/5, F #6's last line and all of F #7 save the last phrase)

- with the resolve to action that dominates the rest of the speech it seems that Macduffe regains self-control and is very strongly intellectual (8/1. the last six lines of the speech - from the last phrase of F #7 on)

- however, that Macduffe's inner turmoil almost bursts through can be seen in that unlike most modern texts, F ungrammatically, sets no punctuation between F #9's lines three and four ('my selfe' and 'Within my Swords length') suggesting that (the fervency of?) Macduffe's avowal is getting the better of him: for clarity most modern texts add a comma, making the moment far more logical than originally set

- the unembellished passages show where he is working at his hardest to control himself no matter what the internal personal cost - from the very opening
  ". All my pretty ones ?"
  through to his refusal to give into tears, no matter what, with just the one incredibly telling word 'feele' breaking F #6's three and a half otherwise unembellished lines
  ". I shall {dispute it like a man} : /But I must also feele it as a man ; /I cannot but remember such things were/That were most precious to me :"
  his calm determination not to give in to his own emotions intensified by the text being set as three (of four) consecutive surround phrases and the momentary breaking of his self control via the impassioned phrase ' : Did heaven looke on', before F #6's last phrase 'And would not take their part' re-establishes unembellished self-control once more

- the remaining three surround phrases all point to key realisations or requests
  ". Sinfull Macduff,/They were all strooke for thee :"
  ": Heaven rest them now ."
  ". But gentle Heavens/Cut short all intermission :"

First Folio

25/ Macduff

1 All my pretty ones?
2 Did you say All?
3 Oh Hell-Kite!
4 All?
5 What, All my pretty Chickens, and their Damme+
At one fell swoope?
6 I shall {dispute it like a man}: x
But I must also feele it as a man; x
I cannot but remember such things were
That were most precious to me: Did heaven looke on,
And would not take their part?
7 Sinfull Macduff,
They were all strooke for thee: + Naught that I am,
Not for their owne demerits, but for mine+
Fell slaughter on their soules: Heaven rest them now.
8 O+ I could play the woman with mine eyes,
And Braggart with my tongue. +
9 But+ gentle Heavens,
Cut short all intermission: Front to Front,
Bring thou this Fiend of Scotland, x and my selfe+
Within my Swords length set him, + if he scape
Heaven forgive him too.

26/ Lady **Yet heere's a spot.** between 5.1.31 - 68

Background: Lady Macbeth is sick. She has been walking and talking in her sleep repeatedly, leaving no doubt as to her complicity in and/or knowledge of the various murders that have enabled Macbeth to become, and then maintain his position as, King. Here she walks once more, not knowing that she is being closely watched by the Doctor and the Gentlewoman who has summoned him.

Style: solo, observed by two hidden watchers

Where: the castle at Dunsinane **To Whom:** self, and the imagined presence of Macbeth

# of Lines: 17 **Probable Timing: 0.55 minutes**

Modern Text

26/ Lady

1 Yet here's* a spot.

2 Out, damned spot ! out, I say !
3 One - Δtwo - Δwhy
then 'tis time to do't*. †
4 Hell is murky.
5 Fie*, my Lord, fie,
a Δsoldier*, and afear'd*? †
6 What need we fear* who knows*
it, when none can call our pow'r* to accompt ? †
7 Yet who
would have thought the old* man to have had so much
blood in him ?

8 The Thane of Fife, had a wife; where is she now?
9 What, will these hands ne'er be clean*?
10 No more o'that
my Δlord, no more o'that; you mar* all with this starting.

11 Here's* the smell of the blood still. †
12 All the per-
fumes of Arabia will not sweeten this little hand.
13 O*, ΔO*, ΔO* !

14 Wash your hands, put on your Δnight-Δgown*,
look* not so pale. †
15 I tell you yet again*, Banquo's buried;
he cannot come out on's grave.

16 To bed, to bed; there's knocking at the gate. †

The large number of major punctuation marks (thirteen, of which only one is emotional), and the pronounced and quick switches between four different patterns of release underscore the Doctor's earlier description of her as being 'troubled with thicke-comming Fancies/That keepe her from her rest.' – for here her mind never stays on one topic or remains in one particular style for more than a brief moment.

- the factual recollections and sometimes their current consequences - F #2 (her attempt to wash the blood off her hands); F #3 (the sound of the all-clear bell to summon them to kill Duncan); F #5 (the recollection of the now murdered Macduffe's wife); #F 7 (the attempt to keep Macbeth from becoming distracted by guilt from their plan); F #8, (the scent of the blood); F #10 (again instructions to Macbeth); F #11 (avoiding discovery by the arrival of Lenox and Macduffe) – are all heightened by being set as surround phrase sentences, as if each recollection is so disturbing as to give her pain – almost as if she were struggling to control each new memory so as not to be swamped by it

- the most disturbing of all the recollections seems to be F #10's last two emotional surround phrases
  " : I tell you yet againe Banquo's buried ; he cannot come out on's grave. "
since they are heightened by being linked by the only semicolon in the speech

- F's occasional onrush, where the juxtaposing of two ungrammatically connected ideas are joined in one sentence, shows where she is almost swamped - especially F #4's chastising of Macbeth plus the amount of blood spilled when Duncan was killed; F #10's ordering Macbeth to tidy himself plus the fact that Banquo cannot rise out of his grave; and F #11's repeated instructions 'to bed' plus 'What's done, cannot be undone'

- the unembellished monosyllabic surround phrases of F #2, ' . Out damned spot : out I say . ', suggest a moment of great determination in her attempt to rid herself of what she must feel would be the only evidence of their crime, while the calm of the almost completely unembellished [6] finale

First Folio

26/ Lady

1 Yet heere's a spot.

2 Out+ damned spot: + out +I say. +
3 One: x Two: x Why
then 'tis time to doo't: Hell is murky.
4 Fye, my Lord, fie,
a Souldier, and affear'd? what need we feare? x who knowes
it, when none can call our powre to accompt: + yet who
would have thought the olde man to have had so much
blood in him. +

5 The Thane of Fife, had a wife: x where is she now?
6 What+ will these hands ne're be cleane?
7 No more o'that
my Lord, no more o'that: x you marre all with this starting.

8 Heere's the smell of the blood still: all the perfumes of Arabia will not sweeten this little hand.
9 Oh, oh, oh. +

10 Wash your hands, put on your Night-Gowne,
looke not so pale: I tell you yet againe+ Banquo's buried;
he cannot come out on's grave.

11 To bed, to bed: x there's knocking at the gate:

{ctd. over}

[6] unembellished save for the capitals at the top of two new ideas 'Come' and 'What's', each of which adds weight to the plea that follows

17 Come, come, come, come, give me your hand. †
18 What's
done cannot be undone.
19 To bed, to bed, to bed.

"To bed, to bed : there's knocking at the gate : Come, come, come, come, give me your hand : What's done, cannot be undone . To bed, to bed, to bed ."
could well suggest that with all she has gone through her energy has at last drained away

12 Come, come, come, come, give me your hand: What's
done,ₓ cannot be undone.
To bed, to bed, to bed.

27/ Macbeth **She should have dy'de heereafter;** 5.3.17 - 28

Background: This is Macbeth's response to the news 'The Queene (my Lord) is dead'.

Style: solo, in front of one other person

Where: the castle at Dunsinane **To Whom:** self, audience, in front of Seyton

# of Lines: 12 **Probable Timing: 0.40 minutes**

Modern Text

27/ Macbeth

1 She should have died* hereafter*;
There would have been* a time for such a word. †
2 To-morrow, and to-morrow, and to-morrow,
Creeps* in this petty pace from day to day,
To the last △syllable of △recorded time;
And all our yesterdays* have lighted △fools*
The way to dusty death.
3 Out, out, brief* △candle ! †
4 Life's but a walking △shadow, a poor* △player,
That struts and frets his hour* upon the △stage,
And then is heard no more.
5 It is a △tale
Told by an △idiot*, full of sound and fury,
Signifying nothing.

- following the announcement of his wife's death, his lack of further words about her need not mean that he is not moved, for the speech opens with two emotional surround phrases (created by the only semicolon of the speech)
  " . She should have dy'de heereafter ; /There would have beene a time for such a word : "
  the emotional semicolon enhanced by the emotion of the first two lines (0/3)

- 'the petty pace' that is to continue 'from day to day' is expressed passsionately (3/3), though very interestingly the preceeding
  " To morrow, and to morrow, and to morrow,"
  that triggers this sequence is eerily and bleakly unembellished, a conclusion matched by his final unembellished summation of the speech

- the sequence continues passionately as he suggests, first, that his life should finish ('Out, out, breefe Candle,') and then in realising that as a consequence, life is but a 'walking Shadow' with a very short life span to come (F #2, 4/3)

- F #3's despairing assessment that life is a 'Tale/Told by an Ideot' is passionate (2/1), and then comes the final unembellished conclusion,
  "full of sound and fury/Signifying nothing."
  as if Macbeth's realisation of life's bleakness is echoed in his delivery

First Folio

27/ Macbeth

1 She should have dy'de heereafter;
There would have beene a time for such a word:
To morrow, and to morrow, and to morrow,
Creepes in this petty pace from day to day,
To the last Syllable of Recorded time: ₓ
And all our yesterdayes,ₓ have lighted Fooles
The way to dusty death.
2 Out, out, breefe Candle,⁺
Life's but a walking Shadow, a poore Player,
That struts and frets his houre upon the Stage,
And then is heard no more.
3 It is a Tale
Told by an Ideot, full of sound and fury⁺
Signifying nothing.

SPEECHES IN ORDER		TIME	PAGE
TIMON OF ATHENS			
#'s 1 - 3: Timon's Generosity			
1/ Timon	Oh no doubt my good Friends, but the Gods	1.00	261
2/ Poet	You see this confluence, this great flood of visitors,	1.45	262
3a/ Senator	And late five thousand : to Varro and to Isidore	0.45	264
b/ Senator	Get on your cloak & haste you to Lord Timon	1.00	265
#'s 4 - 8: Timon's Generosity Leads To Trouble			
4/ Steward	O my good Lord,/At many times	0.45	266
5/ Steward	Lord Lucius and Lucullus, {and the Senators}?	0.50	267
6/ Timon	You Gods reward them :/Prythee man looke cheerely.	1.00	268
7/ {Lucius}	Servilius? You are kindely met sir.	1.15	269
8/ Timon	Let me looke backe upon thee. O thou Wall	2.00	270
#'s 9 - 11: The Apermantus Debates			
9/ Apermantus	This is in thee a Nature but infected,	0.55	272
10/ Apermantus	Thou hast cast away thy selfe, being like thy self	0.45	273
11/ Timon	Would'st thou have thy selfe fall in the confusion	1.10	274
#'s 12 - 17: Timon And His New Found Gold			
12/ Timon	I have enough Gold to make a Whore forsweare	1.30	275
13/ Timon	Thankes I must you con,/That you are Theeves	1.15	276
14/ Painter	As I tooke note of the place, it cannot be farre	1.30	278
15/ Poet	I am thinking/What I shall say I have provided for him:	0.40	279
16/ Poet	Haile worthy Timon, our late Noble Master.	0.40	280
17/ Timon	Most honest men : /Why how shall I requite you?	1.55	281
#'s 18 - 20: The Alcibiades Factor			
18/ 1st Senator	The Senators of Athens, greet thee Timon,	1.15	283
19/ Timon	I love my Country, and am not/One that rejoyces . . .	1.30	284
20/ 1st Senator	Noble, and young ;	2.00	285

SPEECHES BY GENDER

		Speech #(s)
SPEECHES FOR WOMEN (0)		
SPEECHES FOR EITHER GENDER (13)		
Poet	**Traditional:** male, any age **Today:** any age, any gender	#2, #15, #16
Painter	**Traditional:** male, any age **Today:** any age, any gender	#14
Steward	**Traditional:** older male, any age **Today:** any age, any gender	#4, #5
{Lucius}	**Traditional:** male, any age **Today:** any age, any gender	#7
Apermantus	**Traditional:** older male **Today:** any gender, any age – often middle age or older	#9, #10
Senators (x3)	**Traditional:** male, any age **Today:** any age, any gender	#3a, #3b, #18, #20
SPEECHES FOR MEN (or women in an adventurous production) (8)		
Timon	**Traditional:** older male **Today:** male/female of any age	#1, #6, #8, #11, #12, #13, #17, #19

TIMON OF ATHENS

#'s 1 - 3: Timon's Generosity

1/ Timon **Oh no doubt my good Friends, but the Gods** 1.2.88 - 108

Background: At one of his frequent almost potlatch-type banquets, Timon gives praise to his friends. As such, and as an explanation of his personal philosophy, the speech is self-explanatory. That the text is in prose might well suggest that he is overcome by the enormity of the gracious praise from his guests (lip-service as it eventually turns out) which has triggered this speech.

Style: general address to a large group

Where: Timon's home **To Whom:** a large number of guests

# of Lines: 20 **Probable Timing: 1.00 minutes**

Modern Text

1/ Timon

1 O*, no doubt, my good Δfriends, but the Δgods
themselves have provided that I shall have much help*
from you : how had you been* my Δfriends else ?
2 Why
have you that charitable title from thousands,◊ did not
you chiefly* belong to my heart?
3 I have told more of
you to myself*, [than] you can with modesty$_*$ speak* in
your own* behalf*; ◊ and thus far* I confirm* you.
4 O*
you Δgods, think* I, what need we have any Δfriends, if
we should ne'er have need of 'em?
5 They were the most
needless* Δcreatures living, should we ne'er have use for
'em; ◊ Δand would most resemble sweet* Δinstruments
hung up in Δcases, that keeps* [their] sounds to themselves.
6 Why I have often wish'd myself* poorer, that
I might come nearer* to you. †
7 We are borne to do bene-
fits; ◊ and what better or properer can we call our own*
[than] the riches of our Δfriends?
8 O*, what a precious* com-
fort 'tis, to have so many like Δbrothers commanding
one another's Δfortunes !

• Timon's philosophy of friendship, that is to be so rudely shattered later in the play, is underscored by four consecutive emotional surround phrases created by the only semicolons in the speech

"". Oh you Gods (thinke I,) what need we have any Friends ; if we should nere have need of 'em ? They were the most needlesse Creatures living ; should we nere have use for 'em ? "

while the pleasure such friendship yields is neatly encapsulated in the logical (colon created) surround phrases

". Why I have often wisht my selfe poorer, that I might come neerer to you : we are borne to do benefits ."

". Oh joyes, e'ne made away er't can be borne : mine eies cannot hold out water$_x$ me thinks to forget their Faults . "

• his opening passionate belief (F #1, 3/3) that friends are provided by 'the Gods' is heightened by the first surround phrase of the speech ' : how had you beene my Friends else . ' – which is offered as a statement, not as a question as most modern texts suggest by adding a question mark to the end of mt. #1

• the fact that F's sentence that follows, striking in its calmness

"Why have you that charitable title from thousands?"

is not only the sole unembellished passage in the speech but is also regarded by most modern texts as ungrammatical (and therefore rationally joined with the sentence that follows) suggests that Timon is so moved by the idea of friendship and the number of friends present that it is difficult for him to even speak the thought

• but then as Timon confirms those present as belonging to his heart (F #3-5) he becomes highly emotional (0/6 in two and a half lines)

• the emotional surround phrase lead-in to and the celebration of the need for friends turns passionate (5/5, F #6-8), as does the somewhat naive F #10-11 belief of how wonderful it is that so many 'Brothers' are able to command 'one anothers Fortunes' (3/3)

First Folio

1/ Timon

1 Oh+ no doubt+ my good Friends, but the Gods
themselves have provided that I shall have much helpe
from you : how had you beene my Friends else. +
2 Why
have you that charitable title from thousands?
3 Did not
you chiefely belong to my heart?
4 I have told more of
you to my selfe, [then] you can with modestie speake in
your owne behalfe.
5 And thus farre I confirme you.
6 Oh
you Gods ($_x$thinke I,)$_x$ what need we have any Friends;$_x$ if
we should nere have need of 'em?
7 They were the most
needlesse Creatures living;$_x$ should we nere have use for
'em?
8 And would most resemble sweete Instruments
hung up in Cases, that keepes [there] sounds to themselves.
9 Why I have often wisht my selfe poorer, that
I might come neerer to you : we are borne to do benefits.
10 And what better or properer can we call our owne,$_x$
[then] the riches of our Friends?
11 Oh+ what a pretious com-
fort 'tis, to have so many like Brothers commanding
one anothers Fortunes. +

{ctd. over}

9 O*, [joy* e'en made away ere't* can be born* !] † [1]
10 Mine eyes* cannot hold out water, methinks*. †
11 To forget their Δfaults, ◊ I drink* to you .

• though in the midst of this passion both the corollary that he has often wished himself poorer to take advantage of their friendship (F #9) and the peculiarly ungrammatical finale offering breathing/thinking proof of just how moved/disturbed he is as he tries to drink away his joys and tears (F #12-13) are very emotional (0/3, 1/4 respectively)

12 Oh+ [joyes,x e'ne made away er't can be borne]: mine eies cannot hold out water,x+me thinks+ to forget their Faults.
13 I drinke to you.

2/ Poet — You see this confluence, this great flood of visitors,

between 1.1.42 - 83

Background: In this, one of the first speeches in the play, the Poet is talking to the Painter, both of whom are desperate to have Timon become their patron, thus ensuring them a generous income.

Style: as part of a two-handed scene surrounded by a number of people who are not part of the conversation **Where:** Timon's home

To Whom: the Painter, in the presence of other party guests who, bent on their own ventures, are not listening

# of Lines: 36 **Probable Timing: 1.45 minutes**

Modern Text

2/ Poet

1 You see this confluence, this great flood of visitors .†
2 I have, in this rough work*, shap'd out a man
Whom this beneath world doth embrace and hug*
With amplest entertainment . †
3 My free drift
Halts not particularly, but moves itself*
In a wide Δsea of wax; no levell'd malice
Infects one comma in the course I hold,
But flies an Δeagle flight, bold, and forth on,
Leaving no Δtract behind*.
xxxxxxxxxxxxxxxxxxxxxxxxxxxxxxxxxxxxxxxxxxxxxxxxxxxxxxxx
4 You see how all Δconditions, how all Δminds*,
As well of glib and slipp'ry Δcreatures as
Of Δgrave and austere quality*, tender down*
Their services to Lord Timon . †
5 His large Δfortune,
Upon his good and gracious Δnature hanging,
Subdues and properties to his love and tendance
All sorts of hearts; yea, from the glass*-fac'd Δflatterer
To Apemantus, that few things loves better

F's much more onrushed quality (most modern texts splitting F #1 into three, F #2 and #4 into two) and large scale sweeps of release suddenly switching in styles confirm the Poet as an excitable character whose enthusiasms keep threatening to run away with him, especially when the emotional semicolons suddenly appear (outweighing the more logical colons four to two).

• amidst all this artistic purple imagery, the only surround phrases in the speech hint at the mercenary considerations underlining the Poet's true intentions (wishing Timon to become his patron) as he begins to talk of the others who have achieved that desired status

" . Nay {ψ}, but heare me on : /All those which were his Fellowes but of late,/Some better then his valew ; "

• given his later (enthusiastic?) excesses, the Poet opens quite circumspectly with only two releases in just three and half lines, the careful emotion (0/2) supported by the first line - the only unembellished one in the speech - suggesting that he is overawed by the social/financial status of the guests with whom they are mingling and/or may be trying not to draw attention to himself

• but as soon as he begins to describe the 'free drift' of his new 'rough worke' so his intellect is added to the mix (4/2, the onrushed F #1's last five lines)

• yet as he focuses on the vast range of society which 'tender downe/Their services to Lord Timon', especially 'his large Fortune', his intellect really takes over (8/2), at least until he names the misanthropist Apermantus, at which point he becomes highly emotional (3/6, F #2's last four lines), the emotional intensity heightened by the two

First Folio

2/ Poet

1 You see this confluence, this great flood of visitors,
I have+ in this rough worke, shap'd out a man
Whom this beneath world doth embrace and hugge
With amplest entertainment : My free drift
Halts not particularly, but moves it selfe
In a wide Sea of wax, + no levell'd malice
Infects one comma in the course I hold,
But flies an Eagle flight, bold, and forth on,
Leaving no Tract behinde.
xxxxxxxxxxxxxxxxxxxxxxxxxxxxxxxxxxxxxxxxxxxxxxxxxxxxxxxx
2 You see how all Conditions, how all Mindes,
As well of glib and slipp'ry Creatures,x as
Of Grave and austere qualitie, tender downe
Their services to Lord Timon : his large Fortune,
Upon his good and gracious Nature hanging,
Subdues and properties to his love and tendance
All sorts of hearts ; yea, from the glasse-fac'd Flatterer
To Apemantus, that few things loves better
[Then] to abhorre himselfe ; even hee drops downe

[1] there are several glosses of this line, with some modern editions replacing Ff's plural 'joyes' with the singular 'joy' or 'joy's', and altering F1 - 2's 'borne' (with its double connotation of being carried as well as being given birth) to 'born' - i.e. to the single meaning associated with birth: this latter alteration, first set by F3, happens several times throughout the text

[Than] to abhor* himself* ; even he* drops down*
The knee before him, and returns* in peace
Most rich in Timon's nod.

6 {ψ} I have upon a high and pleasant hill
Feign'd Fortune to be thron'd.
7 The Δbase o'th'Δmount
Is rank'd with all deserts, all kind* of Δnatures,
That labor* on the bosom* of this Δsphere
To propagate their states . †
8 Amongst them all,
Whose eyes are on this Δsovereign* Δlady fix'd,
One do I personate of Lord Timon's frame,
Whom Fortune with her Δivory hand wafts to her,
Whose present grace to present slaves and servants
Translates his Δrivals.

9 Nay {ψ}, but hear* me on:
All those which were his Δfellows* but of late -
Some better [than] his value* - on the moment
Follow his strides, his Δlobbies fill with tendance,
Rain* Δsacrificial* whisperings in his ear*,
Make Δsacred even his stirrup*, and through him
Drink* the free Δair*.

semicolons that suddenly appear (save for the general fear of Apermantus' mordant criticism, it is never made clear in the play just what Apermantus has done to him to create such a reaction)

• returning to the theme of his new poem regenerates his passions (5/3, F #3 and the first three lines of F #4) as well as a need for a short break at the end of F #3 (perhaps the appreciation of his own genius in setting 'Fortune on a 'high and pleasant hill' momentarily stops him in his tracks): most modern texts reset F's two short lines (four/six syllables) as one, as shown, thus removing this possible self-admiring moment

• as he reaches the subject of Timon being blessed by Fortune's 'Ivory hand' he becomes profoundly intellectual once more (7/1, F #4's last five lines)

• in finishing, the Poet's explanation that anyone who is fortunate enough to 'follow his [i.e. Timon's] strides' can 'through him/Drinke the free Ayre' is, not surprisingly, emotional (5/9, F #5), within the opening surround phrases urging that the Painter should still 'heare me on' as well as the start of the explanation both pointing to how important the need of Timon's patronage (and thus money) is to him

The knee before him, and returnes in peace
Most rich in Timons nod.

3 {ψ} I have upon a high and pleasant hill
Feign'd Fortune to be thron'd. →
4 The Base o'th'Mount
Is rank'd with all deserts, all kinde of Natures+
That labour on the bosome of this Sphere,$_x$
To propagate their states ; among'st them all,
Whose eyes are on this Soveraigne Lady fixt,
One do I personate of Lord Timons frame,
Whom Fortune with her Ivory hand wafts to her,
Whose present grace,$_x$ to present slaves and servants
Translates his Rivals.

5 Nay {ψ}, but heare me on:
All those which were his Fellowes but of late,
Some better [then] his valew ;$_x$ on the moment
Follow his strides, his Lobbies fill with tendance,
Raine Sacrificiall whisperings in his eare,
Make Sacred even his styrrop, and through him
Drinke the free Ayre.

3a/ Senator **And late five thousand : to Varro and to Isidore** 2.1.1 – 14

3b/ **Get on your cloake, & hast you to Lord Timon** between 2.1.15 - 35

Background: These are the only speeches for the character, the first of Timon's many creditors to have doubts about Timon's ability to meet his debts. They can be joined as one complete speech though they are split in two here as shown below.

Style: initially solo, then as part of a two-handed scene with a virtually silent partner

Where: the Senator's home **To Whom:** initially himself and the audience, then to his servant

Speech 3a: # of Lines: 14 **Probable Timing: 0.45 minutes**

Speech 3b: # of Lines: 20 **Probable Timing: 1.00 minutes**

Modern Text

3a/ Senator

1 And late, five thousand ; to Varro and to Isidore
He owes nine thousand, besides my former sum*,
Which makes it five and twenty.
2 Still in motion
Of raging waste?
3 It cannot hold, it will not.
4 If I want $^{\Delta}$gold, steal* but a beggar's* $^{\Delta}$dog*
And give it Timon, why, the $^{\Delta}$dog* coins* $^{\Delta}$gold.
5 If I would sell my $^{\Delta}$horse and buy twenty moe
Better [than] he, why, give my $^{\Delta}$horse to Timon, ◊
Ask* nothing, give it him, it $^{\Delta}$foals$_{*}$ me straight
And able $^{\Delta}$horses . †
6 No $^{\Delta}$porter at his gate,
But rather one that smiles and still invites
All that pass* by.
7 It cannot hold, no reason
Can sound his state in safety.
8 Caphis ho* ! †
9 Caphis, I say !

- in the midst of an essentially intellectual speech (14/7 overall), the two moments of unembellished total calm could suggest not just concern but also a critical moment of keen analysis as to whether foreclosure on Timon must be made
  "Still in motion/Of raging waste? It cannot hold, it will not."
  "It cannot hold, no reason/Can sound his state in safety."

- thus it's not surprising that the speech starts out with little or no release (2/1, the first four lines, F #1-3)

- but as the Senator starts to voice examples of Timon's generous but foolish profligacy (sending Gold in exchange for the gift of a 'Dogge') he becomes very passionate (5/3, the two lines of F #4), while the exchange of money for a horse becomes highly intellectual, not only in terms of release (7/2, F #5-6) but also by being expressed via three consecutive surround phrases
  ". If I would sell my Horse, and buy twenty moe/Better then he ; why give my Horse to Timon . /Aske nothing, give it him, it Foles me straight/And able Horses : "
  the first two emotionally heightened by being linked via the speech's only semicolon (exasperation? or sarcasm perhaps?)

- and after the unembellished realisation that 'It cannot hold', in calling for his servant the Senator moves into decisive intellectual action (2/0, the short F #8's five words)

First Folio

3a/ Senator

1 And late^{+} five thousand :$_{x}$ to Varro and to Isidore
He owes nine thousand, besides my former summe,
Which makes it five and twenty.
2 Still in motion
Of raging waste?
3 It cannot hold, it will not.
4 If I want Gold, steale but a beggers Dogge,$_{x}$
And give it Timon, why^{+} the Dogge coines Gold.
5 If I would sell my Horse,$_{x}$ and buy twenty moe
Better [then] he;$_{x}$ why^{+} give my Horse to Timon.
6 Aske nothing, give it him, it Foles me straight
And able Horses : No Porter at his gate,
But rather one that smiles,$_{x}$ and still invites
All that passe by.
7 It cannot hold, no reason
Can sound his state in safety.
8 Caphis hoa,$^{+}$
Caphis^{+} I say. $^{+}$

Modern Text

3b/ Senator

1 Get on your cloak* & haste* you to Lord Timon ;
Importune him for my Δmoneys*, be not ceas'd
With slight denial*; nor then silenc'd when
"Commend me to your Δmaster", and the Δcap
Plays* in the right hand, thus - but tell him,
My Δuses cry to me ; I must serve my turn*
Out of mine own* . †
2 His days* and times are past,
And my reliances on his fracted dates
Have smit my credit.
3 I love and honor* him,
But must not break* my back* to heal* his finger.
4 Immediate are my needs, and my relief*
Must not be toss'd* and turn'd to me in words,
But find* supply immediate.
5 Get you gone,
Put on a most importunate aspect,
A visage of demand ; for I do fear*,
When every Δfeather sticks* in his own* wing,
Lord Timon will be left a naked gull,
Which flashes now a Δphœnix . †
6 Get you gone.

7 {T}ake the Bonds along with you,
And have the dates in.

8 Go.

Whereas the previous speech was essentially intellectual, this, the immediate follow-up, is anything but - at least for the first two-thirds, for it starts out passionately (in instructing his servant to go to Timon); then turns emotional as he instructs him how to proceed; and only then does he regain some element of self-control, both intellectually and via unembellished calm, as he expresses his fear for Timon (though whether this is out of respect for Timon or for the more personal fear of losing the money lent to him is up to each actor to decide).

- the speech's only surround phrase ' : but tell him,/My Uses cry to me ; ', its significance heightened by the only emotional semicolon he has, underscores the argument he wishes his servant to use with Timon in order to retrieve his money – and the first two of three unembellished passages 'And my reliances on his fracted dates/Have smit my credit.' (F #1) plus 'Immediate are my needs,' (F #3) suggest that the argument reflects a genuine concern

- the opening order to 'Get on your cloake, & hast you to Lord Timon' and the instruction on how to face him humbly ('the Cap/Playes in the right hand') are passionate (5/4, F #1's first four and a half lines)

- given the fact of F #1's continued onrush suggesting the urgency of the situation (an onrush not supported by most modern texts), it's hardly surprising that advancing the argument to be used becomes emotional (1/3, F #1's next two and a half lines) and then unembellishedly quiet about how Timon's situation has 'smit my credit'

- it's worthwhile noting that his own 'Immediate' needs (as well as his paying 'honour' to Timon) are expressed emotionally without any intellect at all (0/6, F #2-3) – again pointing to a genuine rather than a trumped up need

- with the decision to approach Timon taken, the Senator finally becomes calmer, and after the unembellished advice for his servant to put on an 'importunate aspect,/A Visage of demand' (F #4's first two and half lines), his reflection that 'Lord Timon will be left a naked gull.' ends passionately (4/3)

First Folio

3b/ Senator

1 Get on your cloake,$_x$ & hast you to Lord Timon,+
Importune him for my Moneyes, be not ceast
With slight deniall ; nor then silenc'd,$_x$ when
Commend me to your Master, and the Cap
Playes in the right hand, thus :$_x$ but tell him,
My Uses cry to me ; I must serve my turne
Out of mine owne, his dayes and times are past,
And my reliances on his fracted dates
Have smit my credit.
2 I love,$_x$ and honour him,
But must not breake my backe,$_x$ to heale his finger.
3 Immediate are my needs, and my releefe
Must not be tost and turn'd to me in words,
But finde supply immediate.
4 Get you gone,
Put on a most importunate aspect,
A visage of demand :$_x$ for I do feare+
When every Feather stickes in his owne wing,
Lord Timon will be left a naked gull,
Which flashes now a Phœnix, get you gone.

5 {T}ake the Bonds along with you,
And have the dates in.

6 Go.

#'s 4 - 8: Timon's Generosity Leads To Trouble

4/ Steward **O my good Lord,/At many times I brought in my accompts,** 2.2.132 - 144

Background: Having been put off by Timon's Steward for some time, Timon's creditors have gone so far as to publicly waylay Timon and demand immediate payment (thus embarrassing him in front of his closest friends). Now alone with the Steward, Timon has demanded an explanation, refusing to accept the Steward's explanation that he has tried 'at many leysures' to warn Timon about the perilous state of his finances.

Style: as part of a two-handed scene

Where: outside, close to Timon's home **To Whom:** his employer,

# of Lines: 13 **Probable Timing: 0.45 minutes**

Modern Text

4/ Steward

1 O my good ^Δ^lord,
At many times I brought in my accompts,
Laid them before you ; you would throw them off,
And say you [found] them in mine honesty*. †

2 When for some trifling present you have bid me
Return* so much, I have shook* my head, and wept ;
Yea, 'gainst th'^Δ^authority *of manners, pray'd you
To hold your hand more close . †

3 I did endure*
Not seldom*, nor no slight checks*, when I have
Prompted you in the ebb* of your estate
And your great flow of debts . †

4 My lov'd ^Δ^lord,
Though you hear* now (too late), yet now's* a time :
The greatest of your having, lacks* a half*
To pay your present debts.

Whereas most modern texts set four rational sentences suggesting a character under great control, F sets the speech as one long onrush which suggests that self-control is almost impossible for him to maintain - and F's orthography points to where the control starts to slip.

- as the Steward lays in the needed background that Timon has deflected any earlier attempts to go over the accounts by saying that he trusted the Steward's honesty, he is initially very careful (1/0, F #1's first three and a half lines) - the first of only two marginally intellectual moments

- however, in moving to the awkward matter of his disapproval of Timon giving too much in return for 'some trifling present', he becomes emotional (0/2, the next two lines)

- then, as the Steward reminds Timon that, in attempting to get Timon to face the problem head on he broke the norm of servant-master relationship, comes the other intellectual moment (1/0)

  " : Yea 'gainst th'Authoritie of manners, pray'd you/To hold your hand more close : "
  the recollection intensified by being set as the only surround phrase in the speech

- so far the first seven lines have shown little release (2/2), but now the emotional dam breaks, for the remaining six lines, dealing with the past 'slight checkes' when he pushed Timon too hard and the resultant appalling current situation that his 'having' now 'lackes a halfe,/To pay your present debts.', are highly emotional in comparison with the earlier part of the speech (1/7)

First Folio

4/ Steward

1 O my good Lord,
At many times I brought in my accompts,
Laid them before you,+ you would throw them off,
And say you [sound] them in mine honestie,
When for some trifling present you have bid me
Returne so much, I have shooke my head, and wept : x
Yea+ 'gainst th'Authoritie of manners, pray'd you
To hold your hand more close : I did indure
Not sildome, nor no slight checkes, when I have
Prompted you in the ebbe of your estate, x
And your great flow of debts ; my lov'd Lord,
Though you heare now (too late)+ yet nowes a time,+
The greatest of your having, lackes a halfe,
To pay your present debts.

5/ Steward **Lord Lucius and Lucullus, {and the Senators}? Humh.** between 2.2.196 - 213

Background: Having accepted that he is in financial trouble (see speech #4 above), Timon has decided to dispatch several trusted servants to his closest friends and Senators, all of whom have benefited from his enormous generosity, asking for financial help. However, his personal philosophy as expounded in speech #1 does not seem to be shared by others that the Steward has so far approached on Timon's behalf.

Style: as part of a two-handed scene

Where: outside, close to Timon's home **To Whom:** his employer,

# of Lines: 15 **Probable Timing: 0.50 minutes**

Modern Text

5/ Steward

1 Lord Lucius and Lucullus,{and the Senators}?
2 Humh !

3 I have been* bold
(For that I knew it the most general* way)
To them to use your Δsignet, and your Δname,
But they do shake their heads, and I am here*
No richer in return*.

4 They answer, in a joint* and corporate voice,
That now they are at fall, want Δtreasure, cannot
Do what they would, are sorry*; you are Δhonorable*,
But yet they could have wish'd - they know not -
Something hath been* amiss* - a Δnoble Δnature
May catch a wrench - would all were well - tis pity* -
And so, intending other serious matters,
After distasteful* looks* - and these hard Δfractions,
With certain* half*-caps and cold-moving nods,
They froze me into Δsilence.

- the Steward's initial put down of those Timon has suggested contacting for help is totally intellectual (F #1, 3/0), followed by F #2's unembellished one word monosyllabic release – the orthography suggesting that whatever the 'Humh' signifies it be done quietly, almost as if for the Steward's benefit alone

- the Steward's explanation that he has already approached them in Timon's name is emotional (F #3, 2/4)

- initially his report of their answer is careful, just one intellectual release pointing to their proffered reasons for refusal (lack of 'Treasure') and the fact that everyone answered as one 'joynt' voice (1/1, F #4's first two and a half lines)

- however, his reporting of their avowals of respect for Timon turns emotional (1/3, the next two lines), and as he continues his report, his control is put to the test - as testified by the two emotional surround phrases (unusually heightened by being formed by three successive semicolons, a great rarity in any original Shakespeare printing)

  " ; a Noble Nature/May catch a wrench ; would all were well ; "

  and the emotion is maintained through the remainder of the speech as he describes how, after all the fine words, he was dismissed with 'distastefull lookes' (this description heightened further by being punctuated with the final semicolon of the passage) and 'cold moving nods' (2/5, the last four lines of the speech)

First Folio

5/ Steward

1 Lord Lucius and Lucullus,{and the Senators}?
2 Humh. +

3 I have beene bold
(For that I knew it the most generall way)
To them,+ to use your Signet, and your Name,
But they do shake their heads, and I am heere
No richer in returne.

4 They answer+ in a joynt and corporate voice,
That now they are at fall, want Treaure+ cannot
Do what they would, are sorrie : x you are Honourable,
But yet they could have wisht, they know not,
Something hath beene amisse ; x a Noble Nature
May catch a wrench ; x would all were well ; x tis pitty,
And so+ intending other serious matters,
After distastefull lookes; x and these hard Fractions+
With certaine halfe-caps, x and cold moving nods,
They froze me into Silence.

6/ Timon **You Gods reward them :/Prythee man looke cheerely.** 2.2.213 - 231

Background: The following is Timon's response to the news that the Steward's overtures for financial help (speech #5 above) have been rejected.

Style: as part of a two-handed scene

Where: outside, close to Timon's home **To Whom:** his employee, the Steward

# of Lines: 19 **Probable Timing: 1.00 minutes**

Modern Text

6/ Timon

1 You Δgods, reward them ! †
2 Prithee*, man, look* cheerly*.
3 These old Δfellows*
Have their ingratitude in them Δhereditary :
Their blood is cak'd, 'tis cold, it seldom* flows*;
'Tis lack* of kindly* warmth they are not kind* ;
And Δnature, as it grows* again* toward earth,
Is fashion'd for the journey, dull and heavy.
4 Go to [Ventidius*]. †
5 (Prithee* be not sad,
Thou art true and honest ; Δingeniously I speak*,
No blame belongs to thee . †)
6 [Ventidius*] lately
Buried his Δfather, by whose death he's* stepp'd
Into a great estate . †
7 When he was poor*,
Imprison'd, and in scarcity* of Δfriends,
I clear'd* him with five Δtalents . †
8 Greet him from me,
Bid him suppose some good necessity
Touches his Δfriend, which craves to be remembr'red
With those five Δtalents . †
9 That had, give't these Δfellows*
To whom 'tis instant due.
10 Nev'r speak* or think*
That Timon's fortunes 'mong his Δfriends can sink*.

As with several speeches for many characters in this play, most modern texts set up a far more rational in-control character than F shows, for whereas the onrushed F #3 suggests an enormous urgency when Timon attempts to rectify a financial situation already well out of hand most modern texts split the instructions into six separate and rational logical steps.

- the denunciation of the Senators who have refused to help him starts very emotionally (4/11, the seven lines of F #1-2), the opening release heightened by being set as three consecutive surround 272 phrases
  " . You Gods reward them : /Prythee man looke cheerely . These old Fellowes/ Have their ingratitude in them Hereditary : "
- though the instructions that it is Ventiddius to whom they should turn to start passionately (7/7, F #3's first six and half lines) the (two) emotional opening surround phrases
  " Go to Ventiddius (prythee be not sad,/Thou art true, and honest ; Ingeniously I speake,/No blame belongs to thee :) "
  do not necessarily heighten but point more to Timon's reassuring the Steward of his worth (whether out of kindness and/or need to get him back on track is up to each actor to explore)
- how Ventiddius should be greeted is handled intellectually (3/0, the three lines between F #3's last two pieces of major punctuation) while the notion that the money that Timon expects will result moves him into another emotional surround phrase ' ; that had, give't these Fellowes/To whom 'tis instant due . '
- and the final, as it turns out misguided, belief that all will be well, becomes passionate (2/3, F #4) – though, given the opening attack on the Senators, whether this is genuine or a bluff is up to each actor to decide

First Folio

6/ Timon

1 You Gods+ reward them : +
Prythee+ man+ looke cheerely.
2 These old Fellowes
Have their ingratitude in them Hereditary :
Their blood is cak'd, 'tis cold, it sildome flowes,+
'Tis lacke of kindely warmth,x they are not kinde ;
And Nature, as it growes againe toward earth,
Is fashion'd for the journey, dull and heavy.
3 Go to [Ventiddius] (prythee be not sad,
Thou art true,x and honest ; Ingeniously I speake,
No blame belongs to thee :) [Ventiddius] lately
Buried his Father, by whose death hee's stepp'd
Into a great estate : When he was poore,
Imprison'd, and in scarsitie of Friends,
I cleer'd him with five Talents : Greet him from me,
Bid him suppose,x some good necessity
Touches his Friend, which craves to be remembred
With those five Talents ; that had, give't these Fellowes
To whom 'tis instant due.
4 Nev'r speake,x or thinke,x
That Timons fortunes 'mong his Friends can sinke.

7/ Lucius **Servilius? You are kindely met sir.** between 3.2.27 - 82

Background: A typical rejection for one of Timon's servants searching for financial help, though this is more public than most.

Style: as part of a five handed scene

Where: unspecified, presumably Lucius' home **To Whom:** Timon's servant Servillius, in front of three strangers

# of Lines: 25 **Probable Timing: 1.15 minutes**

Modern Text

7/ **{Lucius}**

1 Servilius?

2 You are kindly* met, sir.

3 {* C}ommend me to thy Δhonorable* virtuous Δlord, my very exquisite Δfriend.

4 Ha? what has he sent?

5 I am so much endear'd* to that Δlord: he's* ever sending. †

6 How shall I thank him, think'st thou?

7 And what has he sent now?

{opens a letter from Tymon}

8 I know his Δlordship is but merry with me;
He cannot want fifty-five hundred Δtalents.

9 What a wicked Beast was I to disfurnish my self against such a good time, when I might ha' shown* myself* Δhonorable*!

10 How unluckily it happ'ned* that I should* Δpurchase the day before for a little part, and undo a great deal* of Δhonor*!

11 Servilius, now before the Δgods, I am not able to do (the more beast [I], I say !) -I was sending to use Lord Timon myself*, these Δgentlemen can witness*; but I would not, for the wealth of Athens, I had done't now.

12 Commend me bountifully to his good Δlordship, and I hope his Δhonor will conceive the fairest of me*, because I have no power to be kind*.

13 And tell him this from me, I count it one of my greatest afflictions, say, that I cannot pleasure such an Δhonorable* Δgentleman.

- as Lucius presumably expects yet another gift from a servant of Timon, it's not surprising that his opening greeting is passionate (3/2, F #1-3)

- his anticipation of some form of gift seems to be heightened by the five surround phrases that follow, first the somewhat unnerving quietness (in its expectation) of F #4's very direct, short, unembellished, monosyllabic double question
  " . Ha? what ha's he sent ? "
  and then the more energetic F #5 (1/2)
  " . I am so much endeered to that Lord ; hee's ever sending : how shall I thank him think'st thou ?"
  (the first two of these fulsome surround phrases of praise are further enhanced in being linked by the first of only two emotional semicolons in the speech)

- F #6's monosyllabic unembellished quiet 'And what has he sent now?' might well suggest that Lucius is now dealing with something unexpected (a letter requesting financial help rather than a gift), for F #7's initial response is purely intellectual as he names the enormity of the sum requested (2/0) - a response heightened by the sudden switch of these two lines being set as verse, the only verse till the end of the speech

- as Lucius starts his (recovered slightly?) prose listing, the first excuses leading to refusal (F #8's currently-I-don't-have-the-cash-because and F #9's I've-just-made-a-purchase-and-so-damaged-my-honour), so his passions swim to the surface (4/4, in four and a half lines)

- with the suggestion that 'I was sending to use Lord Timon my selfe' Lucius seems to take control of himself (5/2, F #10), while F #11's first attempt at dismissing Servilius ('Commend me bountifully') momentarily destroys the control by turning passionate once more (2/2) - which he attempts to counteract with an almost unembellished apology (F #12 - unembellished till the last two words describing Timon as an 'Honourable Gentleman')

First Folio

7/ **{Lucius}** [2]

1 Servilius?

2 You are kindely met+ sir.

3 {* C}ommend me to thy Honourable vertuous Lord, my very exquisite Friend.

4 Ha? what ha's he sent?

5 I am so much endeered to that Lord;+ hee's ever sending: how shall I thank him+ think'st thou?

6 And what has he sent now?

{opens a letter from Tymon}

7 I know his Lordship is but merry with me,+
He cannot want fifty five hundred Talents.

8 What a wicked Beast was I to disfurnish my self against such a good time, when I might ha shewn myselfe Honourable? +

9 How unluckily it hapned,x that I shold Purchase the day before for a little part, and undo a great deale of Honour? +

10 Servilius, now before the Gods+ I am not able to do (the more beast+ [] I say +)+ I was sending to use Lord Timon my selfe, these Gentlemen can witnesse; but I would not+ for the wealth of Athens+ I had done't now.

11 Commend me bountifully to his good Lordship, and I hope his Honor will conceive the fairest of mee, because I have no power to be kinde.

12 And tell him this from me, I count it one of my greatest afflictions+ say, that I cannot pleasure such an Honourable Gentleman.

{ctd. over}

---

[2] here F1 (incorrectly) sets the prefix Lucil. referring to Lucillius (Timon's servant): most modern texts expand F2's Luciu. and assign the prefix to the character who has been the centre point throughout the scene, viz. Lucius

14 Good Servili-
us, will you befriend me* so far*, as to use mine own*
words to him?

[Exit Servil.{ius}]

15 I'll look* you out a good turn*, Servilius.

16 True, as you said, Timon is shrunk* indeed*,
And he that's once denied* will hardly speed*.

- and if the speech had stopped there Lucius might have preserved some semblance of respect, but instead F #13's plea for Servilius to 'befriend mee'; F #14's promise to return the favour in that he will 'looke you out a good turne'; and F #15's remark to the observers that 'Timon is shrunke indeede' are all emotional (3/9 overall), suggesting that the earlier self-control has somewhat disappeared
- and, extraordinarily tellingly, his F #15 amazement at Timon's downfall is further enhanced by being set as a return to verse

13 Good Servili-
us, will you befriend mee so farre, as to use mine owne
words to him?

[Exit Servil.{ius}]

14 Ile looke you out a good turne+ Servilius.

15 True+ as you said, Timon is shrunke indeede,
And he that's once deny'de,x will hardly speede.

8/ Timon **Let me looke backe upon thee. O thou Wall** 4.1.1 – 41

Background: Timon has lost everything. In one final act of defiance he invited all those 'friends' whom he had feasted and gifted for years who in turn rejected him, and, at a supposed feast, threw water and stones in their faces, calling them, among other things, 'Parasites', 'Trencher-friends', and 'Cap and knee-slaves', and then set fire to his home before fleeing. Now, about to leave Athens, these are his final words (in the form of a prayer) to the city and those he thankfully leaves behind.

Style: solo

Where: outside Athens **To Whom:** the city and its inhabitants

# of Lines: 41 **Probable Timing: 2.00 minutes**

Modern Text

8/ Timon

1 Let me look* back* upon thee.

2 O thou Δwall
That girdles in those Δwolves, dive in the earth
And fence not Athens !

3 Matrons, turn* incontinent ! †

4 Obedience, fail* in Δchildren ! †

5 Slaves and Δfools*,
Pluck* the grave wrinkled Senate from the Δbench,
And minister in their steads*! †

6 To general* Δfilths* ◊
Convert o'th'Δinstant, green* Δvirginity !
Do't* in your Δparents' eyes !

7 Bankrupts, hold fast,
Rather [than] render back*, out with your Δknives,
And cut your Δtrusters' throats* !

8 Bound Δservants, steal*;
Large-handed Δrobbers your grave Δmasters are,
And pill by Δlaw.

- in looking back on Athens, Timon's emotions (0/2) are enhanced, opening as he does with a short sentence – the sight presumably enough to move him from a neutral observation into forcing him to start the ensuing 'prayer'
- attacking the basic social order - defense, fidelity ('Matrons turne incontinent'), governance ('Slaves and Fooles' rule instead of the 'wrinkled Senate'), and chastity ('greene Virginity/Doo't in your Parents eyes' – Timon is able to 'pray' intellectually as well as emotionally (12/9 in just the seven lines, F #2-4)
- but as his mind touches how he has been harmed ('Bankrupts . . . cut your Trusters throates' he becomes passionate (2/2, F #5), the horror of what has happened to him and what he wishes for in return

  " . Bankrupts, hold fast/Rather then render backe ; out with your Knives,/And cut your Trusters throates . "

heightened by being set as two emotional surround phrases with the only semicolon in the speech – and in view of how Timon has been financially betrayed by so many people F's punctuation makes good sense here: sadly, most modern texts advance the major punctuation, setting 'Bankrupts, hold fast;/Rather then render backe, out with your Knives', thus making the violence the first focus rather than the financial betrayal

First Folio

8/ Timon

1 Let me looke backe upon thee.

2 O thou Wall
That girdles in those Wolves, dive in the earth,x
And fence not Athens. +

3 Matrons, turne incontinent,+
Obedience+ fayle in Children : + Slaves and Fooles+
Plucke the grave wrinkled Senate from the Bench,
And minister in their steeds,+ to generall Filthes.

4 Convert o'th'Instant+ greene Virginity,+
Doo't in your Parents eyes. +

5 Bankrupts, hold fast+
Rather [then] render backe ; x out with your Knives,
And cut your Trusters throates. +

6 Bound Servants, steale,+
Large-handed Robbers your grave Masters are,
And pill by Law.

9 Maid*, to thy Δmaster's bed,
Thy Δmistress* is o'th' Δbrothel* !
10 [Son] of sixteen,
Pluck* the lin'd* Δcrutch from thy old limping Δsire,
With it, beat* out his Δbrains* !
11 Piety, and Δfear*,
Religion to the Δgods, Δpeace, Δjustice, Δtruth,
Domestic* awe, Δnight-rest, and Δneighborhood*,
Instruction, Δmanners, Δmysteries, and Δtrades,
Degrees, Δobservances, Δcustoms*, and Δlaws*,
Decline to your confounding contraries; ◊
And [let] Δconfusion live ! †
12 Plagues incident to men,
Your potent and infectious Δfevers* heap*
On Athens, ripe for stroke !
13 Thou cold Δsciatica,
Cripple our Δsenators, that their limbs* may halt
As lamely as their Δmanners !
14 Lust, and Δliberty*,
Creep* in the Δminds* and Δmarrows* of our youth,
That 'gainst the stream* of Δvirtue they may strive,
And drown* themselves in Δriot !
15 Itches, Δblains*,
Sow* all th'Athenian bosoms*, and their crop
Be general* Δleprosy* ! †
16 Breath, infect breath,
That their Δsociety (as their Δfriendship) may
Be merely* poison* !
17 Nothing I'll bear* from thee
But nakedness*, thou detestable Δtown* ! [3]
Take thou that too, with multiplying Δbans* ! †
18 Timon will to the Δwoods, where he shall find*
Th'unkindest Δbeast more kinder [than] Δmankind*.
19 The Δgods confound (hear* me, you good Δgods all)
Th'Athenians both within and out that Δwall !
And grant*, as Timon grows*, his hate may grow
To the whole race of Δmankind*, high and low !
20 Amen.

• yet as he incites the male lower orders to steal by the example of 'your grave Masters' who 'pill by Law', and the 'Maide' to fornicate since 'Thy Mistris is o'th'Brothell', despite the extraordinarily strong images, he quickly manages to regain intellectual control (7/3, F #6-7) - which he quickly loses as he returns to the earlier theme of filial ingratitude where, for some reason, he becomes very passionate (3/4 in just the two lines of F #8 – perhaps he regarded some of those he helped – Ventiddius? – as surrogate sons)

• and as Timon prays for all the abstracts that form the glue for social order to 'Decline to your confounding contraries' (F #9) and for 'Confusion' to take their place, to be accompanied by 'Plagues incident to men' (F #10) which he then begins to list in more detail (F #11) so, again, despite the strong images, Timon again becomes intellectual (20/8 in ten lines, with possibly five more capitals referring to key abstract thoughts found at the beginning of verse lines) – the intensity of his desires marked not just by the large number of capitals but also by the very icy calmness of the single unembellished line already quoted, 'Decline to your confounding contraries' - the one thing absolutely necessary for all that he is praying for to occur

• as the surround phrase opening F #10, ' . And yet Confusion live : ' points to the key wish driving him on, it's not surprising that, in listing the long and very specific list of physical and abstract horrors he wishes visited upon the Athenians (F #12-13) he becomes passionate, though the strength of his passion (11/11 in just seven lines) is much more than might be expected

• and he stays equally passionate as he decides/announces his intention to leave everything behind in Athens and live in the woods where he believes he will find 'Th'unkindest Beast, more kinder then Mankinde.' (F #14, 5/6)

• and even with the decision made and the prayer reaching its climax, finishing with the double wish that the 'good Gods' 'confound' Athenians everywhere (not just within Athens) and that his hatred eventually touch all mankind, his intellect is still present alongside the emotion (F #15-16, 6/4) – such passion a frightening thought given the wishes expressed

7 Maide, to thy Masters bed,
Thy Mistris is o'th'Brothell. +
8 [Some] of sixteen,
Plucke the lyn'd Crutch from thy old limping Sire,
With it, beate out his Braines. +
9 Piety, and Feare,
Religion to the Gods, Peace, Justice, Truth,
Domesticke awe, Night-rest, and Neighbour-hood,
Instruction, Manners, Mysteries, and Trades,
Degrees, Observances, Customes, and Lawes,
Decline to your confounding contraries.
10 And [yet] Confusion live : + Plagues incident to men,
Your potent and infectious Feavors,x heape
On Athens+ ripe for stroke. +
11 Thou cold Sciatica,
Cripple our Senators, that their limbes may halt
As lamely as their Manners. +
12 Lust, and Libertie+
Creepe in the Mindes and Marrowes of our youth,
That 'gainst the streame of Vertue they may strive,
And drowne themselves in Riot. +
13 Itches, Blaines,
Sowe all th'Athenian bosomes, and their crop
Be generall Leprosie : + Breath, infect breath,
That their Society (as their Friendship) may
Be meerely poyson. +
14 Nothing Ile beare from thee
But nakednesse, thou detestable Towne,+
Take thou that too, with multiplying Bannes :
Timon will to the Woods, where he shall finde
Th'unkindest Beast,x more kinder [then] Mankinde.
15 The Gods confound (heare me+ you good Gods all)
Th'Athenians both within and out that Wall : +
And graunt+ as Timon growes, his hate may grow
To the whole race of Mankinde, high and low. +
16 Amen.

[3] some modern texts suggest at this point Timon is removing part of his clothing

#'s 9 - 11: The Apermantus Debates

9/ Apermantus **This is in thee a Nature but infected,** 4.3.202 – 218
10/ Apermantus **Thou hast cast away thy selfe, being like thy self** between 4.3.219 - 233

Background: Apermantus is rightly known by all as a cynic; even in his better times Timon has publicly acknowledged that Apermantus 'does neither affect companie/Nor is he fit for't indeed'. Yet Apermantus was concerned for Timon from the start, 'Oh you Gods! What a number of men eats, and he sees 'em not? '. Now, in Timon's self-imposed impoverished exile 'Nothing Ile beare from thee /But nakednesse, thou detestable Towne', Apermantus has joined him in the woods, not to comfort him but to strip him of any self-deception. The following two speeches come from the beginning of the in-the-woods encounter, and, as such, each is self-explanatory.

Style: each as part of a two-handed scene

Where: at Timon's camp in the woods **To Whom:** Timon

Speech 9: # of Lines: 17 **Probable Timing: 0.55 minutes**
Speech 10: # of Lines: 13 **Probable Timing: 0.45 minutes**

Modern Text

9/ Apermantus

1 This is in thee a Δnature but infected,
A poor* unmanly Δmelancholy* sprung
From change of future. [4]
2 Why this Δspade? this place?
This* Δslave-like Δhabit ? and these looks* of Δcare?
3 Thy Δflatterers yet wear* Δsilk*, drink* Δwine, lie* soft,
Hug* their diseas'd Δperfumes, and have forgot
That ever Timon was.
4 Shame not these Δwoods[5]
By putting on the cunning of a Δcarper.
5 Be thou a Δflatterer now, and seek* to thrive
By that which has undone thee; hinge* thy knee,
And let his very breath whom thou'lt observe
Blow off thy Δcap, praise his most vicious strain*,
And call it excellent. †
6 Thou wast told thus;
Thou gav'st thine ears* (like Δtapsters that [bade*]
welcome*)
To Δknaves, and all approachers. †
7 'Tis most just
That thou turn* Δrascal*; hadst thou wealth again*,
Rascals should have't.
8 Do not assume my likeness*.

With thirty-three releases in just seventeen lines it seems that Apermantus is not holding back in letting Timon know what he thinks about his new behaviour – whether this is because his own status as the local misanthrope is challenged, or is an attempt to shock Timon back to reality out of a grudging affection for him, or is simply because he must speak his mind no matter what the circumstances, is up to each actor to explore.

- Apermantus is passionate in ascribing Timon's change as one of infection or 'Melancholly' rather than a true change of heart (2/2, F #1)
- F #2's challenge as to what on earth Timon is doing dressed as he is where he is (with just a spade) is ferociously intellectual (4/1 in two lines)
- F #3's (deliberately tantalising? cruel?) suggestion that Timon's one-time flatterers, still living in the lap of luxury, have forgotten him is passionate (5/5), while calling out Timon to stop his pretence is cuttingly intellectual (2/0, F #4)
- then Apermantus loses some control, for his F #5 jamming together of instructions as how to resolve Timon's current situation with the told-you-so and your-fate-is-well-deserved taunt is not only onrushed – most modern texts reworking it as three more rational sentences – it opens with an emotional (semicoloned) surround phrase telling him to become a 'Flatterer' to undo the damage done to him (by his flatterers!)
- F #5's passionate start (2/3, the first four and half lines) ends with an ugly surround phrase suggestion as how to respond to his flatterers ' : praise his most vicious straine,/And call it excellent : '
- after the icily unembellished ' : thou wast told thus : ', doubly heightened by being set as a monosyllabic surround phrase, Apermantus' passions flow once more (4/5) as he finishes ripping Timon apart, the brevity of the bluntness of the final 'Do not assume my likenesse.' seeming to suggest that this warning is much more than a casual comment or joke

First Folio

9/ Apermantus

1 This is in thee a Nature but infected,
A poore unmanly Melancholly sprung
From change of future.
2 Why this Spade? this place?
This Slave-like Habit,+ and these lookes of Care?
3 Thy Flatterers yet weare Silke, drinke Wine, lye soft,
Hugge their diseas'd Perfumes, and have forgot
That ever Timon was.
4 Shame not these Woods, $_{x}$
By putting on the cunning of a Carper.
5 Be thou a Flatterer now, and seeke to thrive
By that which ha's undone thee; hindge thy knee,
And let his very breath whom thou'lt observe
Blow off thy Cap : $_{x}$ praise his most vicious straine,
And call it excellent : thou wast told thus : $_{x}$
Thou gav'st thine eares (like Tapsters, that [bad] welcom)
To Knaves, and all approachers : 'Tis most just
That thou turne Rascall, $_{x}$ had'st thou wealth againe,
Rascals should have't.
6 Do not assume my likenesse.

[4] though some modern texts agree with Ff and set 'future', one gloss = 'fortune'

[5] though most modern texts agree with Ff and set 'Woods', one gloss = 'weeds'

Modern Text

10/ Apermantus

1 Thou hast cast away thyself*, being like thyself,
A Δmadman so long, now a Δfool* . †
2 What, think'st
That the bleak* Δair*, thy boisterous* Δchamberlain*,
Will put thy shirt on warm*?
3 Will these moist [6] Δtrees,
That have out-liv'd the Δeagle, page thy heels*
And skip when thou point'st out?
4 Will the cold brook*,
Candied with Δice, Δcaudle* thy Δmorning taste
To cure thy o'er-nights surfeit? *
5 Call the Δcreatures
Whose naked Δnatures live in all the spite*
Of wreakful* Δheaven, whose bare unhoused Δtrunks,
To the conflicting Δelements expos'd,
Answer mere* Δnature ; bid them flatter thee.
xxxxxxxxxxxxxxxxxxxxxxxxxxxxxxxxxxxxxxxxxxxxxxxxxxxxxxxxxxxxxxxxxxxxxxxxxxxxxxxxx
6 I love thee better now [than] ere I did.

- Apermantus' opening passionate stripping of Timon's illusions (2/2, F #1's first line and a half) as to any belief he may have of his past or current integrity,
  " . Thou hast cast away thy selfe, being like thy self/A Madman so long, now a Foole : "
  quickly turns to emotion as he challenges Timon as to any expectations he may have as to nature offering him any warmth (1/5, F #1's last two lines)

- and as Apermantus elaborates further his ironic challenge - will the trees obey his every command? will the water turn into a comforting drink to clear his previous night's hangover? - so his passions return (5/4, F #2-3)

- in returning to his ever-present theme of flattery/flatterers and his belief that Timon needs both, his suggestion that Timon call the 'Creatures' that 'Answere meere Nature' becomes slightly more intellectual (6/4, F #4's first four lines)

- then suddenly, having not held back any energy in his attacks, the last line and a half of the speech become totally unembellished - and it is especially surprising that the ending of the flattery attack is so handled, F #4's
  " : bid them flatter thee . "
  even more strikingly powerful for being set as a monosyllabic surround phrase – and whether Apermantus has now gone deliberately quiet to enhance the final knife thrust or is forced into quietness because of Timon's reaction to the ruthless stripping of all his illusions is up to each actor to decide

- and while the final 'I love thee better now, then ere I did' can be triggered by several different possibilities (ranging all the way from sympathy and condolence through to sarcasm and triumph), the essence of F #5 is that, for whatever reason, it is spoken with no extra releases at all

First Folio

10/ Apermantus

1 Thou hast cast away thy selfe, being like thy self +
A Madman so long, now a Foole : what+ think'st
That the bleake ayre, thy boysterous Chamberlaine+
Will put thy shirt on warme?
2 Will these moyst Trees,
That have out-liv'd the Eagle, page thy heeles
And skip when thou point'st out?
3 Will the cold brooke+
Candied with Ice, Cawdle thy Morning taste
To cure thy o're-nights surfet?
4 Call the Creatures,x
Whose naked Natures live in all the spight
Of wrekefull Heaven, whose bare unhoused Trunkes+
To the conflicting Elements expos'd+
Answer meere Nature :x bid them flatter thee.
xxxxxxxxxxxxxxxxxxxxxxxxxxxxxxxxxxxxxxxxxxxxxxxxxxxxxxxxxxxxxxxxxxxxxxxxxxxxxxxxx
5 I love thee better now,x [then] ere I did.

---

[6] though most modern texts agree with Ff and set 'moyst', one gloss = 'moss'd'

11/ Timon **Would'st thou have thy selfe fall in the confusion** between 4.3.234 - 345

Background: Timon eventually gives as good as he gets. Having asked Apermantus what he would do with the world 'if it lay in thy power?' and received the answer 'Give it to the Beasts, to be rid of the men', Timon in turn strips Apermantus of the sense-of-unique-superiority he clings to.

Style: as part of a two-handed scene

Where: at Timon's camp in the woods **To Whom:** Apermantus

# of Lines: 21 **Probable Timing: 1.10 minutes**

Modern Text

11/ Timon

1 Wouldst thou have thyself* fall in the confusion of men, and remain* a Δbeast with the Δbeasts?

2 A beastly Δambition, which the Δgods* grant*
thee t'attain* to !

3 If thou wert the Δlion*, the Δfox would
beguile thee ; if thou wert the Δlamb*, the Δfox* would
eat* thee ; if thou wert the Δfox, the Δlion would suspect
thee, when peradventure thou wert accus'd by the Δass*;
Δif thou wert the Δass*, thy dullness* would torment thee,
and still thou liv'dst but as a Δbreakfast* to the wolf*; ◊ Δif
thou wert the Δwolf*, thy greediness* would afflict thee,
& oft thou shouldst hazard thy life for thy dinner; ◊ Δwert
thou the Δunicorn*, pride and wrath would confound
thee and make thine own* self* the conquest of thy fury;
◊ Δwert thou a Δbear*, thou wouldst be kill'd by the Δhorse :
wert thou a Δhorse, thou wouldst be seiz'd* by the Δleopard ; wert thou a Δleopard, thou wert Δgermane to the
Δlion, and the spots* of thy Δkindred, were Δjurors on thy
life; ◊ all thy safety were remotion and thy defense* absence*.

4 What Δbeast could'st thou be*, that were not subject to a Δbeast ? †

5 And what a Δbeast art thou already, that
seest not thy loss* in transformation !

This is one of the rare times where F sets more sentences than its modern counterpart (what most modern texts set as an onrushed mt. #3 was originally set as four F sentences). However, F's divisions are not so much grammatical, since all four sentences essentially deal with Apermantus' inevitable failure to survive no matter what form of animal he would choose to be. Rather, each new F sentence seems to mark a different internal response from Timon (and hence changes in stylistic release) as to what he, in turn, is now piling onto/stripping away from Apermantus' own self-delusion.

- with all that has been dumped on him by Apermantus (see speeches #9-10 above) it's not surprising that Timon starts out so passionately (15/14, in just the first nine lines, F #1-3), and amidst all the insults it's fascinating that the end of the passion, which focuses essentially on Apermantus' intelligence or lack thereof is enhanced even further by being set as two surround phrases,
  " : If thou wert the Asse, thy dulnesse would torment thee ;
  and still thou liv'dst but as a Breakefast to the Wolfe ."
  their conviction heightened even further by the only emotional semicolon of the speech that links them
- for a moment, as Timon turns to the deadly sins of greed and pride, he becomes quite emotional (2/5, F #4-5)
- then, as he turns his attention to the possibility of Apermantus' death, he manages to regain his self-control (F #6, 9/3)
- and just as Apermantus went deadly quiet in giving what he thought would be Timon's coup-de-grace in the previous speech, Timon follows suit with F #7's
  "All thy safety were remotion, and thy defence absense.'
- while F #8's final triumphant surround phrase flourish becomes passionate once more (#3/2)

First Folio

11/ Timon

1 Would'st thou have thy selfe fall in the confusion of men, and remaine a Beast with the Beasts. +

2 A beastly Ambition, which the Goddes graunt
thee t'attaine to. +

3 If thou wert the Lyon, the Fox would
beguile thee,+ if thou wert the Lambe, the Foxe would
eate thee : x if thou wert the Fox, the Lion would suspect
thee, when peradventure thou wert accus'd by the Asse : x
If thou wert the Asse, thy dulnesse would torment thee ; x
and still thou liv'dst but as a Breakefast to the Wolfe.

4 If
thou wert the Wolfe, thy greedinesse would afflict thee,
& oft thou should'st hazard thy life for thy dinner.

5 Wert
thou the Unicorne, pride and wrath would confound
thee, x and make thine owne selfe the conquest of thy fury.

6 Wert thou a Beare, thou would'st be kill'd by the Horse : x
wert thou a Horse, thou would'st be seaz'd by the Leopard : x wert thou a Leopard, thou wert Germane to the
Lion, and the spottes of thy Kindred, were Jurors on thy
life.

7 All thy safety were remotion, x and thy defence absense.

8 What Beast could'st thou bee, that were not subject to a Beast : and what a Beast art thou already, that
seest not thy losse in transformation. +

#'S 12 - 17: TIMON AND HIS NEW FOUND GOLD

12/ Timon **I have enough Gold to make a Whore forsweare her Trade,** between 4.3.133 - 166

Background: In digging for roots for food, Timon has stumbled across a huge cache of gold. Instead of being overjoyed and rushing back to Athens to pick up his old ways, his hatred of the deceptive, hypocritical element of mankind remains as strong as ever, and he makes plans to use the gold to destroy those who are willing to participate in their own (and others') destruction. In the following sequence, the now exiled Athenian general Alcibiades, once a very close friend, and his army have come across Timon in the woods and offered him money to help, which of course he has refused. Alcibiades has been unjustly treated by the Athenian senators, and has formed an army to rid the city-state of all its corrupt elements. Timon now offers his newly discovered gold to two of the whores that are accompanying the army, in the hope that they will sow destruction in Athens too.

Style: as part of a three-handed scene, in front of a larger listening group **Where:** at Timon's camp in the woods

To Whom: two whores, in front of Alcibiades and his army

# of Lines: 31 **Probable Timing: 1.30 minutes**

Modern Text

12/ Timon

1 {I have e}nough {Δgold} to make a Δwhore forswear* her Δtrade,
And to make Δwhores,[7] a Δbawd.
2 Hold up, you Δsluts,
Your Δaprons mountant. †
3 You are not Δoathable*,
Although I know you'll* swear*, terribly swear*
Into strong shudders and to heavenly Δagues
Th'immortal* Δgods that hear* you.
4 Spare your Δoaths*;
I'll trust to your Δconditions, be whores still.
5 And he whose pious breath seeks* to convert you,
Be strong in Δwhore, allure him, burn* him up,
Let your close fire predominate his smoke,
And be no turn*-coats; yet may your pains* six months
Be quite contrary. †
6 And Δthatch your poor* thin Δroofs*
With burthens of the dead - some that were hang'd,
No matter; wear* them, betray with them. †
7 Whore still,
Paint till a horse may mire* upon your face:
A pox of wrinkles!

F's orthography suggests that while Timon's hatred of the 'Gold' and the idea of whoredom is intellectual, his contempt for the women themselves and their clients is far more personal.

- Timon starts very intellectually with the tempting of the women with the 'Gold' (7/1, the first two and half lines), though F #2's opening surround phrase
  ". Hold up you Sluts/Your Aprons mountant ; "
  suggests an emotional undertow in being set with an emotional semicolon

- which leads to a release of passion as he insults them for their intrinsic untrustworthiness (5/5, the four and lines ending F #2, and F #3), finishing with F #3's double surround phrase finish
  " Spare your Oathes : /Ile trust to your Conditions, be whores still . "

- as he turns his attentions to the threadbare wiles they should use to destroy any who 'seekes to convert you', he starts emotionally (1/3, F #4's first three and a half lines), yet as he returns once more to the women themselves, wishing the same tricks would eventually destroy them in six months time, so his feeling about the women reverts to passion (3/3, the next three lines)

- which climaxes with the three rather ugly surround phrases summarising his disgust of what their eventual trumped up physical appearance will be like, starting with their wearing of wigs made from corpses (often of criminals)
  " : Weare them, betray with them ; Whore still,/Paint till a horse may myre upon your face : /A pox of wrinkles . "

First Folio

12/ Timon

1 {I have e}nough {Gold} to make a Whore forsweare her Trade,
And to make Whores, a Bawd.
2 Hold up+ you Sluts+
Your Aprons mountant; you are not Othable,
Although I know you'l sweare, terribly sweare
Into strong shudders,$_{x}$ and to heavenly Agues
Th'immortall Gods that heare you.
3 Spare your Oathes: $_{x}$
Ile trust to your Conditions, be whores still.
4 And he whose pious breath seekes to convert you,
Be strong in Whore, allure him, burne him up,
Let your close fire predominate his smoke,
And be no turne-coats:$_{x}$ yet may your paines six months
Be quite contrary, And Thatch
Your poore thin Roofes with burthens of the dead,
($_{x}$Some that were hang'd$_{x}$) no matter: $_{x}$
Weare them, betray with them; Whore still,
Paint till a horse may myre upon your face:
A pox of wrinkles. +

{ctd. over}

[7] in *William Shakespeare: A Textual Companion,* op. cit., page 505-6, footnote to line 4.3.135/1563 the editors offer a detailed explanation for their interesting substitution of 'wholesönes a Bawd' (i.e. 'whole sons' for Ff's 'Whores, a Bawd': an earlier, simpler gloss = 'whores abhor'd'

8 Consumptions sow*
In hollow bones of man, strike their sharp* shins*,
And mar* men's spurring.
9 Crack* the Δlawyers voice*,
That he may never more false Δtitle plead*,
Nor sound his Δquillets shrilly ; Δhoar* the Δflamen,
That [scolds] against the quality of flesh
And not believes* himself*.
10 Down* with the Δnose,
Down* with it flat; take the Δbridge quite away
Of him that, his particular to foresee,
Smells* from the general* weal*.
11 Make curl'd-pate Δruffians bald,
And let the unscarr'd Δbraggarts* of the Δwar*
Derive some pain* from you .
12 Plague all,
That your Δactivity may defeat* and quell
The source* of all Δerection.
13 There's more Δgold.
14 Do you damn* others, and let this damn* you,
And ditches grave you all !

the attack heightened by F's irregular verse (7/10/7/8/10 syllables), as if Timon is so disturbed that he cannot maintain the niceties of verse – however most modern texts minimise the irregularities, as the shaded text shows (11/10/11/10)

• Timon voices the longed-for physically destructive effect of their diseases upon their clients quite emotionally (F #5's two lines, 0/4, and F #7's three lines 2/4), while the anticipated results on the psyche of both the Lawyer and the Priest (long-time Shakespeare's favourite targets) as well as on 'Ruffians' and 'Braggerts of the Warre' arouse his passions (F #6, 5/6 and F #8, 3/3)

• and while his final direct curses 'Plague all' (F #9) and 'damne others' and 'damne you' (F #11) remain passionate (2/3), the curse of the gift of 'Gold' is much more deliberate in that is it is handled via a very short intellectual monosyllabic sentence (F #10, 1/0)

5 Consumptions sowe
In hollow bones of man, strike their sharpe shinnes,
And marre mens spurring.
6 Cracke the Lawyers voyce,
That he may never more false Title pleade,
Nor sound his Quillets shrilly : x Hoare the Flamen,
That [scold'st] against the quality of flesh, x
And not beleeves himselfe.
7 Downe with the Nose,
Downe with it flat, take the Bridge quite away
Of him, x that+ his particular to foresee+
Smels from the generall weale.
8 Make curld'pate Ruffians bald+
And let the unscarr'd Braggerts of the Warre
Derive some paine from you.
9 Plague all,
That your Activity may defeate and quell
The sourse of all Erection.
10 There's more Gold.
11 Do you damne others, and let this damne you,
And ditches grave you all. +

13/ Timon **Thankes I must you con,/That you are Theeves profest :** 4.3.425 - 449

Background: Just as Timon bribed the whores to sow destruction in Athens, he now urges some bandits (who attempted to rob him) to do the same thing.

Style: as part of at least a four handed scene **Where:** at Timon's camp in the woods

To Whom: the three bandits listed as speaking, perhaps plus some silent fellows

# of Lines: 25 **Probable Timing: 1.15 minutes**

Modern Text

13/ Timon

1 {ψ} {T}hanks* I must you con,
That you are Δthieves* profess'd*, that you work* not
In holier shapes ; Δfor there is boundless* Δtheft
In limited Δprofessions.
2 Rascal* Δthieves*,
Here's* Δgold.
3 Go, suck* the subtle blood o'th'Δgrape,
Till the high Δfever* seethe* your blood to froth,
And so scape hanging.

This is a fascinating speech for Timon in that it is one of the most relentlessly uncompromising in terms of ongoing passionate release anywhere in the play (37/40 in just twenty-five lines) – suggesting that, rather than being a quiet urging of something Timon has understood for some time (which is usually how it is played, often with bamboozling casual ease to rather stupid members of the lower classes), it may be something that has only just struck him – and the release frenzy may be an attempt to understand as well as to persuade.

• the extra drive of the surround phrases underscores exactly what Timon believes/wants, starting with the passionate F #1 (4/4)

"Thankes I must you con,/That you are Theeves profest : that you worke not /In holier shapes : For there is boundlesse Theft/In limited Professions ."

First Folio

13/ Timon

1 {ψ} {T}hankes I must you con,
That you are Theeves profest : x that you worke not
In holier shapes : x For there is boundlesse Theft
In limited Professions.
2 Rascall Theeves+
Heere's Gold.
3 Go, sucke the subtle blood o'th'Grape,
Till the high Feavor seeth your blood to froth,
And so scape hanging.

4 Trust not the Δphysician*,
His Δantidotes are poison*, and he slays*
Moe [than] you Δrob . †
5 Take wealth and lives together,
Do, [Δvillains,] do, since you protest to do't*◊
Like Δworkmen*. †
6 I'll example you with Δthievery*:
The Δsun's* a Δthief*, and with his great attraction
Robs* the vast* Δsea; ◊ the Δmoon's* an arrant Δthief*,
And her pale fire she snatches from the Δsun*; ◊
The Δsea's a Δthief*, whose liquid Δsurge resolves
The Δmoon* into salt tears*; ◊ the Δearth's a Δthief*,
That feeds and breeds by a composture stol'n*
From gen'ral* excrement ; each thing's a Δthief*.
7 The Δlaws*, your curb* and whip, in their rough power
Has uncheck'd Δtheft .
8 Love not your selves, away,
Rob one another . †
9 There's more Δgold . †
10 Cut throats*,
All that you meet* are Δthieves* . †
11 To Athens go,
Break* open shops*, nothing can you steal*
But Δthieves* do lose* it . †
12 Steal* less*[8] for this I give you,
And Δgold confound you howsoe'er ! †
13 Amen.

and then urging them with the equally passionate end of F #4 and F #5 (7/7)

" : Take wealth, and lives together,/Do [Villaine] do, since you protest to doo't . /Like Workemen, Ile example you with Theevery : /The Sunnes a Theefe, and with his great attraction/Robbes the vaste Sea ."

which leads to

" : each thing's a Theefe . "

with the very last

" : steale lesse, for this I give you,/And Gold confound you howsoere : Amen . "

ending only one of two emotional moments in the speech

- from the opening greeting Timon is passionate (4/3, F#1), which he sustains through F #2's offer of the gold (2/3 in just four words!) and F #3's suggestion that they drink themselves to death (2/2)

- and as he continues, his passion seems intensified by the peculiar onrush of F #4 (5/5) where the suggestion that they don't visit physicians is suddenly jammed together with the idea that they should kill as they steal, the two ideas more rationally separated by most modern texts as separate sentences (perhaps the F setting suggests that if they don't visit physicians they will stay in the drunken fervour wished upon them by Timon in F #3, and thus be more prone to kill)

- as Timon promises 'to example you with Theevery' he moves into four separate sentences (F #5-8) to isolate the thefts of sun, moon, sea, and earth respectively, all still amazingly passionate (16/16 overall): most modern texts regard this as syntactically dreadful and run all four sentences together (mt. #6), more indicative of one long general blurt – however, F's four sentence setting suggests that to Timon each example of theft is very different from the others and/or that he is only just discovering the next idea/example as he finishes the one before

- after his summation of the power of Law as 'uncheck'd Theft' (F #9, 2/2), in once more turning his attention to the Bandits and to humanity in general he becomes predominantly emotional for only the second time in the speech (F #10, 6/10) - his condemnation of them and Athenians in general matching his earlier disgust with the whores and their potential clients (speech #12 above, perhaps his prayer-wish to be able to hate 'the whole race of Mankinde' – speech #8 above - is beginning to take effect)

4 Trust not the Physitian,
His Antidotes are poyson, and he slayes
Moe [then] you Rob : Take wealth,[x] and lives together,
Do+ [Villaine]+ do, since you protest to doo't.
5 Like Workemen, Ile example you with Theevery :
The Sunnes a Theefe, and with his great attraction
Robbes the vaste Sea.
6 The Moones an arrant Theefe,
And her pale fire,[x] she snatches from the Sunne.
7 The Seas a Theefe, whose liquid Surge,[x] resolves
The Moone into Salt teares.
8 The Earth's a Theefe,
That feeds and breeds by a composture stolne
From gen'rall excrement :[x] each thing's a Theefe.
9 The Lawes, your curbe and whip, in their rough power
Ha's uncheck'd Theft.
10 Love not your selves, away,
Rob one another, there's more Gold, cut throates,
All that you meete are Theeves : to Athens go,
Breake open shoppes, nothing can you steale
But Theeves do loose it : steale lesse,[x] for this I give you,
And Gold confound you howsoere : + Amen.

[8] though most modern texts agree with Ff and set 'steale lesse', two glosses set the exact opposite, offering 'steale no lesse' or 'steale not lesse'

14/ Painter **As I tooke note of the place, it cannot be farre** between 5.1.1 – 42

15/ Poet **I am thinking /What I shall say I have provided for him :** between 5.5.32 - 46

Background: In revenge for Timon's dismissal of him, as promised Apermantus has let Athens know that Timon has money once again. The Painter and the Poet are trying to get to him first, and, as such, each of the following speeches are self-explanatory.

Style: each as part of a two-handed scene

Where: in the woods near to Timon's camp **To Whom:** speech #14 the Poet; speech #15 the Painter

Speech 14: # of Lines: 30 **Probable Timing: 1.30 minutes**

Speech 15: # of Lines: 12 **Probable Timing: 0.40 minutes**

Modern Text

[9] **14/ Painter**

1 As I took* note of the place, it cannot be far*
where he abides.

2 {Certain*t}he Δrumor hold{s} for true that he's*
So full of Δgold {.}

3 Alcibiades reports it ;
[Phrinia and Timandra] [10] had Δgold of him.
4 He likewise enrich'd Δpoor* straggling* Δsoldiers* with
Great quantity.
5 'Tis said* he gave unto
His Δsteward a mighty sum*.

6 You shall see him a Δpalm* in Athens again*, and flourish
With the highest. †
7 Therefore, 'tis not amiss*,
We tender our loves to him in this suppos'd
Distress* of his ; it will show honestly in us,
And is very likely to load* our purposes
With what they travail* for, if it be
A just and true report, that goes of his having.

8 {I have nothing to present unto him} at this time
But my Δvisitation ;
Only* I will promise him an excellent Δpiece*.

As they draw near to their quarry, it seems that the Painter can barely contain himself (whether from excitement or exhaustion is up to each actor to decide) for initially there is no consistency in his releases.

- in announcing their closeness he starts emotionally (F #1, 0/2), while F #2's belief thatbif the 'Rumor holds for true', Timon is once more rich is passionate (2/2): and while the initial confirmation (from the two prostitutes, whose names he gets hopelessly wrong) is intellectual (F #3, 3/0), the secondary confirmation from what he has heard from/about the Banditti and Timon's Steward is emotional (2/4 in just the three lines of F #4-5)
- the thought that they should 'tender their loves' because Timon will be 'a Palme in Athens againe' continues the emotion (F #6, 2/6) – the first consistency in the speech
- the realisation that he has nothing to give to Timon seems quite disturbing, for suddenly come four successive surround phrases,
  ". I have nothing to present unto him at this time/But my Visitation : onely I will promise him/An excellent Peece . /Promising, is the verie Ayre o'th'Time ; /It opens the eyes of Expectation . "
- the first two of these surround phrases, how to get out of the problem, are passionate (F #7, 2/2), while the third and fourth, the thought that his solution of 'promising' might just work (heightened by being linked with the emotional semicolon), become intellectual for only the second time in the speech (F #8, 3/1)
- and as the Painter elaborates further on the theme of promising, his astounding dismissal of the value of 'Performance' for being 'ever the duller for his acte' (F #9) and a 'great sicknesse' (the last two lines of F #10) is emotional (1/3 and 2/3 respectively), while the one line of lavish praise of 'Promise'

First Folio

14/ Painter

1 As I tooke note of the place, it cannot be farre
where he abides.

2 {Certaine t}he Rumor hold{s} for true,$_x$
That hee's so full of Gold? {.}

3 Alcibiades reports it :$_x$ [Phrinica and Timandylo]
Had Gold of him.
4 He likewise enrich'd
Poore stragling Souldiers,+ with great quantity.
5 'Tis saide,$_x$ he gave unto his Steward
A mighty summe.

6 You shall see him a Palme in Athens againe,
And flourish with the highest :
Therefore, 'tis not amisse,$_x$ we tender our loves
To him,$_x$ in this suppos'd distresse of his :$_x$
It will shew honestly in us,
And is very likely,$_x$ to loade our purposes
With what they travaile for,
If it be a just and true report, that goes
Of his having.

7 {I have nothing to present unto him} at this time
But my Visitation :$_x$ onely I will promise him
An excellent Peece.

---

[9] all but two lines of the scene in which this speech appears are set in verse: however, only a quarter of the text is set in regular verse: i.e. lines of ten syllables; thus, with less than twenty-five percent of the lines being seen as regular verse, many modern texts set the first 53 lines of the scene, including this speech, as prose (*The Riverside Shakespeare* being a notable exception), and regularise many of the remaining irregular verse lines, presumably arguing 'white space' is responsible for the peculiar Folio layout: the reader is invited to consider whether the irregularities reflect the inner workings of not only the Poet and Painter as they attempt to wheedle Timon out of some of his gold, but also Timon's inner turmoil, dealing as he is for the first time since leaving Athens with members of his one time entourage whom he knows to be untrustworthy

[10] [illegible]

9 Promising is the very* Δair* o'th'Δtime ;
It opens the eyes of Δexpectation.

10 Performance, is ever the duller for his act*,
And but in the plainer and simpler kind* of people,
The deed* of Δsaying is quite out of use.

11 To Δpromise is most Δcourtly and fashionable ;
Performance is a kind* of Δwill or Δtestament
Which argues a great sickness* in his judgment*
That makes it.

12 {ψ} {ψ} Let's seek* him {.}

13 Then do we sin* against our own* estate,
When we may profit meet*, and come too late.

" . To Promise,,x is most Courtly and fashionable ; "
is not only intellectual (2/0) it is heightened both by the extra breath thought (marked ,,x) and by being set as an emotional surround phrase

• and having determined with this wonderfully appalling chop logic that it will be perfectly fine for him to approach Timon with no gift as of yet, both the short monosyllabic sentence suggestion 'Let's seeke him.' and the rhyming couplet maxim/hope that 'we may profit meete' are emotional (0/4, F #11-12)

8 Promising,,x is the verie Ayre o'th'Time ;
It opens the eyes of Expectation.

9 Performance, is ever the duller for his acte,
And but in the plainer and simpler kinde of people,
The deede of Saying is quite out of use.

10 To Promise,,x is most Courtly and fashionable ;
Performance,,x is a kinde of Will or Testament
Which argues a great sicknesse in his judgement
That makes it.

11 {ψ} {ψ} Let's seeke him {.}

12 Then do we sinne against our owne estate,
When we may profit meete, and come too late.

Modern Text

15/ Poet

1 I am thinking
What I shall say I have provided for him . †

2 It must be a personating of himself* :
A Δsatire* against the softness* of Δprosperity,
With a Δdiscovery* of the infinite Δflatteries
That follow youth and opulency*.

3 Nay let's seek* him.

4 Then do we sin* against our own* estate,
When we may profit meet*, and come too late.

5 {ψ}When the day serves before black*-corner'd[11] night ;
Find* what thou want'st, by free and offer'd light.

6 Come.

• as with the Poet's previous speech (#2 above), this too starts very quietly, the unembellished surround phrase first line
" . I am thinking /What I shall say I have provided for him : "
followed by a second almost unembellished surround phrase
" : It must be a personating of himselfe : "
- the opening quietness perhaps suggesting deep concentration, as if the need to find a cogent way to proceed has only just hit him (especially with the short spelling of both 'Discoverie' and 'opulencie')

• in envisaging what the new work shall be ('A Satyre against the softnesse of Prosperity') his intellect takes over (4/2, F #1's last two and half lines), but only momentarily, for once the theme is hit upon, the Poet moves emotionally into action (0/6, the remaining four lines plus two bits of the speech)

• F #2's 'Nay let's seeke him.' is made more urgent by being set as a short, monosyllabic sentence, which then, quite unusually, leads to . . .

• . . . two pairs of rhyming couplets (F #3's 'estate/late', F #4's 'night/light'), the rhyme scheme often associated with heightening the intensity of the moment – perhaps signifying an increased sense of (financially greedy?) purpose on the Poet's part: certainly the second couplet maxim, a variant of the well known motto 'seize the day', seems to be very important to the Poet, for F #4 shows it is as two emotional (semicolon formed) surround phrases

First Folio

15/ Poet

1 I am thinking
What I shall say I have provided for him :
It must be a personating of himselfe :
A Satyre against the softnesse of Prosperity,
With a Discoverie of the infinite Flatteries
That follow youth and opulencie.

2 Nay let's seeke him.

3 Then do we sinne against our owne estate,
When we may profit meete, and come too late.

4 {ψ}When the day serves before blacke-corner'd night ;
Finde what thou want'st, by free and offer'd light.

5 Come.

[11] though most modern texts agree with F and print this as 'blacke-corner'd', one gloss = 'blacke curtain'd'

16/ Poet **Haile worthy Timon, our late Noble Master.** between 5.1.54 - 72

Background: Finally, the Poet and Painter find Timon, little knowing that he has overheard their machinations (speeches #14-15, above). The following is the Poet's opening greeting.

Style: as part of a three-handed scene

Where: at Timon's camp in the woods **To Whom:** Timon, in front of the Painter

# of Lines: 12 **Probable Timing: 0.40 minutes**

Modern Text

16/ Poet

1 Hail* worthy Timon {,}
{ψ} our late Δnoble Δmaster.

2 Sir,
Having often of your open Δbounty tasted,
Hearing you were retir'd*, your Δfriends fall'n* off,
Whose thankless* Δnatures (O abhorred Δspirits !)
Not all the Δwhips* of Δheaven, are large enough - ◊
What, to you,
Whose Δstar*-like Δnobleness* gave life and influence
To their whole being!

3 I am rapt and cannot cover
The monstrous bulk* of this Δingratitude
With any size of words.

4 {ψ} He and myself*
Have travail'd in the great show'r* of your gifts*,
And sweetly felt it.

5 {ψ}We are hither come to offer you our service.

Whereas the Poet's previous pre-planning speech was essentially emotional (#15 above, 4/9) and this appears to be more passionate (13/11), the quick enthusiastic shifts in release-patterns seen in the Poet's earlier speeches (#2 and #15 above) still apply. Here the Poet's opening unbridled intellectual attempt at wooing Timon (10/5 in just the five lines of F #1-2) becomes somewhat more cautious, shifting to emotion (3/5, the four lines from F #3 to the opening of F #5), and then finally goes quiet with the last four lines of the speech – whether it's his own diminishing energy or Timon's unwavering lack of response that causes the speech's progressive wind-down is up to each actor to explore.

- thus the short sentence greeting is strongly intellectual (F #1, 3/1) while the (unexpected?) lack of response from Timon might explain the one word surround phrase " . Sir : " that opens F #2 and, since it is set alone as a one syllable line, the very long pause that comes after before the Poet can continue

- nevertheless, continue he does, intellectually struggling to connect the unconnectable - the idea of Timon's 'Bounty' and the denigrating of those 'Friends falne off' (7/4, F #2)

- the lack of any logical completion to either of F #2's conflicting ideas plus the peculiar setting of a new ungrammatical F #3, together with F #3's starting short (three syllable) line, shows just how much the Poet has lost his way – and sure enough, intellect is replaced by passion (3/3) as he stumbles through the sudden fulsome praise of Timon (F #3) and the attempt to cover up the fact he really is lost for words (F #4) – F #3's confusion is undone by most modern texts adding it to F #2

- but inevitably the Poet cannot stay away from the financial, and with reference to Timon's previous 'guifts' the Poet becomes emotional (0/3, F #5) – and finally (embarrassment? awkwardness? creating a mood of false sincerity? lack of response from Timon?) he becomes unembellishedly quiet in F #6's short sentence offer ('We are hither come/To offer you our service.'), the awkwardness enhanced by the potential pause created by the sentence being set as two short lines (five/seven syllables), a pause removed by most modern texts setting F #6's two short lines as one

First Folio

16/ Poet

1 Haile worthy Timon {,}
{ψ} our late Noble Master.

2 Sir : $_x$
Having often of your open Bounty tasted,
Hearing you were retyr'd, your Friends falne off,
Whose thankelesse Natures (O abhorred Spirits+)
Not all the Whippes of Heaven, are large enough.

3 What, to you,
Whose Starre-like Noblenesse gave life and influence
To their whole being? +

4 I am rapt, $_x$ and cannot cover
The monstrous bulke of this Ingratitude
With any size of words.

5 {ψ} He, $_x$ and my selfe
Have travail'd in the great showre of your guifts,
And sweetly felt it.

6 {ψ}We are hither come
To offer you our service.

17/ Timon **Most honest men :/Why how shall I requite you?** between 5.1.73 - 115

Background: The following is Timon's short-shrift stripping of the effusive, pretentious, and self-serving greeting offered him via speech #16 above.

Style: as part of a three-handed scene

Where: at Timon's camp in the woods **To Whom:** the Poet and Painter

# of Lines: 38 **Probable Timing:** 1.55 minutes

Modern Text

17/ Timon

1 Most honest men ! †
2 Why, how shall I requite you?
3 Can you eat* Δroots and drink* cold water . †
4 No?
5 {ψ} {You'll } what you can {ψ} to do {me} service.

6 Y'are honest men ; y'have heard that I have Δgold,
I am sure you have . †
7 Speak* truth, y'are honest men.

8 Good honest men ! †
9 Thou draw'st a counterfeit*
Best in all Athens; th'art indeed the best,
Thou counterfeit'st* most lively.
10 E'en so sir as I say. –
11 And, for thy fiction,
Why, thy Δverse swells* with stuff* so fine and smooth
That thou art even Δnatural* in thine Δart.
12 But for all this, my honest Δnatur'd friends,
I must needs say you have a little fault ;
Marry, 'tis not monstrous in you, neither wish I
You take much pains* to mend.

13 There's never a one of you but trusts a Δknave
That mightily deceives you.

14 [Ay], and you hear* him cog*, Δsee him dissemble,
Know his gross* patchery, love him, feed* him,
Keep* in your bosom*; yet remain* assur'd
That he's a made-°up ΔΔvillain*.

15 Look* you, I love you well, I'll give you Δgold,
Rid me these Δvillains* from your companies ;
Hang them, or stab them, drown* them in a draught,

• in comparison with his earlier sequences with Apermantus, the whores, and the Banditti (speeches #11 – 13 above), the opening being so controlled, though the subtext of the calm unembellished first five sentences, heightened by much of it being expressed via surround phrases, should delight the audience in awaiting/guessing what is to come and perhaps surprise the Poet and Painter – though they could always put down the quietness to Timon's exhaustion or even, vaingloriously and mistakenly, his relief at their arrival

". Most honest men : /Why how shall I requite you ? . . . /You'll what you can to do {me} service . /Y'are honest men,/Good honest men : . . . / . . . th'art indeed the best,/Thou counterfet'st most lively . "

• whatever releases there are in the opening ten lines are essentially intellectual (5/3, F #1-5), a further sign of Timon's incredible self-control and/or exhaustion

• interestingly, while his handling of the Painter is economic and intellectual (2/0 F #5-6), - the unembellished monosyllabic short F #6 seems to set a finality on that part of the conversation, and . . .

• . . . his response to the Poet is nowhere as self-controlled (3/2, F #7) - and whether this sudden passion is intentionally seductive or somewhat more personal is up to each actor to explore

• Timon manages to regain control (just 1/1 in the four lines of F #8, much of it unembellished once again, as he lays in the idea that)

"I must needs say you have a little fault,/Marry 'tis not monstrous in you,"

• but as he begins his stripping of their pretences, control disappears as his emotions get the better of him (F #9-10, 2/8), with the minute hesitations inherent in the three short lines ending F #9 and opening F #10 (these last two reset as a single eleven syllable line by most modern texts) suggesting that his early struggles to maintain control have very little effect in restraining what is burning underneath

• indeed it may be that Timon recognises this himself, for after the suggestion that 'Ile give you Gold' if they will in removing 'these Villaines from your companies ; /Hang them, or stab them, drowne them in a draught' (passionate for only the second passage in the speech, 2/3, F #11's first three and a half lines), he quietens himself with the second temptation of money

"Confound them by some course, and come to me,/Ile give you gold enough."

First Folio

17/ Timon

1 Most honest men : + →
Why+ how shall I requite you?
2 Can you eate Roots,x and drinke cold water, no?
3 {ψ} {Youle } what you can {ψ} to do {me} service.

4 Y'are honest men,+ →
Y'have heard that I have Gold,
I am sure you have, speake truth, y'are honest men.

5 Good honest men : + Thou draw'st a counterfet
Best in all Athens,+ th'art indeed the best,
Thou counterfet'st most lively.

6 E'ne so sir as I say.
7 And+ for thy fiction,
Why+ thy Verse swels with stuffe so fine and smooth,x
That thou art even Naturall in thine Art.
8 But for all this (xmy honest Natur'd friendsx)
I must needs say you have a little fault,+
Marry+ 'tis not monstrous in you, neither wish I
You take much paines to mend.

9 There's never a one of you but trusts a Knave,x
That mightily deceives you.

10 [I], and you heare him cogge, →
See him dissemble,
Know his grosse patchery, love him, feede him,
Keepe in your bosome,+ yet remaine assur'd
That he's a made-up-Villaine.

11 Looke you,
I love you well, Ile give you Gold
Rid me these Villaines from your companies ;
Hang them, or stab them, drowne them in a draught,

{ctd. over}

Confound them by some course, and come to me,
I'll give you gold enough.

16 You that way, and you this ; but two in ^Δ^company ;
Each man [apart], all single, and alone,
Yet an arch ^Δ^villain* keeps* him company . †

17 [12] If where thou art, two ^Δ^villains* shall not be,
Come not near* him.

18 If thou wouldst not reside*
But where one ^Δ^villain* is, [than] him abandon.

19 Hence, pack*! there's ^Δ^gold; you came for ^Δ^gold, ye slaves. †

20/[13] You have work* for me ; there's payment, hence ! †

21 You are an ^Δ^alcumist, make ^Δ^gold of that . †

22 Out, ^Δ^rascal* dogs*!

• but, once more, the self-control cannot last, for as he separates the two unsuspecting 'Villaines' he has been talking about, with the attempted discipline of F #12's unembellished and then intellectual (0/1) opening surround phrases

" . You that way, and you this : /But two in Company :"[14]

and the unembellished start of the riddle suggesting that each is the 'Villaine'

"Each man [a part], all single, and alone,"

his control blows apart and the next four lines explaining that to avoid the 'Villaine' that Timon has urged them to kill, they have to avoid each other becomes emotionally passionate (3/5, F #12's last two and a half lines and F #13)

• the throwing of the Gold at them (F #14's first three lines), while intellectual (4/2), is heightened by the emotional (in part semicolon created) surround phrase

" ; there's payment, hence,/You are an Alcumist, make gold of that : "

• and passion/emotion takes over once again in the final act of chasing them away (1/2, the last three words of the speech)

Confound them by some course, and come to me,
Ile give you gold enough.

12 You that way, and you this : ~x~ →
But two in Company : ~x~
Each man [a part], all single, and alone,
Yet an arch Villaine keepes him company :
If where thou art, two Villaines shall not be,
Come not neere him.

13 If thou would'st not recide
But where one Villaine is, [then] him abandon.

14 Hence, packe,+ there's Gold,+ you came for Gold+ ye slaves :+
You have worke for me ; there's payment, hence,+
You are an Alcumist, make Gold of that :
Out+ Rascall dogges . +

[12] most modern texts indicate Timon speaks the following sentence to just one of the characters, and the next sentence to the other

[13] from Timon's earlier comments when eavesdropping upon the others, most modern texts indicate he addresses this line to the Poet, and the next to the Painter

[14] the two short lines – six/six syllables - allow time for the symbolic act of the Poet and Painter separating to be done in silence: most modern texts join the two lines together

#'s 18 - 20: The Alcibiades Factor

18/ 1st Senator **The Senators of Athens, greet thee Timon** between 5.1.136 - 166

Background: Totally unexpectedly, representatives of the Athenian Senate appear at Timon's camp, ostensibly to apologise for Athens' earlier rejection of him, proposing to escort him back in triumph. However, as they let slip at the end of the speech, this is only a surface greeting, masking an enormous hidden agenda. Alcibiades' rebellion against Athens is succeeding only too well, and in desperation, the two Senators, representing many of those who ignored Timon in his hour of need, have now come to seduce Timon supposing he will help them to stop the invasion of his one-time friend once he accepts.

Style: as part of a four-handed scene

Where: at Timon's camp in the woods **To Whom:** Timon, in front of his fellow Senator, and Timon's one-time Steward

# of Lines: 24 **Probable Timing: 1.15 minutes**

Modern Text

18/ 1st Senator

1 The Δsenators of Athens greet thee, Timon.

2 The Δsenators with one consent of love
Entreat* thee back* to Athens, who have thought
On special* Δdignities, which vacant lie*,
For thy best use and wearing.

3 {ψ} They confess*
Toward thee forgetfulness* too general* gross*;
Which now the public* Δbody, which doth seldom*
Play the re°canter, feeling in it*self*
A lack* of Timon's aid*, hath [sense] withal*
Of it own* fall,[15] restraining aid* to Timon,
And send forth us, to make their sorrowed render,
Together, with a recompense more fruitful*
[Than] their offense can weigh down* by the Δdram*;
[Ay], even such heaps* and sums* of Δlove and Δwealth
As shall to thee blot out, what wrongs were theirs,
And write in thee the figures of their love,
Ever to read them thine.

4 Therefore so please thee to return* with us
And of our Athens, thine and ours, to take
The Δcaptainship, thou shalt be met with thanks*,
Allow'd* with absolute power, and thy good name
Live with Δauthority*; so soon* we shall drive back*
Of Alcibiades th'approaches wild,
Who, like a Δboar* too savage, doth root up
His Δcountry's* peace.

- the intellectual control of the Sentaor's opening greeting (F #1, 3/0) doesn't last long, for the ensuing smacking-of-bribery statement that 'The Senators, with one consent of love,/Intreate thee backe' becomes passionate (3/4, F #2), - though whether the passion is a result of a deliberate oratorical style in delivering the message, lack of interest from Timon, or having to eat crow in the apology that is about to open F #3 is up to each actor to decide

- certainly from the outset of F #3 the Senator's emotions come enormously into play (3/12, F #3's first five and half lines), from the only surround phrase in the speech
  ". They confesse/Toward thee, forgetfulnesse too generall grosse ; "
  (emotionally intensified by the only semicolon in the speech) through to the seductive explanation that they all have felt 'A lacke of Tymons ayde'

- the ensuing two unembellished phrases suggest dignity
  "And send forth us, to make their sorrowed render ,"
  but then the Senator suddenly seems to lose control with an unexpectedly passionate outburst (3/7 in just thee lines) intensifying F #2's earlier hints of bribery, now offering 'heapes and summes of Love and Wealth' before re-establishing apparent calm with F #3's final two and half line apologia
  "As shall to thee blot out, what wrongs were theirs,/And write in thee the figures of their love,/Ever to read them thine."

- with still no reply from Timon the extra breath-thought (marked ,x) at the end of F #4's first line suggests that the Senator is taking great care to make the bribery offer, now of full leadership in Athens, absolutely clear yet again - the return to careful passion (3/2 in F#4's first four and a half lines) underscoring the need

- and F's orthography suggests that the Senator may momentarily lose control as (following the only colon in the sentence) the subject of Alcibiades is broached, for the first mention of the threat of his invasion is emotional ('so soone we shall drive backe', 0/2), as if he momentarily forgets himself, but then the Senator clamps down and enhances the strong images ('like a Bore too savage') with full intellectual control (3/1, the last two and a half lines of the speech)

First Folio

18/ 1st Senator

1 The Senators of Athens,x greet thee+ Timon.

2 The Senators,x with one consent of love,x
Intreate thee backe to Athens, who have thought
On speciall Dignities, which vacant lye+
For thy best use and wearing.

3 {ψ} They confesse
Toward thee,x forgetfulnesse too generall grosse ;
Which now the publike Body, which doth sildome
Play the re-canter, feeling in it selfe
A lacke of Timons ayde, hath [since] withall
Of it owne fall, restraining ayde to Timon,
And send forth us, to make their sorrowed render,
Together, with a recompence more fruitfull
[Then] their offence can weigh downe by the Dramme,+
[I]+ even such heapes and summes of Love and Wealth,x
As shall to thee blot out, what wrongs were theirs,
And write in thee the figures of their love,
Ever to read them thine.

4 Therefore so please thee to returne with us,x
And of our Athens, thine and ours+ to take
The Captainship, thou shalt be met with thankes,
Allowed with absolute power, and thy good name
Live with Authoritie :x so soone we shall drive backe
Of Alcibiades th'approaches wild,
Who+ like a Bore too savage, doth root up
His Countries peace.

---

[15] though the Ff phrase 'it owne fall' is completely valid, commentators offer various glosses including 'it's' for grammatical correctness plus 'fail' and 'fault'

19/ Timon **I love my Country, and am not/One that rejoyces in the common wracke,** between 5.1.191 - 223

Background: The following is Timon's response once he discovers the true purpose of the Senators' greeting.

Style: as part of a four-handed scene

Where: at Timon's camp in the woods **To Whom:** the two Senators, and Timon's one-time Steward

# of Lines: 32 **Probable Timing: 1.30 minutes**

Modern Text

19/ Timon

1 {ψ} I love my Δcountry, and am not
One that rejoices* in the common wrack*,
As common bruit* doth put it.

2 Commend me to my loving Δcountrymen* - ◊

Commend me to them,
And tell them that, to ease them of their griefs*,
Their fears* of Δhostile strokes, their Δaches losses,
Their pangs of Δlove, with other incident [throes]
That Δnature's fragile Δvessel* doth sustain*
In life's uncertain* voyage, I will some kindness* do them :
I'll teach them to prevent wild* Alcibiades' wrath.

3 I have a Δtree, which grows* here* in my Δclose,
That mine own* use invites me to cut down*,
And shortly must I fell it.
4 Tell my Δfriends,
Tell Athens, in the sequence of degree,
From high to low throughout, that who so please
To stop Δaffliction, let him take his haste,
Come hither, ere my Δtree hath felt the Δaxe,
And hang himself*.
5 I pray you do my greeting.

6 Come not to me again*, but say to Athens,
Timon hath made his everlasting Δmansion
Upon the Δbeached Δverge of the salt Δflood,
Who once a day with his embossed Δfroth
The turbulent Δsurge shall cover ; thither come,
And let my grave-stone be your Δoracle . †
7 Lips*, let four* words go by and Δlanguage end !
What is amiss*, Δplague and Δinfection mend. !
8 Graves only* be men's works*, and Δdeath their gain*! †
9 Sun*, hide thy Δbeams*, Timon hath done his Δreign*.

• Timon's apparently acquiescence opening is emotional (2/4, F #1-2), though, interestingly, his F #2 mention of his 'loving Countreymen' immediately drives him into the unembellished opening of F #3, 'Commend me to them/And tell them,' – as if the very thought of them has caused the quietness (an attempt to maintain self-control perhaps) – though this quiet is extraordinarily brief . . .

• for the F #3 offer of the 'kindnes' he will do them 'to ease them of their greefes' is even more passionate (6/9 in just five and half lines)

• it is possible that he almost gives away the shocking denouement (that they should come and hang themselves) before he intends to, for F #4's first mention of the 'Tree' he must shortly 'fell' is surprisingly emotional (2/4)

• but he recovers intellectual control (F #5, 5/1) as he tantalises them with the thought that those who wish 'To stop Affliction' should come to him – and then drops the bombshell, with the shock of
"; Come hither ere my Tree hath felt the Axe,/And hang himselfe . "
heightened by being set as an emotional (semicolon) surround phrase – a shock which is then maximised by the simple calm of the following unembellished short F #6, 'I pray you do my greeting.', its quietness stressing the absolute deliberateness of the offer (whether the offer is genuine or sarcastic is up to each actor to explore)

• after which Timon becomes surprisingly factual in announcing where his own final resting place is going to be (7/1, F #7's first four and half lines), the intellectual ease a stark contrast to the somewhat startling images

• then, with his final words (an invitation, a curse, and an epitaph) expressed via five consecutive surround phrases, three of which are intensified in part by emotional semicolons,
"; thither come, /And let my grave-stone be your Oracle : /Lippes, let foure words go by, and Language end : /What is amisse, Plague and Infection mend . /Graves onely be mens workes, and Death their gaine ; /Sunne,hide thy Beames, Timon hath done his Raigne ."
his passions subsume him once more (8/9, the last five and a half lines of the speech)

• the setting of his epitaph at the end of F #7 strikingly caps his hatred of all that he now believes Athens stands for: most modern texts remove the onrush by setting it as a more rational separate mt. #8, thus reducing the passionate blurt of the original

First Folio

19/ Timon

1 {ψ} I love my Country, and am not
One that rejoyces in the common wracke,
As common bruite doth put it.

2 Commend me to my loving Countreymen.

3 Commend me to them,
And tell them, x that+ to ease them of their greefes,
Their feares of Hostile strokes, their Aches losses,
Their pangs of Love, with other incident [throwes]
That Natures fragile Vessell doth sustaine
In lifes uncertaine voyage, I will some kindnes do them,+
Ile teach them to prevent wilde Alcibiades wrath.

4 I have a Tree+ which growes heere in my Close,
That mine owne use invites me to cut downe,
And shortly must I fell it.
5 Tell my Friends,
Tell Athens, in the sequence of degree,
From high to low throughout, that who so please
To stop Affliction, let him take his haste ; x
Come hither+ ere my Tree hath felt the Axe,
And hang himselfe.
6 I pray you do my greeting.

7 Come not to me againe, but say to Athens,
Timon hath made his everlasting Mansion
Upon the Beached Verge of the salt Flood,
Who once a day with his embossed Froth
The turbulent Surge shall cover ; thither come,
And let my grave-stone be your Oracle :
Lippes, let foure words go by, x and Language end : +
What is amisse, Plague and Infection mend. +
8 Graves onely be mens workes, and Death their gaine ;+
Sunne, hide thy Beames, Timon hath done his Raigne.

20/ 1st Senator **Noble, and young ;** between 5.4.13 - 54

Background: In his quest to clear Athens of its corrupt elements Alcibiades has reached the gates of the city. The following, pieced together by combining the speeches of two Senators (not necessarily those who failed to bring Timon back, speeches #18-19 above), makes the best of the inevitable situation facing the city-state since non-compliance to Alcibiades' demand 'Descend, and open your uncharged Ports' (i.e. the gates, which now must be unguarded) is out of the question.

Style: public address to one man for the benefit of a larger accompanying group

Where: at Athen's gates **To Whom:** Alcibiades, and his 'powers'

# of Lines: 42 **Probable Timing: 2.00 minutes**

Modern Text

20/ 1st Senator

1 Noble, and young -
When thy first griefs* were but a mere* conceit,
Ere thou hadst power or we had cause of fear*,
We sent to thee, to give thy rages Δbalm*,
To wipe out our Δingratitude, with Δloves
Above their quantity*.

2 So did we woo*
Transformed Timon to our Δcity's* love
By humble Δmessage and by promis'd means*. †

3 We were not all unkind*, nor all deserve
The common stroke of war*.

4 These walls* of ours,
Were not erected by their hands from whom
You have receiv'd* your grief*; Δnor are they such,
That these great Δtow'rs*, trophies*, & Δschools should fall*
For private faults in them.

5 Nor are they living
Who were the motives that you first went out ;
Shame, (that they wanted cunning) in excess*
Hath broke their hearts.

6 March, Δnoble Δlord,
Into our Δcity with thy Δbanners spread*;
By decimation, and a tithed* death,
If thy Δrevenges hunger for that Δfood
Which Δnature loathes, take thou the destin'd tenth,
And by the hazard of the spotted die*
Let die* the spotted.

Once in self-control, F's orthography suggests that the Senator makes very skillful use of quiet moments to place before Alcibiades the key thoughts and/or offers the Athenians are desperate to have him consider. The orthography also shows how long it takes the senator to get to the moment he feels secure enough to employ his rhetorical skills.

• that from the very outset the Senator struggles to deal with the awkwardness of the situation can be seen in

a/ the opening phrase, ' . Noble, and young ; ' is very carefully calm, intensified by being set as an emotional (semicolon formed) surround phrase

b/ though thematically F #1 is of a unity, explaining the background to their first offer for a negotiated peace, there is no stylistic consistency for this first phrase's unembellishment gives way to two lines of emotion (0/3, the not-seen- as-serious-early-stages of the rebellion) and then two and half lines of intellect (3/1, describing what they, as negotiators, were tasked to do)

c/ the strange ungrammatical jamming together of what most modern texts set as two separate sentences mt. #2-3, and the fact that it too switches in style with the similar wooing of Timon being expressed passionately (3/2, F #2's first two and a half lines) and the sudden non-sequitor of pleading innocence/therefore deserving of clemency on the part of (presumably) himself and some of his colleagues being emotional (0/2, F #2's last one and a half lines)

• and this rapid mid-sentence switch of release continues into F #3: whether this is still a sign of awkwardness or the fact that now the Senator has recovered enough to begin to employ his undoubtedly skillful rhetoric is up to each actor to decide, but at least the switches now have more logic to them - for though the corollary that Athens was not built by those who caused Alcibiades' 'greefe' remains emotional (0/3, F #3's first two lines), the urging that the great institutions of Athens should not therefore fall for the faults of the guilty becomes intellectual (4/1, F #3's last two lines)

• then comes a quiet statement - whether intended to calm or offered as a statement of political inevitability (cynical or genuine) – with the indirect hint that they might just have executed his enemies or caused them to commit suicide, almost unembellished (F #4 just 0/1 in three lines)

• and the emotional control continues, for the invitation for Alcibiades to march peacefully 'Into our City' is almost totally intellectual (7/1, the first four lines) –

First Folio

20/ 1st Senator

1 Noble, and young ;x
When thy first greefes were but a meere conceit,
Ere thou had'st power,x or we had cause of feare,
We sent to thee, to give thy rages Balme,
To wipe out our Ingratitude, with Loves
Above their quantitie.

2 So did we wooe
Transformed Timon to our Citties love
By humble Message,x and by promist meanes :
We were not all unkinde, nor all deserve
The common stroke of warre.

3 These walles of ours,
Were not erected by their hands,x from whom
You have receyv'd your greefe :x Nor are they such,
That these great Towres, Trophees, & Schools shold fall
For private faults in them.

4 Nor are they living
Who were the motives that you first went out,+
(xShame+ that they wanted,x cunning+ in excesse,x)
Hath broke their hearts.

5 March, Noble Lord,
Into our City with thy Banners spred,+
By decimation+ and a tythed death ;x
If thy Revenges hunger for that Food
Which Nature loathes, take thou the destin'd tenth,
And by the hazard of the spotted dye,x
Let dye the spotted.

{ctd. over}

7 All have not offended ;
For those that were, it is not square to take
On those that are, Δrevenge ; Δcrimes, like Δlands,
Are not inherited . †
8 Then, dear* Δcountryman*,
Bring in thy ranks*, but leave without thy rage ;
Spare thy Athenian Δcradle and those Δkin
Which in the bluster of thy wrath must fall
With those that have offended ; like a Δshepherd*,
Approach the Δfold and cull th'infected forth,
But kill not [all together] .

9 What thou wilt,
Thou rather shalt enforce* it with thy smile
[Than] hew to't*, with thy Δsword.

10 Set but thy foot
Against our rampir'd* gates and they shall ope,
So thou wilt send thy gentle heart before,
To say thou't enter Δfriendly.

11 Throw thy Δglove,
Or any Δtoken of thine Δhonor* else,
That thou wilt use the wars* as thy redress*
And not as our Δconfusion, Δall thy Δpowers
Shall make their harbor* in our Δtown* till we*
Have seal'd thy full desire.

until the sudden (and perhaps unexpected) emotionally appalling offer to let Alcibiades draw lots to determine 'the destin'd tenth' who still should die (0/2, F #5's last two lines)

• and it seems that this offer of a tenth has a very strong base, for as the Senator elaborates further, the opening

" . All have not offended : /For those that were, it is not square to take /On those that are, Revenge : "

is voiced as two unembellishesd surround phrases (with the exception of the key word 'Revenge'), the quietness adding intensity to the do-not-destroy-everything argument now being advanced, and then the details added in support become strongly intellectual (8/3, F #6's remaining seven lines)

• F #7's ensuing suggestion of how Alcibiades should conquer, by his 'smile' and not his 'Sword', becomes very calm, its almost unembellished quality only broken by the capitalisation of the sentence's last key word 'Sword', . . .

• . . . and F #8's enticement of how easily Alcibiades will be able to enter the city if he does so 'Friendly' is equally careful (1/1), the urging of it having to be promised to be a 'Friendly' act emphasised by the suggestion

" : So thou wilt send thy gentle heart before,/To say thou't enter Friendly . "

being set as a surround phrase

• and then with F #9's demand/plea that Alcibiades pledges now to do so, and the benefits that will thereby ensue, the Senator becomes passionate once more (7/6, whether as a matter of deliberate skillful manipulative rhetoric or out of more personal concerns – nothing else left to offer? fear? - is up to each actor to explore), the two extra breath-thoughts (marked ,$_x$) adding the final tiny much needed details to preserve the appearance of the Athenian Senators' honour (',$_x$ /And not as our Confusion:' and the reassurance of ',$_x$ till we/Have seal'd thy full desire.')

6 All have not offended:
For those that were, it is not square to take
On those that are, Revenge: $_x$ Crimes, like Lands$_x$
Are not inherited, then+ deere Countryman,
Bring in thy rankes, but leave without thy rage,
Spare thy Athenian Cradle,$_x$ and those Kin
Which in the bluster of thy wrath must fall
With those that have offended,+ like a Shepheard,
Approach the Fold,$_x$ and cull th'infected forth,
But kill not [altogether] .

7 What thou wilt,
Thou rather shalt inforce it with thy smile,$_x$
[Then] hew too't, with thy Sword.

8 Set but thy foot
Against our rampyr'd gates,$_x$ and they shall ope : $_x$
So thou wilt send thy gentle heart before,
To say thou't enter Friendly.

9 Throw thy Glove,
Or any Token of thine Honour else,
That thou wilt use the warres as thy redresse,$_x$
And not as our Confusion : $_x$ All thy Powers
Shall make their harbour in our Towne,$_x$ till wee
Have seal'd thy full desire.

SPEECHES IN ORDER		TIME	PAGE
KING LEAR			
#'s 1 - 8: The Division Of The Kingdom			
1/ Lear	Attend the Lords of France & Burgundy, Gloster.	1.00	289
2/ Gonerill	Sir, I love you more then word can weild ÿ matter,	0.30	290
3/ Regan	I am made of that selfe-mettle as my Sister,	0.30	290
4/ Cordelia	Unhappie that I am, I cannot heave/My heart	0.40	291
5/ Lear	Let it be so, thy truth then be thy dowre :	1.00	292
6/ Kent	Be Kent unmannerly, /When Lear is mad	0.55	293
7/ Kent	Fare thee well King, sith thus thou wilt appeare,	0.30	294
8/ Cordelia	I yet beseech your Majesty.	0.40	295
#'s 9 - 13: Edmund's Plot			
9/ Bastard	Thou Nature art my Goddesse, to thy Law	1.10	296
10/ Gloucester	These late Eclipses in the Sun and Moone portend	0.45	297
11/ Bastard	This is the excellent foppery of the world,	1.00	298
12/ Edgar	I heard my selfe proclaim'd,	1.00	299
13/ Bastard	To both these Sisters have I sworne my love :	0.50	300
#'s 14 - 21: The Stripping Down Of Lear			
14/ Gonerill	Did my Father strike my Gentleman ...	0.55	301
15/ Foole	Let me hire him too, here's my Coxcombe.	0.30	302
16/ Gonerill	Not only Sir this, your all-lycenc'd Foole,	0.55	303
17/ Gonerill	I would you would make use of your good wisedome	0.55	304
18/ Lear	Darknesse, and Divels. / Saddle my horses:	0.55	305
19/ Kent	Fellow I know thee. /{Thou'rt a}Knave, a Rascall, ...	0.40	306
20/ Foole	And thou hadst beene set i'th'Stockes for that	0.55	307
21/ Lear	O reason not the need : our basest Beggers	1.10	308
#'s 22 - 24: Madness			
22/ Lear	Blow windes, & crack your cheeks ; Rage, blow	1.00	310
23/ Lear	Let me alone. /Thou think'st 'tis much ...	0.55	311
24/ Foole	This is a brave night to coole a Curtizan :	0.50	312
#'s 25 - 27: Gloucester & Lear			
25/ Edgar	Come on Sir, /Heere's the place : stand still :	0.55	313
26/ Lear	I, every inch a King. /When I do stare, ...	1.00	314
27/ Lear	What, art mad? A man may see how this world goes	1.00	315
#'s 28 - 30: Lear & Cordelia			
28/ Cordelia	Alacke, 'tis he : why he was met even now	0.50	317
29/ Cordelia	O my deere Father, restauration hang	0.50	318
30/ Lear	Howle, howle, howle : O [your] are men of stones,	1.10	319

SPEECHES BY GENDER

		Speech #(s)
SPEECHES FOR WOMEN (9)		
Gonerill	**Traditional & Today:** early middle-aged and older	#2, #14, #16, #17
Regan	**Traditional & Today:** early middle-aged and older	#3
Cordelia	**Traditional & Today:** young woman	#4, #8, #28, #29
SPEECHES FOR EITHER GENDER (0)		
SPEECHES FOR MEN (21)		
Lear	**Traditional & Today:** older male	#1, #5, #18, #21, #22, #23, #26, #27, #30
Foole	**Traditional:** an older male, even though Lear frequently refers to him as 'boy' **Today:** male, any age	#15, # 20, #24
Kent	**Traditional:** older male **Today:** male of any age	#6, #7, #19
Bastard	**Traditional & Today:** young man	#9, #11, #13
Edgar	**Traditional & Today:** young man	#12, #25
Gloucester	**Traditional & Today:** older man with two adult sons	#10

#'S 1 - 8: THE DIVISION OF THE KINGDOM

1/ Lear **Attend the Lords of France & Burgundy, Gloster.** between 1.1.34 - 54

Background: This is Lear's first speech of the play and, on what should be one of the happiest days of his life, it is self-explanatory.

Style: group address

Where: the great hall of Lear's palace **To Whom:** an assembly including his three daughters (Gonerill, Regan, and Cordelia); the husbands of the older two, Albany (married to Gonerill) and Cornwall (husband to Regan); Gloucester and his illegitimate son Edmund; Kent and attendants

# of Lines: 20 **Probable Timing: 1.00 minutes**

Modern Text

1/ Lear

1 Attend the Δlords of France & Burgundy, [Gloucester*].
2 Mean* time we shall* express* our darker purpose.
3 Give me the Δmap there.
4 Know that we have divided
In three our Kingdom*; and 'tis our fast intent,
To shake all Δcares and Δbusiness* from our Δage,
Conferring them on younger* strengths, while we
Unburthen'd crawl* toward death.
5 Our son of [Cornwall*],
And you, our no less* loving Δson* of Albany,
We have this hour* a constant will to publish
Our daughters' several* Δdowers, that future strife
May be prevented now.
6 The Δprinces, France & Burgundy,
Great Δrivals in our youngest* daughter's love,
Long in our Δcourt have made their amorous sojourn*,
And here* are to be answer'd.
7 Tell me, my daughters
(Since now we will divest us both of Δrule,
Interest of Δterritory, Δcares of Δstate),
Which of you shall we say doth love us most,
That we our largest bounty* may extend
Where Δnature doth with merit challenge ?
8 [Goneril*],
Our eldest-born*, speak* first.

In a predominantly intellectual speech (22/14 overall), the two moments of emotion both point to Lear's more personal reaction to the giving away of his throne, F #2's 'Meane time we shal expresse our darker purpose.' (0/2) and the moment when the handing over is about to begin, the speech's final sentence implementing his F #7 suggestion that to get the portion of the country they merit, his three daughters must speak publicly as to how much they love him, 'Gonerill, / Our eldest borne, speake first.' (F #8, 0/3).

- thus, the slightly emotional F #2 notwithstanding, in establishing the required players for the event (France, Burgundy, and the 'Map') Lear starts strongly intellectually (F #1 and #3, 5/0)

- his F #4 announcement of his intentions to (in essence) abdicate is passionate (4/3) and heightened by the opening surround phrase
" . Know, that we have divided/In three our Kingdome : "
and his F #5 follow-up that the Kingdome is being divided so that 'future strife/May be prevented now.' is equally passionate (4/4)

- Lear seems to take intellectual delight in announcing that the reason for the presence of the 'Princes, France & Burgundy' is since they both seek to marry Cordelia (Lear's youngest daughter) and an answer will be forthcoming today (5/2, F #6)

- and it seems that Lear takes equal delight in asking his daughters to speak of their love for him to earn 'our largest bountie' (5/0, F #7), though the actual posing of the question
"Which of you shall we say doth love us most/That we, our largest bountie may extend"
is surprisingly unembellished, and the follow-up, as he asks Gonerill to open the proceedings, is emotional (0/3) – both of which hint that he may not be quite as calm as his opening intellectual request may suggest

First Folio

1/ Lear

1 Attend the Lords of France & Burgundy, [Gloster].
2 Meane time we shal expresse our darker purpose.
3 Give me the Map there.
4 Know,x that we have divided
In three our Kingdome : x and 'tis our fast intent,
To shake all Cares and Businesse from our Age,
Conferring them on yonger strengths, while we
Unburthen'd crawle toward death.
5 Our son of [Cornwal],
And you+ our no lesse loving Sonne of Albany,
We have this houre a constant will to publish
Our daughters severall Dowers, that future strife
May be prevented now.
6 The Princes, France & Burgundy,
Great Rivals in our yongest daughters love,
Long in our Court,x have made their amorous sojourne,
And heere are to be answer'd.
7 Tell me+ my daughters
(Since now we will divest us both of Rule,
Interest of Territory, Cares of State)+
Which of you shall we say doth love us most,
That we,x our largest bountie may extend
Where Nature doth with merit challenge. +
8 [Gonerill],
Our eldest borne, speake first.

2/ Gonerill	**Sir, I love you more then word can weild ÿ matter,**	1.1.54 - 61
3/ Regan	**I am made of that selfe-mettle as my Sister,**	1.1.69 - 76
4/ Cordelia	**Unhappie that I am, I cannot heave/My heart**	between 1.1.91 - 104

Background: The following are the three replies of Lear's daughters to his request 'Which of you shall we say, doth love us most/that we our largest bountie may extend/Where Nature doth with merit challenge'. The replies start first with the eldest daughter Gonerill, and work down to the youngest, and only unmarried child, Cordelia. One note: the last line in the modern text version of speech #4 is taken from the earlier quarto version of the play (titled as the 'History' rather than the 'Tragedy' as in the First Folio.)

Style: one on one address for the larger group to hear

Where: the great hall of Lear's palace **To Whom:** Lear and the assembly including their sisters; Albany and Cornwall; Gloucester and his illegitimate son Edmund; Kent and attendants

Speech 2: # of Lines: 7 **Probable Timing: 0.30 minutes**

Speech 3: # of Lines: 8 **Probable Timing: 0.30 minutes**

Speech 4: # of Lines: 11 **Probable Timing: 0.40 minutes**

Modern Text

2/ Gonerill

1 Sir, I love you more [than] [words] can wield [the] matter,
Dearer* [than] eye-sight, space, and liberty*,
Beyond what can be valued*, rich or rare,
No less* [than] life, with grace, health, beauty, honor;
As much as ^Δ^child* ere lov'd, or ^Δ^father found; ◊
A love that makes breath poor*, and speech unable:
Beyond all manner of so much I love you.

- with so much at stake, not surprisingly the speech is essentially emotional (2/5 overall), yet the unembellished opening
  " Sir, I love you more then word can weild [the] matter,"
  and the final line
  " Beyond all manner of so much I love you."
  point to what great pains she is taking to make sure she is understood and/or that her feelings do not run away with her at the key moment

- thus the flourish of one intellectual/passionate moment
  " : As much as Childe e're lov'd, or Father found . "
  is thrown into enormous relief, especially as it ends F #1 (2/1), and is heightened even more by being the only surround phrase in the speech

First Folio

2/ Gonerill

1 Sir, I love you more [then] [word] can weild [ÿ] matter,
Deerer [then] eye-sight, space, and libertie,
Beyond what can be valewed, rich or rare,
No lesse [then] life, with grace, health, beauty, honor: x
As much as Childe ere lov'd, or Father found.

2 A love that makes breath poore, and speech unable,x
Beyond all manner of so much I love you.

Modern Text

3/ Regan

1 I am made of that self* ° [metal*] as my ^Δ^sister,
And prize me at her worth.

2 In my true heart,
I find* she names my very deed* of love;
Only* she comes too short, that I profess*
Myself* an enemy to all other joys*
Which the most precious square of sense [possesses],
And find* I am alone felicitate
In your dear* Highness* love.

- whether the energy of the release is simply unconscious, or is a deliberate rhetorical ploy, Gonerill's emotional response is even stronger than her sister's (2/11 overall)

- though she cannot overmatch her sister's surround phrase praise, for all she can manage is
  " . In my true heart/I finde she names my very deede of love : "

- and her first unembellished line, 'And prize me at her worth.' also points to the fact that she cannot outpraise Gonerill, though the quiet of the second
  "Which the most precious square of sense professes"
  does call to everyone's attention what is to follow, her protestation that she is happy ('felicitate') only in 'your deere Highnesse love'

First Folio

3/ Regan

1 I am made of that selfe-[mettle] as my Sister,
And prize me at her worth.

2 In my true heart,
I finde she names my very deede of love: x
Onely she comes too short, that I professe
My selfe an enemy to all other joyes,x
Which the most precious square of sense [professes],
And finde I am alone felicitate
In your deere Highnesse love.

Modern Text

4/ Cordelia

1 Unhappy* that I am, I cannot heave
My heart into my mouth . †

2 I love your Majesty
According to my bond, no more nor less*.

3 Good my Lord,
You have begot me, bred me, lov'd me : ◊ I
Return* those duties back* as are right fit,
Obey you, △love you, and most △honor* you .

4 Why have my △sisters △husbands, if they say
They love you all?

5 Happily, when I shall wed,
That △lord, whose hand must take my plight shall carry
Half* my love with him, half* my △care, and △duty* . †

6 Sure I shall never marry like my △sisters,
To love my father all] .

• unlike her sisters, Cordelia makes a very determined attempt to get Lear to understand exactly where she stands, opening with two surround phrases

" . Unhappie that I am, I cannot heave/My heart into my mouth : I love your Majesty/According to my bond, no more nor lesse . "

- her difficulty heightened by the first line being unembellished too, as if she were taking great care as to how she begins so as not to give offence

• thus F #2, outlining what Lear has done for her, is carefully intellectual (1/0)

• but trying to establish publicly what she owes him in return seems very difficult for her, for not only is F #3 passionate overall, its first line, 'I returne those duties backe as are right fit', is emotional (0/2)

• and then the F #4 challenge to her Sisters' integrity and honesty and her F #5 protestation that when she weds, her husband will have half her love (and thus Lear the other) are strongly intellectual (6/2)

First Folio

4/ Cordelia

1 Unhappie that I am, I cannot heave
My heart into my mouth : I love your Majesty
According to my bond, no more nor lesse .

2 Good my Lord,
You have begot me, bred me, lov'd me .

3 I returne those duties backe as are right fit,
Obey you, Love you, and most Honour you .

4 Why have my Sisters Husbands, if they say
They love you all?

5 Happily+ when I shall wed,
That Lord, whose hand must take my plight,x shall carry
Halfe my love with him, halfe my Care, and Dutie,
Sure I shall never marry like my Sisters .
[ ]

5/ Lear **Let it be so, thy truth then be thy dowre :** between 1.1.108 - 129

Background: Prior to Cordelia 's speech (#4 above), Lear had asked her 'What can you say, to draw/A third more opilent then your sisters?', to which she simply replied 'Nothing'. The following is Lear's irate response when Cordelia refuses to soften her stand, despite his warning that 'Nothing will come of nothing, speake againe'.

Style: one on one address for the larger group to hear

Where: the great hall of Lear's palace **To Whom:** Cordelia in front of the assembly which includes Gonerill and Regan; Albany and Cornwall; Gloucester and his illegitimate son Edmund; Kent and attendants

# of Lines: 20 **Probable Timing: 1.00 minutes**

Modern Text

5/ Lear

1 Let it be so, thy truth then be thy dow'r* ! †
2 For by the sacred radiance* of the Δsun*,
The [mysteries] of Hecat* and the night;
By all the operation of the Δorbs*,
From whom we do exist, and cease to be;
Here* I disclaim* all my Δpaternal* care,
Propinquity and property of blood,
And as a stranger to my heart and me
Hold thee from this for ever.
3 The barbarous Scythian,
Or he that makes his generation messes
To gorge his appetite, shall to my bosom*
Be as well neighbor'd*, pitied*, and reliev'd*,
As thou my sometime Δdaughter.
4 I lov'd {you} most, and thought to set my rest
On {your} kind nursery.
5 Hence, and avoid my sight !-†
6 So be my grave my peace, as here I give
Her Δfather's heart from her. †
7 Call France. †
8 Who stirs*?
9 Call Burgundy. †
10 Cornwall and [Albany],
With my two Daughters dow'rs*, digest the third;
Let pride, which she calls, plainness*, marry her.

F's orthography points to moments, perhaps unexpected, when Lear is both affected by his decision to banish Cordelia and unable to establish full control of self and situation.

- the surround phrases point to the determination behind Lear's decision
  " . Let it be so, thy truth then be thy dowre : "
  " . Hence and avoid my sight : /So be my grave my peace, as here I give/Her Fathers heart from her ; call France, who stirres ? "
  with the only emotional semicolon of the speech (ungrammatically) linking the last two, pointing to the pain Lear must be undergoing
- though the speech is often played as one large vocal attack and the overall pattern of more than the first half of the speech is very emotional (6/12, F #1-2), the calm of the unembellished lines point to a man being incredibly quiet at the actual moment of banishing his daughter
  " Propinquity and property of blood,/And as a stranger to my heart and me,/Hold thee from this for ever ."
  and a man hurt to boot
  "I lov'd {you} most, and thought to set my rest/On {your} kind nursery. Hence and avoid my sight:"
- after the mixture of emotion and sudden quiet (the unembellished lines referring to his personal relationship with his daughter) Lear's intellect begins to take over, for, though F #4's instruction to leave is also unembellished, the act of relinquishing 'Her fathers heart' and the instruction to bring in France shows the start of re-establishing control (2/1)
- yet F #5, despite appearing intellectual (5/2), is onrushed, jamming the instructions to 'Cornwall and Albanie' to divide between them the portion that was due to Cordelia together with the instructions to bring in Burgundy, suggesting that control is still somewhat difficult for Lear – yet most modern texts regard the juxtaposition as ungrammatical, and split F #8 into two more rational moments

First Folio

5/ Lear

1 Let it be so, thy truth then be thy dowre : +
For by the sacred radience of the Sunne,
The [miseries] of Heccat and the night : x
By all the operation of the Orbes,
From whom we do exist, and cease to be,
Heere I disclaime all my Paternall care,
Propinquity and property of blood,
And as a stranger to my heart and me,x
Hold thee from this for ever.
2 The barbarous Scythian,
Or he that makes his generation messes
To gorge his appetite, shall to my bosome
Be as well neighbour'd, pittied, and releev'd,
As thou my sometime Daughter.
3 I lov'd {you} most, and thought to set my rest
On {your} kind nursery .
4 Hence+ and avoid my sight :+
So be my grave my peace, as here I give
Her Fathers heart from her; call France, who stirres?
5 Call Burgundy, Cornwall,x and [Albanie],
With my two Daughters Dowres, digest the third,+
Let pride, which she cals plainnesse, marry her {.}

6/ Kent **Be Kent unmannerly,/When Lear is mad** between 1.1.145 - 166
7/ Kent **Fare thee well King, sith thus thou wilt appeare,** 1.1.180 - 187

Background: A true loyalist both to Lear and Cordelia, the nobleman Kent speaks up on her behalf. Speech #6 is Kent's passionate if less than tactful appeal to reason; speech #7 is his final reply, when, as a result of his continued protests, Lear banishes him from Britain on pain of death.

Style: one on one address in front of a larger group for all to hear

Where: the great hall of Lear's palace **To Whom:** Lear, in front of the assembly which includes Cordelia, Gonerill, and Regan; Albany and Cornwall; Gloucester and his illegitimate son Edmund; and attendants

Speech 6: # of Lines: 17 **Probable Timing: 0.55 minutes**
Speech 7: # of Lines: 8 **Probable Timing: 0.30 minutes**

Modern Text

6/ Kent

1 {ψ} {B}e Kent unmannerly,
When Lear is mad. †
2 What wouldest thou do, old man?
3 Think'st thou that duty* shall have dread to speak*
When power to flattery bows*?
4 To plainness* honor's* bound,
When Δmajesty falls to folly. †
5 Reserve thy state,
And in thy best consideration check
This hideous rashness*. †
6 Answer* my life my judgment*;
Thy youngest* Δdaughter does* not love thee least,
Nor are those empty-hearted whose low sounds
Reverb* no hollowness*.

7 My life I never held but as [a] pawn*
To wage against thine enemies, ne'er [fear'd] to lose*it,
Thy safety being motive.

8 Kill thy Δphysician*, and [the] fee bestow
Upon the foul* disease. †
9 Revoke thy gift*,
Or whilst I can vent clamor* from my throat*,
I'll tell thee thou dost evil*.

- Kent opens intellectually (2/0) not so much with a rebuke of Lear but more with the assertion that the situation has forced him to speak as a matter of duty

- then he speaks his mind, but doing so seems to be troubling for him from the outset, for F #2's
  ". Think'st thou that dutie shall have dread to speake ; /When power to flattery bowes ? "
  is not only the first of four successive emotional sentences (0/2), the moment is further heightened by
  a/ the sentence being composed of two emotional surround phrases (created by the speech's only semicolon)
  b/ the two short lines that end this sentence and start the next (6-8/6 syllables), the pause between them perhaps suggesting that he needs a moment to regain self-control before continuing to publicly disagree with and challenge the king

- the remainder of the speech is primarily emotional (3/15, the fourteen lines F #3-5), with the two extra breath-thoughts (marked ,x) towards the end of F #3 underscoring the moments that he feels he must make clearly understood - the offer of his life and the oblique challenge and suggestion (in defence of Cordelia's lack of fulsome praise for her father) that little noise does not signify lack of true feelings

- thus, in this sea of emotion, extra attention should be paid to the quietness of the few unembellished lines, pointing as they do
  a/ the great care with which he pleads with Lear
  'reserve thy state,/And in thy best consideration check thy hideous'
  (and then the key word breaks out of him unchecked, 'rashnesse')
  b/ the equal care with which he tries to make Lear understand
  "Thy safety being motive."

First Folio

6/ Kent

1 {ψ} {B}e Kent unmannerly,
When Lear is mad, what wouldest thou do+ old man?
2 Think'st thou that dutie shall have dread to speake ; x
When power to flattery bowes? →
3 To plainnesse honour's bound,
When Majesty falls to folly, reserve thy state,
And in thy best consideration check
This hideous rashnesse, answere my life,x my judgement :+
Thy yongest Daughter do's not love thee least,
Nor are those empty hearted,x whose low sounds
Reverbe no hollownesse.

4 My life I never held but as [ ] pawne
To wage against thine enemies, nere [feare] to loose it,
Thy safety being motive.

5 Kill thy Physition, and [thy] fee bestow
Upon the foule disease, revoke thy guift,
Or whil'st I can vent clamour from my throate,
Ile tell thee thou dost evill.

Modern Text

7/ Kent

1 Fare thee well, King ; sith thus thou wilt appear*,
Freedom* lives hence, and banishment is here . †

2 [1] The Gods to their dear* shelter take thee, △maid,
That justly think'st and hast most rightly said ! †

3 And your large speeches, may your deeds approve,
That good effects may spring from words of love . †

4 Thus Kent, O △princes, bids you all adieu*,
He'll* shape his old course in a △country new.

While most modern texts present a rational, dignified, four sentence exit by separating the various strands of the farewell (mt. #1 to Lear, #2 to Cordelia, #3 Gonerill and Regan, and #4 to all present), F's one sentence onrush speaks volumes as to how, underneath the rationality, Kent is riding on to an overall wave of sentiment that could well threaten to run away with him.

• thus it's fascinating that within the outpouring each of Kent's separate farewells, each has a separate style of release: the farewell to Lear is slightly emotional (1/2); and though the first line to Cordelia is slightly intellectual (2/1), the second, as well as the subsequent two lines to the (manipulative) sisters, is unembellished - as if he were taking great care not to let his true feelings out?; while, quite fascinatingly, the last two lines show him re-establishing intellectual control (4/2) before leaving

First Folio

7/ Kent

1 Fare thee well+ King,+ sith thus thou wilt appeare,
Freedome lives hence, and banishment is here ;
The Gods to their deere shelter take thee+ Maid,
That justly think'st,x and hast most rightly said : +
And your large speeches, may your deeds approve,
That good effects may spring from words of love :
Thus Kent, O Princes, bids you all adew,
Hee'l shape his old course,x in a Country new.

[1] most modern texts suggest the next two lines are addressed to Cordelia and the following two to her sisters

8/ Cordelia **I yet beseech your Majesty.** 1.1.223 - 233

Background: France and Burgundy, the rival suitors for Cordelia, have been summoned, and informed that if they still wish to marry her there will be no dowry, for 'now her price is fallen' and she should be considered a 'wretch whom Nature is asham'd/Almost t'acknowledge hers'. Here Cordelia asks that the reason for Lear's 'hate' should be made public least she be thought of as having committed some dishonourable act.

Style: one on one address in front of a larger group for all to hear

Where: the great hall of Lear's palace **To Whom:** Lear, in front of the assembly which includes France and Burgundy; Gonerill and Regan; Albany and Cornwall; Gloucester and his illegitimate son Edmund; and attendants

# of Lines: 11 **Probable Timing: 0.40 minutes**

Modern Text

8/ Cordelia

1 I yet beseech your Majesty - ◊
If for I want that glib and oily* Δart
To speak* and purpose not, since what I [well] intend,
I'll do't before I speak* - that you make known*
It is no vicious blot, [murder], or foulness*,
No unchaste action, or dishonored* step,
That hath depriv'd me of your Δgrace and favor*,
But even for want of that, for which I am richer -
A still-soliciting eye, and such a tongue
That I am glad I have not, though not to have it
Hath lost me in your liking.

Cordelia is often played here as level-headed and dry-eyed. Yet F's orthography suggests that it is not until the quiet of the last four unembellished lines of the speech (as she asks that Lear tell Burgundy and France why she is in disfavour - and in doing so asserting that she is proud not to be the flatterer he would wish) that she gains self-control.

• indeed the speech opens ungrammatically, with F's peculiar (slightly intellectual, 1/0) one line sentence suddenly stopping in mid-stream, F's period (changed to a dash in most modern texts) suggesting that she needs a very definite pause before continuing

• in continuing with the public plea that she be known as honourable (not guilty of 'vicious blot, murther, or foulnesse,/No unchaste action or dishonoured step') she becomes very emotional (2/7, F #2's first six lines)

• though she speaks extremely calmly for the last four lines, the two extra breath-thoughts (marked ,x) point to how difficult it is to keep calm when facing the dilemma of professing who and what she is 'Hath lost me in your liking'

First Folio

8/ Cordelia

1 I yet beseech your Majesty.
2 If for I want that glib and oylie Art,x
To speake and purpose not, since what I [will] intend,
Ile do't before I speake, that you make knowne
It is no vicious blot, [murther], or foulenesse,
No unchaste action+ or dishonoured step+
That hath depriv'd me of your Grace and favour,
But even for want of that, for which I am richer,
A still soliciting eye, and such a tongue,x
That I am glad I have not, though not to have it,x
Hath lost me in your liking.

#'s 9 - 13: Edmund's Plot

9/ Bastard **Thou Nature art my Goddesse, to thy Law** 1.2.1 - 22

Background: Also known as the Bastard, this is the illegitimate Edmund's first major speech. Given the fact that, being the elder brother, had he been legitimate he would be the first in line to inherit from his father (together with the jokes made in front of him to Kent about there being 'good sport at his making, and the horson must be acknowledged') the determination in the speech is very understandable.

Style: solo

Where: unspecified, but probably Gloucester's home **To Whom:** direct audience address and self

# of Lines: 22 **Probable Timing: 1.10 minutes**

Modern Text

Edmund as
9/ Bastard

1 Thou, Nature, art my $^{\triangle}$goddess*, to thy $^{\triangle}$law
My services are bound . †
2 Wherefore should I
Stand in the plague of custom*, and permit
The curiosity of $^{\triangle}$nations, to deprive me, ◊
For that I am some twelve or fourteen* $^{\triangle}$moonshines
Lag of a $^{\triangle}$brother?
3 Why $^{\triangle}$bastard?
4 Wherefore base?
5 When my $^{\triangle}$dimensions are as well compact,
My mind* is generous, and my shape as true,
As honest $^{\triangle}$madam's issue?
6 Why brand they us
With $^{\triangle}$base? ◊ with baseness$_{*}$ $^{\triangle}$bastardy*? ◊ $^{\triangle}$base, $^{\triangle}$base?
7 Who, in the lusty$_{*}$ stealth of $^{\triangle}$nature, take
More composition, and fierce quality$_{*}$,
[Than] doth within a dull, stale, tired* bed
Go* to th'creating a whole tribe of $^{\triangle}$fops,
Got 'tween* asleep* and wake?
8 Well then,
Legitimate Edgar, I must have your land . †
9 Our $^{\triangle}$father's love is to the $^{\triangle}$bastard [Edmund]
As to th'legitimate . †
10 Fine word : $^{\triangle}$legitimate !
11 Well, my $^{\triangle}$legitimate*, if this $^{\triangle}$letter speed
And my invention thrive, [Edmund] the base
Shall [top] 'th'$^{\triangle}$legitimate . †
12 I grow, I prosper :
Now, $^{\triangle}$gods, stand up for $^{\triangle}$bastards !

- while the three sentence lead in to the all important question, why should he and all that should be his (at least in his own eyes) be dismissed through the term 'Bastard' is firmly intellectual (7/3, F #1-3), the urgency of the question rides rough-shod over syntactical niceties . . .

- . . . for as set, F #1 is not grammatical: the pledging of himself to nature slips within the same sentence (via a fast-link comma) to his very dangerous challenge (in Elizabethan eyes) to conventional social order – F's drive is very understandable in human terms, yet most modern texts replace the comma by a period, thus starting the question far more rationally

- thus, according to most modern texts, F #2 is also ungrammatical: however, as reset in most modern texts it simply continues to expand upon the question already asked, but as set in F this new sentence in fact answers F #1's rhetorical question with some form of emphasis (with ridicule? scorn? certainly decisively) – since the function of the Elizabethan question mark is that it can serve as an exclamation point

- it would seem that the low status associated with bastardy disturbs him, for the unembellished short F #4, 'Wherefore base?', is very quiet - whether in an attempt to control emotion (little of which has been seen so far in the speech) or out of genuine pain and hurt is up to each actor to explore

- the assertion of himself as equal in every respect to 'honest Madams issue' starts out intellectually (5/2, F 5-8), despite the repetition of the (troubling?) 'Base' ending the sequence, but, as he expands on how it takes 'More composition, and fierce qualitie' to create a bastard than in creating lawfully 'a whole tribe of Fops', so he becomes emotional (2/4, F #9)

- then comes the switch that would cause them great concern if any on-stage character were to overhear it, for the two sentence naked plotting to have Edgar's birthright (F #10-11) is not only far less held in check than most modern texts' rational six sentence setting (suggesting that Edmund is riding almost unfettered the wild horses of his desire), it is also relentlessly intellectual (11/1, the last seven and a half lines of the speech)

- and at last, the determined surround phrases make their appearance, adding almost celebratory weight to his thinking, with
" : fine word : Legitimate . "
" : I grow, I prosper : Now Gods, stand up for Bastards . "

First Folio

Edmund as
9/ Bastard

1 Thou^{+} Nature^{+} art my Goddesse, to thy Law
My services are bound, wherefore should I
Stand in the plague of custome, and permit
The curiosity of Nations, to deprive me?$_{x}$
2 For that I am some twelve,$_{x}$ or fourteene Moonshines
Lag of a Brother?
3 Why Bastard?
4 Wherefore base?
5 When my Dimensions are as well compact,
My minde is generous, and my shape as true^{+}
As honest Madams issue?
6 Why brand they us
With Base?
7 With basenes Barstadie?
8 Base, Base?
9 Who^{+} in the lustie stealth of Nature, take
More composition, and fierce qualitie,
[Then] doth within a dull^{+} stale^{+} tyred bed
Goe to th'creating a whole tribe of Fops^{+}
Got 'tweene a sleepe,$_{x}$ and wake?
10 Well then,
Legitimate Edgar, I must have your land,
Our Fathers love,$_{x}$ is to the Bastard [Edmond],$_{x}$
As to th'legitimate : fine word : Legitimate . $^{+}$
11 Well, my Legittimate, if this Letter speed,$_{x}$
And my invention thrive, [Edmond] the base
Shall [to] 'th'Legitimate : I grow, I prosper :
Now^{+} Gods, stand up for Bastards . $^{+}$

10/ Gloucester **These late Eclipses in the Sun and Moone portend . . .** 1.2.203 - 117

Background: Totally believing Edmund's lies that Edgar, Gloucester's legitimate son, is plotting to take everything away from him, the following is Gloucester's attempt to find supernatural causes to justify all the current aberrant behaviour so apparent throughout court and kingdom.

Style: as part of a two-handed scene

Where: unspecified, but probably Gloucester's home **To Whom:** Edmund the bastard

# of Lines: 14 **Probable Timing: 0.45 minutes**

Modern Text

10/ Gloucester

1 These late Δeclipses in the Δsun and Δmoon* portend no good to us . †
2 Though the wisdom* of Δnature can
reason it thus and thus yet Δnature finds itself* scourg'd
by the sequent effects.
3 Love cools*, friendship falls off,
Δbrothers divide : ◊ in Δcities, mutinies; in Δcountries, discord ; in Δpalaces*, Δtreason ; and the Δbond crack'd, 'twixt
Δson* and Δfather.
4 This villain* of mine comes under the
prediction; there's Δson against Δfather: the ΔKing falls⁎ from
bias* of Δnature ; there's Δfather against Δchild*.
5 We have
seen* the best of our time.
6 Machinations, hollowness*,
treachery⁎, and all ruinous disorders follow us disquietly
to our Δgraves.
7 Find out this Δvillain, [Edmund], it shall lose
thee nothing, do it carefully . †
8 And the Δnoble & true-hear-
ted⁎ Kent banish'd ! his offense, honesty !
9 'Tis strange.

Given the circumstances, it is very surprising that intellect dominates not only overall (24/11) but at almost every moment.

- thus the first assertion of the influences of 'Eclipses' is strongly intellectual (the opening surround phrase, 3/1), while nature's inability to withstand their effects becomes passionate (2/2, F #1's last two lines) - Gloucester's concerned concentration enhanced by the two extra breath-thoughts (marked $_{,x}$) that suddenly appear

- there is no doubt that these portents are very important to Gloucester, for in addition to opening with a concerned surround phrase
  " . These late Eclipses in the Sun and Moone portend no good to us : "
  - and after F #2's short passionate assessment of general decline in human relations (1/1) - there comes what at first seems another very heady section (13/ 5, F #3-4)

- yet this key passage, which rapidly moves from general signs of social revolt to his own particular grief, has enormous emotional underpinnings, for it is couched in no fewer than five emotional surround phrases (created by semicolons)
  " . In Cities, mutinies ; in Countries, discord ; in Pallaces, Treason ; and the Bond crack'd, 'twixt Sonne and Father . This villaine of mine comes under the prediction ; "
  - the emotion giving weight to how very disturbing his intellectual analysis is proving

- the sad reflection that 'We have seene the best of our time.' (F #5) and why (F #6) is the only time the speech becomes emotional (1/2)

- while the call for Edmund to advance himself by finding his brother seems intellectually rational (4/0, F #7), the ungrammatical jamming together of this and the strange banishment of Kent for 'honesty'; the fact that F #7 is totally formed by surround phrases; and that those surround phrases referring to Kent are linked by yet another emotional semicolon; all suggest that Gloucester is not as capable of controlling himself as most modern texts imply

First Folio

10/ Gloucester

1 These late Eclipses in the Sun and Moone portend no good to us : though the wisedome of Nature can
reason it thus$_{,x}$ and thus$_{,x}$ yet Nature finds it selfe scourg'd
by the sequent effects.
2 Love cooles, friendship falls off,
Brothers divide.
3 In Cities, mutinies ; in Countries, dis-
cord ; in Pallaces, Treason ; and the Bond crack'd, 'twixt
Sonne and Father.
4 This villaine of mine comes under the
prediction ; there's Son against Father,+ the King fals from
byas of Nature,+ there's Father against Childe.
5 We have
seene the best of our time.
6 Machinations, hollownesse,
treacherie, and all ruinous disorders follow us disquietly
to our Graves.
7 Find out this Villain+ [Edmond], it shall lose
thee nothing, do it carefully : and the Noble & true-har-
ted Kent banish'd ; + his offence, honesty. +
8 'Tis strange.

11/ Bastard **This is the excellent foppery of the world,** 1.2.118 - 137

Background: This is Edmund's response to Gloucester's explanation for the strangeness of current events (speech #10 above).

Style: solo

Where: unspecified, but probably Gloucester's home **To Whom:** direct audience address, and self

# of Lines: 19 **Probable Timing: 1.00 minutes**

Modern Text

11/ Bastard

1 This is the excellent foppery of the world, that when
we are sick* in fortune - often the surfeits* of our own
behavior* - we make guilty of our disasters the △sun, the
△moon*, and △stars*, as if we were villains* on necessity*,
△fools* by heavenly compulsion, △knaves, △thieves*, and
△treachers by △spherical* predominance; ◊ △drunkards, △li-
ars*, and △adulterers by an enforc'd obedience of △planetary*
influence ; and all that we are evil* in, by a divine thrusting on.

2 An admirable evasion of △whoremaster * man,
to lay his △goatish disposition on the charge of a △star* ! †

3 My father compounded with my mother under the Dragon's tail*, and my △nativity was under Ursa Major, so
that it follows*, I am rough and △lecherous*.

4 [Fut] I should
have been* that I am, had the maidenl'est △star* in the △fir-
mament twinkled on my bastardizing.

ENTER EDGAR

5 Pat ! he comes like the △catastrophe of the old △comedy* . †

6 My △cue is villainous* △melancholy*, with a sigh* like Tom
o'Bedlam.

7 ◊ ______ O these △eclipses do portend these divisions ! △*fa*, △*sol*, △*la*, △*mi**.

Having dedicated his services to the goddess Nature (speech # 9 above), it's hardly surprising that Edmund has little time for the conventional wisdom of predestined planetary influences and their effects on the world of men – though what may be surprising is how lengthy and full of release his rejection of the doctrine turns out to be.

- Edmund's dismissal of his father and the world he represents as seen in the calm unembellished opening of the speech,
  "This is the excellent foppery of the world,"
  might be dismissed as contemptuously easy, except that this, the only unembellished line, triggers a lengthy list of ridiculousness suggesting that he has no time for belief in, as the one emotional surround phrase puts it,
  " ; and all that we are evill in, by a divine thrusting on . "

- that this has probably been a sore point can be seen in the ungrammatical ending of F #1 - as if something in the next set of descriptions coming up ('Lyar' perhaps?) generates in Edmund a need to pause (anger? amusement? despair?) - most modern texts set a comma, allowing the flow to continue into a larger whole much more smoothly

- thus, after the unembellished opening, Edmund starts emotionally (0/2, F #1's first three lines) and then quickly moves into passion as he lists the supposed astrological influences on the world of men (8/6, F #1's last three lines), and, while F #2's ungrammatical dismissal of evil coming from 'an inforc'd obedience of Planetary influence' starts intellectually, the surround phrase already discussed is doubly emotional (0/1)

- Edmund's F #3 five lines (of mockery? amusement? irony?) as he begins to apply this 'Planetary influence' to his own compounding and 'Nativity' are highly intellectual (9/4), but his resultant F #4 terse self-definition becomes passionate (1/1)

- the arrival of his brother (F #5) and the beginning of the plan to ensnare him (F #6-7) is strongly intellectual (10/3) – the assessment of his own inevitable success heightened by the two surround phrases that open F #5
  " . Pat : he comes like the catastrophe of the old Comedie : "

First Folio

11/ Bastard

1 This is the excellent foppery of the world, that when
we are sicke in fortune, often the surfets of our own
behaviour, we make guilty of our disasters,x the Sun, the
Moone, and Starres, as if we were villaines on necessitie,
Fooles by heavenly compulsion, Knaves, Theeves, and
Treachers by Sphericall predominance.

2 Drunkards, Ly-
ars, and Adulterers by an inforc'd obedience of Planatary
influence ; and all that we are evill in, by a divine thrusting on.

3 An admirable evasion of Whore-master-man,
to lay his Goatish disposition on the charge of a Starre,+
My father compounded with my mother under the Dragons taile, and my Nativity was under Ursa Major, so
that it followes, I am rough and Leacherous.

4 [ ] I should
have bin that I am, had the maidenlest Starre in the Firmament twinkled on my bastardizing.

ENTER EDGAR

5 Pat :+ he comes like the Catastrophe of the old Comedie :
my Cue is villanous Melancholly, with a sighe like Tom
o'Bedlam.

6 ______ O these Eclipses do portend these divisions. +

7 Fa, Sol, La, Me.

12/ Edgar **I heard my selfe proclaim'd,** 2.3.1 - 21

Background: Thanks to Edmund's plottings (see speeches #9 and #11 above) and further trickery, Gloucester has given orders that his legitimate son Edgar should be taken prisoner. The following is spoken as Edgar tries to escape.

Style: solo

Where: somewhere in the open **To Whom:** direct audience address, and self

# of Lines: 20 **Probable Timing: 1.00 minutes**

Modern Text

12/ Edgar

1 I heard myself* proclaim'd,
And by the happy hollow of a Δtree
Escap'd the hunt.
2 No Δport is free, no place
That guard and most unusual* vigilance
Does* not attend my taking.
3 Whiles I may scape
I will preserve myself*, and am bethought
To take the basest and most poorest shape
That ever penury, in contempt of man,
Brought near* to beast. †
4 My face I'll grime with filth,
Blanket my loins*, elf* all my hairs* in knots,
And with presented nakedness* outface
The Δwinds* and persecutions of the sky*. †
5 The Δcountry gives me proof* and president
Of Bedlam beggars, who, with roaring voices,
Strike in their numb'd* and mortified Δarms*
Pins, Δwooden*-pricks*, Δnails*, Δsprigs of Δrosemary*;
And with this horrible object, from low Δfarms*,
Poor* pelting Δvillages, Δ[sheep*-Δcotes]*, and Δmills*,
[Sometime] with Δlunatic* bans, sometime with Δprayers*,
Enforce their charity*. †
6 Poor* Turlygod! poor* Tom! †
7 That's something yet: Edgar I nothing am.

Despite the onrushed F #3 which initially suggests that Edgar cannot maintain self control, F's orthography shows far more human dignity than modern rationality does (most modern texts having divided F #3 into five); however, Edgar manages to preserve a strong sense of self-identity despite the difficulties facing him.

- given the circumstances of the hunt all around him, the few releases in the first four and half lines (2/2, F #1-2) could well suggest that Edgar is trying to be as quiet as possible to avoid detection

- Edgar's determination to save himself can be seen in the onrushed F #3's opening surround phrase
  " Whiles I may scape/I will preserve myselfe : "
  and, by the end of the speech, just how much of a non-person he will have to become to do so is just as strongly recognised
  " : poore Turlygod, poore Tom,/That's something yet : Edgar I nothing am . "

- the need to stay quiet to give himself a chance to 'scape' can be seen in F#3's three and a half (almost) unembellished lines as he begins to give voice to his desperate ploy of demeaning disguise
  " and am bethought/To take the basest, and most poorest shape/That ever penury in contempt of man,/Brought neere to beast ; my face Ile grime with filth,"
  unembellished save for the key word 'neere' to describe how close to humiliation he is prepared to go by being no better than a beast (an appalling thought for any Elizabethan)

- emotions swamp him for a moment (1/5) as he begins to picture how he must abuse his physical appearance to the point of dirty nigh-near nakedness (the three lines before F #2's next semicolon)

- then comes a two-fold surprise - first that in the midst of his problems he still has the wit/political sense to find a (comforting? practical?) parallel to his condition in the 'Bedlam beggers' that the 'Country' presents him, and second that, in so doing, he manages to contain his passion with some intellectual control as he lists the 'beggers' appearance and treatment that is shortly to be his (17/13, the last nine lines of the speech)

First Folio

12/ Edgar

1 I heard my selfe proclaim'd,
And by the happy hollow of a Tree,x
Escap'd the hunt.
2 No Port is free, no place
That guard,x and most unusall vigilance
Do's not attend my taking.
3 Whiles I may scape
I will preserve myselfe : x and am bethought
To take the basest,x and most poorest shape
That ever penury+ in contempt of man,
Brought neere to beast ; my face Ile grime with filth,
Blanket my loines, elfe all my haires in knots,
And with presented nakednesse out-face
The Windes,x and persecutions of the skie ;
The Country gives me proofe,x and president
Of Bedlam beggers, who+ with roaring voices,
Strike in their num'd and mortified Armes,x
Pins, Wodden-prickes, Nayles, Sprigs of Rosemarie : x
And with this horrible object, from low Farmes,
Poore pelting Villages, [Sheeps-Coates], and Milles,
[Sometimes] with Lunaticke bans, sometime with Praiers+
Inforce their charitie : poore Turlygod,+ poore Tom,+
That's something yet : Edgar I nothing am.

13/ Bastard **To both these Sisters have I sworne my love :** 5.1.55 - 69

Background: Edmund's trickery didn't stop with getting rid of brother Edgar. He then betrayed his father Gloucester to the Duke of Cornwall who stripped Gloucester of his title and holdings, gave them to Edmund as reward , and then, as the final coup de grace, as punishment blinded Gloucester. But, as the following speech explains, this still isn't enough for Edmund, to whom loyalty means absolutely nothing, for he has wooed both Gonerill and Regan - and they are publicly fighting over him. One note: though Gonerill is still married to the weak Albany, Regan is now a widow (for Cornwall was killed as he blinded Gloucester).

Style: solo

Where: the camp of the English army formed to reject Cordelia's attempt to rescue her father (see speeches #28-29 below) **To Whom:** direct audience address

# of Lines: 15 **Probable Timing: 0.50 minutes**

Modern Text

13/ Bastard

1 To both these △sisters have I sworn* my love ;
Each jealous of the other, as the stung
Are of the △adder.
2 Which of them shall I take?
3 Both? ◊ one? ◊ or neither?
4 Neither can be enjoy'd
If both remain* alive : △to take the △widow*
Exasperates, makes mad her △sister [Goneril],
And hardly shall I carry out my side,
Her husband being alive.
5 Now then, we'll* use
His countenance for the △battle*, which being done,
Let her who would be rid of him devise
His speedy taking off.
6 As for the mercy*
Which he intends to Lear and to Cordelia,
The △battle* done, and they within our power,
Shall never see his pardon ; for my state
Stands on me to defend, not to debate.

F shows the relaxation and occasional flurries of the man who would be alpha-male - though the final moment contemplating the deaths of Lear and Cordelia suggests thathe may not be totally immune to feeling.

- the surround phrases and short sentences neatly encapsulate the love triangle
  " . To both these Sisters have I sworne my love : "

- the (delighted? amazed? mischievous?) passion of this opening line (1/1) is followed by the surprisingly calm detachment (0/1) of
  " . Which of them shall I take? /Both? One? Or neither? Neither can be enjoy'd /If both remaine alive : "
  suggesting more than just a careful analysis (relaxed amusement perhaps?)

- however, the danger of making a play for Cornwall's widow Regan is heightened by being voiced with much release (4/2) in just the next line and half

- yet his ability to maintain strong self-control quickly reasserts itself, for calm detachment reappears in his ensuing unembellished admission that he cannot make a move on Gonerill, 'And hardly shall I carry out my side,/Her husband being alive.'

- . . . at least until after he has used her husband's forces to his own advantage – and though this suddenly admitted subplot is emotional (1/2, F #7's first line) he once more establishes calm detachment as he voices his intention to stand aloof so as not to be incriminated in anything Gonerill might do to her husband Albany,
  "Let her who would be rid of him, devise/His speedy taking off."

- as in his analysis of most of his other male rivals throughout the play for their weaknesses and how to combat them (notably his father and brother Edgar), his dismissal of Albany here is intellectual (3/1, F #8's first three lines) – though the reason for getting rid of Lear and Cordelia (his own advancement) is spoken of icily unembellishedly
  " : for my state,/Stands on me to defend, not to debate . "
  - determination? or perhaps the seriousness in planning the death of a monarch and his daughter, herself the wife of a King, forces him to quiet?

First Folio

13/ Bastard

1 To both these Sisters have I sworne my love : x
Each jealous of the other, as the stung
Are of the Adder.
2 Which of them shall I take?
3 Both?
4 One?
5 Or neither?
6 Neither can be enjoy'd
If both remaine alive : To take the Widdow,x
Exasperates, makes mad her Sister [Gonerill],
And hardly shall I carry out my side,
Her husband being alive.
7 Now then, wee'l use
His countenance for the Battaile, which being done,
Let her who would be rid of him,x devise
His speedy taking off.
8 As for the mercie
Which he intends to Lear and to Cordelia,
The Battaile done, and they within our power,
Shall never see his pardon : x for my state,x
Stands on me to defend, not to debate.

#'s 14 - 21: The Stripping Down Of Lear

14/ Gonerill **Did my Father strike my Gentleman for chiding of his Foole?** between 1.3.1 - 26

Background: As was made clear at the end of the first scene where Lear divested himself of his powers as he divided up his kingdom, Gonerill and Regan are worried about Lear's possible behaviours as he stays with them, carefully referring to the difficulties that might be created by 'the infirmity of his age'. Gonerill is the first to find how prescient her fears were.

Style: as part of a two-handed scene

Where: the palace of Gonerill and Albany **To Whom:** her Steward and right-hand man, Oswald

# of Lines: 18 **Probable Timing: 0.55 minutes**

Modern Text

14/ Gonerill

1 Did my ΔFather strike my Δgentleman
For chi-ding of his Δfool*?

2 By day and night, he wrongs me, every hour*
He flashes into one gross* crime or other
That sets us all at odds. †
3 I'll not endure it. †
4 His Δknights grow riotous, and himself* upbraids* us
On every trifle.
5 When he returns* from hunting,
I will not speak* with him, say I am sick*. †
6 If you come slack* of former services,
You shall do well; the fault of it I'll answer.

7 Put on what weary negligence you please,
You and your Δfellows*; I'd* have it come to question. †
8 If he distaste it, let him to my Δsister,
Whose mind and mine I know in that are one,

{N.B. [2] see below for lines often inserted from the quarto }

Remember what I have said.

9 And let his Δknights have colder looks* among you;
What grows* of it, no matter. †
10 Advise your fellows so. †

Q/F open with either prose or a long (15 syllable) verse line allowing Gonerill's unchecked intelligent indignation (3/1) to break all metric niceties; most modern texts amend the text with the hesitations of two short verse lines (9/6 syllables) presenting a much more controlled lady than was originally set.

- while at first glance her F #2 (1/4) decision to do something about her father's excesses should be emotional, the fact that it is finally voiced as two determined but emotional surround phrases (linked by the first of the three semicolons scattered throughout the speech)
  "; Ile not endure it ; /His Knights grow riotous, and himselfe upbraides us/On every trifle ."
  suggests that perhaps it is not as easy for her to move against her father as some actresses/productions portray

- as she puts the plan into action (F #3) she continues emotionally (0/4), yet the possibility of who should take the blame is voiced very quietly
  'You shall do well, the fault of it Ile answer'
  the unembellishment perhaps suggesting that, in facing the enormity of what she is about to do, she needs to calm both herself and her Steward

- this calmness in turn yields more determined (2/1) surround phrases
  ". Put on what weary negligence you please,/You and your Fellowes : I'de have it come to question ; "
  the idea of forcing the issue heightened by the second emotional semicolon

- apart from the one word 'Sister' (the key word relating to her fellow conspirator in the overall scheme) this determination leads to the three line unembellished
  ". If he distaste it, let him to my Sister,/Whose mind and mine I know in that are one,/Remember what I have said . "
  the quiet once more suggesting the determined need for calming

First Folio

14/ Gonerill

1 Did my Father strike my Gentleman for chi-
ding of his Foole?

2 By day and night, he wrongs me, every howre
He flashes into one grosse crime, or other,
That sets us all at ods: Ile not endure it;
His Knights grow riotous, and himselfe upbraides us
On every trifle.
3 When he returnes from hunting,
I will not speake with him, say I am sicke,
If you come slacke of former services,
You shall do well,+ the fault of it Ile answer.

4 Put on what weary negligence you please,
You and your Fellowes:, I'de have it come to question;
If he distaste it, let him to my Sister,
Whose mind and mine I know in that are one,
Remember what I have said.

5 And let his Knights have colder lookes among
you:, what growes of it+ no matter, advise your fellowes

{ctd. over}

[2] Q sets from what is shown as mt.5 the ensuing text as prose, finishing with the following (which is not set in F)
". . . not to be overruld: idle old man that still would manage those authorities that hee hath given away, now by my life old fooles are babes again, & must be us'd with checkes as flatteries, when they are seene abus'd, remember what I tell you."

{1.5 quarto lines often inserted}

12 I'll write straight to my △sister to hold my [very] course .†
13 Prepare for dinner.

• the final instruction to 'let his Knights have colder lookes among you' while she writes to her Sister is passionate (2/3), and it seems she realises that the forthcoming awkwardness will start once her final instruction ' ; prepare for dinner . ' is given, for it is surprisingly set as yet another emotional surround phrase (perhaps she is somewhat disturbed by what she is putting into action?)

so, Ile write straight to my Sister to hold my[ ] course;
prepare for dinner.

15/ Foole **Let me hire him too, here's my Coxcombe.** between 1.4.95 - 104

Background: The Foole, in the traditional and protected role of not just entertainer but of one expected to comment on the follies of his betters, is unsparing in his chastising of Lear for handing over all his power to his two daughters. The banished Kent, worried about Lear's future, has not left the country as charged but has instead changed his appearance and presented himself to Lear for employment as a common man named Caius. He has just proved his worth by beating Gonerill's Steward for being rude to Lear (the Steward being so instructed by Gonerill - speech #14 immediately above). Lear has now offered 'Caius' a permanent job, occasioning the following from the Foole.

Style: as part of a three-handed scene

Where: in Gonerill's palace **To Whom:** Lear, in front of Kent/Caius

# of Lines: 8 **Probable Timing: 0.30 minutes**

Modern Text

15/ Foole

1 Let me hire him too, here's my △coxcomb*.
2 Sirrah, you were best take my △coxcomb*. [3]
3 Why? for taking ones part that's out of favor* . †
4 Nay, & thou canst not smile as the wind sits, thou'lt catch cold* shortly . †
5 There, take my △coxcomb*. †
6 Why, this fellow has banish'd two on's △daughters, and did the third a blessing against his will ; if thou follow him, thou must needs wear* my △coxcomb*.

Underneath the fooling, the one almost unembellished passage (save for the key word 'colde') points to a very shrewd assessment of the political situation at large
" & thou canst not smile as the wind sits, thou'lt catch colde shortly,"

• thus it's not surprising that overall the speech is passionate (5/7) and that, when the mordant but accurate F #3 analysis on both Lear and the world at large is begun, the Foole indulges in a far more unchecked onrush (whether relaxed or disturbed) than the four sentences of the modern texts allow

• interestingly, many of the longer spellings come at the end of phrases, suggesting a quite pointed delivery designed either to be heard as the performer's final 'ta-da' verbal flourish when a telling point has been made or to sting into reply the listener to whom the barb is directed

First Folio

15/ Foole

1 Let me hire him too, here's my Coxcombe.
2 Sirrah, you were best take my Coxcombe.
3 Why? for taking ones part that's out of favour,
nay, & thou canst not smile as the wind sits, thou'lt catch
colde shortly, there+ take my Coxcombe ; why+ this fellow
ha's banish'd two on's Daughters, and did the third a
blessing against his will,+ if thou follow him, thou must
needs weare my Coxcombe.

[3] one commentator makes the interesting suggestion that this could be spoken to Kent rather than Lear

16/ Gonerill **Not only Sir this, your all-lycenc'd Foole,** between 1.4.201 - 222
17/ Gonerill **I would you would make use of your good wisedome** between 1.4.219 - 252

Background: The Foole has just seen Lear almost play the inferior to a (oft-)frowning Gonerill. Pulling no punches, in Gonerill's presence he has told Lear 'Thou was't a pretty fellow when thou hadst no need to care for her frowning . . . I am better than thou art now, I am a Foole, thou art nothing'. Gonerill now begins to do what she promised in speech #14 - pushing matters to a head because she'll 'not endure it'. Speech #16 deals with the problem in general, while speech #17 proposes some unpleasant remedies.

Style: public address

Where: her palace **To Whom:** Lear, in front of the Foole, Kent/Caius, and Lear's attendants

Speech 16: # of Lines: 18 **Probable Timing: 0.55 minutes**
Speech 17: # of Lines: 18 **Probable Timing: 0.55 minutes**

Modern Text

16/ Gonerill

1 Not only, Δsir, this, your all-licens'd* Fool*,
But other of your insolent retinue
Do hourly* Δcarp* and Δquarrel*, breaking forth
In rank*, and not-to-be endur'd riots. †

2 Sir,◊
I had thought, by making this well known* unto you,
To have found a safe redress*, but now grow fearful*,
By what yourself* too late have spoke and done,
That you protect this course and put it on
By your allowance; which if you should, the fault
Would not scape censure, nor the redresses sleep*,
Which, in the tender of a wholesome weal*,
Might in their working do you that offense*,
Which else were shame, that [than] necessity$_*$
Will call discreet proceeding.

3 I would you would make use of your good wisdom*
(Whereof I know you are fraught) and put away
These dispositions which of late transport you
From what you rightly are.

Though giving the appearance of great verbal control, F shows Gonerill starting to feel the strain, for not only does she open very passionately (5/6 in F #1's four lines) she also ends her first F sentence rather peculiarly. Yet F shows that despite this awkward start, by speech end she manages to salvage at least the appearance of the dignity she feels behooves her position.

• by ending F #1's blunt passionate remonstrance of the riotous behaviour of both the Foole and Lear's retinue with 'Sir.', followed by a period, Gonerill has repeated 'Sir' twice in one sentence, not a normal occurrence for someone in self-control - (Q sets a comma before 'Sir' and no punctuation after, still suggesting a character not in full control: most modern texts start F #2 before 'Sir', and set a comma after – thus showing much more verbal dignity for her than originally intended)

• then, as she rather long-windedly, even awkwardly, explains how she had hoped that her earlier mentioning of this would have rectified matters, all pretence of any intellectual self-control disappears, for her struggles to maintain dignity via five unembellished lines set in two different F #2 series -
"That you protect this course, and put it on/By your allowance, which if you should, the fault/Would not scape censure,"
"Might in their working do you that offence,/Which else were shame, that then necessitie/Will call discreet proceeding ."
is blown apart by her emotions (0/6, F #2's other four and a half lines)

• but it eventually seems that her attempt at dignity succeeds, for F #3's final three and a half line rebuke/appeal for him to put away 'These dispositions' is unembellished save for one keyword, as she appeals to his 'wisedome', though the two extra breath-thoughts (marked $_{,x}$) show that it is a struggle for her to maintain composure

First Folio

16/ Gonerill

1 Not only+ Sir+ this, your all-lycenc'd Foole,
But other of your insolent retinue
Do hourely Carpe and Quarrell, breaking forth
In ranke, and ($_x$not to be endur'd$_x$) riots+ Sir. $_x$

2 I had thought+ by making this well knowne unto you,
To have found a safe redresse, but now grow fearefull+
By what your selfe too late have spoke and done,
That you protect this course,$_x$ and put it on
By your allowance,+ which if you should, the fault
Would not scape censure, nor the redresses sleepe,
Which+ in the tender of a wholesome weale,
Might in their working do you that offence,
Which else were shame, that [then] necessitie
Will call discreet proceeding.

3 I would you would make use of your good wisedome
(Whereof I know you are fraught),$_x$ and put away
These dispositions,$_x$ which of late transport you
From what you rightly are.

Modern Text

17/ Gonerill

1 I would you would make use of your good wisdom*
(Whereof I know you are fraught) and put away
These dispositions which of late transport you
From what you rightly are.

2 I do beseech you
To understand my purposes aright,
As you are Δold and Δreverend, should be Δwise.

3 Here* do you keep* a hundred Δknights and Δsquires,
Men so disorder'd, so debosh'd and bold,
That this our Δcourt, infected with their manners,
Shows* like a riotous Δinn*. †

4 Epicurism* and Δlust
Makes it more like a Δtavern* or a Δbrothel*
[Than] a grac'd Δpalace*.

5 The shame itself* doth speak*
For instant remedy.

6 Be then desir'd
By her, that else will take the thing she begs*,
A little to disquantity your Δtrain*,
And the remainders that shall still depend,
To be such men as may besort your Δage,
Which know themselves and you.

As with the previous speech her calm is difficult to maintain, as the sudden orthographical outburst of F #3 (and the struggles through the remainder of the speech to re-establish public composure) shows.

- starting where the previous speech left off, and repeating the last sentence, the three and a half line rebuke/appeal for Lear to put away 'These dispositions' is unembellished save for the keyword, as she appeals to his 'wisedome', though the two extra breath-thoughts (marked ,x) show that it is a struggle for her to maintain composure

- but F #2 opens with the very determined unembellished surround phrase
"．I do beseech you/To understand my purposes aright : "
which leads to the unequivocally intellectual demand to be 'Wise' (3/0) - which would be fine if she could remain in such control, but she can't

- F #3's onrushed listing of complaints bursts the bubble of her dignity, (9/8 in five and half lines), the only semicolon of the speech underscoring the emotional disgust/contempt/loathing in her 'Taverne . . . Brothell' rather than a 'grac'd Pallace' comparison, the whole a less controlled attack than the two more reasoned sentences used by her modern counterpart

- and emotion is all for her short F #4 'instant remedy' demand (0/2) and for her threat that Lear 'disquantity your Traine' or she 'will take the thing she begges' (0/2, F #5's first two and a half lines)

- then her appearance of dignity is captured once more as F #5's final three line demand that Lear retain only men of a certain 'Age' is unembellished, save for the pertinent word 'Age'
"And the remainders that shall still depend,/To be such men as may besort your Age,/Which know themselves, and you."
- though whether the calm is genuine or enforced is up to each actor to explore

First Folio

17/ Gonerill

1 I would you would make use of your good wisedome
(Whereof I know you are fraught),x and put away
These dispositions,x which of late transport you
From what you rightly are.

2 I do beseech you
To understand my purposes aright : x
As you are Old,x and Reverend, should be Wise.

3 Heere do you keepe a hundred Knights and Squires,
Men so disorder'd, so debosh'd,x and bold,
That this our Court+ infected with their manners,
Shewes like a riotous Inne ; Epicurisme and Lust
Makes it more like a Taverne,x or a Brothell,x
[Then] a grac'd Pallace.

4 The shame it selfe doth speake
For instant remedy.

5 Be then desir'd
By her, that else will take the thing she begges,
A little to disquantity your Traine,
And the remainders that shall still depend,
To be such men as may besort your Age,
Which know themselves,x and you.

18/ Lear **Darknesse, and Divels./Saddle my horses:** between 1.4.252 - 289

Background: The following is Lear's immediate response to Gonerill's scolding proposals of speech #17 above.

Style: public address

Where: Gonerill's palace **To Whom:** Gonerill, in front of the Foole, Kent/Caius, and Lear's attendants

# of Lines: 18 **Probable Timing: 0.55 minutes**

Modern Text

18/ Lear

1 Darkness*, and Δdevils*!
2 Saddle my horses; call my Δtrain* together !
3 Degenerate Δbastard, I'll not trouble thee {.}
4 Hear*, Nature, hear*, dear* goddess*, hear* ! †
5 Suspend thy purpose, if thou didst intend
To make this Δcreature fruitful*. †
6 Into her Δwomb* convey sterility*,
Dry$_*$ up in her the Δorgans of increase,
And from her derogate body never spring
A Δbabe to honor her !
7 If she must teem*,
Create her child* of Δspleen*, that it may live
And be a thwart disnatur'd torment to her.
8 Let it stamp* wrinkles in her brow of youth,
With cadent Δtears* fret Δchannels in her cheeks*,
Turn* all her Δmother's pains* and benefits
To laughter and contempt, Δthat she may feel*
How sharper [than] a Δserpent's tooth it is
To have a thankless* Δchild* ! †
9 - Away, away !

In a speech that is often bellowed from start to finish, F's orthography suggests a couple of moments where Lear's sudden quietness has implications both for what is being said and, eventually, for himself.

- in an already passionate speech (15/22 in eighteen lines) the immense shock to Lear of what Gonerill has demanded of him (speeches #16-17 above) can be seen in the three one line sentences and three surround phrases the first four lines contain, topped off by the veritable explosion (2/5 in just one line) as he begins the onrushed curse contained in F #4
  ". Heare Nature, heare deere Goddesse, heare : "

- in his relentless request to render Gonerill sterile, Lear's onrushed F #4 becomes passionate (4/3), which turns to emotion with F #5's corollary that if she does give birth it should be a 'childe of Spleene' (1/3) until the amazingly quiet explanation why
  "that it may live/And be a thwart disnatur'd torment to her."
  the contrast of which, as the only unembellished passage in the speech, is presumably startling in its icy calmness to everyone present

- but the quiet is only momentary, for Lear's F #6's extending of the curse into wishing upon his daughter 'wrinkles', 'Teares', and her child's 'laughter, and contempt' becomes passionate once more (6/8), the extra breath-thoughts pointing either to his ensuring that every tiny malevolent wish strikes home or to how much the curse is costing him (emotionally or simply in losing control) – with the latter being a possibility since the very last short F #7 'Away, away.' is unembellished – the quietness suggesting that, instead of it being yelled as a climax to the speech as it so often is, Lear has no energy left

First Folio

18/ Lear

1 Darknesse, and Divels. +
2 Saddle my horses:$_x$ call my Traine together. +
3 Degenerate Bastard, Ile not trouble thee {.}
4 Heare+ Nature, heare+ deere Goddesse, heare: +
Suspend thy purpose, if thou did'st intend
To make this Creature fruitfull:
Into her Wombe convey stirrility,
Drie up in her the Organs of increase,
And from her derogate body,$_x$ never spring
A Babe to honor her. +
5 If she must teeme,
Create her childe of Spleene, that it may live
And be a thwart disnatur'd torment to her.
6 Let it stampe wrinkles in her brow of youth,
With cadent Teares fret Channels in her cheekes,
Turne all her Mothers paines,$_x$ and benefits
To laughter,$_x$ and contempt:$_x$ That she may feele,$_x$
How sharper [then] a Serpents tooth it is,$_x$
To have a thanklesse Childe. +
7 Away, away. +

19/ Kent **Fellow I know thee./{Thou'rt a} Knave, a Rascall, an eater of broken meates,** between 2.2.13 - 24

Background: Lear has sent Kent/Caius to Gloucester's palace where, unbeknownst to him, both Cornwall and Regan are journeying. So that Regan will know her mind, and that the plot to strip Lear of large numbers of his train has begun, Gonerill has sent letters by her steward Oswald who, naturally, has followed Regan and Cornwall to Gloucester's home. There Kent/Caius and Oswald meet once more, Kent having tripped him up and beaten him earlier for rudeness to Lear. Kent recognises Oswald, who does not immediately recognise him in return. Here, a series of neutral questions from Oswald have been answered rudely by Kent/Caius, generating the Steward's reasonable question 'Why do'st thou use me thus? I know thee not', which triggers the following.

Style: as part of a two-handed scene

Where: the courtyard of Gloucester's palace **To Whom:** Gonerill's steward, Oswald

# of Lines: 11 **Probable Timing: 0.40 minutes**

Modern Text

19/ Kent

1 Fellow, I know thee.

2 {Thou'rt a}△knave, a △rascal*, an eater of broken meats*;
a base, proud, shallow, beggarly, three-suited hundred-
pound, filthy [worsted*]-stocking knave; a △lily*-livered,
action-taking, whoreson, glass*-gazing, super serviceable,
finical* △rogue; one △trunk*-inheriting slave; one that
wouldst be a △bawd₊ in a way of good service, and art nothing but the composition of a △knave, △beggar, △coward,
△pandar, and the △son* and △heir* of a △mongrel* △bitch;
one whom I will beat* into [clamorous] whining, if thou
deni'st* the least syllable₊ of thy addition.

- Kent's opening unembellished short sentence calm is highly deceptive
- for the explosive F #2 (14/11 in just ten lines) runs the gamut of insulting styles
  - a/ the one line suggestion that the Steward is so low in the pecking order that all he eats are scraps left over after others have eaten is passionate (2/2)
  - b/ that his clothing is that of a servant rather than that of the higher rank of Steward is quietly emotional (0/1)
  - c/ that his nature is that of a 'Lilly-livered . . . Baud' is passionate (4/4)
  - d/ that all his pedigree adds up to is a 'Mungrell Bitch' is highly intellectual/factual (8/3)
- the whole ends with the emotional threat of a beating (0/2), until, as the speech opened, the sudden (and presumably very dangerous) unembellished calm of the last phrase
  "if thou deny'st the least sillable of thy addition'

First Folio

19/ Kent

1 Fellow I know thee.

2 {Thou'rt a} Knave, a Rascall, an eater of broken meates,+
a base, proud, shallow, beggerly, three-suited- hundred
pound, filthy [woosted]-stocking knave,+ a Lilly-livered,
action-taking, whoreson+ glasse-gazing+ super-serviceable+
finicall Rogue,+ one Trunke-inheriting slave,+ one that
would'st be a Baud in a way of good service, and art nothing but the composition of a Knave, Begger, Coward,
Pandar, and the Sonne and Heire of a Mungrill Bitch,+
one whom I will beate into [clamours] whining, if thou
deny'st the least sillable of thy addition.

20/ Foole **And thou hadst beene set i'th'Stockes for that** between 2.4.64 - 85

Background: Kent/Caius' anger with Oswald spilled over to insulting both Cornwall and Regan when they arrived to prevent him from beating Oswald yet again. As a result, despite his protests that he is a representative of the king, Kent has been imprisoned in the stocks overnight. Lear has arrived, but Gonerill's insistence that he reduce his attendant knights has already had effect, for many of his supporters did not make the journey with him. Thus the still stocked Kent asks the Foole 'How chance the king comes with so small a number?', to which the Foole answers thus.

Style: as part of a three-handed scene

Where: in the courtyard of Gloucester's palace **To Whom:** Kent, in front of Lear's Gentleman

# of Lines: 18 **Probable Timing: 0.55 minutes**

Modern Text

20/ Foole

1 And thou hadst been* set i'th'Δstocks* for that question, thou'dst well deserv'd it.

2 All that follow their noses are led by their eyes but blind* men, and there's not a nose among twenty but can smell him that's stinking. †

3 Let go thy hold when a great wheel* runs down* a hill, lest* it break* thy neck* with following; ◊ Δbut the great one that goes upward, let him draw thee after. †

4 When a wise man gives thee better counsel*, give me mine again*, I would [have] none but knaves follow it, since a Δfool* gives it.

5 [4] That Δsir, which serves and seeks* for gain*,
And follows* but for form*,
Will pack*, when it begins to rain*,
And leave thee in the storm*. †

6 But I will tarry, the Δfool* will stay,
And let the wise man fly*. †

7 The knave turns* Δfool* that runs* away,
The Fool* no knave, perdie.

Though the speech is highly emotional (5/22 overall), as with the previous Foole's speech (#15 above), the unembellished lines point to the deeper political message beneath his surface fooling, viz.

"and there's not a nose among twenty, but can smell him that's stinking;"

which is then followed by an emotionally enhanced (by the semicolon) emotionally released surround phrase of explanation (0/4)

"; let go thy hold, when a great wheele runs downe a hill, least it breake thy necke with following."

with the astute logical outcome heightened by being offered as both unembellished and as a surround phrase

". But the great one that goes upward, let him draw thee after :"

- the Foole opens fairly calmly if slightly emotionally (1/3, the first four lines), but his emotions intensify with 'when a great wheele runs downe' it will 'breake thy necke' (0/4, F #2's last two lines)

- the unembellished advice to follow a 'great one' is followed by an emotional kick as to the value of a Foole's advice being better than that of a 'wiseman' (1/3, F #3's last two and half lines)

- with the final doggerel of F #4 being onrushed it seems that the rise and fall of great ones and their followers is disturbing to him – the first four lines referring to fair-weather followers who will leave at the first sign of trouble being very emotional (1/7), while the last four lines praising (his own?) loyalty no matter what is passionate (3/5): F 4#'s onrush suggests that this could well be an improvised piece – by splitting it into three more rational sentences, however, most modern texts seem to have set it as a well crafted ditty (perhaps already composed by another)

First Folio

20/ Foole

1 And thou hadst beene set i'th'Stockes for that question, thoud'st well deserv'd it.

2 All that follow their noses,x are led by their eyes,x but blinde men, and there's not a nose among twenty,x but can smell him that's stinking; let go thy hold,+ when a great wheele runs downe a hill, least it breake thy necke with following.

3 But the great one that goes upward, let him draw thee after: when a wiseman gives thee better counsell+ give me mine againe, I would [hause] none but knaves follow it, since a Foole gives it.

4 That Sir, which serves and seekes for gaine,
And followes but for forme; x
Will packe, when it begins to raine,
And leave thee in the storme,
But I will tarry, the Foole will stay,
And let the wiseman flie:
The knave turnes Foole that runnes away,
The Foole no knave+ perdie.

[4] most modern texts suggest that the following is sung by the Foole

21/ Lear **O reason not the need : our basest Beggers** 2.4.264 - 286

Background: Gonerill has arrived and Regan has publicly taken her side in the argument, going so far as to hold her hand while they argue that Lear needs no attendants at all, never mind the one hundred Lear originally insisted on bringing with him. Finally Regan follows up Gonerill's question 'What need you five and twenty?" with 'What need one?'

Style: initially as part of a three handed scene, for the larger group present to hear

Where: the courtyard of Gloucester's palace **To Whom:** Regan and Gonerill, in front of Albany and Cornwall, Gloucester, Kent, the Foole, Lear's Gentleman, and Gloucester's servants

# of Lines: 22 **Probable Timing: 1.10 minutes**

Modern Text

21/ Lear

1 O, reason not the need! our basest $^{\Delta}$beggars
Are in the poorest thing superfluous. †

2 Allow not $^{\Delta}$nature, more [than] $^{\Delta}$nature needs,
Man's life is cheap* as $^{\Delta}$beast's*.

3 Thou art a $^{\Delta}$lady;
If only* to go warm* were gorgeous,
Why, $^{\Delta}$nature needs not what thou gorgeous wear'st,
Which scarcely keeps* thee warm*. †

4 But for true need -
You $^{\Delta}$heavens, give me that patience, patience I need ! †

5 You see me here*, you $^{\Delta}$gods, a poor* old man,
As full of grief* as age, wretched in both . †

6 If it be you that stirs* these $^{\Delta}$daughters' hearts
Against their $^{\Delta}$father, fool* me not so much
To bear* it tamely; touch me with $^{\Delta}$noble anger,
And let not women's weapons, water drops,
Stain* my man's cheeks* !

7 No, you unnatural* $^{\Delta}$hags,
I will have such revenges on you both
That all the world shall ——— I will do such things -
What they are yet I know not, but they shall ° be
The terrors of the earth! †

8 You think* I'll weep*:
No, I'll not weep*. †

9 I have full cause of weeping.

[Storme and Tempest]

Lear's attempt to reason his way out of the quarrel, at least to begin with, can be seen in the surround phrases that open and close F #1 and open F #2
" . O reason not the need : " & " : Mans life is cheape as Beastes . "
" . Thou art a Lady ; "

- all are heightened - the first, the opening words of the speech, being unembellished, suggesting that Lear attempts to contain himself, at least as he starts; the second, monosyllabic, suggesting that he is going to the heart of the argument without wasting words; the third being enhanced by the (emotional) semicolon (the only one in the speech) that finishes it
- supporting his attempt, these opening four lines are intellectual (5/2)
- yet F #2's onrush (split into four in most modern texts) and ensuing orthography shows just how quickly his reason becomes emotionally swamped (5/10 in F #2's next eight lines) – especially in the fast link connection via a comma where most modern texts start their new mt. #4
- this fast link moment is made even more striking in F, for whereas most modern texts allow what they see as the start of the new sentence 'but for true need' to flow on, F sets it as spilling out from (possibly even as the continuation of) the previous argument, only to have Lear pull himself up by the colon that follows – almost as if he had momentarily lost his way mentally
- as he asks the Heavens to 'touch me with Noble anger' (the end of F #2) and begins to curse both daughters (the first phrase of F #3), his emotion turns to passion (2/3, in three and half lines)
- and then, quite amazingly, in discovering that he cannot formulate what the 'revenges on you both' shall be, he goes absolutely quiet with four unembellished lines
  "I will have such revenges on you both,/That all the world shall I will do such things,/What they are yet, I know not, but they shalbe/The terrors of the earth ? "

First Folio

21/ Lear

1 O^{+} reason not the need : $^{+}$ our basest Beggers
Are in the poorest thing superfluous,
Allow not Nature, more [then] Nature needs: $_{x}$
Mans life is cheape as Beastes.

2 Thou art a Lady;
If onely to go warme were gorgeous,
Why$_{x}$ Nature needs not what thou gorgeous wear'st,
Which scarcely keepes thee warme,$^{+}$ but for true need :$_{x}$
You Heavens, give me that patience, patience I need,$^{+}$
You see me heere ($_{x}$you Gods$_{x}$) a poore old man,
As full of griefe as age, wretched in both,
If it be you that stirres these Daughters hearts
Against their Father, foole me not so much,$_{x}$
To beare it tamely : $_{x}$ touch me with Noble anger,
And let not womens weapons^{+} water drops,
Staine my mans cheekes. $^{+}$

3 No^{+} you unnaturall Hags,
I will have such revenges on you both,$_{x}$
That all the world shall ——— I will do such things,
What they are yet,$_{x}$ I know not, but they shalbe
The terrors of the earth? $^{+}$ you thinke Ile weepe,$^{+}$
No, Ile not weepe, I have full cause of weeping.

[Storme and Tempest]

10 But this heart
Shall, break into a hundred thousand flaws*
Or ere I'll weep*. †
11 O ^fool*, I shall go mad !

[Exeunt]

the question mark at quote's end functioning as the Elizabethan equivalent of an exclamation point, adding even more weight to the dreadful threat

• in finishing, Lear's first mention of his refusal to weep is emotional (0/3, F #3's last line and a half), while the surround phrase ending of the speech vehemently reiterating his refusal becomes passionate once more (F #4, 2/3)

4 But this heart shal break into a hundred thousand flawes
Or ere Ile weepe : O Foole, I shall go mad. +

[Exeunt]

#'s 22 - 24: Madness

22/ Lear **Blow windes, & crack your cheeks ; Rage, blow** between 3.2.1 - 24

Background: Lear has rushed into the storm, any sympathy from his contemporary Gloucester firmly squelched by Cornwall ('My Lord, entreate by no meanes him to stay') and Lear's daughter Regan ('He is attended with a desperate traine,/And what they may incense him to, being apt,/To have his eare abus'd, wisedome bids feare'). In his madness Lear addresses the storm.

Style: essentially solo, in front of one other character

Where: on the heath **To Whom:** the storm, in front of the Foole

# of Lines: 20 **Probable Timing: 1.00 minutes**

Modern Text

22/ Lear

1 Blow, winds*, & crack your cheeks ! †
2 Rage, blow ! †
3 You Δcataracts, and Δhurricanoes⁎, spout,
Till you have drench'd our Δsteeples, [drown'd] the Δcocks*!
4 You Δsulph'rous and Δthought-executing fires,
Vaunt-couriers⁎ of Δoak*-cleaving Δthunder-bolts,
Singe* my white head !
5 And thou, all-shaking Δthunder,
Strike flat the thick* Δrotundity o'th'world !
Crack* Δnature's moulds, all germains* spill at once
That makes ungrateful* Δman !

---

6 Rumble thy bellyful*! †
7 Spit, Δfire ! †
8 Spout*, Δrain*! †
9 Nor Δrain*, Δwind*, Δthunder, Δfire are my Δdaughters . †
10 I tax* not you, you Δelements, with unkindness*; ◊
I never gave you Δkingdom*, call'd you Δchildren ;
You owe me no subscription.
11 Then let fall
Your horrible pleasure.
12 Here* I stand your Δslave,
A poor*, infirm*, weak*, and despis'd old man ;
But yet I call you Δservile Δministers,
That will with two pernicious Δdaughters join*
Your high-engender'd Δbattles* 'gainst a head
So old and white as this.
14 O, ho! 'tis foul*.

The onrush of F #1 and #4 (split into two and four and a half modern sentences respectively) show Lear's exhortations flowing much more easily from him than from his modern counterpart – as a man in full cry, commanding as an equal, rather than one trying to be heard - especially when the intellectualism of the opening two sentences are taken into account (9/4).

- this is not to say that there isn't an undercurrent of emotion as Lear begins to command the elements, for the first words are set in an (emotional) surround phrase, via the first of several semicolons in the speech – though whether this is suggestive of pride, joy, or fear is up to each actor to decide
- F #3's terrifying request to kill (most of? all?) future humanity ('all germains spill at once/That makes ingratefull Man') is spoken passionately (4/4)
- this seems to trigger what could be seen as a brain-storm in Lear, for F #4-5's fixation that, since the elements are not his daughters and he has not given them anything, they thus owe him nothing, is jam-packed with release (10/7 in the first four of five lines), the whole formed by six consecutive surround phrases, the last four of which are again emotional (thanks to the semicolons that link them)
- and then comes a most unexpected calm as he first voices that the elements owe him nothing (F #5's final emotional surround phrase) and then realises/suggests (given the unembellished quality of the short F #6 probably not commands/exhorts) that they 'let fall/Your horrible pleasure'
- F #7's realisation of his weakness and initially describing himself as their 'Slave' – a very different status from the opening of the speech – is emotional (1/4, F #7's first line and a half)
- yet in finishing the speech he changes tactics and attacks the elements demeaning them as 'Servile Ministers', now believing that they 'will with two pernicious Daughters joyne' against him - and his attack is passionate (4/3, the last four lines of the speech)

First Folio

22/ Lear

1 Blow+ windes, & crack your cheeks ; + Rage, blow+
You Cataracts, and Hyrricano's+ spout,
Till you have drench'd our Steeples, [drown] the Cockes.+
2 You Sulph'rous and Thought-executing fires,
Vaunt-curriors of Oake-cleaving Thunder-bolts,
Sindge my white head. +
3 And thou+ all-shaking Thunder,
Strike flat the thicke Rotundity o'th'world,+
Cracke Natures moulds, all germaines spill at once
That makes ingratefull Man. +

---

4 Rumble thy belly full : + spit+ Fire,+ spowt+ Raine : +
Nor Raine, Winde, Thunder, Fire are my Daughters ;
I taxe not you, you Elements+ with unkindnesse.
5 I never gave you Kingdome, call'd you Children ;
You owe me no subscription.
6 Then let fall
Your horrible pleasure.
7 Heere I stand your Slave,
A poore, infirme, weake, and dispis'd old man : x
But yet I call you Servile Ministers,
That will with two pernicious Daughters joyne
Your high-engender'd Battailes,x 'gainst a head
So old,x and white as this.
8 O, ho! 'tis foule.

23/ Lear **Let me alone./Thou think'st 'tis much that this contentious storme** between 3.4.3 - 22

Background: Though Kent/Caius has found a hovel which can give shelter to them all (not realising it is already home to Edgar, disguised as 'Poore Tom' - see speech #12 above), they are still out in the storm. Kent has urged them to enter, but Lear has other thoughts

Style: initially as part of a three-handed scene, then solo

Where: on the heath **To Whom:** Caius/Kent and the Foole, and then alone

# of Lines: 17 **Probable Timing: 0.55 minutes**

Modern Text

23/ Lear

1 Let me alone.
2 Thou think'st 'tis much that this contentious storm*
Invades us to the skin; so 'tis to thee;
But where the greater malady is fix'd,
The lesser is scarce felt.
3 Thou'dst shun a Δbear*,
But if [thy] flight lay toward the roaring Δsea,
Thou'dst meet* the Δbear* i'th'mouth. †
4 When the mind's free,
The body's, delicate: [this] tempest in my mind
Doth from my senses take all feeling else,
Save what beats* there - Δfilial* ingratitude! †
5 Is it not as this mouth should tear* this hand
For lifting food to't*?
6 But I will punish home. †
7 No, I will weep* no more. †
8 In such a night,
To shut me out?
9 Pour* on, I will endure. †
10 In such a night as this?
11 O Regan, Goneril*!
12 Your old kind Father, whose frank* heart gave all -
O, that way madness* lies, let me shun that! †
13 No more of that.

In contrast to the excesses of the previous speech, Lear seems far more contemplative and rational for much of the time (at least in his own mind, though to his listeners the idea he is putting forward may seem peculiar).

- thus F #2's opening four and half lines suggesting that the storm is the lesser 'malady' facing him are essentially unembellished (save for the word 'storme', which is affecting them all)

- the unembellished lines of F #3 outline exactly why
  "when the mind's free/The bodies delicate : the tempest in my mind,/
  Doth from my sences take all feeling else,"
  though F #3's preamble to this and the subsequent explanation, that his mental tempest is 'Filliall ingratitude' is passionate (6/6 overall)

- and then comes another virtually unembellished sentence (F #4, 0/1), picking up his earlier avowal that he will not 'weepe' (the only released word) but punish
  " But I will punish home ; /No, I will weepe no more ; in such a night,/
  To shut me out ? "
  the avowal heightened by being set as three surround phrases and by the quiet with which they are uttered, and yet undercut by the fact that the surround phrases are emotional (set with two semicolons, although grammatically the last one should have been set as a separate sentence)

- this is followed by another surround phrase (short) sentence (F #5) that is equally grammatically mixed,
  " . Poure on, I will endure : /In such a night as this ? "
  the first phrase defying the night, the second again referring to his daughters' treatment of him - this latter again spoken (introspectively?) without embellishment

- and this thought of his daughters seems to trigger his passions for the final F #6) where naming them seems to swamp him (3/3 in two and half lines) until his final unembellished surround phrase order to himself to stop thinking about them ' : No more of that . '

First Folio

23/ Lear

1 Let me alone.
2 Thou think'st 'tis much that this contentious storme
Invades us to the skin+ so :x 'tis to thee,+
But where the greater malady is fixt,
The lesser is scarce felt.
3 Thou'dst shun a Beare,
But if [they] flight lay toward the roaring Sea,
Thou'dst meete the Beare i'th'mouth, when the mind's free
The bodies delicate : [the] tempest in my mind,x
Doth from my sences take all feeling else,
Save what beates there, Filliall ingratitude,
Is it not as this mouth should teare this hand
For lifting food too't?
4 But I will punish home;
No, I will weepe no more; in such a night,
To shut me out?
5 Poure on, I will endure:
In such a night as this?
6 O Regan, Gonerill,+
Your old kind Father, whose franke heart gave all,
O+ that way madnesse lies, let me shun that:
No more of that.

24/ Foole **This is a brave night to coole a Curtizan :** 3.2.79 - 96

Background: Caius (the disguised Kent), has sought and found Lear and the Foole on the heath, and urges them to take shelter. He and Lear have left the stage, leaving the Foole alone to utter the following.

Style: solo

Where: the heath **To Whom:** direct audience address

# of Lines: 16 **Probable Timing: 0.50 minutes**

Modern Text

24/ Foole

1 This is a brave night to cool* a △courtezan*. †

2 I'll speak* a △prophecy₊ ere I go:
When △priests are more in word, [than] matter;
When △brewers mar* their △malt with water;
When [△tailors are their △nobles △tutors];
No △heretics* burn'd, but wenches' suitors₊;
Then shall the △realm* of Albion
Come [into] great confusion. †

3 When every △case in △law is right;
No △squire in debt, nor no poor* △knight;
When △slanders do not live in △tongues;
Nor △cut purses come not to throngs;
When △usurers tell their △gold i'th'△field,
And △bawds* and whores, do △churches build;
Then comes the time, who lives to see't,
That going shall ° be us'd with feet.

4 This prophecy₊ Merlin shall make, for I live before his time.

At last this seems to be the outburst that the smaller political statements embedded in more general fooling seen earlier (speeches #15 and #20 above) have been threatening that it is not as foolish or as innocent a piece of doggerel as is often played, can be seen in

a/ the onrush of F #2 (split into two more rational sentences in most modern texts)

b/ the enormous intellectualism of the speech (25/8 overall)

c/ half of the sixteen lines being set as determined surround phrases

d/ six of the surround phrases being further heightened by (emotional) semicolons

e/ after all the excesses, the final gloomy three line prophecy of England declining to the point that 'going shalbe us'd with feet' is essentially unembellished - with the name 'Merlin' being the only release in (the undercutting/self-excusing/I'm-not-saying-this-but-somebody-else-will) F#2

• that this notion is so disturbing to him can be seen in the shaded F line (a line not found in the quarto)

"Then shal the Realme of Albion, come to great confusion"

being overly long (13 syllables at least), seeming to underscore the Foole's passionate overflow of feeling as he contemplates England's destruction: however, not only do most modern texts split this F-only line in two, so as to maintain the doggerel/'songspiel' style of the speech, but, as shown, some also move it away from the climactic F placement to a weaker position ending the to them more rational position at the end of their (to them) more rationally set mt. #1

First Folio

24/ Foole

1 This is a brave night to coole a Curtizan:
Ile speake a Prophesie ere I go:
When Priests are more in word, [then] matter;
When Brewers marre their Malt with water;
When [Nobles are their Taylors Tutors],+
No Heretiques burn'd+ but wenches Sutors;
When every Case in Law,ₓ is right;
No Squire in debt, nor no poore Knight;
When Slanders do not live in Tongues;
Nor Cut-purses come not to throngs;
When Usurers tell their Gold i'th'Field,
And Baudes,ₓ and whores, do Churches build,+
Then shal the Realme of Albion, come [to] great confusion:
Then comes the time, who lives to see't,
That going shalbe us'd with feet.

2 This prophecie Merlin shall make, for I live before his time.†

#'S 25 - 27: GLOUCESTER & LEAR

25/ Edgar **Come on Sir,/Heere's the place : stand still :** between 4.6.11 - 27

Background: Despite orders to the contrary, Gloucester has helped Lear evade the vengeful forces of Cornwall and Regan who are bent on a 'plot of death' against him. As punishment Cornwall has blinded Gloucester and cast him loose into the countryside. Edgar, still disguised as Poore Tom, has come across his newly blinded father. Gloucester, not recognising his voice, has asked Edgar to escort him to the cliffs at Dover from which he can throw himself in an act of suicide. To save him, Edgar is pretending that they have arrived at the top of the cliffs, when in fact they are perfectly safe elsewhere.

Style: as part of a two-handed scene

Where: near the cliffs at Dover **To Whom:** his blinded father Gloucester

# of Lines: 18 **Probable Timing: 0.55 minutes**

Modern Text

25/ Edgar

1 Come on, Δsir, Δhere's* the place ; stand still . †
2 How fearful*
And dizzy* 'tis, to cast one's eyes so low ! †
3 The Δcrows* and choughs* that wing the midway air*
Show scarce* so gross* as Δbeetles .
4 Half* way down*
Hangs one that gathers Δsampire, dreadful* Δtrade !
Methinks* he seems* no bigger [than] his head .
5 The Δfishermen, that [walk] upon the beach
Appear* like Δmice ; and yond tall Δanchoring Δbark*,
Diminish'd to her Δcock*; her Δcock*, a Δbuoy
Almost too small for sight .
6 The murmuring Δsurge,
That on th'unnumb'red idle Δpebble chafes,
Cannot be heard so high .
7 I'll look* no more,
Least my brain* turn*, and the deficient sight
Topple down* headlong .

8 Give me your hand . †
9 You are now within a foot*
Of th'extreme Δverge . †
10 For all beneath the Δmoon*
Would I not leap* upright .

- most modern texts follow Q and form one line from the opening two short lines of Edgar: the F setting (three/eight syllables) allows for careful 'pretend' maneuvering to convince Gloucester that they are indeed on a hill, a play-acting heightened by the opening also being set as two surround phrases
  " . Come on Sir,/Heere's the place : stand still : "
- this opening care might well explain the remaining onrush of the sentence in that, now having caught his father's attention, by maintaining an unbroken stream of energy he can fool Gloucester into accepting the deception (most modern texts break F #1 into three)

- F #2 and #3 are equally determined, setting up the supposed details of what lies way below via six consecutive surround phrases

- however, whereas the passion of the opening onrushed sentence borders on the emotional (4/6, F #1), as if Edgar were fighting hard not to let his emotions cloud his words and actions, becoming passionate (9/9) by the time of F #2-3's piling on of details

- the sudden intellect of F #4 (2/0) is surprising, but perhaps the newly blinded Gloucester has been trying to use his hearing to verify what Edgar has been talking about - hence the quick unexpected comment that they are too high to hear even the surf

- then, in the attempt to distract his father/prevent him from discovering the ruse, Edgar's F #5 'Ile looke no more' becomes purely emotional (0/4) - though whether this is play-acting emotion or genuine in that the moment for his father to 'leap' is upon them is up to each actor to explore

- and just as he opened, Edgar closes with an onrush as he leads Gloucester to the supposed edge: as such, in addition to the added tension of the onrush (not maintained by most modern texts which often split F #8 in three)
  a/ the opening unembellished monosyllabic surround phrase ' . Give me your hand : ' conveys great care, and the pause that follows the F only setting of this as a short line allows for him to maneuver Gloucester into position
  b/ the rest of the sentence being set as two surround phrases (2/3) points to the determined focus Edgar displays to the very end

First Folio

25/ Edgar

1 Come on+ Sir, →
Heere's the place :x stand still : how fearefull
And dizie 'tis, to cast ones eyes so low,+
The Crowes and Choughes,x that wing the midway ayre
Shew scarse so grosse as Beetles .
2 Halfe way downe
Hangs one that gathers Sampire :x dreadfull Trade :+
Me thinkes he seemes no bigger [then] his head .
3 The Fishermen, that [walk'd] upon the beach
Appeare like Mice :x and yond tall Anchoring Barke,
Diminish'd to her Cocke :x her Cocke, a Buoy
Almost too small for sight .
4 The murmuring Surge,
That on th'unnumbred idle Pebble chafes+
Cannot be heard so high .
5 Ile looke no more,
Least my braine turne, and the deficient sight
Topple downe headlong .

6 Give me your hand :
You are now within a foote of th'extreme Verge :
For all beneath the Moone would I not leape upright .

26/ Lear **I, every inch a King. /When I do stare, see how the Subject quakes.** 4.6.107 - 131

Background: Edgar's trick (speech #25 above) to save Gloucester has worked. In the mean time, Lear, still essentially mad, is running free, and (not necessarily recognising them) has come across Edgar and Gloucester, with the latter exclaiming 'The tricke of that voyce, I do well remember:/Is't not the King?', which triggers the following.

Style: as part of a three-handed scene

Where: near the cliffs at Dover **To Whom:** Gloucester and Edgar

# of Lines: 20 **Probable Timing: 1.00 minutes**

Modern Text

26/ Lear

1 [Ay], every inch a Δking !
2 When I do stare, see how the Δsubject quakes.
3 I pardon that man's life.
4 What was thy cause?
5 Adultery? †
6 Thou shalt not die*. †
7 Die* for Δadultery?
8 No,
The Δwren goes to't*, and the small gilded Δfly
Does* lecher* in my sight.
9 [5] Let Δcopulation thrive ; Δfor Gloucester's bastard Δson
Was kinder to his Δfather [than] my Δdaughters
Got 'tween* the lawful* sheets. †
10 To't*, Δluxury pell-mell, for I lack* Δsoldiers*.
11 Behold yond simpering Δdame,
Whose face between* her Δforks* presages Δsnow ;
That minces Δvirtue, & do's shake the head
To hear* of pleasure's name - ◊
The Δfitchew nor the soiled* horse goes to't*
With a more riotous appetite. †
12 Down* from the [waist] Δthey are Centaurs*,
Though Δwomen all above ;
But to the Δgirdle do the Δgods inherit,
Beneath is all the Δfiends : ◊Δthere's hell, there's darkness*,
There is the sulphurous pit, burning, scalding,
Stench, consumption. †

In an already disturbed speech (especially seen in the switches between verse and prose), F's orthography reveals just where and how Lear's distress gets the better of him, as well as when he controls himself – though at times that control reveals some very ugly convictions.

- in opening as a King, Lear seems well in control, for the first two sentences of status assertion are intellectual (2/0); playing at magnanimity,
  "I pardon that mans life. What was thy cause?"
  Lear becomes unembellished, as if the imagined case deserved quiet, close attention
- then, as sexual disgust begins to hit home (much of the theme of the rest of the speech) his passion surfaces (1/2), heightened by F #5 being set as three surround phrases
  " . Adultery ? thou shalt not dye : dye for Adultery ? "
- but in keeping the examples away from his own direct sphere, talking about the world of animals and Gloucester's 'bastard Son', he stays intellectual (6/2, F #6 and all but the last line of F #7), but as soon as he turns to his own daughters and the attack on all women, so he becomes passionate (12/12, eight lines in all, the last line of F #7 to all but the last line of F #10)
- the whole attack can be summed up
  a/ by F #7's opening surround phrase ' . Let Copulation thrive : '
  b/ by the fact that from the opening of F #9's attack on all women
  " . Behold yond simpering Dame, whose face betweene her Forkes presages Snow ; "
  the verse he has hitherto spoken disintegrates to much less gracious prose (at least in F)
  c/ by the fact that from this moment, the final ten and a half lines of the speech are set as twelve successive surround phrases, eight of which are heightened by (emotional) semicolons

First Folio

26/ Lear

1 [I], every inch a King. +
2 When I do stare, see how the Subject quakes.
3 I pardon that mans life.
4 What was thy cause?
5 Adultery? thou shalt not dye : dye for Adultery?
6 No, the Wren goes too't, and the small gilded Fly
Do's letcher in my sight.
7 Let Copulation thrive : x
For Gloucesters bastard Son was kinder to his Father,x
[Then] my Daughters got 'tweene the lawfull sheets.
8 Too't Luxury pell-mell, for I lacke Souldiers.
9 Behold yond simpering Dame, whose face betweene her
Forkes presages Snow ; that minces Vertue, & do's shake
the head to heare of pleasures name.
10 The Fitchew,x nor
the soyled Horse goes too't with a more riotous appetite : Downe from the [waste] Δthey are Centaures, though
Women all above : x but to the Girdle do the Gods inherit, beneath is all the Fiends.
11 There's hell, there's darkenes,
there is the sulphurous pit ; x burning, scalding, stench,

[5] though Q1/Ff set this passage as prose, several modern texts set it as verse: however, as with speech #26 above, given the vehemence and horror of the images, the descent of Lear into prose seems very viable theatrically

13 Fie*, fie, fie ! pah, pah ! †
Give me an Δounce of Δcivet ; good Δapothecary,
Sweeten my imagination*. †
14 There's money for thee.

- sadly, the appalling description 'but to the Girdle do the Gods inherit, beneath is all the Fiends' is heightened even more by being totally intellectual (3/0), while the explanation
  ". There's hell, there's darkenes, there is the sulphurous pit ;
  burning, scalding, stench, consumption : "
  is even more disturbing since it is set as two unembellished emotional surround phrases

- while the desire to 'sweeten my immagination' turns intellectual once more (6/2, F #11's last two lines)

consumption: Fye, fie, fie; + pah, pah: + Give me an Ounce of Civet ; good Apothecary+ sweeten my immagination : There's money for thee.

27/ Lear **What, art mad? A man may see how this world goes, with no eyes.** between 4.6.150 - 172

Background: Whether recognising that Gloucester is blind or not, Lear has demanded that Gloucester read a challenge (whether actual or not, and specifically to whom, is up to each production to decide). Gloucester has declared 'Were all thy Letters Sunnes, I could not see', explaining that he can only see the world 'feelingly', which occasions the following from Lear.

Style: as part of a three-handed scene

Where: near the cliffs at Dover **To Whom:** Gloucester and Edgar

# of Lines: 20 **Probable Timing: 1.00 minutes**

Modern Text

27/ Lear

1 What, art mad?
2 A man may see how this world
goes, with no eyes.
3 Look* with thine ears*; Δsee how
yond Δjustice rails* upon yond simple thief*.
4 Hark* in
thine ear*: Δchange places, and handy-dandy, which is
the Δjustice, which is the thief*?
5 Thou hast seen* a Δfar-
mer's dog* bark* at a Δbeggar {,} †
{a}nd the Δcreature run from the Δcur ? †
6 There thou
might'st behold the great image of Δauthority*: a Δdog's*
obey'd in Δoffice.[6]
7 Thou, Δrascal* Δbeadle, hold thy bloody hand ! †
8 Why dost thou lash that Δwhore?

It seems that Lear has grown as politically shrewd as his Foole (see speeches #15, #20, and #24 above), and F's orthography clearly delineates the few moments where he loses control and, more especially, when the seriousness of what he believes forces him to utter quiet. One note: F does not follow Q/most modern texts in suddenly setting verse at mt.8/F #6 – presumably the images are so disturbing that they don't warrant the F Lear is moving into a state of grace.

- the opening unembellished calm (F #1-2) underscores Lear's amazing political philosophy, ' . What, art mad ? A man may see how this world goes, with no eyes . ', which he then goes on to expound with great determination . . .

- . . . via nine successive surround phrases, F #3-5
  a/ F #3's command to 'Looke with thine eare : ' is emotional (2/4)
  b/ the suggestion that there is no difference between 'the Justice' and 'the theefe' is passionate (5/6, F #4's first three lines)
  c/ but one of the central tenets of his new-found belief in the corruption of those at the top, the demeaning putdown of 'the great image of Authoritie' (the end of F #4) plus the abuse of office by 'the Rascall Beadle'(F #5), is astoundingly intellectual (8/1 in just three lines)

First Folio

27/ Lear

1 What, art mad?
2 A man may see how this world
goes, with no eyes.
3 Looke with thine eares : x See how
yond Justice railes upon yond simple theefe.
4 Hearke in
thine eare : Change places, and handy-dandy, which is
the Justice, which is the theefe : + Thou hast seene a Far-
mers dogge barke at a Beggar {,}
{a}nd the Creature run from the Cur : + there thou
might'st behold the great image of Authoritie, + a Dogg's
obey'd in Office.
5 Thou, Rascall Beadle, hold thy bloody
hand : + why dost thou lash that Whore?

{ctd. over}

[6] though Q1/Ff set this passage as prose, several modern texts set it as verse: however, as with speech #26 above, given the vehemence and horror of the images, the descent of Lear into prose seems very viable theatrically

9 Strip thy own* back*,
Thou hotly lusts to use her in that kind
For which thou whip'st her.
10 The Δusurer hangs the Δcozener.
11 Thorough tatter'd clothes* [small] Δvices do appear*;
ΔRobes and Δfurr'd gowns* hide all.
12 [Plate sin] with Δgold,
And the strong Δlance of Δjustice hurtless* breaks*;
ΔArm* it in rags*, a Δpigmy's* straw does* pierce it.
13 None does* offend, none, I say none, I'll able 'em. †
14 Take that of me, my Δfriend, who have the power
To seal* th'accusers lips.
15 Get thee glass*-eyes,
And like a scurvy Δpolitician, seem*
To see the things thou dost not.

- yet as in the previous speech (#26 above) the momentary return to adultery (F #6) becomes emotional (0/2)
- then it's quickly back to intellect as he baldly states that the person who hangs an anti-social being is just as anti-social as the being they hang (the very short F #7, 2/0)
- and as Lear turns to the appearance of Justice being just that, appearance only, masking all sorts of 'Vices' beneath and easily broken (F #8-9) so the passion of his belief sweeps in, both in terms of release (8/7 in just four lines), but also in that it is expressed yet again via four successive surround phrases
- the opening of his F #10 (sad?) conclusion that since Justice is so corrupt, 'None do's offend' is offered almost as calmly as he began the speech, but the emotion underneath it is underscored by the sentence being set as two emotional surround phrases (linked by the only semicolon in the speech), the first heightened even further by being unembellished
- while the final 'gift' to Gloucester of this insight is offered passionately (2/3, the last three lines following F #10's semicolon)

6 Strip thy owne
backe, thou hotly lusts to use her in that kind,x for which
thou whip'st her.
7 The Usurer hangs the Cozener.
8 Tho
rough tatter'd cloathes [great] Vices do appeare :x Robes,x
and Furr'd gownes hide all.
9 [Place sinnes] with Gold, and
the strong Lance of Justice,x hurtlesse breakes :x Arme it in
ragges, a Pigmies straw do's pierce it.
10 None do's offend,
none, I say none, Ile able 'em; take that of me+ my Friend,
who have the power to seale th'accusers lips.
11 Get thee
glasse-eyes, and like a scurvy Politician, seeme to see the
things thou dost not.

#'S 28 - 30: LEAR & CORDELIA

28/ Cordelia **Alacke, 'tis he : why he was met even now** between 4.4.1 - 20

Background: Learning of her father's treatment by her sisters, his current condition, and the threatened civil war between Albany and Cornwall, Cordelia has lead a troop of French forces to rectify the situation for both family and country. This is the first speech assigned to her after her return to Britain.

Style: address to a small group in front of a larger one

Where: the French encampment near Dover **To Whom:** a small group of Gentlemen in front of soldiers

# of Lines: 16 **Probable Timing: 0.50 minutes**

Modern Text

28/ Cordelia

1 Alack*, 'tis he ! †
2 Why, he was met even now
As mad as the vex'd Δsea, singing aloud*,
Crown'd with rank* [Δfemiter], and furrow-weeds,
With [Δhardocks], Δhemlock*, Δnettles, Δcuckoo-flowers*,
Darnel*, and all the idle weeds* that grow
In our sustaining Δcorn*.
3 A [Δcentury] send forth ;
Search every Δacre in the high-grown* field,
And bring him to our eye.
4 What can man's wisdom*
In the restoring his bereaved Δsense ? †
5 He that helps* him, Δtake all my outward worth.

6 All blest Δsecrets,
All you unpublish'd Δvirtues of the earth
Spring with my tears*; be aidant*, and remediate
In the Δgood man's [distress] ! †
7 Seek*, seek* for him,
Least his ungovern'd rage dissolve the life
That wants the means* to lead* it.

That the surround phrase ' . Alacke, tis he : ' opens the speech suggests just how much Cordelia has hoped for the discovery of her father's whereabouts: the fact that it is the only non-emotional surround phrases of six in the speech, and that orthographically the finish of the speech is highly emotional (1/6 the last three and half lines), shows just what effect the long sought for news has on her.

- thus, now knowing his general whereabouts, the order to search for him (F #2) and the promise to reward handsomely anyone who can cure him (F #3), while passionate (3/3), are set as four successive emotional surround phrases
  " . A Centery send forth ; /Search every Acre in the high-growne field,/And bring him to our eye . What can mans wisedome/In the restoring his bereaved Sense ; he that helpes him,/Take all my outward worth . "
- also emotional is the climax to her F #4 prayer to the 'Vertues of the earth'
  " ; be aydant, and remdiate/In the Goodmans [desires/distress] : "
- as the speech opens, the facts of her flower-crowned father are passionate (F #1, 7/8)
- as described above, the surround phrase orders to find him and offer of a reward to anyone who can cure him are passionate (3/3)
- and, for the only moment in the speech, in beginning her F #4 prayer, the naming of what she is appealing to, the 'blest Secrets' and 'Vertues of the earth', she is intellectually focused (2/0, the first line and a half) – but as she voices her request and then urges her followers to find her father before his 'rage, dissolve the life', intellect virtually disappears and she becomes highly emotional (1/6)

First Folio

28/ Cordelia

1 Alacke, 'tis he : + why+ he was met even now
As mad as the vext Sea, singing alowd,
Crown'd with ranke [Fenitar], and furrow weeds,
With [Hardokes], Hemlocke, Nettles, Cuckoo flowres,
Darnell, and all the idle weedes that grow
In our sustaining Corne.
2 A [Centery] send forth ;
Search every Acre in the high-growne field,
And bring him to our eye.
3 What can mans wisedome
In the restoring his bereaved Sense ; he that helpes him,
Take all my outward worth.

4 All blest Secrets,
All you unpublish'd Vertues of the earth
Spring with my teares ; be aydant, and remediate
In the Goodmans [desires] : seeke, seeke for him,
Least his ungovern'd rage,x dissolve the life
That wants the meanes to leade it.

29/ Cordelia **O my deere Father, restauration hang** between 4.7.25 - 43

Background: Cordelia's men have finally found her father, and in his maddened state have brought Lear back to camp in an effort to cure him. All medical preliminaries have been completed and now comes the dangerous and delicate moment when Lear has to be awoken to see whether the treatment has been successful or not.

Style: one on one in front of a small supportive group

Where: the French encampment near Dover **To Whom:** her father, in front of Kent, a Gentleman (sometimes referred to as 'Doctor'), and servants who have brought in Lear.

# of Lines: 16 **Probable Timing: 0.50 minutes**

Modern Text

29/ Cordelia

1 O my dear* $^{\Delta}$father, restoration* hang
Thy medicine on my lips*, and let this kiss*
Repair* those violent harms* that my two $^{\Delta}$sisters
Have in thy $^{\Delta}$reverence made.

2 Had you not been$_{*}$ their $^{\Delta}$father, these white flakes
Did challenge pity* of them.
3 Was this a face
To be oppos'd against the [warring] winds*?
4 [To stand against the deep dread-bolted thunder?
In the most terrible and nimble stroke
Of quick cross lightning? to watch - poor perdu ! -
Within this thin helm?]
5 Mine $^{\Delta}$enemy's$_{*}$ dog*,
Though he had bit me, should have stood that night
Against my fire, and wast thou fain* (poor* $^{\Delta}$father)
To hovel* thee with $^{\Delta}$swine and $^{\Delta}$rogues forlorn*
In short and musty straw?
6 Alack*, alack*,
'Tis wonder that thy life and wits at once
Had not concluded all.

7 How does my $^{\Delta}$royal* $^{\Delta}$lord?
8 How fares your Majesty?

The fact that there is no major punctuation suggests that this is essentially a stream of consciousness speech, each thought triggered by the one previous, by Lear's appearance, or by (non-)reaction to what she's saying. One note, the shaded passage shown in the modern text comes from the quarto version of the play, and was not set in F.

- the only unembellished lines (the latter part of F #5) point to from where the impetus for her speech stems
  " 'Tis wonder that thy life and wits, at once/Had not concluded all . "
- Cordelia's opening wish that her kisses could be the medicine to cure the ravages her sisters have made on Lear's 'reverence' is emotional (F #1, 3/6)
- her wonder that anyone could harm such an old man (F #2); throw him to the mercy of the winds (F #3); and make him 'hovell' with 'Swine and Rogues folorne', treating him worse that 'Mine Enemies dogge' (F #4), is expressed passionately (5/7)
- the precursor to the unembellished passage is emotional (0/2, the opening of F #5)
- and then, in questioning him directly (F #6-7) two things happen: first she becomes intellectual for the first time in the speech (2/1) and, second, the two short lines (5 or 6/6 syllables) set for Cordelia allow an understandable hesitation between the first and second questions: most modern texts follow Q and set a single line of verse, thus robbing her of the hesitation

First Folio

29/ Cordelia

1 O my deere Father, restauration hang
Thy medicine on my lippes, and let this kisse
Repaire those violent harmes$_{,x}$ that my two Sisters
Have in thy Reverence made.

2 Had you not bin their Father, these white flakes
Did challenge pitty of them.
3 Was this a face
To be oppos'd against the [jarring] windes?
[ ]
4 Mine Enemies dogge, though he had bit me,
Should have stood that night against my fire,
And was't thou faine (poore Father)
To hovell thee with Swine and Rogues forlorne$_{,x}$
In short$_{,x}$ and musty straw?
5 Alacke, alacke,
'Tis wonder that thy life and wits$_{,x}$ at once
Had not concluded all.

6 How does my Royall Lord? →
7 How fares your Majesty?

30/ Lear **Howle, howle, howle : O [your] are men of stones,** between 5.3.258 - 312

Background: In the ensuing battle between Cordelia's forces and the recently-combined forces of Albany and the late Cornwall (his forces now led by Edmund, since Cornwall's death - mortally wounded during his blinding of Gloucester), Cordelia and Lear have been captured and jailed. With peace now established and in a final act of justice, Albany has turned on Edmund, working it so that Edmund must duel to the death with his wronged brother Edgar. As he lies dying, Edmund reveals that he has given instructions that a Captain be sent to kill Lear and Cordelia - and before the order can be reversed Lear enters with the apparently dead Cordelia in his arms.

Style: general address and also one on one to various individuals within the group

Where: the battlefield **To Whom:** Albany, Kent, Edgar, the dead Cordelia, with bodies of Regan and Gonerill to one side

# of Lines: 22 **Probable Timing: 1.10 minutes**

Modern Text

30/ Lear

1 Howl*! howl*! howl* ! [howl !]†
2 O, [you are] men of stones ! †
3 Had I your tongues and eyes, I'ld use them so
That Δheavens vault should crack . †
4 She's gone for ever !
5 I know when one is dead, and when one lives;
She's dead as earth . †
6 Lend me a Δlooking-glass*,
If that her breath will mist or stain* the stone,
Why then she lives.
7 This feather stirs, she lives ! †
8 If it be so,
It is a chance which do's redeem* all sorrows*
That ever I have felt.
9 A plague upon you, Δmurderers*, Δtraitors all ! †
10 I might have sav'd her, now she's gone for ever ! †
11 Cordelia, Cordelia, stay a little.
12 Ha !
13 What is't thou say'st*?
14 Her voice was ever soft,
Gentle, and low, an excellent thing in woman.
15 I kill'd the Δslave that was a-hanging thee.
16 And my poor* Δfool* is hang'd !
17 No, no, no life !
18 Why should a Δdog, a Δhorse, a Δrat, have life,
And thou no breath at all?

The fact that so much of this speech is unembellished is usually taken for granted, given that Lear is so close to death; has exerted himself beyond all belief by killing 'the Slave that was a hanging thee'; and carried his dead daughter from the prison. What is worth exploring is that, since virtually all of the unembellishment centers solely on the dead Cordelia (whereas most of the circumstances of her death, his questioning why she had to die, and his requests for help to see if she is actually dead are the moments that are released), the quiet may not be simple exhaustion but more moments of quiet conversation/ observation with and about the most beloved of his children. Also, F's onrush (14 sentences in comparison to modern texts' 21) suggests at times a Lear less controlled than his modern counterpart.

- what is even more fascinating is that most of these moments of calm are further heightened by being set either as surround phrases or short sentences, adding extra weight to whatever he believes/says
  - " : she's gone for ever . /I know when one is dead, and when one lives,/She's dead as earth : "
  - " . This feather stirs, she lives : "
  - " . A plague upon you . . . / I might have sav'd her, now she's gone for ever . "
  - " . Ha : /What is't thou saist ? Her voice was ever soft,/Gentle, and low, an excellent thing in woman . "
  - " . Thou'lt come no more,/Never, never, never, never, never . "
  - " . Do you see this ? "
- when he's not quiet, the battle between intellect and emotion rages and his moods change very swiftly, as with the thrice repeated and, not surprisingly, totally emotional (0/3) opening 'howle' being followed by an intellectual accusation/explanation as to why those he is addressing are 'men of stones' (2/0, the remainder of F #1)
- after F #2's first calm statement that Cordelia's dead, the sudden ungrammatical request for a 'Looking-glasse' to see if her breath will cloud it is passionate (2/2, F #2's last two lines)
- after F #3's (astonished? dumbfounded?) mistaken belief that 'This feather stirs', his response is emotional (0/2, F #3's last two lines)

First Folio

30/ Lear

1 Howle,+ howle,+ howle+ []: + O+ [your] are men of stones,+
Had I your tongues and eyes, Il'd use them so,x
That Heavens vault should crack : she's gone for ever.+
2 I know when one is dead, and when one lives,+
She's dead as earth : Lend me a Looking-glasse,
If that her breath will mist or staine the stone,
Why then she lives.
3 This feather stirs, she lives : + if it be so,
It is a chance which do's redeeme all sorrowes
That ever I have felt.
4 A plague upon you+ Murderors, Traitors all,+
I might have sav'd her, now she's gone for ever :
Cordelia, Cordelia, stay a little.
5 Ha : +
What is't thou saist?
6 Her voice was ever soft,
Gentle, and low, an excellent thing in woman.
7 I kill'd the Slave that was a hanging thee.
8 And my poore Foole is hang'd : + no, no, no life?+
9 Why should a Dog, a Horse, a Rat+ have life,
And thou no breath at all?

{ctd. over}

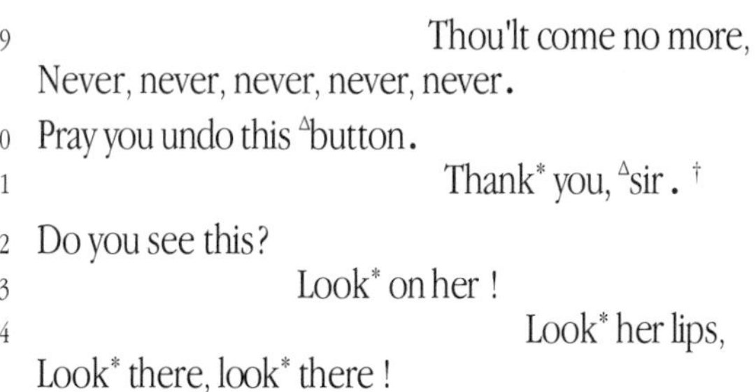

19 Thou'lt come no more,
Never, never, never, never, never.
20 Pray you undo this △button.
21 Thank* you, △sir. †
22 Do you see this?
23 Look* on her!
24 Look* her lips,
Look* there, look* there!

- F #4's (unjustified) attack on them for being 'Murderers, Traitors all' is passionate (2/1), while its plea for Cordelia to stay is intellectual (3/0, including the first word of F #4's last line)

- F#7's short announcement of killing the man that hanged her is also intellectual (1/0), while F #8's statement that she is dead becomes passionate once more (1/2)

- sadly, F #9's querying as to why creatures should live while she does not is totally intellectual (3/0) – as if there were no escaping this question

- and following the passionate request of F #11-12 (2/1) to undo 'this Button' – presumably to help him breathe - his final words pointing to her lips are emotional (0/4, F #13-14), the crux of whether he dies believing her to be alive or not never definitively answered

10 Thou'lt come no more,
Never, never, never, never, never.
11 Pray you undo this Button.
12 Thanke you+ Sir,
Do you see this?
13 Looke on her?+
14 Looke her lips,
Looke there, looke there. +

CORIOLANUS

SPEECHES IN ORDER

Speech	First line	TIME	PAGE
#'s 1 - 4: The Family			
1/ Volumnia	I pray you daughter sing, or expresse your selfe	1.10	323
2/ Volumnia	Me thinkes, I heare hither your Husbands Drumme:	0.45	324
3/ Valeria	Come, lay aside your stitchery, I must have you	0.50	325
4/ Martius	What's the matter you dissentious rogues	1.10	326
#'s 5 - 8: The Political Climate			
5/ Menenius	Why Masters, my good Friends, mine honest ...	0.50	328
6/ Menenius	Either you must/Confesse your selves wondrous	2.00	329
7/ Brutus	All tongues speake of him, and the bleared sights	1.00	331
8/ Menenius	I am knowne to be a humorous Patritian, and	0.55	332
#'s 9 - 10: The War, And Auffidius			
9/ Auffidius	The Towne is ta'ne./'Twill be deliver'd backe ...	1.15	333
10/ Cominius	If I should tell thee o're this thy dayes Worke,	1.30	334
#'s 11 - 17: Roman Conflict			
11/ Brutus	I heard him sweare/Were he to stand for Consull,	1.00	336
12/ Coriolanus	Shall remaine?/Heare you this Triton	2.30	337
13/ Coriolanus	Let them pull all about mine eares, present me	0.50	339
14/ Volumnia	Pray be counsail'd;/I have a heart as little apt as yours,	1.10	340
15/ Volumnia	Now it lyes you on to speake to th'people:	0.55	341
16/ Volumnia	I pry thee now, my Sonne,/Goe to them,	0.55	342
#'s 17 - 21: Exile And Revenge			
17/ Coriolanus	You common cry of Curs, whose breath I hate,	0.50	343
18/ Auffidius	Oh Martius, Martius;	2.15	344
19/ 2nd Servingman	Wee shall have a stirring World againe:	0.35	346
20/ Cominius	Oh you have made good worke.	0.55	347
21/ Cominius	He would not seeme to know me.	1.30	348
#'s 22 - 25: The Final Tragedy			
22/ Auffidius	All places yeelds to him ere he sits downe,	1.30	349
23/ Volumnia	Oh no more, no more: /You have said you will not ...	1.55	351
24/ Volumnia	Nay, go not from us thus:	2.40	353
25/ Auffidius	Read it not Noble Lords, /But tell the Traitor	1.00	355

SPEECHES BY GENDER

Character	Description	Speech #(s)
SPEECHES FOR WOMEN (8)		
Volumnia	**Traditional & Today:** older woman with son and young grandson	#1, #2, #14, #15, #16, #23, #24
Valeria	**Traditional & Today:** female, any age	#3
SPEECHES FOR EITHER GENDER (3)		
Brutus	**Traditional:** male, any age **Today:** any age, any gender	#7, #11
2nd Servingman	**Traditional:** male, any age **Today:** any age, any gender	#19
SPEECHES FOR MEN (13)		
Coriolanus	**Traditional & Today:** late-young/early middle-aged military man	#4, #12, #13, #17
Menenius	**Traditional & Today:** late middle-aged man, and older	#5, #6, #8
Cominius	**Traditional & Today:** middle-aged and older military man	#10, #20, #21
Auffidius	**Traditional & Today:** late-young/early middle-aged military man	#9, #18, #22, #24

CORIOLANUS

#'s 1 - 4: The Family

1/ Volumnia **I pray you daughter sing, or expresse your selfe** between 1.3.1 - 25

2/ Volumnia **Me thinkes, I heare hither your Husbands Drumme :** between 1.3.29 - 44

Background: Volumnia, Martius' mother, is a war-hawk, and proud of her son's accomplishments and reputation as a military killing machine; Virgilia, Martius' wife, is the exact opposite. As they await news of the latest Roman war against Auffidius and the Volsces, the tension and differences between them are very apparent. Speech #1 is a clear statement of Volumnia's personal philosophy; speech #2 shows her war-like imagination.

N.B. 'Valeria', referred to in the last sentence of speech #2, is a Roman matron ('the Moone of Rome: Chaste as the Isicle') who has come to call.

Style: as part of a two-handed scene, in front of a Gentlewoman

Where: Volumnia's home **To Whom:** her daughter-in-law Virgilia

Speech 1: # of Lines: 21 **Probable Timing: 1.10 minutes**

Speech 2: # of Lines: 14 **Probable Timing: 0.45 minutes**

Modern Text

1/ Volumnia

1 I pray you daughter, sing, or express* yourself*
in a more comfortable sort. †
2 If my Δson* were my Δhus-
band, I should freelier rejoice* in that absence wherein
he won* Δhonor [than] in the embracements of his Δbed
where he would show* most love.
3 When yet he* was but
tender-bodied, and the only* Δson* of my womb; when
youth with comeliness* pluck'd all gaze his way; when
for a day of Δkings' entreaties a Δmother should not sell, him
an hour* from her beholding; I, considering how Δhonor*
would become such a person, that it was no better [than]
Δpicture-like to hang by th'wall, if renown* made it not
stir*, was pleas'd to let him seek* danger where he was
like to find* fame. †
4 To a cruel* Δwar* I sent him, from
whence he return'd, his brows* bound with Δoak*.
5 I tell
thee, Daughter, I sprang not more in joy at first hearing
he was a Δman-child, [than] now in first seeing he had pro-
v'd* himself* a man.

6 Hear* me pro-

Volumnia's joy in her son and contempt of the softer aspects of life are clearly expressed in the language of the speech, and F's orthography seems to reveal just how (unhealthily) deep that joy lies.

- the emotional underpinnings to Volumnia's fixation on son Martius can be seen in F #2's emotional (semicolon created) surround phrases
  " . When yet hee was but tender-bodied, and the onely Sonne of my womb ; when youth with comelinesse pluck'd all gaze his way ; "
  and her pride in him can be seen in the final surround phrase of the same sentence
  " : To a cruell Warre I sent him, from whence he return'd, his browes bound with Oake . "

- whatever Volumnia's emotional attitude (0/2) towards her daughter-in-law (scorn? impatience?), it is heightened by her first words of the speech being set as a surround phrase, while her belief in 'Honor' above all is is expressed intellectually (5/3, F #1's remaining three lines) - the extra breath-thoughts that suddenly appear (marked ,x) could well point to her scorn of setting importance in the 'embracements of his Bed,x', but they could also mark her personal excitement in the joy of war and of her son in war

- Volumnia's setting up of how when Martius was a youth, she as 'a Mother should not sel him an houre from her beholding' is passionate (3/5, F #2's first four lines); her extended belief 'how Honour' was nothing if 'renowne made it not stirre' (2/5, F #2's next four lines) is emotional; while passion sweeps in once more

First Folio

1/ Volumnia

I pray you daughter+ sing, or expresse your selfe
in a more comfortable sort: If my Sonne were my Husband, I should freelier rejoyce in that absence wherein
he wonne Honor,x [then] in the embracements of his Bed,x
where he would shew most love.
2 When yet hee was but
tender-bodied, and the onely Sonne of my womb; when
youth with comelinesse pluck'd all gaze his way; when
for a day of Kings entreaties,x a Mother should not sel him
an houre from her beholding; I+ considering how Honour
would become such a person, that it was no better [then]
Picture-like to hang by th'wall, if renowne made it not
stirre, was pleas'd to let him seeke danger,x where he was
like to finde fame: To a cruell Warre I sent him, from
whence he return'd, his browes bound with Oake.
3 I tell
thee+ Daughter, I sprang not more in joy at first hearing
he was a Man-child, [then] now in first seeing he had proved himselfe a man.

4 Heare me pro-
fesse sincerely,+ had I a dozen sons+ each in my love alike,

{ctd. over}

fess* sincerely : had I a dozen sons, each in my love alike,
and none less* dear* [than] thine and my good Martius, I
had rather had eleven die* Δnobly for their Δcountry* [than]
one voluptuously surfeit₊ out of Δaction.

in her expressing what this belief inevitably ensured - that, despite his youth, 'To a cruell Warre I sent him' (3/4 in just the last line and a half of F #2)

• Volumnia's F#3 comparing of her joy at her son's proof of manhood through war to that of his birth is still passionate, though more relaxed (2/2)

• and, as in F #1, though F 4's sudden and grammatically unnecessary extra breath-thoughts might simply show just how carefully Volumnia is pointing out to Virgilia the depth of her (sacrificial) patriotism, since so much of F #2 has been spent on the (excitement?) joy that Coriolanus brings her, this may be as revelatory of the depth of her need to live through him and his victories, as it is of her beliefs – the whole being expressed in high passion once more (4/6 in just four lines)

and none lesse deere [then] thine,ₓ and my good Martius, I
had rather had eleven dye Nobly for their Countrey,ₓ [then]
one voluptuously surfet out of Action.

Modern Text

2/ Volumnia

1 Methinks* I hear* hither your Δhusband's Δdrum*;
See him pluck* [Aufidius] down* by th'hair*;
As children from a Δbear*, the [Volsces] shunning him. †
2 Methinks* I see him stamp* thus, and call thus :
"Come on, you Δcowards, you were got in fear*,
Though you were borne in Rome !" †
3 His bloody brow
With his mail'd hand then wiping, forth he goes,
Like to a Δharvest- man [that's] task'd to mow*
Or all or lose* his hire*.
4 {Blood} more becomes a man
[Than] gilt his Δtrophy₊.
5 The breasts₊ of Hecuba,
When she did suckle Hector, look'd not lovelier
[Than] Hector's forehead when it spit forth blood
At Grecian sword, ◊[Δcontemning]. †
6 Tell Valeria
We are fit to bid her welcome.

F's opening onrush shows just how focused Volumnia can become when she envisages her son in battle, possibly ungrammatically so (most modern texts reduce her fixation by splitting F #1 into three).

• whether done to disconcert the squeamish Virgilia or out of a genuine enthusiasm, Volumnia's emotionally passionate war envisionings (7/11, F #1's first five and a half lines) are driven even harder by the first three lines being set as surround phrases
" . Me thinkes, I heare hither your Husbands Drumme : /See him plucke Auffidius downe by th'haire : /(As children from a Beare) the Volces shunning him : "

• then, as with the previous speech, as she reaches the climax of the battle - her son cutting through the enemy 'Like to a Harvest man, that{'s} tasked to mowe' - extra breath thoughts (marked ,ₓ) appear, either underscoring each tiny point or suggestive that she needs the extra breath to control her excitement (for certainly the releases in F #1's last three lines are much fewer, 1/3)

• for the remainder of the speech Volumnia's fixation on the beauty of battle becomes totally intellectual (6/0, the fives lines F #2-4)

• however, with the first word of F #4 ('Contenning', equivalent of 'despising' or 'scorning') seemingly more related to the previous sentence than to what follows, it could well be that Volumnia has given up on getting any form of meaningful response from her daughter-in-law and abruptly instructs the Servant to bring in her friend without bothering to start a new sentence: most modern texts remove this possibility by setting the word at the end of the previous sentence

First Folio

2/ Volumnia

1 Me thinkes,ₓ I heare hither your Husbands Drumme : ₓ
See him plucke [Auffidius] downe by th'haire : ₓ
(ₓAs children from a Beareₓ) the [Volces] shunning him :
Me thinkes I see him stampe thus, and call thus,+
Come on+ you Cowards, you were got in feare+
Though you were borne in Rome ; + his bloody brow
With his mail'd hand,ₓ then wiping, forth he goes+
Like to a Harvest man,ₓ [that] task'd to mowe
Or all,ₓ or loose his hyre.
2 {Blood} more becomes a man
[Then] gilt his Trophe.
3 The brests of Hecuba+
When she did suckle Hector, look'd not lovelier
[Then] Hectors forhead,ₓ when it spit forth blood
At Grecian sword. ₓ
4 [Contenning], tell Valeria
We are fit to bid her welcome.

3/ Valeria **Come, lay aside your stitchery, I must have you . . .** between 1.3.69 - 101

Background: Valeria has come to tempt Volumnia and Virgilia to accompany her out into Rome, and while Volumnia is more than willing, Virgilia stubbornly is not.

Style: as part of a three-handed scene, in front of two others

Where: Volumnia's home **To Whom:** Volumnia, Virgilia, and an Usher and a Gentlewoman in Valeria's employ

# of Lines: 16 **Probable Timing: 0.50 minutes**

Modern Text

3/ Valeria

1 Come, lay aside your stitchery, I must have you
play the idle △houswife* with me this afternoon*.

2 Fie*, you confine yourself* most unreasonably . †

3 You would be another Penelope: yet they say, all
the [yarn*]she spun in [Ulysses'] absence, did but fill [Ithica]
full of △moths*.

4 In truth la, go with me, and I'll tell you excellent
news* of your △husband.

5 Verily, I do not jest with you ; there came news*
from him last night.

6 In earnest, it's true; I heard a Senator* speak* it.

7 Thus it is: the [Volsces] have an △army forth ; against [whom]
Cominius the △general* is gone, with one part of our Roman* power.

8 Your Lord and Titus Lartius are set down
before their △city* [Corioles] ; they nothing doubt prevailing, and to make it brief* △wars*.

9 This is true, on mine
△honor, and so I pray go with us.

F's orthography reveals Valeria using, whether consciously or no, certain patterns of relaxation and release to maintain herself as the centre of attention and get her way.

- Valeria's attitude towards Virgilia can be seen quite clearly in the surround phrase rebukes opening F #2
  " . Fye, you confine your selfe most unreasonably :
  {y}ou would be another Penelope : "

- Virgilia's love of being the first to know/disseminate the latest news can be seen in the five consecutive surround phrases from F #4 to the first phrase of F #6
  " . Verily I do not jest with you : there came newes from him last night . In earnest it's true ; I heard a Senatour speake it . Thus it is : "
  - the unembellished calm of the third and fifth (pertaining to the news being 'true' and setting up her delivery) perhaps a deliberate ploy to make herself the centre of attention by going very quiet (especially when being 'true' is underscored by the phrase ending with an emotional semicolon)

- while her opening request for Virgilia to leave the home and accompany her is relatively relaxed (1/3, the first three lines), her rebuke when obviously refused becomes strongly intellectual in her classical comparison to Penelope (4/2, the last two and half lines of F #2)

- as with the opening temptation to leave the house, so the second temptation/bribe that she will tell Virgilia news of her husband if she does is also a little more emotional (2/4, the four and a half lines of F #3 to the first phrase of F #6)

- and as befits the build-up her information is delivered with great intellectual enthusiasm (11/4, in just four lines, F #6-7)

- while F #5's earlier quietness in avowing 'it's true' is seen again in the same reassurance ending the speech (1/0, F #8)

First Folio

3/ Valeria

1 Come, lay aside your stitchery, I must have you
play the idle Huswife with me this afternoone.

2 Fye, you confine your selfe most unreasonably:
{y}ou would be another Penelope: yet they say, all
the [yearne] she spun in [Ulisses] absence, did but fill [Athica]
full of Mothes.

3 In truth la+ go with me, and Ile tell you excellent
newes of your Husband.

4 Verily+ I do not jest with you : x there came newes
from him last night.

5 In earnest+ it's true; I heard a Senatour speake it.

6 Thus it is: the [Volcies] have an Army forth, against [whó]
Cominius the Generall is gone, with one part of our Romane power.

7 Your Lord,x and Titus Lartius,x are set down
before their Citie [Carioles],+ they nothing doubt prevailing, and to make it breefe Warres.

8 This is true+ on mine
Honor, and so I pray go with us.

4/ Martius **What's the matter you dissentious rogues** between 1.1.164 - 189

Background: These are Martius' first words in the play, little caring that he is inflaming once again a group of rebellious citizens who have only just been calmed by his much more diplomatic mentor, Menenius (see speeches #5-6 below). As such they reveal his completely undemocratic and right-wing approach to the under-classes.

Style: general group address

Where: a street in Rome **To Whom:** an unspecified number of Citizens close to revolt, in front of his mentor, the senator Menenius

# of Lines: 23 **Probable Timing: 1.10 minutes**

Modern Text

4/ Martius

1 What's the matter, you dissentious rogues,
That rubbing the poor* Δitch of your Δopinion,
Make your selves Δscabs ?

2 What would you have, you
Δcurs*,
That like nor Δpeace nor Δwar*?
3 The one affrights you,
The other makes you proud.
4 He that trusts to you,
Where he should find* you Δlions*, finds* you Δhares;
Where Δfoxes, Δgeese . †
5 You are no surer, no,
[Than] is the coal* of fire upon the Δice,
Or Δhailstone in the Δsun.
6 Your Δvirtue is
To make him worthy whose offense⁎ subdues him,
And curse that Δjustice did it.
7 Who deserves Δgreatness⁎
Deserves your Δhate; and your Δaffections are
A sick ° man's Δappetite, who desires most that
Which would increase his evil*.
8 He that depends
Upon your favors* swims* with fins* of Δlead*,
And hews* down* Δoaks* with rushes.
9 Hang ye ! †
10 Trust ye?
11 With every Δminute you do change a Δmind*,
And call him Δnoble, that was now your Δhate;
Him vile*, that was your Δgarland.

F's orthography reveals Coriolanus/Martius' fatal flaw – not knowing when to reign himself in - for orthographically this speech falls into two parts, a perfectly rational if very tough opening political assessment, admittedly tinged by personal disgust, which then spills into a much less controlled and politically inept group character assassination and attack.

- the foundation of Martius/Coriolanus' disgust with the 'dissentious rogues' (the commoners) can be seen in the (for him dangerously quiet) unembellished dismissal of their response to 'Peace' and 'Warre', for
  " . The one affrights you,/The other makes you proud . "
  and thus his attitude to them (the 'Curres') throughout is ' . Hang ye : '
- the opening of the speech, essentially a dismissal of them all for their Cowardice, is strongly intellectual (20/8, the thirteen and half lines of F #1-6) – his anger strongly channeled by the surround phrases that open F #4
  " . He that trusts to you,/Where he should finde you Lyons, findes you Hares : /Where Foxes, Geese you are : "
- the sequence ends with F #6's three surround phrases driving home of how out of step they are with those that would maintain Rome's greatness
  " . Who deserves Greatnes,/Deserves your Hate : and your Affections are /A sickmans Appetite ; who desires most that/Which would encrease his evill . "
  and though the sentence seems intellectual (4/1), the fact that the last two phrases are linked by the only emotional semicolon in the speech suggests that there is a much deeper set of feelings lurking just below his words
- and if he had been able to reign himself in and finish here, the diatribe could have been accepted as harsh (and perhaps valid) political criticism – but he can't and it isn't . . .
- . . . for F #7's attack on their steadfastness is suddenly emotional (2/7), and he needs two extra breath-thoughts (marked , $_x$), either to control himself or to ensure that every tiny detail of his attack is driven home

First Folio

4/ Martius

1 What's the matter+ you dissentious
rogues+
That rubbing the poore Itch of your Opinion,
Make your selves Scabs. +

2 What would you have, you
Curres,
That like nor Peace,$_x$ nor Warre?
3 The one affrights you,
The other makes you proud.
4 He that trusts to you,
Where he should finde you Lyons, findes you Hares: $_x$
Where Foxes, Geese you are:$_x$ No surer, no,
[Then] is the coale of fire upon the Ice,
Or Hailstone in the Sun.
5 Your Vertue is,$_x$
To make him worthy, whose offence subdues him,
And curse that Justice did it.
6 Who deserves Greatnes,$_x$
Deserves your Hate:$_x$ and your Affections are
A sickmans Appetite;$_x$ who desires most that
Which would encrease his evill.
7 He that depends
Upon your favours,$_x$ swimmes with finnes of Leade,
And hewes downe Oakes,$_x$ with rushes.
8 Hang ye:+ trust ye?
9 With every Minute you do change a Minde,
And call him Noble, that was now your Hate: $_x$
Him vilde, that was your Garland.

12 What's the matter,
That in these several* places of the Δcity$_{*}$
You cry against the Δnoble Senate, who
(Under the Δgods) keep* you in awe, which else
Would feed* on one another?

• and even though he recovers some intellectual control in the attack on them for 'With every Minute you do change a Minde' (F #9, 5/2), his demand to know why they have the temerity to 'cry against the Noble Senate' becomes passionate (F #10, 4/3) - matching his earlier passion in F #2 when he first demanded to know what they 'would have' (3/2)

10 What's the matter,
That in these severall places of the Citie,$_{x}$
You cry against the Noble Senate, who
(Under the Gods) keepe you in awe, which else
Would feede on one another?

#'s 5 - 8: The Political Climate

5/ Menenius **Why Masters, my good Friends, mine honest/Neighbours,** between 1.1.62 – 78
6/ Menenius **Either you must/Confesse your selves wondrous Malicious,** between 1.1.87 - 155

Background: The rebellious citizens, part of at least two groups simultaneously airing their grievances publicly to gain attention from the authorities, have been careful to state that they are at the point of revolt because of 'hunger for Bread, not in thirst for Revenge'. They claim that the current famine, and the hoarding of the grain by the aristocrats so as to force up prices, are the root of their problems. Prior to Martius' undiplomatic interference (speech #4 above) Menenius, according to the citizens 'one that hath alwayes lov'd the people', has been sent to calm the group down. The following are his attempts so to do. Speech #5 deals with the overall problem, and speech #6 attempts to point out the citizens' place in the overall scheme of Roman social organization.

Style: general group address

Where: a street in Rome **To Whom:** an unspecified number of Citizens close to revolt

Speech 5: # of Lines: 16 **Probable Timing: 0.50 minutes**

Speech 6: # of Lines: 40 **Probable Timing: 2.00 minutes**

Modern Text

5/ Menenius

1 Why, $^{\triangle}$masters, my good $^{\triangle}$friends, mine honest $^{\triangle}$neighbors*,
will you undo yourselves?

2 I tell you $^{\triangle}$friends, most charitable care
Have the $^{\triangle}$patricians of you . †
3 For your wants, ◊
Your suffering in this dearth, you may as well
Strike at the $^{\triangle}$[heavens] with your staves as lift them
Against the Roman $^{\triangle}$state, whose course will on
The way it takes, cracking ten thousand $^{\triangle}$curbs*
Of more strong link* asunder* [than] can ever
Appear* in your impediment.
4 For the $^{\triangle}$dearth,
The $^{\triangle}$gods, not the $^{\triangle}$patricians, make it, and
Your knees to them (not arms*) must help*.
5 Alack*,
You are transported by $^{\triangle}$calamity
[Thither*] where more attends you, and you slander
The $^{\triangle}$helms* o'th $^{\triangle}$state, who care for you like $^{\triangle}$fathers,
When you curse them as $^{\triangle}$enemies.

In his initial attempt to quieten the potentially rebellious citizens, Menenius' political skill is so clearly evident - refusing to move into any emotional or sustained intellectual release until absolutely necessary.

- thus his concern that they might 'undo your selves' (F #1), his reassurance that the nobles ('Patricians') have 'most charitable care . . . for your wants' (F #2), and that the citizens might 'as well/Strike at the Heaven . . . as . . . the Roman State' (F #3), are all very carefully intellectually advanced (8/1, the first seven and a half lines of the speech)
- then comes his first emotional release (1/4) in predicting the chaos (an Elizabethan fear) that could only ensue from such a striving (the last two lines of F #30 – and this coincides with what most modern texts regard as an ungrammatical period ending F #2, perhaps suggesting that Menenius shows himself so moved by their appearance and grievances (whether genuinely or no) that he is forced to take a break here before continuing: most modern texts establish a more logical situation, placing the period three words earlier, after 'you', and set a comma here in its place
- in explaining that it is not the Patricians' fault, Menenius becomes passionate for the only time in the speech (F #4, 3/2) – whether the passion is genuine urging or deliberate rhetoric to give the appearance of urging to move the crowd is up to each actor to decide
- and now comes the strong and concentrated intellectual release as he fears for them being 'transported by Calamity' (F #5, 5/2), and as if to push his concern home even more, the speech ends with the first and only surround phrase
  " ; who care for you like Fathers,/When you curse them, as Enemies . "
  - it's concern underscored by being led into by the only emotional semicolon in the speech

First Folio

5/ Menenius

1 Why^{+} Masters, my good Friends, mine honest
Neighbours, will you undo your selves?

2 I tell you Friends, most charitable care
Have the Patricians of you for your wants.
3 Your suffering in this dearth, you may as well
Strike at the [Heaven] with your staves,$_{x}$ as lift them
Against the Roman State, whose course will on
The way it takes: $_{x}$ cracking ten thousand Curbes
Of more strong linke assunder,$_{x}$ [then] can ever
Appeare in your impediment.
4 For the Dearth,
The Gods, not the Patricians^{+} make it, and
Your knees to them (not armes) must helpe.
5 Alacke,
You are transported by Calamity
[Thether],$_{x}$ where more attends you, and you slander
The Helmes o'th State;$_{x}$ who care for you like Fathers,
When you curse them,$_{x}$ as Enemies.

Modern Text

6/ Menenius

1 Either you must
Confess* yourselves wondrous Δmalicious,
Or be accus'd of Δfolly.
2 I shall tell you
A pretty Δtale . †
3 It may be you have heard it,
But since it serves my purpose, I will venture
To [stale't] a little more.

4 There was a time when all the body's$_*$ members
Rebell'd against the Δbelly; thus accus'd it:
That only* like a Δgulf* it did remain*
I'th mid'st* a th'body, idle and unactive,
Still cupboarding* the Δviand, never bearing
Like labor* with the rest, where th'other Δinstruments
Did see and hear*, devise, instruct, walk*, feel*,
And mutually participate, did minister
Unto the appetite and affection common
Of the whole body . †
5 The Δbelly answer'd - ◊

"True is it my incorporate Δfriends," (quoth he),
"That I receive the general* Δfood at first
Which you do live upon; and fit it is,
Because I am the Δstore-house and the Δshop
Of the whole Δbody.
6 But, if you do remember,
I sent it through the Δrivers of your blood,
Even to the Δcourt, the Δheart, to th'seat* o'th'Δbrain*,
And, through the Δcranks*[1] and Δoffices of man,
The strongest Δnerves and small inferior* Δveins*
From me receive that natural* competency$_*$
Whereby they live.
7 And though that all at once" -
You, my good Friends, this says* the Δbelly, mark* me.

8 "Though all at once cannot
See what I do deliver out to each,

[1] most modern texts agree with Ff and set 'cranks': one modern gloss = 'ranks'

Menenius' manipulative story-telling skills are evident throughout, with even his apparent syntactical untidiness at the end of F #3 probably deliberate rather than evidence of his being overwhelmed by the current situation.

- as with his first speech (#3 above), Menenius starts quite carefully and with little emotional release (3/1, the five lines of F #1-2): indeed, the offer to tell the 'pretty Tale' is made without any embellishment at all
  "it may be you have heard it,/But since it serves my purpose, I will venture/To [scale't] a little more."
  though whether the quiet is a rhetorical attempt, to seduce the audience, or a matter of enforcing calm on himself so as not to appear too eager or genuine casualness, is up to each actor to explore
- Menenius opens his 'Tale' very carefully (F #3 1/0), his once-upon-a-time build-up enhanced by being set as two emotional surround phrases
  " . There was a time, when all the bodies members/Rebell'd against the Belly ; thus accus'd it : "
- with the accusation then explored in great detail very emotionally (3/9, F #3's next six and a half lines)
- fascinatingly, though modern texts regard the semicolon ending this passage and the punctuation thereafter as ungrammatical, as a good story teller F's setting
  "Unto the appetite ; and affection common/Of the whole body, the Belly answer'd . "
  establishes far more anticipation in the listeners than the modern texts' resetting
  "Unto the appetite and affection common/Of the whole body. The belly answer'd - "
- then, again, a fine example of the story-teller's art, it seems at first Menenius intellectually agrees with the body's members' (and thus by parallel the Citizens') complaints (F #4, 5/1)
- but as he explains why the Belly/Senate should have the best of everything, he becomes passionate for the first time in the speech (13/10, the eleven lines, F #5-7)

First Folio

6/ Menenius

1 Either you must
Confesse your selves wondrous Malicious,
Or be accus'd of Folly.
2 I shall tell you
A pretty Tale, it may be you have heard it,
But since it serves my purpose, I will venture
To [scale't] a little more.

3 There was a time,$_x$ when all the bodies members
Rebell'd against the Belly; thus accus'd it:
That onely like a Gulfe it did remaine
I'th midd'st a th'body, idle and unactive,
Still cubbording the Viand, never bearing
Like labour with the rest, where th'other Instruments
Did see,$_x$ and heare, devise, instruct, walke, feele,
And mutually participate, did minister
Unto the appetite; $_x$ and affection common
Of the whole body, the Belly answer'd.

4 True is it my incorporate Friends+ (quoth he)+
That I receive the generall Food at first
Which you do live upon: $_x$ and fit it is,
Because I am the Store-house,$_x$ and the Shop
Of the whole Body.
5 But, if you do remember,
I sent it through the Rivers of your blood+
Even to the Court, the Heart, to th'seate o'th'Braine,
And+ through the Crankes and Offices of man,
The strongest Nerves,$_x$ and small inferiour Veines
From me receive that naturall competencie
Whereby they live.
6 And though that all at once+
($_x$You+ my good Friends, this sayes the Belly,$_x$) marke me.

7 Though all at once,$_x$ cannot
See what I do deliver out to each,

{ctd. over}

Yet I can make my Δaudit* up, that all
From me do back* receive the [Δflour] of all,
And leave me but the Δbran."
9 What say you to't*?

10 The Δsenators of Rome are this good Δbelly,
And you the mutinous Δmembers: Δfor examine
Their Δcounsels* and their Δcares; digest* things rightly
Touching the Δweal* a'th Δcommon, you shall find*
No public* benefit which you receive
But it proceeds or comes from them to you,
And no way from yourselves.
11 What do you think*,
You, the great Δtoe of this Δassembly?

• then, superbly changing tactics, Menenius first goes very quiet in asking for their response (the unembellished, very short, monosyllabic F #8), and then, in drawing the parallel between the 'Tale' and the current situation in Rome, thereby drawing attention to the danger that they could be in for being seen as 'mutinous', he becomes strikingly intellectual (7/1, F #9's first two and a half lines), driving the issue home with the two surround phrases via which this parallel is pushed

" . The Senators of Rome, are this good Belly,/And you the mutinous Members : For examine/Their Counsailes, and their Cares ; "

• and his final platitude that everything done for the 'Weale a'th'Common' (the last four and half lines of F #9) and challenge to a supposed citizen leader (F #10) for an answer is passionate (4/5) – and even here his manipulative skills are cunningly evident, for the lead in to the Senators digesting 'things rightly' is via the emotional semicolon (a nice potentially seductive touch perhaps), while assuring them that the

"benefit which you receive/But it proceeds, or comes from them to you,/And no way from your selves ."

is, as befits such matters of state, appropriately solemnly unembellished

Yet I can make my Awdit up, that all
From me do backe receive the [Flowre][2] of all,
And leave me but the Bran.
8 What say you too't?

9 The Senators of Rome,$_{x}$ are this good Belly,
And you the mutinous Members: For examine
Their Counsailes,$_{x}$ and their Cares; disgest things rightly,,
Touching the Weale a'th Common, you shall finde
No publique benefit which you receive
But it proceeds,$_{x}$ or comes from them to you,
And no way from your selves.
10 What do you thinke?+
You, the great Toe of this Assembly?

[2] Ff = 'Flowre', most modern texts = 'flour' which somewhat spoils the double meaning

7/ Brutus **All tongues speake of him, and the bleared sights** between 2.1.205 - 223

Background: To satisfy the rebellious people five Tribunes, or representatives, have been appointed to speak on their behalf. This does not sit well with Martius whose reaction was, 'Sdeath,/the rabble should first have unroo'(f)t the city/Ere so prevayl'd with me;'. That it does not sit well with Martius, and like thinkers, is well known to two of the Tribunes. One of these Tribunes, Brutus is here analysing the situation with his colleague Sicinius. The 'him' spoken of in the first line is Martius, who has returned to Rome with a hero's welcome, receiving the 'Oaken Garland' for the third time, and adding to his name Caius Martius a third word,'Coriolanus', to celebrate and commemorate his single-handed capture of the Volscian city of Corioles.

Style: as part of a two-handed scene

Where: a Roman street **To Whom:** a fellow Tribune Sicinius

# of Lines: 19 **Probable Timing: 1.00 minutes**

Modern Text

7/ Brutus

1 All tongues speak* of him, and the bleared sights
Are spectacled to see him.
2 Your prattling* △nurse
Into a rapture lets her △baby cry*
While she chats him; the △kitchen △malkin pins*
Her richest △lockram 'bout her reechy* neck*,
Clamb'ring the △walls to eye him; △stalls, △bulks*, △windows*,
Are smother'd up, △leads* fill'd, and △ridges hors'd
With variable △complexions, all agreeing
In earnestness* to see him. †
3 Seld-shown* △flamens*
Do* press* among the popular △throngs, and puff*
To win* a vulgar station; our veil'd* △dames
Commit the △war* of △white and △damask* in
Their nicely gawded △cheeks* toth'wanton spoil
Of Phoebus' burning △kisses - such a pother*
As if that whatsoever △god, who leads* him
Were slily* crept into his human* powers,
And gave him graceful* posture.
4 {ψ} Our △office may, during his power, go* sleep*.

F's onrushed F #2 (split into two more rational litanies of complaint by most modern texts) and two (shaded) passages of irregular lines imply a character not in full control of himself – and the orthography suggests when the breakdown occurs, as Brutus begins to describe how everywhere everyone is 'In earnestnesse to see him', i.e Coriolanus.

- with its very quiet start (F #1 slightly emotional, 0/1; F#2's first two lines slightly intellectual, 2/0) it seems that Brutus is just beginning to notice what is taking place around them, or, given the excesses later in the speech, is trying very hard not to let his antipathy towards Coriolanus get in the way of analysing the current political danger
- but as Brutus describes how even the lowest are dressing up to see Coriolanus, so his releases start to flow - though he still manages some self control (4/2 in just F #2's next two lines, between the first two colons) it is a control undercut by being set as three irregular lines (7/8/6 syllables, suggesting that Brutus struggles to retain self-composure)
- then, as he describes/imagines people scrambling to see Coriolanus from every possible vantage point, his full flow turns passionate (4/4, the next three and half lines), leading to the only surround phrase in the speech " ; all agreeing/In earnestnesse to see him : " - heightened by starting with the only emotional semicolon in the speech
- the fact that even Priests ('Flamins') are struggling with the 'popular Throngs' creates an (amazed? horrified? despairing?) emotional response (2/5, F #2's next two lines), while the observation that the better sort of women ('our veyl'd Dames') are attracted toward Coriolanus triggers an enormously passionate reaction (7/6 in just the next three lines) - the slightly irregular structure (9/11 syllables) showing another imbalance as he describes the women's reactions
- and his accurate summation that, since Coriolanus is now being idolized as something more than human, their new 'Office' may 'goe sleepe' is highly emotional once more (2/6, the last four and half lines of the speech)

First Folio

7/ Brutus

1 All tongues speake of him, and the bleared sights
Are spectacled to see him.
2 Your pratling Nurse
Into a rapture lets her Baby crie, x
While she chats him: x the Kitchin Malkin pinnes
Her richest Lockram 'bout her reechie necke,
Clambring the Walls to eye him: x
Stalls, Bulkes, Windowes, are smother'd up,
Leades fill'd, and Ridges hors'd
With variable Complexions; x all agreeing
In earnestnesse to see him: seld-showne Flamins
Doe presse among the popular Throngs, and puffe
To winne a vulgar station: x our veyl'd Dames
Commit the Warre of White and Damaske
In their nicely gawded Cheekes, x toth'wanton spoyle
Of Phoebus burning Kisses: x such a poother, x
As if that whatsoever God, who leades him, x
Were slyly crept into his humane powers,
And gave him gracefull posture.
3 {ψ} Our Office may, during his power, goe sleepe.

8/ Menenius **I am knowne to be a humorous Patritian, and** 2.1.47 - 65

Background: The Senator Menenius, a cagey politician, has very little time for the upstart Tribunes, especially Brutus and Sicinius. The following stems from their first lengthy on-stage meeting. Menenius pulls no punches, either about himself or, especially, in his opinion of the two Tribunes.

Style: as part of a three-handed scene

Where: a street in Rome **To Whom:** the Tribunes Brutus and Sicinius

# of Lines: 18 **Probable Timing: 0.55 minutes**

Modern Text

8/ Menenius

1 I am known* to be a humorous Δpatrician*, and one that loves a cup of hot Δwine with not a drop of allaying* Tiber in't; Δsaid to be something imperfect in favoring* the first complaint, hasty and Δtinder-like upon* to trivial* motion; Δone that converses more with the Δbuttock* of the night [than] with the forehead* of the morning.

2 What I think, I utter, and spend my malice in my breath.

3 Meeting two such Δweals*men as you are (I cannot call you Lycurguses*,) if the drink* you give me touch my Δpalate* adversely, I make a crooked face at it † .

4 I [cannot] say your Δworships* have deliver'd the matter well, when I find* the Δass* in compound, with the Δmajor part of your syllables; ◊ Δand though I must be content to bear* with those, that say you are reverend grave men, yet they lie* deadly that tell you have good faces . †

5 If you see this in the Δmap of my Δmicrocosm*, follows* it that I am known* well enough too?

6 What harm* can your beesom* Δconspectuities glean* out of this Δcharacter*, if I be known* well enough too ?

In the midst of discussing what other people say about him and his demeanor and behaviour, Menenius' F #2 self-description, whether truthful or not, is notable for its unembellished quietness in describing himself as a no-nonsense plain-dealer

"What I think, I utter, and spend my malice in my breath."

- especially since he uses this to challenge the tribunes at speech's end.

- his reputation as quaint drink-loving noble is described quite factually (F #1's first two and a half lines, 3/2); that he is quick-tempered over trivialities is less easily handled (2/3, the next two lines); and then the emotional passion turns to intellectual passion as he mentions his reputation for preferring late nights to early mornings (2/1, F #1's last line and half)
- following his F #2 unembellished self-description as a plain-dealer, he proves exactly that - the deceptive quiet of the previous sentence blown apart by his passionate judgement that, because of their pronouncements, he regards each of the Tribunes as an 'Asse' (6/5, the five lines of F #3)
- having become passionate, his control begins to slip - at least according to the emotional F #4 (2/5) - for he jumps quite peculiarly via a fast-link comma from the idea that, even if he puts up with others who say the Tribunes are 'reverend grave men' they lie who say that, to challenging them to say what that tells them about him: (most modern texts remove this weirdness - drunk? angry over 'triviall motion'? - by setting a grammatically correct new sentence (mt. #5)
- and his emotions still dominate as F #5 intensifies his previous challenge - this time for them to make some political/personal capital of his insults (2/5)

First Folio

8/ Menenius

1 I am knowne to be a humorous Patritian, and one that loves a cup of hot Wine,$_x$ with not a drop of alaying Tiber in't: $_x$ Said,$_x$ to be something imperfect in favouring the first complaint, hasty and Tinder-like uppon,$_x$ to triviall motion: $_x$ One,$_x$ that converses more with the Buttocke of the night,$_x$ [then] with the forhead of the morning.

2 What I think, I utter, and spend my malice in my breath.

3 Meeting two such Weales men as you are (I cannot call you Licurgusses,) if the drinke you give me,$_x$ touch my Palat adversly, I make a crooked face at it, I [can] say,$_x$ your Worshippes have deliver'd the matter well, when I finde the Asse in compound, with the Major part of your syllables.

4 And though I must be content to beare with those, that say you are reverend grave men, yet they lye deadly,$_x$ that tell you have good faces, if you see this in the Map of my Microcosme, followes it that I am knowne well enough too?

5 What harme can your beesome Conspectuities gleane out of this Charracter, if I be knowne well enough too. +

#'S 9 - 10: THE WAR, & AUFFIDIUS

9/ Auffidius **The Towne is ta'ne./Twill be deliver'd backe on good Condition.** between 1.10.1 - 27

Background: Auffidius is Martius/Coriolanus' Volscian enemy-state equivalent, in Martius' words 'a Lion/That I am proud to hunt'. Martius has beaten him in a fair fight five times in a row, and Auffidius is now determined to win by fair means, or foul, no matter how foul those means may be.

Style: as part of a two-handed scene

Where: away from the battlefield **To Whom:** his Lieutenant

# of Lines: 26 **Probable Timing: 1.15 minutes**

Modern Text

9/ Auffidius

1 The △town* is ta'en!
2 {ψ} 'Twill be deliver'd back* on good △condition.
3 Condition?
4 I would I were a Roman, for I cannot,
Being a [Volsce], be that I am.
5 Condition?
6 What good △condition can a △treaty* find*
I'th'part that is at mercy? †
7 Five times, Martius,
I have fought with thee; so often hast thou beat me;
And wouldst do* so, I think*, should we encounter
As often as we eat*.
8 By th'△elements,
If e'er again* I meet him beard to beard,
He's mine, or I am his. †
9 Mine △emulation
Hath not that △honor in't it had; △for where
I thought to crush him in an equal* △force,
True △sword to △sword, I'll potch* at him some way,
Or △wrath or △craft may get him.
10 {He's} △bolder {than the devil*},
though not so subtle. †
11 My valor's poison'd
With only* suff'ring stain* by him; for him
Shall fly* out of itself*. †
12 Nor sleep* nor sanctuary,
Being naked, sick*, nor △fane* nor △capitol*,
The △prayers of △priests nor times of △sacrifice,
Embarquements all of △fury, shall lift up
Their rotten △privilege* and △custom* 'gainst
My hate to Martius.

Underneath all the releases, the occasional unembellished lines clearly illustrate the problems eating away at him while the surround phrases elaborate the lengths to which he will go to solve them once and for all.

- the first unembellishment focuses twice on the fact that, as the defeated, they will have to agree to terms to have their capital city returned to them
  ". Condition ? " (twice, the short F #3 and F #5)
  then, the quiet deals with the tarnishing of his own personal reputation, enhanced by being set as two surround phrases
  " ? five times, Martius,/I have fought with thee ; so often hast thou beat me : "
  moving to the determination to battle him to the ultimate end
  " He's mine, or I am his : "
  even if it means breaking all chivalric beliefs
  "were it/At home, . . ./would I/Wash my fierce hand in's heart."
- the remaining surround phrases point to the depth of his disturbance
  " : Mine Emulation/Hath not that Honor in't it had : "
  " : Ile potche at him some way,/Or Wrath, or Craft may get him . He's Bolder than the divell,/ though not so subtle : my valors poison'd,/With onely suff'ring staine by him : "
  " ; nor Phane, nor Capitoll,/The Prayers of Priests, nor times of Sacrifice : "
- in determining the loss of the town, Auffidius is passionate (F #1-2, 2/2), and then becomes very controlled as he fixates on the appalling fact that to get it back they will have to abide by imposed 'Conditions' (F #3 through to F #6's first three lines being a mixture of unembellished lines and intellect, 5/1)
- for the first time in the speech, F #6's ending is emotional (0/3) as he voices how he would always be beaten no matter how many times he faced Martius/Coriolanus in a fair fight
- thus Auffidius' determination to beat Martius even if it takes 'Craft' is the more shocking for being so avowedly and determinedly intellectual (F #7, 10/3)
- and though his initial analysis of the reputations of both of them is emotional (1/7, F #8's first four lines - highly damaging for himself), his further elaboration of how far he is prepared to go to destroy Martius – even in a Church or at his brother's home- matches the earlier intellectualism of F #7 (12/5, the last seven lines of the speech)

First Folio

9/ Auffidius

1 The Towne is ta'ne. +
2 {ψ} 'Twill be deliver'd backe on good Condition.
3 Condition?
4 I would I were a Roman, for I cannot,
Being a [Volce], be that I am.
5 Condition?
6 What good Condition can a Treatie finde
I'th'part that is at mercy? five times, Martius,
I have fought with thee; so often hast thou beat me: x
And would'st doe so, I thinke, should we encounter
As often as we eate.
7 By th'Elements,
If ere againe I meet him beard to beard,
He's mine, or I am his: Mine Emulation
Hath not that Honor in't it had: x For where
I thought to crush him in an equall Force,
True Sword to Sword: x Ile potche at him some way,
Or Wrath, x or Craft may get him.
8 {He's} Bolder {than the divell},
though not so subtle: my valors poison'd, x
With onely suff'ring staine by him: + for him
Shall flye out of it selfe, nor sleepe, x nor sanctuary,
Being naked, sicke; x nor Phane, x nor Capitoll,
The Prayers of Priests, x nor times of Sacrifice: x
Embarquements all of Fury, shall lift up
Their rotten Priviledge, x and Custome 'gainst
My hate to Martius.

{ctd. over}

13 Where I find* him, were it
At home, upon my Δbrother's Δguard, even there,
Against the hospitable Δcanon, would I
Wash my fierce hand in's heart.

9 Where I finde him, were it
At home, upon my Brothers Guard, even there+
Against the hospitable Canon, would I
Wash my fierce hand in's heart.

10/ Cominius **If I should tell thee o're this thy dayes Worke,** between 1.9. 1 – 66

Background: Having won the town of Corioles single-handedly and defeated Auffidius in hand-to-hand combat, Martius is singled out for fulsome praise in front of the assembled forces - an honour that doesn't sit too well with him. Nevertheless, Cominius, his senior general, insists that Martius stay and hear himself lauded.

Style: one on one address for the benefit of a very large group in attendance

Where: at the Roman camp close to Corioles **To Whom:** Martius, soon to be named Coriolanus, in front of the victorious Roman forces

# of Lines: 30 **Probable Timing: 1.30 minutes**

Modern Text

10/ Cominius

1 If I should tell thee o'er this thy day's* Δwork*,
Thou't not believe* thy deeds: but I'll report it
Where Δsenators shall mingle tears* with smiles;
Where great Δpatricians shall attend and shrug,
I'th'end admire; where Δladies shall be frighted,
And gladly quak'd, hear* more; where the dull Δtribunes,
That with the fusty* Δplebeians* hate thine Δhonors,
Shall say against their hearts, "We thank* the Δgods
Our Rome hath such a Δsoldier*".

2 You shall not be
The Δgrave of your deserving; Rome must know
The value of her own*. †

3 'Twere a Δconcealment*
Worse [than] a Δtheft, no less* [than] a Δtraducement,
To hide your doings, and to silence that
Which, to the spire and top of praises* vouch'd,
Would seem* but modest; therefore I beseech you,
In sign* of what you are, not to reward
What you have done, before our Δarmy* hear* me.

4 {O}f all the Δhorses -
Whereof we have ta'en good, and good store - of all
The Δtreasure in this field achieved* and Δcity*,

We render you the Δtenth, to be ta'en forth,
Before the common distribution, at

Throughout, the extra breath-thoughts (marked , $_x$) suggest that Cominius ensures that even the tiniest of points will be recognised by the soldiers listening.

- Cominius opens carefully but passionately (4/5, the first five and half lines), the first surround phrase
  ". If I should tell thee o're this thy dayes Worke,/Thou't not beleeve thy deeds : "
  a very true statement, since Martius has won the town of Corioles single-handedly, and the ease of the opening is enhanced by the only other surround phrase of praise which ends this section
  " : where Ladies shall be frighted,/And gladly quak'd, heare more : "

- the teasing praise then turns to intellect (scorn? laughter at?) as he damns the 'dull Tribunes' and the 'fustie Plebeans' (the commoners) who, despite their hatred of Martius, will have to praise him (6/2, F #1's last three lines)

- the ensuing irregular Ff sequence (7/11/9/9/7 syllables) seems to suggest an awkwardness for Cominius, with
  a/ a hesitation before starting
  b/ irregular lines to start getting the argument across
  c/ a pause either before or after the dishonourable images of 'Theft' 'Traducement'
  all indicative that he is trying to forestall Martius' potential refusal for any further public praise or reward: the modern restructuring (11/10/11/11 syllables) glosses over the irregularity and thus gives the appearance of balance where none was originally set
  d/ the irregularity and the subsequent fulsome conclusion beseeching Coriolanus to allow both praise and reward is passionate (5/7, F #2)

First Folio

10/ Cominius

1 If I should tell thee o're this thy dayes Worke,
Thou't not beleeve thy deeds: but Ile report it,$_x$
Where Senators shall mingle teares with smiles,+
Where great Patricians shall attend,$_x$ and shrug,
I'th'end admire: $_x$ where Ladies shall be frighted,
And gladly quak'd, heare more: $_x$ where the dull Tribunes,
That with the fustie Plebeans,$_x$ hate thine Honors,
Shall say against their hearts, We thanke the Gods
Our Rome hath such a Souldier.

2 You shall not be the Grave of your deserving,+
Rome must know the value of her owne:
'Twere a Concealement worse [then] a Theft,
No lesse [then] a Traducement,
To hide your doings, and to silence that,$_x$
Which+ to the spire,$_x$ and top of prayses vouch'd,
Would seeme but modest: $_x$ therefore I beseech you,
In signe of what you are, not to reward
What you have done, before our Armie heare me.

3 {O}f all the Horses,
Whereof we have ta'ne good, and good store+ of all,$_x$
The Treasure in this field atchieved,$_x$ and Citie,

We render you the Tenth, to be ta'ne forth,
Before the common distribution,

Your only* choice*.

5 Therefore be it known*,
As to us, to all the Δworld, Δthat Caius Martius
Wears* this Δwar's* Δgarland; in token of the which,
My Δnoble Δsteed, known* to the Δcamp*, I give him,
With all his trim belonging; and from this time,
For what he did before Corioles, call him,
With all th'applause and Δclamor of the Δhost*,
Marcus Caius Coriolanus!
6 Bear*
Th'addition Δnobly ever!

passionate (5/7, F #2)

- the initial announcement of the reward, one tenth of all the horses and spoils taken from the city, is intellectual (4/1, F #3's first three and half lines), while the capper, that he should choose without restriction before anyone else, is announced emotionally (0/2, the last line and a half) – the sudden switch in style perhaps suggesting that this 'first choice' is a most unusual perk
- then, in awarding Martius the laurel wreath of victory; giving him his own horse; and renaming him as Coriolanus Cominius is resoundingly intellectual (16/7, F #4-5), the few emotional (longer spelling) releases supporting the award of the laurel wreath ('Weares this Warres Garland') and the gift of the horse which is 'knowne to the Campe'
- to end the speech F sets a seventeen syllable line, suggesting a triumphant build for the listening soldiers to hail Martius by his new name, which most modern texts reset as ten/seven syllables as shown, thus spoiling Cominius' obvious excitement - also most modern texts change Ff's question mark to an exclamation point, though in Elizabethan orthography the question mark served both functions

At your onely choyse.

4 Therefore be it knowne,
As to us, to all the World, That Caius Martius
Weares this Warres Garland: x in token of the which,
My Noble Steed, knowne to the Campe, I give him,
With all his trim belonging; and from this time,
For what he did before Corioles, call him,
With all th'applause and Clamor of the Hoast,
Marcus Caius Coriolanus. +
5 Beare th'addition Nobly ever? +

#'S 11 - 17: ROMAN CONFLICT

11/ Brutus **I heard him sweare/Were he to stand for Consull, never would he** between 2.1.231 - 253

Background: As a follow up to his analysis of the 'hero-Martius-now-named-Coriolanus' (speech #7 above), Brutus now begins to define possible tactical probes to exploit any weakness in Coriolanus in order to prevent Coriolanus from becoming a political figure in Rome.

Style: as part of a two-handed scene

Where: a Roman street **To Whom:** a fellow Tribune Sicinius

# of Lines: 19 **Probable Timing: 1.00 minutes**

Modern Text

11/ Brutus

1 I heard him swear*,
Were he to stand for Δconsul*, never would he
Appear* i'th'Δmarket place, nor on him put
The Δnapless* Δvesture of Δhumility*,
Nor showing* (as the manner is) his Δwounds
[To th'Δpeople], beg* their stinking Δbreaths.

2 It was his word. †
3 O*, he would miss* it
Rather [than] carry it Δbut by the suit* of the Δgentry to him,
And the desire of the Δnobles.

4 So it must fall out
To him, or our Δauthorities, for an end.

5 We must suggest the Δpeople in what hatred
He still hath held them ; that to's power he would
Have made them Δmules, silenc'd their Δpleaders, and
Dispropertied their Δfreedoms*, holding them,
In human* Δaction and Δcapacity*,
Of no more Δsoul* nor fitness* for the Δworld
[Than] Δcamels* in [the] Δwar*, who have their Δprovand
Only* for bearing Δburthens, and sore blows*
For sinking under them.

Unlike the earlier frustrated Brutus who could only observe and not plan (speech #7 above), here F reveals when and how quickly the intellectual political analyst and planner quality of Brutus becomes subsumed in passion and not emotion as before.

- their whole plan of campaign can be summed up in the second surround phrase in the speech
  " . We must suggest the People, in what hatred/He still hath held them : "
- his F #1 focus on one key earlier comment by Coriolanus that can be used against him (that he would never succumb to an essential requirement of becoming Consul - dressing in the traditional rags of humility and enduring the people's gaze and questioning) is intellectual (8/4)
- initially, it's almost as if Brutus cannot believe Coriolanus actually vowed this, for F #2 opens with the monosyllabic unembellished surround phrase, ' . It was his word : '
- as Brutus realises the vehemence of Coriolanus' refusal (in not bending even to the requests of the Nobles and gentry to follow tradition) he becomes (excitedly?) passionate (F #2, 2/3) ...
- ... which quickly subsides as he recognises what they are up against, his statement of it's-him-or-us being bleakly intellectual (1/0, F #3)
- as he plans the main thrust of the disinformation they will feed their followers (we, and therefore you, will be powerless), he begins intellectually (4/1, F #4's first three and a half lines), and then, as he embellishes it to the image of the people being no better than 'Cammels in their Warre' in that they will be overworked and beaten, he becomes very passionate (8/7, F #4's last five lines)

First Folio

11/ Brutus

1 I heard him sweare+
Were he to stand for Consull, never would he
Appeare i'th'Market place, nor on him put
The Naples Vesture of Humilitie,
Nor shewing (as the manner is) his Wounds
[Toth'People], begge their stinking Breaths.

2 It was his word:
Oh+ he would misse it,x rather [then] carry it,x
But by the suite of the Gentry to him,
And the desire of the Nobles.

3 So it must fall out
To him, or our Authorities, for an end.

4 We must suggest the People,x in what hatred
He still hath held them: x that to's power he would
Have made them Mules, silenc'd their Pleaders,
And dispropertied their Freedomes; x holding them,
In humane Action,x and Capacitie,
Of no more Soule,x nor fitnesse for the World,x
[Then] Cammels in [their] Warre, who have their Provand
Onely for bearing Burthens, and sore blowes
For sinking under them.

12/ Coriolanus **Shall remaine?/Heare you this Triton of the Minnoues?** between 3.1.88 - 170

Background: Brutus and Sicinius have attacked very shrewdly Coriolanus in public, informing the Senators accompanying him that 'The People are incens'd against him', and 'cry you mockt them', especially since 'When Corne was given them gratis, you repin'd,/Scandal'd the Suppliants for the People, call'd them/Time-pleasers, flatterers, foes to Noblenesse'. They have done so banking on Coriolanus' notorious temper getting the better of him - which it does, and, despite warnings from his more politically astute advisors, Coriolanus insists on speaking his mind, revealing much more than simply strong right-wing leanings - leanings sufficient for much of his support to melt away.

Style: public address to a large group

Where: a street in Rome **To Whom:** the Senators at large, including Menenius and Cominius, the Tribunes Brutus and Sicinius, and the people

# of Lines: 52 **Probable Timing: 2.30** minutes

Modern Text

12/ Coriolanus

1 Shall remain*?

2 Hear* you this Triton of the Δminnows*?

3 Mark* you
His absolute "Δshall"?

4 "Shall"?

5 O [Δgood] but most unwise Δpatricians ! why,
You grave but reakless* Δsenators, have you thus
Given [Hydra] here* to choose an Δofficer,
That with his peremptory "Δshall", being but
The horn* and noise o'th'Δmonster's, wants not spirit
To say he'll* turn* your Δcurrent in a ditch,
And make your Δchannel* his?

6 If he have power,
Then vale your Δignorance; [3] Δif none, awake
Your dangerous Δlenity . †

7 If you are Δlearn'd,
Be not as common Δfools*; if you are not,
Let them have Δcushions by you .

8 You are Δplebeians,
If they be Δsenators; and they are no less*,
When, both your voices blended, the great'st taste
Most palates* theirs.

9 They choose their Δmagistrate,
And such a one as he, who puts his "Δshall",
His popular "Δshall, against a graver Δbench
[Than] ever frown'd in Greece.

In a very long speech Coriolanus seems to keep his emotions in check almost throughout, or at least match them with his relentless intellect so that his passion shines through in all his fervent beliefs as to the duty of Rome's nobles to cherish the power that they have been given, not for themselves but for the good of the State – yet F's orthography reveals that in this passion his potential for fascism overcomes him at the very last moment as his emotions finally take over.

- Coriolanus' initial response to what he regards as Sicinius' (a commoner) insolence is passionate (3/4, F #1-3)

- the quiet of the unembellished 'Shall? O God!' follows - which though quiet, is emphasised by both the question mark serving as an exclamation mark and the very rare, for an Elizabethan text, exclamation point, suggesting that his astonishment could be directed inward

- the ensuing surround phrase
  " ! but most unwise Patricians : "
  sets up the beginning of a long passionate harangue (8/6, the remainder of F #5) asking why the nobles have appointed commoners as Tribunes who could take over the nobles' power

- then, in piling detail upon detail in an attempt to get the Senators to take back their power before it's too late, not only does his intellect reign supreme (14/3, F #6-8), but the first five lines are also driven home by five consecutive surround phrases urging the argument to its fullest
  " . If he have power,/Then vale your Ignorance : If none, awake/Your dangerous Lenity : If you are Learn'd, /Be not as common Fooles ; if you are not, /Let them have Cushions by you . You are Plebeians,/If they be Senators : "

First Folio

12/ Coriolanus

1 Shall remaine?

2 Heare you this Triton of the Minnoues?

3 Marke you
His absolute Shall?

4 Shall?

5 O [God!] but most unwise Patricians: + why+
You grave,x but wreaklesse Senators, have you thus
Given [Hidra] heere to choose an Officer,
That with his peremptory Shall, being but
The horne,x and noise o'th'Monsters, wants not spirit
To say,x hee'l turne your Current in a ditch,
And make your Channell his?

6 If he have power,
Then vale your Ignorance: x If none, awake
Your dangerous Lenity: If you are Learn'd,
Be not as common Fooles; if you are not,
Let them have Cushions by you.

7 You are Plebeians,
If they be Senators: x and they are no lesse,
When+ both your voices blended, the great'st taste
Most pallates theirs.

8 They choose their Magistrate,
And such a one as he, who puts his Shall,
His popular Shall, against a graver Bench
[Then] ever frown'd in Greece.

{ctd. over}

[3] Ff = 'Ignorance', some modern texts = 'impotence'

10 By Jove himself*,
It makes the Δconsuls base; and my Δsoul* aches*
To know, when two Δauthorities are up,
Neither Δsupreme*, Δhow soon* Δconfusion
May enter 'twixt the gap of Δboth, and take
The one by th'other.

---

11 What may be sworn* by, both Δdivine and Δhuman*,
Seal* what I end withal*!
12 This double worship,
[Where one] part do's disdain* with cause, the other
Insult without all reason; where Δgentry, Δtitle, wisdom*,
Cannot conclude but by the yea and no
Of general* Δignorance - it must omit
Real* Δnecessities, and give way the while
To unstable Δslightness*.
13 Purpose so barr'd, it follows*
Nothing is done to purpose.
14 Therefore beseech you,
You that will be less* fearful* [than] discreet;
That love the Δfundamental* part of Δstate
More [than]you doubt the change on't; Δthat prefer*
A Δnoble Δlife, before a Δlong, and Δwish
To jump* a Δbody with a dangerous Δphysic*
That's sure of death without it - at once pluck* out
The Δmultitudinous Δtongue; let them not lick*
The sweet which is their poison*.
15 Your dishonor
Mangles true judgment*, and bereaves the Δstate
Of that Δintegrity which should become't*;
Not having the power to do the good it would,
For th'ill which doth control't*.

---

16 What should the people do with these bald Δtribunes?
On whom depending, their obedience fails*
To'th'greater Δbench. †
17 In a Δrebellion,
When what's not meet, but what must be, was Δlaw,
Then were they chosen; in a better hour*,
Let what is meet be said* it must be meet,
And throw their power i'th'dust.

• having thoroughly trashed the choice of Sicinius as the Commoners' representative and the danger that he represents to the seemingly uncaring/unaware nobles, Coriolanus becomes passionate as he turns to both the insult to the Consular post to which he has just been appointed and the 'Confusion' that it is inevitably going to create (8/5, F #9), with his opinions again driven home by the surround phrase that opens the sentence

" . By Jove himselfe,/It makes the Consuls base ; "

the phrase heightened even more by being set with the first of two emotional semicolons in the sentence

• in moving to take an oath to validate all that he has said, he becomes very emotional (2/4, F #10)

• though his ensuing attack on the danger of two opposing factions with equal powers ('This double worship') begins quite carefully (0/1, F #11's first two lines), his concern that the 'Gentry' will have to give way becomes passionate (5/4, F #11's last four lines), which in turn leads to a hushed statement of what this will lead to, the short almost unembellished

" . Purpose so barr'd, it followes,/Nothing is done to purpose . "

• beseeching those who 'love the Fundamentall part of State' to be 'lesse fearefull' begins emotionally (2/3, F #13's first three lines) but the intellectual appeal to their nobility (5/3, F #13's next three lines) doesn't last long, for the appeal to pull out the 'Multitudinous Tongue' (i.e. the tribunes Brutus and Sicinius) becomes passionate once more (2/3, F #13's last two lines)

• his statement that the Nobles' 'dishonor . . . bereaves the State' remains passionate (2/2, F #14) – and the point that their current inaction has made them essentially politically impotent is heightened via the sentence's final surround phrase

" : Not having the power to do the good it would/For th'ill which doth controul't . "

• amazingly after all the passion, in finishing Coriolanus attempts to re-establish a strong sense of self-control for a moment: but while his suggestion that if the people continue to owe obedience to the Tribunes, they may fail in their duty 'To'th'greater Bench' may seem logical (3/1), the lesson he draws from this is extraordinarily dangerous . . .

• . . . for the careful and unemotional drive of the surround phrase

: When what's not meet, but what must be, was Law,/Then were they chosen : "

leads to the appalling fascist suggestion that, since it is now a 'better houre', the only course of action to defang the Tribunes is for the Nobles to arbitrarily 'throw their power i'th'dust' (i.e the Tribunes' power) . . .

• . . . with his intellect being subsumed by emotion (0/2) as he finishes the last two and half lines of the long convoluted speech

9 By Jove himselfe,
It makes the Consuls base; and my Soule akes
To know, when two Authorities are up,
Neither Supreame; How soone Confusion
May enter 'twixt the gap of Both, and take
The one by th'other.

---

10 What may be sworne by, both Divine and Humane,
Seale what I end withall. +
11 This double worship,
[Whereon] part do's disdaine with cause, the other
Insult without all reason:$_x$ where Gentry, Title, wisedom+
Cannot conclude,$_x$ but by the yea and no
Of generall Ignorance, it must omit
Reall Necessities, and give way the while
To unstable Slightnesse.
12 Purpose so barr'd, it followes,$_x$
Nothing is done to purpose.
13 Therefore beseech you,
You that will be lesse fearefull,$_x$ [then] discreet,+
That love the Fundamentall part of State
More [then] you doubt the change on't: $_x$ That preferre
A Noble life, before a Long, and Wish,$_x$
To jumpe a Body with a dangerous Physicke,$_x$
That's sure of death without it: $_x$ at once plucke out
The Multitudinous Tongue,+ let them not licke
The sweet which is their poyson.
14 Your dishonor
Mangles true judgement, and bereaves the State
Of that Integrity which should becom't: $_x$
Not having the power to do the good it would+
For th'ill which doth controul't.

---

15 What should the people do with these bald Tribunes?
On whom depending, their obedience failes
To'th'greater Bench, in a Rebellion: $_x$
When what's not meet, but what must be, was Law,
Then were they chosen: $_x$ in a better houre,
Let what is meet,$_x$ be saide it must be meet,
And throw their power i'th'dust.

13/ Coriolanus **Let them pull all about mine eares, present me** between 3.2.1 - 16

Background: The public anti-Coriolanus sentiment has grown so strong that his supporters know the only way to try to save him is by suggesting that they will bring him to the 'Market place' 'in peace,/Where he shall answer by a lawfull forme/(In peace) to his utmost perill'. There's just one snag, Coriolanus is not prepared to back down or apologise from the sentiments earlier expressed (speech #12 immediately above).

Style: group address and one on one in front of the group

Where: Volumnia's home **To Whom:** the nobles supporting Coriolanus, and then his mother Volumnia

# of Lines: 15 **Probable Timing: 0.50 minutes**

Modern Text

13/ Coriolanus

1 Let them pull all about mine ears*, present me
Death on the Δwheel*, or at wild* Δhorses' heels,
Or pile ten hills* on the Tarpeian Δrock*,
That the precipitation might down* stretch
Below the beam* of sight, yet will I still
Be thus to them.

2 I muse my Δmother
Does* not approve me further, who was wont
To call them Δwoollen* Δvassals*, things created
To buy and sell with Δgroats, to show bare heads
In Δcongregations to yawn*, be still, and wonder,
When one but of my ordinance stood up
To speak* of Δpeace or Δwar*.

3 I talk* of you :
Why did you wish me milder?

4 Would you have me
False to my Δnature?

5 Rather say, I play
The man I am.

The entrenchment of Coriolanus' belief that he will never change is underscored by the monosyllabic, emotional (created by the only semicolon), single surround phrase in the speech, vowing that no matter what the common people do to him ' ; yet will I still /Be thus to them . ' and by the final monosyllabic sentence refusing to be false to his nature, 'Rather say, I play/The man I am.'

- thus as he starts to make his I-am-I declaration, it's not surprising that the speech opens emotionally (4/8, F #1's opening four and half lines)

- fascinatingly, before his mother's entry, his expression that he is wondering why 'my Mother/Do's not approve me further' in his scornful put-down of the common people when so often she has done the same is fully released, and quite intellectually-passionate (7/4, in the six lines of F #2)

- yet when Volumnia enters he clamps down on both his sentence lengths (now becoming very short) and releases, which he almost completely eradicates

- F #3 is emotional only in the first phrase when he admits 'I talke of you' (0/1), and then he becomes completely quiet in the unembellished asking why she wishes him milder (a far cry from the passion of the previous sentence when she wasn't present)

- his F #4 challenge as to whether she wishes him to be false is only slightly more released, this time intellectually (1/0)

- and his final self-definition is quietly defiant, as unembellished as the self definition which ended F #1 before his mother joined them

First Folio

13/ Coriolanus

1 Let them pull all about mine eares, present me
Death on the Wheele, or at wilde Horses heeles,
Or pile ten hilles on the Tarpeian Rocke,
That the precipitation might downe stretch
Below the beame of sight; x yet will I still
Be thus to them.

2 I muse my Mother
Do's not approve me further, who was wont
To call them Wollen Vassailes, things created
To buy and sell with Groats, to shew bare heads
In Congregations, x to yawne, be still, and wonder,
When one but of my ordinance stood up
To speake of Peace, x or Warre.

3 I talke of you,+
Why did you wish me milder?

4 Would you have me
False to my Nature?

5 Rather say, I play
The man I am.

14/ Volumnia **Pray be counsail'd ;/I have a heart as little apt as yours,** between 3.2.28 - 57
15/ Volumnia **Now it lyes you on to speake to th'people :** 3.2.52 - 69
16/ Volumnia **I pry thee now, my Sonne,/Goe to them, with this Bonnet in thy hand,** between 3.2.73 - 92

Background: It was his mother's ambition which caused Coriolanus to seek political office, and now Volumnia attempts to counsel her son as to what he must do to retrieve the situation. Speech #14 is her immediate response to his opening outburst of speech #13, a theoretical approach based on practical necessity; speech #15, starting with the same sentence as ends the previous speech, shows the wide gulf between her expectations and his, for to her the end justifies the means, lying and all; and speech #16 is her attempt to coach him in the exact method of self-abasing behaviours he needs must go through if he is to succeed.

Style: one on one address in front of a small group

Where: Volumnia's home **To Whom:** Coriolanus, in front of his supporting nobles, and Menenius and the more cautious Senators

Speech 14: # of Lines: 21 **Probable Timing: 1.10 minutes**
Speech 15: # of Lines: 18 **Probable Timing: 0.55 minutes**
Speech 16: # of Lines: 18 **Probable Timing: 0.55 minutes**

Modern Text

14/ Volumnia

1 Pray be counsell'd* . †

2 I have a heart as little apt as yours,
But yet a brain*, that leads* my use of △anger
To better vantage.

---

3 You are too absolute,
Though therein you can never be too △noble,
But when extremities speak*.

4 I have heard you say
Honor and △policy, like unsever'd △friends,
I'th'△war* do grow together ; grant that, and tell me
In △peace what each of them by th'other lose*
That they combine not there?

---

5 If it be △honor in your △wars* to seem*
The same you are not, which, for your best ends,
You adopt your policy: △how is it less* or worse
That it shall hold △companionship in △peace
With △honor*, as in △war*, since that to both
It stands in like request.

---

6 Now it lies* [on you] to speak*
To th'people; not by your own* instruction,
Nor by th'matter which your heart prompts you,
But with such words that are but roted*
In your △tongue, though but △bastards and △syllables
Of no allowance, to your bosom's* truth.

The drive of her speech can be boiled down to the contents of two of the surround phrases, the opening emotional (ending with the semicolon)
" . Pray be counsail'd ; "
and the overview of what she wants him to do
" . Now it lyes on you to speake to th'people : "

• her unembellished lines, presumably deliberately quiet to ensure that he listens to what she has to say, add flesh to the argument,

a/ first talking of their own superiority to the common folk
"I have a heart as little apt as yours,"
"You are too absolute,/Though therein you can never be too . . ."
the quiet broken by the key word separating them from the hoi polloi, 'Noble'

b/ then reminding him that he has already practiced deceit in war, seeming to be
"The same you are not, which for your best ends/You adopt your policy : "

c/ and that the current situation demands he do the same now as a civilian
"Not by your owne instruction, nor by'th'matter/Which your heart prompts you,"

• with so much at stake, it's not surprising that her preamble though careful is somewhat emotional (2/4, the first five and half lines, F #1-2)

• in starting her argument proper, using his own words against him ('Honor and Policy' serve well in war), she is staunchly intellectual (5/2)

• turning to a concept that embraces them all, 'Honor', she passionately asks why he cannot follow the same philosophy here (7/5, F #4), the capper being quietly driven home as an emotional and unembellished surround phrase
" ; since that to both/It stands in like request . "

• and in establishing the need for him to lie, and not to be disconcerted by it since the words would be 'but Bastards, and Syllables/Of no allowance' she moves toward emotion once more (F #5, 3/5) , though this may not be easy for her to put forward, for the middle of F #5's irregular four line structure (11/9/8/8 syllables as shaded) seems to suggest that Volumnia carefully gathers herself before beginning this very tricky stage of the argument to her recalcitrant son (for some reason the modern texts set a different awkwardness, as shown)

First Folio

14/ Volumnia

Pray be counsail'd;
I have a heart as little apt as yours,
But yet a braine, that leades my use of Anger
To better vantage.

---

2 You are too absolute,
Though therein you can never be too Noble,
But when extremities speake.

3 I have heard you say,x
Honor and Policy, like unsever'd Friends,
I'th'Warre do grow together: x Grant that, and tell me
In Peace,x what each of them by th'other loose,x
That they combine not there?

---

4 If it be Honor in your Warres, to seeme
The same you are not, which+ for your best ends+
You adopt your policy: How is it lesse or worse
That it shall hold Companionship in Peace
With Honour, as in Warre; x since that to both
It stands in like request.

---

5 Now it lyes [you on] to speake to th'people: x
Not by your owne instruction, nor by'th'matter
Which your heart prompts you, but with such words
That are but roated in your Tongue; x
Though but Bastards,x and Syllables
Of no allowance, to your bosomes truth.

Modern Text

15/ Volumnia

1 Now it lies* [on you] to speak*
To th'people; not by your own* instruction,
Nor by th'matter which your heart prompts you,
But with such words that are but roted*
In your Δtongue, though but Δbastards and Δsyllables
Of no allowance, to your bosom's* truth.

2 Now, this no more dishonors you at all
[Than] to take in a Δtown* with gentle words,
Which else would put you to your fortune and
The hazard of much blood.

3 I would dissemble with my Δnature where
My Δfortunes and my Δfriends at stake requir'd
I should do so in Δhonor.

4 I am in this
Your Δwife, your Δson*, Δthese Δsenators, the Δnobles;
And you will rather show* our general* Δlouts*
How you can frown*, [than] spend a fawn* upon 'em
For the inheritance of their loves and safeguard$_*$
Of what that want might ruin*.

Starting from just before where the previous speech ended, F's orthography shows that while Volumnia may have difficulty in opening, it seems she successfully manages to get back on intellectual track – only to lose control (whether deliberately or not) at the very last moment.

- establishing the need for him to lie, and not to be disconcerted by it since his words would be 'but Bastards, and Syllables of no allowance', she opens emotionally (F #1, 3/5), though this may not be easy for her to put forward, for
  - a/ the kernel of her argument is expressed as an opening surround phrase " . Now it lyes on you to speake to th'people : "
  - b/ the irregular four line structure in the middle of F #1 (11/9/8/8 syllables as shaded) seems to suggest that Volumnia is carefully gathering herself before beginning this very tricky stage of the argument, and . . .

- . . . F #2's unembellished lines (save for the one word 'Towne', which points to the military comparison with which she is trying to draw a parallel) show her trying to head off any suggestion from Coriolanus that her advice may be dishonourable
  "Now, this no more dishonors you at all,/Then to take in a Towne with gentle words,/Which else would put you to your fortune, and/The hazard of much blood . "

- having launched herself fully into attack-mode, her initial follow-up to the non-dishonourable argument (that she would do anything for Friends in the name of 'Honor') is totally intellectual (4/0, F #3) - as is the first line and half of F #4's claim (5/1) that in this she is speaking for all that should be dear to him ('Wife', Sonne', 'These Senators', 'Nobles')

- but then her control shatters for her emotion spills over as she accuses him of being unwilling to show the 'generall Lowts' anything other than a 'frowne', (1/5, F #4's last three and a half lines), though whether this is a deliberate ploy to shame him or a genuine loss of control is up to each actor to explore . . .

- . . . and the extra breath-thoughts that have been scattered throughout the speech (marked ,$_x$) suddenly gather together in this unexpected cluster of releases – though whether this is because she is trying to ensure every distasteful point is rammed home or is trying to prevent herself from losing control altogether is again up to each actor to explore

First Folio

15/ Volumnia

1 Now it lyes [you on] to speake to th'people: $_x$
Not by your owne instruction, nor by'th'matter
Which your heart prompts you, but with such words
That are but roated in your Tongue; $_x$
Though but Bastards,$_x$ and Syllables
Of no allowance, to your bosomes truth.

2 Now, this no more dishonors you at all,$_x$
[Then] to take in a Towne with gentle words,
Which else would put you to your fortune,$_x$ and
The hazard of much blood.

3 I would dissemble with my Nature,$_x$ where
My Fortunes and my Friends at stake,$_x$ requir'd
I should do so in Honor.

4 I am in this
Your Wife, your Sonne:$_x$ These Senators, the Nobles,+
And you,$_x$ will rather shew our generall Lowts,$_x$
How you can frowne, [then] spend a fawne upon 'em,$_x$
For the inheritance of their loves,$_x$ and safegard
Of what that want might ruine.

Modern Text

16/ Volumnia

1 I [prithee*] now, my △son*,
Go* to them, with this △bonnet in thy hand,
And thus far* having stretch'd it (here be with them),
Thy △knee bussing the stones (for in such business*
Action is eloquence, and the eyes of th'ignorant
More learned [than] the ears*), waving thy head,
Which often thus correcting thy stout heart,
Now humble as the ripest Mulberry
That will not hold the handling**:** or say to them,
Thou art their △soldier*, and being bred in broils*,
Hast not the soft way which, thou dost confess*,
Were fit for thee to use as they to claim*,
In asking their good loves, but thou wilt frame
Thyself*, forsooth, hereafter theirs, so far*,
As thou hast power and person**.**

2 Prithee* now,
Go*, and be rul'd **;** although I know thou hadst rather
Follow thine △enemy* in a fiery* gulf*
[Than] flatter him in a △bower**.**

This, the most onrushed of the three speeches is the least intellectual of her attempts at persuasion (7/15 overall).

- thus it's fascinating that, instead of reasoning with him, she now tries begging him ('I [prythee] now my Sonne,') and starts out passionately (3/3, F #1's first three and half lines) as she advises him about the general humbling demeanor he should adopt
- then the explanation as to why adopting the right physical presence is key is a very careful mixture of the unembellished ('Action is eloquence, and the eyes of th'ignorant /More learned . . .') and emotion (1/2, the five lines of F #2 between the two colons)
- in advising him what to say if he does have to talk, she becomes more emotional (1/6 the remaining six lines of F #1) now with virtually no unembellishment – perhaps she is worried that his mouth will run away with him yet again
- though verbally repeated in almost the same form as F #1's opening request (here 'Prythee now'), F #2's opening surround phrase quickly turns from plea to emotional command ('Goe, and be rul'd :', 0/1, F #2's second line)
- while the final sop to his dignity - that she understands how he would rather be doing anything else - is passionate (2/1, the last two lines of the speech)

First Folio

16/ Volumnia

1 I [pry thee] now, my Sonne,
Goe to them, with this Bonnet in thy hand,
And thus farre having stretcht it (here be with them)+
Thy Knee bussing the stones**:** x for in such businesse
Action is eloquence, and the eyes of th'ignorant
More learned [then] the eares,+ waving thy head,
Which often thus correcting thy stout heart,
Now humble as the ripest Mulberry,x
That will not hold the handling**:** or say to them,
Thou art their Souldier, and being bred in broyles,
Hast not the soft way,x which+ thou do'st confesse+
Were fit for thee to use,x as they to clayme,
In asking their good loves, but thou wilt frame
Thy selfe (xforsoothx) hereafter theirs+ so farre,
As thou hast power and person**.**

2 Prythee now,
Goe, and be rul'd**:** x although I know thou hadst rather
Follow thine Enemie in a fierie gulfe,x
[Then] flatter him in a Bower**.**

#'S 17 - 21: EXILE AND REVENGE

17/ Coriolanus — You common cry of Curs, whose breath I hate, — 3.3.118 - 135

Background: All the appeasing advice of speeches #14-16 above has gone for naught, for once in the market place Coriolanus' short temper has got the best of him again, and he has insulted both the people and the Tribunes yet again. Sicinius has therefore pronounced Coriolanus' exile, or worse ('In the name a'th'people,/And in the power of us the Tribunes, wee/(Ev'n from this instant) banish him our Citie/In perill of precipitation/From off the Rocke Tarpeian, never more/To enter our Rome gates./I'th'Peoples name,/I say it shall bee so). The following is Coriolanus' reply.

Style: public address

Where: the Market-place **To Whom:** all present, supporters and foes alike

# of Lines: 16 **Probable Timing:** 0.50 minutes

Modern Text

17/ Coriolanus

1 You common cry of Δcurs, whose breath I hate
As reek* a'th'rotten Δfens*, whose loves I prize
As the dead Δcarcasses* of unburied men
That do corrupt my Δair* - I banish you !
And here* remain* with your uncertainty*!

2 Let every feeble Δrumor shake your hearts !
Your Δenemies, with nodding of their Δplumes,
Fan you into despair* ! †

3 Have the power still
To banish your Δdefenders, till at length
Your ignorance (which finds* not till it feels*,
Making but reservation of yourselves,
Still your own* Δfoes) deliver you as most
Abated Δcaptives to some Δnation
That won* you without blows*! †

4 Despising,
For you, the Δcity,◊ thus I turn* my back*;
There is a world elsewhere.

Having been tricked into anger, far from abasing himself, Coriolanus' initiates an unrelenting passionate attack (14/14 overall), and though seemingly logical, F's orthography reveals two rather surprising moments at speech's end.

- the initial passionate attack (8/7, F #1 and the first two and a half lines of F #2, seven and a half lines in all) is heightened by four surround phrases
  " . You common cry of Curs, whose breath I hate, /As reeke a'th'rotten Fennes : . . . : I banish you, And heere remaine with your uncertaintie . /Let every feeble Rumor shake your hearts : /Your Enemies, with nodding of their Plumes/Fan you into dispaire : "

- and even when the drive of the surround phrases stops, the continuation of the onrushed F #2 condemning the Citizens to have all the 'power still/To banish your Defenders' so that these 'Curs' can become 'most abated Captives, to some Nation/That wonne you without blowes' still remains passionate (6/5, F #2's last seven lines)

- then according to F it seems that Coriolanus finally loses self-control, for, whereas most modern texts start their final sentence logically with the phrase 'despising/For you the City', relating it to how Coriolanus feels about them, F, ungrammatically in the opinion of most modern editors, sets the phrase at the end of the may-you-become-captives sequence, thus attaching it to whichever Nation captures them, suggesting that the captors will hate Rome because of the common folk that now dominate it

- this triggers an emotional start to his farewell, with F #3 being set as two emotional surround phrases
  " . Thus I turne my backe ; /There is a world elsewhere . "
  the emotion of the first phrase intensified by the releases (0/2)

- but, in a moment of supreme self-control, his very last words before leaving, 'There is a world elsewhere.', display enormous and perhaps surprising dignity, for they are completely unembellished

First Folio

17/ Coriolanus

1 You common cry of Curs, whose breath I hate,x
As reeke a'th'rotten Fenne: x whose Loves I prize,x
As the dead Carkasses of unburied men,x
That do corrupt my Ayre: I banish you,+
And heere remaine with your uncertaintie. +

2 Let every feeble Rumor shake your hearts: +
Your Enemies, with nodding of their Plumes+
Fan you into dispaire: + Have the power still
To banish your Defenders, till at length
Your ignorance (which findes not till it feeles,
Making but reservation of your selves,
Still your owne Foes) deliver you
As most abated Captives,x to some Nation
That wonne you without blowes,+ despising+
For you+ the City.

3 Thus I turne my backe;
There is a world elsewhere.

18/ Auffidius **Oh Martius, Martius ;** between 4.5.101 - 147

Background: Coriolanus, banished from Rome, has made his way to the home of his old adversary Auffidius, where he has made an honourable offer to a dishonourable man (see speech #9 above). The offer is simply, "use me" ('For I will fight/Against my Cankred Countrey, with the Spleene/Of all the under Fiends'), or "kill me" 'I also am/longer to live most wearie: and present/My throat to thee, and to thy ancient Malice: which not to cut would show thee but a Foole'. The following is Auffidius' reply, who, as it turns out, wants to do both.

Style: one on one address, perhaps in front of a third party

Where: presumably outside Auffidius' home (the courtyard perhaps) **To Whom:** Coriolanus, perhaps in front of the 2nd Servingman

# of Lines: 47 **Probable Timing: 2.15 minutes**

Modern Text

18/ Auffidius

1 O* Martius, Martius ! †
2 Each word thou hast spoke hath weeded from my heart
A root* of Δancient Δenvy.
3 If Jupiter
Should from yond cloud* speak* divine things,
And say "'Tis true", I'd* not believe* them more
[Than] thee, all-Δnoble Martius.
4 Let me twine
Mine arms* about that body, where against
My grained Δash an hundred times hath broke,
And scarr'd the Δmoon* with splinters. †
5 Here* I cleep
The Δanvil* of my Δsword, and do contest
As hotly, and as Δnobly with thy Δlove
As ever in Δambitious strength I did
Contend against thy Δvalor*.
6 Know thou first,
I lov'd the Δmaid I married; never man
Sigh'd truer breath; ◊ but that I see thee here*,
Thou Δnoble thing, more dances my rapt heart
[Than] when I first my wedded Δmistress* saw
Bestride my Δthreshold.
7 Why, thou Mars, I tell thee,
We have a Δpower on foot*; and I had purpose
Once more to hew thy Δtarget from thy Δbrawn*,
Or lose* mine Δarm* for't. †

The speech is one of the most clever pieces of extended deception and manipulation in the play – with, save for the first two sentences, Auffidius' emotions very rarely breaking through: instead the speech is orthographically full of intellect and quiet, the passion reserved for the military images which (presumably) he believes would capture Martius' interest.

- though Auffidius' opening welcome seems strongly intellectual, (7/2, F #1-2), it is in part composed of three emotional (semicoloned) surround phrases, suggesting hidden depths beneath, and the first two of F #1
  " . Oh Martius, Martius ; /Each word thou hast spoke, hath weeded from my heart/A roote of Ancient Envy . "
  are very surprising in view of his earlier vow to destroy Coriolanus by any means (speech # 9 above)

- while his request to embrace Coriolanus (or rather Martius as he insists on calling him) is passionate (2/2, F #3's first three lines) . . .

- as he does so, he becomes intellectual once more, both in
  a/ the public statement of offering him as intense a love as he one time offfered 'Ambitious strength' (6/3, F #3's last four lines)
  b/ the follow-up that he's as pleased to see Martius as he was the first night he saw his just wedded bride (4/1, F #4-5)

- in informing Martius of his and the Volscian intent to invade Italy and face him in combat once more, Auffidius opens very passionately (5/4 in just the first three lines of F #6), heightened by the speech's first logical surround phrase ' . Why, thou Mars I tell thee,/We have a Power on foote : '

- then, in a seeming side-bar, as Auffidius focuses on the previous encounters in which Martius defeated him 'twelve severall times', he becomes very emotional (3/9, F #6's last five and half lines)

- the somewhat surprising statement that they would fight Rome even if there were 'no other quarrell else' than Martius' banishment begins intellectually (3/1, the first three lines of F #7) . . .

First Folio

18/ Auffidius

1 Oh Martius, Martius; +
Each word thou hast spoke,$_x$ hath weeded from my heart
A roote of Ancient Envy.
2 If Jupiter
Should from yond clowd speake divine things,
And say 'tis true; $_x$ I'de not beleeve them more
[Then] thee+ all-Noble Martius.
3 Let me twine
Mine armes about that body, where against
My grained Ash an hundred times hath broke,
And scarr'd the Moone with splinters: heere I cleep
The Anvile of my Sword, and do contest
As hotly, and as Nobly with thy Love,$_x$
As ever in Ambitious strength,$_x$ I did
Contend against thy Valour.
4 Know thou first,
I lov'd the Maid I married: $_x$ never man
Sigh'd truer breath.
5 But that I see thee heere+
Thou Noble thing, more dances my rapt heart,$_x$
[Then] when I first my wedded Mistris saw
Bestride my Threshold.
6 Why, thou Mars+ I tell thee,
We have a Power on foote: $_x$ and I had purpose
Once more to hew thy Target from thy Brawne,
Or loose mine Arme for't: Thou hast beate mee out

8 Thou hast beat* me* out
Twelve several* times, and I have nightly since
Dreamt of encounters 'twixt thyself* and me;
We have been* down* together in my sleep*,
Unbuckling △helms*, fisting each other's △throat,
And wak'd half* dead with nothing.
9 Worthy Martius,
Had we no other quarrel* else to Rome but that
Thou art thence △banish'd, we would muster all
From twelve to seventy⁎, and pouring* △war*
Into the bowels of ungrateful* Rome,
Like a bold Flood o'er-beat* [4].
10 O*, come, go in,
And take our △friendly △senators by'th'hands,
Who now are here*, taking their leaves of me*,
Who am prepar'd against your △territories,
Though not for Rome itself*.

---

11 Therefore, most absolute △sir, if thou wilt have
The leading of thine own* △revenges, take
Th'one half* of my △commission, and set down* -
As best thou art experienc'd, since thou know'st
Thy △country's⁎ strength and weakness* -thine own ways⁎:
Whether to knock* against the △gates of Rome,
Or rudely visit them in parts remote,
To fright them, ere destroy.
12 But come in,
Let me commend thee first to those that shall
Say yea to thy desires.
13 A thousand welcomes! †
14 And more a △friend [than] ere an enemy⁎;
Yet, Martius, that was much.
15 Your hand; most welcome!

- . . . but then the idea of battle and entering Rome like a 'bold Flood' quickly becomes passionate (3/4, F #7's last two lines), as does the offer to come in and greet the Volscian Senators (4/4, F #8)

- the first part of the seemingly amazing generous offer of half Auffidius' commission if Martius 'wilt have/The leading of thine owne Revenges' is also passionate (3/3, F #9's first three lines)

- and the reason for the generosity becomes quickly apparent, for Auffidius makes it clear that in return they will want to know 'Thy Countries strength and weaknesse' - this being as equally passionate as the offer (lines five and six of F #9, 3/2)

- neatly interspersed are carefully unembellished pointers as to the purpose of the invasion
  "As best thou art experienc'd, since thou know'st"
  whether to attack Rome directly,
  "Or rudely visit them in parts remote,/To fright them, ere destroy."
  the quietness thus seems either intended to make it absolutely clear what knowledge is expected of Martius', or to not put him off by becoming over-excited

- and, surprisingly, this quietness continues – again perhaps Auffidius is attempting to ensure that he does not overwork his hand as he offers
  "But come in, /Let me commend thee first, to those that shall/Say yea to thy desires . A thousand welcomes,/ . . . / . Your hand : most welcome ."

- the only time he breaks this is in his F #11 reassurance that Martius is welcome as a 'Friend' (3/0), interesting in that it is carefully intellectual, as if he were still trying to ensure that his emotions don't break through

Twelve severall times, and I have nightly since
Dreamt of encounters 'twixt thy selfe and me: x
We have beene downe together in my sleepe,
Unbuckling Helmes, fisting each others Throat,
And wak'd halfe dead with nothing.
7 Worthy Martius,
Had we no other quarrell else to Rome, x but that
Thou art thence Banish'd, we would muster all
From twelve, x to seventie: x and powring Warre
Into the bowels of ungratefull Rome,
Like a bold Flood o're-beate.
8 Oh+ come, go in,
And take our Friendly Senators by'th'hands+
Who now are heere, taking their leaves of mee,
Who am prepar'd against your Territories,
Though not for Rome it selfe.

---

9 Therefore+ most absolute Sir, if thou wilt have
The leading of thine owne Revenges, take
Th'one halfe of my Commission, and set downe+
As best thou art experienc'd, since thou know'st
Thy Countries strength and weaknesse, thine own waies+
Whether to knocke against the Gates of Rome,
Or rudely visit them in parts remote,
To fright them, ere destroy.
10 But come in,
Let me commend thee first, x to those that shall
Say yea to thy desires.
11 A thousand welcomes,+
And more a Friend, x [then] ere an Enemie,+
Yet+ Martius+ that was much.
12 Your hand: x most welcome. +

[4] Ff = 'o're-beate', some modern texts = 'o're-bear't'

19/ 2nd Servingman **Wee shall have a stirring World againe :** between 4.5.218 - 229

Background: News of the unholy alliance between the Roman Coriolanus and the Volscian Auffidius (joined in the common end to destroy both Italy and Rome) spreads very quickly among Auffidius' closest servants.

Style: as part of a three handed scene

Where: in or just outside Auffidius' home **To Whom:** his fellow servants

# of Lines: 10 **Probable Timing: 0.35 minutes**

Modern Text

19/ 2nd Servingman

1 {ψ} {W}e* shall have a stirring $^{\Delta}$world again*. †

2 This peace is nothing but to rust $^{\Delta}$iron, increase* $^{\Delta}$tailors*, and breed $^{\Delta}$ballad-makers.

3 {ψ} Let me have $^{\Delta}$war*, say I, it exceeds peace as far* as day does$_{*}$ night; $^{\Delta}$it's sprightly, [waking], audible, and full of $^{\Delta}$vent.

4 Peace is a very $^{\Delta}$apoplexy, $^{\Delta}$lethargy$_{*}$, mull'd, deaf*, [sleepy], insensible, a getter of more bastard $^{\Delta}$children [than] war's* a destroyer of $^{\Delta}$men.

5 'Tis so, and as war's*, in some sort, may be said* to be a $^{\Delta}$ravisher, so it cannot be denied but peace is a great maker of $^{\Delta}$cuckolds.

Whether this servant is an ex-military man or merely a cheated husband, his views on peace and war are strongly expressed.

- the opening four consecutive surround phrases underscore the war-mongering nature of the servant, his passionate enthusiastic desire for 'a stirring World againe' being so expressed (6/6, F #1-2)
- his F #3 all encompassing dismissal of 'Peace' is initially intellectual (4/2)
- and, at least according to the orthography and repeated image of F #4, the peace's deleterious effect on sexual mores is what he dislikes most, for his final denunciation of peace 'as a great maker of Cuckolds' is passionate (2/2)

First Folio

19/ 2nd Servingman

1 {ψ} {W}ee shall have a stirring World againe: This peace is nothing,$_{x}$ but to rust Iron, encrease Taylors, and breed Ballad-makers.

2 {ψ} Let me have Warre, say I, it exceeds peace as farre as day do's night: $_{x}$ It's sprightly^{+} [walking], audible, and full of Vent.

3 Peace,$_{x}$ is a very Apoplexy, Lethargie, mull'd, deafe, [sleepe], insensible, a getter of more bastard Children,$_{x}$ [then] warres a destroyer of Men.

4 'Tis so, and as warres^{+} in some sort^{+} may be saide to be a Ravisher, so it cannot be denied,$_{x}$ but peace is a great maker of Cuckolds.

20/ Cominius **Oh you have made good worke.** between 4.6.80 - 99

Background: This is the general Cominius' first direct attack on the Tribunes as being directly responsible for the Coriolanus-Auffidius invading army which, as has been reported, 'Rages/Upon our Territories, and have already/O're-borne their way, consum'd with fire, and tooke/What lay before them', for 'All the Regions/Do smilingly Revolt, and who resists/Are mock'd for valiant Ignorance,/And perish constant Fooles'.

Style: small group address

Where: unspecified, perhaps a public street where Citizens, Messengers, the Tribunes, and Senators can encounter each other **To Whom:** Menenius, Sicinius, Brutus 'with others'

# of Lines: 18 **Probable Timing: 0.55 minutes**

Modern Text

20/ Cominius

1 O* you have made good work*!

2 You have holp to ravish your own* daughters, &
To melt the Δcity* Δleads* upon your pates,
To see your Δwives dishonor'd* to your Δnoses - ◊
Your Δtemples burned in their Δcement*, and
Your Δfranchises, whereon you stood, confin'd
Into an Δauger's* bore*.

3 {ψ} You have made fair* work* {.}

4 {ψ} Martius {is} join'd* [wi'th] [Volscians].

5 He is their Δgod ; he leads them like a thing
Made by some other Δdeity [than] Δnature,
That shapes man Δbetter ; and they follow him
Against us Δbrats, with no less* Δconfidence,
[Than]Δboys* pursuing Δsummer Δbutterflies,
Or Δbutchers killing Δflies*.

6 {ψ} You have made good work*,
You and your Δapron men; you,$_x$ that stood so much
Upon the voice* of occupation, and
The breath of Δgarlic*-eaters !

7 He'll* shake your Rome about your ears*.

F's orthography, especially the almost complete lack of surround phrases, reveals a character who, in speaking more from the point of immediate release rather than from a preplanned speech/report and despite being very shaken, tries to present the dreadful facts without his emotions getting in the way – and also shows where and why Cominius is not always successful.

- that the normally phlegmatic Cominius opens emotionally should be enough to shock his listeners (F #1, 0/2), and if it doesn't, the passion behind his subsequent images of sexual and property destruction that their actions may have caused should (F #2, 4/4)

- F's orthography then suggests that he manages to get control of himself, for F #3's detailed images of property destruction (places of religion and business) are spoken of more intellectually (4/2)

- the opening pattern of emotion leading to passion is seen once more, the repeated attack on the Tribunes for making 'faire worke' being emotional (0/2, F #4) and the announcement why, 'Martius is joyn'd with Volceans.', is passionate (2/2)

- then Cominius manages to regain intellectual control again, with the details of how Martius/Coriolanus is being followed as a 'God' and treating the Italian/Roman opposing forces as 'Butchers killing Flyes [5] ' spelled out in great detail without emotion getting in the way (11/3, F #6's five and half lines)

- with the third ironic accusation of the work the tribunes have wrought comes the only surround phrase in the speech

  " . You have made good worke/You and your Apron men : "

  and with this, passion returns once more (2/3, F #7)

- while the final short sentence prophecy of Rome's destruction turns to the emotional (1/2, F #8)

First Folio

20/ Cominius

1 Oh+ you have made good worke. +

2 You have holp to ravish your owne daughters, &
To melt the Citty Leades upon your pates,
To see your Wives dishonour'd to your Noses.

3 Your Temples burned in their Ciment, and
Your Franchises, whereon you stood, confin'd
Into an Augors boare.

4 {ψ} You have made faire worke {.}

5 {ψ} Martius {is} joyn'd [with] [Volceans].

6 He is their God,$_x$ he leads them like a thing
Made by some other Deity [then] Nature,
That shapes man Better :$_x$ and they follow him
Against us Brats, with no lesse Confidence,
[Then] Boyes pursuing Summer Butter-flies,
Or Butchers killing Flyes.

7 {ψ} You have made good worke,
You and your Apron men :$_x$ you, that stood so much
Upon the voyce of occupation, and
The breath of Garlicke-eaters. +

8 Hee'l shake your Rome about your eares.

---

[5] Ff = 'Flyes': many commentators, cogently arguing that Compositor B repeated the word from the end of the previous line, offer 'sheep' and 'pigs' as viable alternatives

21/ Cominius **He would not seeme to know me.** between 5.1.8 - 74

Background: The Roman citizens are taking no responsibility for Coriolanus' exile, laying the blame firmly on the Tribunes. In desperation, Cominius, Martius/Coriolanus' one-time senior general, has been sent to plead with Coriolanus to spare Rome. The following is his report of what (didn't) happen.

Style: small group address

Where: unspecified, perhaps a council chamber **To Whom:** Menenius, Sicinius, Brutus 'with others'

# of Lines: 28 **Probable Timing: 1.30 minutes**

Modern Text

21/ Cominius

1 He would not seem* to know me.

2 Yet one time he did call me by my name. †

3 I urg'd our old acquaintance, and the drops
That we have bled together.

4 Coriolanus
He would not answer too; Δforbade, all Δnames;
He was a kind* of Δnothing, Δtitleless*,
Till he had forg'd himself* a name a'th'fire
Of burning Rome.

5 I minded him, how Δroyal* 'twas to pardon
When it was less* expected.

6 He replied*,
It was a bare petition of a Δstate
To one whom they had punish'd.

7 I offered to awaken his regard
For's private Δfriends.

8 His answer to me was,
He could not stay to pick* them, in a pile
Of noisome* musty Δchaff*.

9 He said 'twas folly
For one poor* grain* or two, to leave unburnt
And still to nose th'offense*.

10 I tell you, he does sit in Δgold, his eye
Red as 'twould burn* Rome; and his Δinjury
The [jailer] to his pity*.

11 I kneel'd before him;
'Twas very faintly he said "Rise"; dismiss'd, me
Thus with his speechless* hand.

12 What he would do

F's orthography reveals some very surprising moments where Cominius seems so shocked by his (lack of ?) reception and subsequent words from Coriolanus that he can hardly give voice to what happened.

- the speech opens very carefully (0/1, the first four and half lines)

- but a very unusual F setting, three consecutive unembellished surround phrases (from the top of F #2 to the opening of F #3) underscore Cominius' shock of rejection
  " . Yet one time he did call me by my name : /I urg'd our old acquaintance, and the drops/That we have bled together. Coriolanus/He would not answer too : "
- which leads to a intellectual flurry (5/3, F #3's last three lines) as he describes Coriolanus refusing to answer to any title 'Till he had forg'd himselfe a name a'th'fire/ Of burning Rome'

- Coriolanus' refusal to pardon the 'State' is reported passionately (2/3, F #4-5), while his refusal to spare any former private friends, regarding them as 'one poore graine or two' unfortunately swamped in a pile 'Of noysome musty Chaffe', is not surprisingly reported emotionally (2/5, F #6-8)

- then comes a sequence of six consecutive passionate surround phrases driving home what did occur (5/4, F #9 to the opening of F #11)
  " . I tell you, he doe's sit in Gold, his eye/Red as 'twould burne Rome : and his Injury/The Gaoler to his pitty. I kneel'd before him, /'Twas very faintly he said Rise : dismist me/Thus with his speechlesse hand. What he would do/He sent in writing after me : what he would not, Bound with an Oath to yeeld to his conditions : "
  the firmness of Coriolanus' decision, '.What he would do/He sent in writing after me :', heightened by also being unembellished

- thus Cominius now suggests that the only hope left for Rome is a plea from Coriolanus' mother Volumnia, and does so very passionately (4/6, in just two and half lines between F #11's last two colons), with F's two irregular lines (13/13 syllables as shaded) only adding to his passion – however, most modern texts reset the two lines as three (6/10/10), creating a pause and then regularity instead of F's original almost uncontrolled flow

- and the final words of the speech are a suggestion that they all go and wish Volumnia success, and, not surprisingly, the wish is emphasised by being set as yet another (slightly emotional, 0/1) surround phrase
  " : therefore let's hence,/And with our faire intreaties hast them on. "

First Folio

21/ Cominius

1 He would not seeme to know me.

2 Yet one time he did call me by my name:
I urg'd our old acquaintance, and the drops
That we have bled together.

3 Coriolanus
He would not answer too: x Forbad all Names,+
He was a kinde of Nothing, Titlelesse,
Till he had forg'd himselfe a name a'th'fire
Of burning Rome.

4 I minded him, how Royall 'twas to pardon
When it was lesse expected.

5 He replyed+
It was a bare petition of a State
To one whom they had punish'd.

6 I offered to awaken his regard
For's private Friends.

7 His answer to me was+
He could not stay to picke them, in a pile
Of noysome musty Chaffe.

8 He said, x 'twas folly
For one poore graine or two, to leave unburnt
And still to nose th'offence.

9 I tell you, he doe's sit in Gold, his eye
Red as 'twould burne Rome: x and his Injury
The [Gaoler] to his pitty.

10 I kneel'd before him,+
'Twas very faintly he said Rise: x dismist me
Thus with his speechlesse hand.

11 What he would do

He sent in writing after me; what he would not,
Bound with an △oath to yield* to [no] conditions;
So that all hope is vain*,
Unless* his △noble △mother and his △wife,
Who, as I hear*, mean* to solicit* him
For mercy to his △country*. †
13 Therefore let's hence,
And with our fair* △entreaties hast them on.

He sent in writing after me: $_x$ what he would not,
Bound with an Oath to yeeld to [his] conditions: $_x$
So that all hope is vaine, unlesse his Noble Mother, $_x$
And his Wife, who ($_x$as I heare$_x$) meane to solicite him
For mercy to his Countrey: therefore let's hence,
And with our faire intreaties hast them on.

#'S 22 - 25: THE FINAL TRAGEDY

22/ Auffidius **All places yeelds to him ere he sits downe,** 4.7.28 - 57

Background: Though the invasion of Italy is proceeding well (see the background to speech #20 above), Auffidius still intends to pull Coriolanus down when the time is right.

Style: as part of a two-handed scene

Where: the Volscian camp near Rome **To Whom:** Auffidius' Lieutenant

N.B. the speech is more of a construct than most, in that it is a combination of two speeches in the same short scene, sentences #2-4 from the first speech, sentences #1, 5-6 from the second

# of Lines: 30 **Probable Timing: 1.30 minutes**

Modern Text

22/ Auffidius

1 All places yields* to him ere he sits down*,
And the △nobility of Rome are his. †
2 The △senators and △patricians love him too;
The △tribunes are no △soldiers, and their people
Will be as rash in the repeal*, as hasty
To expel* him thence.
3 I think* he'll* be to Rome
As is the [△osprey] to the △fish, who takes it
By △sovereignty of △nature.
4 First, he was
A △noble servant to them, but he could not
Carry his △honors even*. †
5 Whether [t'was] △pride,
Which out of daily* △fortune ever taints
The happy man; whether [defect] of judgment*,

There seems to be a see-saw struggle between Auffidius' intellect, so good in analysing situations, and his emotions, which seem to come to the fore whenever Coriolanus' successes are considered.

- thus, after the opening one line emotional outburst (0/2) as to the success Coriolanus has already had, Auffidius' ability to quickly analyse the situation can be seen both in F #1's terse surround phrases
  " : The Senators and Patricians love him too : /The Tribunes are no Soldiers : "
and in the strong intellect of lines two to four (6/0) that accompanies it
- yet the realisation of what will probably happen, essentially further success for Coriolanus, is also emotional (0/2, F #1's last two and half lines)
- the realisation that Coriolanus will lead them all to victory does not lead to more emotion: the idea of his swallowing Rome as 'the Aspray to the Fish' is instead handled intellectually (5/2, F #2) – perhaps the soldier within Auffidius recognises the value in what should inevitably occur

First Folio

22/ Auffidius

1 All places yeelds to him ere he sits downe,
And the Nobility of Rome are his:
The Senators and Patricians love him too: $_x$
The Tribunes are no Soldiers: $_x$ and their people
Will be as rash in the repeale, as hasty
To expell him thence.
2 I thinke hee'l be to Rome
As is the [Aspray] to the Fish, who takes it
By Soveraignty of Nature.
3 First, he was
A Noble servant to them, but he could not
Carry his Honors eeven: whether ['was] Pride+
Which out of dayly Fortune ever taints
The happy man; whether [detect] of judgement,

{ctd. over}

To fail* in the disposing of those chances
Which he was △lord of; or whether △nature,
Not to be other [than] one thing, not moving*
From th'△casque* to th'△cushion, but commanding peace
Even with the same austerity and garb*
As he controll'd the war*; ◊ △but one of these
(As he hath spices of them all, not all,
For I dare so far* free him) made him fear'd,
So hated, and so banish'd; but he ha's a △merit
To choke* it in the utt'rance. †
6 So our [△virtues],
Lie in th'interpretation of the time,
And power, unto itself* most commendable,
Hath not a △tomb* so evident as a △chair*
T'extol* what it hath done.

7 One fire drives out one fire; one △nail*, one △nail*;
Rights by rights fouler, [6] strengths by strengths do fail*.

8 Come, let's away. †
9 When, Caius, Rome is thine,
Thou art poor'st of all; then shortly art thou mine.

• in analysing why, despite his 'Soveraignty of Nature', Coriolanus was forced to leave Rome, and therefore searching for a possible defect, Auffidius becomes passionate (8/6, F #3's first eight lines) until he realises that the defect was probably an inability to differentiate between the public behaviour best suited to peace and that suited to war – the realisation being completely emotional (0/2, F #3's last two lines)

• and this realisation brings him to a virtually unembellished section as he explores this potentially fatal flaw further (F #4's first three lines)
" . But one of these/(As he hath spices of them all) not all,/For I dare so farre free him, made him fear'd, /So hated, and so banish'd:"
unembellished save for the word 'farre' (a grudging acknowledgement that Coriolanus is not completely inept)

• which in turn leads to the shrewdly passionate surround phrase assessment (1/1) that Coriolanus' military success will usually lead people to excuse his less than gracious public behaviour, ' : but he ha's a Merit/To choake it in the utt'rance : '

• and this leads to a sudden frenzy of different releases
a/ the intellectual one and a half line recognition that they must bide their time in order to pull Coriolanus down (2/0)
b/ leading to F #4's final realisation that excessive praise (extolling) of whoever sits in the 'Chaire' will lead eventually to their downfall (2/4, F #4's emotional last three and half lines)
c/ which leads to a passionate maxim of three successive emotional surround phrases promising to outdo Coriolanus by any means possible (2/3, F #5)
d/ followed in turn by three more surround phrases, the last two again emotionally underpinned by the semicolon, intellectually vowing to take down Coriolanus but not until after he has taken Rome (2/0) – the intensity of the vow enhanced even further by the first and last surround phrases being quietly spoken without any embellishment

To faile in the disposing of those chances
Which he was Lord of: x or whether Nature,
Not to be other [then] one thing, not mooving
From th'Caske to th'Cushion: x but commanding peace
Even with the same austerity and garbe, x
As he controll'd the warre.
4 But one of these
(As he hath spices of them all) x not all,
For I dare so farre free him, + made him fear'd,
So hated, and so banish'd: x but he ha's a Merit
To choake it in the utt'rance: So our [Vertue],
Lie in th'interpretation of the time,
And power+ unto it selfe most commendable,
Hath not a Tombe so evident as a Chaire
T'extoll what it hath done.

5 One fire drives out one fire; one Naile, one Naile;
Rights by rights fouler, strengths by strengths do faile.

6 Come+ let's away: when+ Caius+ Rome is thine,
Thou art poor'st of all; then shortly art thou mine.

[6] Ff = 'fouler', some modern texts = 'falter' or 'founder'

23/ Volumnia **Oh no more, no more :/You have said you will not grant us any thing :** between 5.3.86 - 125

24/ Volumnia **Nay, go not from us thus :** 5.3.131 - 182

Background: Both Cominius (speech #21 above) and Menenius have failed to turn Coriolanus away from his intention to destroy Rome. As a final ploy his mother Volumnia (accompanied by his wife Virgilia, his young son, and the respected Roman matron Valeria) have come to beseech him to spare the city. Speech #23 stems from his firm opening 'Do not bid me/Dismisse my soldiers, or capitulate/Againe, with Romes Mechanickes'. Since Coriolanus does not answer speech #22, both Virgilia and his son openly defy him, leading him to attempt to leave with 'Not of a womans tendernesse to be,/Requires nor childe, nor womans face to see:/I have sate too long', triggering Volumnia's speech #24.

Style: one on one address in front of a small group of both Romans and Volscians

Where: the Volscian camp outside Rome **To Whom:** her son Coriolanus, in front of her fellow Romans Virgilia, Valeria and Coriolanus' young son and attendants; and the Volscian Auffidius

Speech 23: # of Lines: 38 **Probable Timing: 1.55 minutes**

Speech 24: # of Lines: 52 **Probable Timing: 2.40 minutes**

Modern Text

23/ Volumnia

1 O* no more, no more ! †

2 You have said you will not grant us any thing;
For we have nothing else to ask* but that
Which you deny already. †

3 Yet we will ask*,
That if you[7] fail* in our request, the blame
May hang upon your hardness*, therefore hear* us.

4 Should we be silent & not speak, our Δraiment
And state of Δbodies would bewray what life
We have led since thy Δexile.

5 Think* with thyself*
How more unfortunate [than] all living women
Are we come hither; since that thy sight, which should
Make our eyes* flow with joy, hearts* dance with comforts,
Constrains* them weep*, and shake with fear* & sorrow*,
Making the Δmother, wife, and Δchild* to see
The Δson*, the Δhusband, and the Δfather tearing
His Δcountry's* bowels out. †

6 And to poor* we
Thine enmities most capital*; Δthou barr'st us

Though often played as a fine example of controlled debate by a ruthless woman with a steel-trap mind, F's orthography reveals a woman fighting very hard to maintain self-control in an appallingly difficult situation, and often not succeeding.

- despite the fact that three determined surround phrases open the speech, this may not be the way she intended to handle the situation – for
  - a/ her short line (five syllables) start is a response to an unexpected overlylong line of denial from her son (at least seventeen syllables), the pause before she begins to speak suggesting that his outburst has taken her aback more than a little
  - b/ the few releases the surround phrases contain are emotional (0/2) and not intellectual
  - c/ F #1 is onrushed (most modern texts splits it into two)
- the emotion continues as she states that despite his denial, she/they will attempt to reason with him (0/4, F #1's last two and half lines)
- and then, if only momentarily, her intellect takes over as she suggests that their clothing and health would speak to their distress even if they were 'silent' (3/0, F #2)
- then, whether as an act of deliberate rhetoric or genuine emotional lack of control, the onrushed F #3 starts emotionally as she describes their dilemma in seeing him as their country's enemy (0/5, the first fourlines), and then she regains her reasoning to brilliantly play upon the familial impact of his actions ('Mother, wife and Childe' linked to

First Folio

23/ Volumnia

1 Oh no more, no more: +
You have said you will not grant us any thing: $_x$
For we have nothing else to aske,$_x$ but that
Which you deny already: yet we will aske,
That if you faile in our request, the blame
May hang upon your hardnesse, therefore heare us.

2 Should we be silent & not speak, our Raiment
And state of Bodies would bewray what life
We have led since thy Exile.

3 Thinke with thy selfe,$_x$
How more unfortunate [then] all living women
Are we come hither; since that thy sight, which should
Make our eies flow with joy, harts dance with comforts,
Constraines them weepe, and shake with feare & sorow,
Making the Mother, wife, and Childe to see,$_x$
The Sonne, the Husband, and the Father tearing
His Countries Bowels out; and to poore we
Thine enmities most capitall: $_x$ Thou barr'st us

{ctd. over}

[7] Ff's meaning makes sense, and single mindedly points to Coriolanus as the sole creator of the potential failure , via 'you'/'your': some modern texts alter Ff's 'you' to 'we'

Our prayers to the △gods, which is a comfort
That all but we enjoy.
7 For how can we,
Alas! how can we, for our △country pray,
Whereto we are bound, together with thy victory,
Whereto we are bound ? †
8 Alack*, or we must lose*
The △country*, our dear* △nurse, or else thy person,
Our comfort in the △country.
9 We must find*
An evident △calamity, though we had
Our wish, which side should win; ◊ for either thou
Must as a △foreign* △recreant be led
With △manacles through[8] our streets, or else
Triumphantly tread* on thy △country's* ruin*,
And bear* the △palm* for having bravely shed
Thy △wife and △children's blood. †
10 For myself*, △son*,
I purpose not to wait* on △fortune, till
These wars* determine. †
11 If I cannot persuade* thee
Rather to show* a △noble grace to both parts,
[Than] seek* the end of one, thou shalt no sooner
March to assault thy △country [than]to tread*
(Trust to't*, thou shalt not) on thy △mother's womb*
That brought thee to this world.

him not as a soldier but as 'Sonne, the Husband, and the Father'), (9/2, in four and half of F #3's final five and half lines) – though in the midst of the intellect comes an emotional (semicoloned) surround phrase (0/2)

" ; and to poore we/Thine enmities most capitall : "

underscoring yet again the personal stresses his family is undergoing

- now F's sentence structure shows a very aggressive, if not grammatical, stage in her argument, with the onrush of F #4 stressing the personal dilemma far more than the rational two sentences of mt. #7-8 and the short F #5 not only stressing the inevitable 'calamity' but also setting up the personal catastrophes that may follow in the onrushed F #6

- continuing the argument on the personal level ('how can we' pray for you or for our Country), F #4 starts with no fewer than five consecutive surround phrases, heightened even more by being unembellished save for the key word linking/separating their family, 'Country' – the calm suggesting either the importance of this moment to the logic of her reasoning or that she is trying very hard to maintain control

- in voicing the 'evident Calamity' of the loss of him or the Country her passions brush her intellect aside (5/4, the last two lines of F #4 and the first of F #5)

- then comes the speech's last quiet moment, the acknowledgement that they will lose out 'though we had/Our wish, which side should win.' - the bleak unembellished realisation heightened by being monosyllabic

- and her passions sweep in once more (14/13, F #6) as she paints the accurate, if melodramatic, images of the inevitable result for one or other of them (his defeat ensuring that he will 'as a Forraine Recreant be led/With Manacles through our streets'; his victory leading him to 'treade . . . on thy Mothers wombe') unless he 'shew a Noble grace to both parts'

Our prayers to the Gods, which is a comfort
That all but we enjoy.
4 For how can we? x
Alas! how can we, for our Country pray? x
Whereto we are bound, together with thy victory: x
Whereto we are bound: x Alacke, or we must loose
The Countrie+ our deere Nurse, or else thy person+
Our comfort in the Country.
5 We must finde
An evident Calamity, though we had
Our wish, which side should win.
6 For either thou
Must as a Forraine Recreant be led
With Manacles through our streets, or else
Triumphantly treade on thy Countries ruine,
And beare the Palme, x for having bravely shed
Thy Wife and Childrens blood: For my selfe, Sonne,
I purpose not to waite on Fortune, till
These warres determine: If I cannot perswade thee, x
Rather to shew a Noble grace to both parts,
[Then] seeke the end of one; x thou shalt no sooner
March to assault thy Country, x [then] to treade
(Trust too't, thou shalt not) on thy Mothers wombe
That brought thee to this world.

W [8] Ff = 'through', some modern texts = 'thorough', so as to establish a full ten syllable line

Modern Text

24/ Volumnia

1 Nay, go not from us thus. †
2 If it were so, that our request did tend
To save the Romans*, thereby to destroy
The [Volsces] whom you serve, you might condemn* us
As poisonous* of your Δhonor*.
3 No, our suit*
Is that you reconcile them: Δwhile the [Volsces]
May say, "This mercy we have show'd*," the Romans*,
"This we receiv'd"; and each in either side
Give the Δall-hail* to thee, and cry, "Be Δblest
For making up this peace!"
4 Thou know'st, great Δson*,
The end of Δwar's* uncertain*; but this certain*,
That, if thou conquer Rome, the benefit
Which thou shalt thereby reap*, is such a name
Whose repetition will be dogg'd with Δcurses;
Whose Δchronicle thus writ: "The man was Δnoble,
But with his last Δattempt he wip'd it out,
Destroy'd his Δcountry, and his name remains*
To th'ensuing Δage abhorr'd."
5 Speak* to me, Δson. †
6 Thou hast affected the [fine] strains* of Δhonor,
To imitate the graces of the Δgods: ◊
To tear* with Δthunder the wide Δcheeks* a'th'Δair*,
And yet to [charge] thy Δsulphur* with a Δbolt*
That should but rive an Δoak*.
7 Why dost not speak*?
8 Think'st thou it Δhonorable* for a Δnoble ° man
Still to remember wrongs?
9 Daughter, speak* you;
He cares not for your weeping.
10 Speak* thou, Δboy;
Perhaps thy childishness* will move him more
[Than] can our Δreasons.
11 There's no man in the world
More bound to's Δmother, yet here* he let's me prate
Like one i'th'Δstocks*.

F's orthography delineates amazing surges of control and passion, marking when Volumnia can still advance her argument and when her son's avowed silence finally gets to her – but even when she loses control, the smaller variations in F's releases still show her struggling to get him to agree as well as the costs the struggle has upon her.

- it seems that, Volumnia has regained some of her debating abilities at the last moment in the scene, for each of her first three sentences open with surround phrases pressing home the key points she wants to make
  " : Nay, go not from us thus : " (F #1)
  " : No, our suite/Is that you reconcile them : While the Volces/May say, this mercy we have shew'd : " (F #2)
  " . Thou know'st (great Sonne)/The end of Warres uncertaine : " (F #3)

- yet it seems that her inner self-control has not yet been established, for
  a/ her passionate disclaimer (3/4) that she is not aiming to save Rome by destroying the Volces (the end of F #1 and the first line of F #2) is followed by
  b/ an intellectual urging that the Volces can claim they have shown mercy (2/0, F #2's second surround phrase)
  c/ leading to passion as she appeals to his vanity in claiming both sides can say (as almost to a God?) 'All-haile to thee, and cry be Blest/ For making up this peace' (3/2, F #2's last three and a half lines)

- once the idea of uncertainty in war is stated very passionately via F #3's opening surround phrase (2/3), she very cleverly (and strongly intellectually, 8/3) suggests that there is one certainty - if he is victorious in destroying Italy, he will ensure that his once 'Noble' name will be 'abhorr'd'

- the onrushed F #4, with its opening surround phrase
  " . Speake to me Son : "
speaks volumes as to her growing sense of frustration/desperation, and now, for the rest of the speech, his lack of reply creates a huge change in her pattern of release, for . . .

- . . . the next twenty-eight and a half lines (the twelve sentences F #4-15), save for two moments - F #8 and F #12 - release nothing but passion (30/28)

- the first moment where this pattern breaks comes with the extra drive of the surround phrase urging of Coriolanus' wife to speak (F #8)
  " . Daughter, speake you : /He cares not for your weeping . "
with emotions lightly dominating the first phrase (0/1) - and (despairing? encouraging?) unembellished quiet underscoring the second – both perhaps suggesting that Volumnia momentarily does not know how to proceed

First Folio

24/ Volumnia

1 Nay, go not from us thus:
If it were so, that our request did tend
To save the Romanes, thereby to destroy
The [Volces] whom you serve, you might condemne us
As poysonous of your Honour.
2 No, our suite
Is that you reconcile them: While the [Volces]
May say, this mercy we have shew'd: x the Romanes,
This we receiv'd, + and each in either side
Give the All-haile to thee, and cry+ be Blest
For making up this peace. +
3 Thou know'st (x great Sonne x)
The end of Warres uncertaine: x but this certaine,
That+ if thou conquer Rome, the benefit
Which thou shalt thereby reape, is such a name
Whose repetition will be dogg'd with Curses: x
Whose Chronicle thus writ, + The man was Noble,
But with his last Attempt, x he wip'd it out: x
Destroy'd his Country, and his name remaines
To th'insuing Age, x abhorr'd.
4 Speake to me + Son:
Thou hast affected the [five] straines of Honor,
To imitate the graces of the Gods.
5 To teare with Thunder the wide Cheekes a'th'Ayre,
And yet to [change] thy Sulphure with a Boult
That should but rive an Oake.
6 Why do'st not speake?
7 Think'st thou it Honourable for a Nobleman
Still to remember wrongs?
8 Daughter, speake you: x
He cares not for your weeping.
9 Speake thou+ Boy, +
Perhaps thy childishnesse will move him more
[Then] can our Reasons.
10 There's no man in the world
More bound to's Mother, yet heere he let's me prate
Like one i'th'Stockes.

{ctd. over}

12 - Thou hast never in thy life
Show'd* thy dear* △mother any courtesy*,
When she, poor* △hen, fond of no second brood,
Has cluck'd thee to the △wars*, and safely* home
Loaden* with △honor.
13 Say my △request's unjust,
And spurn* me back*; △but if it be not so
Thou art not honest, and the Gods will plague thee
That thou restrain'st from me the △duty which
To a △mother's part belongs.
14 He turns* away . †
15 Down, △ladies; let us shame him [ ] with our knees . †
16 To his surname Coriolanus longs more pride
[Than] pity* to our △prayers.
17 Down*! an end,
This is the last.
18 So, we will home to Rome,
And die* among our △neighbors*. †
19 - Nay, behold's! †
20 This △boy, that cannot tell what he would have,
But kneels* and holds up hands for fellowship,
Does reason our △petition with more strength
[Than] thou hast to deny't.
21 - Come, let us go. †
22 This △fellow had a [Volscian] to his △mother ;
His △Wife is in Corioles, and his[9] △child*
Like him by chance. †
23 - Yet give us our dispatch . †
24 I am hush'd until* our △city be afire,
And then I'll speak a little.

- the second break, a demand for some definitive response to the logic of her argument, once more starts with emotion within a surround phrase
  " . Say my Request's unjust,/And spurne me backe : "
  (F #12's first line, 1/20), which she then twists back to the two themes she has relentlessly pushed throughout - dishonesty/nobility, and his duty to her as a mother - but this time she does so intellectually (4/0), not all emotionally or passionately as elsewhere in the speech - an amazing twist given all she has gone through - and a great credit to her loyalty to Rome

- and when all else fails, her determination to win even by self-abasement is highlighted, for the commands from this proud woman for them all to kneel are all couched via surround phrases
  " . He turnes away : Down Ladies : " (F #13)
  " . Downe : " (F #14)
  and when this doesn't work, there comes the very bleak monosyllabic unembellished surround phrase that finishes F #14
  " : an end,/This is the last . "

- the statement of failure, couched in their returning to Rome to die (F #15) and rejection of him as a family member (F #16), whether genuine or a desperate last melodramatic rhetorical attempt to sway him, are again heightened by surround phrases
  " . So, we will home to Rome/And dye among our Neighbours : "
  " . Come, let us go : /This Fellow had a Volcean to his Mother : /His Wife is in Corioles, and his Childe/Like him by chance : yet give us our dispatch : /I am husht untill our City be afire, & then Ile speak a little "

- and whether through fatigue or just realising that there is little point in raising her voice, several of the key 'departure' surround phrases are unembellished too, 'So, we will home to Rome', and 'Come, let us go', & 'yet give us our dispatch'

- however, the more melodramatic of the surround phrases (their death (2/2) and Rome being 'ablaze' (1/1) are emotional, while the dismissal of Coriolanus as a family member is ferociously intellectual (6/1, lines two and three of F # 16)

- the last line of the speech is peculiarly set by F as an eighteen syllable line with no final punctuation: naturally most modern texts correct it as shown, though in human terms F's final outburst is very understandable

11 Thou hast never in thy life,ₓ
Shew'd thy deere Mother any curtesie,
When she (ₓpoore Henₓ) fond of no second brood,
Ha's cluck'd thee to the Warres:ₓ and safelie home
Loden with Honor.
12 Say my Request's unjust,
And spurne me backe:ₓ But,+ if it be not so
Thou art not honest, and the Gods will plague thee
That thou restrain'st from me the Duty,ₓ which
To a Mothers part belongs.
13 He turnes away:
Down+ Ladies:ₓ let us shame him [with him]with our knees
To his sur-name Coriolanus longs more pride
[Then] pitty to our Prayers.
14 Downe:+ an end,
This is the last.
15 So, we will home to Rome,
And dye among our Neighbours: Nay, behold's,+
This Boy+ that cannot tell what he would have,
But kneeles,ₓ and holds up hands for fellowship,
Doe's reason our Petition with more strength
[Then] thou hast to deny't.
16 Come, let us go:
This Fellow had a [Volcean] to his Mother:ₓ
His Wife is in Corioles, and his Childe
Like him by chance: yet give us our dispatch:
I am husht untill our City be afire, & then Ile speak a little

[9] Ff = 'his', some modern texts = 'this'

25/ Auffidius **Read it not Noble Lords,/But tell the Traitor** between 5.6.83 - 119

Background: Coriolanus, acceding to his mother's request, has turned back from Rome and returned to Volscia, knowing that this will probably lead to his death ('Oh my Mother, Mother: Oh!/You have won a happy victory to Rome./But for your Sonne, beleeve it: Oh beleeve it,/Most dangerously you have with him prevail'd,/If not most mortall to him'). Back in Volscia, as he presents to the leading Senators an extremely favourable peace proposal for the Volscians already agreed to by the Romans, Coriolanus' prescience proves correct.

Style: a general as well as one on one address

Where: at the Volscian Senate **To Whom:** the Volscian Senators and Coriolanus

# of Lines: 20 **Probable Timing: 1.00 minutes**

Modern Text

25/ Auffidius

1 Read it not, Δnoble Δlords,
But tell the Δtraitor {Martius}, in the highest degree
He hath abus'd your Δpowers.

2 [Ay*] Martius, Caius Martius ! †

3 Dost thou think*
I'll grace thee with that Δrobbery, thy stol'n* name
Coriolanus, in Corioles?

4 You Δlords and Δheads a'th'Δstate, perfidiously
He has betray'd your business*, and given up
For certain* drops of Δsalt, your Δcity Rome,
I say "your Δcity", to his Δwife and Δmother,
Breaking his Δoath and Δresolution like
A twist of rotten Δsilk*, never admitting
Counsel* a'th'war*; Δbut at his Δnurse's tears*
He whin'd and roar'd away your Δvictory,
That Δpages blush'd at him, and men of heart
Look'd wond'ring each at others.

5 Why, Δnoble Δlords,
Will you be put in mind* of his blind* Δfortune,
Which was your shame, by this unholy Δbraggart,
'Fore your own* eyes and ears*?

6 {ψ} Let him die* for't.

In a speech where Auffidius no longer has to hold back, it is remarkable how carefully he handles the destruction of Coriolanus, keeping his emotions in check virtually throughout – with the only break in his intellectual control coming at the very end of the speech.

- F #1's opening denial/challenge to Martius is totally intellectual (5/0)
- Auffidius' onrushed F #2 denial of even Martius' new-given name at the Volscian expense, 'Coriolanus' is also highly intellectual (7/2)
- and the intellet continues in the lengthy unflattering description to the Volscian Senators of how Martius gave away 'your City Rome' for 'certaine drops of Salt', i.e. 'his Nurses teares' (referring to his mother Volumnia) . . .
- . . . with the two F only colons adding extra strength to the key descriptions ': I say your City' and ': But at his Nurses teares', and thus heightening the overall intellect of the F #3 sentence (16/6)
- fascinatingly, the one clustered release of (emotional) long spellings seems to point to his own loss of face in being excluded from the campaign plans, for the release underscores Coriolanus' 'never admitting/Counsaile a'th'warre : ' (0/2)
- however, having made his report/attack, Auffidius' plea for action (F #4) is passionate (4/4)
- while the final plea for the long hoped for end to all his waiting and watching is the short emotional monosyllabic
"Let him dye for't." (F #5, 0/1)

First Folio

25/ Auffidius

1 Read it not+ Noble Lords,
But tell the Traitor {Martius}+ in the highest degree
He hath abus'd your Powers.

2 [I] Martius, Caius Martius : + Do'st thou thinke
Ile grace thee with that Robbery, thy stolne name
Coriolanus+ in Corioles?

3 You Lords and Heads a'th'State, perfidiously
He ha's betray'd your businesse, and given up
For certaine drops of Salt, your City Rome : x
I say your City+ to his Wife and Mother,
Breaking his Oath and Resolution,x like
A twist of rotten Silke, never admitting
Counsaile a'th'warre : x But at his Nurses teares
He whin'd and roar'd away your Victory,
That Pages blush'd at him, and men of heart
Look'd wond'ring each at others.

4 Why+ Noble Lords,
Will you be put in minde of his blinde Fortune,
Which was your shame, by this unholy Braggart?x
'Fore your owne eyes,x and eares?

5 {ψ} Let him dye for't.

SPEECHES IN ORDER		TIME	PAGE
ANTHONY & CLEOPATRA			
#'s 1 - 4: Anthony Seen In Decline			
1/ Cæsar	You may see Lepidus, and henceforth know,	1.30	357
2/ Ventidius	Oh Sillius, Sillius,/I have done enough.	1.10	359
3/ Charmian	L. Alexas, sweet Alexas, most anything Alexas,	0.35	360
4/ Soothsayer	Would I had never come from {Egypt}, nor you	0.45	361
#'s 5 - 12: Anthony And His Women, Cleopatra, Fulvia And Octavia			
5/ Enobarbus	When she first met Marke Anthony, she purst	2.30	362
6/ Enobarbus	{If} Fulvia is dead, . . .	0.35	364
7/ Agrippa	Give me leave Cæsar. /Thou hast a Sister . . .	1.00	365
8/ Cleopatra	Pray you stand farther from mee.	1.10	366
9/ Cleopatra	Oh Charmion: /Where think'st thou he is now?	0.50	367
10/ Anthony	Oh thou day o'th'world,/Chaine mine arm'd necke,	0.55	368
11/ Cleopatra	I dreampt there was an Emperor Anthony.	0.55	369
#'s 12 - 13: Politics			
12/ Anthony	Nay, nay Octavia, not onely that,	1.15	370
13/ Cæsar	Why have you stoln upon us thus? you come not	0.45	372
#'s 14 - 18: Anthony, Cleopatra & Cæsar			
14/ Anthony	I have offended Reputation,	1.15	373
15/ Thidias	So. Thus then thou most renown'd, Cæsar intreats,	0.55	375
16/ Anthony	You have beene a boggeler ever,	1.10	376
17/ Enobarbus	Yes like enough: hye battel'd Cæsar will	0.50	377
18/ Cæsar	He calles me Boy, and chides as he had power	0.50	378
#'s 19 - 21 : Downfall Of Enobarbus & Anthony			
19/ Enobarbus	Alexas did revolt, and went to Jewry on	0.55	379
20/ Anthony	Unarme Eros, the long dayes taske is done,	1.00	380
21/ Anthony	Since Cleopatra dyed,/I have liv'd in such dishonour,	1.30	381
#'s 22 - 26: Cleopatra's Downfall			
22/ Cleopatra	Noblest of men, woo't dye?	0.35	383
23/ Cleopatra	No more but in a Woman, and commanded	1.00	384
24/ Cleopatra	See Cæsar: Oh behold, /How pompe is followed:	1.30	385
25/ Cleopatra	He words me Gyrles, he words me,	1.15	386
26/ Cleopatra	Give me my Robe, put on my Crowne, I have	1.35	388

SPEECHES BY GENDER

		Speech #(s)
SPEECHES FOR WOMEN (9)		
Cleopatra	**Traditional:** middle aged woman, and older **Today:** early middle aged woman, and older	#8, #9, #11, #22, #23, #24, #25, #26
Charmian	**Traditional & Today:** younger woman	#3
SPEECHES FOR EITHER GENDER (2)		
Soothsayer	**Traditional:** male, any age **Today:** any age, any gender	#4
Agrippa	**Traditional:** male, any age **Today:** any age, any gender	#7
SPEECHES FOR MEN (15)		
Cæsar	**Traditional & Today:** male, from young to early middle age (always younger than Anthony)	#1, #13, #18
Anthony	**Traditional & Today:** middle-aged man and older	#10, #12, #14, #16, #20, #21
Enobarbus	**Traditional & Today:** older military male	#5, #6, #17, #19
Thidias	**Traditional & Today:** male, any age	#15
Ventidius	**Traditional & Today:** military man of any age	#2

ANTHONY & CLEOPATRA

#'S 1 - 4: ANTHONY SEEN IN DECLINE

1/ Cæsar **You may see Lepidus, and henceforth know,** between 1.4.1 - 33

Background: Of the three partners that ruled the Roman world, two, Cæsar and Anthony, have fallen out, with the third, Lepidus, who while supporting Cæsar is by no means as rabidly anti-Anthony as Cæsar is. The following is Cæsar's first speech and somewhat puritanical assessment of Anthony's current behaviour in Egypt.

Style: as part of a two handed scene in front of a small group

Where: Cæsar's palace **To Whom:** Lepidus, in front of their respective 'traines'

# of Lines: 27 **Probable Timing: 1.30 minutes**

Modern Text

1/ Cæsar

1 You may see, Lepidus, and henceforth know,
It is not Cæsar's △natural* vice to hate
[Our] great △competitor.
2 From Alexandria
This is the news*; △he fishes, drinks*, and wastes
The △lamps* of night in revel*; △is not more manlike
[Than] Cleopatra; nor the △queen* of Ptolomy
More △womanly [than] he; ◊ △hardly gave audience △or
[Vouchsafe'd] to think* he had △partners.
3 You shall find* there
A man, who is [th'abstract] of all faults,
That all men follow.

4 Let's grant* it is not
Amiss* to tumble on the bed of Ptolomy,
To give a △kingdom* for a △mirth, to sit
And keep the turn* of △tippling* with a △slave,
To reel* the streets at noon*, and stand the △buffet
With knaves that [smell*] of sweat*: △say this becomes* him
(As his composure must be rare indeed
Whom these things cannot blemish), yet must Anthony
No way excuse his [soils], when we do bear*
So great weight in his lightness*.
5 If he fill'd
His vacancy* with his △voluptuousness*,
Full surfeits* and the dryness* of his bones
Call on him for't.

Though initially appearing rational, Cæsar's orthography suggests that this is only skin-deep, and that his fixation on Anthony drives him at times into some most unexpected personal releases, for at least thirteen of the twenty-five and a half lines break the ten syllable metrical norm (though the poets would suggest many of these irregular lines could be eradicated by traditional poetic analyses).

- in the opening of his anti-Anthony diatribe, Cæsar seems to be well in control, the only slight blemish in the intellectual opening (4/1, F #1) being the extra breath-thought (marked ,x) before the idea of 'hate' is voiced vis-a-vis the man he cannot even name

- but the news of Anthony's revelling in Egypt seems to disturb him more than somewhat, for the whole of F #2 is composed of four surround phrases, with the revelry itself dismissed passionately (3/4)
  "From Alexandria/This is the newes : He fishes, drinkes, and wastes/The Lampes of night in revell : "
  the last two, the fact of Anthony's not living up to the ideals of a Roman Soldier, handled much more intellectually (5/1)
  ". . . : Is not more manlike/Then Cleopatra : nor the Queene of Ptolomy/More Womanly then he . "

- then comes F #3, which modern texts regard as ungrammatical in that it contains no active verb – but as a pointer to what has really upset Cæsar (being ignored) it has no parallel, especially in its quiet intellectualism (0/1), the calmest moment in the speech so far

- and the calm extends into the slightly emotional quiet dismissal of Anthony on all grounds (F #4, 0/1), especially when the final phrase "who is th'abstracts of all faults,/That all men follow." is unembellished (perhaps the assessment is so troublesome to him that it is difficult to say the words – especially when F's irregular (shaded) lines suggest it is F #4's concentration on Anthony's faults that breaks the metre the most (11/10/12), unlike the modern rewrite at the end of mt. #2 (12/2/9) which emphasises his lack of partnership

First Folio

1/ Cæsar

1 You may see+ Lepidus, and henceforth know,
It is not Cæsars Naturall vice,x to hate
[One] great Competitor.
2 From Alexandria
This is the newes :x He fishes, drinkes, and wastes
The Lampes of night in revell :x Is not more manlike
[Then] Cleopatra :x nor the Queene of Ptolomy
More Womanly [then] he.
3 Hardly gave audience
[Or vouchsafe] to thinke he had Partners.
4 You
Shall finde there a man, who is [th'abstracts] of all faults,
That all men follow.

5 Let's graunt it is not
Amisse to tumble on the bed of Ptolomy,
To give a Kingdome for a Mirth, to sit
And keep the turne of Tipling with a Slave,
To reele the streets at noone, and stand the Buffet
With knaves that [smels] of sweate : Say this becoms him
(As his composure must be rare indeed,
Whom these things cannot blemish)+ yet must Anthony
No way excuse his [foyles], when we do beare
So great waight in his lightnesse.
6 If he fill'd
His vacancie with his Voluptuousnesse,
Full surfets,x and the drinesse of his bones,x
Call on him for't.

{ctd. over}

6 But to confound such time
That drums* him from his sport and speaks* as loud*
As his own* △state and ours, 'tis to be chid -
As we rate △boys* who, being mature in knowledge,
Pawn* their experience to their present pleasure,
And so rebel* to judgment*.

• once Cæsar returns to Anthony's appetite for sex, drink, and food, he suddenly explodes in passion (8/7, F #5's first seven and a half lines), ending emotionally with the firm belief that Anthony cannot excuse himself for such 'lightnesse', especially when Cæsar and Lepidus have to pick up the slack (0/3, F #5's last one and half lines)

• and in a complex finale, Cæsar's suggestion that while Anthony's excesses would normally be sufficient rebuke (F #6), when both his and Cæsar's reputation are at stake, he must be 'chid : /As we rate Boyes' (F #7) is highly emotional (3/9 the last eight lines of the speech) – the F only colon after 'chid' adding extra emphasis to the rebuke Cæsar feels must be made, an emphasis most modern texts wipe out by setting no punctuation between the words

7 But to confound such time,$_x$
That drummes him from his sport,$_x$ and speakes as lowd
As his owne State,$_x$ and ours, 'tis to be chid : $_x$
As we rate Boyes,$_x$ who⁺ being mature in knowledge,
Pawne their experience to their present pleasure,
And so rebell to judgement.

2/ Ventidius **Oh Sillius, Sillius,/I have done enough.** between 3.1.11 - 37

Background: This is the only speaking scene for Ventidius, a loyal Anthony supporter and highly successful general. At the moment of his great triumph in the battle of Parthia, he explains his very pragmatic approach to the potential dangers of perceived success and over-achieving should he outshine Anthony's accomplishments and/or reputation.

Style: as part of a two handed scene in front of a celebratory group

Where: unspecified, but presumably the battlefield at Parthia **To Whom:** Sillius, one of his officers

# of Lines: 23 **Probable Timing: 1.10 minutes**

Modern Text

2/ Ventidius

1 O* [Silius], [Silius],
I have done enough; ◊ △a lower place, note well,
May make too great an act.
2 For learn* this, [Silius] :
Better to leave undone, [than] by our deed
Acquire too high a △fame when him we serves away.
3 Cæsar and Anthony have ever won*
More in their officer, [than] person.
4 Sossius
One of my place in Syria, his △lieutenant,
For quick* accumulation, of renown*,
Which he achiev'd* by th'minute, lost his favor*.
5 Who does i'th'△wars* more [than] his △captain* can
Becomes his △captain's* △captain*; and △ambition
(The △soldier's* virtue) rather makes choiceof loss*
[Than] gain* which darkens him.
6 I could do more to do [Antonius] good,
But 'twould offend him; ◊ △and in his offense
Should my performance perish.

7 I'll humbly signify, what in his name,
That magical* word of △war*, we have effected ;
How with his △banners, and his well paid ranks,
The ne'er-yet-beaten △horse of Parthia
We have jaded out o'th'△field.

8 On, there, pass* along!

In a speech that is often played calmly, as befits a man with such a shrewd political understanding, F's orthography reveals both the moment when Ventidius' passions get the better of him, and the superb way in which he is able to clamp down on his feelings and regain a public demeanor of apparent equilibrium.

- it seems that Ventidius needs to gain Sillius' attention, for there is a strong passionate demand in the opening three words (2/3), but then . . .

- . . . his urgent lesson in realpolitick is spoken very quietly - the theory
  " . I have done enough . /A lower place note well/May make too great an act . . .
  / Better to leave undone, then by our deed/Acquire too high a Fame,
  when him we serves away . "

  the unembellishment suggesting either great seriousness, as befits such a pragmatic philosophy, or great care to ensure that he is not overheard (with the one word breaking the calm, 'Fame', being the very thing that could bring great trouble to them both)

- the lesson to be drawn from Ventidius' calm statement of his belief-system is initially put forward with careful intellect (4/2, F #3-4), but the recollection of his military colleague Sossius who was once Anthony's lieutenant seems to cause him problems, for while he maintains his intellectual drive in introducing Sossius (3/0, F #5's first one and a half lines), the mention of his fate, falling out of favour because of his 'quicke accomulation of renowne,' swiftly turns completely emotional (0/4, F #5's last two lines)

- this suddenly leads to a very passionate and unexpected outburst (given the tenor of the speech so far) as he dwells on the dangers that 'Ambition', which should be 'The Souldiers vertue', more likely leading to his 'losse' (6/7 in just the three and a half lines of F #6)

- then, quite superbly, Ventidius manages to calm himself as he concisely extends the philosophy to the current situation, this unembellished, save for the name of Anthony, practical application (1/0, F #7-8) matching the quiet theoretical statements of F #2-3 above
  " I could do more . . . good/But 'twould offend him. And in his offence,/
  Should my performance perish."

- and so, not surprisingly, the explanation that follows of what Ventidius will do ('humbly signifie' what they have achieved in Anthony's name) is firmly intellectual (5/2, F #9)

First Folio

2/ Ventidius

1 Oh [Sillius], [Sillius],
I have done enough.
2 A lower place+ note well+
May make too great an act.
3 For learne this+ [Sillius],+
Better to leave undone, [then] by our deed
Acquire too high a Fame,x when him we serves away.
4 Cæsar and Anthony,x have ever wonne
More in their officer, [then] person.
5 Sossius
One of my place in Syria, his Lieutenant,
For quicke accomulation of renowne,
Which he atchiv'd by'th'minute, lost his favour.
6 Who does i'th'Warres more [then] his Captaine can,x
Becomes his Captaines Captaine :x and Ambition
(The Souldiers vertue) rather makes choise of losse
[Then] gaine,+ which darkens him.
7 I could do more to do [Anthonius] good,
But 'twould offend him.
8 And in his offence,x
Should my performance perish.

9 Ile humbly signifie what in his name,
That magicall word of Warre+ we have effected, +
How with his Banners, and his well paid ranks,
The nere-yet beaten Horse of Parthia,x
We have jaded out o'th'Field.

10 On+ there, passe along. +

3/ Charmian **L. Alexas, sweet Alexas, most anything Alexas,** between 1.2.1 - 27

Background: While the atmosphere in both Rome (speech #1 above) and on the battle-field in Anthony's name (speech #2) is naturally highly male, the atmosphere in Cleopatra's court in Egypt where Anthony is currently ensnared is very different. The following is the opening scene for one of Cleopatra's closest women, Charmian, and as such is both self-explanatory and highly indicative of the sensuality into which Anthony, according to Cæsar, is abandoning himself.

Style: as part of a two-handed scene in front of others

Where: in Cleopatra's court **To Whom:** the (male) Egyptian Alexas, in front of Charmian's fellow Egyptian gentlewoman Iras and the eunuch Mardian, with the Soothsayer and the Romans Enobarbus, Lamprius, Rannus, and Lucillius, close at hand

# of Lines: 10 **Probable Timing: 0.35 minutes**

Modern Text

3/ Charmian

1 [Lord] Alexas, sweet Alexas, most any ° thing Alexas,
almost most absolute Alexas, where's the Δsoothsayer
that you prais'd so to ° th'Δqueen*?
2 O* that I knew* this
Δhusband, which, you say, must [charge] his Δhorns* with
Δgarlands !
3 Good now, some excellent Δfortune ! †
4 Let me*
be married to three Δkings in a forenoon*, and Δwidow*
them all. †
5 Let me have a Δchild* at fifty, to whom Herod*
of Jewry may do Δhomage.
6 Find* me to marry* me with
Octavius Cæsar, and companion me with my Δmistress*.
7 {ψ} I love long life better [than] Δfigs.

F's orthography suggests that Charmian's switches in style reveal a character with a splendidly quicksilver mind, rich in imagination.

- Charmian's verbal seduction of Alexas opens very intellectually (6/1, F #1)
- which is quickly swallowed by her passion as she longs to know who is going to be the husband that she intends to cheat upon (F #2, 3/3)
- her profound wish for good luck is underscored by being set as the only surround phrase in the speech
  " . Good now some excellent Fortune : "
  and by her passions that continue to roll as she exuberantly dreams of being married to 'three Kings in a forenoone and Widdow them all' (3/3, the two lines between F #3's two colons)
- but as she extends her dreams to the possibly blasphemous wish of being worshiped by Kings for having a 'Childe at fifty' or of being married to Octavius Cæsar and thus becoming a 'companion . . . with my Mistris', she becomes as strongly intellectual as in the opening (9/3, in just four lines, the last line and a half of F #3 and all F #4-5)

First Folio

3/ Charmian

1 [L.] Alexas, sweet Alexas, most anything Alexas,
almost most absolute Alexas, where's the Soothsayer
that you prais'd so to'th'Queene?
2 Oh that I knewe this
Husband, which+ you say, must [change] his Hornes with
Garlands. +
3 Good now+ some excellent Fortune: + Let mee
be married to three Kings in a forenoone, and Widdow
them all: Let me have a Childe at fifty, to whom Herode
of Jewry may do Homage.
4 Finde me to marrie me with
Octavius Cæsar, and companion me with my Mistris.
5 {ψ} I love long life better [then] Figs.

4/ Soothsayer **Would I had never come from {Egypt}, nor you** between 2.3.12 - 31

Background: Anthony has been manipulated into returning to Rome for a conciliatory meeting with Cæsar and Lepidus to join forces to deal with the threat from Pompey. During the meeting Anthony has been further manipulated into agreeing to a marriage of convenience with Cæsar's sister Octavia as a symbol of reconciliation (see speech #7 below). The following is the Egyptian soothsayer's frank response to Anthony's blunt question, 'Now Sirrah: you do wish your selfe in Egypt?'.

Style: as part of a two handed scene

Where: unspecified, perhaps Cæsar's palace in Rome **To Whom:** Anthony

# of Lines: 14 **Probable Timing: 0.45 minutes**

Modern Text

4/ Soothsayer

1 Would I had never come from {Egypt}, nor you
thither .

2 But yet hie you to Egypt again*.

3 O [Antony], stay not by {Cæsar's} side . †

4 Thy Δdaemon, that thy spirit which keeps* thee, is
Noble, Δcourageous, high unmatchable,
Where Cæsar's is not; ◊ Δbut near* him, thy Δangel*
Becomes a [feared], as being o'er-powr'd : therefore
Make space enough between* you .

5 If thou dost play with him at any game,
Thou art sure to lose*; Δand of that Δnatural* luck*,
He beats thee 'gainst the odds*.

6 Thy Δlustre thickens
When he shines by . †

7 I say again*, thy spirit
Is all afraid* to govern* thee near* him ;
But he [away,] 'tis Δnoble.

Though often regarded as a mystical character in full control of himself and the situation, here F's orthography suggests that, while the Soothsayer may start out this way, what he fears will happen for Anthony causes him great personal problems (distress? sadness? fear?).

- the Soothsayer's regret at having left Egypt and at Anthony's ever finding his way there, as well as his warning for Anthony not to stay by Cæsar's side is strongly intellectual (7/2 in the five and half lines, F #1-3)
- and his concern for Anthony seems heightened by F's setting no punctuation at the end of the Soothsayer's first line of F #3, as if the urgency of what he needs to say forces him to rush on unchecked - most modern texts remove this concern by adding a grammatically correct period
- having voiced the concern that Anthony's noble spirit will inevitably be damaged since 'Cæsars is not', the Soothsayer not only becomes very emotional for the rest of the speech as he explains how Cæsar will win (5/12, eight lines F #4-6), but every single detail to the end of the speech is driven home by being set as eight consecutive surround phrases

First Folio

4/ Soothsayer

1 Would I had never come from {Egypt}, nor you
thither .

2 But yet hie you to Egypt againe.

3 O [Anthony])$_x$ stay not by {Cæsar's} side
Thy Daemon+ that thy spirit which keepes thee, is
Noble, Couragious, high unmatchable,
Where Cæsars is not.

4 But neere him, thy Angell
Becomes a [feare] : + as being o're-powr'd,+ therefore
Make space enough betweene you.

5 If thou dost play with him at any game,
Thou art sure to loose :$_x$ And of that Naturall lucke,
He beats thee 'gainst the oddes.

6 Thy Luster thickens,$_x$
When he shines by : I say againe, thy spirit
Is all affraid to governe thee neere him : $_x$
But he [alway]+ 'tis Noble.

#'s 5 - 11: ANTHONY AND HIS WOMEN, CLEOPATRA, FULVIA, & OCTAVIA

5/ Enobarbus **When she first met Marke Anthony, she purst** between 2.2.186 - 239

Background: Though now supporting different sides, once the formal military discussions between their leaders have concluded (see background to speech #4 above) the three friends, Enobarbus (essentially Anthony's confidant, military advisor, and generally his right hand man), Agrippa and Mecenas (both Cæsar loyalists), now alone, have a chance to catch up on the gossip, which of course centers on how Cleopatra managed to ensnare Anthony.

Style: as part of a three-handed scene

Where: Cæsar's palace **To Whom:** Agrippa and Mecenas

# of Lines: 50 **Probable Timing: 2.30 minutes**

Modern Text

5/ Enobarbus

1 When she first met Mark* [Antony], she purs'd
up his heart upon the River of [Cydnus].

2 I will tell you . †

3 The △barge she sat in, like a burnish'd △throne,
Burnt on the water. †

4 The △poop* was beaten △gold,
Purple the △sails*, and so perfumed that
The △winds* were love-△sick* ◊ △with them; the △oars*
were △silver,
Which to the tune of flutes kept stroke, and made
The water which they beat* to follow faster,
As amorous of their strokes.

5 For her own* person,
It beggard₊ all description₊: she did lie*
In her △pavilion* °-cloth of △gold, of △tissue -
O'er-picturing that Venus, where we see
The fancy₊ outwork* △nature.

6 On each side her
Stood pretty △dimpled △boys*, like smiling Cupids,
With divers-color'd* △fans*, whose wind* did seem*
To [glow] the delicate cheeks* which they did cool*,
And what they undid did.

7 Her [△gentlewomen], like the Nereides,
So many △mermaids*, tended her i'th'eyes,
And made their bends adornings.

8 At the △helm* ◊
A seeming △mermaid* steers*; △the △silken △tackle
Swell with the touches of those △flower-soft hands,
That yarely frame the office.

In describing the first meeting of Anthony and Cleopatra and the hold she has on him, though often in control, Enobarbus' orthography reveals his own emotional fascination with Cleopatra as well as his ability to be affected by women in general.

• establishing where the lovers met, and her throne-like barge, Enobarbus opens very factually (6/1, in the casualness of F #1's prose and the first two lines of F #2, now in verse)

• but the amount of wealth on display still seems burned in his memory – for the description of 'the Poope was beaten Gold' and 'the Owers were Silver' is very passionate (7/5, the last two lines of F #2 and the first of F #3) – the enormity of the memory heightened by

a/ a surround phrase, ' : the Poope was beaten Gold,/Purple the sailes : '

b/ the pause between the short line ending F #2 and the one opening F #3

c/ the fact that the description of the oars starts as a new sentence, thus emphasising his need for two separate sentences (F #2 and #3) to establish the amazing display

- most modern texts wipe out the last two hints by joining the two short lines as one and changing the period to major punctuation at a different point in the phrase, as shown

• and the sensuality of the moment is emphasised by the final emotional (semicoloned) surround phrase that ends F #3's description of the water responding ' ; As amorous of their strokes . '

• the description of Cleopatra and her self-presentation as 'O're-picturing Venus' is passionate (5/4, F #4), as is the description of the 'pretty Dimpled Boyes, like smiling Cupids' (4/3, F #5's first two lines) – while the recollection of the (sensual) effect of their fanning Cleopatra moves Enobarbus to emotion (0/4, F #5's last two lines)

• by leaving the entrancing subject of Cleopatra on the barge, Enobarbus seems to regain some element of self control for the description of her women as the 'Nereides' (sea-nymphs) or 'Mer-maides'; the tackle swelling like silk; and the perfume drifting from the barge, for all are described intellectually (11/5, F #6 - 9) – though the presence of all the women, especially in power positions, still seems to throw him, for the fact that

" At the Helme . A seeming Mer-maide steeres : "

is very strangely punctuated, the resilience of the memory very much intensified with the F only period after 'Helme' and the surround phrase that follows

First Folio

5/ Enobarbus

1 When she first met Marke [Anthony], she purst
up his heart upon the River of [Sidnis].

2 I will tell you,
The Barge she sat in, like a burnisht Throne+
Burnt on the water: the Poope was beaten Gold,
Purple the Sailes: x and so perfumed that
The Windes were Love-sicke. →

3 With them+ the Owers were Silver,
Which to the tune of flutes kept stroke, and made
The water which they beate, x to follow faster; x
As amorous of their strokes.

4 For her owne person,
It beggerd all discription,+ she did lye
In her Pavillion, cloth of Gold, of Tissue,
O're-picturing that Venus, x where we see
The fancie out-worke Nature.

5 On each side her, x
Stood pretty Dimpled Boyes, like smiling Cupids,
With divers coulour'd Fannes whose winde did seeme, x
To [glove] the delicate cheekes which they did coole,
And what they undid did.

6 Her [Gentlewoman], like the Nereides,
So many Mer-maides+ tended her i'th'eyes,
And made their bends adornings.

7 At the Helme.

8 A seeming Mer-maide steeres: x The Silken Tackle, x
Swell with the touches of those Flower-soft hands,
That yarely frame the office.

9 From the △barge
A strange invisible perfume hits the sense
Of the adjacent △wharfs*.
10 The △city* cast
Her people out upon her; and [Antony]
Enthron'd i'th'△market-place, did sit alone,
Whistling to th'air*, which, but for vacancy*,
Had gone to gaze on [Cleopatra] too,
And made a gap in △nature.

---

11 Upon her landing, [Antony] sent to her,
Invited her to △supper. †
12 She replied*
It should be better he became her guest;
Which she entreated. †
13 Our △courteous [Antony],
Whom ne'er the word of "No" woman heard* speak*,
Being barber'd ten times o'er, goes to the △feast,
And for his ordinary, pays* his heart,
For what his eyes eat* only*.

---

14 I saw her once
Hop forty △paces through the public* street*;
And having lost her breath, she spoke, and panted,
That she did make defect, perfection,
And, breathless*, pour* breath forth.

---

15 {ψ} {[Antony]} will not {leave her}:
Age cannot wither her, nor custom* stale
Her infinite variety. †
16 Other women cloy
The appetites they feed*, but she makes hungry
Where most she satisfies; ◊ △for [vilest*] things
Become themselves in her, that the holy △priests
Bless* her when she is △riggish.

• the memory of Anthony's sitting alone 'i'th'Market-place', the crowd abandoning him to see Cleopatra (F #10), her suggesting that he become her guest for 'Supper' rather than she his, and Anthony's making himself as presentable as possible by 'being barber'd 'ten times o're' (the first six lines of F #11) is also handled intellectually (10/4 in all)

• however, the seemingly innocent event from which all the subsequent love-related troubles sprang is expressed as a surround phrase

" : she replyed,/It should be better, he became her guest : "

as is the inevitable result

" ; And for his ordinary, paies his heart,/For what his eyes eate onely . "

this last description heightened by being emotional (0/2) and enhanced by being an emotional (semicoloned) surround phrase too

• in returning to the subject of Cleopatra, Enobarbus becomes emotional again as he describes her ability to 'make defect, perfection' (F #12, 1/4)

• the strength of his belief that

" . Anthony will not leave her : /Age cannot wither her, nor custome stale/ Her infinite variety : "

is underscored by being set as two surround phrases, intensified further by being spoken so quietly as to be almost unembellished (0/1, the first two and a half lines of F #13)

• and the reasons why (that Cleopatra is unique in making men want more of her no matter how much they have of her and that she is so entrancing that even the Priests bless her no matter what she does) are spoken of passionately (2/2, the last four lines of the speech)

9 From the Barge
A strange invisible perfume hits the sense
Of the adjacent Wharfes.
10 The Citty cast
Her people out upon her :ₓ and [Anthony]
Enthron'd i'th'Market-place, did sit alone,
Whistling to'th'ayre :ₓ which+ but for vacancie,
Had gone to gaze on [Cleopater] too,
And made a gap in Nature.

---

11 Upon her landing, [Anthony] sent to her,
Invited her to Supper: she replyed,ₓ
It should be better,ₓ he became her guest :ₓ
Which she entreated, our Courteous [Anthony],
Whom nere the word of no woman hard speake,
Being barber'd ten times o're, goes to the Feast; ₓ
And for his ordinary, paies his heart,
For what his eyes eate onely.

---

12 I saw her once
Hop forty Paces through the publicke streete,+
And having lost her breath, she spoke, and panted,
That she did make defect, perfection,
And+ breathlesse+ powre breath forth.

---

13 {ψ} {[Anthony]} will not {leave her }:
Age cannot wither her, nor custome stale
Her infinite variety: other women cloy
The appetites they feede, but she makes hungry,ₓ
Where most she satisfies.
14 For [vildest] things
Become themselves in her, that the holy Priests
Blesse her,ₓ when she is Riggish.

6/ Enobarbus **{If} Fulvia is dead,** 1.2.158 - 170

Background: Well before the manipulated marriage of convenience to Cæsar's sister Octavia, (see background to speech #4, and the text speech #7), news has arrived that Fulvia, Anthony's separated wife who, without Anthony's support or encouragement, has been waging war against Cæsar, has died. The following is Enobarbus' frank assessment suggesting the death is a blessing, for now there is nothing to hinder Anthony's relationship with Cleopatra.

Style: as part of a two-handed scene

Where: Cleopatra's palace **To Whom:** Anthony

# of Lines: 10 **Probable Timing: 0.35 minutes**

Modern Text

6/ Enobarbus {ψ}

1 {If} Fulvia is dead,
{,w}hy, sir, give the △gods a thankful* △sacrifice. †

2 When it pleaseth their △deities to take the wife of a man
from him, it shows* to man the △tailors of the earth; comforting therein, that when old* △robes are worn* out,
there are members to make new.

3 If there were no more
△women but Fulvia, then had you indeed* a cut, and the
case to be lamented. †

4 This grief* is crown'd with △conso-
lation: your old △smock* brings forth* a new △petticoat*,
and indeed the tears* live in an △onion that should water
this sorrow.

Whether this is intended to jolt Anthony out of his current somber mood, or as a tease, or a matter of plain-speaking to get Anthony to understand the realpolitick of the situation (after all, Anthony and Fulvia were separated and she had damaged his standing with Cæsar by waging war against him), given the circumstances, Enobarbus offers more releases than might be expected.

- the pragmatic (cynical?) opening surround phrase suggesting thanks
  " . If Fulvia is dead,/why sir, give the Gods a thankefull Sacrifice : "
  is intellectual (3/1)
- in suggesting that the Gods are merely giving Anthony a chance to get himself a new wife (if 'olde Robes are worne out, there are members to make new.') he turns passionate (3/3, F #1's last three and a half lines)
- and though his consolation/elaboration becomes more prosaic ('This greefe is crown'd with Consolation, your old Smocke brings foorth a new Petticoate'), Enobarbus still remains passionate (7/6, F #2)

First Folio

6/ Enobarbus {ψ}

1 {If} Fulvia is dead,
{,w}hy+ sir, give the Gods a thankefull Sacrifice:
when it pleaseth their Deities to take the wife of a man
from him, it shewes to man the Tailors of the earth:x comforting therein, that when olde Robes are worne out,
there are members to make new.

2 If there were no more
Women but Fulvia, then had you indeede a cut, and the
case to be lamented: This greefe is crown'd with Consolation,+ your old Smocke brings foorth a new Petticoate,
and indeed the teares live in an Onion,x that should water
this sorrow.

7/ Agrippa **Give me leave Cæsar./Thou hast a Sister by the Mothers side, admir'd** between 2.2.116 - 138

Background: Anthony has returned to Rome for a meeting with Cæsar and Lepidus to explore joining forces to deal with a possible invasion threat from Pompey. To ease the public appearance of tension between Cæsar and Anthony, and since Anthony is now a widower following Fulvia's death, Agrippa, one of Cæsar's shrewdest advisors, makes an audacious proposal - marriage between Anthony and Cæsar's sister Octavia (the 'Sister' referred to in the first line).

Style: as part of a general address, initially directed towards one man

Where: a meeting place in Rome, possibly the Senate **To Whom:** initially Cæsar, then Anthony in front of Lepidus, Enobarbus, Ventidius, and Mecenas

# of Lines: 20 **Probable Timing: 1.00 minutes**

Modern Text

7/ Agrippa

1 Give me leave, Cæsar - ◊

Thou hast a Δsister by the Δmother's side,
Admir'd Octavia. †

2 Great Mark [Antony]
Is now a widower *{,}

{Though} if [Cleopatra] heard {me, my}[reproof*]
Were well deserved of rashness*.

3 To hold you in perpetual* amity*,
To make your Δbrothers, and to knit your hearts
With an un-slipping knot, take [Antony]
Octavia to his wife; whose beauty claims*
No worse a husband [than] the best of men;
Whose Δvirtue, and whose general* graces speak*
That which none else can utter.

4 By this marriage,
All little Δjealousies*, which now seem* great,
And all great fears*, which now import their dangers,
Would then be nothing.

5 [Truths] would be tales,
Where now half* tales be [truths]. †

6 Her love to both,
Would each to other and all loves to both
Draw after her.

7 Pardon what I have spoke,
For 'tis a studied, not a present thought,
By duty ruminated.

That Agrippa realises he is making a very delicate proposal can be seen not just in F #2's surround phrases in which the names of Octavia and Anthony are first linked, but also in the onrush of both the sentences, and the fact that its two lines are longer than normal (12/13-15 syllables) – if indeed F #2 is verse, for it could well be set as prose as is F #3, which if it is, would suggest that Agrippa is being very careful not to draw too much attention to himself or his proposal just yet.

- the speech opens very factually, again suggesting that Agrippa is being careful not to let any emotion bleed into the suggestion (7/1, F's first four lines, save for the factually correct reminder to Anthony that he is a 'widdower'); it's only with the last line of F #2's sly dig about Cleopatra that the emotion intensifies (0/2)

- the actual proposal that 'to make you Brothers . . . , take Anthony,/Octavia to his wife' is slightly passionate (2/1), while the praise of both parties, enhanced by the opening surround phrase
" : whose beauty claimes/No worse a husband then the best of men : "
and the claim that the marriage would put to rest 'All little Jelousies . . . And all great feares' is emotional (1/5, F #3's last two and a half lines and all of F #4)

- then, for the last two sentences, Agrippa becomes very quiet once more (0/1, the five lines of F #5-6) and, since this starts before his F #6 apology for perhaps overstepping his authority, it could well be that so far the reactions of Anthony and Cæsar (and even Octavia should she be onstage too) to Agrippa's proposal are less than encouraging

- one note: the single release in the last five lines seems to be very important to Agrippa, for it underscores his reference to the hope that the 'halfe' truths which have plagued relationships between Octavius and Anthony to date will be eradicated by the suggested marriage - and the idea is even further heightened by being set as F #5's opening surround phrase
" . Truth's would be tales,/Where now halfe tales be truth's : "

First Folio

7/ Agrippa

1 Give me leave+ Cæsar.

2 Thou hast a Sister by the Mothers side, admir'd
Octavia: Great Mark [Anthony] is now a widdower {,}

{Though} if [Cleopater] heard {me, my}
[proofe] were well deserved of rashnesse.

3 To hold you in perpetuall amitie,
To make your Brothers, and to knit your hearts
With an un-slipping knot, take [Anthony],$_{x}$
Octavia to his wife:$_{x}$ whose beauty claimes
No worse a husband [then] the best of men:$_{x}$ whose
Vertue, and whose generall graces,$_{x}$ speake
That which none else can utter.

4 By this marriage,
All little Jelousies+ which now seeme great,
And all great feares, which now import their dangers,
Would then be nothing.

5 [Truth's] would be tales,
Where now halfe tales be [truth's]: her love to both,
Would each to other,$_{x}$ and all loves to both
Draw after her.

6 Pardon what I have spoke,
For 'tis a studied+ not a present thought,
By duty ruminated.

8/ Cleopatra **Pray you stand farther from mee.** between 1.3.18 - 39

Background: This is found in the first on-stage scene between Anthony and Cleopatra, with Cleopatra publicly chastising Anthony for being supposedly at his wife's Fulvia's beck and call, not yet knowing that Anthony has just received news of Fulvia's death. (For a happier moment between the two lovers, see speech #10 below.)

Style: one on one address in front of a larger group

Where: Cleopatra's palace **To Whom:** Anthony, in front of Charmian, Alexas, and Iras

# of Lines: 22 **Probable Timing: 1.10 minutes**

Modern Text

8/ Cleopatra

1 Pray you stand farther from me*.

2 I know by that same eye there's* some good news.
3 What says* the married woman, you may go*?
4 Would she had never given you leave to come !
5 Let her not say 'tis I that keep* you here*,
I have no power upon you ; Δhers you are.

6 O*, never was there Δqueen*
So mightily betrayed ! yet at the first
I saw the Δtreasons planted.

7 Why should I think you can be mine, & true
(Though you in swearing shake the Δthroned* Δgods)
Who have been false to Fulvia?
8 Riotous madness*,
To be entangled with those mouth-made vows*,
Which break* themselves in swearing !

9 Nay, pray you seek* no color* for your going,
But bid farewell, and go*. †
10 When you sued staying,
Then was the time for words; Δno going then ;
Eternity was in our Δlips* and Δeyes,
Bliss* in our brows* bent ; none our parts so poor*
But was a race of Δheaven.
11 They are so still,
Or thou, the greatest Δsoldier* of the world,
Art turn'd the greatest Δliar*.

Here Cleopatra displays an interesting tactic, speaking very quietly, and without embellishment, just before hitting out at Anthony - though eventually her emotions and passions break through.

- thus
  - a/ the calm F #2 leads to F #3's attack on him as a married man
  - b/ the calm of F #4 leads to F #5's attack on Fulvia and Anthony's relationship with her
  - c/ the calm first line of F #7 leads to the rest of the sentence's berating him for being false to his previous impassioned oaths
  - d/ and the unembellished two short lines of F #9 'When you sued staying,/Then was the time for words' moves directly into reminding (berating?) him for the words and looks that were then exchanged between Anthony and herself

- amidst the (tactical? attempting to control emotions?) calm, some of Cleopatra's emotions still leak through (F #1, 0/1; F #3, 0/2)

- then, as she claims that Anthony never really belonged to her and that she has been 'betrayed' as she knew would happen from the outset of their relationship, not only do her passions get the better of her (3/3, F #5-6), much of her attack is also driven home by the three surround phrases

  " : Hers you are . /Oh never was there Queene/So mightily betrayed : yet at the first/I saw the Treasons planted . "

- the only time she becomes intellectual is in her denial of the value of his oaths which, when made, threatened to 'shake the Throaned Gods' (3/1, F #7) – and the fact that the lines ending F #7 and the one starting F #8 are short (7 or 8/4 or 5 syllables) allows Cleopatra a significant pause before continuing – whether the pause is deliberately oratorical to allow the sting (playful or otherwise) of her public rebuke to strike home or because she is genuinely upset is up to each actor to explore (the choice is not available in most modern texts, which set the two lines as one)

- that this may be genuine might be seen in the emotion that then follows, both in
  - a/ her F #8 dismissal of her relationship with him as 'Riotous madnesse' and the F #9 opening surround phrase telling him to go (0/6)
  - b/ following the short unembellished lines (themselves suggestive of difficulty in continuing without a pause for self-control) the sudden enormously passionate explosion as she recalls their passionate words, looks, and kisses of love that are 'a race of Heaven', and should still be unless he has become 'the greatest Lyar' (6/6, the last five lines of the speech)

First Folio

8/ Cleopatra

1 Pray you stand farther from mee.

2 I know by that same eye ther's some good news.
3 What sayes the married woman + you may goe?
4 Would she had never given you leave to come. +
5 Let her not say 'tis I that keepe you heere,
I have no power upon you :x Hers you are.

6 Oh+ never was there Queene
So mightily betrayed : + yet at the first
I saw the Treasons planted.

7 Why should I think you can be mine, & true,x
(Though you in swearing shake the Throaned
Gods)
Who have been false to Fulvia? →
8 Riotous madnesse,
To be entangled with those mouth-made vowes,
Which breake themselves in swearing. +

9 Nay+ pray you seeke no colour for your going,
But bid farewell, and goe : →
When you sued staying,
Then was the time for words :x No going then,+
Eternity was in our Lippes,x and Eyes,
Blisse in our browes bent :x none our parts so
poore,x
But was a race of Heaven.
10 They are so still,
Or thou+ the greatest Souldier of the world,
Art turn'd the greatest Lyar.

9/ Cleopatra **Oh Charmion :/Where think'st thou he is now?** 1.5.18 - 34

Background: With Anthony's return to Rome for military discussions, Cleopatra cannot keep him out of her mind. The speech is self-explanatory, the second part added from a speech coming somewhat later in Anthony's absence.

Style: one on one address for the benefit of the rest of the small group

Where: Cleopatra's palace **To Whom:** Charmian, Iras, and the eunuch Mardian

# of Lines: 16 **Probable Timing: 0.50 minutes**

Modern Text

9/ Cleopatra

1 O* [Charmian] !
Where think'st thou he is now?
2 Stands he, or sits he?
3 Or does he walk*?
4 Or is he on his Δhorse?
5 O* happy horse, to bear* the weight of [Antony]!
6 Do bravely, Δhorse, for wot'st thou whom thou mov'st* ?
The demi°-Atlas of this Δearth, the Δarm*
And Δburgonet* of men.
7 He's* speaking now,
Or murmuring, "Where's my Δserpent of old [Nile] ?"
(For so he calls* me .)†
8 Now I feed* myself*
With most delicate poison*.
9 Think* on me,
That am with Phœbus' amorous pinches black*,
And wrinkled deep* in time ?
10 Broad-fronted Cæsar,
When thou wast here* above the ground, I was
A morsel* for a Δmonarch*; and great Pompey
Would stand and make his eyes grow in my brow;
There would [he anchor his] Δaspect, and die*
With looking on his life.

Fs orthography shows how Cleopatra's thoughts of love, coloured by her concerns about her age, her (fading?) beauty, and Anthony's absence run the complete gamut from the opening brief moments of intellect and quietness through to emotion and passion - and not always where expected.

- in addition to the words/images themselves, the intensity of Cleopatra's longing is underscored
  - a/ by the shortness of the first five sentences
  - b/ their mixture of unembellishment and passion (3/4)
  - c/ F #1's first words heightened by being set as two surround phrases
  - d/ apart from the name 'Charmion', the first four sentences are expressed as monosyllables
  - e/ F #5 ending with a very rare (for Elizabethan/Jacobean texts) exclamation mark (which emphasises then exclamation even more)
- her speaking to the horse she imagines carrying Anthony, ordering it to 'Do bravely' since it is carrying 'The demy-Atlas of this Earth', is strongly released (slightly more intellectually than emotionally, 5/3, F #6's three lines)
- her imagining Anthony murmuring his desire for her is passionate (2/1, the first two lines of F #7)
- then she becomes highly emotional as she realises, via the surround phrase " : Now I feede my selfe/With most delicate poyson . " calling out to him that he should think of her - even though she is not the - Elizabethan - concept of true beauty either in age or skin tone - (2/6, the last line of F #7 and all of F #8)
- and perhaps stimulated by these thoughts of love she recalls how she was worthily the focus of attention with her previous great partners, Cæsar and Pompey (F #9), and not surprisingly she becomes passionate once more (4/4)

First Folio

9/ Cleopatra

1 Oh [Charmion] : +
Where think'st thou he is now?
2 Stands he, or sits he?
3 Or does he walke?
4 Or is he on his Horse?
5 Oh happy horse+ to beare the weight of [Anthony]!
6 Do bravely+ Horse, for wot'st thou whom thou moov'st,+
The demy Atlas of this Earth, the Arme
And Burganet of men.
7 Hee's speaking now,
Or murmuring, where's my Serpent of old [Nyle],+
(For so he cals me:) Now I feede my selfe
With most delicate poyson.
8 Thinke on me+
That am with Phœbus amorous pinches blacke,
And wrinkled deepe in time. +
9 Broad-fronted Cæsar,
When thou was't heere above the ground, I was
A morsell for a Monarke: x and great Pompey
Would stand and make his eyes grow in my brow,+
There would [be anchor this] Aspect, and dye
With looking on his life.

10/ Anthony **Oh thou day o'th'world,/Chaine mine arm'd necke, leape thou, Attyre and all** between 4.7.13 - 39

Background: The following shows the lovers' relationship in all its glory, despite the desperate circumstances. With Pompey murdered by his own man the coalition between Anthony and Cæsar has fallen apart (at Cæsar's instigation) as has the marriage of convenience between Anthony and Octavia. Now, despite an almost continual losing series of skirmishes; betrayed by the flight of the Egyptian navy and beset by desertions, including that of Enobarbus'; Anthony has finally won a battle and presents Scarrus, to whom much of the credit for victory belongs, for Cleopatra's praise.

Style: as part of a four-handed scene

Where: Cleopatra's palace **To Whom:** Cleopatra in front of Scarrus and Eros

# of Lines: 18 **Probable Timing: 0.55 minutes**

Modern Text

10/ Anthony

1 O* thou day o'th'world,
Chain* mine arm'd neck*, leap* thou, △attire* and all,
Through proof* of △harness* to my heart, and there
Ride on the pants triumphing !

2 [My] △nightingale,
We have beat* them to their △beds.
3 What, △girl*, though grey
Do something* mingle with our younger* brown, yet ha' we
A △brain* that nourishes our △nerves, and can
Get goal* for goal* of youth.

4 Give me thy hand . †
5 Through Alexandria make a jolly △march,
Bear* our hack'd △targets, like the men that owe them.
6 Had our great △palace* the capacity
To △camp* this host*, we all would sup together,
And drink* △carouses* to the next day's* △fate,
Which promises △royal* peril*.
7 Trumpeters*,
With brazen din* blast you the △city's* ear*,
Make mingle with our rattling* △taborines*,
That heaven and earth may strike their sounds together,
Applauding our approach.

That this is just one long stream of consciousness rather than a preplanned speech can be seen in the fact that, most unusual for any Shakespearean speech, it contains no heavy punctuation and thus no surround phrases.

- save for the very last wonderfully unembellished phrase in which he invites Cleopatra to become as one with his heart, Anthony's opening F #1 rush of adulation/fulsome praise of her is highly emotional (2/7)

- not surprisingly, the announcement that their forces have defeated Cæsar's (F #2-3) is passionate (5/5), the victory's enormity heightened by the short pauses offered by the three short lines (7/4/7 syllables, ending F #1 and forming all of F #2), each allowing tiny hesitations for the news to be delivered and/or to sink in and/or for Cleopatra to do as he suggested and jump into his arms

- then his enthusiasm begins to build,
  a/ while the initial suggestion that they march through Alexandria in celebration is intellectual (F #4, 3/1)
  b/ the wish that immediately follows, that the 'Pallace' were big enough for all the forces to feast and drink together, moves toward emotion (F #5, 5/8)
  c/ and the order for the 'Trumpetters' to give sign of their success to the city at large is emotional (2/5, F #6's first two and half lines)

- but, very surprisingly, the last two lines of the speech supposedly capping the whole speech
  "That heaven and earth may strike their sounds together,/ Applauding our approach."
  are completely unembellished, which perhaps suggests that the enormity of what has occurred has just struck home and that this is a moment of almost religious thanks (or that Cleopatra is proving too heavy for him and he can hardly talk!)

First Folio

10/ Anthony

1 Oh thou day o'th'world,
Chaine mine arm'd necke, leape thou, Attyre and all+
Through proofe of Harnesse to my heart, and there
Ride on the pants triumphing. +

2 [Mine] Nightingale,
We have beate them to their Beds. →
3 What+ Gyrle, though gray
Do somthing mingle with our yonger brown, yet ha we
A Braine that nourishes our Nerves, and can
Get gole for gole of youth.

4 Give me thy hand,
Through Alexandria make a jolly March,
Beare our hackt Targets, like the men that owe them.
5 Had our great Pallace the capacity
To Campe this hoast, we all would sup together,
And drinke Carowses to the next dayes Fate+
Which promises Royall perill.
6 Trumpetters+
With brazen dinne blast you the Citties eare,
Make mingle with our ratling Tabourines,
That heaven and earth may strike their sounds together,
Applauding our approach.

11/ Cleopatra **I dreampt there was an Emperor Anthony.** between 5.2.76 - 94

Background: Conclusively beaten by Cæsar's forces, in part thanks to a second naval desertion by the Cleopatra-led Egyptian fleet, and lied to (at Cleopatra's insistence) and therefore believing that Cleopatra is dead, Anthony clumsily committed suicide and died a painful death. Despite Cæsar's promises of friendship and respect, Cleopatra's private quarters have been invaded by Roman forces, and she and her women are now essentially (well-treated) prisoners. Dolabella, one of Cæsar's loyal supporters, one of many that Cleopatra was advised by the dying Anthony not to trust[1], has just joined her, and she has essentially refused to acknowledge his opening greetings, challenging him instead with the rather oblique 'You laugh when Boyes or Women tell their Dreames,/Is't not your tricke?'

Style: as part of a five-handed scene, initially directed to one man

Where: private quarters in Cleopatra's palace **To Whom:** Dolabella, in front of Charmian, Iras, and the eunuch Mardian

# of Lines: 18 **Probable Timing: 0.55 minutes**

Modern Text

11/ Cleopatra

1 I dreamt* there was an Emperor [Antony].
2 O* such another sleep*, that I might see
But such another man !
3 His face was as the Δheav'ns, and therein stuck*
A Δsun* and Δmoon*, which kept their course, & lighted
The little ΔO, th'earth.
4 His legs* bestrid the Δocean, his rear'd arm*
Crested the world, Δhis voice* was propertied
As all the tuned Δspheres, and that to Δfriends;
But when he meant to quail* and shake the Δorb*,
He was as rattling⁎ Δthunder.
5 For his Δbounty,
There was no winter in't; ◊ an [autumn t'was]
That grew the more by reaping. †
6 His delights
Were Δdolphin-like, they show'd* his back* above
The Δelement they liv'd in. †
7 In his Δlivery
Walk'd Δcrowns* and Δcrownets; Δrealms & Δislands were
As plates dropp'd⁎ from his pocket.
8 Thinke you there was or might be such a man
As this I dreamt* of?

F #7's final emotional orthography (0/2) as she asks Dolabella whether such a man as she has extolled could exist is most surprising, and this is the crux of the speech – for if she is in control throughout, it could be a direct challenge to Dolabella to deny it if he dare, but if she has lost self-control, it could be that she is seeking help in deciding whether she has 'dreampt' all this, or not.

- the first thoughts of her now dead Anthony are passionate (5/6, the first four lines of the speech), the first two sentences, attesting that will be no-one like him again, heightened by being short
- F #3's hyperbole that the 'Sunne and Moone' were embodied in him 'which kept their course, & lighted/The little o'th'earth' finishes without embellishment, suggesting that the magnificence of her dream and the memories so triggered have quietened her down completely
- then in her F #4 painting of him as a super-being her passions flow back in (6/5), heightened by the two surround phrases
  ". His legges bestrid the Ocean, his rear'd arme/Crested the world : His voyce was propertied/As all the tuned Spheres, and that to Friends : "
- as she turns from his physical attributes to his generosity and influence on those around him (F #5-6), though the hyperbole continues, she moves from passion to strong intellect in just six lines (11/2), as if these were more substantial memories (based on fact perhaps?)
- though most modern texts regard F #5 as ungrammatical and add it to the information that follows, F Cleopatra's singling out of Anthony's 'Bounty' being so generous that it never ceased as a separate sentence points to just how fundamental a memory this is for her to cling to
- and the fact that F #6 is expressed as both onrushed and set as four consecutive surround phrases shows how deeply these memories are etched (and perhaps just how much need she has of them at this moment)

First Folio

11/ Cleopatra

1 I dreampt there was an Emperor [Anthony].
2 Oh such another sleepe, that I might see
But such another man. +
3 His face was as the Heav'ns, and therein stucke
A Sunne and Moone, which kept their course, & lighted
The little o+'th'earth.
4 His legges bestrid the Ocean, his rear'd arme
Crested the world :ₓ His voyce was propertied
As all the tuned Spheres, and that to Friends : ₓ
But when he meant to quaile,ₓ and shake the Orbe,
He was as ratling Thunder.
5 For his Bounty,
There was no winter in't.
6 An [Anthony it was],ₓ
That grew the more by reaping : His delights
Were Dolphin-like, they shew'd his backe above
The Element they liv'd in : In his Livery
Walk'd Crownes and Crownets : Realms & Islands were
As plates dropt from his pocket.
7 Thinke you there was,ₓ or might be such a man
As this I dreampt of?

---

[1] as it turns out, Dolabella can be trusted, while the one person Anthony suggests she can trust, Proculeius, proves as double-faced as the rest of Cæsar's entourage

#'s 12 - 13: Politics

12/ Anthony **Nay, nay Octavia, not onely that,** between 3.4.1 - 38

Background: Despite the marriage of convenience between Anthony and Octavia supposedly cementing the new-alliance between Cæsar and Anthony, distrust is still rampant between the two men. Here Anthony explains his side of the disagreement .

Style: as part of a two-handed scene

To Whom: Octavia **Where:** unspecified, but presumably Anthony's private chambers in (as some modern texts suggest) Athens

# of Lines: 24 **Probable Timing: 1.15 minutes**

Modern Text

12/ Anthony

1 Nay, nay, Octavia, not only* that -
That were excusable, that, and thousands more
Of semblable import - but he hath wag'd
New Δwars* 'gainst Pompey; ◊ Δmade his will, and read it,
To public* ear*;
Spoke scantly of me ; when perforce he could not
But pay me terms* of Δhonor*, cold and sickly
He vented [them,] most narrow measure lent me ;
When the best hint was given him, he not [took't],
Or did it from his teeth.

2 Gentle Octavia,
Let your best love draw to that point which seeks
Best to preserve it . †
3 If I lose* mine Δhonor*,
I lose* myself*; better I were not yours
[Than yours] so branchless*.
4 But as you requested,
Yourself* shall go between's . †
5 The mean* time, Δlady,
I'll raise the preparation of a Δwar*
Shall stain* your Δbrother . †

With all of his vocal releases elsewhere, the unembellished phrases within the first twelve lines of this speech assume prime significance, for they point to matters which are so disturbing to him and his thought processes (see footnote #2) that he becomes uncharacteristically quiet.

- even from the outset it seems that Anthony has been holding himself back until now
  " That were excusable, that and thousands more/Of semblable import,"
  for now, as affects Anthony himself, Octavius has
  "Made his will and read it,/ . . . spoke scantly of me,"
  and, when by rights Octavius should have payed him 'tearmes of Honour',
  " : cold and sickly/He vented [then] most narrow measure : lent me,/ When the best hint was given him : he not [look't],/Or did it from his teeth ."[2]
- as regards Octavia, caught between loyalty to her brother (Octavius) and her new husband (Anthony), Anthony is very sympathetic
  "Let your best love draw to that point which seeks/Best to preserve it"
- with all this occurring within the first twelve lines, the two outbursts assume equal importance – Octavius' breaking faith with Pompey being the first disturbing factor (the passionate F #1, 3/2) and Octavius' insult to Anthony the second (the emotional opening to F #2, 1/4)
- following a very quiet unembellished two line appeal to Octavia that opens F #3 (1/0) Anthony sums up his dilemma superbly (and very emotionally, 1/5) in the determined surround phrases that conclude the sentence

First Folio

12/ Anthony

1 Nay, nay+ Octavia, not onely that,
That were excusable, that+ and thousands more
Of semblable import, but he hath wag'd
New Warres 'gainst Pompey.
2 Made his will, and read it,
To publicke eare,+ spoke scantly of me,+
When perforce he could not
But pay me tearmes of Honour :x cold and sickly
He vented [then]+ most narrow measure :x lent
me,+
When the best hint was given him :x he not [look't],
Or did it from his teeth.

3 Gentle Octavia,
Let your best love draw to that point which seeks
Best to preserve it ; if I loose mine Honour,
I loose my selfe :x better I were not yours
[Then your] so branchlesse.
4 But as you requested,
Your selfe shall go between's, the meane time+ Lady,
Ile raise the preparation of a Warre
Shall staine your Brother, make your soonest hast,+

---

[2] this passage has been subject to much examination and revision: notably

a/ F's first two short lines (9/6 syllables) are often restructured with little advantage (to 4/11 syllables as shown) and there has been much repunctuation and rephrasing - of the two most common one is set above, the other as set below

To publicke eare:
Spoke scantly of me: when perforce he could not
But pay me tearmes of Honour, cold and sickly
He vented them*; most narrow measure lent me:
When the best hint was given him, he not look't*,
Or did it from his teeth.

b/ as the [ ] show in the body of the text above (in the footnote quote by the *), there have been two word substitutions 'them' for F's 'then', and 'not took't' for F's 'not look't': while the modern alterations serve both to clarify and tidy the passage grammatically, F's setting could suggest that Anthony is so upset he is unable to talk clearly about the situation

6 Make your soonest haste* ;
So your desires are yours.

7 When it appears* to you where this begins,
Turn* your displeasure {Cæsar's} way, for our faults
Can never be so equal* that your love
Can equally move with them.

8 Provide your going,
Choose your own* company, and command what cost
Your heart [has] mind too.

" ; if I loose mine Honour,/I loose my selfe : better I were not yours/
[Than yours] so branchlesse . "

• his agreeing to Octavia's request that she act as intermediary in an attempt to maintain peace between the two men is passionate (3/4, F #4) - perhaps a further indication of the struggle within him, for while tacitly acknowledging her worth he also tells her that he will be preparing for a war that 'Shall staine your Brother' – an awkwardness evident in his onrushed ungrammatical fast-link via the unembellished comma ending to the sentence
", make your soonest hast/So your desires are yours."
which most modern texts set as a much more rational separate mt. #6

• the awkwardness seems to continue into the emotional summing up and farewell, for while the suggestion that she should consider Cæsar more at fault is strongly released (1/3, F #5), the actual farewell is very subdued (0/1, F #6) - and whether the quietness is because of her reaction to what he has just said about her brother or because Anthony doesn't really know how to say goodbye is up to each actor to explore

So your desires are yours.

5 When it appeeres to you where this begins,
Turne your displeasure {Cæsar's} way, for our faults
Can never be so equall,$_{x}$ that your love
Can equally move with them.

6 Provide your going,
Choose your owne company, and command what cost
Your heart [he's] mind too.

13/ Cæsar **Why have you stoln upon us thus? you come not** 3.6.40 - 55

Background: At Octavia's request she has journeyed back to her brother in Rome as a 'most weake . . . reconciler', hoping to bring peace between Cæsar and Anthony. The following is Cæsar's immediate reaction to her, in his eyes, under-heralded and inadequately ceremonial appearance.

Style: one on one in front of a larger group

Where: Rome, perhaps at Cæsar's palace **To Whom:** his sister Octavia, in front of her 'traine' and Agrippa and Mecenas

# of Lines: 14 **Probable Timing: 0.45 minutes**

Modern Text

13/ Cæsar

1 Why have you stol'n upon us thus? †
2 You come not
Like Cæsar's $^{\triangle}$sister.
3 The wife of [Antony]
Should have an $^{\triangle}$army for an $^{\triangle}$usher, and
The neighs* of $^{\triangle}$horse to tell of her approach,
Long ere she did appear*; ◊ $^{\triangle}$the trees by th'way
Should have borne men, and expectation fainted,
Longing for what it had not ; ◊ $^{\triangle}$nay, the dust
Should have ascended to the $^{\triangle}$roof* of $^{\triangle}$heaven,
Rais'd by your populous $^{\triangle}$troops*. †
4 But you are come
A $^{\triangle}$market-maid to Rome, and have prevented
The ostentation of our love, which, left unshown*,
Is often left unlov'd. †
5 We should have met you
By $^{\triangle}$sea, and $^{\triangle}$land, supplying every $^{\triangle}$stage
With an augmented greeting.

Given the enormity of the images, the fact that Octavius is far more intellectual than emotional virtually throughout (15/5) suggests that he is holding himself in check for some reason (trying not to upset his beloved sister perhaps) – yet at times emotion and passion do break through, giving the lie to his self-control.

- the shock of the perceived insult to him, as well as her, in her lack of a flamboyant entourage can be seen in the surround phrases that open the speech, especially the first which is both monosyllabic and unembellished - as if Octavius can barely find his voice – while the second finishes with two final words of intellectual flourish (2/0) of (prideful?) self-definition

- his intellect continues in the description of what Octavia should have, 'an Army for an Usher', (3/0, F #2's first line and half), and the suggestion that the 'neighes of Horse' from far away and a route crowded with people even hanging in the trees should mark her arrival turns slightly emotional (1/2, the last two lines of F #2, and F #3)

- while grandiose notion that the dust of those accompanying her 'Should have ascended to the Roofe of Heaven' turns passionate (3/2, F #4's first two lines)

- but in returning to the perceived insult of Anthony's not allowing her sufficient public display, 'you are come/A Market-maid to Rome', and explaining how he would have received her, 'supplying every Stage/With an augmented greeting.', Octavius regains almost full mental discipline (6/1)

- the one slip into emotion (0/1), heightened by being set as an emotional (semicoloned) surround phrase, concerns his belief of how (his) love should be shown as a matter of 'ostentation'

  " ; which left unshewne,/Is often left unlov'd : "

- and that he so quickly recovers intellectual equilibrium underscores his (desire to be seen as in?) self-control

First Folio

13/ Cæsar

1 Why have you stoln upon us thus? you come not
Like Cæsars Sister.
2 The wife of [Anthony]
Should have an Army for an Usher, and
The neighes of Horse to tell of her approach,
Long ere she did appeare.
3 The trees by th'way
Should have borne men, and expectation fainted,
Longing for what it had not.
4 Nay, the dust
Should have ascended to the Roofe of Heaven,
Rais'd by your populous Troopes: But you are come
A Market-maid to Rome, and have prevented
The ostentation of our love; $_{x}$ which^{+} left unshewne,
Is often left unlov'd: we should have met you
By Sea, and Land, supplying every Stage
With an augmented greeting.

#'s 14 - 18: Anthony, Cleopatra, & Cæsar

14/ Anthony **I have offended Reputation,/A most unnoble swerving.** between 3.11.49 - 74

Background: Anthony has abandoned all hope of victory, going so far as to tell his closest 'Friends, come thither,/ . . . I/Have lost my way for ever. I have a shippe,/Laden with Gold, take that, divide it: flye,/And make your peace with Cæsar'. Though responsible for the current defeat (see the opening to the background of speech #11), Cleopatra has been persuaded by her attendants to comfort Anthony. Initially he has refused to even acknowledge her presence, and when finally forced to deal with her, the following is his response.

Style: essentially one on one in front of a small group

Where: unspecified, somewhere in Alexandria **To Whom:** Cleopatra, in front of Charmian and Eros, as well as Anthony's attendants

# of Lines: 24 **Probable Timing: 1.15 minutes**

Modern Text

14/ Anthony

1 I have offended Δreputation,
A most unnoble swerving.

2 O*, [whither] hast thou lead me, Egypt ? †
3 See
How I convey my shame out of thine eyes
By looking back* what I have left behind*
'Stroy'd in dishonor.

4 Egypt, thou knew'st too well
My heart was to thy Δrudder tied* by'th'strings,
And thou should'st [tow] me after.
5 O'er my spirit
[Thy] full supremacy$_{*}$ thou knew'st, and that
Thy beck* might from the bidding of the Δgods
Command me*.

6 Now I must
To the young man send humble Δtreaties, dodge
And palter in the shifts of lowness$_{*}$, who
With half* the bulk* o'th'world play'd$_{*}$ as I pleas'd,
Making and marring Δfortunes.
7 You did know
How much you were my Δconqueror, and that
My Δsword, made weak* by my affection, would
Obey it on all cause.

8 Fall not a tear*, I say, one of them rates
All that is won* and lost . †
9 Give me a kiss*. †
10 Even this repays* me.

With no major punctuation appearing until after nineteen lines, it seems that the early part of the speech is a stream of consciousness, without forethought or re-analysis: however, the appearance of the surround phrases marks his struggle to cope with the realities of defeat -eventually by avoiding them.

- in realising just how much this ignoble defeat will crush his reputation Anthony opens quietly intellectually (1/0, F #1's first line) and, with his subsequent comment of how 'unnoble' he now appears being unembellished, it would seem that he is shaken to the core by what has just occurred

- in his emotional acknowledgment that Cleopatra's full 'supremacie' 'O're my spirit' ensured his 'heart was to thy Rudder tyed by'th'strings' (3/6, F #2-4) he is careful not to blame her, clearly stating via another set of unembellished phrases
"see/How I convey my shame,$_{x}$ out of thine eyes"
with the extra breath-thoughts (marked ,$_{x}$) adding clarity to his exoneration for all to hear

- the only moments of (tired?) passion in the speech come as Anthony realises he must abase himself ('shifts of lownes') and 'send humble Treaties' to Octavius, his vanquisher (F #5), and in his F #6 acknowledgement for a second time of her sway over him, 'You did know/How much you were my Conqueror' (4/3)

- his F #7 attempt to stop her tears and mend the bridges between them by kissing her, suggesting that just a single 'kisse/Even this repayes me', is emotional (1/4), and that he is genuine can be seen in the surround phrases which form the sentence
" . Fall not a teare I say, one of them rates/All that is wonne and lost : Give me a kisse,/Even this repayes me . "

- the setting of the shaded passage is very different in the two texts - and F's three line irregular setting (5 or 6/10/8 syllables) is masterly - the pause of the first short line allows Anthony time for the kiss's effect before continuing, the second to realise the depths of his own depression before telling Cleopatra of his feelings: most modern texts regularise (not particularly successfully) the passage as shown (11 or 12/10/12 syllables), basically substituting a two line blurt for F's struggle

- also, with Anthony's F #8 emotional enquiry (1/2) as to the whereabouts of the 'Schoolemaster' (who has been acting as his ambassador to Cæsar), F becomes onrushed (two sentences as opposed to most modern texts' six)

First Folio

14/ Anthony

1 I have offended Reputation,
A most unnoble swerving.

2 Oh+ [whether] hast thou lead me+ Egypt, see
How I convey my shame,$_{x}$ out of thine eyes,$_{x}$
By looking backe what I have left behinde
Stroy'd in dishonor.

3 Egypt, thou knew'st too well,$_{x}$
My heart was to thy Rudder tyed by'th'strings,
And thou should'st [stowe] me after.
4 O're my spirit
[The] full supremacie thou knew'st, and that
Thy becke,$_{x}$ might from the bidding of the Gods
Command mee.

5 Now I must
To the young man send humble Treaties, dodge
And palter in the shifts of lownes, who
With halfe the bulke o'th'world plaid as I pleas'd,
Making,$_{x}$ and marring Fortunes.
6 You did know
How much you were my Conqueror, and that
My Sword, made weake by my affection, would
Obey it on all cause.

7 Fall not a teare+ I say, one of them rates
All that is wonne and lost : Give me a kisse,
Even this repayes me.

{ctd. over}

11 We sent our ^Δ^schoolmaster*,
Is 'a come back*?
12 Love, I am full of ^Δ^lead .†
13 Some ^Δ^wine
Within there, and our ^Δ^viands ! †
14 Fortune knows*
We scorn* her most when most she offers blows*.

• as he abandons his attempts to be a strategist, the large-scale onrush of F #9's three surround phrases occur, marking a huge struggle between his depression ' . Love I am full of Lead : ' and his attempts to cheer himself up by calling for wine – the start of the struggle (3/0), while the rhyming couplet maxim with which he ends, attempting to defy Fortune's 'blowes', turns emotional (1/3)

8 We sent our Schoolemaster, is a come backe?
9 Love+ I am full of Lead : some Wine
Within there, and our Viands : Fortune knowes, x
We scorne her most, x when most she offers blowes.

15/ Thidias **So./Thus then thou most renown'd, Cæsar intreats, . . .** between 3.13.52 - 82

Background: In accordance with Cæsar's mysogonic view of women (who in his eyes 'are not/In their best Fortunes strong; but want will perjure/The ne're touched Vestall'), the 'cunning' Thidias has been sent to Egypt in order to 'From Anthony winne Cleopatra' by promising 'what she requires'. This is how Thidias begins.

Style: one on one, in front of a small group

Where: Cleopatra's palace **To Whom:** Cleopatra, in front of Charmian, Iras, and Anthony's right-hand man, Enobarbus

# of Lines: 18 **Probable Timing: 0.55 minutes**

Modern Text

15/ Thidias

1 So.

2 Thus then, thou most renown'd : Cæsar entreats*
Not to consider in what case thou stand'st
Further then he is [Cæsar].

3 He knows* that you [embraced] not [Antony]
As you did love, but as you fear'd him.

4 The scar's* upon your Δhonor, therefore, he
Does pity*, as constrained blemishes,
Not as deserved.

5 Shall I say to Cæsar
What you require of him ? for he partly begs*
To be desir'd to give.

6 It much would please him,
That of his Δfortunes you should make a staff*
To lean* upon; ◊ but it would warm* his spirits
To hear* from me you had left [Antony],
And put yourself* under his shroud*,
The universal Δlandlord .

7 'Tis your Noblest course .†

8 Wisdom* and Δfortune combating* together,
If that the former dare but what it can,
No chance may shake it.

9 Give me grace to lay
My duty* on your hand.

F's orthography suggests that Thidias is a very clever negotiator, knowing when to apply pressure and when to pull back so as to leave his words to speak for themselves.

- Thidias' first attempt at reassuring Cleopatra that all she should think of is Cæsar's protection is carefully intellectual (F #2, 2/0)
- the attempt to pry her away from Anthony, you-didn't-embrace-him-out-of-love-but-fear, (F #3) and the explanation that Cæsar pities the 'the scarre' on her 'Honor' as an undeserved 'blemishes' (F #4) is passionate (2/3)
- Thidias' F #5 attempt to get her to commit herself continues passionately (1/1), the demand of the surround phrases ' . Shall I say to Cæsar,/What you require of him : for he partly begges/To be desir'd to give.' adding great pressure
- while the seductive image 'of his Fortunes you should make a staffe' (F #6) coupled with F #7's suggestion that it would 'warme his spirits/To heare . . . you had left Anthony,/And put your selfe under his shrowd' are advanced emotionally (3/6)
- for the last phase of his pressure he cleverly runs the full gamut of releases, quickly changing from one style to another
  a/ he briefly returns to intellect for the very naked suggestion of the surround phrase ' . 'Tis your Noblest course : ' (1/0, F #8's first line)
  b/ then turns to emotion (1/2) for the suggestion that it would smack of 'Wisdome and Fortune combatting together'
  c/ while the conclusion urging that 'Wisedome' should be her unshakeable guide
  "If that the former dare but what it can,/No chance may shake it."
  is very cleverly totally unembellished
- the fact that his final request to kiss her hand is also unembellished suggests that this could be more than mere diplomacy, but rather asking her to display a tacit agreement to his suggestions – and whether it is spoken quietly so as not to break the seductive spell he thinks he may have weaved or so as not to offend Cleopatra is up to each actor to explore

First Folio

15/ Thidias

1 So.

2 Thus then+ thou most renown'd,+ Cæsar intreats,$_x$
Not to consider in what case thou stand'st
Further then he is [Cæsars].

3 He knowes that you [embrace] not [Anthony]
As you did love, but as you feared him.

4 The scarre's upon your Honor, therefore+ he
Does pitty, as constrained blemishes,
Not as deserved.

5 Shall I say to Cæsar,$_x$
What you require of him : + for he partly begges
To be desir'd to give.

6 It much would please him,
That of his Fortunes you should make a staffe
To leane upon.

7 But it would warme his spirits
To heare from me you had left [Anthony],
And put your selfe under his shrowd, the universal Landlord.

8 'Tis your Noblest course :
Wisedome and Fortune combatting together,
If that the former dare but what it can,
No chance may shake it.

9 Give me grace to lay
My dutie on your hand.

16/ Anthony **You have beene a boggeler ever,** between 3.13.110 - 131

Background: Realising that the 'cunning' Thidias is attempting to drive a wedge between Cleopatra and Anthony, and concerned that Cleopatra may be considering Cæsar's overtures, Enobarbus has brought Anthony in to see Thidias' proceedings, which, unfortunately for Thidias, involves kissing Cleopatra's hand as Anthony enters.

Style: one on one for the benefit of the small group

Where: Cleopatra's palace **To Whom:** in front of Cleopatra, Charmian and Iras, Enobarbus and, eventually, a servant

# of Lines: 22 **Probable Timing: 1.10 minutes**

Modern Text

16/ Anthony

1 You have been* a boggeler ever,
But when we in our viciousness* grow hard
(O* misery on't !) the wise Δgods seel* our eyes ;
In our own* filth drop our clear* judgments*; make us
Adore our errors; laugh at's while we strut
To our confusion.

2 I found you as a Δmorsel*, cold upon
Dead Cæsar's Δtrencher ; Δnay, you were a Δfragment
Of Gneius Pompey's* - besides what hotter hours*
Unregist'red in vulgar Δfame, you have
Luxuriously pick'd* out; ◊ for I am sure,
Though you can guess* what Δtemperance should be,
You know not what it is.

3 To let a Δfellow that will take rewards
And say, "God quit you !" be familiar with
My play-fellow, your hand, this Δkingly Δseal*
And plighter of high hearts !
4 O that I were
Upon the hill of Basan, to outroar*
The horned Δherd* ! †
5 For I have savage cause,
And to proclaim* it civilly were like
A halter'd neck* which does* the Δhangman thank*
For being yare about him.
6 Is he whipt?

Quite fascinatingly, though clearly outraged, after the first emotional explosion much of Anthony's attack turns to intellect, stripping Cleopatra's reputation with pointed barbs rather than a generalised emotional wash – though, as ever, F's orthography shows where his control eventually breaks down.

- Anthony's outraged sense of sexual propriety leads to an enormously emotional opening harangue (1/8, F #1's first four lines), though he regains an icy (and thus inherently dangerous) calm line and half in finishing F #1

- as he turns to a virulent description of what she was when he found her, F #2's opening
  " . I found you as a Morsell, cold upon/Dead Cæsars Trencher : "
  the image is driven home by both the intellect involved (3/1) and by being set as a surround phrase

- the intellect continues as he attacks her previous relationships not only as 'a Fragment/Of Gneius Pompeyes', but also with those 'Unregistred in vulgar Fame', and her inability to practice 'Temperance' (6/3, the last three lines of F #2 and all of F #3) – the power of the insult made even stronger by being set as two sentences instead of the onrushed mt. #2

- and though his intellectual attack continues (F #4, 4/1) as he berates her for allowing Thidias, whom Anthony regards as an errand boy ('a Fellow that will take rewards'), to kiss her hand, the description of her hand as
  " ; this Kingly Seale,/And plighter of high hearts . "
  being set as an emotional surround phrase (created by the only semicolon in the speech) hints at the depths of feeling he is struggling to contain

- which he fails to contain, for he becomes passionate in wishing that he could roar out his anger at being made (as he mistakenly thinks) a cuckold (3/4, F #5) – the three extra breath-thoughts (marked , $_x$) that suddenly appear marking his fury at having to 'proclaime it civilly' instead (perhaps voicing the indignity is almost literally choking him)

- after everything that has gone on before, the icy calm of the final monosyllabic unembellished short sentence 'Is he whipt?' should strike fear into all listening, waiting for the explosion that will probably follow soon after

First Folio

16/ Anthony

1 You have beene a boggeler ever,
But when we in our viciousnesse grow hard
(Oh misery on't+) the wise Gods seele our eyes+
In our owne filth,$_x$ drop our cleare judgements,+
make us
Adore our errors,+ laugh at's while we strut
To our confusion.

2 I found you as a Morsell, cold upon
Dead Cæsars Trencher :$_x$ Nay, you were a Fragment
Of Gneius Pompeyes, besides what hotter houres
Unregistred in vulgar Fame, you have
Luxuriously pickt out.
3 For I am sure,
Though you can guesse what Temperance should be,
You know not what it is.

4 To let a Fellow that will take rewards,$_x$
And say, God quit you,+ be familiar with
My play-fellow, your hand ;$_x$ this Kingly Seale,$_x$
And plighter of high hearts. +
5 O that I were
Upon the hill of Basan, to out-roare
The horned Heard,+ for I have savage cause,
And to proclaime it civilly,$_x$ were like
A halter'd necke,$_x$ which do's the Hangman thanke,$_x$
For being yare about him.
6 Is he whipt?

17/ Enobarbus **Yes like enough : hye battel'd Cæsar will** between 3.13.29 - 46

18/ Cæsar **He calles me Boy, and chides as he had power** between 4.1.1 – 16 + 4.6.7 - 9

Background: In a show of old-fashioned chivalry, Anthony has sent a challenge of single hand-to-hand combat to Cæsar. The following are two of the only-to-be-expected pragmatic (if not downright cynical) responses. Speech #17 is Enobarbus' immediate reaction once Anthony comes up with the idea, while speech #18 is Cæsar's initial assessment of the situation.

Style: speech #17, solo; speech #18, as part of a three-handed scene in front of a larger group

Where: speech #17, palace; speech #18, Cæsar's camp, presumably near Alexandria **To Whom:** speech #17, audience address; speech #18, Agrippa and Mecenas, in front of their army

Speech 17: # of Lines: 15 **Probable Timing: 0.50 minutes**

Speech 18: # of Lines: 15 **Probable Timing: 0.50 minutes**

Modern Text

17/ Enobarbus

1 Yes, like enough ! high*-battled* Cæsar will
Unstate his happiness*, and be △stag'd to th'show*
Against a △sworder !
2 I see men's △judgments* are
A parcel* of their △fortunes, and things outward
Do draw the inward quality after them,
To suffer all alike . †
3 That he should dream*,
Knowing all measures, the full Cæsar will
Answer his emptiness* ! †
4 Cæsar, thou hast subdu'd*
His judgment* too.

---

5 Mine honesty and I begin* to square . †
6 The △loyalty well held to △fools* does make
Our △faith mere* folly ; yet he that can endure
To follow with △allegiance* a fall'n* △lord
Does conquer him that did his △master conquer,
And earns* a place i'th'△story.

The onrush of F #2 and #3 (most modern texts splitting them in three and two respectively) suggests that the current situation is somewhat troubling for Enobarbus - though the speech's two key surround phrases show quite clearly that he has lost none of his keen, shrewd, (and cynical?) political acumen.

- he gets right to the point with a curt dismissal of Cæsar's accepting Anthony's idea of hand to hand combat with ' . Yes like enough : ', with the full impact of the surround phrase thought heightened by being unembellished

- Enobarbus then jumps into passion as he elaborates why – Cæsar not being fool enough to risk his 'happinesse' to fight against 'a Sworder'

- and the passion continues (3/4, F #2's first five lines) as he voices how in the world at large 'mens Judgements are/A parcell of their Fortunes', which leads inevitably to the (sad? disturbing?) recognition that in the current situation vis-à-vis Anthony
  " ; Cæsar thou hast subdu'de/His judgement too . "
  the disturbing thought underscored by being the only emotional (semicoloned) surround phrase in the speech

- Enobarbus' passion continues as he realises that, despite his own 'honesty', he is beginning to question whether his 'Loyalty' to Anthony is that exhibited by 'Fooles' (3/3, F #3's first two and a half lines)

- yet at the crucial moment, in concluding (at least for now) that keeping 'Allegeance' with 'a falne Lord' in fact conquers the conqueror and earns he who keeps that allegiance everlasting fame ('a place i'th'Story), he reigns in his passions and establishes a modicum of intellectual self-control (4/2, F #3's last three and half lines)

First Folio

17/ Enobarbus

1 Yes+ like enough : + hye battel'd Cæsar will
Unstate his happinesse, and be Stag'd to'th'shew
Against a Sworder. +
2 I see mens Judgements are
A parcell of their Fortunes, and things outward
Do draw the inward quality after them+
To suffer all alike, that he should dreame,
Knowing all measures, the full Cæsar will
Answer his emptinesse ;+ Cæsar+ thou hast subdu'de
His judgement too.

---

3 Mine honesty,$_x$ and I,$_x$ beginne to square,
The Loyalty well held to Fooles,$_x$ does make
Our Faith meere folly ;$_x$ yet he that can endure
To follow with Allegeance a falne Lord,$_x$
Does conquer him that did his Master conquer,
And earnes a place i'th'Story.

Modern Text

18/ Cæsar

1 He calls* me Δboy, and chides as he had power
To beat* me out of Egypt.
2 My Δmessenger
He hath whipt with Δrods, dares me to personal Δcombat, ◊
Cæsar to [Antony]. †
3 Let the old Δruffian know
I have many other ways* to die*; mean* time
Laugh at his Δchallenge.

4 Let our best heads know
That to-morrow, the last of many Δbattles*
We mean* to fight.
5 Within our Δfiles there are,
Of those that serv'd [Mark* Antony] but late,
Enough to fetch him in.

one sentence insert from Act 4 Scene 6
6 {Go charge Agrippa,
Plant those that have revolted in the [Δvan],
That [Antony] may seem* to spend his Δfury
Upon himself*. }

7 See it done,
And Δfeast the Δarmy ; we have store to do't*,
And they have earn'd the waste.
8 Poor* [Antony]!

F's orthography shows Octavius' mercurial nature, his switches in style matching his equally swift switches from topic to topic.

- Octavius' assessment/response to Anthony's message/challenge opens passionately (F #1, 2/2)

- but his description of what happened to his unfortunate diplomat Thidias is purely intellectual (F #2, 3/0) - whether this denotes (amused?) acceptance or his reading of the information for the first time is up to each actor to explore

- normally set as the end to the previous sentence by most modern texts, the ungrammatical start to F #3 ('Cæsar to Anthony') could well support (amused again?) amazement or disbelief, especially since the information contained in the passionate sentence it opens (3/3, F #3)
  " . Cæsar to Anthony : let the old Ruffian know,/I have many other wayes to dye : meane time/Laugh at his Challenge . "
is heightened by being set as three consecutive surround phrases, the only ones in the speech

- F #4's determination that tomorrow will be 'the last of many Battailes' is slightly emotional (1/2) - while the strategically brilliant if heartless idea of gaining advantage by putting all of the men that have deserted Anthony in the front line of the troops that will now oppose him is highly intellectual (7/3, F #5-6) – and whether this is a cold-hearted factual suggestion or a sudden new idea is up to each actor to explore

- the final instruction to feed the Army before the battle is still slightly intellectual (2/1, F #7)

- and, perhaps surprisingly, so is the final two word sentence about Anthony - though again whether this is in anticipation of Octavius' expected victory or a final comment on Anthony's message/challenge that was so easily dismissed earlier is a matter for actor exploration and choice

First Folio

18/ Cæsar

1 He calles me Boy, and chides as he had power
To beate me out of Egypt.
2 My Messenger
He hath whipt with Rods, dares me to personal Combat.
3 Cæsar to [Anthony] : let the old Ruffian know,ₓ
I have many other wayes to dye :ₓ meane time
Laugh at his Challenge.

4 Let our best heads know,ₓ
That to morrow, the last of many Battailes
We meane to fight.
5 Within our Files there are,
Of those that serv'd [Marke Anthony] but late,
Enough to fetch him in.

one sentence insert from Act 4 Scene 6
6 {Go charge Agrippa, ₓ
Plant those that have revolted in the [Vant],
That [Anthony] may seeme to spend his Fury
Upon himselfe. }

7 See it done,
And Feast the Army,+ we have store to doo't,
And they have earn'd the waste.
8 Poore [Anthony]. +

#'s 19 - 21: Downfall Of Enobarbus & Anthony

19/ Enobarbus **Alexas did revolt, and went to Jewry on** between 4.6.10 - 38

Background: As have many of his colleagues (and superiors, including royalty), Enobarbus has abandoned Anthony and joined Cæsar's forces. The following is triggered by Cæsar's pre-battle instructions 'Plant those that have revolted in the Vant,/That Anthony may seeme to spend his Fury/Upon himselfe', as well as by the surprising news that instead of confiscating the treasure, Anthony has sent all Enobarbus' worldly goods to him, earning the sobriquet of one of Cæsar's soldiers 'Your Emperor/Continues still a Jove'.

Style: solo

Where: Cæsar's camp somewhere near Alexandria **To Whom:** self, and direct audience address

# of Lines: 18 **Probable Timing:** 0.55 minutes

Modern Text

19/ Enobarbus

1 Alexas did revolt, and went to Jewry on
Affairs* of [Antony], there did [persuade]
Great Herod to incline himself* to Cæsar,
And leave his Δmaster Anthony; ◊ for this pains*
Cæsar hath hang'd him. †
2 [Canidius] and the rest
That fell away, have entertainment, but
No honorable* trust. †
3 I have done ill,
Of which I do accuse myself* so sorely
That I will joy no more.

~~~~~~~~~~~~~~~~~~~~~~~~~~~~~~

4 I am alone the Δvillain* of the earth,
And feel* I am so most.
5 O* [Antony],
Thou Δmine of Δbounty, how would'st thou have paid*
My better service, when my turpitude
Thou dost so Δcrown* with Δgold!
6 This blows* my heart**.†
7 If swift thought break* it not, a swifter mean*
Shall out-strike thought, but thought will do't*, ◊ I feel*.†
8 I fight against thee? †
9 No, I will go seek*
Some Δditch, wherein to die*; the foul'st best fits
My latter part of life.

Within the intellectual analysis and the emotional realisations underscoring his own act of disloyalty, the few unembellished passages underscore Enobarbus' depth of self-loathing.

- in assessing the fate of Alexas, a colleague and fellow-deserter, Enobarbus opens analytically-intellectually (6/3, F #1), while the surround phrase recollection
  " . For this paines/Cæsar hath hang'd him : "
  plunges him into passion (2/2, F #2's first three lines) as he explores this and the lack-of-trust shown to other fellow-deserters, including Camindius
- which in turn leads to the first very quiet self-accusation
  "I have done ill,/Of which I do accuse my selfe so sorely,/That I will joy no more."
  the only word breaking the lack of release being the crucial 'my selfe', while F #3's condemnation of himself as 'the Villaine of the earth' turns emotional (1/2)
- in contrast, his F #4 praise of Anthony as 'the Mine of Bounty' becomes more intellectual (5/3)
- not surprisingly, Enobarbus' ensuing grief is expressed emotionally (F #5, 0/4), intensified by being set as two surround phrases
  " . This blowes my hart,/If swift thought breake it not : a swifter meane/Shall out-strike thought, but thought will doo't . "
- and F #6's relating of his grief to the practical reality of the current situation is also heightened by three consecutive surround phrases, at first passionately (2/3, the first three phrases)
  " . I feele /I fight against thee : No I will go seeke/Some Ditch, wherein to dye : "
  and then bleakly unembellished for the final self disgusted assessment of his own worth
  " : the foul'st best fits/My latter part of life . "

First Folio

19/ Enobarbus

1 Alexas did revolt, and went to Jewry on
Affaires of [Anthony], there did [disswade]
Great Herod to incline himselfe to Cæsar,
And leave his Master Anthony.
2 For this paines,x
Cæsar hath hang'd him: [Camindius] and the rest
That fell away, have entertainment, but
No honourable trust: I have done ill,
Of which I do accuse my selfe so sorely,x
That I will joy no more.

~~~~~~~~~~~~~~~~~~~~~~~~~~~~~~

3 I am alone the Villaine of the earth,
And feele I am so most.
4 Oh [Anthony],
Thou Mine of Bounty, how would'st thou have payed
My better service, when my turpitude
Thou dost so Crowne with Gold. +
5 This blowes my hart,
If swift thought breake it not:x a swifter meane
Shall out-strike thought, but thought will doo't.
6 I feele +
I fight against thee:x No+ I will go seeke
Some Ditch, wherein to dye:x the foul'st best fits
My latter part of life.

20/ Anthony **Unarme Eros, the long dayes taske is done,** 4.14.35 - 54

21/ Anthony **Since Cleopatra dyed,/I have liv'd in such dishonour, that the Gods** between 4.14.55 - 93

Background: These are Anthony's responses following Mardian's (false) news of Cleopatra's death (see background to speech #11 above). Speech #20 is a general assessment of his personal state, while speech #21 deals with his reminding his man Eros of an earlier promise to help Anthony commit suicide.

Style: partially a three-handed, also two-handed and solo sequence

Where: near Alexandria **To Whom:** speech #20, Eros, with the second part of the first sentence to Mardian, self, and the absent Cleopatra; speech #21, Eros

Speech 20: # of Lines: 20 **Probable Timing: 1.00 minutes**
Speech 21: # of Lines: 30 **Probable Timing: 1.30 minutes**

Modern Text

20/ Anthony

1 Unarm*[3], Eros, the long day's* task* is done,
And we must sleep*. †
2 That thou depart'st hence safe
Does pay thy labor* richly : Δgo.

[exit Mardian]

3 Off, pluck* off,
The seven-fold shield of Ajax cannot keep*
The battery from my heart.
4 O*, cleave, my sides !
5 Heart, once be stronger [than] thy Δcontinent,
Crack* thy frail* Δcase !
6 Apace, Eros, apace. †
7 No more a Δsoldier. †
8 Bruised pieces*, go,
You have been‸ Δnobly borne.
9 - From me awhile.

[exit Eros]

10 I will o'er-take thee, Cleopatra, and
Weep* for my pardon.
11 So it must be, for now
All length is Δtorture ; since the Δtorch is out,
Lie* down* and stray no farther.
12 Now all labor*
Mars* what it does : yea, very force entangles
Itself* with strength. †
13 Seal* then, and all is done.
14 Eros!

There seem to be two sets of energy for Anthony - the releases one would expect given the enormity of the situation; the loss of the final battle; his decision to no longer be called a soldier; and his plan to join the supposedly dead Cleopatra by committing suicide, and then sudden clusters of surround phrase energy suggesting that a certain fervor has taken hold of him in his understanding and/or plans.

the orthography of the onrushed F #1 shows Anthony struggling with a series of thoughts that threaten to swamp him, with

a/ F #1, set as three separate surround phrases, shows how driven he is

b/ the ungrammatical connection of Anthony's emotional call for Eros to help to unarm him (1/4, the first line and a half) coupled via the first colon to the passionate chasing away of Cleopatra's eunuch Mardian (2/1, F #1's last line) suggests that Anthony is not yet in full control of himself

c/ that Mardian's final dismissal is via the capitalised one word monosyllabic surround phrase ' : Go . ' suggests that an extraordinary amount of energy is being directed towards the unfortunate message-bearer

• Anthony's response to the removal of his armour (F #2) and exclamation as Eros continues (F #3) is emotional (1/3), while the exhortation for his 'Heart' to 'cracke thy fraile Case' is passionate (2/2, F #4)

• F #5's urgency for the last piece of armour to be removed, and then taken away with the rest since he no longer regards himself as a soldier (3/1 in just two lines), the clear intellectualism of which is heightened by the three successive surround phrases

" . Apace Eros, apace ; /No more a Soldier : bruised peeces go,/You have bin/Nobly borne . "

the first two of which are emotionally charged by being linked with the (emotional) semicolon – not surprising considering that he is acknowledging/watching the disappearance of his (adult) life

First Folio

20/ Anthony

1 Unarme+ Eros, the long dayes taske is done,
And we must sleepe : That thou depart'st hence safe
Does pay thy labour richly : Go.

[exit Mardian]

2 Off, plucke off,
The seven-fold shield of Ajax cannot keepe
The battery from my heart.
3 Oh+ cleave+ my sides. +
4 Heart, once be stronger [then] thy Continent,
Cracke thy fraile Case. +
5 Apace+ Eros, apace ;
No more a Soldier : bruised peeces+ go,
You have bin Nobly borne.
6 From me awhile.

[exit Eros]

7 I will o're-take thee+ Cleopatra, and
Weepe for my pardon.
8 So it must be, for now
All length is Torture :‸ since the Torch is out,
Lye downe and stray no farther.
9 Now all labour
Marres what it does : yea, very force entangles
It selfe with strength : Seale then+ and all is done.
10 Eros?+

[3] some modern texts add 'me', Ff omit the word

15 - I come my △queen*! -
16 Eros! -
17 Stay for me! †
18 Where △souls* do couch on △flowers, we'll* hand in hand,
And with our sprightly △port make the △ghosts* gaze:
Dido and her Æneas shall want △troops*,
And all the haunt be ours.

• thus F #6's quietly unembellished monosyllabic order/request to Eros 'From me awhile.' is testimony to the impact that this farewell-to-arms is having on him

• the decision to commit suicide so as to join the (supposedly) dead Cleopatra is passionate (3/3, F #7-8), with the F #8 reasons intensified by being set as surround phrases – as is his emotional realisation that to do anything other than commit suicide is simply a waste of energy (F #9, 1/4)

• with this realisation Anthony's desire to expedite matters is seen in the three short sentences that follow - the double request for Eros' return and the assurance to Cleopatra that he is coming to her (F #10-12)

• in finishing, following his F #13 opening unembellished monosyllabic plea for Cleopatra to wait for him, his final address to Cleopatra, envisioning how they will be together, and how, when together, their 'sprightly Port make the Ghostes gaze', is splendidly passionate (6/4, F #13)

11 I come my Queene. +
12 Eros?+
13 Stay for me,+
Where Soules do couch on Flowers, wee'l hand in hand,
And with our sprightly Port make the Ghostes gaze:
Dido,$_x$ and her Æneas shall want Troopes,
And all the haunt be ours.

Modern Text

21/ Anthony

1 Since Cleopatra died*
I have liv'd in such dishonor* that the △gods
Detest my baseness*.
2 I, that with my △sword
Quarter'd the △world, and o'er green* Neptune's back*
With △ships made △cities, condemn* myself* to lack*
The △courage of a △woman - less* △noble mind*
[Than] she which by her death our Cæsar tells*,
"I am △conqueror of myself* ".
3 Thou art sworn*, Eros,
That when the exigent should come, which now
Is come indeed, △when I should see behind* me
Th'inevitable prosecution of
Disgrace and horror, that on my command,
Thou then wouldst kill me.
4 Do't*, the time is come.†
5 Thou strik'st not me, 'tis Cæsar thou defeat'st.
6 Put color* in thy △cheek*.
7 Eros,
Wouldst thou be window'd in great Rome, and see
Thy △master thus with pleach'd △arms*, bending down*
His corrigible neck*, his face subdu'd*

From a very difficult to speak opening of self-condemnation, Anthony eventually gains sufficient self-control to make a determined and reasoned appeal for Eros to kill him, as Eros has sworn to do – and has already been greatly rewarded for making that oath.

• the six extra breath-thoughts (marked ,$_x$) scattered throughout the first two sentences suggest that Anthony is having enormous difficulty in voicing (the reasons for) his self-disgust

• his opening suggestion that he has sunk so low that 'the Gods/Detest my basenesse' is passionate (2/3, F #1) , and, while the momentary recollection/ brag of his one time greatness turns intellectual (5/2, F #2's first two lines), the return via the emotional semicolon to his earlier self-condemnation reignites his earlier passion (5/7, F #2's last three lines)

• though he seems to be carefully passionate as he reminds Eros of his one-time oath that he would kill Anthony if ever the need arose (F #3, 2/2), two small cracks in the orthography suggest the strain within

a/ the lines spelling out why such an act is necessary are unembellished "Th'inevitable prosecution of disgrace and horror,/That on my command, thou then would'st kill me."
the quiet seemingly underscoring the determination of the moment with great calm, yet

b/ F sets the first line as a tremendous rush of fifteen syllables, suggesting that calm may be spoken but that the thought certainly is not

First Folio

21/ Anthony

1 Since Cleopatra dyed,$_x$
I have liv'd in such dishonour,$_x$ that the Gods
Detest my basenesse.
2 I, that with my Sword,$_x$
Quarter'd the World, and o're greene Neptunes backe
With Ships,$_x$ made Cities;$_x$ condemne my selfe,$_x$ to lacke
The Courage of a Woman, lesse Noble minde
[Then] she which by her death,$_x$ our Cæsar telles+
I am Conqueror of my selfe.
3 Thou art sworne+ Eros,
That when the exigent should come, which now
Is come indeed:$_x$ When I should see behinde me
Th'inevitable prosecution of disgrace and horror,
That on my command, thou then would'st kill me.
4 Doo't, the time is come: Thou strik'st not me,
'Tis Cæsar thou defeat'st.
5 Put colour in thy Cheeke.
6 Eros,
Would'st thou be window'd in great Rome, and see
Thy Master thus with pleacht Armes, bending downe
His corrigible necke, his face subdu'de

{ctd. over}

To penetrative shame, whilst the wheel'd seat*
Of [Δfortunate] Cæsar drawn* before him, branded
His Δbaseness* that ensued ?

8 Come then ; for with a wound I must be cur'd.
9 Draw that thy honest Δsword, which thou hast worn*
Most useful* for thy Δcountry.

10 When I did make thee free, swor'st [thou] not then
To do this when I bade₊ thee?
11 Do it at once,
Or thy precedent Δservices are all
But accidents unpurpos'd.
12 Draw, and come.

13 {ψ} Let it do at once
The thing why thou hast drawn* it.

14 Now, Eros.

• the urging of F #4-5's 'Doo't', is similarly off-balance, with a short line (9 syllables) opening the out-of-kilter monosyllabic surround phrase command 'Doo't, the time is come : ' and a long line (twelve syllables) adding extra drive to the urgency of the emotional short sentence demand 'Put colour in thy Cheeke.' (F #7, 1/2)

• with Eros not yet responding (indicated by the short one syllable line opening F #6), Anthony's reminder of the disgrace both of them would face in Rome is offered passionately (6/7), which is a great contrast . . .

• . . . to the very quiet and thus determinedly unembellished monosyllabic surround phrase sentence that follows
" . Come then : for with a wound I must be cur'd . "
the quietness perhaps suggesting an attempt to steady Eros' nerves/resolve,

• it seems he cannot remain calm, for his F #8 request for Eros to draw his sword is very passionate for just a line and a half (2/2)

• but quite superbly, Anthony manages to restore the appearance of calm for the rest of the speech (just 2/1 for the five sentences that make up the last six lines)

• thus the reminder that Eros was created a free-man in return for swearing to this (F #9) and F #11's request 'Draw, and come.' are completely unembellished, Anthony presumably believing that the words reminding him of his oath should themselves drive Eros to do as he is obliged

• and the words that break the calm, F #10's 'Services' and F #12's pointing to the fact that Eros has already 'drawne' the sword are the key words necessary to push the point(s) home

To penetrative shame ; ₓ whil'st the wheel'd seate
Of [Fortune] Cæsar drawne before him, branded
His Basenesse that ensued. +

7 Come then : ₓ for with a wound I must be cur'd.
8 Draw that thy honest Sword, which thou hast worne
Most usefull for thy Country.

9 When I did make thee free, swor'st [ÿ] not then
To do this when I bad thee?
10 Do it at once,
Or thy precedent Services are all
But accidents unpurpos'd.
11 Draw, and come.

12 {ψ} Let it do at once
The thing why thou hast drawne it.

13 Now+ Eros.

#'S 22 - 26: CLEOPATRA'S DOWNFALL

22/ Cleopatra **Noblest of men, woo't dye?** 4.15.59 - 68

23/ Cleopatra **No more but in a Woman, and commanded** 4.15.73 - 91

Background: The dying Anthony has been lifted 'aloft' to join Cleopatra in the comparative safety of her monument. Speech #22 is triggered by his last words in the play, 'Now my spirit is going,/I can no more'. At the end of speech #22 scholarly assessment rightly suggests that Cleopatra faints, and speech #23 are her first words on regaining consciousness, triggered by Iras' attempt to awaken her, 'Royall Egypt: Empresse'.

Style: one on one, and small group address

Where: Cleopatra's monument **To Whom:** the dying Anthony, and her women Charmian & Iras

Speech 22: # of Lines: 10 **Probable Timing: 0.35 minutes**

Speech 23: # of Lines: 19 **Probable Timing: 1.00 minutes**

Modern Text

22/ Cleopatra

1 Noblest of men, woo't die*?
2 Hast thou no care of me ? †
3 Shall I abide
In this dull world, which in thy absence is
No better [than] a △sty*?
4 O*, see, my women:
The △crown* o'th'earth doth melt.
5 My △lord!
6 O*, wither'd is the △garland of the △war*,
The △soldier's* pole is fall'n* ! †
7 Young △boys* and △girls*
Are level* now with men; △the odds* is gone,
And there is nothing left remarkable*
Beneath the visiting △moon*. [4]

F's orthography suggests that while Cleopatra may be able to stay in control as the speech starts, the onrush of F #2 shows her control beginning to slip, and her fight to remain so fails once the enormous gap of what is left in his absence hits home – the onrush of the passionate F #5 suggesting that she can no longer stop herself from venting her grief.

• the essence of Cleopatra's love and loss can be seen in the (desperate?) quiet unembellishment of the onrushed F #3, especially when the icy calm is broken by the very last word that sums up her vision of the world without him, describing it with sudden passion as a 'Stye'

" . Hast thou no care of me, shall I abide/In this dull world, which in thy absence is/No better then a Stye ? "

• her recognition of the enormity of his death not simply to her but to all the civilized world is heightened via surround phrases

" . Oh see my women : /The Crowne o'th'earth doth melt . "

" . Oh wither'd is the Garland of the Warre,/The Souldiers pole is falne : young Boyes and Gyrles/Are levell now with men : "

• not surprisingly, the speech opens emotionally, (0/1, the short F #1), and, after the unembellishment continues emotionally into F #4's recognition of his death (1/3)

• and thus the rest of the speech turns resolutely passionate (F #5, 7/10)

First Folio

22/ Cleopatra

1 Noblest of men, woo't dye?
2 Hast thou no care of me,+ shall I abide
In this dull world, which in thy absence is
No better [then] a Stye?
3 Oh+ see+ my women:
The Crowne o'th'earth doth melt.
4 My Lord?+
5 Oh+ wither'd is the Garland of the Warre,
The Souldiers pole is falne: + young Boyes and Gyrles
Are levell now with men:x The oddes is gone,
And there is nothing left remarkeable
Beneath the visiting Moone.

---

[4] most modern texts indicate that here Cleopatra faints

Modern Text

23/ Cleopatra

1 No more but [e'en] a Δwoman, and commanded
By such poor* passion as the Δmaid that Δmilks*
And [does] the meanest chares.
2 It were for me
To throw my Δsceptre* at the injurious Δgods,
To tell them that this Δworld did equal* theirs*
Till they had stol'n* our Δjewel*.
3 All's but naught:
Patience is sottish, and impatient does
Become a Δdog* that's mad. †
4 Then is it sin*
To rush into the secret house of death
Ere death dare come to us?
5 How do you, Δwomen?
6 What, what, good cheer*!
7 Why, how now, Charmian?
8 My Δnoble Δgirls*!
9 Ah, Δwomen, women!
10 Look*
Our Δlamp* is spent, it's out.
11 Good sirs, take heart,
We'll* bury him; Δand then, what's brave, what's Δnoble,
Let's do't* after the high Roman fashion,
And make death proud to take us.
12 Come, away,
This case of that huge Δspirit now is cold.
13 Ah, Δwomen, Δwomen!
14 Come, we have no Δfriend
But Δresolution, and the briefest* end.

Orthographically it would seem that once Cleopatra reaches the understanding that, with Anthony's death, it may well be time to 'rush into the secret house of death', the decision brings her the intellectual self-control that she has been struggling to re-establish – though what she now expresses with such conviction may seem overkill, literally, to any outsider.

- that Cleopatra is having difficulty in expressing herself can be seen in the four extra breath thoughts (marked ,$_x$) that are found towards the end of each of the first three sentences, suggesting that each of the last thoughts (she is no better than a milk-maid; the loss/theft of Anthony; and the thought of suicide) are causing her great distress

- that she is trying with difficulty to maintain self-control at the opening of the speech can be seen in the quick switches in style
  a/ she is passionate in equating (demeaning?) herself to the 'Maid' that 'doe's the meanest chares', since they are both moved by 'poore passion', (F #1, 3/2)
  b/ though she is intellectual in recognising the futility of berating the 'Gods' (2/1, F #2's first two lines), in voicing the reason for berating them - for stealing Anthony ('our Jewell') - she turns to emotion (2/4)

- with the bleak monosyllabic surround phrase recognition
  ". All's but naught :/ Patience is sottish, and impatient does/Become a Dogge that's mad : "
leading to the idea of seeking death, she becomes passionate, (F #3, 6/5)

- then, as she tries to comfort and refocus the attention of her 'Women' so that they can deal with Anthony's death (F #4-9), the extra breaths disappear, suggesting that she is now regaining some form of self-control – however, the short sentences through which her instructions/suggestions are imparted and the continuing passion (6/4) suggest that this control does not come easily

- having caught everyone's attention, it seems that her final set of statements are well reasoned (8/3 overall, F #10-13) but, while a brief touch of emotion (rather than intellect) is to be expected in her instructions to the male attendants that she and her women will bury Anthony (0/1) . . .

- . . . the fact that her suggestions that
  a/ the women should commit suicide since Anthony's 'huge Spirit now is cold'
  b/ and that they have 'no Friend/But Resolution'
are so strongly intellectual should give warning that while she believes that she is in control of herself in going to the ends she is proposing, her decisions and reasoning have little base in sanity (or reality) in the eyes of any neutral observer

First Folio

23/ Cleopatra

1 No more but [in] a Woman, and commanded
By such poore passion,$_x$ as the Maid that Milkes,$_x$
And [doe's] the meanest chares.
2 It were for me,
To throw my Scepter at the injurious Gods,
To tell them that this World did equall theyrs,$_x$
Till they had stolne our Jewell.
3 All's but naught:
Patience is sottish, and impatient does
Become a Dogge that's mad: Then is it sinne,$_x$
To rush into the secret house of death,$_x$
Ere death dare come to us. +
4 How do you+ Women?
5 What, what+ good cheere?+
6 Why+ how now+ Charmian?
7 My Noble Gyrles?+
8 Ah+ Women, women!
9 Looke
Our Lampe is spent, it's out.
10 Good sirs, take heart,
Wee'l bury him :$_x$ And then, what's brave, what's Noble,
Let's doo't after the high Roman fashion,
And make death proud to take us.
11 Come, away,
This case of that huge Spirit now is cold.
12 Ah+ Women, Women!
13 Come, we have no Friend
But Resolution, and the breefest end.

24/ Cleopatra **See Cæsar : Oh behold,/How pompe is followed :** between 5.2.150 - 179

Background: Cleopatra supposedly has presented to Cæsar a schedule 'of Money, Plate, & Jewels/I am possesst of, 'tis exactly valewed'. However, her treasurer Seleucus informs the assembled Romans that she has kept back 'Enough to purchase what you have made known'. While Cæsar is not in the least put out ('Nay blush not Cleopatra, I approve/Your wisedome in the deede'), Cleopatra, as the following shows, most definitely is.

Style: essentially to two different people in front of a larger group

Where: Cleopatra's private quarters in the now captured palace at Alexandria **To Whom:** Cæsar and Seleucas, in front of Charmian, Iras. and Mardian, and the Romans Dolabella, Gallus, Mecenas, and others of Cæsar's 'traine'

# of Lines: 30 **Probable Timing: 1.30 minutes**

Modern Text

24/ Cleopatra

1 See, Cæsar ! †
2 O*, behold,
How pomp* is followed ! †
3 Mine will now be yours,
And should we shift estates, yours would be mine.
4 The ingratitude of this Seleucus does
Even make me wild*!
5 O* Slave, of no more trust
[Than] love that's hir'd* !
6 What, goest thou back* ? †
7 [Thou] shalt
Go back*, I warrant thee; but I'll catch thine eyes
Though they had wings.
8 Slave, Δsoulless* Δvillain, Δdog !
9 O rarely base!
10 O Cæsar, what a wounding shame is this,
That thou vouchsafing here* to visit me,
Doing the Δhonor* of thy Δlordliness*
To one so meek*, that mine own* Δservant should
Parcel* the sum* of my disgraces by
Addition of his Δenvy !
11 Say, good Cæsar,
That I some Δlady trifles have reserv'd,
Immoment toys*, things of such Δdignity*
As we greet modern* Δfriends withal*, and say
Some Δnobler token I have kept apart
For Livia and Octavia, to induce

While F's orthography initially suggests that Cleopatra is using all of her wiles to maintain some status in what is essentially a hopeless situation, the changes in style, especially towards the end of the speech, suggest moments where the reality of her newly conquered status intrudes.

- her attempt at verbally wooing/bamboozling/even seducing Octavius opens passionately (3/2) and is heightened by F #1 being set as three consecutive surround phrases
  " . See Cæsar : Oh behold,/How pompe is followed : Mine will now be yours, /And should we shift estates, yours would be mine . "
- while her attack on Seleucus, her whistle-blowing treasurer, is also passionate (5/4, F #2-6), at key moments she knows exactly when to pull back - for while the insults are full of release (F #2-3 and F #5), her F #4 threats of action against him are very quiet (venomous? or full of promise?), and the quiet of the final assessment, F #6's very short unembellished 'O rarely base !', is intensified by the very rare (for Elizabethan/early Jacobean printings) exclamation mark
- after the shredding of Seleucus, Cleopatra's initial attempt at salvaging the situation (both in terms of regaining her reputation and keeping the held back funds) is urged on the concept of honour (' a wounding shame'; 'the Honour of thy Lordlinesse'; 'the summe of my disgraces'; the 'Addition of his Envy') the whole offered with much passion (5/7, F #7) - though whether this is genuine or a rhetorical device to win by style if not by solid argument is up to each actor to explore
- the flimsy factual excuse of keeping the money for gifts, especially to Livia and Octavia (Octavius' wife and sister), is offered highly intellectually (9/3, F #8), though its onrush and the sudden appearance of two surround phrases at the very end of the sentence
  " . The Gods ! it smites me/Beneath the fall I have . "
  suggests that the fact of Seleucus' self-serving betrayal has really struck home, especially with the setting of the speech's second (rare) exclamation mark
- and so the last onrushed dismissal of Seleucus returns to passion (F #9, 3/3), intensified by a final surround phrase to drive home the ultimate insult
  " : Wer't thou a man,/Thou would'st have mercy on me . "

First Folio

24/ Cleopatra

1 See+ Cæsar : + Oh+ behold,
How pompe is followed : + Mine will now be yours,
And should we shift estates, yours would be mine.
2 The ingratitude of this Seleucus,x does
Even make me wilde. +
3 Oh Slave, of no more trust
[Then] love that's hyr'd?+
4 What+ goest thou backe,+ [ÿ] shalt
Go backe+ I warrant thee :x but Ile catch thine eyes
Though they had wings.
5 Slave, Soule-lesse,+ Villain, Dog. +
6 O rarely base!
7 O Cæsar, what a wounding shame is this,
That thou vouchsafing heere to visit me,
Doing the Honour of thy Lordlinesse
To one so meeke, that mine owne Servant should
Parcell the summe of my disgraces,x by
Addition of his Envy. +
8 Say (xgood Cæsarx)
That I some Lady trifles have reserv'd,
Immoment toyes, things of such Dignitie
As we greet moderne Friends withall, and say
Some Nobler token I have kept apart
For Livia and Octavia, to induce

{ctd. over}

Their mediation, must I be unfolded
With one that I have bred ? †
12 The ^Δgods! it smites me
Beneath the fall I have.
13 [5] Prithee* go hence,
Or I shall show* the ^Δcinders* of my spirits
Through th'^Δashes of my chance. †
14 Wer't thou a man,
Thou wouldst have mercy on me.

15 Be it known that we, the greatest are mis-thought,
For things that others do; and when we fall,
We answer other's merits in our name,
Are therefore to be pitied*.

• the ending to the speech is somewhat surprising, for, though convoluted, the final appeal for understanding/pity is completely unembellished and opens with a surround phrase – which, while being yet another rhetorical ploy - going quiet so as to seem humble, could also be seen as the reality of Cleopatra's powerlessness hitting home at last, so the game-playing has stopped and the final lines

" . Be it known, that we the greatest are mis-thoght/For things that others do : and when we fall,/We answer others merits, in our name/Are therefore to be pittied . "

may well be a genuine statement from a suddenly very emotionally drained and tired woman

Their mediation, must I be unfolded
With one that I have bred: The Gods! it smites me
Beneath the fall I have.
9 Prythee go hence,
Or I shall shew the Cynders of my spirits
Through th'Ashes of my chance: Wer't thou a man,
Thou would'st have mercy on me.

10 Be it known,ₓ that we⁺ the greatest are mis-thoght
For things that others do:ₓ and when we fall,
We answer others merits,ₓ in our name⁺
Are therefore to be pittied.

25/ Cleopatra **He words me Gyrles, he words me,** 5.2.190 - 232

Background: Despite Cæsar's public proclamation 'Make not your thoughts our prison: No deere Queen/For we intend so to dispose you, as/Your selfe shall give us counsell', Cleopatra does not trust him. The following are her first words as soon as she and her entourage are left alone.

Style: as part of a four-handed scene

Where: Cleopatra's private quarters in the now captured palace at Alexandria **To Whom:** Charmian, Iras, and the eunuch Mardian

# of Lines: 24 **Probable Timing: 1.15 minutes**

Modern Text

25/ Cleopatra

1 He words me, ^Δgirls*, he words me,
That I should not be ^Δnoble to myself*.

2 Now, Iras, what think'st thou?
3 Thou, an Egyptian ^Δpuppet, shall be shown*
In Rome as well as I. †
4 Mechanic* ^Δslaves
With greasy* ^Δaprons, ^Δrules, and ^Δhammers shall
Uplift us to the view.
5 In their thick* breaths*,
Rank* of gross* diet*, shall we be enclouded*,
And forc'd to drink* their vapor*.

Cleopatra's ability to assess information and take charge when necessary is clearly seen here, F's orthography suggesting that, though her emotions threaten to swamp her early in the speech, intellectual strength comes to the fore, and, once she reaches the key decision of how to proceed, her passions rather than diverting her, give her energy and drive as she prepares for the final, to her, joyous outcome.

• Cleopatra's realisation that she is being lied to is passionate (F #1, 2/2)

• stressing to Iras the indignancy that she believes they will be subjected to is underscored by the short F #2 and the opening surround phrase of F #3

" . Thou, an Egyptian Puppet shall be shewne/In Rome as well as I : "

the whole very clearly intellectually understood and argued (9/3, F #2-3) – though the onrushed F #3 suggests that she is losing just a little self-control

• and then her self-control seems to have a momentary melt down, for F #4's revulsion as she imagines the breaths of those who will gaze on them ('the thicke breathes' of the 'Mechanicke Slaves') is totally emotional (0/8)

First Folio

25/ Cleopatra

1 He words me⁺ Gyrles, he words me,
That I should not be Noble to my selfe.

2 Now⁺ Iras, what think'st thou?
3 Thou, an Egyptian Puppet⁺ shall be shewne
In Rome as well as I: Mechanicke Slaves
With greazie Aprons, Rules, and Hammers shall
Uplift us to the view.
4 In their thicke breathes,
Ranke of grosse dyet, shall we be enclowded,
And forc'd to drinke their vapour.

[5] most modern texts indicate this is addressed to Seleucus

6 Nay, 'tis most certain*, Iras. †
7 Saucy* Δlictors
Will catch at us like Δstrumpets, and scald Δrhymers*
Ballad's [ ] out a Δtune.
8 The quick* Δcomedians
Extemporally will stage us, and present
Our Alexandrian Δrevels: [Antony]
Shall be brought drunken forth, and I shall see
Some squeaking Cleopatra Boy my greatness*
I'th'posture of a Δwhore.

9 Nay, that's certain*.

10 Now, Charmian!
Show* me, my Δwomen, like a Δqueen*; Go fetch
My best Δattires*.
11 I am again* for [Cydnus]
To meet* [Mark* Antony].
12 Sirrah* Iras, go. †
13 Now, Δnoble Charmian, we'll* dispatch indeed*,
And when thou hast done this chare, I'll give thee leave
To play till Δdoomsday *. †
14 Bring our Δcrown* and all.

• the certainty of their humiliation is driven home by the surround phrase that opens F #5, ' . Nay, 'tis most certaine Iras : ', which in turn leads to detailing further inescapable unpleasantries, their being called 'Strumpets'; made the subjects of ballads; made the butt of improvisational 'Comedians'; with Anthony presented as a drunk and herself as a 'Whore'; - and it seems these appalling thoughts are burned into her brain, for this is all spelled out with ferocious intellect (12/3, F #5-6)

• the repetition of the certainty of it all is emphasised now by an emotional short three word sentence, F #7's 'Nay that's certaine.' (0/1), which then pushes her into a very swift decision, marked by F #8's even shorter 'Now Charmian.'

• her decision to reassert her true regal status is intellectual (5/2, F #8-9), with the two surround phrases of F #9 stressing the importance of her instructions

" . Shew me my Women like a Queene : Go fetch/My best Attyres . "

• in announcing her intention to commit suicide so as 'To meete Marke Anthony' (F #10) and busying her people in preparation for the event (F #11) Cleopatra becomes passionate (8/7 overall), her need to be seen as a Queen at the point of death stressed by the final surround phrase with its extra wonderfully defining breath-thought (marked ,x)

" : bring our Crowne,x and all . "

the complete certainty of her actions underscored by the onrush of F #11 (usually split into three more grammatically correct sentences by most modern texts)

5 Nay, 'tis most certaine+ Iras: sawcie Lictors
Will catch at us like Strumpets, and scald Rimers
Ballads [us] out a Tune.
6 The quicke Comedians
Extemporally will stage us, and present
Our Alexandrian Revels: [Anthony]
Shall be brought drunken forth, and I shall see
Some squeaking Cleopatra Boy my greatnesse
I'th'posture of a Whore.

7 Nay+ that's certaine.

8 Now+ Charmian. +
9 Shew me+ my Women+ like a Queene:x Go fetch
My best Attyres.
10 I am againe for [Cidrus],x
To meete [Marke Anthony].
11 Sirra Iras, go
(xNow+ Noble Charmian, wee'l dispatch indeede,)x
And when thou hast done this chare, Ile give thee leave
To play till Doomesday: bring our Crowne,x and all.

26/ Cleopatra **Give me my Robe, put on my Crowne, I have** between 5.2.280 - 313

Background: With her fears of the public humiliations that await her being confirmed by the Roman Dolabella, Cleopatra is preparing to take her own life by snake-bite. Already the asps, the 'pretty worme of Nylus . . ./That killes and paines not', have been smuggled in to her, and she has her woman dress her 'like a Queene' in her 'best Attyres' in which she will once more 'meete Marke Anthony'. The following are her last words in the play.

Style: as part of a three-handed scene

Where: Cleopatra's private quarters in the now captured palace at Alexandria **To Whom:** Charmian & Iras

# of Lines: 32 **Probable Timing: 1.35 minutes**

Modern Text

26/ Cleopatra

1 Give me my △robe, put on my △crown*, I have
Immortal* longings in me.
2 Now no more
The juice* of Egypt's △grape shall moist* this lip.
3 Yare, yare, good Iras; quick*. †
4 Methinks* I hear*
[Antony] call; I see him rouse* himself*
To praise my △noble △act.
5 I hear* him mock
The luck* of Cæsar, which the △gods give men
To excuse their after wrath.
6 Husband, I come !†
7 Now to that name, my △courage prove my △title !
8 I am △fire and △air*; my other △elements
I give to baser life.
9 So, have you done?
10 Come then, and take the last warmth of my △lips*.
11 Farewell, kind* Charmian, Iras, long farewell.[6]
12 Have I the △aspic* in my lips*?
13 Dost fall?
14 If thou and △nature can so gently part,
The stroke of death is as a △lover's pinch,
Which hurts, and is desir'd.
15 Dost thou lie* still?
16 If thus thou vanishest, thou tell'st the world
It is not worth leave-taking.

The speech falls into five basic parts; passion in the dressing/readying herself for the event; relative calmness in the first set of farewells; a mixture of responses with the unexpected death of Iras; passion again at taking the first of the poisonous snakes; and a final sense of calm – and though such a journey is not entirely unexpected, F's orthography shows the unexpected highs and/or swift changes which point to Cleopatra's brilliance, both in mind and spirit.

- the first third of the speech, the urging of and preparation for the final act of suicide, is passionate (10/11 overall in just seven and a half lines, F #1-4)

- whether it's because of her longing to join Anthony as quickly as possible or to ensure that she can proceed before Cæsar's representatives can stop her, her F #3 urging for more speed is underscored by being both slightly onrushed and set as four consecutive surround phrases
  " . Yare, yare, good Iras ; quicke : Me thinkes I heare/Anthony call : I see him rowse himselfe/To praise my Noble Act . "
  the opening heightened even more by being linked with the (emotional) semicolon

- then, in assuring dead Anthony that she is about to join him (F #5) and in the realisation that she is now composed of the more dashing brilliant elements that make up a human being (F #6's 'Fire , and Ayre') she regains self-control (5/1), with four more consecutive surround phrases
  " . Husband, I come : /Now to that name, my Courage prove my Title . / I am Fire, and Ayre ; my other Elements/I give to baser life . "
  emphasising just how confident she is in her choice of actions (F #5) and even more so in what she is becoming (the emotional surround phrases of F #6)

- her F #7 question/realisation that her (physical state of) dress as a queen finally matches her desires and intentions is remarkable in the fact that it is so quiet (an unembellished monosyllabic very short sentence, 'So, have you done?')

- and this now leads to the moment of farewell where initially very little need be said, as the next four short sentences (F #8-11) suggest – though, despite the lack of verbal flourish, the passion is still there (4/4 overall)

First Folio

26/ Cleopatra

1 Give me my Robe, put on my Crowne, I have
Immortall longings in me.
2 Now no more
The juyce of Egypts Grape shall moyst this lip.
3 Yare, yare, good Iras; quicke: Me thinkes I heare
[Anthony] call:$_{x}$ I see him rowse himselfe
To praise my Noble Act.
4 I heare him mock
The lucke of Cæsar, which the Gods give men
To excuse their after wrath.
5 Husband, I come: +
Now to that name, my Courage prove my Title. +
6 I am Fire,$_{x}$ and Ayre; my other Elements
I give to baser life.
7 So, have you done?
8 Come then, and take the last warmth of my Lippes.
9 Farewell+ kinde Charmian, Iras, long farewell.
10 Have I the Aspicke in my lippes?
11 Dost fall?
12 If thou,$_{x}$ and Nature can so gently part,
The stroke of death is as a Lovers pinch,
Which hurts, and is desir'd.
13 Dost thou lye still?
14 If thus thou vanishest, thou tell'st the world,$_{x}$
It is not worth leave-taking.

---

[6] most modern texts indicate that here Iras 'falls and dies'

17 This proves me base. †

18 If she first meet* the △curled Anthony,
He'll* make demand of her, and spend that kiss*
Which is my heaven to have.

19 Come, thou mortal wretch,[7]
With thy sharp* teeth this knot intrinsicate
Of life at one untie*. †

20 Poor* venomous △fool*,
Be angry, and dispatch.

21 O* couldst thou speak*,
That I might hear* thee call great Cæsar △ass*
Unpolicied!

22 Peace, peace! †

23 Dost thou not see my △baby at my breast,
That sucks* the △nurse asleep*?

24 As sweet* as △balm*, as soft as △air*, as gentle - ◊
O [Antony]!

25 Nay, I will take thee too: ◊ [8]
What should I stay ——

- after F #10's 'Have I the Aspicke in my lippes?', following the death of Iras there are quick shifts in style (F #10 emotional, the unembellished F #11, F #12 intellectual; and F #13 slightly emotional): given the circumstances the releases are very few (2/1 in three and a half lines of F #12 - 13), suggesting that Cleopatra still has a firm grip on the situation

- and indeed, the next observation at the easiness of Iras' death is extraordinary in that it is unembellished
  "If thus thou vanishest, thou tell'st the world, /It is not worth leave-taking."
  perhaps suggesting that it simply confirms in her mind the correctness of her decision

- whether meant as a whimsical remark to ease the tragedy of the situation or indicating a genuine fear, the thought that Iras may thus receive Anthony's kiss of welcome instead of her is passionate (F #15, 2/3)

- the moment of taking up the first Asp is emotional (0/2, F #16's first two lines), with the urging of it to strike heightened by being set as a surround phrase, the first part of the phrase very passionate (2/2), and the second and third calmly unembellished ' : Poore venomous Foole,/Be angry, and dispatch."

- the moment of her F #17 triumph over Cæsar is splendidly emotional (2/4, in just one and a half lines)

- F #18's short unembellished surround phrase opening ('Peace, peace :') could either be to Charmian or to the first Asp, while the description of the Asp as a child that kills is very passionate (4/5 in just the last two lines of F #18 and the single line of #19)

- with the rare (for Elizabethan/early Jacobean printings) exclamation mark ending F #20 it seems that at last the first Asp has struck

- which could well lead to the calmness of the last two unembellished sentences (F #21-22), as there is either now no need for any extra releases, or that such releases are impossible if the poison spreads as quickly as it should

15 This proves me base:
If she first meete the Curled Anthony,
Hee'l make demand of her, and spend that kisse
Which is my heaven to have.

16 Come+ thou mortal wretch,
With thy sharpe teeth this knot intrinsicate,$_{x}$
Of life at one untye: Poore venomous Foole,
Be angry, and dispatch.

17 Oh+ could'st thou speake,
That I might heare thee call great Cæsar Asse,$_{x}$ unpolicied.+

18 Peace, peace:+
Dost thou not see my Baby at my breast,
That suckes the Nurse asleepe. +

19 As sweete as Balme, as soft as Ayre, as gentle.

20 O [Anthony]!

21 Nay+ I will take thee too.

22 What should I stay ——

[7] most modern texts indicate Cleopatra takes an asp from the basket and puts it to her breast
[8] most modern texts indicate Cleopatra takes another asp and places it on her arm

SPEECHES IN ORDER		TIME	PAGE
CYMBELINE			
#'s 1 - 4: A Bad Situation At Home			
1/ Imogen	A Father cruell, and a Stepdame false,	0.30	391
2/ Queene	No, be assur'd you shall not finde me (Daughter)	0.45	392
3/ Cloten	If she be up, Ile speake with her: if not	0.45	393
4/ 2nd Lord	That such a craftie Divell as is his Mother	0.45	394
#'s 5 - 9: A Foolish Wager With An Unscrupulous Man			
5/ Iachimo	You must not so farre preferre {your Lady}, 'fore ours	1.40	395
6/ Iachimo	What are men mad? Hath Nature given them eyes	0.55	397
7/ Iachimo	Had I this cheeke/To bathe my lips upon: . . .	0.55	398
8/ Iachimo	The Crickets sing, and mans ore-labor'd sense	2.00	399
9/ Iachimo	Your Lady,/Is one of the fayrest that I have . . .	1.35	401
#'s 10 - 18: With Potentially Disasterous Results			
10/ Posthumus	Is there no way for Men to be, but Women	1.45	402
11/ Pisanio	How? of Adultery? Wherefore write you not	1.10	404
12/ Imogen	A Letter from my Lord Leonatus.	0.45	406
13/ Imogen	Oh for a Horse with wings: Hear'st thou Pisanio?	1.40	407
14/ Imogen	False to his Bed? What is it to be false?	1.10	409
15/ Pisanio	What shall I need to draw my Sword, the Paper	0.30	410
16/ Imogen	Come Fellow, be thou honest,/Do thou thy Masters	1.40	410
17/ Imogen	I see a mans life is a tedious one,	1.30	412
18/ Belarius	How hard it is to hide the sparkes of Nature?	1.30	414
#'s 19 - 20: Complications Via Cloten			
19/ Cloten	I love, and hate her: for she's Faire and Royall,	0.35	415
20/ Cloten	I am neere to'th'place where they should meet,	1.15	416
#'s 21 - 22: An Unscrupulous Step-Mother			
21/ Queene	I wonder, Doctor,/Thou ask'st me such a Question:	0.45	417
22/ Queene	Weepes she still (saist thou?)	2.00	418
#'s 23 - 24: Leads To Further Complications			
23/ Arviragus	The Bird is dead/That we have made so much on.	1.10	420
24/ Imogen	Yes Sir, to Milford-Haven, which is the way?	2.00	422
# 25: The Italian Invasion			
25/ Cymbeline	You must know,/Till the injurious Romans, did extort	1.15	424

SPEECHES BY GENDER

		Speech #(s)
SPEECHES FOR WOMEN (10)		
Imogen	**Traditional & Today:** young woman	#1, #12, #13, #14, #16, #17, #24
Queene	**Traditional & Today:** woman with an adult son	#2, #21, #22
SPEECHES FOR EITHER GENDER (1)		
2nd Lord	**Traditional:** male, any age **Today:** any age, any gender	#4
SPEECHES FOR MEN (14)		
Cloten	**Traditional & Today:** a young man	#3, #19, #20
Iachimo	**Traditional & Today:** a young to middle-aged male	#5, #6, #7, #8, #9
Posthumus	**Traditional & Today:** a young man	#10
Pisanio	**Traditional:** older male **Today:** male, any age, often middle-aged and older	#11, #15
Arviragus	**Traditional & Today:** young male	#23
Belarius	**Traditional & Today:** male old enough to be 'father' to two young men	#18
Cymbeline	**Traditional & Today:** male old enough to have a teenage daughter	#25

CYMBELINE

#'s 1 - 4: A Bad Situation At Home

1/ Imogen **A Father cruell, and a Stepdame false,** 1.6.1 - 9

Background: This is Imogen's summation of her own situation. Given that her father (the King, Cymbeline) has just banished her newly wed husband, Posthumus, and she does not trust her step-mother, the speech is self-explanatory.

Style: solo

Where: somewhere in the palace **To Whom:** direct audience address

# of Lines: 9 **Probable Timing: 0.30 minutes**

Modern Text

1/ Imogen

1 A △father cruel*, and a △step-dame false,
A △foolish △suitor to a △wedded △lady
That hath her △husband banish'd. †
2 O, that △husband! †
3 My supreme* △crown* of grief*, and those repeated
Vexations of it.
4 Had I been* thief-stol'n*,
As my two △brothers, happy! but most miserable
Is the [desire] that's glorious.
5 Blessed be those,
How mean* soe'er, that have their honest wills,
Which seasons comfort.
6 Who may this be?
7 Fie*!

The opening intellectual clarity of the speech (7/1, the first two and a half lines), the fact that F #2 is made up of two surround phrases, and the monosyllabic brevity of F #4 (unembellished) and #5 all point to a woman seriously analysing her self and state rather than just a melodramatic bleat as it often comes out.

- the passion associated with the last two lines of F #1 and the surround phrases of F #2 (5/5 in all), followed by her relative quiet in the last three and a half lines (0/2), underscores how important this analysis is to her and how devastating the interruption (the arrival of Iachimo) could be

First Folio

1/ Imogen

1 A Father cruell, and a Stepdame false,
A Foolish Suitor to a Wedded-Lady, x
That hath her Husband banish'd: + O, that Husband, +
My supreame Crowne of griefe, and those repeated
Vexations of it.
2 Had I bin Theefe-stolne,
As my two Brothers, happy: + but most miserable
Is the [desires] that's glorious.
3 Blessed be those +
How meane so ere, that have their honest wills,
Which seasons comfort.
4 Who may this be?
5 Fye. +

2/ Queene **No, be assur'd you shall not finde me (Daughter)** between 1.1.70 - 83

Background: The Queene is Imogen's step-mother, and, as later revealed, wants her own son Cloten to marry Imogen to strengthen her own hold on the 'Brittish Crowne'. Thus her kindness to the just married Imogen and therefore-banished Posthumus is merely a mask, and, once the Queene leaves, it is almost certain that she straightway informs the king, Imogen's father, where Imogen and Posthumus are so that he can break up their being together.

Style: as part of a three-handed scene

Where: somewhere in the palace **To Whom:** Imogen and Posthumus

# of Lines: 13 **Probable Timing: 0.45 minutes**

Modern Text

2/ Queene

1 No, be assur'd you shall not find* me, △daughter,
After the slander of most △step△mothers,
Evil*-ey'd unto you.
2 You're my △prisoner, but
Your [△jailer]shall deliver you the keys*
That lock* up your restraint.
3 For you, Posthumus,
So soon* as I can win th'offended King,
I will be known* your △advocate. †
4 Marry, yet
The fire of △rage is in him, and 'twere good
You lean'd unto his △sentence, with what patience
Your wisdom* may inform* you.
5 You know the peril*. †
6 I'll fetch a turn* about the △garden, pitying*
The pangs of barr'd △affections, though the King
Hath charg'd you should not speak* together.

So much release within a short speech (13/12 in just thirteen lines) suggests a character working far harder than might be thought necessary for the purposes of mere reassurance.

- while the only surround phrase of the speech, F #4's ' . You know the perill : ', might suggest a genuine reason for the Queene's apparent concern, given the lack of urgency elsewhere and the underlying manipulatory qualities of the character, it is likely that the excesses relate more to her own agenda than genuine concern

- hence the onrushed F #3, referring to the 'Rage' of the 'King', might well be intended to discombobulate Imogen and her out of favour husband Posthumus rather than to calm them down

- thus throughout the capitals are very careful to point to the low status of Imogen ('Daughter' as 'Prisoner') and the power the Queene has over her (both as 'Step-Mother' and 'Gaolor')

First Folio

2/ Queene

1 No, be assur'd you shall not finde me ($_x$Daughter$_x$)
After the slander of most Step-Mothers,
Evill-ey'd unto you.
2 You're my Prisoner, but
Your [Gaoler] shall deliver you the keyes
That locke up your restraint.
3 For you+ Posthumus,
So soone as I can win th'offended King,
I will be knowne your Advocate: marry+ yet
The fire of Rage is in him, and 'twere good
You lean'd unto his Sentence, with what patience
Your wisedome may informe you.
4 You know the perill:
Ile fetch a turne about the Garden, pittying
The pangs of barr'd Affections, though the King
Hath charg'd you should not speake together.

3/ Cloten **If she be up, Ile speake with her : if not** 2.3.64 - 76

Background: Encouraged by his mother and step-father King Cymbeline, Cloten still insists on wooing Imogen, even though she's married and cannot stand him. The following occurs after his early morning serenade outside Imogen's window (musicians and all), has failed to yield any response.

Style: solo

Where: outside Imogen's bedroom window or door **To Whom:** direct audience address

# of Lines: 13 **Probable Timing: 0.45 minutes**

Modern Text

3/ Cloten

1 If she be up, I'll speak* with her ; if not,
Let her lie* still and dream*. †
2 By your leave ho* ! †
3 I know her women are about her ; what
If I do line one of their hands ? †
4 'Tis △gold
Which buys* admittance (oft it doth), yea, and makes
Diana's △rangers false themselves, yield* up
Their △deer* to th'stand o'th'△stealer ; and 'tis △gold
Which makes the △true ° man kill'd and saves the △thief*;
Nay, sometime hangs both △thief* and △true man. †
5 What
Can it not do, and undo*?
6 I will make
One of her women △lawyer to me, for
I yet not understand the case myself*.
7 By your leave.

For an early morning speech, the onrushed nature of F #1 (split into five sentences by most modern texts) and the three surround phrases opening F #1 plus the two closing it point to just how much unchecked release accompanies anything that Cloten tries to achieve . . .

• . . . although it does seem that he occasionally tries to rein himself in, as when trying to work out just how to get to Imogen

"I know her women are about her : what/If I do line one of their hands,"

one of his very few unembellished moments in the play – though it immediately leads to enormous excesses in his cynical assumption that 'Gold' will lead to betrayal anywhere (9/6 the last six lines of F #1)

• and it could be that this intellectual spurt in working things out exhausts him, for the final decision to get 'One of her women Lawyer for me' is, for him, remarkably unreleased (1/1, the last three lines of the speech)

First Folio

3/ Cloten

1 If she be up, Ile speake with her : x if not+
Let her lye still, x and dreame : by your leave hoa,+
I know her women are about her : x what
If I do line one of their hands,+ 'tis Gold
Which buyes admittance (oft it doth)+ yea, and makes
Diana's Rangers false themselves, yeeld up
Their Deere to'th'stand o'th'Stealer : x and 'tis Gold
Which makes the True-man kill'd, x and saves the Theefe
: x
Nay, sometime hangs both Theefe, x and True-man : what
Can it not do, and undoo?
2 I will make
One of her women Lawyer to me, for
I yet not understand the case my selfe.
3 By your leave.

4/ 2nd Lord **That such a craftie Divell as is his Mother** 1.6.52 - 65

Background: This less than hopeful assessment of the complete familial situation comes from one of the two Lords whose main assignations seems to be trying to keep Cloten out of the continual quarrels he tends to generate and minimising the damages when the quarrels actually occur .

Style: solo

Where: somewhere in the palace **To Whom:** direct audience address

# of Lines: 14 **Probable Timing: 0.45 minutes**

Modern Text

4/ 2nd Lord

1 That such a crafty* Δdevil* as is his Δmother
Should yield the world this Δass*! Δa woman, that
Bears* all down* with her Δbrain*, and this her Δson*
Cannot take two from twenty, for his heart,
And leave eighteen*.
2 Alas poor* Princess*,
Thou divine Imogen, what thou endur'st,
Betwixt a Δfather by thy Δstep-dame govern'd,
A Δmother hourly* coining* plots, Δa Δwooer
More hateful* [than] the foul* expulsion is
Of thy dear* Δhusband, ◊ [than] that horrid Δact
Of the divorce he'ld* make . †
3 The Δheavens hold firm*
The walls of thy dear* Δhonor*; ◊ keep* unshak'd
That Δtemple, thy fair* mind, that thou mayst* stand
T'enjoy thy banish'd Δlord and this great Δland !

Presumably attendant on Clotens' every whim, and now alone, the 2nd. Lord can express his frustration without fear of reprisal and does so (20/20 in just fourteen lines), the relative lack of punctuation pointing much more to simple release rather than determined analysis.

- the occasional exasperation can be seen in the capitalised indefinite article that comes immediately after the colon in both F #1 and #2

- the first two extra breath-thoughts (marked , x) point to the Lord's need to either control himself and/or find the means to express his amazement as to Cloten's (mathematical) stupidity (F #1) and his presumably appalling behaviour as a 'Wooer' (F #2) , while the third (F #3) connects two vastly disparate thoughts, pointing to a momentary loss of composure (though most modern texts regard this moment as ungrammatical and repunctuate for more rationality, as shown)

- given the appalling situation Britain finds itself in the play (de facto ruled by the Queene in place of the sickly and irascible Cymbeline, and threatened with invasion from Italy), the final surround phrase ' : and this great Land . ' is not merely a jingoistic piece of posturing but rather points to a very determined love and concern for the country

First Folio

4/ 2nd Lord

1 That such a craftie Divell as is his Mother
Should yeild the world this Asse : + A woman, that
Beares all downe with her Braine, and this her Sonne, x
Cannot take two from twenty+ for his heart,
And leave eighteene.
2 Alas poore Princesse,
Thou divine Imogen, what thou endur'st,
Betwixt a Father by thy Step-dame govern'd,
A Mother hourely coyning plots : x A Wooer, x
More hatefull [then] the foule expulsion is
Of thy deere Husband.
3 [Then] that horrid Act [1]
Of the divorce, x heel'd make the Heavens hold firme
The walls of thy deere Honour.
4 Keepe unshak'd
That Temple+ thy faire mind, that thou maist stand
T'enjoy thy banish'd Lord : x and this great Land. +

---

[1] this and the next full line raise serious grammatical problems: most modern texts do not reproduce the F 1-3 period (or any punctuation at all) and end the sentence on the next line after 'make' (omitting the comma between 'divorce' and 'heel'd): the modern text thus reads

Of thy dear husband than that horrid act
Of the divorce hel'd make. The heavens hold firm

if one keeps the F layout as is, while acknowledging the modern restructuring is correctly grammatical, in F the 2nd Lord's rhetoric could be seen as momentarily failing

#'s 5 - 9: A Foolish Wager With An Unscrupulous Man

5/ Iachimo **You must not so farre preferre {your Lady}, 'fore ours of/Italy.** between 1.4.65 - 168

Background: Once in Italy, Posthumus has been drawn into an international 'argument . . . in praise of our Country-Mistresses' in which, according to a Frenchman, Posthumus has maintained Imogen to be above all others in terms of 'Faire, Vertuous, Wise, Chaste, Constant, Qualified, and lesse attemtible then any, the rarest of our Ladies in Fraunce'. This triggers the following from the Italian Iachimo.

Style: as part of a six-handed scene

Where: the house of Philario, who has befriended Posthumus **To Whom:** Posthumus, in front of Philario, a Frenchman, a Spaniard and a Dutchman

# of Lines: 33 **Probable Timing: 1.40 minutes**

Modern Text

5/ Iachimo

1 You must not so far* prefer* {your Δlady} 'fore ours of
Italy.

2 I have seen*, as that Δdiamond of yours outlustres* many I
have beheld, I could not [but] believe* she excelled many
.†

3 But I have not seen* the most precious* Δdiamond that is,
nor you the Δlady.

4 {Y}ou
know strange Δfowl* light upon neighboring* Δponds.

5 Your Δring may be stol'n* too : so your brace of unpriz-
able* Δestimations, the one is but frail* and the other Δcasu-
al*. †

6 A cunning Δthief*, or a (that way) accomplish'd
Δcourtier, would hazard* the winning both of first and
last.

7 With five times so much conversation, I should
get ground of your fair* Δmistress*; make her go back*, e-
ven to the yielding, had I admittance, and opportunity*
to friend.

8 I dare thereupon pawn* the moi'ty* of my Δe-
state, to your Δring, which in my opinion o'er-values it
something. †

9 But I make my wager rather against your
Δconfidence, [than] her Δreputation; ◊ Δand to bar* your of-

No matter how quickly the situation may get out of hand, the seriousness behind the challenge of seducing Posthumus' wife Imogen is emphasised by the calm of F #9's unembellished phrases 'provided, $_x$ I have your commendation, $_x$ for my more free entertainment.', especially when underscored by two F only extra breath thoughts.

- and the earlier specific details of the challenge are handled almost as quietly (F #5, 1/2)
  "With five times so much conversation, I should get ground of your faire Mistris ; make her go backe, even to the yeilding, had I admittance, and opportunitie to friend . "
  with the sexual crudity of 'backe', her enhanced description as 'faire', and the capitalisation of the short-spelled 'Mistris' being the key words that break the calm

- the passion of the ten lines (F #1-5) preamble to F #6's setting forth of the financial details of his challenge (12/16) suggests that Iachimo has been quite stung by Posthumus' claims of the women of Britain's fidelity, the long spelled words all tending to be (deliberately?) insultingly provocative

- initially the elaboration of the challenge maintains the passion (4/5, F #6-7), but when further financial details are discussed and the depth of the bet (seduction of Imogen) is specified, the passion gives way to intellect (5/1, F #8)

First Folio

5/ Iachimo

1 You must not so farre preferre {your Lady},$_x$ 'fore ours of
Italy.

2 I have seene+ as that Diamond of yours out-lusters many I
have beheld, I could not [ ] beleeve she excelled many:
but I have not seene the most pretious Diamond that is,
nor you the Lady.

3 {Y}ou
know strange Fowle light upon neighbouring Ponds.

4 Your Ring may be stolne too,+ so your brace of unprize-
able Estimations, the one is but fraile,$_x$ and the other Casu-
all; .[2] A cunning Thiefe, or a (that way) accomplish'd
Courtier, would hazzard the winning both of first and
last.

5 With five times so much conversation, I should
get ground of your faire Mistris; make her go backe, e-
ven to the yeilding, had I admittance, and opportunitie
to friend.

6 I dare thereupon pawne the moytie of my E-
state, to your Ring, which in my opinion o're-values it
something: but I make my wager rather against your
Confidence, [then] her Reputation.

7 And to barre your of-
fence heerein to, I durst attempt it against any Lady in
the world {,}

{ctd. over}

[2] F1 sets two pieces of punctuation: F2 and most modern texts omit the semicolon

fence herein* too*, I durst attempt it against any ^Δ^lady in the world {,}

{even y}ours, whom in constancy* you think* stands so safe.
10 I will lay you ten [thousand] ^Δ^ducats* to your ^Δ^ring, that, commend me to the ^Δ^court where your ^Δ^la-
dy is, with no more advantage [than] the opportunity* of a
second conference, and I will bring from thence that ^Δ^honor of hers which you imagine so reserv'd.

11 {ψ} If I bring you no sufficient testimony that I have enjoy'd the dearest* bodily part of your ^Δ^mistress*, my ten thousand ^Δ^ducats* are yours,
so is your ^Δ^diamond too. †
If I come off, and leave her in
12 such honor* as you have trust in, ^Δ^she* your jewel*, this your ^Δ^jewel*, and my ^Δ^gold are yours - provided I have your commendation for my more free entertainment.

last sentences slightly reshaped 13 Your hand - a ^Δ^covenant. †
14 We* will have these things set down* by lawful* ^Δ^counsel* {,} I will fetch my ^Δ^gold, and straight away for Britain*.

• that this is not a casual challenge even for Iachimo can be seen not just in the extra breath thoughts ending F #8

"and I will bring from thence, x that Honor of hers, x which you imagine so reserv'd. "

but especially in the four successive surround phrases ending F #9 and the fifth opening F #10 (which appear only now, after twenty-seven lines)

" : my ten thousand Duckets are yours, so is your Diamond too : if I come off, and leave her in such honour as you have trust in ; Shee your Jewell, this your Jewell, and my Gold are yours : provided, I have your commendation, for my more free entertainment. Your hand, a Covenant : "

with the emotional underscoring following the semicolon summing up the whole bet

" ; Shee your Jewell, this your Jewell, and my Gold are yours : "

and very passionately too (4/3 in just ten words), not surprising when so much money and reputation are at stake

• while the passion that accompanies this final flourish (11/10, F #9-10) points to the demand and pressure that Iachimo puts on Posthumus (and perhaps himself)

{even y}ours, whom in constancie you thinke stands so safe.
8 I will lay you ten [thousands] Duckets to your Ring, that⁺ commend me to the Court where your Lady is, with no more advantage [then] the opportunitie of a second conference, and I will bring from thence, x that Honor of hers, x which you imagine so reserv'd.

9 {ψ} If I bring you no sufficient testimony that I have enjoy'd the deerest bodily part of your Mistris : x my ten thousand Duckets are yours, so is your Diamond too : if I come off, and leave her in such honour as you have trust in ; x Shee your Jewell, this your Jewell, and my Gold are yours : x provided, x I have your commendation, x for my more free entertainment.

last sentence slightly reshaped 10 Your hand, a Covenant : wee will have these things set downe by lawfull Counsell {,} I will fetch my Gold, and straightaway for Britaine .

6/ Iachimo **What are men mad? Hath Nature given them eyes** between 1.6.32 - 50
7/ Iachimo **Had I this cheeke/To bathe my lips upon : this hand, whose touch,** between 1.6.99 - 117

Background: Arriving in Britain, Iachimo wastes no time in attempting to win his bet to seduce Imogen, making his overtures at their very first meeting. Each speech is self-explanatory, the first general speech of amazement implying Posthumus' foolishness in choosing another and the second far more intimate and specific.

Style: as part of a two-handed scene

Where: somewhere in the palace **To Whom:** Imogen

Speech 6: # of Lines: 18 **Probable Timing: 0.55 minutes**
Speech 7: # of Lines: 18 **Probable Timing: 0.55 minutes**

Modern Text

6/ Iachimo

1 What, are men mad?
2 Hath Δnature given them eyes
To see this vaulted Δarch and the rich Δcrop
Of Δsea and Δland, which can distinguish 'twixt
The fiery* Δorbs* above, and the twinn'd Δstones
Upon the number'd [3] Δbeach, and can we not
Partition make with Δspectacles so precious*
Twixt fair* and foul*?

3 It cannot be i'th'eye : for Δapes and Δmonkeys
'Twixt two such Δshe's would chatter this way, and
Contemn* with mows* the other ; ◊ Δnor i'th'judgment :
For Δidiots in this case of favor* would
Be wisely definite* : Δnor i'th'Δappetite : ◊
Sluttery, to such neat* Δexcellence oppos'd,
Should make desire vomit emptiness*,
Not so allur'd to feed.

4 The Δcloyed will,
That satiate yet unsatisfied* desire, that Δtub
Both fill'd and running - Δravening first the Δlamb*,
Longs after for the Δgarbage.

Iachimo's first (and in terms of imagery, very dense) attempts at softening up Imogen for seduction show great skill, for not only is the overall speech strongly intellectual (21/10 in just seventeen lines), four of the six sentences open with great bite: F #1 is a very short sentence, monosyllabic and unembellished; F #3 and #4 open out with unembellished surround phrases; and F #6's strong imagery of sexual corruption is composed totally of (three) surround phrases.

- the fact that most modern texts create a single mt. #3 offers an onrushed blurt instead of allowing each of F #3, #4, and #5 to stand independently: thus most modern Iachimos already seem to be on a roll whereas their original counter-part seems to be working far harder-in an attempt to get his overly-dense imagery understood
- the five extra breath-thoughts scattered through the piece (marked ,x) add extra support to the original Iachimo's extra hard work
- the only crack in the intellectual barrage is in F #5 (1/2) as he begins to become somewhat more specific, comparing Posthumus' supposed object of dalliance ('Sluttery') to the purity of Imogen (described as 'Excellence')

First Folio

6/ Iachimo

1 What+ are men mad?
2 Hath Nature given them eyes
To see this vaulted Arch,x and the rich Crop
Of Sea and Land, which can distinguish 'twixt
The firie Orbes above, and the twinn'd Stones
Upon the number'd Beach, and can we not
Partition make with Spectacles so pretious
Twixt faire,x and foule?

3 It cannot be i'th'eye : for Apes,x and Monkeys
'Twixt two such She's,x would chatter this way, and
Contemne with mowes the other.

4 Nor i'th'judgment :
For Idiots in this case of favour,x would
Be wisely definit : Nor i'th'Appetite.

5 Sluttery+ to such neate Excellence,x oppos'd+
Should make desire vomit emptinesse,
Not so allur'd to feed.

6 The Cloyed will : x
That satiate yet unsatisfi'd desire, that Tub
Both fill'd and running : x Ravening first the Lambe,
Longs after for the Garbage.

[3] Ff = 'number'd', some modern texts = 'unnumber'd'

Modern Text

7/ Iachimo

1 Had I this cheek*
To bath* my lips upon; this hand, whose touch
(Whose every touch) which force the Δfeeler's soul*
To th'oath of loyalty; ◊ Δthis object, which
Takes prisoner the wild motion of mine eye,
[Fixing] it only* here*; should I (damn'd [4] then)
Slaver* with lips* as common as the stairs*
That mount the Capitol*; Δ join* grips* with hands
Made hard with hourly* falsehood* (falsehood* , as
With labor*); then by-peeping in an eye
Base and illustrious as the smoky* light
That's fed with stinking Δtallow: it were fit
That all the plagues of Δhell should at one time
Encounter such revolt.

2 {ψ} {Your} Lord, I fear*,
Has forgot Britain*.
3 And himself*. †
4 Not I
Inclin'd to this intelligence, pronounce
The Δbeggary of his change; but 'tis your Δgraces
That from my mutest Δconscience to my tongue
Charms* this report out.

That the intellect of the first seduction attempt (speech #6, 21/10) may not have gone down as well as expected is shown by the totally different set of releases in this second speech (5/15 in the first two sentences, 5/4 in the last two).

- the differences are especially apparent as the speech opens, for as Iachimo starts to zero in on Imogen herself (her 'cheeke' and 'hand'), F #1's surround phrase start is far more emotional than anything in the previous speech (1/3) - and this is just the prelude to the middle of F #2
- having moved his focus from her cheek to her hand and wishing to expand further, he needs a new sentence (ungrammatical as far as most modern texts are concerned) - the move at first causes him to go enormously quiet (F #2's first line and half opening without embellishment)
- unlike the first speech, here the imagery has been clear, at least until now – but then he returns to incredible complexity as he hints at Posthumus' supposed brushes with prostitutes, bursting into a huge emotional release (2/11, F #2's next four and half lines) as he laments how her hand has been/might be cheapened
- though he manages to calm down somewhat by the end of the sentence (perhaps for effect, pretending that he has been moved at the thought of Posthumus' foolishness - 2/1, F #2's last four and a half lines) the complex imagery still remains
- however, in stating directly that Posthumus has forgotten Britain and, by implication, thus Imogen herself, Iachimo manages to regain his initial simplicity
- and as he does so, passion returns (5/4, F #3-4), the final extra breath-thoughts in the penultimate line (marked , x) suggesting (whether truthfully or for effect) his (supposed?) awkwardness/embarrassment in having to be the bearer of such disquieting news

First Folio

7/ Iachimo

1 Had I this cheeke
To bathe my lips upon: x this hand, whose touch, x
(Whose every touch) which force the Feelers soule
To'th'oath of loyalty. [5]
2 This object, which
Takes prisoner the wild motion of mine eye,
[Fiering] it onely heere,+ should I (damn'd then)
Slavver with lippes as common as the stayres
That mount the Capitoll: x Joyne gripes, x with hands
Made hard with hourely falshood (falshood+ as
With labour:) x then by peeping in an eye
Base and illustrious as the smoakie light
That's fed with stinking Tallow: it were fit
That all the plagues of Hell should at one time
Encounter such revolt.

3 {ψ} {Your} Lord, I feare
Has forgot Brittaine.
4 And himselfe, not I
Inclin'd to this intelligence, pronounce
The Beggery of his change: x but 'tis your Graces
That from my mutest Conscience, x to my tongue, x
Charmes this report out.

---

[4] F = 'damn'd', one modern gloss offers 'dampn'd'

[5] Ff set a period, as if Iachimo needs an extra moment to control himself: most modern texts reduce the need by setting a semicolon

8/ Iachimo **The Crickets sing, and mans ore-labor'd sense** 2.2.9 - 51

Background: With Imogen repelling him so strongly, Iachimo seems to have resoundingly lost his bet. However, he managed to lie his way out of public denunciation by explaining that he couldn't believe Posthumus' description of Imogen's beauty and chastity and just had to test it for himself, and claiming Posthumus was lucky to have such a wife. Imogen is pacified, but Iachimo is not. Determined to win by fair means or foul, he asked whether a trunk full of gifts for the Emperor from 'Some dozen Romanes of us, and your lord/(The best Feather of our wing)' might for safety be kept in Imogen's room for the night. She has agreed, but the trunk rather than full of gifts, is full of Iachimo, and out he steps to note intimate details of Imogen and her room that he hopes will convince Posthumus that Imogen is unchaste and so win the bet deceitfully.

Style: solo

Where: Imogen's bed-chamber **To Whom:** self, audience, and the sleeping Imogen

# of Lines: 42 **Probable Timing: 2.00 minutes**

Modern Text

8/ Iachimo

1 The △crickets sing, and mans o'er-labor'd sense
Repairs* itself* by rest. †
2 Our Tarquin* thus
Did softly press* the △rushes ere he waken'd
The △chastity, he wounded.
3 Cytherea,
How bravely thou becom'st thy △bed ! fresh △lily*,
And whiter [than] the △sheets* ! †
4 That I might touch ! †
5 But kiss*, one kiss* !
6 Rubies unparagon'd,
How dearly* they [6] do't* ! †
7 'Tis her breathing that
Perfumes the △chamber thus. †
8 The △flame o'th'△taper
Bows* toward her, and would under-peep* her lids, ◊
To see th'inclosed △lights, now △canopied
Under these windows*, △white and △azure lac'd
With △blue* of △heaven's own* tinct.
9 But my design* ◊
To note the △chamber, I will write all down*:
Such and such pictures; △there the window; such
Th'adornment* of her △bed; the △arras, △figures,
Why, such and such; and the △contents o'th'△story.

The need for success and the strains he is undergoing, especially since he is so attracted to her beauty (F #2-3) is underscored with seven of the first eight phrases of the opening three sentences being set as surround-phrases – emphasised even more with the opening surround phrases of F #2, his first sight of her in her sleepwear, being linked with the speech's first emotional semicolon.

- the opening (awkward?) climbing out of the trunk and orienting himself is passionate (F #1, 5/4), while the first sight of Imgen on the bed and the focus on her lips, wanting a 'kisse, one kisse.' from those 'Rubies unparagon'd', turns emotional (F #2 and the first phrase of F #3, 3/6 in less than four lines)

- then, perhaps as if he were trying to control himself, his further longings inspired by her breath (the remainder of F #3), and his ungrammatical (at least according to most modern texts) F #4 desire to see her eyes, Iachimo becomes intellectual (10/5)

- with F #5 set as a separate sentence, unlike most modern texts, it seems that the original Iachimo has far more difficulty than his modern counterpart in pulling himself away from Imogen's body to make notes of the room

- his noting of the room seems to be quite excited, for not only is it highly intellectual (7/2, F #6), it is also completely created by four surround phrases
" . To note the Chamber, I will write all downe, /Such, and such pictures :
There the window, such /Th'adornement of her Bed ; the Arras,
Figures,/Why such, and such : and the Contents o'th'Story."

- and the intellect continues, momentarily, as he is attracted once more to the sleeping Imogen (F #7, 3/1), but this quickly turns to passion as he begs that sleep possess her still (F #8, 4/3)

First Folio

8/ Iachimo

1 The Crickets sing, and mans ore-labor'd sense
Repaires it selfe by rest: Our Tarquine thus
Did softly presse the Rushes,x ere he waken'd
The Chastitie he wounded.
2 Cytherea,
How bravely thou becom'st thy Bed; + fresh Lilly,
And whiter [then] the Sheetes: + that I might touch,+
But kisse, one kisse. +
3 Rubies unparagon'd,
How deerely they doo't: + 'Tis her breathing that
Perfumes the Chamber thus: the Flame o'th'Taper
Bowes toward her, and would under-peepe her lids. [7]
4 To see th'inclosed Lights, now Canopied
Under these windowes, White and Azure lac'd
With Blew of Heavens owne tinct.
5 But my designe.
6 To note the Chamber, I will write all downe,+
Such,x and such pictures: x There the window,+ such
Th'adornement of her Bed; the Arras, Figures,
Why+ such,x and such: x and the Contents o'th'Story.

{ctd. over}

[6] though most modern texts agree with Ff and print this as 'they', one interesting gloss = 'they'd', and in applying the conditional tense to the verb (making the kiss imagined at some point in the future) it removes the need for Iachimo to actually kiss Imogen here and now

[7] F sets a period, as if Iachimo is struck dumb by the sight of her even with her eyes closed, the new sentence wanting even more: most modern texts reset the period as a comma, thus reducing both the moment and the need

10 Ah, but some natural* notes about her △body,
Above ten thousand meaner △moveables
Would testify⁎, t'enrich mine △inventory⁎.

11 O sleep*, thou △ape of death, lie* dull upon her,
And be her △sense but as a △monument,
Thus in a △chapel* lying !

12 Come off, come off; [8]
As slippery as the Gordian ° knot was hard !

13 'Tis mine, and this will witness* outwardly,
As strongly as the Conscience does⁎ within,
To th'madding of her △lord.

14 On her left breast⁎
A mole △cinque-spotted, △like the △crimson drops
I'th'bottom* of a △cowslip*.

15 Here's* a △voucher,
Stronger [than] ever △law could make; this △secret
Will force him think* I have pick'd the lock and ta'en
The treasure of her △honor*.

16 No more: to what end?

17 Why should I write this down* that's riveted,
Screw'd to my memory⁎ ?

18 She hath been⁎ reading late,
The △tale of Tereus : here* the leaf's* turn'd down*
Where Philomele gave up.

19 I have enough ;
To th'△trunk* again*, and shut the spring of it.

20 Swift, swift, you △dragons of the night, that dawning
May [bare]* the △raven's eye ! †

21 I lodge in fear*;
Though this a heavenly △angel*, hell is here*.

[Clocke strikes]

22 One, two, three: time, time !

- while F #9's attempt to get her bracelet is very quiet, the two (emotional) surround phrases suggest that it takes a great deal of effort/concentration on his part to succeed
- the ungrammatical final surround phrase of F #10 , ' : To'th'madding of her Lord', climaxing his passionate triumph (2/1) is totally understandable, though highly diminished by most modern texts' repunctuation
- the continued surround phrase excitement in spotting the 'Cinque-spotted' birth-mark 'On her left brest' in no way diminishes the intellect within the passion (8/5, F #11-12)
- then momentary calm kicks in, (F #13 -14, 0/1) - afraid that his excitement will awake her perhaps, or maybe he is just plain exhausted)
- his momentary calm disappears and he becomes passionate once more (7/9 overall in just six and a half lines) as he
  - a/ returns to Imogen's body once more (F #15)
  - b/ tears himself away from her yet again (F #16)
  - c/ and especially F #17's three surround phrase prayer for the night to end
- while the final F #18 horror of entering the trunk again is quadruply weighted by being a short sentence, monosyllabic, unembellished, and created by two surround phrases

7 Ah, but some naturall notes about her Body,
Above ten thousand meaner Moveables
Would testifie, t'enrich mine Inventorie.

8 O sleepe, thou Ape of death, lye dull upon her,
And be her Sense but as a Monument,
Thus in a Chappell lying. +

9 Come off, come off;
As slippery as the Gordian-knot was hard. +

10 'Tis mine, and this will witnesse outwardly,
As strongly as the Conscience do's within: x
To'th'madding of her Lord.

11 On her left brest
A mole Cinque-spotted: x Like the Crimson drops
I'th'bottome of a Cowslippe.

12 Heere's a Voucher,
Stronger [then] ever Law could make; this Secret
Will force him thinke I have pick'd the lock,x and t'ane
The treasure of her Honour.

13 No more: to what end?

14 Why should I write this downe,x that's riveted,
Screw'd to my memorie. +

15 She hath bin reading late,
The Tale of Tereus,xx heere the leaffe's turn'd downe
Where Philomele gave up.

16 I have enough,x
To'th'Truncke againe, and shut the spring of it.

17 Swift, swift, you Dragons of the night, that dawning
May [beare] the Ravens eye: + I lodge in feare, +
Though this a heavenly Angell: x hell is heere.

[Clocke strikes]

18 One, two, three: time, time. +

[8] most modern texts explain that Iachimo is removing Posthumus' bracelet from Imogen's arm

9/ Iachimo **Your Lady,/Is one of the fayrest that I have look'd upon** between 2.4.31 - 91

Background: Back in Italy, Iachimo goes ahead with his deception to win the bet (see background to speeches #5-8 above)

Style: as part of a three-handed scene

Where: the house of Philario, who has befriended Posthumus **To Whom:** Posthumus, in front of Philario

# of Lines: 32 **Probable Timing: 1.35 minutes**

Modern Text

9/ Iachimo

1 Your Δlady,
Is one of the fairest* that I have look'd upon . †

2 I'll make a journey twice as far*, t'enjoy
A second night of such sweet shortness* which
Was mine in Britain*, for the Δring is won* {,}
Your Δlady being so easy.

3 {ψ} Had I not brought
The knowledge of your Δmistress* home, I grant
We were to question farther, but I now
Profess* myself* the winner of her Δhonor,
Together with your Δring; and not the wronger
Of her or you, having proceeded but
By both your wills*.

4 {ψ} My Δcircumstances,
I will confirm* with oath.

5 First, her Δbed-chamber
(Where I confess* I slept not, but profess*
Had that was well worth watching), it was hang'd
With Δtapestry* of Δsilk* and Δsilver; the Δstory
Proud Cleopatra, when she met her Roman,
And [Cydnus] swell'd above the Δbanks*, or for
The press* of Δboats* or Δpride.

6 A piece* of Δwork*
So bravely done, so rich, that it did strive
In Δworkmanship* and Δvalue, which I wonder'd
Could be so rarely and exactly wrought,
[Such] the true life on't was ——

7 The Δchimney
Is Δsouth the Δchamber, and the Δchimney-piece*
Chaste Dian bathing. †

Iachimo seems to take great care in tantalising Posthumus (8/9 in the twelve and half lines of F #1-3) before moving onto the 'proof', but once the proof is begun, releases, especially intellectual, come thick and fast (29/14, in the final nineteen lines, F #4-8).

- however, underpinning the apparent opening care are wonderful cracks heralding the onslaught that is to come, as with
  - a/ the lack of punctuation at the end of F#1's second line, allowing an onrush from Imogen's beauty (mt. #1) straight into his suggestion that he would journey twice as far for a similar happy conquest (mt. #2)
  - b/ the extra breath-thought (marked , x) leading the sudden verbal flourish claiming victory at the end of F #1, ', x which/Was mine in Britaine, for the Ring is wonne,/Your Lady being so easy.' (3/2, almost a third of all the opening releases in just a line and a half)
  - c/ F #2's two emotional semicolons emphasising his professing himself as the victor
    "; but I now/Professe my selfe the winner of her Honor,/Together with your Ring ;"
- the initial description of Imogen's overall bed-chamber (F #4) is splendidly intellectual (11/6), with two extra breath-thoughts (marked , x) adding to the tiny extra tormenting details of the 'Tapistry'
- though the continued excessive praise of the work that opens F #5 is passionate (3/3), for some reason F #5's last two lines
  "which I wonder'd/Could be so rarely, and exactly wrought/[Since] the true life on't was —— "
  are unembellished (play acting at being so struck perhaps, possibly to infuriate Posthumus even more)
- and then as he adds detail upon detail, of the Chimney and the 'Roofe o'th'Chamber', so his intellect sweeps back in for the rest of the speech (15/4, the last nine lines), with the unusual surround phrase emphasis about 'chaste Dian, bathing'
  " : never saw I figures/So likely to report themselves ; "
  perhaps designed to destroy Postumus by besmirching the idea of (Imogen's) chastity even more, especially since the surround phrase ends with an emotional semicolon

First Folio

9/ Iachimo

1 Your Lady,
Is one of the fayrest that I have look'd upon
Ile make a journey twice as farre, t'enjoy
A second night of such sweet shortnesse, x which
Was mine in Britaine, for the Ring is wonne {,}
Your Lady being so easy.

2 {ψ} Had I not brought
The knowledge of your Mistris home, I grant
We were to question farther; x but I now
Professe my selfe the winner of her Honor,
Together with your Ring; and not the wronger
Of her, x or you+ having proceeded but
By both your willes.

3 {ψ} My Circumstances+
I will confirme with oath.

4 First, her Bed-chamber
(Where I confesse I slept not, but professe
Had that was well worth watching)+ it was hang'd
With Tapistry of Silke, x and Silver,+ the Story
Proud Cleopatra, when she met her Roman,
And [Sidnus] swell'd above the Bankes, or for
The presse of Boates, x or Pride.

5 A peece of Worke
So bravely done, so rich, that it did strive
In Workemanship, x and Value, which I wonder'd
Could be so rarely, x and exactly wrought+
[Since] the true life on't was ——

6 The Chimney
Is South the Chamber, and the Chimney-peece
Chaste Dian, x bathing: never saw I figures

{ctd. over}

8 Never saw I figures
So likely to report themselves. †
9 The Δcutter
Was as another Δnature, dumb*, outwent her,
Motion and Δbreath left out.

10 The Δroof* o'th'Δchamber
With golden Δcherubins is fretted.
11 Her Δandirons
(I had forgot them) were two winking Cupids
Of Δsilver each on one foot* standing, nicely
Depending on their Brands.

So likely to report themselves; the Cutter
Was as another Nature+ dumbe, out-went her,
Motion,x and Breath left out.

7 The Roofe o'th'Chamber,x
With golden Cherubins is fretted.
8 Her Andirons
(I had forgot them) were two winking Cupids
Of Silver,x each on one foote standing, nicely
Depending on their Brands.

#'s 10 - 18: With Potentially Disastrous Results

10/ Posthumus **Is there no way for Men to be, but Women** 2.5.1 - 35

Background: Iachimo's trickery has succeeded only too well (see speech #9 immediately above) and a distraught Posthumus has rushed out of the room alone ('Quite besides/The government of Patience'), having agreed Iachimo has won, with the implication that his beloved wife Imogen is, apparently, unchaste.

Style: solo

Where: somewhere in or Philario's home **To Whom:** self and audience

# of Lines: 35 **Probable Timing: 1.45 minutes**

Modern Text

10/ Posthumus
1 Is there no way for Δmen to be, but Δwomen
Must be half*-workers?
2 We are Δ[bastards all],
And that most venerable man which I
Did call my Δfather, was I know not where
When I was stamp'd.
3 Some Δcoiner* with his Δtools*
Made me a counterfeit; yet my Δmother seem'd
The Dian of that time. †
4 So doth my Δwife
The Δnonpareil* of this.
5 O* Δvengeance, Δvengeance!
6 Me of my lawful* pleasure she restrain'd,
And pray'd me oft forbearance; did it with

The only thing here that might save Posthumus in a modern audience's eyes is that his youthful excesses seem more foolish (melodramatically self-indulgent?) than spiteful - and no matter how foolish an audience may adjudge Posthumus both for believing Iachimo's faked proof of Imogen's lack of chastity and for his final conclusions, there is no doubt how painfully explosive this speech is for him, especially when he finally envisions the physical encounter that supposedly took place (F #7 on).

- the imagined unchaste encounter has a heightened emotional intensity of six semicolons, the first three dealing with Imogen (F #5, #7, and #8) and the final three dealing with the supposed infidelity of women in general (all in F #9)
- yet the speech starts relatively calmly, with intellect controlling the (perhaps face-saving) suggestion that all men, including his father, can be so deceived (F #1-2, 4/1)

First Folio

10/ Posthumus
1 Is there no way for Men to be, but Women
Must be halfe-workers?
2 We are [all Bastards],
And that most venerable man,x which I
Did call my Father, was,x I know not where
When I was stampt.
3 Some Coyner with his Tooles
Made me a counterfeit: x yet my Mother seem'd
The Dian of that time: so doth my Wife
The Non-pareill of this.
4 Oh Vengeance, Vengeance!
5 Me of my lawfull pleasure she restrain'd,
And pray'd me oft forbearance: x did it with

A pudency* so Δrosy* the sweet view on't
Might well have warm'd old* Saturn*; Δthat I thought her
As Δchaste as unΔsunn'd Δsnow.
7 O*, all the Δdevils*!
8 This yellow [Jachimo], in an hour* - was't not?
Or less* - at first?
9 Perchance he spoke not, but
Like a full -Δacorn'd Δboar*, a [German one],
Cried* "ΔO *! " and mounted; found no opposition
But what he look'd for should oppose and she
Should from encounter guard.
10 Could I find* out
The Δwoman's part in me - for there's no motion
That tends to vice in man, but I affirm*
It is the Δwoman's part: be it Δlying, note it,
The woman's: Δflattering, hers; Δdeceiving, hers;
Lust, and rank* thoughts, hers, hers: Δrevenges hers:
Ambitions, Δcovetings, change of Δprides, Δdisdain*,
Nice-longing, Δslanders, Δmutability,
All Δfaults that name [9], nay, that Δhell knows*,
Why hers, in part, or all; but rather, all;
For even to Δvice
They are not constant, but are changing still:
One Δvice, but of a minute old, for one
Not half* so old as that.
11 I'll write against them,
Detest them, curse them; yet 'tis greater Δskill
In a true Δhate, to pray they have their will:
The very Δdevils* cannot plague them better.

• but the thought of his mother being unfaithful sends Posthumus over the edge, with the passion of F #3 (6/3) being intensified by three successive surround phrases – leading to the amazingly powerful release of the short F #4's 'Oh Vengeance, Vengeance!' (2/1 in three words, with the added power of the rare – for an original text – exclamation mark)

• the remembrance of how she swore him to chastity continues his passion (5/3, F #5) so that the apparent modesty of how she worked him 'with/A pudencie so Rosie' still seems to have a tremendous impact on him, short spelled as it is, and the effect she had on him then still seems to disturb him with the two unusual F only short lines

"Might well have warm'd olde Saturne;
That I thought her"

suggesting that he needs to pause (for self-control) before continuing - a control which doesn't last, for there comes yet another exclamation marked short sentence explosion (F #6), 'Oh, all the Divels!'

• initially, and not surprisingly, the powerfully imagined act of intercourse is very passionate (4/5, F #7 plus the two lines opening F #8), but then turns deathly quiet as he imagines Imogen's compliance

"; found no opposition/But what he look'd for, should oppose, and she/Should from encounter guard."

• though the long unflattering F #9, exploring the supposed frailty of women, seems profoundly intellectual (16/6), there are definite cracks within the process, most notably

a/ the hammer blows of the five successive surround phrases which suddenly appear in the middle of the sentence
": be it Lying, note it,/ The womans : Flattering, hers ; Deceiving, hers : /Lust, and ranke thoughts, hers, hers : Revenges hers : "

b/ the long irregular (shaded) line, where F's fourteen or fifteen syllables suggest that his thoughts are in danger of running away with him, even if just for a moment

• that he is a very young man flailing in his misery can be clearly seen in F #10's rather ridiculous speech-ending conclusion, the foolish chop-logic of which, though seeming intellectual (3/1), is made even more over-blown by the sentence being created by three successive surround phrases

A pudencie so Rosie,ₓ the sweet view on't
Might well have warm'd olde Saturne; →
That I thought her
As Chaste,ₓ as un-Sunn'd Snow.
6 Oh, all the Divels!
7 This yellow [Iachimo]+ in an houre, was't not?
Or lesse; ₓ at first?
8 Perchance he spoke not, but
Like a full Acorn'd Boare, a [Jarmen on],
Cry'de oh,+ and mounted; found no opposition
But what he look'd for,ₓ should oppose,ₓ and she
Should from encounter guard.
9 Could I finde out
The Womans part in me, for there's no motion
That tends to vice in man, but I affirme
It is the Womans part: be it Lying, note it,
The womans: Flattering, hers; Deceiving, hers: ₓ
Lust, and ranke thoughts, hers, hers: Revenges hers:
Ambitions, Covetings, change of Prides, Disdaine,
Nice-longing, Slanders, Mutability; ₓ
All Faults that name, nay, that Hell knowes,
Why hers, in part, or all: ₓ but rather+ all+ For even to Vice
They are not constant, but are changing still; +
One Vice, but of a minute old, for one
Not halfe so old as that.
10 Ile write against them,
Detest them, curse them: ₓ yet 'tis greater Skill
In a true Hate, to pray they have their will:
The very Divels cannot plague them better.

[9] because F set only a four foot, eight syllable line, various glosses to F1's 'that name' include a) F2 = 'may be nam'd' b) some modern texts = 'man can' c) other modern texts = 'man may'

11/ Pisanio **How? of Adultery? Wherefore write you not** 3.2.1 - 22

Background: As a consequence of Iachimo's 'proof' the distraught Posthumus has written to his servant Pisanio, stating Imogen is an adulteress, commanding Pisanio to lure Imogen away from the protection of the palace and then kill her. Pisanio, who is equally devoted to both of them, cannot believe the news.

Style: solo

Where: somewhere in the palace **To Whom:** self and direct audience address

# of Lines: 22 **Probable Timing: 1.10 minutes**

Modern Text

11/ Pisanio

1 How? of △adultery?
2 Wherefore write you not
What △monsters her accuse?
3 Leonatus!
O* △master, what a strange infection
Is fall'n* into thy ear*!
4 What false Italian
(As poisonous* tongu'd as handed) hath prevail'd
On thy too ready hearing?
5 Disloyal*?
6 No.
7 She's punish'd for her △truth, and undergoes,
More △goddess*-like [than] △wife-like, such △assaults
As would take in some △virtue.
8 O* my △master,
Thy mind to [her's] is now as low* as were
Thy △fortunes.
9 How? ◊ that I should [murder] her,
Upon the △love and △truth and △vows* which I
Have made to thy command?
10 I, her?
11 Her blood?
12 If it be so, to do good service, never
Let me be counted serviceable.
13 How look* I
That I should seem* to lack* humanity
So much as this △fact comes to?
14 "Do't*; △the △letter ◊
That I have sent her, by her own* command
Shall give thee opportunity*."

One of the two small unembellished passages points to the determined loyalty and profound sense of morality that imbues Pisanio throughout 'I her ? Her blood ? /If it be so, to do good service, never/Let me becounted serviceable.' (F #11-13); the other, towards the end of F #3 and F #4, points to his wisdom in not totally blaming Posthumus but rather realising how badly the boy has been tricked: 'what a strange infection/Is falne into thy eare? . . . / . . . hath prevail'd/On thy too ready hearing?'

- the enormous impact of Posthumus' request can be seen in the opening three sentences, two of which are short, F #1 and F#2, and two of which, F #1 and #3, are created by surround phrases
- his opening struggle to understand what is going on starts intellectually (F #1-2, 2/0), but the moves into emotion (F #3-4, 2/4), which is intensified emotion in the one word F #5
- and while his F #7 recognition that 'She's punish'd for her Truth" seems clearly intellectual (5/1), the emotional underpinnings are enormous, the whole sentence being formed by three emotional (semicolon created) surround phrases
- that he is having enormous difficulties in reconciling/coming to terms with Imogen's 'Goddesse-like' qualities, Posthumus' 'lowe' 'mind' and 'Fortunes', and his own dilemma can be seen both in the five extra breath-thoughts (marked , $_x$) that suddenly cluster (F #7-10), and in the short sentences F #8-10 (including F #10's two emotional surround phrases)
- this struggle leads to the unembellished moral statement referred to in the opening above (F #11-13)
- then Pisanio seems to be torn apart in attempting to balance the terse somewhat intellectual surround phrase command from Posthumus (2/1, F #15's, ' . Doo't: The Letter . ') with his own emotional sense of self (F #14's 1/3), asking how could he 'seeme to lacke humanity'
- in what has been an essentially restrained speech, in his sense of helplessness and hopelessness he suddenly breaks into enormous passion as he takes his frustration out on the letter in the three surround phrase (two emotional) F #17, (4/4 in just three lines) . . .

First Folio

11/ Pisanio

1 How? of Adultery?
2 Wherefore write you not
What Monsters her accuse?
3 Leonatus: +
Oh Master, what a strange infection
Is falne into thy eare?+
4 What false Italian,$_x$
(As poysonous tongu'd,$_x$ as handed) hath prevail'd
On thy too ready hearing?
5 Disloyall?
6 No.
7 She's punish'd for her Truth; $_x$ and undergoes$_x$
More Goddesse-like,$_x$ [then] Wife-like; $_x$ such Assaults
As would take in some Vertue.
8 Oh my Master,
Thy mind to [her],$_x$ is now as lowe,$_x$ as were
Thy Fortunes.
9 How?
10 That I should [murther] her,
Upon the Love,$_x$ and Truth,$_x$ and Vowes; $_x$ which I
Have made to thy command?
11 I+ her?
12 Her blood?
13 If it be so, to do good service, never
Let me be counted serviceable.
14 How looke I,$_x$
That I should seeme to lacke humanity,$_x$
So much as this Fact comes to?
15 [10] Doo't: $_x$ The Letter.
16 *That I have sent her, by her owne command,* $_x$

[10] most modern texts add a stage direction that Pisanio is now reading from the letter, and that as a consequence the words 'Doo't' and 'The Letter' are phrases within the letter

15 O* damn'd paper,
Black* as the △ink* that's on thee ! †
16 Senseless* baube,
Art thou a △feodary* for this △act, and look'st
So △virgin-like without?
17 Lo*, here she comes.

• . . . which makes the monosyllabic almost unembellished short sentence recovery of F #18 even more remarkable

shall give thee opportunitie .
17 Oh damn'd paper,
Blacke as the Inke that's on thee :+ senselesse bauble,
Art thou a Fœdarie for this Act ; x and look'st
So Virgin-like without?
18 Loe+ here she comes.

12/ Imogen **A Letter from my Lord Leonatus.** between 3.2.25 - 39
13/ Imogen **Oh for a Horse with wings : Hear'st thou Pisanio?** between 3.2.48 - 82

Background: To lure Imogen away (see background to speech #10 above), Posthumus (surnamed Leonatus, hence the reference) has sent her a letter saying that he is in 'Cambria, at Milford Haven' - that is, in the very furthest parts of Wales. Not realising that anything is amiss, Imogen's delight knows no bounds either before she opens the letter, speech #12, or, especially, once she learns how soon they supposedly can be together again, speech #13.

Style: both as part of a two-handed scene

Where: somewhere in the palace **To Whom:** Pisanio

Speech 12: of Lines: 14 **Probable Timing: 0.45 minutes**
Speech 13: of Lines: 34 **Probable Timing: 1.40 minutes**

Modern Text

12/ Imogen

1 {ψ} {A} Letter from my Δlord Leonatus .

2 O*, learn'd indeed were that Δastronomer
That knew the Δstars*, as I his Δcharacters;
He'ld* lay the Δfuture open.
3 You good Δgods,
Let what is here* contain'd, relish* of Δlove,
Of my Δlord's health, of his content - yet not
That we two are asunder ; let that grieve him:
Some griefs* are med'cinable, that is one of them,
For it doth physic* Δlove - of his content,
All but in that !
4 Good Δwax, thy leave. †
5 Blest be
You Δbees that make these Δlocks* of counsel !
6 Lovers
And men in dangerous Δbonds* pray not alike ;
Though Δforfeitors* you cast in prison, yet
You clasp* young Cupid's Δtables. †
7 Good Δnews*, Δgods! [11]

Not surprisingly, the preamble before opening the letter from her banished husband (spinning out the anticipation for as long as possible perhaps) is passionate: what might be surprising is that she manages to channel her emotion throughout so that it is more intellect than emotion that drives the speech (20/13 overall).

- Imogen's only purely intellectual moment is the opening realisation that it is a letter from Posthumus (3/0, F #1)

- and in the midst of her passion is the one very quiet unembellished surround phrase wish that he misses her as much as she him, hoping that, while he will write of 'his content',
  " : yet not /That we two are asunder, let that grieve him ; "
  - the semicolon pointing to the emotional longing beneath the quietness

- that her eagerness may be getting the better of her prudence can be seen in the last two onrushed F sentences, F #4's blessing of the 'Bees' that made the 'Wax' that sealed the letter and F #5's prayer for 'good Newes Gods': most modern texts split each into two more grammatically correct sentences

- and her fervency in this is underscored by F #4 being composed of surround phrases, as is F #5's final wish for ' : good Newes Gods . '

First Folio

12/ Imogen

1 {ψ} {A} Letter from my Lord Leonatus .

2 Oh, learn'd indeed were that Astronomer
That knew the Starres, as I his Characters,+
Heel'd lay the Future open.
3 You good Gods,
Let what is heere contain'd, rellish of Love,
Of my Lords health, of his content : x yet not
That we two are asunder,+ let that grieve him ; +
Some griefes are medcinable, that is one of them,
For it doth physicke Love, of his content,
All but in that. +
4 Good Wax, thy leave : blest be
You Bees that make these Lockes of counsaile. +
5 Lovers, x
And men in dangerous Bondes pray not alike,+
Though Forfeytours you cast in prison, yet
You claspe young Cupids Tables : good Newes+ Gods.+

[11] most modern texts explain that now Imogen reads the letter

Modern Text

13/ Imogen

1 O* for a △horse with wings ! †

2 Hear'st thou, Pisanio?

3 He is at Milford-Haven. †

4 Read, and tell me
How far* 'tis thither.

5 If one of mean* affairs*
May plod it in a week*, why may not I
Glide thither in a day?

6 Then, true Pisanio,
Who long'st like me, to see thy △lord; who long'st,
(O* let me bate !) - but not like me - yet long'st,
But in a fainter kind* - ◊ O* not like me,
For mine's beyond, beyond - say, and speak* thick*
(Love's △counsellor* should fill the bores of hearing,
To th'smothering of the △sense), how far* it is
To this same blessed Milford.

7 And by th'way
Tell me how Wales was made so happy as
T'inherit* such a △haven.

8 But first of all,
How we may steal* from hence; and for the gap
That we shall make in △time, from our hence-going,
[To] our return*, to excuse. †

9 But first, how get hence.

10 Why should excuse be born* or ere begot?

11 We'll* talk* of that hereafter*.

12 Prithee* speak*,
How many [score] of △miles may we well [ride]
Twixt hour* and hour*?

13 {One score ?}

14 Why, one that rode to's △execution*, △man,
Could never go so slow. †

15 I have heard of △riding wagers,
Where △horses have bin nimbler [than] the △sands
That run i'th'△clocks behalf *.

16 But this is △fool'ry* . †

17 Go, bid my △woman feign* a △sickness*, say
She'll* home to her △father; and provide me presently

With its various onrushes and quick switches in style, the shape of the speech and thus its releases as set in F is very different from that which most modern texts present: while both Imogens are excited and free-flowing, F's releases seem to suggest the excitement of a much younger woman than her modern counterpart.

- the opening excitement is both palpable, with F #1-2 formed by surround phrases, and intellectual in her joyful demands and recognition (6/2), and then turns quickly to emotion to open F #3 (0/3)

- but the unembellished quietness at the end of F #3
  "why may not I/Glide thither in a day?"
  underscores her longing for him, the longing ('long'st like me . . ./. . . yet long'st') even more marked by being contained within the two emotional (semicolon created) surround phrases of F #4

- not surprisingly in her unfocussed expressions of ongoing delight and demands for information, passion breaks through (7/8, F #4-6), the scattershot thinking heightened by all of F #4 and the start of F #5 being formed by six successive surround phrases

- it seems that Imogen finally manages to concentrate on the key matter, 'How we may steale from hence', and she becomes more controlled in her releases as she does (1/2, F #7) though her fierce intellect/logic makes itself felt once more with the sentence underscored by opening and closing with logical (colon created) surround phrases

- but very quickly, without waiting for a reply, her emotions take over once again with another series of disjointed thoughts (1/8, F #8-10)

- her incredulous dismissal of the miles Pisanio suggests their daily journey will cover starts with the short monosyllabic unembellished F #11 repetition of his 'One score?' and then plunges into intellect as she rips apart the slowness of his proposal (6/1, F #12) and then orders him to get a disguise from one of her servants (9/3, F #13)

- the apparent imperiousness of her final passage of commands is very marked in most modern texts, which set them as seven separate sentences (mt. #14-19): however, F sets the orders as just four sentences (F #12-15) that seem to be much more the excited enthusiasm of a young girl whose desire to see her husband can excuse almost anything, especially when six more surround phrases, including all of the last sentence, are involved

First Folio

13/ Imogen

1 Oh for a Horse with wings: + Hear'st thou+ Pisanio?

2 He is at Milford-Haven: Read, and tell me
How farre 'tis thither.

3 If one of meane affaires
May plod it in a weeke, why may not I
Glide thither in a day?

4 Then,$_x$ true Pisanio,
Who long'st like me, to see thy Lord; who long'st
(Oh let me bate+)+ but not like me: $_x$ yet long'st+
But in a fainter kinde.

5 Oh not like me: $_x$
For mine's beyond, beyond: $_x$ say, and speake thicke
(Loves Counsailor should fill the bores of hearing,
To'th'smothering of the Sense)+ how farre it is
To this same blessed Milford.

6 And by'th'way
Tell me how Wales was made so happy,$_x$ as
T'inherite such a Haven.

7 But first of all,
How we may steale from hence: $_x$ and for the gap
That we shall make in Time, from our hence-going,
[And] our returne, to excuse: but first, how get hence.

8 Why should excuse be borne or ere begot?

9 Weele talke of that heereafter.

10 Prythee speake,
How many [store] of Miles may we well [rid]
Twixt houre,$_x$ and houre?

11 {One score ?}

12 Why, one that rode to's Excution+ Man,
Could never go so slow: I have heard of Riding wagers,
Where Horses have bin nimbler [then] the Sands
That run i'th'Clocks behalfe.

13 But this is Foolrie,
Go, bid my Woman faigne a Sicknesse, say
She'le home to her Father; and provide me presently

{ctd. over}

A $^{\Delta}$riding-$^{\Delta}$suit, $^{\Delta}$no costlier [then] would fit
A $^{\Delta}$franklin's huswife.

---

18 I see before me, $^{\Delta}$man; nor here*, [nor] here*,
Nor what ensues, but have a $^{\Delta}$fog in them
That I cannot look* through.
19 Away, I prithee*,
Do as I bid thee. †
20 There's no more to say:
Accessible is none but Milford way.

A Riding Suit: $_{x}$ No costlier [then] would fit
A Franklins Huswife.

---

14 I see before me ($_{x}$Man)$^{+}$ nor heere, [not] heere; $_{x}$
Nor what ensues^{+} but have a Fog in them
That I cannot looke through.
15 Away, I prythee,
Do as I bid thee: There's no more to say:
Accessible is none but Milford way.

14/ Imogen — **False to his Bed? What is it to be false?** — between 3.4.40 - 64

15/ Pisanio — **What shall I need to draw my Sword, the Paper** — 3.4.32 - 39

16/ Imogen — **Come Fellow, be thou honest,/Do thou thy Masters bidding.** — between 3.4.64 - 98

Background: Once Pisanio and Imogen have arrived in Wales he shows her the 'adultery/kill her' letter from Posthumus (see speech #11 above). Each speech is self-explanatory. One note: in speech #16, sentence #6's 'Soft, soft, wee'l no defence' refers to something literally blocking access of a sword to her heart, that something being, as sentence #7 explains, all the love letters from Posthumus that she has brought with her on the journey.

Style: as part of a two-handed scene, though speech #14 is essentially solo

Where: somewhere in Wales, some distance from Milford Haven **To Whom:** speech #15, Pisanio essentially to himself; speeches #14 and 16, Imogen to Pisanio

Speech 14: # of Lines: 23 **Probable Timing: 1.10 minutes**

Speech 15: # of Lines: 8 **Probable Timing: 0.30 minutes**

Speech 16: # of Lines: 34 **Probable Timing: 1.40 minutes**

Modern Text

14/ Imogen

1 False to his Δbed?
2 What is it to be false?
3 To lie* in watch there, and to think* on him?
4 To weep* 'twixt clock and clock?
5 If sleep charge Δnature,
To break* it with a fearful* dream* of him,
And cry myself* awake?
6 That's false to's bed? ◊ is it?
7 I false?
8 Thy Δconscience witness* ! †
9 [Jachimo],
Thou didst* accuse him of Δincontinency*;
Thou then look'dst like a Δvillain*; now, methinks*
Thy favors* good enough.
10 Some Δjay of Italy
(Whose mother was her painting) hath betray'd*him. †
11 Poor* I am stale, a Δgarment out of fashion,
And for I am richer [than] to hang by th'walls*,
I must be ripp'd*. †
12 To pieces* with me !†
13 O*!
Men's Δvows* are women's Δtraitors.
14 All good seeming,
By thy revolt, ΔO* Δhusband, shall be thought
Put on for Δvillainy; not born* where't grows*,
But worn* a Δbait* for Δladies.

Imogen's repetitions of the accusation against her, 'What is it to be false?' (F #2); 'That's false to's bed?' (F #6); 'Is it?' (F #7); 'I false?' (F #8), are triply remarkable for their quietness, their being voiced as monosyllables, and their being contained in extraordinarily short sentences – though whether this is as a result of the shock of thinking she was coming to a love rendezvous only to discover that she is to be killed or stems from her strength strength of mind and dignity of self is up to each actress to decide.

- the devastating effect of the circumstances facing her can be seen in the fact that of thirteen sentences overall six of Imogen's first seven are short, and that there are twelve surround phrases in the remaining nineteen lines of the speech

- as she begins her attempt to understand what has happened, emotions are naturally interspersed with her (enforced?) calmness (2/7, F #1-8)

- then passion rips through the rest of the speech, (19/21 in nineteen lines)

- as she believes Iachimo's earlier accusations of Posthumus' lack of fidelity to her (speeches #6-7 above) and that Posthumus, and therefore she, have been betrayed by 'Some Jay of Italy', the passion starts, heightened by four successive surround phrases (6/5, F #9 and the first line and a half of F #10)

- her passionate despairing cry ending F #10 ' : To peeces with me : Oh ! / Mens Vowes are womens Traitors' (4/3) is equally heightened by two more surround phrases and the very rare (for an original text) exclamation mark

- indeed, save for the opening of F #10, the rest of the speech, despairing of the dishonesty of men, is set as six successive surround phrases

First Folio

14/ Imogen

1 False to his Bed?
2 What is it to be false?
3 To lye in watch there, and to thinke on him?
4 To weepe 'twixt clock and clock?
5 If sleep charge Nature,
To breake it with a fearfull dreame of him,
And cry my selfe awake?
6 That's false to's bed?
7 Is it?
8 I false?
9 Thy Conscience witnesse : + [Iachimo],
Thou didd'st accuse him of Incontinencie,+
Thou then look'dst like a Villaine : x now, me thinkes
Thy favours good enough.
10 Some Jay of Italy
(Whose mother was her painting) hath betraid him :
Poore I am stale, a Garment out of fashion,
And for I am richer [then] to hang by th'walles,
I must be ript : To peeces with me : + Oh!
Mens Vowes are womens Traitors.
11 All good seeming+
By thy revolt (xoh Husbandx) shall be thought
Put on for Villainy; not borne where't growes,
But worne a Baite for Ladies.

{ctd. over}

15 True honest men being heard, like false Æneas,
Were in his time thought false; and Sinon's* weeping
Did scandal* many a holy tear*, took* pity*
From most true wretchedness*.
16 So thou, Posthumus,
Wilt lay the Δleaven on all proper men;
Goodly and gallant shall be false and perjur'd
From thy great fail*. †

• three of these surround phrasesare further heightened by being emotional - the thought that men's goodness is simply a 'Baite for Ladies' (the end of F #11), a principle which she then applies to Posthumus (the whole of the final F #13)

• the speech finishes with a colon in F, suggesting that, though silent, her mental processes are still continuing: most modern texts end the speech with a conventional period, removing the possibility that this final thought might be so highly disturbing to her that she is forced to break off in mid-stream

12 True honest men being heard, like false Æneas,
Were in his time thought false:$_{x}$ and Synons weeping
Did scandall many a holy teare: $_{x}$ tooke pitty
From most true wretchednesse.
13 So thou, Posthumus+
Wilt lay the Leaven on all proper men;
Goodly,$_{x}$ and gallant,$_{x}$ shall be false and perjur'd
From thy great faile:

Modern Text

15/ Pisanio

What shall I need to draw my Δsword, the Δpaper
Hath cut her throat already*!
2 No, 'tis Δslander,
Whose edge is sharper [than] the Δsword, whose tongue
Outvenoms* all the Δworms* of Nile*, whose breath
Rides on the posting winds* and doth belie*
All corners of the Δworld.
3 Kings, Δqueens*, and Δstates,
Maids*, Δmatrons, nay, the Δsecrets of the Δgrave
This viperous slander enters.

That this is not premeditated speech, but instead springs forth almost unchecked, can be seen in the lack of any major punctuation.

• the opening and closing are strongly intellectual
a/ F #1's specific recognition of Imogen's plight (2/0)
b/ F #3's more general realisation that slander affects everyone (7/2, if the first word of the opening two lines, 'Kings' and 'Maides', are included for their importance to the debate)

• however, F #2's recognition of the all-ranging power and devastation of 'Slander' is deeply passionate (5/5 in just four lines)

First Folio

15/ Pisanio

1 What shall I need to draw my Sword, the Paper
Hath cut her throat alreadie?+
2 No, 'tis Slander,
Whose edge is sharper [then] the Sword, whose tongue
Out-venomes all the Wormes of Nyle, whose breath
Rides on the posting windes,$_{x}$ and doth belye
All corners of the World.
3 Kings, Queenes, and States,
Maides, Matrons, nay+ the Secrets of the Grave
This viperous slander enters.

Modern Text

16/ Imogen

1 Come, Δfellow, be thou honest,
Do thou thy Δmaster's bidding.
2 When thou seest him,
A little witness* my obedience.
3 Look*
I draw the Δsword myself*, take it, and hit
The innocent Δmansion of my Δlove, my Δheart. †
4 Fear* not, 'tis empty of all things but Δgrief*. †
5 Thy Δmaster is not there, who was indeed*
The riches of it.
6 Do his bidding, strike. †
7 Thou mayst be valiant in a better cause,
But now thou seem'st a Δcoward.

Facing death, Imogen's overall passion is not surprising (36/31) yet it is somewhat deceiving, for there are passages when her intellectual strength momentarily gains the upper hand, only to be subsumed by moments of raw emotion – the whole being one huge struggle to maintain some form of balance, which, amazingly, she manages to achieve by speech's end.

• given the circumstances, the enormity of the opening five sentences demanding that Pisanio kill her according to Posthumus' instructions are amazingly disciplined, with only two passages showing any emotional cracks
a/ the opening surround phrase of F #5 ' . Why, I must dye : ' (0/1)
b/ F #3's last two and a half lines suggesting that Pisanio strike her heart, explaining via the surround phrase 'Feare not, 'tis empty of all things,$_{x}$ but Greefe : ' (2/3) – her 'Greefe' heightened by the extra breath thought (marked ,$_{x}$)

• that the control doesn't come without a struggle can be seen in the two short sentences that open the speech and the two emotional (semicolon created) surround phrases forming the otherwise controlled F #4

First Folio

16/ Imogen

1 Come+ Fellow, be thou honest,
Do thou thy Masters bidding.
2 When thou seest him,
A little witnesse my obedience.
3 Looke
I draw the Sword my selfe, take it, and hit
The innocent Mansion of my Love ($_{x}$my Heart:$_{x}$)
Feare not, 'tis empty of all things,$_{x}$ but Greefe:
Thy Master is not there, who was indeede
The riches of it.
4 Do his bidding, strike,
Thou mayst be valiant in a better cause; $_{x}$
But now thou seem'st a Coward.

8 Why, I must die*;
And if I do not by thy hand, thou art
No △servant of thy △master's.
9 Against △self*-slaughter,
There is a prohibition so △divine,
That cravens my weak* hand. †
10 Come, here's* my heart:
Something's [a-fore't*]. † [12]
11 Soft, soft, we'll* no defense*,
Obedient as the △scabbard.
12 What is here*? †
13 The △scriptures of the △loyal* Leonatus,
All turn'd to △heresy*?
14 Away, away,
Corrupters of my △faith! you shall no more
Be △stomachers to my heart. †
15 Thus may poor* △fools*
Believe* false △teachers. †
16 Though those that are betray'd*
Do feel* the △treason sharply*, yet the △traitor
Stands in worse case of woe.
17 And thou, Posthumus,
That didst* set up my disobedience 'gainst the King
My △father, and [make] me put into contempt the suits*
Of △princely fellows*, shalt hereafter* find*
It is no act* of common passage, but
A strain* of △rareness*; and I grieve* myself*
To think*, when thou shalt be disedg'd by her
That now thou tirest* on, how thy memory
Will then be pang'd by me.
18 Prithee* dispatch,
The △lamb* entreats the △butcher.
19 Where's* thy knife?
20 Thou art too slow to do thy △master's bidding
When I desire it too.

" . Do his bidding, strike,/Thou mayst be valiant in a better cause ;
/But now thou seem'st a Coward . "

• her F #6 denunciation of suicide and preparation to bare her heart is doubly reinforced by passion (5/4), and by ending with three consecutive surround phrases

• the discovery of her husbands love-letters next to her heart and her rejection of them and him starts out intellectually (16/10, F #7 to the first three lines of F #9), the one surround phrase marking the depth of her realisation as to how foolish she has been
" : thus may poore Fooles/Beleeve false Teachers : "

• yet her love is so strong that, though facing her own death, she is primarily concerned with the sadness Posthumus will inevitably face thereafter - and is amazingly emotional in the process (1/9, F #9's last five lines)

• however, though starting passionately (2/2, F #10) Imogen regains her control and dignity (1/0, F #11-12), even to the extent of her calmly asking
" . Wher's thy knife ? "
being heightened by being the only unembellished passage in the speech, and the question is further heightened by being set as a monosyllabic short sentence, again the only one in the speech

5 Why, I must dye: x
And if I do not by thy hand, thou art
No Servant of thy Masters.
6 Against Selfe-slaughter,
There is a prohibition so Divine,
That cravens my weake hand: Come, heere's my heart:
Something's [a-foot]: Soft, soft, wee'l no defence,
Obedient as the Scabbard.
7 What is heere,
The Scriptures of the Loyall Leonatus,
All turn'd to Heresie?
8 Away, away+
Corrupters of my Faith,+ you shall no more
Be Stomachers to my heart: thus may poore Fooles
Beleeve false Teachers: Though those that are betraid
Do feele the Treason sharpely, yet the Traitor
Stands in worse case of woe.
9 And thou+ Posthumus,
That didd'st set up my disobedience 'gainst the King
My Father, and [makes] me put into contempt the suites
Of Princely Fellowes, shalt heereafter finde
It is no acte of common passage, but
A straine of Rarenesse: x and I greeve my selfe, x
To thinke, when thou shalt be disedg'd by her, x
That now thou tyrest on, how thy memory
Will then be pang'd by me.
10 Prythee dispatch,
The Lambe entreats the Butcher.
11 Wher's thy knife?
12 Thou art too slow to do thy Masters bidding
When I desire it too.

[12] most modern texts explain that in preparing herself for death she discovers (at least one) letter(s) from Posthumus next her heart: also, while Ff = 'a-foot', some modern texts = 'a-for't'

17/ Imogen **I see a mans life is a tedious one,** 3.6.1 - 27

Background: As the loyal Pisanio explained, he had no intention of killing Imogen, but instead has brought her to Wales so that she can disguise herself as a boy (to that end he has brought with him the necessary clothes). That way, she can present herself for employment to the Roman Ambassador who will be at 'Milford-Haven/To-morrow' and, once back in Italy, she can get close to Posthumus' residence to see him 'As truely he mooves'. Imogen has disguised herself, but, unfortunately, has lost her way.

Style: solo

Where: near the cave of Belarius, which is referred to from sentence #9 onwards **To Whom:** direct audience address

# of Lines: 27 **Probable Timing: 1.30 minutes**

Modern Text

17/ Imogen

1 I see a mans life is a tedious one,
I have tir'd* myself*; and for two nights together
Have made the ground my bed.
2 I should be sick*,
But that my resolution helps* me. †
3 Milford,
When from the Δmountain* top Pisanio show'd thee,
Thou wast within a ken*.
4 O* Jove, I think*
Foundations fly* the wretched: such, I mean*,
Where they should be reliev'd*.
5 Two Beggars told me
I could not miss* my way.
6 Will poor* Δfolks* lie*,
That have Δafflictions on them, knowing 'tis
A punishment or Δtrial*?
7 Yes; no wonder,
When Δrich-ones scarce tell true.
8 To lapse in Δfullness*
Is sorer, [than] to lie* for Δneed*; and Δfalsehood*
Is worse in Δkings, [than] Δbeggars.
9 My dear* Δlord,
Thou art one o'th'false Δones. †
10 Now I think* on thee,
My hunger's gone; but even before, I was
At point to sink* for food.
11 But what is this?
12 Here* is a path to't*; 'tis some savage hold. †
13 I were best not call; I dare not call; yet Δfamine
Ere clean* it o'er-throw Δnature, makes it valiant.

Imogen's determination to come to some form of understanding is underscored by both the enormous number of surround phrases (twenty-five at the most conservative count) and the relative shortness of the sentences when compared to most other speeches in the play. Thus it's not surprising that overall the speech is passionate (30/35).

- however, Imogen opens emotionally as she bewails what has recently happened to her (4/11, F #1-3); then, in discussing falsehood, passion takes over (10/8, F #4-7); which is maintained as she turns to thoughts of her husband, both good and bad (3/3 F #8)
- her initial response to the cave is intellectual (7/4, F #9-11) as she debates what to do; then, in taking verbal action by calling out, she becomes totally emotional (0/5, F #12-14), followed by a wonderfully quiet (terrified?) response when there is no answer to her challenge (F #15-16) – and while her decision to enter the cave starts passionately (3/3, F #17), her final prayer for help is totally intellectual (2/0, F #18)
- the fact that there is a huge struggle between her logical self and her emotions can be seen in that while fifteen of the surround phrases are logical (colon created) the remaining ten are all formed, in part, by the emotional semicolons
- the logical surround phrases all support her play-long determination to find/create maxims, both personal and 'society-in-general-based', to help her gain understanding and/or control of what she is facing, as with the three personal maxims with which she opens

  ". I see a mans life is a tedious one,/I have tyr'd my selfe : and for two nights together/Have made the ground my bed . I should be sicke, /But that my resolution helpes me : "

  then continuing with the more general F #3

  ". Oh Jove, I thinke/Foundations flye the wretched : such I meane, /Where they should be releev'd . "

  followed by F #7's generality moving in to her own F #8 circumstances

  ". To lapse in Fulnesse/Is sorer, [then] to lye for Neede : and Falshood/ Is worse in Kings, [then] Beggers . My deere Lord,/Thou art one o'th'false Ones : "

First Folio

17/ Imogen

1 I see a mans life is a tedious one,
I have tyr'd my selfe: x and for two nights together
Have made the ground my bed.
2 I should be sicke,
But that my resolution helpes me: Milford,
When from the Mountaine top,x Pisanio shew'd thee,
Thou was't within a kenne.
3 Oh Jove, I thinke
Foundations flye the wretched: such + I meane,
Where they should be releev'd.
4 Two Beggers told
me,x
I could not misse my way.
5 Will poore Folkes lye +
That have Afflictions on them, knowing 'tis
A punishment,x or Triall?
6 Yes; no wonder,
When Rich-ones scarse tell true.
7 To lapse in Fulnesse
Is sorer, [then] to lye for Neede: x and Falshood
Is worse in Kings, [then] Beggers.
8 My deere Lord,
Thou art one o'th'false Ones: Now I thinke on thee,
My hunger's gone; but even before, I was
At point to sinke,x for food.
9 But what is this?
10 Heere is a path too't: x 'tis some savage hold:
I were best not call; I dare not call: x yet Famine
Ere cleane it o're-throw Nature, makes it valiant.

14 Plenty* and Δpeace breeds Δcowards; Δhardness* ever
Of Δhardiness* is Δmother.

15 Ho*! who's here*?

16 If any thing that's civil*, speak*; if savage,
Take or lend.

17 Ho*!

18 No answer?

19 Then I'll enter.

20 Best draw my Δsword; and if mine Δenemy
But fear* the Δsword like me, he'll* scarcely* look* on't.

21 Such a Δfoe, good Δheavens !

and even when she is facing danger (F #10 onwards) her surround phrase maxims still flow when referring to her cowardice being challenged by need

" : yet Famine/Ere cleane it o're-throw Nature, makes it valiant . /Plentie, and Peace breeds Cowards : Hardnesse ever/Of Hardinesse is Mother . "

• the emotional surround phrases all deal with the tremendous impact the current circumstances are having on her, whether for the worse, as with Posthumus' disloyalty (F #6)

' . Yes ; no wonder,/When Rich-ones scarse tell true . "

or the better effects thinking of him can still have on her (F #8)

" : Now I thinke on thee,/My hunger's gone ; but even before, I was/At point to sinke, for food ."

or with the immediate problem of finding shelter in what may be a dangerous place (F #10, #13, and #17)

" : I were best not call ; I dare not call : "

" . If any thing that's civill, speake ; if savage,/Take, or lend . "

" . Best draw my Sword ; and if mine Enemy/But feare the Sword like me, hee'l scarsely looke on't. "

11 Plentie,x and Peace breeds Cowards :x Hardnesse ever
Of Hardinesse is Mother.

12 Hoa?+ who's heere?

13 If any thing that's civill, speake; if savage,
Take,x or lend.

14 Hoa?+

15 No answer?

16 Then Ile enter.

17 Best draw my Sword; and if mine Enemy
But feare the Sword like me, hee'l scarsely looke on't.

18 Such a Foe, good Heavens . +

18/ Belarius **How hard it is to hide the sparkes of Nature?** 3.3.79 - 107

Background: Belarius is in fact a one-time general of Cymbeline's, then known as Morgan. The two boys known as Polidore and Cadwal, who believe he is their father, are in fact Cymbeline's two sons Guiderius and Arviragus, and thus Imogen's long lost brothers. In praising the boys, Belarius/Morgan explains how all three of them are where they are and how the two boys come to believe who they are.

Style: solo

Where: outside their cave **To Whom:** direct audience address

# of Lines: 30 **Probable Timing: 1.30 minutes**

Modern Text

18/ Belarius

1 How hard it is to hide the sparks* of Δnature!

2 These Δboys* know little they are Δsons* to'th'King,
Nor Cymbeline dreams* that they are alive.

3 They think* they are mine, and though train'd up thus meanly*
I'th'Δcave, [wherein theyΔ bow], their thoughts do hit,
The Δroofs* of Δpalaces, and Δnature prompts them
In simple and low* things to Δprince it much
Beyond the trick* of others.

4 This [Polydore],
The heir* of Cymbeline and Britain*, who
The King his Δfather call'd Guiderius - ◊ Jove !
When on my three-foot stool* I sit and tell
The warlike feats I have done, his spirits fly* out
Into my Δstory ; say , "Thus mine Δenemy fell,
And thus I set my foot* on's neck*," even then
The Δprincely blood flows* in his Δcheek+ , he sweats
Strains* his young* Δnerves, and puts himself* in posture
That acts my words.

5 The younger* Δbrother, [Cadwal],
Once Arviragus, in as like a figure
Strikes life into my speech, and shows* much more
His own* conceiving*.

6 [13] - Hark*, the Δgame is rous'd ! - †

7 O* Cymbeline, Δheaven and my Δconscience knows*
Thou didst* unjustly banish me ; whereon
At three and two years* old, I stole these Δbabes,

With so few pieces of major punctuation (just three), no surround phrases, and the late onrush (F #7-8, each split in two by most modern texts), it seems that this is more a stream of consciousness release than a series of premeditated thoughts (perhaps he is delighted to have adult company - the audience - to talk to for the first time in ages).

- the one moment where F includes an extra sentence (F #5) adds extra dimension to Morgan/Belarius' pride and joy in detailing the reactions of the older Prince (Paladour/Guiderius), the new sentence suggesting even more relish than before

- the speech opens passionately (17/12, F #1-4) as he reveals the true nature of Cymbeline's sons who regard him as their father – and they are emphasised not only by the pause inherent in the two short lines opening F #3 (sadness that they are not his perhaps?) but also by the two extra breath thoughts (marked ,$_{x}$) that single out the image underscoring their inner nature, viz. ',$_{x}$ to Prince it,$_{x}$'

- the pride in Guiderius starts out intellectually (4/2, the last line of F #4 and the first three lines of F #5) but then turns emotional (4/7, F #5's last four lines) as he describes Guiderius' thrilled reactions to tales of battle

- a similar pattern occurs as he describes the younger prince, Cadwall/Arviragus (3/1, F #6's first two lines, 0/3 the last one)

- though supposedly moving onto the hunt for food, the memory of the injustices done to him by Cymbeline and the resultant absconding with the boys moves Belarius to passion (F #7, 7/7), though the memory of their deceased Nurse (and presumably his partner) and of their honouring her manages to bring him back to a more even keel (6/2, F #8-9)

First Folio

18/ Belarius

1 How hard it is to hide the sparkes of Nature?+

2 These Boyes know little they are Sonnes to'th'King,
Nor Cymbeline dreames that they are alive.

3 They thinke they are mine, →
And though train'd up thus meanely
I'th'Cave, [whereon the Bowe]+ their thoughts do hit,
The Roofes of Palaces, and Nature prompts them
In simple and lowe things,$_{x}$ to Prince it,$_{x}$ much
Beyond the tricke of others.

4 This [Paladour],
The heyre of Cymbeline and Britaine, who
The King his Father call'd Guiderius.

5 Jove,+
When on my three-foot stoole I sit,$_{x}$ and tell
The warlike feats I have done, his spirits flye out
Into my Story : $_{x}$ say+ thus mine Enemy fell,
And thus I set my foote on's necke, even then
The Princely blood flowes in his Cheeke, he sweats,$_{x}$
Straines his yong Nerves, and puts himselfe in posture
That acts my words.

6 The yonger Brother+ [Cadwall],
Once Arviragus, in as like a figure
Strikes life into my speech, and shewes much more
His owne conceyving.

7 Hearke, the Game is rows'd,+
Oh Cymbeline, Heaven and my Conscience knowes
Thou didd'st unjustly banish me : $_{x}$ whereon
At three,$_{x}$ and two yeeres old, I stole these Babes,

---

[13] several scholars have problems in accepting the text from here to the end of the speech as vintage Shakespeare: at best they suggest it arose as a Shakespearean afterthought, at worst it is not Shakespearean at all: (one critic goes as far as to doubt the authenticity of the whole scene): see William Shakespeare: A Textual Companion, op. cit., page 607, notes re. lines 3.3.99 - 107/1454 – 1462

Thinking to bar* thee of Δsuccession, as
Thou refts me of my Δlands.
8 Euriphile,
Thou wast their Nurse ; they took thee for their mother,
And every day do honor to her grave. †
9 Myself*, Belarius, that am [Morgan] call'd,
They take for Δnatural* Δfather.
10 - The Δgame is up.

Thinking to barre thee of Succession, as
Thou refts me of my Lands.
8 Euriphile,
Thou was't their Nurse,+ they took thee for their mother,
And every day do honor to her grave:
My selfe+ Belarius, that am [Mergan]† call'd+
They take for Naturall Father.
9 The Game is up.

#'s 19 - 20: Complications Via Cloten

19/ Cloten **I love, and hate her: for she's Faire and Royall,** 3.5.70 - 80

Background: Learning that Imogen has fled, Cloten is more determined than ever to lay his hands on her - especially since in an earlier scene she told him, as he says later in this speech, 'shee held the very Garment of Posthumus, in more respect than my Noble and naturall person'.

Style: solo, and as part of a two-handed scene

Where: somewhere in the palace **To Whom:** direct audience address, and to Pisanio

# of Lines: 10 **Probable Timing: 0.35 minutes**

Modern Text

19/ Cloten

I love, and hate her ; for she's Δfair* and Δroyal*,
And that she hath all courtly parts more exquisite
[Than] Δlady, Δladies, Δwoman, from every one
The best she hath, and she*, of all compounded,
Outsells* them all.
2 I love her therefore, but
Disdaining me and throwing Δfavors* on
The low Posthumus slanders so her judgment*
That what's else rare, is chok'd*; and in that point
I will conclude to hate her, nay indeed*,
To be reveng'd upon her.
3 For, when Δfools* shall ——

ENTER PISANIO

Who is here*?

For such a normally blustering character the moments of calm in this speech - ' . I love, and hate her : ' (the surround phrase opening the speech), 'And that she hath all courtly parts more exquisite . . .' (middle of F #1), 'I love her therefore,' (opening F #2), and 'and in that point/I will conclude to hate her, . . ./To be reveng'd upon her.' (ending F #2) - all point to Cloten not only understanding his feelings but also no longer deceiving himself and, far more dangerously, coming instead to a firm resolution of how he will proceed.

- in this new state, following the surprise of the unembellished first phrase, comes an even more surprising intellectual rather than emotional assessment of how Imogen surpasses all other women (5/2, the next two lines of F #1)
- however, he then resorts to his more traditional emotion as he suggests that Imogen 'out-selles' all other women (0/2, to end of F #1)
- and the remainder of the speech, dealing with his eventual revenge on her for disdaining him in preference for Posthumus inevitably turns passionate (3/5, F #2-3)

First Folio

19/ Cloten

1 I love, and hate her : $_x$ for she's Faire and Royall,
And that she hath all courtly parts more exquisite
[Then] Lady, Ladies, Woman, from every one
The best she hath, and shee+ of all compounded+
Out-selles them all.
2 I love her therefore, but
Disdaining me,$_x$ and throwing Favours on
The low Posthumus,$_x$ slanders so her judgement,$_x$
That what's else rare, is choak'd: $_x$ and in that point
I will conclude to hate her, nay indeede,
To be reveng'd upon her.
3 For, when Fooles shall ——

ENTER PISANIO

Who is heere?

20/ Cloten **I am neere to'th'place where they should meet,** 4.1.1 - 25

Background: Under duress and believing Imogen to be long gone as planned, Pisanio has told Cloten where he had left her. Unfortunately, Cloten has journeyed to Wales with nothing but vengeance on his mind ('unfortunately', for in a moment Cloten is extremely rude to, and challenges, Guiderius/Polidore to a duel, which he loses, and is beheaded as a result).

Style: solo

Where: near the cave of Belarius **To Whom:** direct audience address

# of Lines: 24 **Probable Timing: 1.15 minutes**

Modern Text

20/ Cloten

1 I am near* to th'place where they should meet,
if Pisanio have mapp'd it truly*.
2 How fit his Δgarments
serve me!
3 Why should his Δmistress*, who was made by him
that made the Δtailor*, not be fit too? ◊ Δthe rather (saving
reverence of the Δword) for 'tis said* a Δwoman's fitness*
comes by fits. †
4 Therein I must play the Δworkman. †
5 I dare
speak* it to myself*, for it is not Δvainglory* for a man,
and his Δglass* to confer in his own* Δchamber - I mean*,
the Δlines of my body are as well drawn* as his; no less*
young, more strong, not beneath him in Δfortunes, beyond him in the advantage of the time, above him in
Δbirth, alike conversant in general* services, and more remarkable* in single oppositions; yet this imperseverant
Δthing loves him in my despite*.
6 What Δmortality* is!
7 Posthumus, thy head, which now is growing upon* thy
shoulders, shall within this hour* be off, thy Δmistress* enforced, thy Δgarments cut to pieces* before [her] face: and
all this done, spurn* her home to her Δfather, who may
(happily) be a little angry for my so rough usage; but my
Mother, having power of his testiness*, shall turn* all into my commendations.
8 My horse is tied* up safe, out,
Δsword, and to a sore purpose! †
9 Fortune put them in to my
hand! †
10 This is the very description of their meeting place,
and the Δfellow dares not deceive me.

Cloten's envy/jealousy of Imogen's husband Posthumus is highly emotional, for the three (emotional) semicolons

" ; I meane,/the Lines of my body are as well drawne as his ; "

" ; yet this imperseverant/Thing loves him in my despight . "

underscore his murderous intentions.

- it's not surprising, since he thinks he is close to achieving both Posthumus' death and the ravishing of Imogen, at the opening of the speech he is somewhat passionate (4/3, F #1-3), and the shortness of the sentences suggest control is somewhat of a struggle for him

- F #4's opening lack of grammar (according to most modern texts) emphasises the crudity of his sexual joke, and the onrush that ensues as he focuses on Posthumus becomes much more passionate (13/14 – F #4 through to the first three lines of F #6)

- though the (despairing? bemused?) short-spelled short sentence F #5 summary
" . What Mortalitie is ! "
is momentarily intellectual (1/0) which immediately dissipates, for the final imagining of his triumph over Imogen is passionate (2/3, the end of F #6)

- yet danger lies in the fact that he becomes intellectual in checking that everything is ready once more (5/1, F #7), the move to action enhanced by the fervent surround phrase wish
" : Fortune put them in to my hand : "

First Folio

20/ Cloten

1 I am neere to'th'place where they should meet,
if Pisanio have mapp'd it truely.
2 How fit his Garments
serve me?+
3 Why should his Mistris+ who was made by him
that made the Taylor, not be fit too?
4 The rather (saving
reverence of the Word) for 'tis saide a Womans fitnesse
comes by fits: therein I must play the Workman, I dare
speake it to my selfe, for it is not Vainglorie for a man,
and his Glasse,x to confer in his owne Chamber; x I meane,
the Lines of my body are as well drawne as his; no lesse
young, more strong, not beneath him in Fortunes, beyond him in the advantage of the time, above him in
Birth, alike conversant in generall services, and more remarkeable in single oppositions; yet this imperseverant
Thing loves him in my despight.
5 What Mortalitie is!
6 Posthumus, thy head (xwhich now is growing uppon thy
shouldersx) shall within this houre be off, thy Mistris in-
forced, thy Garments cut to peeces before [thy] face: and
all this done, spurne her home to her Father, who may
(happily) be a little angry for my so rough usage: x but my
Mother+ having power of his testinesse, shall turne all into my commendations.
7 My Horse is tyde up safe, out+
Sword, and to a sore purpose: + Fortune put them in to my
hand: + This is the very description of their meeting place+
and the Fellow dares not deceive me.

#'s 21 - 22: An Unscrupulous Step-Mother

21/ Queene **I wonder, Doctor,/Thou ask'st me such a Question:** 1.5.5 - 23

Background: The malevolent Queene (see background to speech #2 above) has asked Doctor Cornelius for 'drugges'. He in turn asked 'without offence/(My Conscience bids me aske) wherefore you have/Commanded me of these most poysonous compounds,/which are the moovers of a languishing death:/But though slow, deadly'. The following is her reply.

Style: as part of a two-handed scene

Where: outdoors in the gardens or woods near to the palace **To Whom:** Dr. Cornelius

# of Lines: 14 **Probable Timing: 0.45 minutes**

Modern Text

21/ Queene

1 I wonder, △doctor,
Thou ask'st me such a △question. †
2 Have I not been*
Thy △pupil* long?
3 Hast thou not learn'd me how
To make △perfumes? ◊ △distill? ◊ △preserve? ◊ △yea so,
That our great King himself* doth woo me oft
For my △confections?
4 Having thus far* proceeded
(Unless* thou think'st me devilish*) is't not meet*
That I did amplify$_*$ my judgment* in
Other △conclusions?
5 I will try the forces
Of these thy △compounds on such △creatures as
We count not worth the hanging (but none human*),
To try the vigor* of them, and apply
Allayments to their △act, and by them gather
Their several* virtues and effects.

The direct shortness of sentences F #2-5 and the surround phrase composition of F #1 show the Queene's magnificent understanding of the Machiavellian-type principle that 'attack is the best form of defence', an attack manifested even more by the onrush of F #1.

- not surprisingly, the challenges to the Doctor with which she opens the speech shows her in splendid intellectual control (7/2, F #1-5): as set, the much more deliberate rational F challenges presents the Doctor a far more difficult task if he were to think of answering her – unfortunately, the separate challenges of F #3-5 are rolled into one more generalised longer modern sentence (mt. #3)

- then, when she dares him to openly state that she is 'divellish' in her experiments, she becomes emotional (1/5, F #6) – though whether this is genuine or merely a superb rhetorical ploy to prevent the Doctor from opening his mouth is up to each actress to explore

- and finally, in explaining (untruthfully, as later events in the play show) that she wants the noxious substances for animal experimentation only, she becomes passionate (3/3, F #7) - though again whether through deliberate choice or genuine release is up to actress to decide

First Folio

21/ Queene

1 I wonder, Doctor,
Thou ask'st me such a Question: Have I not bene
Thy Pupill long?
2 Hast thou not learn'd me how
To make Perfumes?
3 Distill?
4 Preserve?
5 Yea so,
That our great King himselfe doth woo me oft
For my Confections?
6 Having thus farre proceeded,$_x$
(Unlesse thou think'st me divellish) is't not meete
That I did amplifie my judgement in
Other Conclusions?
7 I will try the forces
Of these thy Compounds,$_x$ on such Creatures as
We count not worth the hanging (but none humane)+
To try the vigour of them, and apply
Allayments to their Act, and by them gather
Their severall vertues,$_x$ and effects.

22/ Queene **Weepes she still (saist thou?)** 1.5.46 - 74

Background: Hoping to destroy the liaison between Imogen and Posthumus by either bribing their go-between, the servant Pisanio, or giving him the dangerous drugs she believes Cornelius has just given her (see speech #20 immediately above) so as to poison him, the Queene moves into the attack - first enquiring apparently solicitously as to Imogen's current state.

Style: as part of a two-handed scene

Where: outdoors in the gardens or woods near to the palace **To Whom:** Pisanio

# of Lines: 39 **Probable Timing: 2.00 minutes**

Modern Text

22/ Queene

1 Weeps* she still, say'st* thou?
2 Dost thou think* in time
She will not quench, and let instructions enter
Where Δfolly now possesses?
3 Do thou work*. †
4 When thou shalt bring me word she loves my Δson*,
I'll tell thee on the instant thou art then
As great as is thy Δmaster - Δgreater, for
His Δfortunes all lie* speechless*, and his name
Is at last gasp*.
5 Return* he cannot, nor
Continue where he is. †
6 To shift his being
Is to exchange one misery with another,
And every day that comes comes to decay
A day's* work*[14] in him.
7 What shalt thou expect
To be depender on a thing that leans*?
Who cannot be new built, nor has no Δfriends
So much as but to prop him?
8 [15] Thou tak'st up
Thou know'st not what; Δbut take it for thy labor*. †
9 It is a thing I made, which hath the King
Five times redeem'd from death.
10 I do not know
What is more Δcordial*.
11 Nay, I prithee* take it,

No matter how gentle or friendly the Queene may appear on the surface, that she is used to command/having her way can be seen in that all six surround phrases in this speech open sentences.

- in addition, three of them are actual orders, no matter how seductively urged, viz.
  ". Do thou worke : " (F #3)
  ". Tell thy Mistris how/The case stands with her : doo't, as from thy selfe . " (F #19);
  a fourth is information attempting to get Pisanio to desert Posthumus
  ". Returne he cannot, nor/Continue where he is : " (F #4)
  a fifth begins a (somewhat clumsy) bribe
  ". Thou tak'st up/Thou know'st not what : " (F #6)
  while the sixth, when she is finally left alone, is an immediate explosive dismissal of Pisanio as
  ". A slye, and constant knave,/Not to be shak'd : " (F #13)

- her attempt to discover just how distraught Imogen might be at the separation is passionate, as is her straight-to-the-point attempt to win Pisanio to her side (F #1-3, 5/7) – though her follow up dismissal of his current employer, Posthumus, turns emotional (2/4, F #4-5), the extra breath-thought in the final line (marked , x) driving home the fact of Posthumus' isolation (and thus uselessness) even more
  : nor ha's no Friends/So much, x as but to prop him?"

- and the initial temptation/offering to Pisanio of the (as she believes) poisoned cordial remains passionate (3/2, F #6-7)

- but once Pisanio displays reluctance in taking it, the Queene's pushing it at him - with the condition that he work on Imogen to get her to understand how delicate her situation will be if she insists on clinging to the now banished Posthumus - turns emotional (3/8, F #8-9)

- when this doesn't necessarily work she switches to intellect as she promises to intercede with the King to procure advancement for Pisanio (2/0, F #10's first two lines), which she quickly follows up with emotion as she adds the enticement of her own financial help (0/4, F #10's last two lines plus F #11-12)

First Folio

22/ Queene

1 Weepes she still (x saist thou? x) →
2 Dost thou thinke in time
She will not quench, and let instructions enter
Where Folly now possesses?
3 Do thou worke:
When thou shalt bring me word she loves my Sonne,
Ile tell thee on the instant, x thou art then
As great as is thy Master : x Greater, for
His Fortunes all lye speechlesse, and his name
Is at last gaspe.
4 Returne he cannot, nor
Continue where he is: To shift his being, x
Is to exchange one misery with another,
And every day that comes, x comes to decay
A dayes worke in him.
5 What shalt thou expect
To be depender on a thing that leanes?
Who cannot be new built, nor ha's no Friends
So much, x as but to prop him?
6 Thou tak'st up
Thou know'st not what : x But take it for thy labour,
It is a thing I made, which hath the King
Five times redeem'd from death.
7 I do not know
What is more Cordiall.
8 Nay, I prythee take it,
It is an earnest of a farther good

[14] though most modern texts agree with F and print this as 'worke', one interesting gloss = 'worth'

[15] most modern texts add the stage direction that the Queene deliberately drops the box of drugs given her by Cornelius

It is an earnest of a farther good
That I mean* to thee.
12 Tell thy Δmistress* how
The case stands with her ; do't*, as from thyself*. †
13 Think* what a chance thou [hangest] on, but think*
Thou hast thy Δmistress* still, ; to boot*, my Δson*,
Who shall take notice of thee.
14 I'll move the King
To any shape of thy Δpreferment, such
As thou'lt desire ; and then myself*, I chiefly*,
That set thee on to this desert, am bound
To load* thy merit richly.
15 Call my women.

[Exit Pisanio {momentarily}]

16 Think* on my words. [16]
17 A sly* and constant knave,
Not to be shak'd ; the Δagent for his Δmaster,
And the Δremembrancer of her to hold
The hand-fast to her Δlord.
18 I have given him that,
Which if he take, shall quite unpeople her
Of Δleigers* for her Δsweet*; and which she after
Except she bend her humor, shall be assur'd
To taste of too.
19 Fare thee well, Pisanio; ◊
Think* on my words.

• when alone (as Pisanio goes to fetch her women), though her intellect takes over as she expresses her dislike of Pisanio (4/1, F #13), her telling the audience the true nature of the (poisoned) cordial turns to passion again (2/2, the first two lines of F #14)

• in the midst of this sudden sweep of personal revelations, what is frightening are the moments of calm – for both the dismissal of Pisanio
" . . . a constant knave,/Not to be shak'd : "
and the nature of the poison
"I have given him that,/Which if he take, shall quite unpeople her/ . . . and which, she after/Except she bend her humor, shall be assur'd/To taste of too ."
reveal a woman very firm in her attitudes and intents

• and even in the final moment of the speech she is still trying to work on Pisanio, as both the final two short sentences (F #15-16) and the extra spelling weight on 'Thinke on my words.' attest

That I meane to thee.
9 Tell thy Mistris how
The case stands with her : x doo't, as from thy selfe ;
Thinke what a chance thou [changest] on, but thinke
Thou hast thy Mistris still,+ to boote, my Sonne,
Who shall take notice of thee.
10 Ile move the King
To any shape of thy Preferment, such
As thou'lt desire : x and then my selfe, I cheefely,
That set thee on to this desert, am bound
To loade thy merit richly.
11 Call my women.

[Exit Pisanio {momentarily}]

12 Thinke on my words.
13 A slye,x and constant knave,
Not to be shak'd : x the Agent for his Master,
And the Remembrancer of her,x to hold
The hand-fast to her Lord.
14 I have given him that,
Which if he take, shall quite unpeople her
Of Leidgers for her Sweete : x and which,x she after
Except she bend her humor, shall be assur'd
To taste of too.
15 Fare thee well, Pisanio.
16 Thinke on my words.

[16] most modern texts place Pisanio's exit here, half a line later than Ff: this seems somewhat arbitrary - after all the Queene could be calling after him as he leaves

#'S 23 - 24: LEADS TO FURTHER COMPLICATIONS

23/ Arviragus **The Bird is dead/That we have made so much on.** between 4.2.197 - 229

Background: Imogen, discovered sleeping in their cave by Belarius/Morgan, Arviragus/Cadwal, and Guiderius/Polidore, has been adopted by them (thanks to her disguise they believe her to be a young boy). As the Queene planned (speech #22 above), Pisanio handed Imogen the drugs given the Queene by Dr. Cornelius and, being sick, Imogen has taken them. What the Queene didn't know was that Cornelius, not trusting her, only gave her a very powerful death-like sleeping potion, one that would eventually wear off. Belarius/Morgan, Arviragus/Cadwal, and Guiderius/Polidore have discovered Imogen in her drug induced state, and believe her/him to be dead, as the following, spoken by the younger of the two brothers, shows

Style: as part of a three-handed scene

Where: outside the cave of Belarius **To Whom:** Belarius/Morgan and Guiderius/Polidore

# of Lines: 23 **Probable Timing: 1.10 minutes**

Modern Text

23/ Arviragus

1 The Δbird is dead
That we have made so much on.
2 I had rather
Have skipp'd, from sixteen* years* of Δage, to sixty,
To have turn'd my leaping time into a Δcrutch,
[Than] have seen* this.

3 {ψ} {I} found {ψ} him stark*, as you see;
Thus smiling, as some Δfly had tickled slumber,
Not as death's dart being laugh'd at; his right Δcheek*
Reposing on a Δcushion {,}

{o}'th'floor+ ;
His arms* thus leagu'd. †
4 I thought he slept, and put
My clouted* Brogues from off my feet*, whose rudeness*
Answer'd my steps too loud*.

5 With fairest* Δflowers
Whilst Δsummer* lasts and I live here*, Fidele,
I'll sweeten thy sad grave. †
6 Thou shalt not lack*
The Δflower that's like thy face, ◊ pale primrose, nor
The azur'd Δharebell, like thy Δveins*; no, nor
The leaf* of Δeglantine, whom not to slander,
Outsweet'ned not thy breath. †

The attempt to stay rational throughout sometimes seems too much for the younger of the two brothers, for the onrush at the end of F #3 (set as a separate modern sentence, mt. #4); the unusual punctuation at the end of F #4 which suggests that the (supposed) death is getting the better of Arviragus, and he needs the break to regain self-control: and the ensuing onrush of F #5, which jams together both flowers and birds, all point to his repeated inability to maintain grammatical dignity and/or self control – yet, to his credit, there are no swamping emotional semicolons anywhere in the speech, suggesting that whatever breakdowns he may be experiencing, he is eventually able to control them

- the opening dreadful statement is purely intellectual (1/0, F #1)
- then passion sweeps in (4/5) with both Arviragus' sense of loss (F #2) and his first description of finding the (supposedly) dead Imogen/Fidele (the first three lines of F#3), the passion heightened by the passage being set as four consecutive surround phrases
  "I had rather/Have skipt from sixteene yeares of Age, to sixty : / To have turn'd my leaping time into a Crutch,/[Then] have seene this . /{I} found him starke, as you see : /Thus smiling, as some Fly had tickled slumber,/Not as deaths dart being laugh'd at : "
- not surprisingly though emotion suddenly takes over as Arviragus tells of the final details of her/him (dead) on the floor (3/7, the last line of F #3 through F #4) and . . .
- . . . once the listing of the flowers to strew on the grave is initiated so passion returns (16/12, the remaining eleven lines of the speech), with the aforementioned lack of grammar breaking up his F #4 statement of intent

First Folio

23/ Arviragus

1 The Bird is dead
That we have made so much on.
2 I had rather
Have skipt from sixteene yeares of Age, to sixty : x
To have turn'd my leaping time into a Crutch,
[Then] have seene this.

3 {ψ} {I} found {ψ} him starke, as you see: x
Thus smiling, as some Fly had tickled slumber,
Not as deaths dart being laugh'd at: x his right Cheeke
Reposing on a Cushion {,}

{o}'th'floore: x
His armes thus leagu'd, I thought he slept, and put
My clowted Brogues from off my feete, whose rudenesse
Answer'd my steps too lowd.

4 With fayrest Flowers
Whil'st Sommer lasts, x and I live heere, Fidele,
Ile sweeten thy sad grave: thou shalt not lacke
The Flower that's like thy face.
5 Pale-Primrose, nor
The azur'd Hare-bell, like thy Veines: x no, nor
The leafe of Eglantine, whom not to slander,
Out-sweetned not thy breath: the Raddocke would

7 The △raddock[17] * would
With △charitable bill (△O* bill, sore shaming
Those rich-left heirs* that let their Fathers lie*
Without a △monument!), bring thee all this,
Yea, and furr'd △moss* besides.
8 When △flowers* are
none,
To [winter-gowne] thy △corse* ——

With Charitable bill (Oh bill+ sore shaming
Those rich-left-heyres,x that let their Fathers lye
Without a Monument+)+ bring thee all this,
Yea, and furr'd Mosse besides.
6 When Flowres are none+
To [winter-ground] thy Coarse ——

[17] Ff = 'Raddocke', some modern texts = 'Ruddocke' (a name for the English bird, the robin redbreast)

24/ Imogen **Yes Sir, to Milford-Haven, which is the way?** 4.2.291 - 332

Background: Following the memorial service (see speech #23 immediately above) the supposedly dead Imogen and the headless Cloten, dressed in her husband Posthumus' clothes (see speeches #19-20 above) have been laid out to rest on a bed of flowers. Imogen slowly awakes from the drug's effects, fully dressed and very confused.

Style: solo

Where: outside the cave of Belarius **To Whom:** self, and audience, and the dead body (whom she mistakes for her husband since it is dressed in his clothes)

# of Lines: 42 **Probable Timing: 2.00 minutes**

Modern Text

24/ Imogen

1 Yes, Δsir, to Milford-Haven, which is the way?
2 I thank* you . †
3 By yond bush? †
4 Pray how far* thither*?
5 'Ods pittikins! can it be six* mile yet?
6 I have gone all night . †
7 'Faith, I'll lie* down* and sleep*.
8 But soft ! no Δbedfellow ! [18]
9 O* Δgods, and Δgoddesses!
10 These Δflow'rs* are like the pleasures of the Δworld;
This bloody man, the care on't.
11 I hope I dream*;
For so I thought I was a Δcave-keeper,
And Δcook* to honest Δcreatures.
12 But 'tis not so . †
13 'Twas but a bolt of nothing, shot at nothing,
Which the Δbrain* makes of Δfumes.
14 Our very eyes,
Are sometimes like our Δjudgments*, blind*.
15 Good faith,
I tremble still with fear*; but if there be
Yet left in Δheaven, as small a drop of pity*
As a Δwren's eye, fear'd Δgods, a part of it !
16 The Δdream's* here* still; even when I wake, it is
Without me, as within me; x not imagin'd, felt.
17 A headless* man?
18 The Δgarments of Posthumus?

To her enormous credit, instead of giving way to emotion in the face of the most appalling circumstances, much of Imogen's voicings are determined attempts to understand what has occurred rather than bemoan it.

- that Imogen's gradual awakening is far from peaceful can be seen both in the fact that the first six sentences are either short (F #5 and #6) or composed of nine successive surround phrases (F #1-4), and in the passion released therein (7/7 in just five lines), ending in the rare (for an original text) exclamation mark

- that the impact the awakening has on her is equally disturbing yet somewhat more difficult to shake can be seen in her mind taking over (7/4, F #7-9) and in that each of F #7-9 opens with a surround phrase - referring first to the blood (F #7), then to ' . I hope I dreame :' (F #8), and then to the realisation she is not dreaming (F #9)

- her propensity to create maxims (in the hope that the headless man will disappear) leads to more passion (5/4, F #10-11), and, following her first emotional realisation that her hope has proven groundless (1/2, the first phrase of the three surround phrases forming F #12), the horror of it is then spoken so quietly, without any embellishment

  " : even when I wake it is/Without me, as within me : not imagin'd, felt . "

  though whether this is through an inability to voice her thoughts or a determined effort to establish some form of self-control is up to each actress to explore

First Folio

24/ Imogen

1 Yes+ Sir, to Milford-Haven, which is the way?
2 I thanke you: by yond bush? pray how farre thether?
3 'Ods pittikins: + can it be sixe mile yet?
4 I have gone all night: 'Faith, Ile lye downe, x and sleepe.
5 But soft; + no Bedfellow?+
6 Oh Gods, and Goddesses!
7 These Flowres are like the pleasures of the World;
This bloody man+ the care on't.
8 I hope I dreame: x
For so I thought I was a Cave-keeper,
And Cooke to honest Creatures.
9 But 'tis not so:
'Twas but a bolt of nothing, shot at nothing,
Which the Braine makes of Fumes.
10 Our very eyes,
Are sometimes like our Judgements, blinde.
11 Good faith+
I tremble still with feare: x but if there be
Yet left in Heaven, as small a drop of pittie
As a Wrens eye; x fear'd Gods, a part of it . +
12 The Dreame's heere still: x even when I wake+ it is
Without me, as within me: x not imagin'd, felt.
13 A headlesse man?
14 The Garments of Posthumus?

---

[18] most modern texts rightly suggest this is when she sees the body, but readers/actors should note that she doesn't say anything about it being headless or dressed in Posthumus' clothes for another twelve lines

19 I know the shape of's Δleg*: this is his Δhand,
His Δfoot* Δmercurial*, his martial* Δthigh,
The brawns* of Hercules; but his Δjovial* face ! †
20 [Murder] in heaven?
21 How? †
22 'Tis gone.
23 Pisanio,
All Δcurses madded Hecuba gave the Greeks*,
And mine to boot, be darted on thee ! †
24 Thou,
Conspir'd with that Δirregulous devil *Cloten,
Hath here* cut off my Δlord.
25 To write and read
Be henceforth treacherous !
26 Damn'd Pisanio
Hath with his forged Δletters (damn'd Pisanio!)
From this most bravest vessel* of the world
Struck* the main* top!
27 O* Posthumus, alas,
Where is thy head? †
28 Where's that?
29 Ay* me! where's that?
30 Pisanio might have kill'd thee at the heart
And left [thy] head on.
31 How should this be ? †
32 Pisanio?
33 'Tis he, and Cloten. †
34 Malice and Δlucre in them
Have laid this Δwoe here*.
35 O*, 'tis pregnant, pregnant!
36 The Δdrug* he gave me, which he* said was precious
And Δcordial* to me, have I not found it
Murd'rous to th'Δsenses?
37 That confirms* it home. †
38 This is Pisanio's deed*, and Cloten. †
39 O*!
Give color* to my pale cheek* with thy blood,
That we the horrider may seem* to those
Which chance to find* us.[19]
40 O*, my Δlord! my Δlord! [20]

• while the recognition of Posthumus' clothes is intellectual (F #14, 2/0) the (incorrect) conclusion that the 'headlesse man' is therefore her husband is, not surprisingly, highly passionate (7/6, in just the first three lines of F #15), the passion heightened by being set as five consecutive surround phrases

" . I know the shape of's Legge : this is his Hand : /His Foote Mercuriall : his martiall Thigh/The brawnes of Hercules : but his Joviall face ——"

• but then, and all credit to her, instead of giving way to emotion, her next seven lines (the end of F #15 through to the first line and a half of F #19) are a battle between intellect (9/2) and unembellished control as she attempts to come to some understanding of the appalling evidence in front of her (the word 'Curses' included in the following to give context to the quote

" - Murther in heaven ? How ? 'tis gone . Pisanio,/All Curses . . . And mine to boot, be darted on thee : . . . /To write, and read,/Be henceforth treacherous . "

• at last, in bemoaning the apparent fate of Posthumus, 'the bravest vessell of the world', so her emotions sweep in (1/5, the last line and a half of F #19 through to F #21)

• amazingly, she regains control once more and, though the conclusions she comes to are totally incorrect, her process seems quite rational, for the F #22 statement that Pisanio could have killed Posthumus without beheading him is completely unembellished, while the subsequent (as it turns out erroneous) conclusion that Pisanio has joined forces with the much loathed Cloten is strongly intellectual (5/1, F #23-24)

• the apparent evidence of Pisanio's guilt (the drugged cordial which he, not knowing of its sleep-inducing properties, gave her) is spoken of passionately (6/7, F #25 through to the first two lines and a half of F #27)

• while the daubing of herself with what she believes to be her husband's blood is totally emotional (0/4, F #27's last two and a half lines), the passion of her final cry of 'Oh, my Lord! my Lord!' (2/1, F #28) is once more heightened by the setting of two more (rare) exclamation marks, made even more weighty by the monosyllabic short sentence

15 I know the shape of's Legge: this is his Hand: x
His Foote Mercuriall: x his martiall Thigh+
The brawnes of Hercules: x but his Joviall face —— +
[Murther] in heaven?
16 How? 'tis gone.
17 Pisanio,
All Curses madded Hecuba gave the Greekes,
And mine to boot, be darted on thee: + thou+
Conspir'd with that Irregulous divell Cloten,
Hath heere cut off my Lord.
18 To write,x and read,x
Be henceforth treacherous. +
19 Damn'd Pisanio,x
Hath with his forged Letters (damn'd Pisanio+)
From this most bravest vessell of the world
Strooke the maine top!
20 Oh Posthumus, alas,
Where is thy head? where's that?
21 Aye me! where's that?
22 Pisanio might have kill'd thee at the heart,x
And left [this] head on.
23 How should this be, Pisanio?
24 'Tis he, and Cloten: Malice,x and Lucre in them
Have laid this Woe heere.
25 Oh+ 'tis pregnant, pregnant!
26 The Drugge he gave me, which hee said was precious
And Cordiall to me, have I not found it
Murd'rous to'th'Senses?
27 That confirmes it home:
This is Pisanio's deede, and Cloten: Oh!+
Give colour to my pale cheeke with thy blood,
That we the horrider may seeme to those
Which chance to finde us.
28 Oh, my Lord! my Lord!+

[19] most modern texts add the stage direction that here Imogen smears her cheeks with blood [20] most modern texts suggest Imogen faints and/or falls on the body

25: The Italian Invasion

25/ Cymbeline **You must know,/Till the injurious Romans, did extort** between 3.1.46 - 85

Background: In a sub-plot not explored in these speeches, England and Italy are on the brink of, and by the fifth act of the play go to, war. The following is King Cymbeline's response to the Roman Ambassador Lucius' demand for the annual tribute of three thousand pounds.

Style: public address nominally to one man, for the benefit of the whole group

Where: the British court **To Whom:** Lucius, the Roman Ambassador, in front of the Queene, Cloten, and English lords, as well as Lucius' attendants

# of Lines: 26 **Probable Timing: 1.15 minutes**

Modern Text

25/ Cymbeline

1 You must know,
Till the injurious Romans did extort
This Δtribute from us, we were free.
2 Cæsar's Δambition,
Which swell'd so much that it did almost stretch
The sides o'th'Δworld, against all color* here*
Did put the yoke* upon's; which to shake off
Becomes a warlike people, whom we reckon
Ourselves to be. †
3 We do ◊ Δsay then to Cæsar,
Our Δancestor was that Mulmutius which
Ordain'd our Δlaws*, whose use the Δsword of Cæsar
Hath too much mangled, whose repair* and franchise
Shall (by the power we hold) be our good deed,
Though* Rome be therefore* angry.
4 Mulmutius made our laws*
Who was the first of Britain* which did put
His brows* within a golden Δcrown* and call'd
Himself* a Δking.

5 Thou art welcome, Caius . †
6 Thy Cæsar Δknighted me; my youth I spent
Much under him ; of him I gather'd Δhonor*,
Which he, to seek* of me again*, perforce,
Behooves me keep* at utterance.
7 I am perfect
That the Pannonians and Dalmatians for
Their Δliberties are now in Δarms*, a Δpresident
Which not to read* would show* the Britains* cold. †
8 So Cæsar shall not find* them.

In a speech of bold defiance to a representative of a probably superior military power, it is not surprising that there are at least fourteen extra breath-thoughts (marked , $_x$) scattered throughout – which points to both Cymbeline's care in defying Rome and his precarious health (presumably the Queene's poison, which (as revealed at the end of the play) she has been steadily administering to him so that she can take over the throne after his death, has begun its subtle work).

- despite the two semicolons within the first three sentences, the speech opens with Cymbeline at his intellectual best (12/5) – the only emotional break being the reference to Rome enslaving Britaine
  " against all colour heere,/Did put the yoake upon's ; " (0/3)

- the reason for defying Rome is made abundantly clear by the unembellished passage
  " ; which to shake off/Becomes a warlike people, whom we reckon/Our selves to be, we do . "
  heightened by being set up by the emotional semicolon: the fact that the calm might be difficult to maintain can be seen in F's setting of ', we do.' which most modern texts consider ungrammatical – instead they put a period before this phrase and either let Cymbeline start a new sentence 'We do say then to . . . ' or else reassign the phrase as a two word sentence 'We do.' spoken by 'All' the English

- it seems that strain then gets the better of him, whether through ill-health or because of the powerful circumstances, for Cymbeline's consistency and control begin to disappear
  a/ the recognition of Mulmutius as the first British law-maker is passionate (3/5, F #4)
  b/ while the welcome to his Roman friend/now adversary is intellectual (3/0, the first line of F #5), the recollection of the good times with Cæsar is quietly but purposefully, even emotionally, invoked via the unembellished
  " ; my youth I spent/Much under him : "
  c/ and the recollection of the 'Honour' then garnered is emotional (1/4) the remainder of F #5

- while the recognition of current military rebellion against Rome by the Pannonians and Dalmations is spoken of intellectually (4/1, F #6's first two and a half lines), the spur to British resolve so created is uttered passionately (3/3, F #6's last two and a half lines)

First Folio

25/ Cymbeline

1 You must know,
Till the injurious Romans,$_x$ did extort
This Tribute from us, we were free.
2 Cæsars Ambition,
Which swell'd so much,$_x$ that it did almost stretch
The sides o'th'World, against all colour heere,$_x$
Did put the yoake upon's; which to shake off
Becomes a warlike people, whom we reckon
Our selves to be, we do.
3 Say then to Cæsar,
Our Ancestor was that Mulmutius,$_x$ which
Ordain'd our Lawes, whose use the Sword of Cæsar
Hath too much mangled; $_x$ whose repayre,$_x$ and franchise,$_x$
Shall (by the power we hold) be our good deed,
Tho Rome be therfore angry.
4 Mulmutius made our lawes
Who was the first of Britaine,$_x$ which did put
His browes within a golden Crowne,$_x$ and call'd
Himselfe a King.

5 Thou art welcome+ Caius,
Thy Cæsar Knighted me; my youth I spent
Much under him: $_x$ of him,$_x$ I gather'd Honour,
Which he, to seeke of me againe, perforce,
Behooves me keepe at utterance.
6 I am perfect,$_x$
That the Pannonians and Dalmatians,$_x$ for
Their Liberties are now in Armes: $_x$ a President
Which not to reade,$_x$ would shew the Britaines cold:
So Cæsar shall not finde them.

9 I know your △master's pleasure and he mine:
All the △remain* is "Welcome ! "

- and while F #7's surround phrase summary
  "I know your Masters pleasure, and he mine :'
is quietly intellectual (1/0), the final courtesy seems either genuine in its quiet surround phrase passion (1/1) or perhaps is a polite refusal to say more
  " : All the Remaine, is welcome . "

7 I know your Masters pleasure,$_x$ and he mine:
All the Remaine,$_x$ is welcome. +

BIBLIOGRAPHY

The most easily accessible general information is to be found under the citations of *Campbell*, and of *Halliday*. The finest summation of matters academic is to be found within the all-encompassing *A Textual Companion*, listed below in the first part of the bibliography under *Wells, Stanley and Taylor, Gary* (eds.)

Individual modern editions consulted are listed below under the separate headings 'The Complete Works in Compendium Format' and 'The Complete Works in Separate Individual Volumes,' from which the modern text audition speeches have been collated and compiled.

All modern act, scene, and/or line numbers refer the reader to *The Riverside Shakespeare*, in my opinion still the best of the complete works, despite the excellent compendiums that have been published since.

The F/Q material is taken from a variety of already published sources, including not only all the texts listed in the 'Photostatted Reproductions in Compendium Format' below, but also earlier individually printed volumes, such as the twentieth century editions published under the collective title *The Facsimiles of Plays from The First Folio of Shakespeare* by Faber & Gwyer, and the nineteenth century editions published on behalf of The New Shakespere Society.

The heading 'Single Volumes of Special Interest' is offered to newcomers to Shakespeare in the hope that the books may add useful knowledge about the background and craft of this most fascinating of theatrical figures.

PHOTOSTATTED REPRODUCTIONS OF THE ORIGINAL TEXTS IN COMPENDIUM FORMAT

Allen, M.J.B. and K. Muir, (eds.). *Shakespeare's Plays in Quarto*. Berkeley: University of California Press, 1981.

Blaney, Peter (ed.). *The Norton Facsimile (The First Folio of Shakespeare)*. New York: W.W.Norton & Company, Inc., 1996 (see also Hinman, below).

Brewer D.S. (ed.). *Mr. William Shakespeare's Comedies, Histories & Tragedies, The Second/Third/Fourth Folio Reproduced in Facsimile.* (3 vols.), 1983.

Hinman, Charlton (ed.). *The Norton Facsimile (The First Folio of Shakespeare)*. New York: W.W.Norton & Company, Inc., 1968.

Kökeritz, Helge (ed.). *Mr. William Shakespeare's Comedies, Histories & Tragedies*. New Haven: Yale University Press, 1954.

Moston, Doug (ed.). *Mr. William Shakespeare's Comedies, Histories, and Tragedies*. New York: Routledge, 1998.

MODERN TYPE VERSION OF THE FIRST FOLIO IN COMPENDIUM FORMAT

Freeman, Neil. (ed.). *The Applause First Folio Of Shakespeare In Modern Type*. New York & London: Applause Books, 2001.

MODERN TEXT VERSIONS OF THE COMPLETE WORKS IN COMPENDIUM FORMAT

Craig, H. and D. Bevington (eds.). *The Complete Works of Shakespeare*. Glenview: Scott, Foresman and Company, 1973.

Evans, G.B. (ed.). *The Riverside Shakespeare*. Boston: Houghton Mifflin Company, 1974.

Wells, Stanley and Gary Taylor (eds.). *The Oxford Shakespeare, William Shakespeare, the Complete Works, Original Spelling Edition*, Oxford: The Clarendon Press, 1986.

Wells, Stanley and Gary Taylor (eds.). *The Oxford Shakespeare, William Shakespeare, The Complete Works, Modern Spelling Edition*. Oxford: The Clarendon Press, 1986.

MODERN TEXT VERSIONS OF THE COMPLETE WORKS IN SEPARATE INDIVIDUAL VOLUMES

The Arden Shakespeare. London: Methuen & Co. Ltd., Various dates, editions, and editors.

Folio Texts. Freeman, Neil H. M. (ed.) Applause First Folio Editions, 1997, and following.

The New Cambridge Shakespeare. Cambridge: Cambridge University Press. Various dates, editions, and editors.

New Variorum Editions of Shakespeare. Furness, Horace Howard (original editor.). New York: 1880, Various reprints. All these volumes have been in a state of re-editing and reprinting since they first appeared in 1880. Various dates, editions, and editors.

The Oxford Shakespeare. Wells, Stanley (general editor). Oxford: Oxford University Press, Various dates and editors.

The New Penguin Shakespeare. Harmondsworth, Middlesex: Penguin Books, Various dates and editors.

The Shakespeare Globe Acting Edition. Tucker, Patrick and Holden, Michael. (eds.). London: M.H.Publications, Various dates.

SINGLE VOLUMES OF SPECIAL INTEREST

Baldwin, T.W. *William Shakespeare's Petty School*. 1943.

Baldwin, T.W. *William Shakespeare's Small Latin and Lesse Greeke*. (2 vols.) 1944.

Barton, John. *Playing Shakespeare*. 1984.

Beckerman, Bernard. *Shakespeare at the Globe, 1599-1609*. 1962.

Berryman, John. *Berryman's Shakespeare*. 1999.

Bloom, Harold. *Shakespeare: The Invention of the Human*. 1998.

Booth, Stephen (ed.). *Shakespeare's Sonnets*. 1977.

Briggs, Katharine. *An Encyclopedia of Fairies*. 1976.

Campbell, Oscar James, and Edward G. Quinn (eds.) . *The Reader's Encyclopedia OF Shakespeare. 1966.*

Crystal, David, and Ben Crystal. *Shakespeare's Words: A Glossary & Language Companion. 2002.*

Flatter, Richard. *Shakespeare's Producing Hand*. 1948 (reprint).

Ford, Boris. (ed.). *The Age of Shakespeare*. 1955.

Freeman, Neil H.M. *Shakespeare's First Texts*. 1994.

Greg, W.W. *The Editorial Problem in Shakespeare: A Survey of the Foundations of the Text*. 1954 (3rd. edition).

Gurr, Andrew. *Playgoing in Shakespeare's London*. 1987.

Gurr, Andrew. *The Shakespearean Stage, 1574-1642*. 1987.

Halliday, F.E. *A Shakespeare Companion* . 1952.

Harbage, Alfred. *Shakespeare's Audience*. 1941.

Harrison, G.B. (ed.). *The Elizabethan Journals*. 1965 (revised, 2 vols.).

Harrison, G.B. (ed.). *A Jacobean Journal*. 1941.

Harrison, G.B. (ed.). *A Second Jacobean Journal*. 1958.

Hinman, Charlton. *The Printing and Proof Reading of the First Folio of Shakespeare*. 1963 (2 vols.).

Joseph, Bertram. *Acting Shakespeare*. 1960.

Joseph, Miriam (Sister). *Shakespeare's Use of The Arts of Language*. 1947.

King, T.J. *Casting Shakespeare's Plays*. 1992.

Lee, Sidney and C.T. Onions. *Shakespeare's England: An Account Of The Life And Manners Of His Age*. (2 vols.) 1916.

Linklater, Kristin. *Freeing Shakespeare's Voice*. 1992.

Mahood, M.M. *Shakespeare's Wordplay*. 1957.

O'Connor, Gary. *William Shakespeare: A Popular Life*. 2000.

Ordish, T.F. *Early London Theatres*. 1894. (1971 reprint).

Rodenberg, Patsy. *Speaking Shakespeare*. 2002.

Schoenbaum. S. *William Shakespeare: A Documentary Life*. 1975.

Shapiro, Michael. *Children of the Revels*. 1977.

Simpson, Percy. *Shakespeare's Punctuation*. 1969 (reprint).

Smith, Irwin. *Shakespeare's Blackfriars Playhouse*. 1964 .

Southern, Richard. *The Staging of Plays Before Shakespeare*. 1973.

Spevack, M. *A Complete and Systematic Concordance to the Works Of Shakespeare*. 1968–1980 (9 vols.).

Tillyard, E.M.W. *The Elizabethan World Picture*. 1942.

Trevelyan, G.M. (ed.). *Illustrated English Social History*. 1942.

Vendler, Helen. *The Art of Shakespeare's Sonnets*. 1999.

Walker, Alice F. *Textual Problems of the First Folio*. 1953.

Walton, J.K. *The Quarto Copy of the First Folio*. 1971.

Warren, Michael. *William Shakespeare, The Parallel King Lear 1608–1623*.

Wells, Stanley and Taylor, Gary (eds.). *Modernising Shakespeare's Spelling, with Three Studies in The Text of Henry V*. 1975.

Wells, Stanley. *Re-Editing Shakespeare for the Modern Reader*. 1984.

Wells, Stanley and Gary Taylor (eds.). *William Shakespeare: A Textual Companion*. 1987.

Wright, George T. *Shakespeare's Metrical Art*. 1988.

HISTORICAL DOCUMENTS

Daniel, Samuel. *The Fowre Bookes of the Civile Warres Between The Howses Of Lancaster and Yorke*. 1595.

Holinshed, Raphael. *Chronicles of England, Scotland and Ireland*. 1587 (2nd. edition).

Halle, Edward. *The Union of the Two Noble and Illustre Famelies of Lancastre And Yorke*. 1548 (2nd. edition).

Henslowe, Philip: Foakes, R.A. and Rickert (eds.). *Henslowe's Diary*. 1961.

Plutarch: North, Sir Thomas (translation of a work in French prepared by Jacques Amyots). *The Lives of The Noble Grecians and Romanes*. 1579.

APPENDIX 1: GUIDE TO THE PHOTOSTATS OF THE EARLY TEXTS

A QUARTO (Q)

A single text, so called because of the book size resulting from a particular method of printing. Eighteen of Shakespeare's plays were published in this format by different publishers at various dates between 1594–1622, prior to the appearance of the 1623 Folio. An extremely useful collection of them is to be found in: Allen, Michael J.B., and Kenneth Muir (eds.), *Shakespeare's Plays In Quarto,* Berkeley: University of California Press. 1981.

THE FIRST FOLIO (F1)[1]

Thirty-six of Shakespeare's plays (excluding *Pericles* and *Two Noble Kinsmen*, in which he had a hand) appeared in one volume, published in 1623. All books of this size were termed Folios, again because of the sheet size and printing method, hence this volume is referred to as the First Folio. For publishing details see Bibliography, 'Photostated Reproductions of the Original Texts.'

THE SECOND FOLIO (F2)

Scholars suggest that the Second Folio, dated 1632 but perhaps not published until 1640, has little authority, especially since it created hundreds of new problematic readings of its own. Nevertheless more than 800 modern text readings can be attributed to it. The most recent reproduction is Brewer, D.S. (ed.). *Mr. William Shakespeare's Comedies, Histories & Tragedies, the Second Folio Reproduced in Facsimile*. Dover. Boydell & Brewer Ltd., 1985.

The Third Folio (1664) and the Fourth Folio (1685) have even less authority, and are rarely consulted except in cases of extreme difficulty.

THE THIRD FOLIO (F3)

The Third Folio, carefully proofed (though apparently not against the previous edition), takes great pains to correct anomalies in punctuation ending speeches and in expanding abbreviations. It also introduced seven new plays supposedly written by Shakespeare, only one of which, Pericles, has been established as such. The most recent reproduction is, Brewer, D.S. (ed.). *Mr. William Shakespeare's Comedies, Histories & Tragedies, The Third Folio Reproduced in Facsimile*, Dover. Boydell & Brewer Ltd., 1985.

THE FOURTH FOLIO (F4)

Paradoxically, while the Fourth Folio was the most carefully edited of all, its concentration on grammatical clarity and ease of comprehension by its readers at the expense of faithful reproduction of F1 renders it the least useful for those interested in the setting down on paper of Elizabethan theatre texts. The most recent reproduction is, Brewer, D.S. (ed.). *Mr. William Shakespeare's Comedies, Histories & Tragedies, The Fourth Folio Reproduced in Facsimile,* Dover. Boydell & Brewer Ltd., 1985.

---

[1] for a full overview of the First Folio see the monumental two volume work by Charlton Hinman, *The Printing And Proof Reading Of The First Folio Of Shakespeare.* (2 volumes). Oxford: Clarendon Press. 1963., and W.W Greg. *The Editorial Problem In Shakespeare: A Survey Of The Foundations Of The Text.* Oxford: Clarendon Press. 1954 (3rd. edition).; for a brief summary, see the forty-six page publication from, Peter W.M. Blayney, *The First Folio Of Shakespeare*: Washington, D.C: Folger Library Publications. 1991.

APPENDIX 2: WORD, WORDS, WORDS

PART ONE: VERBAL CONVENTIONS (and how they will be set in the Folio Text column)

"THEN" AND "THAN"

These two words, though their neutral vowels sound different to modern ears, were almost identical to Elizabethan speakers and readers, despite their different meanings. F and Q make little distinction between them, setting them interchangeably. The original setting will be used, and the modern reader should soon get used to substituting one for the other as necessary.

"I," "AY," AND "AYE"

F/Q often print the personal pronoun "I" and the word of agreement "aye" simply as "I." Again, the modern reader should quickly get used to this and make the substitution when necessary. The reader should also be aware that very occasionally either word could be used and the phrase make perfect sense, even though different meanings would be implied.

"MY SELFE/HIM SELFE/HER SELFE" VERSUS "MYSELF/HIMSELF/HERSELF"

Generally F/Q separate the two parts of the word, "my selfe" while most modern texts set the single word "myself." The difference is vital, based on Elizabethan philosophy. Elizabethans regarded themselves as composed of two parts, the corporeal "I," and the more spiritual part, the "self." Thus, when an Elizabethan character refers to "my selfe," he or she is often referring to what is to all intents and purposes a separate being, even if that being is a particular part of him- or herself. Thus soliloquies can be thought of as a debate between the "I" and "my selfe," and, in such speeches, even though there may be only one character on-stage, it's as if there were two distinct entities present.

UNUSUAL SPELLING OF REAL NAMES, BOTH OF PEOPLE AND PLACES

Real names, both of people and places, and foreign languages are often reworked for modern understanding. For example, the French town often set in F1 as "Callice" is usually reset as "Calais." F will be set as is.

NON-GRAMMATICAL USES OF VERBS IN BOTH TENSE AND APPLICATION

Modern texts 'correct' the occasional Elizabethan practice of setting a singular noun with plural verb (and vice versa), as well as the infrequent use of the past tense of a verb to describe a current situation. The F reading will be set as is, without annotation.

ALTERNATIVE SETTINGS OF A WORD WHERE DIFFERENT SPELLINGS MAINTAIN THE SAME MEANING

F/Q occasionally set what appears to modern eyes as an archaic spelling of a word for which there is a more common modern alternative, for example "murther" for murder, "burthen" for burden, "moe" for more, "vilde" for vile. Though some modern texts set the F1 (or alternative Q) setting, others modernise. F1 will be set as is with no annotation.

ALTERNATIVE SETTINGS OF A WORD WHERE DIFFERENT SPELLINGS SUGGEST DIFFERENT MEANINGS

Far more complicated is the situation where, while an Elizabethan could substitute one word formation for another and still imply the same thing, to modern eyes the substituted word has a entirely different meaning to the one it has replaced. The following is by no means an exclusive list of the more common dual-spelling, dual-meaning words

anticke-antique	mad-made	sprite-spirit
born-borne	metal-mettle	sun-sonne
hart-heart	mote-moth	travel-travaill
human-humane	pour-(powre)-power	through-thorough
lest-least	reverent-reverend	troth-truth
lose-loose	right-rite	whether-whither

Some of these doubles offer a metrical problem too, for example "sprite," a one syllable word, versus "spirit." A potential problem occurs in *A Midsummer Nights Dream*, where the modern texts set Q1's "thorough," and thus the scansion pattern of elegant magic can be established, whereas F1's more plebeian "through" sets up a much more awkward and clumsy moment.

The F reading will be set in the Folio Text, as will the modern texts' substitution of a different word formation in the Modern Text column. If the modern text substitution has the potential to alter the meaning (and sometimes scansion) of the line, it will be noted accordingly.

PART TWO: WORD FORMATIONS COUNTED AS EQUIVALENTS FOR THE FOLLOWING SPEECHES

Often the spelling differences between the original and modern texts are quite obvious, as with "she"/"shee". And sometimes Folio text passages are so flooded with longer (and sometimes shorter) spellings that, as described in the General Introduction, it would seem that vocally something unusual is taking place as the character speaks.

However, there are some words where the spelling differences are so marginal that they need not be explored any further. The following is by no means an exclusive list of words that in the main will not be taken into account when discussing emotional moments ("Russian" or "Volcanic" Shakespeare) in the various commentaries accompanying the audition speeches.

(modern text spelling shown first)

and - & apparent - apparant briars - briers choice - choise defense - defence debtor - debter enchant - inchant endurance - indurance ere - e'er expense - expence has - ha's heinous - hainous I'll - Ile increase - encrease	murder - murther mutinous - mutenous naught - nought obey - obay o'er - o're offense - offence quaint - queint reside - recide Saint - S. sense - sence sepulchre - sepulcher show - shew solicitor - soliciter sugar - suger	tabor - taber ta'en - tane than - then theater - theatre then - than uncurrant - uncurrent venomous - venemous virtue - vertue weight - waight

APPENDIX 3:
THE PATTERN OF MAGIC, RITUAL & INCANTATION

THE PATTERNS OF "NORMAL" CONVERSATION

The normal pattern of a regular Shakespearean verse line is akin to five pairs of human heart beats, with ten syllables being arranged in five pairs of beats, each pair alternating a pattern of a weak stress followed by a strong stress. Thus, a normal ten syllable heartbeat line (with the emphasis on the capitalised words) would read as

weak - STRONG, weak - STRONG, weak - STRONG, weak - STRONG, weak - STRONG
(shall I com------PARE thee TO a SUMM-------ers DAY)

Breaks would either be in length (under or over ten syllables) or in rhythm (any combinations of stresses other than the five pairs of weak-strong as shown above), or both together.

THE PATTERNS OF MAGIC, RITUAL, AND INCANTATION

Whenever magic is used in the Shakespeare plays the form of the spoken verse changes markedly in two ways. The length is usually reduced from ten to just seven syllables, and the pattern of stresses is completely reversed, as if the heartbeat was being forced either by the circumstances of the scene or by the need of the speaker to completely change direction. Thus in comparison to the normal line shown above, or even the occasional minor break, the more tortured and even dangerous magic or ritual line would read as

STRONG - weak, STRONG - weak, STRONG - weak, STRONG
(WHEN shall WE three MEET a-------GAINE)

The strain would be even more severely felt in an extended passage, as when the three weyward Sisters begin the potion that will fetch Macbeth to them. Again, the spoken emphasis is on the capitalised words and the effort of, and/or fixed determination in, speaking can clearly be felt.

THRICE the BRINDed CAT hath MEW"D
THRICE and ONCE the HEDGE-Pigge WHIN"D
HARPier CRIES, 'tis TIME, 'tis TIME.

UNUSUAL ASPECTS OF MAGIC

It's not always easy for the characters to maintain it (as with Pucke in *A Midsummer Nights Dream*, speech #34, and especially Prospero in *The Tempest*, speech #4). And the magic doesn't always come when the character expects it (as with the Duke in *Measure For Measure*, speech #12, or Prospero in *The Tempest*, speech #3). What is even more interesting is that while the pattern is found a lot in the Comedies, it is usually in much gentler situations, often in songs (*Two Gentlemen of Verona*, *Merry Wives of Windsor*, *Much Ado About Nothing*, *Twelfth Night*, *The Winters Tale*) and/or simplistic poetry (*Loves Labours Lost* and *As You Like It*), as well as the casket sequence in *The Merchant of Venice*.

It's too easy to dismiss these settings as inferior poetry known as doggerel. But this may be doing the moment and the character a great disservice. The language may be simplistic, but the passion and the magical/ritual intent behind it is wonderfully sincere. It's not just a matter of magic for the sake of magic, as with Pucke and Oberon enchanting mortals and Titania; or Prospero controlling the elements; or the weyward Sisters; or even Macbeth attempting to control the denizens of the 'half' and spirit worlds. It's a matter of the human heart's desires too.

And though none of the following speeches are included in these volumes, no wonder magic is used by, among others: Dumaine, the youngest Navarre lover in *Loves Labours Lost*, in his poetry when worshipping a lady for whom Jove himself would deny his godhood and turn 'mortall for thy Love'; Phebe in *As You Like It,* wondering whether Ganymede, the disguised Rosalind, is a 'god, to Shepherd turn'd?'; and Orlando, also in *As You Like It,* when writing paons of praise to Rosalind suggesting that she is composed of the best parts of the mythical heroines because

THEREfore HEAVen NATure CHARG"D
THAT one BODie SHOULD be FILL"D
WITH all GRACes WIDE enLARG"D

And what could be better than Autolycus (*The Winters Tale*) using magic in his opening song as an extra enticement to trap the unwary into buying all his peddler's goods, ballads, and trinkets.

To help the reader, most magic/ritual lines will be bolded in the Folio text version of the speeches.